Mass Communication Law and Ethics

Mass Communication Law and Ethics

Roy L. Moore
University of Kentucky

LEA LAWRENCE ERLBAUM ASSOCIATES, PUBLISHERS
1994   Hillsdale, New Jersey   Hove, UK

Lawrence Erlbaum Associates, Inc., Publishers
365 Broadway
Hillsdale, New Jersey 07642

Library of Congress Cataloging-in-Publication Data
Moore, Roy L.
   Mass communication law and ethics / by Roy L. Moore.
     p. cm. — (Communication textbook series. Mass
communication)
   Includes index.
   ISBN 0-8058-0240-1
   1. Mass media — Law and legislation — United States.
2. Journalistic ethics — United States. 3. Law and ethics.
I. Title. II. Series.
KF2750.M66 1993
343.7309'9 — dc20
[347.30399]   93-4453
                           CIP

Books published by Lawrence Erlbaum Associates are printed
on acid-free paper, and their bindings are chosen for strength
and durability.

Printed in the United States of America
10 9 8 7 6 5 4 3 2 1

Contents

Preface

A survey of 145 mass media law instructors in 1987 found that although two thirds of the respondents devoted 10% or less of their courses to ethics, they overwhelmingly agreed that ethics should be a significant part of teaching media law. Almost half said ethics is a necessary corollary to law but that legal topics should not be dropped to make room. A similar percentage said that they distinguish in class between legal boundaries and standards of ethics in determining appropriate media conduct.

Mass Communication Law and Ethics is the first book to explicitly combine law and ethics rather than separate them as is traditionally done. Many journalism and mass communication programs now include "ethics" in the title for the media law course — a recognition that their graduates must be grounded in ethics and that a combined course is the most feasible and effective way of accomplishing this goal. Sadly, most students complete their degrees with limited, if any, understanding of the symbiotic relationship between media law and ethics. Each chapter in this book includes a discussion of the ethical dimensions of that specific legal topic to demonstrate where the law ends and ethics begins. For example, although the First Amendment protects a reporter who publishes a rape victim's name from a public record, such disclosure is unethical in the eyes of many journalists. Appropriating another writer's ideas in a story is not copyright infringement so long as only ideas but not expressions are used, but is such conduct ethical? Snapping photos of a severely injured child being pulled from an automobile accident is generally not invasion of privacy, but most media outlets would refrain from publishing or broadcasting the blood and gore out of respect for the child and the family. The moral is that comprehension of the law is only the first step. Every journalist must establish a personal code of ethics, but the standards can best be understood within the context of mass media law. The question should not be "How do I avoid a lawsuit?" but rather "How do I do what is right?" Answering the latter question is often more difficult than ascertaining the appropriate legal principle, but we must, as professional communicators, be able to affirmatively respond to both queries. Mass communication law and media ethics are inseparable and complement one another in a way that makes the bond between them far stronger than the base on which they stand individually.

My thanks to everyone who has adopted this book. I encourage you to let me know your comments and criticisms so the next edition will be even better.

I also wish to thank each of the following for their contributions to this work: my wife, Pam, and my son, Derek, for their patience, love, and understanding during the 4 long years in which the book was written; to Esther Edwards and John Clark for their assistance with preparing the manuscript; to the anonymous reviewer for constructive comments that made the book much stronger; to all of my colleagues for their encouragement; and, finally, to the staff at Lawrence Erlbaum, including Hollis Heimbouch and Robin Weisberg, for their excellent advice and cooperation.

—*Roy L. Moore*

The American Legal System and the Judicial Process

1 Codes of Ethics and Sources and Types of U.S. Law

As early as the third grade, children are taught the structure of the U.S. government, including our tripartite system and the relationship of each branch to the law. Yet few adults, except those directly involved in the judicial system—such as lawyers and judges—actually comprehend the intricacies of our unique system of government and its laws.

A survey commissioned by the Hearst Publishing Corporation[1] for the bicentennial of the adoption of the U.S. Constitution found that almost two-thirds of the respondents wrongly believed the Constitution established English as the official language, and more than one-fourth confused the purpose of the Constitution with the purpose of the Declaration of Independence.[2] In a 1990 national poll by The Thomas Jefferson Center for the Protection of Free Expression,[3] 63.7 percent of those interviewed said they did not feel the government would be violating free speech if it told everyone, including those who spoke Spanish, that English was the official language.

Information overload may be the culprit for some of the confusion and lack of knowledge about our system of government. For example, elementary and secondary school courses in U.S. government typically emphasize that federal and state legislators pass bills that become statutes once signed by the head of government or when a veto is overridden by the legislature, that state and federal courts interpret the laws, and that members of the executive branch are responsible for enforcing the laws. Yet in this day and age of administrative law and an occasional activist court, the concept of separation of powers may be a gross oversimplification of how the government functions in the real world.

When most individuals conceptualize law, they focus on statutory or constitutional law, ignoring the source of law that has had the greatest impact on our legal history — common law. Administrative law is rarely mentioned and equity law is virtually unknown, except among legal experts. Yet these sources of law constitute "the law" as much as statutes do.

This chapter examines the sources and categories of U.S. law from the U.S. Constitution's Bill of Rights to equity. Traditional categories of law, such as civil versus criminal and tort versus contract, are also distinguished as a background for later chapters that analyze specific court cases.

Each chapter of this book, including this chapter, attempts to proceed at least one step beyond the law into the realm of media ethics, which has become as important today as the law in news gathering and reporting. The public no longer expects the mass media to simply stay within the boundaries of the law but also to be objective and unbiased in their presentation of the news and to adhere to standards of professional conduct that ensure fairness.

CONSTITUTIONAL LAW

The Federal Constitution

Almost any elementary school student knows that the U.S. Constitution is the supreme law of the land, but relatively few people are familiar with the document's major provisions, in spite of the massive educational campaigns conducted in the midst of the bicentennial and postbicentennial celebrations.

More than 200 years ago, the authors of the Constitution debated the numerous proposed provisions in the document, very few of which actually survived to become incorporated into the final draft. The general consensus among the delegates indicated that only a strong central government could overcome the serious problems that had quickly doomed the Articles of Confederation. Although there was some strong disagreement, the representatives as a whole felt that such a strong central government had the best chance of maintaining unity and coordination among the individual states and commonwealths.

However, the conveners felt even more strongly that no one interest or person, including the head of state, should be accorded supreme authority over the federal government. Thus a separation of powers, similar to the structure already established in a majority of the constitutions of the 13 original states, was created.

The idea of branches of government acting as checks and balances on one another had wide support at the constitutional convention in 1787 and still can claim strong backing today, but the implementation of that concept is as controversial now as it was then. Those concerns today are expressed in the form of complaints about gross inefficiency and the erosion of states' rights and individual liberties.

The Constitution both limits and defines the powers of federal government, but it is principally an outline of the structure, powers, limitations and obligations of government. Most of the details are left to statutory, common and sometimes equity law.

The first 10 amendments to the Constitution, commonly known as the Bill of Rights, clearly have had the most significant impact on individual privileges such as freedom of speech and freedom of the press guaranteed by the First Amendment, along with freedom of religion.

The academic and professional debate over any significance of the position of the First Amendment in the Bill of Rights — that is, whether first in line means freedom of speech, press and religion take priority over other rights in the Constitution when there is real conflict — has been intense in the last few decades. As discussed later in Chapter 9, according to the general view of the U.S. Supreme Court during the so-called Burger era (when Warren Burger was chief justice of the United States, 1968–1986) and now during the William H. Rehnquist reign, the First Amendment rights are not to be favored over other individual rights granted in the Constitution.

The Bill of Rights did not even become an official part of the Constitution until December 15, 1791, more than three years after the Constitution became official and more than two years after the first U.S. Congress had convened, the first president had been inaugurated, and a federal court system with a U.S. Supreme Court had been created by Congress!

The original Constitution had to be formally approved by the state legislatures (with reluctance by a few states); but how can the Constitution be changed? Constitutional amendments may be proposed in one of three ways: (a) by two-thirds vote of each house of Congress, (b) by request of two-thirds of the state legislatures to call a convention, or (c) by congressional approval to call a convention. The traditional approach has been the first one. These methods are only the first step in the process of altering the Constitution. The Constitution cannot be officially amended until a specific proposed amendment has been ratified. Ratification can be accomplished in two ways: (a) by approval of three-fourths of the state legislatures (after two-thirds vote of each house of Congress), or (b) by approval of three-fourths of the state constitutional conventions (after Congress calls for a convention or two-thirds of the state legislatures call for a convention). Surprisingly, the Constitution itself does not specify how a constitutional convention would be restructured nor even how the delegates to it would be selected.

The last amendment to the Constitution to be ratified was the Twenty-Seventh Amendment in 1992: "No law, varying the compensation for the services of the Senators and Representatives, shall take effect, until an election of Representatives shall have intervened." This amendment was one of the 12 articles proposed by James Madison in 1789, 10 of which made up the Bill of Rights.[4] It forbids Congress from passing any pay raise or decrease that would take effect before the next election of the House of Representatives. Michigan signed on as the necessary 38th state for ratification on May 7, 1992, more than 200 years after the amendment was originally proposed. Four other amendments without a specific deadline are awaiting ratification, including one calling for a new constitutional convention, which has now been approved by 32 of the required 34 states. (Three of the 34, however, have rescinded their approval.) Prior to 1992, the Twenty-sixth Amendment was the last to get the nod. It forbids the states and the federal government from denying any citizen, 18 years of age or older, the right to vote in state and federal elections. All attempts to amend the Constitution since 1971 had been unsuccessful, including the so-called Equal Rights Amendment ("Equality of rights under the law shall not be denied or abridged by the United States or by any state on account of sex"), which died in 1982 when it fell three states short of the 38 required for ratification within the time frame (including one extension) specified by Congress.

State Constitutions

State constitutions are also an important source of U.S. law because they serve as the supreme law in a particular state except when they are in direct conflict with the U.S. Constitution or with valid federal statutes — that is, federal statutes that do not conflict with the U.S. Constitution and that fall within a power enumerated under the Constitution or permitted under the preemption doctrine that allows the federal government to preclude state and local governments from directly regulating certain activities, such as interstate commerce, considered to be national in nature.[5]

Most state constitutions require that a specified percentage (usually two-thirds or three-fourths) of those voting in that election approve any proposed amendments to the state constitution, which are placed on the ballot after approval by the state legislature. Most state constitutions also provide for a state constitutional convention to consider amendments. Although the U.S. Constitution has never been rewritten, several states in recent years have approved new state constitutions. For example, the Georgia electorate approved a new state constitution in 1982 that became effective in 1983.

How does one find state and federal constitutional law? Tracking down the specific constitutions is as easy as a trip to a local library; knowing their meaning is another matter. Constitutions focus on the basic issues of government authority, functions and organization, as well as fundamental rights and limitations, and thus their interpretation is often a burdensome task that state and federal courts must constantly tackle. It is essential that anyone attempting to ascertain the meaning of a state or federal constitutional provision consult appropriate statutes because they often pick up where the constitutions stop and yet cannot conflict with the constitutions) and case law, where the courts have exercised the authority granted them to interpret constitutional law.

In *Marbury V. Madison* (1803),[6] the U.S. Supreme Court, in a landmark decision written by Chief Justice John Marshall, established the authority of the federal judiciary to determine the constitutionality of congressional actions, thereby effectively establishing the U.S. Supreme Court as the final arbiter or interpreter of the U.S. Constitution. The highest appellate court in each state (usually called the Supreme Court, although in some states such as New York the highest court may be called by another name) is generally the final arbiter of the meaning of that state's constitution.

STATUTORY LAW

Laws in this country fall within a hierarchy of authority with constitutional law at the top, just above statutory law. Statutes take priority over all other types of law, except constitutional law. For example, unless a federal statute is determined to conflict with the U.S. Constitution by a court of competent jurisdiction (ultimately, the U.S. Supreme Court if it exercises its discretion to decide the case, as explained in Chapter 2), that statute is presumed valid and preempts any *conflicting* administrative, common or equity law — local, state or federal.

Although the process of altering state constitutions and the federal constitution can be long and cumbersome, enacting statutes can be a relatively simple process, in spite of the fact that committees and subcommittees often bog down the procedures. Most law today is statutory; statutes can deal with problems never anticipated by the framers of the Constitution and can be considerably more flexible because they have the ability to deal with *future* problems and very complex issues.

Legislative bodies, the source of all statutes and ordinances, number in the thousands and include city councils, county commissions, state legislatures and Congress. All possess, with constitutional and other limitations, the authority to regulate social actions that may range from setting the maximum fine for a particular type of parking violation (although not for a specific offender, of course) to ratifying an international nuclear arms agreement.

All statutes, whether civil or criminal, are compiled in some official form so that affected individuals and organizations can have access to them. The typical university law library or courthouse contains myriad volumes of these written laws. The most convenient way of locating a particular statute is to consult the specific "code" in which that type of statute is collected. For example, federal statutes can be found in the official *United States Code*

(U.S.C.) and in two commercially published codes, *United States Code Annotated* (U.S.C.A.) and *United States Code Service* (U.S.C.S.).

These codified texts conveniently arrange statutes by subject matter (such as copyright, obscenity, criminal acts, etc.) rather than chronologically. State laws are also codified under various names such as "(State) Revised Statutes" or "(State) Code Annotated." Statutes can also be found chronologically by date of enactment in session laws. For example, federal session laws are compiled in *Statutes at Large*.

The role of the courts in statutory law is actually quite similar to that played in constitutional law. Contrary to popular belief, most statutes (state, federal and local) are never challenged as unconstitutional. However, most courts have the authority to determine the constitutionality of statutes and, perhaps more significantly, to interpret statutes. The judicial process is examined in Chapter 3, but it should be noted here that the federal courts, including the U.S. Supreme Court and most state courts, are prohibited from considering "political questions" because they can involve a usurpation of executive or legislative authority. Such disputes are characterized as "nonjusticiable" because they do not concern real and substantial controversies but are merely hypothetical or abstract.

For instance, a U.S. District Court (the primary trial court in the federal system, as explained in Chapter 2) could not determine in advance whether a proposed federal statute would be constitutional or unconstitutional even if Congress requested the court to do so. Even the U.S. Supreme Court, the highest appellate court in the country, could not entertain the case because there are no "real parties in interest" already directly affected by the proposed law.

ADMINISTRATIVE LAW

Although constitutional and statutory law prevail when they are in conflict with administrative law, administrative law is playing an increasingly important role as society grows more complex. Administrative law is quite simply that "body of law created by administrative agencies in the form of rules, regulations, orders and decisions."[7] Examples of such administrative agencies at the federal level are the Federal Communications Commission (which has primary authority over nearly all forms of broadcasting and telecommunications, including commercial broadcasting, cable television, satellites and interstate telephone communications), the Federal Trade Commission, the Interstate Commerce Commission, the Social Security Administration, the Veterans Administration and the Department of Education. Every state has similar agencies such as a department of transportation, an office of consumer protection and an insurance commission.

Each administrative agency (whether state, federal, or local) was created by a legislative act or acts and is responsible for implementing the so-called enabling legislation that created the agency as well as creating rules and regulations and issuing orders and decisions to carry out the legislative intent of the statutes. Thus these agencies typically perform both quasi-legislative and quasi-judicial functions — that is, creating laws in the form of rules and regulations and applying the law through case decisions. Occasionally, administrative agencies lock horns with the very legislatures that created them — such as the battle in the late 1970s between the Federal Trade Commission and Congress over proposed restrictions on television advertising aimed at young children. This issue, which was revived again in 1991, is discussed in Chapter 5, which also reviews the process by which agencies enact rules and regulations and make case decisions.

Finding a specific administrative law, especially at the federal level, is a fairly simple task. If you know the approximate date a rule was promulgated, consult the *Federal Register* (Fed. Reg.), where federal administrative rules and regulations are published chronologically. Otherwise, check the *Code of Federal Regulations* (C.F.R.) under the specific topic.

While most states publish their administrative rules and regulations in some official format, some do not. In the latter case, it may be necessary to contact the agency itself. Every state or local administrative agency is required, at a minimum, to make its rules and regulations available in some form so those individuals and entities they regulate will have constructive notice. In some cases, there may be a charge for the complete set of rules and regulations, although a few states provide a free set to anyone upon request and many provide free copies to news organizations.

All federal administrative decisions (both interpretative and enforcement) are available from the agencies themselves. Several agencies — such as the Federal Trade Commission, the Federal Communications Commission and the Interstate Commerce Commission — publish their own rules, which are also available through commercial publishers. An excellent general source for federal administrative agency and major federal and state trial and appellate court decisions affecting mass communication is the unofficial loose-leaf service, *Media Law Reporter*, published by the Bureau of National Affairs (BNA). The BNA, Commerce Clearinghouse (CCH) and Prentice-Hall (P-H) publish a wide variety of loose-leaf reporters on a broad range of topics, including mass communication, copyright, trademarks, antitrust and trade regulations and so on. These services are especially useful in updating the law because they are published on a regular schedule, usually weekly or monthly.

COMMON LAW

When the United States declared independence in 1776, all of the statutory and the case law of England and the colonies prior to that time became the "common law." This type of law still exists today, although its significance has declined considerably over the decades.

Whereas written laws in 13th- and 14th- century England could handle most problems, such statutes could not deal adequately and effectively with all disputes. Gradually, English courts, with the support of the monarchy, began basing some decisions solely on prevailing customs and traditions. These decisions blossomed into an expanding body of law that eventually became known as common law.

Inconsistencies naturally arose in this corpus of law because it was grounded in specific court decisions, rather than legislation. But these conflicts were gradually ironed out as decisions by more influential courts became precedents that effectively bound other courts to follow certain recognized legal principles. As the British colonists came to America, these precedents were generally accepted as American law as well. Common law thus adhered to the doctrine of *stare decisis*, discussed in the next chapter.

Common law is often called "judge-made law" and "case law," although these terms do not represent the total picture when it comes to common law. Judges, at least in theory, do not make law; they merely decide or ascertain the appropriate law and apply it to the given situation. In other words, the role of the judge is to determine the specific legal principle or principles appropriate to the particular case at hand, whether based on constitutional, statutory or common law. Critics sometimes characterize this responsibility as "discovering the law." Common law is based on previous cases, if they exist, but statutory law and constitutional law are occasionally not based on prior decisions.

One way to understand the nature of the common law is to realize that this body of law fills in the gaps left by statutory and constitutional law but is *always* inferior to statutes and the Constitution. If a conflict occurs between common law and constitutional law or between common law and statutory law, common law gives way.

Tracking down common law is sometimes difficult. The only official source is court decisions, which are generally collected in two forms — case reporters which are organized chronologically, and case digests, which are organized by topics. Every major federal court has at least one official or one unofficial case reporter for its decisions. U.S. Supreme Court cases are officially published by volumes in *United States Reports* (U.S.) and unofficially in *Supreme Court Reporter* (S.Ct.) by West Publishing and in *United States Supreme Court Reports Lawyers' Edition* (L.Ed. and L.Ed.2d) by Lawyers Cooperative Publishing Company.

"Official" means the reporter was published with government approval. "Unofficial" reporters are usually more comprehensive and informative than the "official" reporters because they typically include the complete text of a decision *plus* useful annotations not found in the "official" reporters.

U.S. Court of Appeals decisions from all 12 circuits (see Fig. 2.2) are published in the *Federal Reporter* (F.2d) by West. Prior to 1932, U.S. District Court decisions were also reported in the *Federal Reporter*, but since 1932, these decisions have appeared in West's *Federal Supplement* (F.Supp.). Most court decisions, whether state or federal, are not based on common law, and thus these reporters serve primarily as sources for cases dealing with statutory and constitutional law. Unfortunately, the only accurate and effective way to find the common law is by sorting through the cases in the reporters or digests, when they are available.

The highest appellate court in every state has at least one official reporter, and most have at least one unofficial reporter. All but a few states also report cases for their intermediate appellate courts. Reporters generally are not available for trial level courts, although more populous states, such as New York and California, publish at least some trial court decisions.

Most state appellate court decisions can be found in regional reporters published by West. For example, Georgia cases are in the South Eastern reporter, and Kentucky cases can be found in the South Western reporter. As noted earlier, reporters organize cases chronologically. Cases are also complied by topics in digests, which are very convenient to consult because they are divided into hundreds of legal subjects. West, for example, uses a "Key Word" scheme that makes cases very accessible.

A typical court decision, whether trial or appellate, usually touches on several topics and thus, if cited, can be readily tracked in a digest. Several digests are published for the federal courts, including *United States Supreme Court Digest* by West and *United States Supreme Court Digest, Lawyers Edition* by Lawyers Cooperative. Although these two digests contain only U.S. Supreme Court cases, summaries of decisions of all federal courts can be found in a series of digests published by West.[8]

EQUITY LAW

Although equity law falls at the bottom in the hierarchy of laws, it plays an important role in our judicial system, especially in communication law.

Equity law in this country can be traced to British courts of chancery that developed primarily during the 14th and 15th centuries. Over the decades, aggrieved individuals found that courts of law (i.e., common law) were often too rigid in the kinds of actions they could consider and the remedies they could provide. For example, courts of common law adhered to the maxim that damages (money) could right any wrong. But in many instances, such as disputes over land ownership, damages simply were not adequate. Parties then would appeal to the king for justice because the sovereign was above the law. Eventually, the king created special courts of chancery that could be used when a remedy at law was not available or was inadequate or unfair. One of the great strengths of equity law was that it could provide preventive action.

Whereas courts of law and courts of equity were separate in England for many centuries, today they are merged procedurally in the British courts and in all federal and nearly all state courts in the United States. Thus plaintiffs seeking equitable relief generally will file suit in the same court as they would in seeking a remedy at law. In fact, the suit could include a request for both relief at law and at equity or for either (for example, for equity or, in the alternative, for damages.) As discussed in the next chapter, however, some lower level or "inferior" courts in some states have either limited or no power of equity (i.e., authority to grant equitable relief.)

There are several major differences between equity law and common law that can be confusing to the uninitiated. Reporters, editors and other journalists who cover the courts are all too often unfamiliar with these crucial distinctions, leading to inaccurate and sometimes downright misleading information in stories.

First, equity decisions are strictly discretionary. As explained in Chapter 2, in many civil actions (this term is defined shortly), a court of law is required (usually by statute) to hear and render a decision in a particular case. On the other hand, courts of equity are generally not bound to hear any specific case. This discretionary power sometimes frustrates parties who feel they have strong justification for equitable relief, but are nevertheless unsuccessful in convincing a court of equity to entertain the case. For example, the equity court may simply dismiss the case as more appropriate for a court of law, or even grant damages at law while denying any equitable relief when both damages and an equitable remedy have been sought.

Second, there are certain recognized principles or maxims that equity follows but that are not applicable to actions at law. These include (a) "equity acts in personam," (b) "equity follows the law," (c) "equity looks upon that as done which ought to have been done," and (d) "equity suffers not a right without a remedy."[9]

"Equity acts in personam" means simply that equity courts grant relief in the form of judicial decrees rather than the traditional damages granted in courts of law. For example, a court of equity could issue an injunction (the different types of injunctions are examined in Chapter 3) prohibiting a credit bureau from disseminating further information about a particular consumer or, conversely, ordering the bureau to disclose its records to the consumer whom it had investigated. That same court could order an employer to rehire a fired employee or command an individual or company to comply with the terms of a contract (i.e., granting specific performance, as discussed in Chapter 3).

An example of the use of equity in communication law is a U.S. District Court ordering the Federal Trade Commission to reveal records requested by a media organization under the federal Freedom of Information Act.

"Equity follows the law" is the idea that equity courts will follow substantive rules already established under common law, where those rules are applicable. This does not mean, however, that equitable relief must be analogous to relief at law. Equity simply takes over where the common law ends.

One of the real limitations (although some litigants may justifiably perceive it as an advantage) of equity is that it will render relief, especially in contractual disputes, based on that which would be available if the final actions anticipated by the parties had occurred exactly as the parties would have expected them to be executed, *not* as the parties would actually have performed! This principle is congruent with the notion that equity decisions are based on fairness or justice, not according to strict rules of law. Thus "equity looks upon that as done which ought to have been done."

Even today remedies at law can be harsh, unjust, inappropriate or totally lacking, but "equity suffers not a right without a remedy." Whereas, generally, only money damages *per se* are available at law, equity can be broad and flexible. For example, a client who had contracted with the owner to purchase a unique or a very rare manuscript could seek an order for specific performance, which, if granted, would compel the owner to transfer possession and title (ownership) to the client. A court of law would be confined to monetary damages even though money would clearly be inadequate.

Third, equity cases are usually not tried before a jury. There are rare exceptions, such as divorce cases in Georgia (remember divorces are granted in the form of decrees) and in cases in which advisory juries are impaneled. For instance, in *Penthouse v. McAuliffe* (1981),[10] a U.S. District Court judge in Atlanta, Georgia, ruled that the X-rated version of the movie *Caligula* was not obscene because it had serious political and artistic value and did not appeal to prurient interests. Bob Guiccione, owner and publisher of *Penthouse* magazine, had purchased the rights to distribute the film in the United States, but prior to showing the film in Georgia, had sought in equity court a declaration that the film was not obscene and a permanent injunction prohibiting the county solicitor general (prosecuting attorney) from bringing criminal suit against him or anyone else involved with distributing or showing the film. On the advice of the jury, who viewed the movie and heard the evidence presented by attorneys for both sides, the judge declared the film was not obscene. (The judge did not grant the request for the injunction because he felt that declaring the movie was not obscene was tantamount to preventing any criminal actions against it.) Obviously Judge Richard C. Freeman was not bound by the advice of the jury (which can be impaneled in such cases under the Federal Rules of Civil Procedure), but he apparently felt this body of citizens was in the best position of evaluating whether the work violated contemporary community standards (a finding of fact under obscenity laws, as discussed in Chapter 11).

Juries may also be used in those cases in which the primary issue to be decided is one of law, although collateral issues and/or relief sought may be in equity.[11]

Finally, court procedures in equity courts differ somewhat from those in courts of law even though equity and common law courts have been merged. Reporters, editors and other journalists need to understand these distinctions when covering equity cases, but the details are beyond the scope of this book. A number of excellent references on equity are available, including Childres and Johnson's *Equity, Restitution and Damages*[12] and Shoben and Tabb's *Remedies.*[13]

CIVIL VERSUS CRIMINAL LAW

One of the most confusing concepts in our judicial system is civil law. Whereas the U.S. judicial system is based on common law, many other Western countries, such as Germany and France, and the state of Louisiana have judicial systems based on a civil code. Most of the civil code systems can trace their origins to the Roman Empire, in particular the Justinian Code (A.D. 529) and its successors (complied into the *Corpus Juris Civilis*).

The civil law of France was known as the "Code Civil," which later became the "Code Napoleon," from which most of the Louisiana Civil Code is derived.

There are other types of judicial systems, such as that of Vatican City, which is based on so-called ecclesiastical law or "religious" or "church law." Iran's law is also primarily ecclesiastical.

The confusion over civil law arises from the fact that legal actions in our common law system can be either civil or criminal. Civil law or actions in this sense refers to that body of law dealing with those cases in which an individual or legal entity (such as a corporation or partnership or even a governmental agency) is requesting damages or other relief from another individual or entity. Examples of civil actions are divorce, child custody, libel (except criminal libel), invasion of privacy (in most instances) and copyright infringement. The vast majority of court cases are civil, even though criminal cases tend to attract the most attention in the mass media.

A local, state or federal government can bring action against an individual or organization for the commission of a crime or crimes such as murder, burglary, rape and assault. (This can sometimes be a civil action as well.)

The judicial processes involved in criminal and civil cases differ substantially, as described in Chapter 3. Both state courts and federal courts have separate rules of procedure and separate rules of evidence in civil and criminal cases.

Whether a case is civil or criminal is not always readily apparent from the lineup of the litigants. Whereas the government (whether state or federal) is always the plaintiff (the party bringing the suit) in criminal cases, the government can be a plaintiff or a defendant (the party against whom the action is being brought) in a civil case. One easy way of making the distinction is to look at the possible result if the defendant loses. An individual can rarely be incarcerated in a civil action, except for civil contempt of court, as discussed in Chapter 2. On the other hand, the major objectives in a criminal case are to determine guilt or innocence and then to punish the guilty. Punishment can include fines, incarceration (jail and/or prison) and even execution for the commission of certain felonies. The primary purposes in civil actions are also to determine the guilt or innocence of the defendant and then to provide relief, when warranted, for the aggrieved plaintiff(s). Relief in a civil case can also include equity, of course. It should also be noted that punishment can be meted out in civil cases in the form of punitive damages (usually for intentional torts), but the punishment would not include incarceration (except for civil contempt).

TORTS VERSUS CONTRACTS

Civil actions (as defined earlier) are generally classified as arising either *ex contractu* (breach of contract) or *ex delicto* (tort). For example, a publisher who failed to properly (i.e., in good faith) market an author's work when the publisher had made a binding promise to do so could be held liable for damages at law to the author or, if warranted, ordered to perform the terms of the contract (specific performance). Such actions would be classified as *ex contractu* (breach of contract).

A newspaper that published false and defamatory information about an individual could be held liable for harm to the person's reputation. Such an action would be *ex delicto* (in tort).

A tort is simply "a private or civil wrong or injury, other than breach of contract, for which the court will provide a remedy in the form of an action for damages."[14]

The three basic elements of any tort action are (a) a legal duty owed a plaintiff by the defendant, (b) infringement on a legal right of the plaintiff by the defendant and (c) harm resulting from that infringement.

ETHICAL STANDARDS AND CODES OF ETHICS

Journalists who are content to "do my job" by simply reporting the facts and avoiding controversy and legal pitfalls will soon find themselves without much to communicate. It is difficult enough to escape legal sanctions, but it is virtually impossible to eschew ethical dilemmas.

The world was shocked in April 1981 when *Washington Post* editors announced they were returning a Pulitzer Prize for feature writing a mere two days after reporter Janet Cooke's story about an eight-year-old, third-generation heroin addict had captured journalism's top award. The newspaper's internal investigation, prompted by questions from other journalists about inconsistencies in the story and discrepancies in Cooke's biographical sketch that appeared with the sponsor's announcement of the prizes. The *Post's* inquiry revealed that Cooke had falsified much of the information in the story, including "Jimmy," whom the reporter confessed was a composite of young drug addicts described by social workers whom she had interviewed. The newspaper was severely criticized for publishing the story without knowing "Jimmy's" true identity, but managed to regain some of its credibility among at least some critics when it published a full disclosure of the details of the hoax in a report written by its ombud.[15]

Although it is rare for a journalist to have to return a Pulitzer Prize, the circumstances surrounding the Cooke episode are not all that unusual. Editors naturally rely on the word of their reporters, but there are times when journalists must be called to task before their stories hit the front pages. However, there are relatively few guidelines on what is ethical and what is unethical. Janet Cooke may have been as sincere in her belief that a composite was acceptable as editor Ben Bradlee was in his position that the story was wrong. (We still don't know the identity of Bob Woodward and Carl Bernstein's "deep throat," who helped the former *Washington Post* reporters earn a Pulitzer for the Watergate investigations that led to President Richard M. Nixon's downfall in 1974.)

Codes of ethics, unlike the law, are generally so nonspecific that even their staunchest advocates differ on how they would apply them and in their interpretations of their meaning. These codes, however, are useful as guidelines and certainly better than having no standards. The most widely known codes among mass communication professionals are (a) the *Society of Professional Journalists Code of Ethics*,[16] (b) the *American Society of Newspaper Editors Statement of Principles*, (c) the *Associated Press Managing Editors Code of Ethics*, (d) *Declaration of Principles of the Public Relations Society of America*, (e) *Standards of Practice of the American Association of Advertising Agencies* (f) the *Statement of Principles of Radio and Television Broadcasting* of the National Association of Broadcasters, (g) *the Code of Broadcast News Ethics of Radio-Television News Directors Association* and (h) *National Press Photographers, Inc. Code of Ethics*.

A few media outlets such as the *New York Times* and the *Washington Post* have developed their own codes of ethics, but such codes are more the exception than the rule. Even when there are codes, there is no assurance that the journalists supposedly bound by them are even familiar with their provisions and even less likelihood that they will abide by them even when they have read them. The problem is not that journalists are unethical or unwilling to honor codes of ethics—most journalists hold high ethical standards and try to abide by them—but rather that media professionals constantly face such a barrage of ethical dilemmas. Should rape victims be identified? Should a misspelled name that is accidentally published be corrected? What about an incorrect age? Should sports writers and broadcasters be allowed to accept free tickets to sporting events they cover? Are there circumstances under which the face of a corpse should be shown? Should media ads be screened prior to dissemination to ensure they are not misleading or deceptive? Some of the major television cable networks permit ads for "psychic advisers" — available via 900 toll numbers to counsel callers on matters from their love lives to the stock market — and "infommercials" for the usual get-rich-quick schemes (program-length commercials, as discussed in Chapter 5.)

SUMMARY

There are five major categories of law under our common law judicial system that form a hierarchy of authority: Constitutional law is at the top, followed by statutory law, administrative rules and regulations, common law and, finally, equity. The courts play a major role in the development of each type of law. Two of the most important roles are interpreting constitutional and statutory law and determining the constitutionality of statutes and administrative law.

The task of tracking down a particular law can range from simply reading the U.S. Constitution or a state constitution to getting a copy of a local ordinance. It is also important to check an official or unofficial reporter or a digest and read the case law, especially that of higher appellate courts such as the U.S. Supreme Court and the highest appellate court in a particular state.[17]

Civil cases are generally those in which a plaintiff (an individual, organization or government agency) requests damages and/or equitable relief from a defendant. Such cases can be either *ex contractu* (breach of contract) or *ex delicto* (tort). When the state (government) brings action against an individual or organization for the commission of a crime or crimes, the case is known as a criminal suit, and the penalties can range from a small fine to incarceration or even death for certain felonies.

Tracking down the sources for standards of ethics, on the other hand, is no easy task. Indeed, most of what we know about media ethics has been acquired with experience, although there are a few professional codes that provide some guidance. Unfortunately, these codes are typically so vague and general that yes or no answers are usually impossible. Perhaps this happenstance has been created more by the diversity of the mass media than by any unwillingness of journalists to come to grips with ethics. Thus it is not surprising that, according to one study, codes apparently do not have a direct impact on journalists' decisions.[18]

2 The U.S. Legal System

While the structure, functions and procedures of our judicial systems (federal and state) can be confusing, complex and even intimidating to the layperson, journalists must be familiar with not only the basics but with some of the intricacies as well. There are at least three major reasons for acquiring this knowledge.

First, all of the major news media are devoting substantially more coverage to judicial decisions and proceedings, especially civil and criminal trials and criminal pretrial proceedings, and to appellate court rulings. Some of this increased coverage can probably be explained by the series of U.S. Supreme Court decisions favoring greater access of the public and the press to the judicial process, as discussed in Chapter 9. Another explanation for the increase may be the fact that nearly all states now provide for regular access of video, film and still cameras to criminal and, in some cases, civil trials. It is certainly not unusual on an average weekday to see at least two or three stories in the local daily newspaper and on the local television newscasts focusing on a civil or criminal proceeding.

Major U.S. Supreme Court cases are usually decided each week the court is in session from the first Monday in October until late June or early July. These decisions frequently lead radio and television newscasts, including those of the major networks, and receive front-page attention in major dailies. Occasionally, even lower federal and state appellate court decisions attract headlines.

Second, the trend toward more specialized beats, such as consumer reporting and legal affairs, has accelerated the need for journalists to have a broad base of legal knowledge. For example, professional athletes and team owners and managers frequently engage in legal battles over contracts, antitrust issues and even potential liability for personal injuries suffered by spectators. The professional sports writer who can not distinguish a *judgment non obstante veredicto* from a *directed verdict* or a *summary judgment* from a *summary jury* may not be able to write a complete story about a major league baseball player's suit against a team mascot for injuries suffered in a home plate collision. Not only should the writer understand and know how to explain to the readers the issues being litigated in such a suit, but the person should also comprehend the basis or bases on which the case was decided at trial and later on appeal.

Third, significantly more communications law now involves court decisions than in the past. In fact, much of our knowledge of communications law is derived from cases decided in the last two decades in which trial and appellate courts have either established constitutional boundaries and limitations; interpreted federal or state statutes; or set, affirmed or rejected precedents at common law. In other words, law (whether constitutional, statutory, administrative, common or equity) usually has little meaning until an appropriate court or courts interpret the law and thus ultimately determine its impact.

Attorneys, judges and other legal experts sometimes hurl criticism and scorching comments at the press for what they perceive as weak, inaccurate and even distorted coverage of court cases. A law degree is not necessary for journalists to understand the judicial system, but they must possess a thorough and comprehensive background of the system and its processes. This chapter and Chapter 3 are designed to arm the reader with that information. As you struggle with the sometimes complex terms and concepts in this chapter, indeed throughout the text, remember that no journalist has ever faced a firing squad for possessing too much legal knowledge, but all too many of them have fallen prey to misusing and misunderstanding the law and legal matters and consequently endured the wrath of their peers, their readers and their sources.

THE FEDERAL COURT SYSTEM

Although we usually refer to *the* U.S. judicial system, there are actually 51 separate and distinct judicial systems. Each state has its own, and there is an independent federal judicial system.

As Figure 2.1 illustrates, there are three basic levels of courts in the federal system—U.S. District Courts, U.S. Courts of Appeals and the U.S. Supreme Court. Other specialized courts—such as U.S. Tax Court, U.S. Claims Court and U.S. Court of International Trade—are also part of the federal system, but these courts are rarely connected with communication law, and thus are not discussed here.[1]

The "work horse" or primary trial court in the federal system is the U.S. District Court. Every state has at least one such court and most states have two

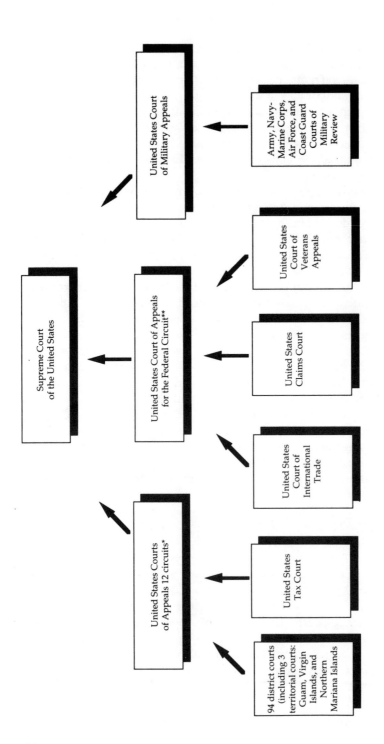

FIG. 2.1. The U.S. Court system.

* The 12 regional courts of appeals also review cases from a number of federal agencies.
** The Court of Appeals for the Federal Circuit also receives cases from the International Trade Commission, the Merit Systems Protection Board, the Patent and Trademark Office, and the Board of Contract Appeals.

or more, with highly populated states such as California, Texas, and New York with as many as four. Each district court serves a specific geographic area in that state (or can include an entire state, as in the case of Massachusetts, which has only one federal district court.) Altogether, there are 94 federal judicial districts and the number of judges in each ranges from 1 to 27, with fewer than 600 judges total.

A specific U.S. District Court is designated by the region it serves: for example, U.S. District Court for the Northern District of Georgia, U.S. District Court for the Eastern District of Kentucky, U.S. District Court for the Central District of California or U.S. District Court for the District of Massachusetts.

Before we examine the federal courts in more detail, seven concepts need to be explained — *venue, jurisdiction, diversity, trial court, appellate court, facts* and *law.*

As mentioned previously, U.S. District Courts are primarily trial courts. A *trial court*, also known as a court of original jurisdiction, is the court in which litigation in a case is likely to be initiated, and if an actual trial occurs, the court in which the trial will occur. Jury trials, discussed in the next chapter, take place only in trial courts. The primary purposes of any civil or criminal trial, whether a bench (judge only, no jury) or a jury trial, are (a) to seek to determine the *facts* in the case (similar to the traditional who, what, when, where, why and how used to organize a news story), (b) to ascertain the appropriate *law* or legal principles (whether constitutional, statutory, common or administrative law) in the case and (c) to apply those principles to the facts as determined at trial. As you will see in the next chapter, the function of a jury in a jury trial is to decide the facts and then apply the law, as ascertained by the judge, to those facts.

Although numerous studies have shown that most of the federal courts and many state courts are understaffed and overloaded with cases, the vast majority of both civil and criminal cases never go to trial. Only approximately 10 percent of all criminal cases ever come to trial because 60 percent of criminal cases result in a guilty plea and 30 percent are dismissed prior to a trial.[2] It is probably safe to assume that at least 90 percent of all civil cases are settled prior to trial as well.

What about appeals? If one were to gauge the percentage of cases that are appealed by the proportion of news stories that deal with appeals versus those covering trials, it would appear that a substantial percentage of civil and criminal cases are appealed. Even television shows and movies dealing with the law are replete with lawyers and their clients asserting, "I'm appealing this one." Fortunately, the fantasy world of television law does not match the real world of law or our courts would have to operate much differently.

A relatively small percentage of civil and criminal cases are appealed even though criminal defendants generally have a statutory or constitutional right to at least one appeal in almost all cases when they lose at trial. Both defendants and plaintiffs in civil cases have such a right. (It should be noted, however, that a higher percentage of criminal convictions than civil decisions are appealed.) In a civil case, usually only the losing side will appeal the decision, but in rare cases a plaintiff who is dissatisfied with the amount of damages awarded, for example, may appeal to a higher court (such as the U.S. Court of Appeals in the federal system) for a new trial on the basis that the damages awarded were inadequate. For instance, a libel plaintiff granted only nominal damages may appeal the jury or judge's decision even though that party technically won the case. In that same situation, the defendant may appeal the decision in hopes of having the verdict overturned.

Most appeals are made on grounds of either (a) errors in court procedures, such as presentation of evidence or jury instructions, or (b) errors in substantive law by the court, such as the judge applying the wrong criteria for determining whether a plaintiff is a public figure in a libel suit.

The appeal rights are considerably different in criminal cases than in civil cases. If an accused criminal is acquitted, the prosecution is prohibited from appealing the court's decision, whether by a judge or a jury even if new evidence against the defendant for the same crime(s) emerges later. The Fifth Amendment to the U.S. Constitution specifically prohibits double jeopardy ("nor shall any person be subject for the same offence to be twice put in jeopardy of life or limb"). Double jeopardy applies only to criminal charges, and a person acquitted of a particular crime can still be successfully sued for a similar civil offense using the same or similar evidence presented in the criminal suit. This seemingly strange situation occurs because the common standard of proof in civil cases is preponderance of the evidence rather than beyond a reasonable doubt, as explained in the next chapter.

If convicted, the criminal defendant can appeal the trial court's decision on grounds that range from violation of the Sixth Amendment right "to a speedy and public trial, by an impartial jury of the State and district wherein the crime shall have been committed" to failure of the state (i.e., the prosecutor) to prove its case beyond a reasonable doubt. (For example, prejudicial pretrial or during trial publicity, examined in Chapter 9, can be shown to have violated a defendant's Sixth Amendment right to an impartial jury.)

Once the defendant (now the appellant or petitioner) files an appeal, that individual effectively waives a claim of double jeopardy. Appellate courts lack authority to ascertain guilt or innocence because this determination is a question of fact for the trial court, not a question of law. Thus the appellate court could order a new trial, pending further appeals, but it cannot declare the appellant guilty or not guilty.

Therefore, the criminal defendant granted a new trial by the appellate court could be retried for the same offense(s), but any new trial would have to follow closely the guidelines or standards established by the appellate court.

For instance, three men sentenced to die by a Georgia trial court in the murder of six members of the same family were granted new trials by an 11th Circuit U.S. Court of Appeals more than 14 years after their convictions because of "prejudicial pretrial publicity." One of the men was reconvicted three years after the original convictions were overturned by the federal appellate court and again given the death sentence after a jury trial. A second defendant received a life sentence after a jury deadlocked on the death penalty. The third man also faced only a life sentence because the county prosecutor did not seek the electric chair for him, thanks to a new state statute prohibiting the execution of mentally retarded defendants.

A filtering process further assures that higher appellate courts, such as state supreme courts and the U.S. Supreme Court, consider a very small percentage of cases from lower appellate and trial courts. As indicated later in this chapter, the U.S. Supreme Court can exercise its discretion and refuse to hear most appeals. Thus it typically grants full-scale review to no more than about 150 to 200 of the approximately 5,000 cases appealed to it each year. By comparison, in 1990, some 31 million civil and criminal cases were filed in state courts. And for the year ending on June 30, 1991, the U.S. District Courts decided 211,713 civil cases and 41,569 criminal cases; the U.S. Courts of Appeals handed down decisions in 41,414 cases in the same year.[3]

The Georgia case (popularly known as the "Alday family murders" case) illustrates another major appellate right of convicted criminals. A defendant convicted in any **state** court may appeal to a **federal** court (either the Court of Appeals or the Supreme court) through a writ of habeas corpus on grounds that the person's constitutional rights (typically Fifth or Sixth Amendment rights) were violated during the judicial process that led to conviction. If it believes such grounds may exist, the federal court has the discretion to hear the appeal and to order a new trial in state court, if warranted. All the federal court needs to do to hear the appeal is to simply issue the writ of habeas corpus, which then requires police to release the prisoner until the legality of the detention can be established.

In the so-called Dr. Sam Sheppard[4] case analyzed in Chapter 9, the U.S. Supreme Court granted a writ of habeas corpus when it agreed to hear Sheppard's appeal of a murder conviction on grounds of prejudicial publicity. The osteopath had been serving 12 years of a life sentence in an Ohio state prison but was freed, pending the outcome of a new trial, when the court issued the writ and overturned his conviction. Even the highest court in the land, like all appellate courts, lacks the authority to decide a defendant's guilt or innocence. Thus the Supreme Court could merely order Sheppard freed until a new trial could be conducted. Previous appeals by Sheppard and his lawyers had failed, including one made earlier to the Supreme Court. Sheppard was ultimately acquitted at trial by a state jury, but his fate is unusual because most individuals who win new trials in criminal cases are subsequently found guilty again.

VENUE VERSUS JURISDICTION

No state or federal court has the authority to render a judgment unless it has both *jurisdiction* and *venue* in the case. Jurisdiction, the legal right of a court to exercise authority in a particular case, is an enormously complex concept that has been the subject of many scholarly books, treatises and law review articles. Attorneys have to be familiar with such terms as pendent, ancillary, concurrent and primary jurisdiction, but, for our purposes, only *personal* and *subject matter jurisdiction* are relevant.

Personal jurisdiction (also called *in personam jurisdiction*) is the authority of the court over a defendant in a given case. Unless the court possesses personal jurisdiction over the defendant, the court cannot effect a binding judgment against that individual or other entity. The federal and state rules regarding personal jurisdiction can be highly complex, especially in their application, but one of the viable grounds for appeal by a defendant in a civil case can be that the trial court lacked in personam jurisdiction.

In the case of property, whether personalty (such as an automobile or a book) or realty (land and that which is attached to it such as a building), the court must also have jurisdiction *in rem* before it can establish the rightful ownership of that property when there is a dispute.

Jurisdiction of the subject matter ("subject matter jurisdiction") is simply the power of the court to hear a particular type of case. Most state court systems include a two-tiered trial court structure. Usually the system includes a lower trial court with *limited jurisdiction* that can adjudicate only those civil cases in which the amount in dispute is less than a specified monetary sum and/or only certain criminal cases such as misdemeanors (but no felonies). A higher trial court typically has *general jurisdiction* or the authority to hear all civil and criminal cases that can be tried in that court system, including those that could have been heard in the lower trial court (but which the higher trial court permitted to bypass the lower court).

Examples of subject matter are divorce, equity, felonies, misdemeanors, child custody and contracts. Even if a particular court could have personal jurisdiction over the parties to the suit, the court cannot hear that case unless it also has subject matter jurisdiction. On rare occasions, an appellate court will reverse a trial court decision on grounds that the lower court lacked jurisdiction (either personal or subject matter). Usually it is clear which specific court (or courts) has jurisdiction, but the U.S. Supreme Court and other appellate courts have struggled for decades with the issue of jurisdiction, especially *jurisdiction in personam*.

Venue, a relatively simple concept compared to jurisdiction, is the county or other geographical area where a case is to be litigated. Journalists often confuse jurisdiction with venue, but the concepts are *not* synonymous. An easy way to remember the difference is to keep in mind that venue bears only on the specific geographic location where the case is to be tried or recall that venue is derived from the French, *venire* ("a coming"), and the Latin, *venire* ("to come").

Ascertaining proper venue involves two major steps. First, a determination must be made of which particular type of court has both personal and subject matter jurisdiction to hear the case. (In diversity cases and in a limited number of other types of cases, as discussed in the next chapter, both a state court and a U.S. District Court may have jurisdiction. Thus the case could be heard in either court but not both.)

In a libel suit, for instance, in which a citizen in Tennessee is suing a newspaper whose primary place of business is in Alabama, a U.S. District Court in Tennessee would likely have both personal and subject matter jurisdiction. Once a judicial determination has been made that a U.S. District Court has such jurisdiction, the question of venue faces the court and the parties. In the vast majority of cases, this question is easily resolved. In the libel case at hand, the U.S. District Court in Alabama whose geographic authority included the city or town in which the newspaper is published would have venue authority. As discussed in Chapter 7, venue in such a libel suit **could** (but not necessarily **would**) lie in another U.S. District Court, such as the plaintiff's state of residence or domicile (Tennessee in this case), if a substantial number of copies of the newspaper were distributed there. Venue could also lie in an Alabama or Tennessee state trial court (assuming that court had jurisdiction).

In summary, think of *jurisdiction* as the authority of a specific type of court such as a state *circuit* court as opposed to a state *district* court, for example, to hear the particular subject matter(s) in the case (for instance, worker's compensation or divorce) **and** the authority over the parties in the suit (especially the defendant). *Venue* is simply the specific court, from a geographic perspective, of that type or level of court (U.S. District Court, state superior court, etc.) in which the case can be litigated.

These distinctions are not trivial. Thus a reporter writing a news story about an invasion of privacy suit should be specific in citing the court on first reference: for example, the "U.S. District Court for the Eastern District of Kentucky" or the "Fulton County (Georgia) Superior Court" and not simply "in a federal court" or "in a superior court."

Here's one more tip for covering court stories. Federal prosecutors in criminal cases generally must try a defendant in the district where the crime occurred, as required under the Sixth Amendment discussed earlier. This constitutional restriction on venue, however, does not prevent a defendant from being granted, upon request, a change to the same type or level of court in another location *within that state*. By requesting this voluntary change of venue, the defendant effectively waives a Sixth Amendment right to be tried in the state or district where the crime was allegedly committed. A change of venue is usually granted by the judge when adverse pretrial and/or during trial publicity is likely to interfere with the defendant's Sixth Amendment "right to a speedy and public trial, by an impartial jury," often characterized as the right to a fair trial. On rare occasions, a change of venue would be made when important witnesses in a civil or criminal case would have difficulty appearing.

Most state constitutions or statutes have venue requirements similar to those under federal law. Although subject matter and personal jurisdiction can usually be challenged during an appeal even though they were unchallenged earlier, any objections to a court's venue must be established by the defendant early in the suit (usually no later than in a pretrial motion to dismiss or in the answer) or be deemed waived.

Can a trial court choose not to hear a civil suit even though the court meets all of the statutory and constitutional requirements for venue? In relatively rare situations in which another trial court satisfies all of the venue requirements *and* in which a clearly more convenient forum than that selected by the plaintiff can be found, a court may invoke a judicial doctrine known as *forum non conveniens*, a discretionary power of the court to decline jurisdiction. This power can be invoked only when (a) a defendant files a motion to dismiss based on *forum non conveniens*, (b) the plaintiff's forum is clearly inconvenient for the litigants and/or witnesses, and (c) there is another forum in which the suit can be brought. *Forum non conveniens* is always discretionary on the part of the court, and thus the judge could still permit the case to be heard even if all of the aforementioned conditions were met. In fact, many states have statutes that prohibit a court from granting a motion to dismiss on grounds of *forum non conveniens* if the plaintiff is a legal resident of the state in which the suit has been brought.

Forum non conveniens per se is no longer a real issue in the federal courts because Congress codified the doctrine in what is known as a *transfer statute*. Under 28 U.S.C.A. §1404, a federal trial court can transfer a case to another court within the same court system in which the suit could have been filed originally. Obviously, the other court would also have to have both proper jurisdiction and venue in the case. There are two major differences, however, between the traditional *forum non conveniens* and transfer — either side may request a transfer and the cause of action is not dismissed and then brought again in the new court when there is a transfer, as it is done for *forum non conveniens*. However, transfers can only occur when the two courts involved are in the same system. Thus *forum non conveniens* would have to be used for changing from a federal court to a state court or vice versa, and for changing from a court in one state to one in another state.

TRANSITORY VERSUS LOCAL CAUSES OF ACTION

In civil cases in state courts, lawsuits can be distinguished as either *transitory* or *local*. If a cause of action is deemed local, the plaintiff can file suit only in the specific court designated by statute or by a provision in the state constitution. Local actions nearly always involve real property, whether the dispute is over ownership, alleged trespassing or damage to real property. Thus the suit must be brought in the county in which the property is located.

Transitory causes of action, on the other hand, can be brought in "any court of general jurisdiction in any district wherein the defendant can be found and served with process" (i.e., with the complaint or petition).[5] Transitory actions do require what is commonly called "minimum contacts" in the case of a foreign corporation or a nonresident defendant. ("Foreign," by the way, means out-of-state, not just out-of-the-country.) The U.S. Supreme Court first adopted the "minimum contacts" test for assuring due process for in personam jurisdiction in 1945 in *International Shoe Company v. Washington*.[6] In a series of cases since *International Shoe*,[7] the Court has established minimum contacts, "fair play" and "substantial justice" as the constitutional standard for personal jurisdiction.

Because the test of minimum contacts is quite complex, we forgo further discussion for now, but this topic reappears in Chapter 7, thanks to two major 1984 U.S. Supreme Court libel decisions.

THE U.S. COURT OF APPEALS

As discussed earlier, appellate courts such as the U.S. Court of Appeals are not trial courts but merely serve to consider appeals from trial courts. Such appeals are usually based on alleged violations of procedural and/or substantive law. State and federal appeals courts generally have three basic options with any appeal they hear: (a) **affirm** or reverse the criminal or civil verdict or judgment of the lower trial court, (b) **dismiss** the appeal or (c) **remand** (send back) the case to the trial court for further consideration (usually for proceedings consistent with the appellate court's decision). The court also has the option of reversing the trial court decision but sending the case back with an order to dismiss.

The federal court system, as shown in Fig. 2.2, features 13 intermediate Courts of Appeals, each of which has limited jurisdiction over a specific geographical area or *circuit*. Eleven of these circuits are numbered, but one is designated the U.S. Court of Appeals for the District of Columbia Circuit (no number). The 13th circuit, the Court of Appeals for the Federal Circuit, is the only federal appellate court, other than the U.S. Supreme Court, with national jurisdiction. The geographic areas of the 11 numbered circuits varies from three to nine states. These 11 plus the D.C. Circuit handle approximately 33,000 appeals each year,[8] the vast bulk of which is from the lower district courts, U.S. Tax Court and federal administrative agencies.

The Court of Appeals for the Federal Circuit has *exclusive appellate jurisdiction* over some 15 specific types of cases, such as final decisions of the

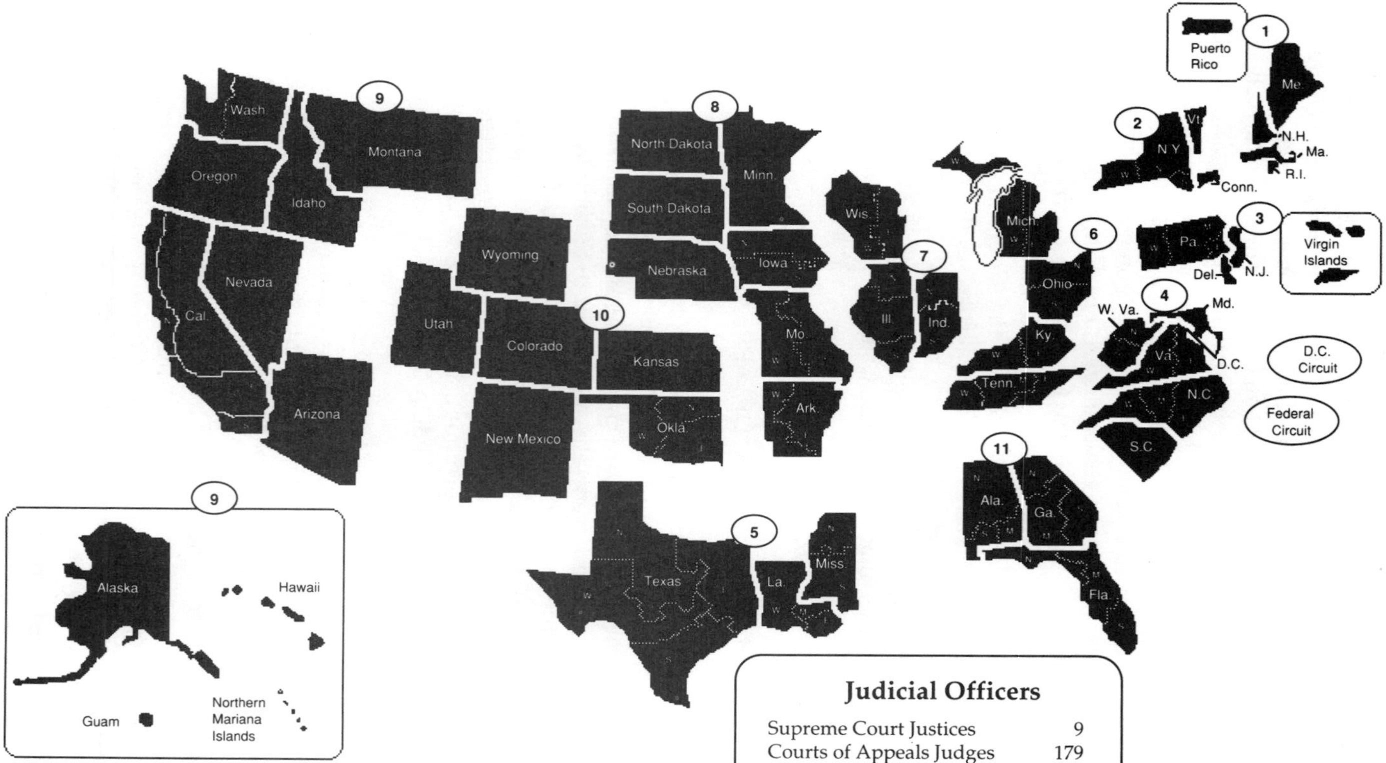

Judicial Officers

Supreme Court Justices	9
Courts of Appeals Judges	179
District Judges	649
Bankruptcy Judges	291
Magistrate Judges	
Full-time	345
Part-time	124

FIG. 2.2. Number and composition of federal judicial circuits.

28

U.S. Claims Court and the Court of International Trade, and most patent appeals. *Exclusive jurisdiction* (whether original or appellate) is, as the term implies, the power of that specific court to hear and decide that particular matter to the exclusion of any other court. *Nonexclusive jurisdiction* means, of course, that one or more other courts could hear the case, although not at the same time. All of the federal courts have original and exclusive jurisdiction over certain types of cases, such as violations of federal laws, but this jurisdiction varies from court to court. For example, the federal courts have original and exclusive jurisdiction over all controversies between two or more states. Federal courts also have *concurrent jurisdiction* with state courts in certain types of cases, such as those involving *diversity* or actions between citizens of different states, as described in the next chapter.

THE U.S. SUPREME COURT

Certainly no court in this country, and probably in the world, has attracted more media and public attention than the U.S. Supreme Court. In the 1988 U.S. presidential election, for example, both the Republican candidate, Vice President George Bush, and the Democratic candidate, Massachusetts' Governor Michael Dukakis, frequently discussed their views on the type of justices that should be appointed to the court. In the second and last televised debate between the presidential nominees, Bush and Dukakis sparred over the qualifications to be considered by the President in nominating justices to the court. (The debate also touched on the selection process for other federal judges.) Four years later, in 1992, President Bush and Democratic nominee Bill Clinton renewed the debate over U.S. Supreme Court justices, intensified by the Court's 5–4 decision in June in *Planned Parenthood v. Casey*,[9] which upheld several state restrictions on abortion, including a 24-hour waiting period. President Bush's two appointees to the Court – Associate Justice David Souter (who replaced William J. Brennan, Jr., in 1990) and Associate Justice Clarence Thomas (who filled the slot of the retired Thurgood Marshall in 1991) – made pivotal votes in important decisions, including those with a First-Amendment focus. When conservative Associate Justice Byron White announced in March 1993 that he was retiring at the end of the Court's 1992–1993 term, President Clinton spent five months deciding on his nominee to replace Justice White. On August 10, Ruth Bader Ginsberg became the 107th Supreme Court justice, the second woman on the Court. She was the first justice nominated by a Democratic President in 26 years. A look at the history and the constitutional authority of the court indicates such intense interest and attention may be justified.

Distinguishing Characteristics
of the U.S. Supreme Court

The U.S. Supreme Court is unique in several significant ways. First, it is the only court specifically established by the U.S. Constitution. As noted earlier,

Article 3, §1 of the Constitution creates "one supreme Court," while granting Congress the authority to ordain and establish "inferior courts," if it so chooses. Thus Congress could constitutionally abolish all of the federal courts except the Supreme Court. As noted previously, the Supreme Court does have original jurisdiction over specific types of cases enumerated in Article 3, §2(2), but the Court functions primarily as an appellate court. Typically, the Court apparently decides one or two original jurisdiction cases each nine-month term, although there have been several terms in this decade when the Court has decided none.

In contrast, under its appellate jurisdiction, the Court usually hears oral arguments and issues decisions for about 200 cases each term from the approximately 5,000 it is formally requested to consider.[10]

Second, the U.S. Supreme Court, as one of the three branches of government (along with the President and Congress) both interprets and applies the U.S. Constitution in cases in which the other branches play a role. In other words, the Court is the final arbiter of the Constitution. This authority is quite wide-ranging and has invoked considerable controversy over the years, but especially in the last two decades. The debate is usually framed in terms of a "liberal versus a conservative court" but really revolves around the issue of whether the Court merely interprets the law or both interprets and makes the law. Former President Ronald Reagan was particularly proud of the fact that he had been able to select (with approval of the U.S. Senate) Chief Justice William H. Rehnquist (who had been nominated as Associate Justice during President Richard M. Nixon's reign) and Associate Justices Sandra Day O'Connor, Antonin Scalia and Anthony M. Kennedy.[11] President George Bush, as indicated earlier, had the opportunity to nominate two Associate Justices—Souter in 1990 and Thomas the next year.[12] President Clinton has had the opportunity to appoint only one justice so far—Ruth Bader Ginsberg.

Third, the process by which the Supreme Court reviews cases is intricate but fascinating. Whereas other federal courts and some state courts may follow some of the steps followed by the Supreme Court in its decision making, the process, as a whole, is rather unique. There are three ways in which a case can be heard on appeal by the Court—*direct appeal*, *writ of certiorari* and *certification*. The grounds on which each of these types of appeals can be heard are enumerated in Title 28 of the U.S. Code Annotated.

Mandatory versus Discretionary Jurisdiction

Until 1988, under Title 28 and other federal statutes, some litigants had, theoretically, a right to have an appeal heard by the Supreme Court. For example, if a U.S. Court of Appeals held that a state statute or treaty was invalid because it violated the Constitution, laws or treaties of the United States, the state had a statutory right to have the case ultimately decided by the

Supreme Court. A similar right existed if the state's highest appellate court held the statute or treaty unconstitutional. For at least the last half century, however, the Supreme Court rejected the vast majority of such appeals "for want of a properly presented federal question" or "because of the inadequacy of the record"[13] or other basis. Thus a seemingly obligatory appeal was, in practice, discretionary.

In 1988, the picture changed dramatically for mandatory jurisdiction. For almost a decade Congress tried unsuccessfully to grant the unanimous request of the U.S. Supreme Court that it be given greater choice in selecting cases for review. More specifically, the justices called for Congress to essentially kill the body's mandatory jurisdiction. With the support of the Reagan administration, Chief Justice Rehnquist and various legal organizations such as the American Bar Association, a bill passed Congress that granted the Court's wish. Congressman Robert Kastenmeier (D-Wis.), chairman of the House subcommittee on courts, characterized the new statute as the "most significant jurisdictional reform affecting the high court in over 60 years."[14]

Over the years Congress had narrowed or eliminated various mandatory appeals that ranged from antitrust cases to suits contesting the constitutionality of state and federal statutes, but it took the 1988 legislation to kill nearly all appeals based on mandatory jurisdiction. To understand the real impact of this statute, one must realize that during its 1987–1988 term, the Court handled 248 mandatory appeals, with 206 being decided summarily (i.e., without full briefing or oral argument), including 120 dismissed for lack of jurisdiction and 83 for lack of a federal question.[15] Thirty-two of the appeals were actually accepted for review, none of which the Court would have had to have decided if the 1988 legislation had been in effect at that time.[16] Remember that the court typically decides only about 200 cases on the merits each term, which means that about one-fifth of the load was mandatory jurisdiction. It should also be noted that these summary decisions were nevertheless binding on state and other federal courts because they had been decided on the merits. Thus typically the lower courts would have little or no guidance beyond the vote of the Court.

The 1988 law, which amended or repealed several sections of Title 28, did not eliminate all mandatory jurisdiction. Specific appeals under the Civil Rights and Voting Rights Acts and the Presidential Election Campaign Act retain their mandatory status.[17]

The 1988 law left intact another way in which the court could hear an appeal—*certification*. Under §1254(3) of Title 28, questions of law in any civil or criminal case can be certified by a court of appeals to the Supreme Court. For example, if a U.S. Court of Appeals is uncertain about the constitutionality of a new federal criminal statute, it can certify this question of law to the Supreme Court for a determination. As with all other judicial cases, there must be a real case in controversy; the federal courts, including the Supreme Court, are prohibited from deciding purely political questions because they are not "justiciable" matters for the courts.

Writ of Certiorari

By far the most common way and now virtually the only way cases are heard by the Supreme Court is *writ of certiorari*. There are three major situations in which the Court will hear an appeal under this writ: before or after judgment or decree in a civil or criminal case in a court of appeals; final judgments or decrees of a state's, Puerto Rico's or DC's highest appellate court involving the constitutionality of a state or federal treaty or statute or any title, right or privilege claimed under the U.S. Constitution; and certain types of decisions by the U.S. Court of Military Appeals. Most states have abandoned this discretionary writ in their courts, but Congress and the Supreme Court continue to cling to what many legal critics contend is an outmoded process.

"Granting cert" (press and legal shorthand for granting a writ of certiorari) is a relatively simple process by which the Supreme Court (after agreeing to hear a case) formally orders the lower appellate court to certify the record and then turn it over to the Supreme Court. As discussed later, denial by the Supreme Court of the request to issue the discretionary writ is tantamount to a denial of the party's appeal.

Certiorari begins when an attorney for one side in a case (nearly always the losing side) files a written petition with the Supreme Court. Such petitions can be filed in other courts, but they are much less common now than in the past. Under a working rule adopted by the court and known as the "rule of four," four justices must agree to hear the appeal before the Court will review the lower court decision. This rule is based on the belief that a legal question is substantial enough to be considered when at least four members are willing to grant a writ of certiorari. When four votes are not available, which occurs about 90 percent of the time, the petition is thereby denied and the lower court (i.e., the last court in which the appeal was decided) ruling stands. Although news stories occasionally unintentionally mislead the public into believing otherwise, denial does not necessarily mean that the Court agrees with the lower court decision but merely that the justices did not feel the appeal warranted their attention, probably because of the lack of a major legal issue. When the Court declines to hear an appeal, it is both inaccurate and unethical to publish or broadcast that the Court "upheld" the lower court decision.

Appellate Briefs and Oral Arguments

If the Court votes to hear the case, the writ is then issued and a tentative date is set for oral arguments. Prior to the oral hearing, however, the attorneys for the two sides are required by a specified deadline to submit written briefs detailing their positions and arguments. A well-written *appellate brief* will normally contain an extended statement of the issues involved, a summary of the facts in the trial court case, relevant laws, arguments based on the law and trial and appellate court decisions that support that position and a summary of and justification for the particular relief sought.

The form and often the content of appellate briefs are usually dictated by the particular court hearing the appeal, and the U.S. Supreme court is no exception. There are other types of briefs, such as a trial brief, but these are not the same as appellate briefs. Although they presumably summarize, appellate briefs are rarely "brief" and are typically quite lengthy and detailed. The briefs are presumably read by all of the justices before the oral arguments, which typically last 30 minutes for each side. The Court is quite strict about the time frame, and the justices, including the Chief Justice, will often interrupt the presenting attorneys arguments with questions, which can be quite pointed, while the time is running. It is not unusual, in a major case, for the attorney to fail to complete oral arguments because of these interruptions. Except in very rare cases, such as those involving sensitive national security matters, the oral arguments are open to the press and to the public, unlike Supreme Court deliberations, which are always secret.

Deliberations

Later, the justices deliberate in chambers to hammer out a decision. The sessions are so secret that even the law clerks and assistants are excluded. The discussion begins with the Chief Justice enunciating his views (although usually not his vote), followed by the Associate Justices in order of seniority (highest to lowest) on the Court. According to books purporting to offer insights into the Court such as Bob Woodward's *The Brethren*, the views and subsequent votes sometimes change as they attempt to forge a majority opinion. Tentative votes are usually taken first, but when the final vote is made, the justices state their decisions beginning with the justice with the shortest tenure on the court on up to the most senior, with the Chief Justice voting last in the case of a tie. If the Chief Justice is a member of the majority in the decision, he or she has the option of writing the majority opinion or designating the justice who will write the opinion. If the Chief Justice is in the minority, the most senior justice in the majority can write the opinion or select the justice to do so.

Types of Opinions

Initially, the draft of a majority opinion is written, usually with the assistance of law clerks, and then circulated to the other members, including those in the minority. Each justice has the option of (a) agreeing with the majority opinion,

(b) writing a separate *concurring opinion* agreeing with the conclusions, outcome or result of the majority opinion but disagreeing with the majority's reasons or rationale, (c) writing a *dissenting opinion* disagreeing with the majority opinion's conclusions, outcome, reasons and rationale, or (d) concurring with the majority in part and dissenting in part. For the latter, the justice agrees with a portion or portions of the majority opinion but disagrees with another portion or portions.

Majority opinions are ideal because they can establish a *precedent* to guide future cases, but sometimes justices cannot reach a majority opinion or they may wish to merely issue a brief majority opinion. When less than a majority of justices join an opinion but more than in any concurring opinion, a *plurality opinion* occurs. Plurality opinions never establish precedents, but they sometimes influence lower court decisions, as witnessed by the Supreme Court's three-justice plurality decision in *Rosenbloom v. Metromedia*,[18] a 1971 libel case. Although the Court explicitly rejected the plurality decision three years later, many lower courts, especially trial courts, adopted the rule cited in the plurality opinion that the actual malice rule of *New York Times v. Sullivan*[19] included "involuntary public figures." Another type of opinion worthy of attention is the *per curiam opinion*. Occasionally, the Supreme Court will issue an unsigned opinion written by one or more justices but representing the views of the whole Court rather than by one particular justice. (Other appellate courts also issue this type of opinion.) Such per curiam opinions are usually brief because they require the agreement of each justice. There are many theories about why the Court issues per curiam opinions, which include the desire by each justice not to have his or her name specifically attached to the opinion (the opinion is simply "by the Court"). Per curiam decisions, even in First Amendment cases, are fairly uncommon, but they have occurred in major media law cases, such as the famous "Pentagon Papers" case[20] discussed in Chapter 4.

A final option of the Court is a *memorandum decision* in which the Court gives its ruling in the case but offers no opinion. It should be noted that a memorandum decision is technically not a judgment but merely an announcement of the Court's vote. Such decisions, which can be rather frustrating for litigants who are looking for precise answers, are becoming more common as the workload of the Court continues to increase each year.

Terms of Service on the Court

Much of aura surrounding the Supreme Court can be attributed to the fact that justices are appointed for life[21] and can be removed from office only upon impeachment. Many justices have served on the Court until their deaths, with some staying on the Court even in their 80s. Although there have been instances in which suggestions have been made that particular justices be impeached, such as Michigan Congressman Gerald Ford's[22] campaign to have Associate Justice William O. Douglas impeached in the late 1960s, only one U.S. Supreme Court Justice has ever been impeached. The U.S. House of Representatives impeached Associate Justice Samuel Chase (not to be confused with Samuel P. Chase, who joined the Court later and served as Chief Justice) in 1804 for his political activities outside the courtroom while he was still serving on the Court. The U.S. Senate, however, could not muster enough votes to convict him.[23]

In recent years, the trend has been for the President to nominate relatively young justices to serve on the Court in order to ensure that a conservative majority sits on the Court for many years to come, regardless of who may become President later. For example, Associate Justice Clarence Thomas, the only African-American serving on the Court, was 43 when he was approved 52–48 to succeed Associate Justice Thurgood Marshall in October 1991 by the Senate in one of the closest votes in Supreme Court history. His nomination by President George Bush was extremely controversial because of his staunchly conservative views; the Senate approved the chief executive's choice in spite of an unprecedented Senate Judicial Committee extended hearing over University of Oklahoma Law Professor Anita Hill's sexual harassment allegations.

Size of the Court

One common myth about the Supreme Court specifies that the U.S. Constitution requires the court to have nine justices. In fact, the Constitution does not provide for any specific number; instead Congress was left with the task of setting the number. Before Congress set the number in 1867 at nine (which has continued to today), the number of justices on the Court changed six times and ranged from 6 to 10. As of the publication date of this book, 107 justices have served on the Court, 16 of whom have been Chief Justice, including the current Chief Justice, William H. Rehnquist. Only five Associate Justices later became Chief Justice.

According to another myth, President Franklin Delano Roosevelt appointed the most members to the Court. Actually, President George Washington holds the record because he appointed the six original justices plus another four during his second term. President Roosevelt is second, however, because he appointed eight justices and selected Associate Justice Harlan Fiske Stone as Chief Justice. President Ronald Reagan appointed three justices and picked Associate Justice Rehnquist as Chief Justice. President George Bush, as already discussed, had the chance to appoint two Associate Justices, and President Clinton has appointed one so far.

The Court's Schedule

The Supreme Court adheres to a rather strict schedule. Each annual session begins on the first Monday in October and typically ends by the July 4 holiday.

Court sessions alternate among hearings, delivering opinions and recesses. Hearings and opinions are known as "sittings." The usual rotation between sittings and recess is every 2 weeks. Opinions are written during the recesses. The sittings begin at 10:00 a.m. each day and typically end by 3:00 p.m. About two dozen cases are heard during each sitting, but the Court conducts other business during this time; it may release a list of orders, admit new attorneys to the Court bar and release opinions. Opinions are not announced in advance, and thus reporters and others covering the Court do not know which opinions will be released on any given day, lending an element of surprise to the proceedings. (Oral arguments, of course, and some of the other business are announced in advance.) Public sessions are conducted only on Mondays, Tuesdays and Wednesdays. During May and June, the last two months of its sessions, the Court conducts no other public business except to announce opinions. When the last opinion has been announced, usually in late June, the Court recesses until the following October. It should be noted, however, that during the summer hiatus numerous petitions for review and motions are processed.

Mootness, Ripeness and Standing

Before this discussion of the Supreme Court ends, three more terms need to be explained—*mootness*, *ripeness* and *standing*. Legal scholars sometimes refer to these concepts as the three horsemen. *Mootness* refers to the refusal of a court to hear a case when the outcome has already been determined, and thus any decision by the Court would have no impact on the case. In other words, the Court will not decide "dead" or merely academic issues. From time to time, the Supreme Court will deny certiorari in a case on the grounds that the issue in the case is nonjusticiable. The basis for this refusal is, once again, that Article III, 2, of the U.S. Constitution restricts all federal courts, including the U.S. Supreme Court, to real "cases" and "controversies." For example, a fired government "whistleblower" who sues his federal employer for violating his First Amendment rights but subsequently settles out-of-court will not be permitted to continue his suit simply to have the Court determine whether his rights were violated even if any claim for damages is sought. In most cases, the death of a plaintiff does *not* render a suit moot. For example, if a plaintiff in a libel suit dies before the case comes to trial or dies while a case is being appealed, the legal representative(s) can continue the case on the victim's behalf.

A second obstacle that may confront litigants or appellants in a case is lack of *ripeness*. Citing Article III, §2, the Court will sometimes refuse to hear a case because it feels the controversy is not ready ("ripe") for review. The rationale for this "ripeness doctrine" is to prevent courts from engaging in premature, abstract or political decisions. For example, a newspaper that wanted to challenge the constitutionality of a *proposed* federal law restricting access to government records would not be able to have its case decided because this issue is not ripe for consideration. Instead of hearing the suit, the Court would dismiss it and probably note that the newspaper must wait until the law is enacted *and* the paper is actually denied access and thus suffers some harm or abridgement of its First Amendment rights.

Finally, litigants in federal court must have *standing* to avail themselves of justice in the federal courts. Standing has been interpreted to mean a plaintiff must have suffered actual injury or be threatened with injury in the case of governmental action. In other words, this "standing to sue" doctrine requires that a party be "sufficiently affected so as to insure that a justiciable controversy is presented to the court."[24]

For example, suppose Congress passes a new law permitting states to impose taxes on newspapers that endorse political candidates. Such a discriminatory law would clearly be unconstitutional in light of a series of U.S. Supreme Court decisions, as discussed in Chapter 4. However, assume that no state enacts this type of tax, even though authorized by Congress. Could a newspaper successfully sue Congress on grounds of a violation of First Amendment rights in enacting the law? The answer is probably no because the newspaper has suffered no harm and thus lacks standing. There is a slim chance the paper could sue on the basis of threatened harm, but the threat is so minimal in this case that the suit would still likely fail. Or assume that a state does pass the tax but that the newspapers choose not to file suit. Instead an enraged "taxpayer" sues the state. Will the taxpayer suit be tried? Very unlikely because standing is lacking. Furthermore, nearly all of "taxpayer suits" (in which the status of the plaintiff is simply that of a taxpayer) have been dismissed for lack of standing.

STATE COURT SYSTEMS

If you intend to become a practicing journalist, you should thoroughly review your state court system. State and federal courts play an increasingly important role in news and newsgathering, and thus it is not unusual now for most reporters, editors and writers to occasionally cover a court decision or a trial, regardless of the specific "beat" assigned.

A state court is a hierarchy—that is, organized by levels from limited or general jurisdiction trial courts to intermediate appellate courts to the highest appellate court (usually, but not always, called the supreme court). The review process is quite similar to that of the federal courts, discussed earlier, with the higher courts having the power to review and, of course, reverse lower court decisions.

Although the federal court system and the 50 individual state court systems are independent, there are links that allow cases to flow from one to the other, especially between the federal and state courts. Although most cases that move from one court system to another are cases being appealed from a state court to a federal court (nearly always to the U.S. Supreme Court), on rare occasions court in one state may refuse to hear a case on grounds that a court in another state is the more appropriate or convenient forum. In other relatively rare cases, a court in one state may invoke the law of another state under a doctrine known as *choice of law*, which arises when a determination must be made as to which state's laws apply when there is a conflict between the two states' laws.

For example, suppose a sports celebrity sues a food conglomerate for using her picture and name to sell one of its popular cereals. The company has headquarters in Atlanta, the ads appear primarily in New York, and the celebrity resides in Oklahoma. If the case is tried in Oklahoma, whose appropriation (the alleged tort committed here) laws will prevail if the laws of the three states involved conflict with each other? As any other state court would do under the circumstances, the Oklahoma court would apply its own conflict of law rules to make that determination.[25]

The final matter to consider about state courts is their relationship to the federal courts, including interpreting federal laws such as the U.S. Constitution. As is pointed out in the next chapter, state courts in some circumstances have the authority to interpret and apply federal laws, including the U.S. Constitution. Although the Supreme Court, as mentioned earlier, has declared that it will be the final arbiter of the meaning of the U.S. Constitution, state courts can indeed decide cases involving the Constitution and even federal statutes when Congress has specifically permitted state courts to interpret and apply federal laws. On the other hand, federal courts will apply state laws in certain types of cases, such as those involving diversity (in which the parties are residents of different states; discussed in the next chapter).

SUMMARY

The federal court and most state courts have three basic levels — a general trial court, an intermediate appellate court and a supreme court. The primary trial court in the federal system is the U.S. District Court. Trial courts determine the facts in a case, ascertain the appropriate law or legal principles and then apply the law to the facts. Appellate courts, such as the U.S. Court of Appeals and the U.S. Supreme Court, merely hear appeals from cases tried in the trial courts and thus do not conduct trials, except in those rare instances in which a court has original jurisdiction. Appellate courts do not determine guilt or innocence.

Before a federal or state court can hear a case, it must have both jurisdiction and venue. Jurisdiction includes both personal and subject matter jurisdiction. In civil cases in state courts, suits are classified as either transitory or local.

The U.S. Supreme Court is the only federal court created by the U.S. Constitution. This court is the final arbiter of the Constitution and hears cases by direct appeal, writ of certiorari and certification. Virtually all appeals heard by the court are now by writ of certiorari since a 1988 federal statute eliminated nearly all mandatory jurisdiction by the U.S. Supreme Court. But before a case can be heard by the court by writ of certiorari, at least four justices must agree to consider the appeal. If at least five justices agree, a majority opinion is reached and a precedent can be established. A plurality opinion (one written by less than a majority) never sets a precedent. Other types of decisions are per curiam opinions and memorandum decisions. If a case is moot or not ripe, or if the parties have no standing, the Court will refuse to hear the case per Article III, §2, of the U.S. Constitution.

It is imperative that journalists and aspiring journalists be familiar with legal concepts, judicial principles and the structure of the state and federal court systems to ensure that their stories are accurate and complete. Media consumers have already been confused and even misled in television shows and novels about lawyers and the courts, with a few notable exceptions such as the Court TV cable network.

3 The Judicial Process

Thanks to television shows such as "L.A. Law" and "The People's Court" and cable television networks such as Court TV, U.S. audiences have become more familiar with the judicial process. Unfortunately, much of the information gleaned from at least some of the shows is distorted and sometimes downright wrong. In "The People's Court," for example, there are no attorneys and Judge Wopner plays an active role in questioning the witnesses and the parties. Although the proceedings bear at least vague similarities to the fairly informal proceedings in most small claims courts, anyone who spends a day or so observing a real courtroom quickly realizes there are differences between television law and real-world law.[1] Any aspiring journalist should spend at least one day watching the proceedings of each of the major courts (state and federal) in the region to acquire some sense of how the judicial process functions.

The purpose of this chapter is to introduce you to the basics of the judicial process, including a description of a typical civil lawsuit and trial and a typical criminal lawsuit and trial. Put aside any images you may have from television shows and movies—you are now in the real world of law. As in the previous chapter, you encounter some strange, new terms in this chapter. Take them to heart because you may find them indispensable later if you become a practicing journalist. You will also be introduced to important ethical considerations, especially in covering criminal cases.

THE CIVIL LAWSUIT

As mentioned earlier, the vast majority of lawsuits never reach trial but are either dropped by the plaintiff or settled out-of-court by the parties. The courts could never handle the load if all or even half of all cases went to trial because they are extremely busy processing and ruling on motions and other pretrial proceedings. Most cases resolved in the courts are civil cases, although criminal cases often attract the most intense media attention. In 1990, for instance, 18.4 million of the 31 million suits filed in state courts around the country were civil.[2]

In the federal courts, the Federal Rules of Civil Procedure and the Federal Rules of Evidence (which also apply to criminal cases) generally dictate the procedures and rules governing civil litigation, both for actions within the courtroom and for those outside the courtroom. Most states have either adopted the federal rules for their state courts or use similar rules with modifications. This chapter relies primarily on the federal rules, but you should consult your own state's rules if you plan to cover state courts.

The Complaint

A civil suit typically is formally initiated with the filing of a legal document known as a *complaint*. The primary purposes of the complaint are to give the defendant notice and to inform the person or organization of the nature and basic facts of the case. A complaint states the specific claim(s) against the defendant, the basis on which the court can exercise jurisdiction over the case, the basic facts, and the particular relief sought (which need not be stated in specific dollar amounts but instead can indicate the type of damages requested, such as punitive and actual).

All of the claims are mere allegations and should never be cited in a news story without attribution and qualification. For example, if a plaintiff says in a complaint that her telephone was wiretapped by the defendant without her permission, do not assume that her statement is a proven fact. Instead, you should note in the story: "According to a complaint filed today in state circuit court, Jane Smith's home telephone was bugged by her ex-husband. Mrs. Smith is seeking $125,000 for alleged invasion of privacy."

A complaint in a civil suit is nearly always a public document and thus available under state and federal open records laws. Simply go to the clerk for the appropriate court and ask to see the case files. If you have a case number, you will save some search time, but court clerks are usually quite helpful in tracking down particular documents if you at least have a name of one of the parties. Local attorneys, who can often be found perusing documents in the courthouse, can also be helpful, but the best way to learn the system is to practice a few trial runs before you have to find a document under deadline pressures.

Once the complaint has been filed, the court clerk will issue a signed *summons* with the seal and name of the court. Under the federal rules, called the *Federal Rules of Civil Procedure*, the summons must also contain the name and address of the plaintiff's attorney, the time frame within which the defendant must respond under the federal rules and a statement that if the defendant fails to answer ("appear and defend"), judgment by default will be entered against the defendant.[3] Under the federal rules, the complaint and the summons must be served together[4] in person by an individual who is not a party to the suit and who is at least 18 years of age.[5] Service can also be made under certain conditions by a U.S. marshal, deputy marshal or other person specially appointed by the court for that purpose.[6] Personal (i.e., in hand) service to the named defendant is known as *actual service*. It is usually not necessary that the defendant be served so long as a "person of suitable age and discretion" within the dwelling is handed the copy.[7] Appointed agents and individuals specified under the law can be served in lieu of the actual defendant in some cases, and federal and state agencies can sometimes be served via certified mail.[8] Service methods such as mail and delivery to an agent or other representative are called *substituted service*. The rules are quite complex because they are designed to assure compliance with the due process clause of the Fourteenth Amendment to the U.S. Constitution. The rules are also complicated by the fact that each local federal district court can set its own rules and because state statutes frequently come into play in federal courts because the federal rules permit federal courts to adopt local (i.e., state) rules for service. In some very limited circumstances, *constructive service*, service via publication in an official organ, is permitted—such as when a defendant cannot be found, or actual or substituted service is not possible.

Filing a complaint is obviously a very serious matter because the allegations become public record and therefore subject to public scrutiny. Thus there are sanctions for individuals and their attorneys who file frivolous or unsubstantiated claims. Rule 11 of the Federal Rules of Civil Procedure requires that every "pleading, motion and other paper of a party represented by an attorney" be signed by at least one attorney. With the signature, attorneys certify that they have read the document and have made a "reasonable inquiry" into the merits of the case to assure that the pleading or motion "is well grounded in fact and is warranted by existing law or a good faith argument for the extension, modification, or reversal of existing law."[9] There are various sanctions, including fines, that the court can exercise when the judge believes the rule has been violated.

During the last several years, Congress has added more teeth to the rule, including revisions in 1983 and 1987. Also, federal judges have been enforcing the rule more rigorously. The result has been a noticeable increase in the number of attorneys being sanctioned and considerable controversy among legal authorities over how and when the rule should be enforced. Because attorneys are certifying that their purpose in filing the suit or motion is not "for any improper purpose, such as to harass or to cause unnecessary delay or needless increase in the cost of litigation,"[10] it is not unusual now for federal judges to cite delaying tactics and harassment in imposing fines. Many states have adopted the federal rules, complete with Rule 11, for their courts, and most of the other states have at least a parallel rule.

Another remedy for the problem of frivolous lawsuits that can be more effective than Rule 11 sanctions, when available, is malicious prosecution of a civil suit, which requires that the defendent win the original suit and prove that the plaintiff had no probable cause in initiating legal action.

The Answer

The next typical step in a civil suit is the filing of an *answer* by the defendant. Under the federal rules, a defendant generally has 20 days from time of service to file an answer or other appropriate *pleadings*. If the defendant is the United States or a federal officer or agency, the maximum time for an answer is 60 days. Similar time constraints apply in most state courts, although the periods do vary among states.

The defendant has a host of options in answering the plaintiff's complaint. These options are generally not mutually exclusive and thus can be used alternatively or in combination. The primary purpose of the answer, also called the defendant's responsive pleading, is to counteract the plaintiff's allegations. In other words, the defendant should demonstrate why the plaintiff should not prevail. The defendant can also enter various denials, as discussed shortly, plead an affirmative defense and even file a *counterclaim*, asking for damages from the plaintiff or other individuals or entities.

Denials

Denials fall into five general categories: general, specific, qualified, insufficient knowledge and denial on information and belief. A *general denial*, asserting that **all** of the averments in the complaint are false, was once rather commonly used. But, because Rule 8(b) now requires that "denials shall fairly meet the substance of the averments denied,"[11] general denials are rare in the federal courts today. Typically, the defendant will file a *specific denial*, which designates the specific statements and/or paragraphs being denied and, usually, the specific statements and paragraphs being admitted. Under Rule 4(d), if the defendant does not deny those averments "to which a responsive pleading is required" (except the amount of damage), they are deemed to have been admitted.[12] In other words, those allegations and other statements made by the plaintiff in the complaint that are not denied by the defendant are generally considered to have been admitted by the defendant. There are certain exceptions to this rule, but these are beyond the scope of this book.

An example of a specific denial would be a media defendant in an invasion of privacy suit denying that it had subjected the plaintiff to public ridicule when it published a story about his financial dealings. On the other hand, the paper would probably admit that the story was actually published on December 30, 1993, and that it contained the statements cited in the complaint.

Another fairly common type of denial is a *qualified denial* in which the defendant denies some but not all of the statements in particular paragraphs or denies a portion of a specific sentence but admits other portions.

The federal courts and most state courts also allow a defendant to make a denial on the basis that the person or company "is without knowledge or information sufficient to form a belief as to the truth of an averment."[13] Attorneys are justifiably cautious about asserting this type of denial because of the requirements of Rule 11, discussed earlier.

Finally a defendant may make a *denial on information and belief*, on grounds that only second-hand information on the truth or falsity of the allegations is available at the time the answer is filed. It is unusual to see this type of denial in media law cases.

It is fairly common for defendants, including those in media law cases, such as libel and invasion of privacy suits, to include affirmative defenses in lieu of or in addition to denials in the answer. An *affirmative defense* is, in effect, saying that defendant admits that the plaintiff's allegations are true (for purposes of the defense only), but that there are additional facts that, when proven, will mean dismissal of the suit. There is a wide range of affirmative defenses with such technical names as assumption of risk, accord and satisfaction and estoppel, but the most common asserted in media law cases is the *statute of limitations*, which is the specified time period during which that particular cause of action must be filed after the right to sue occurs. In other words, if the suit is not filed within that time frame, the court will automatically dismiss the case when it is filed later. For example, the typical statute of limitations for a libel or invasion of privacy suit is one year, although some states have longer periods. Under Rule 8(c), if affirmative defenses are to be asserted by the defendant, they must be included in the answer or be effectively waived. Affirmative defenses usually do not play a major role in media law cases, although you should be alert to them because when they are available, they can have a significant impact on the case—for example, permitting the judge to dismiss the suit before trial. As you will learn in the next section, affirmative defenses can be particularly determinative in criminal cases, where many such defenses can be invoked.

Counterclaims

One more item sometimes included in the answer is the counterclaim. The *counterclaim* is simply a claim made by the defendant against the plaintiff, which, if proven, could cancel or decrease the amount of damages to which the plaintiff would be entitled. For example, if a defendant in an auto accident (personal injury) case also suffered personal injuries and property damage, he or she could file a counterclaim against the plaintiff, alleging that the plaintiff was at fault and therefore should be required to pay damages to the defendant. Counterclaims are relatively rare in media law cases, especially in libel and invasion of privacy. Counterclaims is a fairly complex topic, as demonstrated by the fact that Federal Rule 13 includes six major types.[14] Counterclaims can be filed with the answer or as a separate document. If a counterclaim is filed, the plaintiff is generally required to respond in the same matter as any defendant would to a claim and thus must follow the usual procedural rules.

Motions in General

The next step for both sides is usually filing motions, which is known as challenging the pleadings. Although journalists sometimes confuse pleadings with motions, the two processes are not the same. Pleadings are always written statements of fact and/or law filed by the parties, whereas motions are requests ("applications") made to a judge or a court. Under Rule 7 of the Federal Rules of Civil Procedure, pleadings are limited to the complaint, answer and, if appropriate, a reply to a counterclaim; an answer to a cross-claim (a claim by co-defendants or co-plaintiffs against one another rather than someone on the other side); and a third-party answer (if a third-party complaint has been filed).[15]

Although the federal rules and most state rules are rather strict about the types of pleadings that can be made, those same rules are quite flexible in allowing rather liberal supplementation or amendment of pleadings, in contrast to the old days of common law pleadings when the requirements were rather rigid. The idea of modern pleadings is to allow cases to be tried on their merits, not on technicalities.

Motions are typically filed throughout the judicial process, including during and after the trial, but there are some specific motions that are commonly filed pretrial. Space limitations do not permit a discussion of all of these motions, but it is important that you be familiar with the most common ones.

Pretrial Motions

The two most common pretrial motions in mass communication law suits, especially libel and invasion of privacy cases, are the motion to dismiss and the motion for summary judgment. A *motion to dismiss* simply requests that the court dismiss the case because the plaintiff has failed in the pleadings "to state a claim upon which relief can be granted."[16] In other words, the defendant is contending that there is no legally sound basis for the plaintiff's suit, even if all of the allegations made by the plaintiff are true. The defendant is, of course, not admitting that the allegations are true, but is, in effect, saying, "Even if the plaintiff were to prove all of the facts, so what?" This motion is commonly referred to as a 12(b)(6) motion (the number designated under the federal rules) by lawyers in the federal courts. A similar one is available in the state courts.

Here's an extreme but useful hypothetical case in which the motion to dismiss would almost certainly be granted. Suppose a newspaper reader is highly offended by a full-color picture of a child dying from starvation in the arms of its mother during a drought in Somalia on the front page of the Sunday "Lifestyle" section. The reader is so offended by the picture that she instantly experiences a psychological breakdown. She recovers long enough to see an attorney, who files suit on her behalf, claiming intentional infliction of emotional distress. No doubt, this woman has suffered emotional damages as a direct result of the publication of this photograph, and yet we know her suit will be immediately dismissed. Why? There is simply no legal basis for her suit. Therefore, the judge will grant the newspaper's motion to dismiss.

There are other bases on which a case can be dismissed at this stage, or later under some conditions, including lack of subject matter jurisdiction, improper venue, lack of personal jurisdiction and insufficiency of service of process (all discussed in Chapter 2).

A second common motion filed by a defendant in a media law case is the *motion for summary judgment*. This motion is discussed in more detail in Chapter 7 because it is a much-debated topic in libel and was the focus of a 1986 U.S. Supreme Court libel decision.[17] Briefly, this motion is frequently filed in libel suits when there is no dispute between the parties over the substantive facts in the case, but the two sides differ on the applicable law. A summary judgment has the major advantage that it is made **prior to the trial**. Thus a potentially expensive trial is avoided, saving both sides considerable time and money. Why then is there so much controversy over this type of judgment? As you will see in Chapter 7, summary judgments are far more likely to be decided in favor of defendants, whereas full-blown trials in libel and invasion of privacy suits are much more likely to result in an award of damages for the plaintiff, especially if the trial were before a jury.

Keep in mind that a summary judgment can be granted only when the judge or court is convinced that there is no dispute of facts, only a difference regarding the law. Even though a summary judgment is made without a trial, it is a binding decision and thus can be appealed to a higher (i.e., appellate) court. A motion of summary judgment can usually be made anytime after the pleadings have been closed, including up to the time of the trial, so long as the motion is made "within such time as not to delay the trial."[18]

Although the motion to dismiss and most other pretrial motions are granted based on the pleadings alone, the court is not limited to the pleadings when making a summary judgment but can certainly consider other evidence. In fact, under the federal rules, if matters outside the pleadings are presented to the court in making a decision on whether to grant a motion for judgment on the pleadings, the motion is automatically converted into a motion for summary judgment.[19]

One caution: Do not confuse a summary judgment with a summary jury trial. They are not the same. Summary jury trials are reviewed later in this chapter.

Two other less common motions need to be briefly considered. A *motion for more definite statement* would be filed when a pleading such as a complaint or answer is "so vague or ambiguous that a party cannot reasonably be required to frame a responsive pleading."[20] The idea is that the party filing the motion cannot make sense of the particular contentions of the other side, whether factual or legal, and thus those statements must be made clear before the party can be expected to respond to them.

Finally, the *motion to strike* is sometimes used. This is a request that the court strike (i.e., delete) certain statements from the pleadings, including "any insufficient defense or any redundant, immaterial, impertinent, or scandalous matter."[21] If the court rules in favor of the party filing the motion, the statements will be officially struck from the records.

Discovery in General

The next step in the judicial process, which has no exact parallel even though it is permitted on a limited basis in a criminal case (discussed shortly), is *discovery*. This is the much-publicized, formal process by which each side "discovers" the information and evidence to be presented at trial by the other side. The primary purpose of this often lengthy and expensive process is to avoid surprises at the trial itself. In a nutshell, when both sides do their homework, there are likely to be very few, if any, surprises at trial. Although surprise witnesses and last-minute revelations pervade television shows and theatrical movies with law themes, the real world is much different. You have probably heard the axiom for lawyers: Don't ask a question of a witness at trial to which you don't already know the answer. Those answers are already known, thanks to discovery. A check of any of the recent issues of law journals, such as *Trial* and the *American Bar Association Journal*, will usually reveal several articles on discovery, a clear indication of the importance of this process. There are literally dozens of how-to books on discovery and numerous workshops focus on the topic every year.

Ideally, most of the discovery process takes place extrajudicially, that is, outside the courtroom. This is made possible by the very liberal discovery rules adopted by the federal courts and by most state courts. Twelve of the 86 *Federal Rules of Civil Procedure* deal directly with discovery. Although sometimes complex, they are designed to facilitate the process, not to make it more difficult. The rules are also geared toward keeping discovery from becoming unreasonably long or unduly burdensome. Federal Rule 26(b)(1) specifically permits a court to limit the frequency or use of discovery methods under certain conditions, and Rule 26(f) grants a judge the authority to require attorneys to appear at a discovery conference at which the judge can impose limitations on discovery, including time. In fact, several of the U.S. District Courts now have adopted rules limiting time for discovery, as have numerous state courts. In the past, discovery occupied so much time that what was supposed to be a battle of the facts and the "wits" became an endurance contest instead. The picture has dramatically changed in the last decade or so, but discovery still remains the most time-consuming and expensive part of the civil judicial process most of the time, with the trial often being an anticlimax.

Federal Rule 37 permits the court to impose various sanctions from attorney's fees and other expenses to contempt of court for parties, witnesses and attorneys who fail to appear at or to cooperate in discovery when ordered to do so.

Depositions

The two most common methods of discovery are depositions and interrogatories, with depositions clearly leading the pack. A *deposition* is technically any out-of-court statement made under oath by a witness for use at trial or for preparing for trial. This device is by far the most expensive of the two but, as you may have guessed, the most useful and effective. Generally, either side may depose the other side and any witnesses. For example, a plaintiff in a copyright infringement suit would almost certainly orally depose the defendant and vice versa. (Depositions can be done orally or in writing, but are usually done orally.)

The procedure would be for the plaintiff's attorney to file a formal "notice of deposition" with the defendant's attorney, specifying the exact day, time and location. Because both sides have the right to be present during the deposition, attorneys for both are usually present. The plaintiff's attorney would then question (conduct a "direct examination" of) the defendant under oath. The party or witness being deposed is administered the oath, usually by an independent court reporter, at the beginning of the deposition. No judge is present, but a court reporter hired by the deposing attorney records the proceedings. Depositions can be taken via phone as well and many state and all federal courts now permit them to be taken with new technologies such as satellite television[22] and videotaping.

The primary purpose of depositions is to enable the attorney to learn **before trial** the content of the testimony that witness will offer **at trial**. For example, if a defense attorney in a libel suit wants to know what the plaintiff's expert witness is going to testify at trial about the defendant's alleged negligence, the lawyer would depose that witness in advance. This information would be particularly useful in deciding how to use one's own expert witnesses, who would likely be deposed by the plaintiff's attorney.

The procedure in an oral deposition is relatively simple. The witness and his or her attorney or the attorney representing the side using the witness at trial appear at the designated time and place. Very often the deposition is taken in a law office, usually the office of the attorney who is deposing the witness, although this can certainly vary. After the usual courtesy introductions, the court reporter then swears in the witness. The witness is questioned by the deposing attorney (a process known as direct examination), with the attorney for the other side present only to object if the questioning becomes improper — such as when the deposing attorney poses a question that would require a lay witness to assert a legal opinion or when the deposing attorney badgers the witness.

It is not unusual for even expert witnesses to find a deposition stressful because the questioning can be rather intense and long. Once the deposing attorney has completed questioning, the opposing attorney has the option of conducting a cross-examination of the witness. Unlike in the trial itself in which cross-examination is conducted by the attorney representing the side opposite the one that called the witness, cross-examination in a deposition is typically conducted by the attorney who has selected that witness to testify at trial. Cross-examination is particularly important when the direct-examination has severely damaged the credibility of the witness and thus some "restoration" is in order, or when the deposing attorney has failed to elicit information that could be favorable to the other side.

Interrogatories

Interrogatories are written questions submitted to an adverse party to be answered under oath. The procedure is for the attorney interrogating the witness to submit a series of questions in writing to the opposing party or a witness for the opposing party through the opposing party's attorney. Federal Rule 33 permits only parties to be deposed, not other witnesses, and requires that the interrogatories be written under oath. The attorney for the party being questioned is permitted to work with the party in composing the answers, although all answers must represent the views and direct knowledge of the party. A few state jurisdictions permit interrogatories to be taken of all witnesses, not just parties, but most follow the federal model.

The major advantage of interrogatories is the cost. They are much less expensive to administer than depositions. However, you get what you pay for, as the old saying goes. It is very easy for a party to manipulate answers or to be evasive, and because the questions are prepared in advance without benefit of previous answers, it is difficult to anticipate the party's answers. Thus interrogatories are used principally as a means of getting the discovery process started. Because of the burdensome nature of interrogatories, attorneys can make objections in lieu of answers if reasons are also provided. Conversely, an attorney submitting an interrogatory can request that the judge order that an answer be given or that a party who refuses to cooperate in an interrogatory be forced to respond.[23] Most federal district courts have now adopted local rules that permit the judge to limit the number of questions submitted.

Written Depositions

Written depositions ("depositions upon written questions") are sometimes confused by journalists with interrogatories, but they are not the same. Unlike interrogatories, which are limited to parties, written depositions can be submitted to any witness, including a party to the suit. They are much less expensive than oral depositions because no attorneys need to be present, and they can be answered over a longer period.

In the case of a written deposition, the deposing attorney submits a list of proposed questions to the attorney for the other side who then makes any objections known and submits proposed questions for cross-examination. The witness then appears before a court reporter, usually in the home or office of the witness rather than in an attorney's office, and answers the questions under oath. The answers are, of course, recorded by the reporter and the word-for-word transcript is then made available to the attorneys for both sides. Obviously, the process takes some time, but the witness does have the opportunity to prepare responses. Thus written depositions are almost never taken of parties or of major witnesses.

Except for accepting motions or considering objections to the scope or conduct of the process, the court is rarely involved in discovery, especially in the federal system. The idea is for the attorneys to cooperate in seeing that each side is fully informed before trial. In most cases, an attorney has no obligation to make information available to the other side unless the opponent has made a formal request, but counsel does have a duty to provide such information, once requested. There are exceptions to this requirement, as discussed shortly, but most attorneys cooperate with one another, even though they represent clients on different sides.

Witnesses are important in any case, but witnesses alone are usually not sufficient to build the case. Discovery also permits access to and copying of documents and other evidence. The usual procedure for obtaining documents and other items from a party is for the attorney to file a formal request through the attorney for the other side that specifies the documents or other materials sought. The federal rules and all state court rules also permit an attorney for one side to have the party on the other side submit to a physical examination under certain circumstances, such as when the party's physical or mental condition is an issue in the case.

Subpoenas

For nonparties, a subpoena is traditionally used to compel them to testify or to produce documents or other materials. If a witness is to appear to simply testify and not to bring documents or other physical evidence, an ordinary *subpoena* would be issued, notifying the witness of the specific time and place and the type of information sought. If the witness is to produce "books, papers, documents, or tangible things," a *subpoena duces tecum* would be served on that individual. The process of serving a subpoena or a subpoena duces tecum is fairly similar to that of serving a complaint and summons. In the federal courts, a federal marshal, deputy marshal or anyone who is not a party to the suit and is at least 18 years old simply delivers the subpoena to the witness. In the federal courts, all subpoenas must be issued by the district court clerk.[24] The power of the federal district courts to subpoena nonparty witnesses extends within a 100-mile radius of the court. There is no 100-mile limit for parties. The subpoena power of state courts traditionally resides within the state boundaries, although all states have some form of a long-arm statute, as mentioned in the previous chapter, which permits personal jurisdiction, including subpoena powers, beyond the borders under certain conditions.

The rules for subpoenaing witnesses and documents for a hearing or trial is similar to that of the authority for subpoenas for depositions. Both federal rules and state rules allow courts to cite individuals for contempt for failing to comply with a valid subpoena. However, those same rules permit a subpoenaed witness to make objections, usually in writing, within a specified period—typically 10 days, which the court would ultimately decide whether to sustain or overrule.[25]

Journalists, as pointed out in Chapter 9, have been plagued in recent years by a considerable increase in the number and scope of subpoenas, both in civil and criminal cases. This is a rather complicated matter, so further discussion is deferred until that chapter. Suffice it to say that all journalists, whether or not they cover the courts, must have a strong, basic knowledge of subpoenas because they are routinely called and forced to testify and produce documents, despite the vehement and vociferous protests of their employers and news organizations. There is no federal shield law to protect journalists and state shield laws, where they exist, are often ineffective in offering protection.

One type of protection that journalists sometimes successfully seek is a protective order. Federal Rule 26(c) allows a court to issue a *protective order* "to protect a party or person from annoyance, embarrassment, oppression, or undue burden or expense." The court has several options on the impact of such an order, including prohibiting the discovery entirely, allowing the discovery only under certain terms and conditions and limiting the scope of the discovery matters.[26]

Although there are various constitutional, statutory and common law rights of public and press access to court documents, no such rights have been established thus far for access to discovery materials, including depositions. On rare occasions, courts will order that the transcript of a deposition be made public, but usually only when a strong public interest — such as the fact that the government is a party in the suit — is involved. Thus depositions are almost always conducted in private, with journalists and the public having no access to the proceedings or to the transcripts.

Privileged Discovery

In general, any relevant evidence can be discovered; there are certain exceptions, however. The federal rule notes, "It is not ground for objection that the information sought will be inadmissible at the trial if the information sought appears reasonably calculated to lead to the discovery of admissible evidence."[27] The two major exceptions are privilege, including attorney–client privilege, and attorney work-product. *Privileged communications* are statements made within a particular context or relationship and are protected from disclosure because the nature of that relationship is so sacred that the benefits of disclosure (namely, revelation of the truth) are outweighed by the need to preserve that type of relationship. Typical protected relationships are attorney–client, husband–wife, physician–patient, and clergy–penitent.

Federal and state rules of evidence, rather than rules of civil procedure, govern when privileged communications are permitted — that is, when the content of such communication does not have to be disclosed. For example, the federal courts and all state courts protect attorney–client communications, although the protection is not absolute, whereas some state courts do not have physician–patient privilege, which is available in the federal courts. Reporter-source privilege exists in some form in more than half of the states, but the federal courts do not recognize this privilege, although, as outlined in Chapter 9, the federal Privacy Protection Act of 1980 does offer some procedural protection for federal and state searches for evidence held by journalists.

Finally, the *attorney work-product doctrine*, recognized in most states and now incorporated in the Federal Rules of Evidence, places strict limits on the discovery of information specifically prepared for litigation or for trial by a party or a party's attorney.[28] In fact, the federal rule offers absolute protection "against disclosure of the mental impressions, conclusions, opinions, or legal theories of an attorney or other representative of a party concerning the litigation."[29] For other types of information prepared for litigation or trial, the side seeking the information must clearly demonstrate that it has a "substantial need" for the materials in preparing its case and is unable to get the information or its equivalent without "undue hardship."[30]

Pretrial Conferences

The debate among legal scholars and jurists over the appropriate point at which a case should come into focus so the issues and facts are gelled or at least clear to both sides and the court has been going on for many decades. Some courts have opted for rigid pleadings, an approach designed to hone the issues and facts early in the case. The federal courts and many state courts have chosen more liberal pleadings, but obviously at some point the issues and facts must congeal. The pretrial conference is typically the point at which the judge begins to establish firm control over the case by requiring the attorneys to establish time parameters for pretrial proceedings and/or agree on undisputed facts or issues. Most judges hold several pretrial conferences with the attorneys in the case, but two types of pretrial conferences are frequently employed in the federal courts. After all the initial pleadings have been filed, a *scheduling and planning conference* is usually held among the judge or magistrate and attorneys for both sides to establish time limits for various proceedings, including discovery, and to schedule dates for further pretrial conferences.[31]

The second type of pretrial conference is the *issue conference*. The attorneys and the judge hammer out the issues and facts in the case so an agreement can be reached on undisputed facts and law, also known as *stipulations*. The primary purpose is to narrow the case to the point at which either an out-of-court settlement can be reached or, at the very least, the issues and the facts in the case are crystallized so that the trial itself can focus on important matters and not be bogged down with trivial and undisputed points.

Some judges apply more pressure than others, but all of them are certainly interested in having the case settled before trial, if possible. As discussed in the previous chapter, most courts are overloaded with cases, and trials can be quite expensive. Thus it is not unusual for a case to be settled before trial.

One type of pretrial conference is nearly always required by federal district court judges—the *final pretrial conference*. Federal Rule 16(d) provides that this conference be held close to the time of the trial and that a plan for the trial be established by this point. Cases are sometimes settled at this conference, but the chances of a settlement have usually decreased by this point; both sides have probably expended considerable time and expense and virtually all that remains is the trial itself.

After the final pretrial conference, the judge will issue pretrial orders, including a list of trial witnesses, stipulations and other agreements reached at the conference.[32] Under the federal rules, the pretrial orders can be changed only "to prevent manifest injustice."[33]

THE CIVIL TRIAL

The vast majority of cases, for one reason or another, do not make it to the trial stage. But once the case is placed on the court's trial docket with a specific date set, the wheels of justice begin moving again. It is not unusual for at least one *continuance*, or postponement, to occur, before the trial itself begins.

Both civil and criminal cases can be tried before a jury and a judge or before a judge alone. The latter is known as a *bench trial*. Obviously, jury trials are substantially more time consuming and expensive, both for the parties and for the court, but many litigants and their attorneys prefer jury trials. Although there are varying reasons for this preference, there seems to be a widespread belief among trial lawyers and their clients that juries will render better or fairer verdicts.

The general rules of order are virtually the same for jury versus bench trials, regardless of the jurisdiction. Rather than separate the two types of trials, this chapter analyzes them together and notes differences, where applicable.

According to the Seventh Amendment to the U.S. Constitution, "In suits at common law, where the value in controversy shall exceed twenty dollars, the right of trial by jury shall be preserved." Although this right to a trial by jury is binding only on the federal government, not on the states, every state recognizes such a right in its own constitution or by statute. The difficulty lies in knowing what suits existed at common law in determining when the right can be invoked. In 1970,[34] the U.S. Supreme Court, for the first time, enunciated a constitutional test for deciding when the right exists. Whereas discussion of the test is beyond the scope of this text, it should be noted that it focuses on whether the issue in the case is primarily equitable or legal. As discussed in Chapter 1, there are no jury trials in equity cases, but cases can get complicated when they appear to involve both issues of law and of equity. The Supreme Court has adopted the rule that when a legal and an equitable claim are intertwined, the legal issue will be tried first by the jury (if a jury trial is chosen) and then the equitable claim will be tried by the judge alone.[35]

When most people hear the term *officers of the court*, they immediately think of judges, clerks and bailiffs. The judge, of course, presides over the trial, and the *court clerk* helps the judge administer and keep track of the trial, including the various exhibits. The *bailiff* has the responsibilities of maintaining order in the courtroom, calling witnesses, escorting the jury and, in some jurisdictions, administering the oaths to witnesses and jurors. Few know that lawyers are also officers of the court and are thereby bound by its rules and procedures.

Jury Selection

One of the most critical stages in a jury trial is the jury selection process. In the past, courts and legislators paid relatively little attention to the process as a whole, although everyone knew that successful jury selection was extremely important in the trial. In recent years, jury selection has become a hot topic, with several U.S. Supreme Court decisions considering different aspects of the process. Two of the most important decisions came in the early 1970s. In 1970, the Supreme Court held that nonunanimous verdicts in criminal cases did not violate the Sixth Amendment.[36] Three years later, the Court ruled that less-than-12-member (in this case, 6-member) juries were permissible in civil cases.[37] The court has yet to determine whether nonunanimous verdicts in civil cases are constitutional and whether less-than-12-member juries are acceptable in criminal cases, although it is likely the court would rule favorably in both situations, if given the opportunity to decide.

As a result of these decisions, many jurisdictions, including the federal courts, are now routinely opting for 6-member juries because of the savings in time and expense. More and more states are also allowing, either by experiment or by statute, jury verdicts based on agreement of three-fourths or five-sixths of the members, especially in civil and misdemeanor cases.

In both civil and criminal cases, jurors are selected at random from a pool or list (also called *venire facias*), usually compiled from property tax rolls, automobile registration lists and voter registration printouts. In the federal district courts, potential jurors are chosen at random solely from voter lists. A court official, usually a jury commissioner, appointed by the judge initially screens the prospective jurors to narrow the list down to only qualified and eligible individuals. For example, jurors in federal cases must be residents of the district where the case is tried. Until the last decade or so, a fairly long list of occupational exemptions allowed many people to escape serving as jurors. People in these occupations — physicians, teachers, students and lawyers, for example — were never prevented from serving, but they were merely allowed to exempt themselves. Many of them exercised the exemption because serving usually meant taking time from work with little or no pay.

In the 1970s, however, many states began revising their statutes to eliminate or severely limit exemptions, and legal organizations such as the American Bar Association advocate elimination of all automatic excuses and exemptions.[38]

Once the *array*, as it is sometimes known, of qualified *veniremen* (prospective jurors) is in order, the process of selecting the actual jurors for trial begins. On rare occasions, an attorney will move that the court disqualify the entire array because the list was compiled in violation of some constitutional or statutory right. For example, the list may have somehow excluded all minority group members. Any systematic exclusion of a particular community group could be grounds for violation of that defendant's Sixth Amendment right in a criminal case to a trial by an impartial jury of the state or district where the alleged crime was committed or, in the case of a civil suit, the Seventh Amendment right of trial by jury. The motion in such a case is known as *challenge to the array*, and is more likely to occur in a criminal suit.

The jury selection process begins when panels (usually 12 people at a time) of individuals selected from the array are called. With each panel, the court clerk calls the set of names and then has the individuals sit in the jury box.

After offering the panel a brief overview of the case, the judge then asks that any juror who feels unable to serve for any reason to make it known. Occasionally, potential jurors will be excluded at this point for poor health, personal acquaintance with one of the parties or another basis.

The next step in the process varies, depending on the particular jurisdiction. In *voir dire* the potential jurors are questioned about a variety of matters from their names and occupations to their views on this type of case. Until recent years, most federal judges have conducted the voir dire themselves, preventing the attorneys from playing an active role, except for giving them opportunity to provide the court with potential questions in advance. On the other hand, most state courts allow the attorneys to do most of the questioning.

The types of questions that can be asked, whether by the attorneys or by the judge, can be highly personal and intimate. For example, one federal judge says he often asks potential jurors during voir dire about their religion, the magazines they read, the bumper stickers on their cars, whether they or friends abuse drugs, political parties to which they belong and whether they live with anyone.[39]

There have been dozens of legal treatises and hundreds of articles published about voir dire. For example, a few years ago *Trial*, the journal of the Association of Trial Lawyers of America, featured two articles: "Effective Voir Dire"[40] and "What Makes Jurors Tick?"[41] The first article advocates six basic communication skills for lawyers to use for effective voir dire: openness, empathy, attentiveness, warmth, identification and receptiveness, as well as the use of disclosure reciprocity, positive reinforcement and modeling to "facilitate juror self-disclosure."[42] The latter article discusses matters such as attention span, memory problems and Psychological Anchors (a trademark of Litigation Sciences, a corporation that claims to have conducted in-depth interviews of more than 14,000 actual and "surrogate" jurors throughout the country).[43] Indeed there are several companies offering advice on jury selection, some of which will, for a fee, sit with counsel during voir dire to observe the verbal and nonverbal communication of the prospective jurors and make recommendations regarding which jurors should be struck during the peremptory challenges, discussed shortly. Most attorneys no doubt still rely on experience and instinct or "gut feelings" in their juror challenges, but scientific techniques are making headway in the process, as indicated by the growing use by attorneys of psychological and sociological experts (and occasionally even communication specialists) for consultation during voir dire.

The major goal of voir dire is to weed out those prospective jurors who may have biases or prejudices that would prevent them from making a fair and independent decision in the case. After a panel has been questioned, the attorney for either side can request the judge to dismiss individuals *for cause*. Suppose in a libel case against a newspaper a prospective juror indicates during voir dire that she believes newspapers never tell the truth and are always out to get prominent people. The defense attorney would clearly have grounds for asking the court to dismiss the individual for cause, and this request would very likely be granted.

Judges and attorneys are not necessarily looking for uninformed jurors but for fair and impartial jurors. For instance, in a 1985 bribery case, an Indianapolis, Indiana, newspaper correspondent[44] was allowed to serve as a juror despite the fact that she had written a story on the charges, had done two profiles of the defendant (a city judge) and knew the prosecutor, defense attorney and some of the major witnesses in the case.[45] After the trial, she wrote a Sunday article about her experience.

Only the judge can dismiss jurors for cause, but this can be done either at the request of an attorney or on the judge's own initiative. There is no limit on the number of individuals an attorney can challenge for cause, nor on the number of dismissals a judge can make.

The judge will continue calling prospective jurors until a panel of qualified jurors twice the size of the jury (including alternate jurors) actually needed for trial has survived voir dire without dismissal for cause. If there are to be 12 jurors at trial plus one alternate, the final panel would have 26 members. In highly publicized cases in which there is concern about juror pretrial exposure to potentially highly prejudicial information in the mass media, voir dire can take days or even months. Typically, the process occupies only a few hours.

Art, science and gut instinct tend to play a major role in the next step of the jury selection process—*peremptory challenges*. In civil cases, each side usually gets to "strike" (i.e., make a peremptory challenge of) an equal number of jurors. The attorney can excuse a juror for any or no reason. In fact, the attorney need not state a reason. There is an exception, however, to the general rule that peremptory challenges can be made for any reason. In 1986 in *Batson v. Kentucky*,[46] the U.S. Supreme Court held that the equal protection clause of the Fourteenth Amendment to the U.S. Constitution[47] prohibits a prosecutor in a criminal trial from exercising peremptory challenges against jurors solely because of race or because the attorney believed that members of that racial group would not be able to render a fair and impartial decision.[48]

While *Batson* dealt with a criminal case, one legal writer and judge[49] predicts the decision "will forever change for the better the jury selection process in criminal, and possibly, civil trials.[50] At the present time, racial exclusion is the only ground on which an attorney cannot exercise a peremptory challenge. In *Batson* the Court expressed no view on whether Sixth Amendment rights were involved, even though the case was appealed on Sixth Amendment grounds.[51]

Different jurisdictions have different rules regarding the number of peremptory challenges permitted by each, with some states, for example, permitting a criminal defendant to strike more jurors than the prosecutor, but the number of challenges in civil cases tends to be the same for both sides. All jurisdictions do limit the total number of peremptory challenges, however, unlike challenges for cause.

Once the two sides have exercised their strikes, the jurors, including any alternates, are sworn in by the court clerk. Those who were not selected are then permitted to leave.

Ethical Concerns in Covering Juries

As discussed in Chapter 9, the U.S. Supreme Court in 1984 unanimously held that there was a "presumptive openness" in voir dire so that the press and the public had a constitutional right to attend, except in rare circumstances.[52] Thus journalists frequently cover jury selection, especially in cases with strong public interest. One of the ethical concerns facing journalists is whether to publish names and other personal information about jurors, including potentially embarrassing facts that may have been disclosed during voir dire. Although a few judges have been known to impose prior restraint on reporters by issuing "gag orders" that forbid publication of names and other information about jurors, such orders are, in all likelihood, unconstitutional (discussed in the next chapter). However, reporters and other journalists have a professional obligation to consider the impact on readers and on viewers and on the subjects of their stories. Most media outlets choose not to publish personal information about jurors because such information is not essential to covering a trial and because some individuals may be adversely affected by disclosure. Very careful thought should always be given to the ethical dimensions of covering a trial.

Sequestration

Both witnesses and the jury can be *sequestered* during the trial, whether civil or criminal. Witnesses are sequestered by keeping them separated and out of the courtroom except when giving their testimony. The idea is to prevent one witness from being influenced by the testimony of a previous witness. In reality, sequestration of witnesses probably does not work so well because witnesses have often seen the depositions of the witness on the stand, especially in the case of an expert witness. But some judges apparently feel more comfortable separating witnesses than allowing them to interact. By the way, parties (who can also be witnesses) have a constitutional right to be present during trial and thus cannot be involuntarily sequestered.

Sequestration of the jury is a somewhat different process. The jurors are allowed to interact with one another, but are not allowed to talk with other people, except under highly supervised circumstances. Sequestered jurors are kept together, usually in a local hotel, where they eat together, watch television programs and read newspapers. All of their media content is edited so any prejudicial news is not disseminated to the jurors. Most juries are not sequestered, although the practice is gaining popularity, if recent news stories are an accurate indicator. More than anything else, jury sequestration is aimed at ensuring a fair trial by keeping the members from being exposed to *outside* prejudicial information. Obviously, the jurors are hearing and seeing biased, or at least one-sided, information in the courtroom as both sides try to sway them, but this material is presented as evidence, following strict rules to ensure fairness and relevance.

Opening Statements and Burden of Proof

The trial itself begins with opening statements by each side. In a civil suit, the plaintiff's attorney is first, whereas in a criminal suit the prosecutor goes first. According to the rule, the party with the burden of proof begins the trial. *Burden of proof* is a term frequently confused with *standard of proof*. Both are evidentiary terms whose impact is dictated by the appropriate rules of evidence (civil v. criminal). State and federal rules of evidence place an affirmative duty on the party initiating the suit (the plaintiff in a civil case or the prosecuting attorney in a criminal case) to prove the facts on a particular issue.

For example, in a libel suit, the plaintiff has the burden of proving that the necessary elements of this tort occurred — defamation, identification, publication and, sometimes, special damages. The plaintiff also has the burden of showing the defendant was at fault by acting with negligence or with actual malice, depending on the status of the plaintiff and the jurisdiction, and that harm occurred as a result. In a criminal suit, the prosecutor must prove that the necessary elements of the particular crime or crimes, with which the defendant is charged, occurred.

Standard of proof, a related but much different concept than burden of proof, is the extent or degree to which the evidence must be demonstrated by the party having the burden of proof. For most torts, the standard of proof is "a preponderance of the evidence," although occasionally other standards, such as "clear and convincing evidence," apply. In criminal prosecutions, the standard is always "beyond a reasonable doubt." Figure 3.1 illustrates the concept.

No case would ever require proof beyond all doubt nor would any suit be permitted to go forward with absolutely no evidence, but it is clear, as the chart illustrates, that preponderance of the evidence is a lower evidentiary standard than clear and convincing evidence, which is a lower standard than beyond a reasonable doubt. Please note that preponderance of the evidence is definitely a burden on the plaintiff because the standard requires that the greater weight of the evidence be in favor of the plaintiff. If a judge (in a bench trial) or jury is convinced that the evidence is a dead heat for the two sides, the

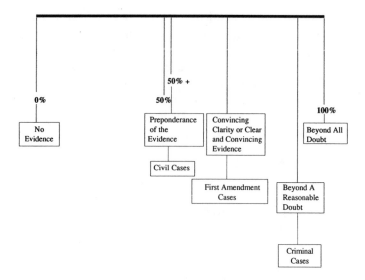

FIG. 3.1. Burden of proof.

judge or jury ("trier of fact") must find in favor of the defendant. In other words, 50/50 is not enough for the plaintiff; the person must be at least slightly ahead.

Under the civil and criminal rules of evidence, *opening statements* cannot be argumentative but must be confined to the facts to be proven at trial. News stories sometimes call opening statements "opening arguments," but such reference is inaccurate. Opening statements are usually relatively brief (typically 30 to 45 minutes for each side), although some courts impose time limits to avoid lengthy statements. The tendency of some lawyers to be long in their opening statements is probably linked to the widespread belief, bolstered by a few scientific studies and pronouncements by some experienced attorneys, that most jurors have made up their minds by the end of the opening statements. Donald E. Vinson, founder of Litigation Sciences, Inc., contends that the most significant information should appear early early in the trial and thus in the opening statements.[53]

Opening statements are always optional, but it is rare for an attorney not to make an opening statement, except in those jurisdictions that allow the defense attorney to postpone opening statements until the plaintiff's attorney or the prosecutor has presented that side.

Evidence is the core of any trial, and thus the rules of evidence, both criminal and civil, are enormously complex. Many lawyers will tell you the most difficult topic in law school was Evidence, especially Hearsay. (Not surprisingly, this topic is probably the most dreaded on the state bar exams.) An indication of this complexity is the fact that there are not only strict, complicated rules about *what kinds* of evidence can be presented, but also even stricter rules about *how* the evidence can be presented! In addition there are so many exceptions to the general rule of *hearsay evidence* (secondhand information—i.e., information *not* based on personal knowledge but instead on communication from a third party) that some law professors are fond of saying the exceptions actually swallow the rule.

Presentation of Evidence

After each side has presented an opening statement, the heart and soul of the trail begins—the presentation of evidence. Opening statements may have an impact on the trial, but the evidence is what the jury or judge weighs in reaching a verdict. Evidence comes in two types and two forms. When most people think of evidence as presented at trial, they probably think of what is known as *direct evidence*, which *Black's Law Dictionary* defines as "that means of proof which tends to show the existence of a fact in question, without the intervention of the proof of any other fact."[54] In other words, direct evidence directly proves a fact without having to be tied to other facts or presumptions. The best examples of direct evidence are oral testimony from an eyewitness, a confession (in a criminal case) or an admission (in a civil or criminal case) and a murder weapon.

The other type of evidence is, as you probably guessed, *indirect evidence*, also known as *circumstantial evidence*. *Black's Law Dictionary* defines circumstantial evidence as "testimony not based on actual personal knowledge or observation of the facts in controversy, but other facts from which deductions are drawn, showing indirectly the facts sought to be proved."[55] In other words, indirect evidence consists of facts that must be proven by inference or by implication. Examples in an invasion of privacy suit in which a defendant is accused of taping a private phone conversation (a tort known as "intrusion") would be the receipts showing the defendant had purchased such equipment and the fact that he or she been fired from a previous job for listening in on other employees' phone conversations. Examples in a criminal case would be the physical appearance of the scene of a crime.

The two forms of evidence are oral testimony of witnesses and exhibits, including documents. Both direct and indirect evidence can be presented in either form.

Direct Examination versus Indirect Examination

Under the federal and state rules of civil procedure and criminal procedure, the side with the evidentiary burden of proof—plaintiff in civil and state in criminal—begins the presentation of evidence. This is accomplished by calling witnesses for *direct examination*, or questioning by the attorney for the side who has called that witness. Beginning journalists sometimes confuse "direct examination" with "direct evidence." They are not the same. Keep in mind that direct examination deals with the interrogation process, whereas direct evidence relates to a type of evidence. The confusion arises from the fact that in a direct examination, the attorney can have the witness offer both direct and indirect evidence.

Direct examinations are usually fairly straightforward, with the attorney asking questions designed to get the witness to make factual statements, identify documents, photos or other physical items to be introduced into evidence. The particular rules of evidence (state or federal) dictate what evidence can be introduced and how and even the forms and types of questions that can be asked. For example, *leading questions*, which suggest a specific answer, are not permitted under most circumstances in direct examination. In fact, Rule 611 (c) of the Federal Rules of Evidence says that leading questions "should not be used on the direct examination of a witness except as may be necessary to develop the witness' testimony." Exceptions include hostile witnesses[56] and questions designed to elicit basic information such as a witness' name, age and address.

The plaintiff or state (in a criminal case) presents its witnesses first. After each witness is sworn in and questioned by the attorney, the defense attorney has the opportunity to conduct a *cross-examination* of that witness. Unlike in direct examination, during cross-examination leading questions are not only permitted but expected. "Ordinarily leading questions should be permitted on cross-examination," according to Rule 611 (c) of the Federal Rules of Evidence. All states have similar rules permitting this type of interrogation. Cross-examinations are generally "limited to the subject matter of the direct examination and matters affecting the credibility of the witness,"[57] so attorneys conducting them feel they have to use leading questions if they are to accomplish their primary goal of destroying the witness' previous testimony during direct examination and, if possible, making the witness give testimony favorable to their side. Another goal of cross-examination, especially with expert witnesses, is to *impeach* or destroy the credibility (not just the content) of the witness.

Cross-examination has become an art that few attorneys probably feel they have ever fully mastered, but nevertheless is often critical to a case, especially in media law suits such as those for libel and invasion of privacy. One litigation expert, Professor James W. McElhaney of the Case Western University School of Law, advises attorneys not only to ask leading questions in cross-examination but also to ask very short questions, use simple words, use headlines and to get one fact straight at a time.[58] According to McElhaney, "Cross-examination is not for the witness. It is for you. It is your opportunity to present your side of the witness' story, punctuated by the witness' reluctant agreement that what you say is true."[59]

To help you understand the difference between leading versus nonleading questions, here are some examples of how the same information could be sought, using both types of questions:

nonleading	*leading*
1. How many years have you been a reporter?	1. You've been a reporter only two years, haven't you?
2. How reliable was John Jones as a confidential source?	2. You had reason to believe John Jones lied, didn't you?
3. When, if ever, do you record your phone conversations?	3. Don't you routinely record your phone conversations?

As mentioned earlier, hearsay testimony is generally not admissible, although there are many exceptions. In fact, the federal rules of evidence specifically cite 24 exceptions, even when the declarant is available to testify, including a catchall "other" category.[60] There are five categories of exceptions if the declarant is unavailable as a witness.[61] Even hearsay within hearsay is permitted under certain circumstances![62] Journalists sometimes get "trapped" by making statements under the pressure or heat of the moment that come back to haunt them. For example, a reporter writing a story about a politician who is allegedly a drug trafficker may accidentally blurt out that he knows the person is a crook and all that's left is to prove it. That statement could be admitted as either an "excited utterance" (an exception to the general hearsay rule) or possibly as an "admission by a party-opponent"[63] (which the federal rules do not even consider as hearsay anyway). *The moral of the story is to be very careful at all times about what you say because your statements may come back to haunt you later in a libel or invasion of privacy suit.*

The opposing counsel can always object to the court during direct examination and cross-examination when impermissible questions are asked or irrelevant evidence is being sought. If the judge overrules the objection, the witness is allowed to answer the question, but the judge's ruling may be the basis for an appeal if an unfavorable verdict is rendered. If the judge sustains the objection, the attorney may either rephrase the question or start another line of questioning.

Cross-examination

After a witness has been directly examined by the attorney who called him or her and then cross-examined by the attorney for the other side, the attorney who called can then conduct a re-direct examination, followed by a re-cross-examination by the other side. Both steps are optional, although a re-cross cannot be conducted unless a prior direct examination has been done. It should be noted that the re-cross can be followed by another re-direct and so on, but such exchanges are rare, and the judge has the authority to end the process when deemed appropriate. Re-direct and re-cross-examinations are usually short, if they are conducted at all, because they can deal only with matters handled in the preceding step.

Motions for Directed Verdict
versus Judgment Notwithstanding the Verdict

Once the plaintiff or state (in a criminal suit) has rested its case after calling all of its witnesses, which have also been cross-examined, and so on, the defendant can (and usually does) make an oral *motion* for a *directed verdict*. This motion is made outside the hearing of the jurors in a jury trial and can be made in both civil and criminal cases. In a criminal case, however, it is usually a motion to dismiss because acquittal in a criminal case either by a judge or a jury is final and the Fifth Amendment bars double jeopardy ("nor shall any person be subject for the same offence to be twice put in jeopardy of life or limb").

The concept of directed verdict is sometimes difficult for beginning journalists to understand, especially when coupled with the concept of *judgment notwithstanding the verdict*, also called *non obstante veredicto* or *jnov*. The two concepts, directed verdict and jnov, are the same, except for the timing. If the judge in a civil case determines *before* the jury renders a verdict that there is either (a) insufficient evidence for a case to go to the jury or (b) the evidence is so compelling that any reasonable person would clearly find for the plaintiff, the judge will issue a directed verdict. If the judge makes this determination *after* the jury has rendered a verdict, a jnov is issued. Obviously, a directed verdict or a jnov in a civil case can be in favor of either the defendant or the plaintiff. If the evidence is sufficiently weak so there is no question of fact for the jury to decide, the directed verdict will be for the defendant. If the evidence is so compelling that there is also no question of fact for the jury, the directed verdict or jnov will be in favor of the plaintiff.

Within the same jurisdiction, the test the judge applies is the same for both the directed verdict and the jnov, but, to add to the confusion, there are two different tests. Most jurisdictions, including the federal courts, now apply the *substantial evidence test*. When a motion for a directed verdict or a jnov is made, the judge is required to look at all of the evidence but view it in the light most favorable to the side *not* requesting the directed verdict or jnov, also called the "nonmovant." If there is not enough evidence that would allow a jury to find in favor of the side not making the motion, the judge will then deny the motion for the directed verdict or jnov. The second test, which is used in a minority of jurisdictions, is the *scintilla test*, which allows the judge to deny the motion if there is *any* evidence whatsoever to warrant jury consideration.

One of the confusing aspects of the directed verdict and the jnov is the timing. The directed verdict may first be made by the defendant right after the plaintiff or state has rested its case. In a civil case, as mentioned earlier, the plaintiff must prove the case by a preponderance of the evidence, not beyond a reasonable doubt, as in a criminal case. How then would a judge be able to grant a directed verdict before the defendant has ever presented that side? Recall that the plaintiff or state has the burden of proof. If the proof is so weak that reasonable minds would not differ, the judge can obviously rule in favor of the defendant even though the defendant has not presented that side because there is so little evidence for the defendant to counter anyway. The defendant, of course, has no reason to contest the judgment because it favors that party.

Why can't a directed verdict be issued in favor of the plaintiff after the plaintiff has rested that side of the case? Even if the evidence is overwhelming, the defendant must be allowed to counter this evidence with other evidence, which may very well substantially negate the plaintiff's case.

If a directed verdict and a jnov are granted on the same basis, then why would a judge wait until a jury had rendered its verdict before issuing a jnov? At first analysis, there would appear to be no real reason; one major purpose of issuing the directed verdict when it is warranted is to save the expense and time of continuing the trial. By waiting until the jury has made its decision, the judge would certainly defeat this purpose. However, many judges prefer to allow the jury to deliberate even though they know they would overturn a verdict if the jury did not decide in favor of the "correct" party for whom the judge would issue the directed verdict.

There are two major reasons for this preference. First, the jury may very well decide in favor of the "correct" side, thus negating the need for a jnov. The typical juror feels frustration and, perhaps, anger when she or he is brought back from a recess—after hearing the plaintiff (or state) present its side or hearing both sides in a civil suit when the directed verdict is in favor of the plaintiff—and dismissed because there is no need to deliberate. Second, the odds of a directed verdict being overturned by an appellate court are typically much higher than that for a jnov. In fact, even if a jnov is overturned on appeal, all the appellate court must do is to reinstate the jury's decision. If a directed verdict is overturned on appeal, there is no jury verdict to reinstate, and thus a new trial will be necessary.

Two more points need to be made about directed verdicts and jnovs. First, the jury may never know that a jnov has been issued overturning its verdict because there is a period, usually 10 to 20 days after the jury's verdict, during which the motion can be filed, and the judge has some time to consider whether to grant the motion. Unless the judge's decision is reported in the media, the jurors will likely never learn their decision was overruled. Second, the federal courts and most state courts do not allow a jnov unless the side requesting it has previously made, at the appropriate time, a motion for a directed verdict.[64]

Assuming no directed verdict is granted in favor of the defendant after the plaintiff or state (in a criminal case) has presented all of its witnesses and the defendant has had the opportunity to cross-examine each of those witnesses, the defense then calls its witnesses. The process is exactly the same as before, except that the defendant conducts a direct examination of each witness, followed by the plaintiff's cross-examination, the defendant's re-direct (if exercised) and so on. It is quite possible that the plaintiff or state may have already called some of the witnesses testifying on behalf of the defense. If so, the plaintiff is permitted to ask leading questions, even though conducting a direct examination. For example, in a libel or invasion of privacy case, the plaintiff's attorney may wish to build the case with testimony from the reporters who wrote the story, the managing editor, the copy desk chief and other journalists in an attempt to establish negligence or even actual malice from the beginning and thus form a strong impression on the jury.

Expert Witnesses

Both sides may call expert witnesses, hired to offer their opinions on a particular aspect of the case. By definition, expert witnesses must possess special skills and/or knowledge not held by the average person but gained through specialized experience or education or a combination of both. In other words, the expert witness must be qualified to testify on the particular issue. For example, a professor of journalism may be hired in a libel case by the defendant to testify that the reporter was not negligent and that the story was not published with actual malice, just as the plaintiff could hire a similar expert to offer evidence that there was negligence or actual malice. An example in a criminal case would be a forensic psychiatrist hired by the prosecutor to testify that the defendant was mentally competent to stand trial.

Expert witnesses are usually paid for their services, and their fees generally range from $50 to several hundred dollars an hour plus expenses. Although the importance of expert witnesses varies from case to case (in both civil and criminal cases), it is sometimes the expert with the strongest testimony who makes such a positive impression on the jury or judge (in a bench trial) that the decision sways in favor of the party for whom the testimony is being offered. In most cases, however, the experts cancel out one another in the eyes of the jury. Thus it is not all that unusual for the attorneys for both sides to forego the experts.

The judge plays a major role in the conduct of any trial, including ruling on whether a particular piece of evidence is admissible under the federal or state rules of evidence. The difficulty is assuring that jurors do not hear inadmissible evidence; probably all too often, however, the inadmissible evidence is heard by the jury anyway because the other side is unable to object until after-the-fact. The judge must then admonish the jury to disregard the inadmissible evidence. Is such an admonition effective? If one study is any indication, the answer is "probably not." An American Bar Foundation researcher[65] found in an experiment with more than 500 adults called to jury duty in Cook County, Illinois, that jurors' decisions in a hypothetical civil case involving clear police misconduct in a raid were affected by the evidence police did or did not find. Even though the "jurors" were instructed by the "judge" to disregard the inadmissible evidence, their decision was affected by that evidence. Even the amount of damages was affected by the illegally obtained evidence, apparently because the information remembered by the jurors during their deliberations was influenced by what the police found. For example, the study's participants who heard that the fruits of the illegal search included evidence that the plaintiff was guilty of selling heroin awarded the plaintiff an average of $7,359 in punitive damages versus an average of $23,585 if the evidence indicated the plaintiff was *innocent* of possession of marijuana.[66]

Closing Arguments

In both civil and criminal cases, the case ends with *closing arguments* by both sides. The opening statements, as mentioned earlier, are summaries of the facts to be presented, *not* arguments; the closing comments can, and indeed nearly always are, arguments designed to sway the jury to that particular side. Even though some studies indicate that jurors often make up their minds during the opening statements, attorneys know that closing arguments can play a key role in influencing the jurors, especially those who may still be undecided after hearing all of the evidence. Thus, it is not unusual, especially in civil cases, for the attorneys to make strong, emotional appeals. Indeed, some of the most colorful and memorable statements from great lawyers such as Clarence S. Darrow — who unsuccessfully defended public school teacher John T. Scopes in the famous Tennessee "Monkey" trial over the teaching of evolution — have come from closing arguments.

In fact, unless the opposing side objects, judges in both civil and criminal cases are generally lax in what they permit attorneys to say in closing. Rule 61 of the Federal Rules of Civil Procedure and a very similar Rule 61 of the Federal Rules of Criminal Procedure are usually cited as the basis for ignoring potential errors in closing arguments because "the court at every stage of the proceeding must disregard any error or defect in the proceeding which does not affect the substantial rights of the parties."[67] Consider the excerpts from the following closing arguments made by the plaintiff's attorney in a libel suit discussed in Chapter 7:

Since he talked with you about the University of Georgia and when he was there, I think I likewise have a right to mention to you briefly that I probably have known Wally Butts longer than any man in this case. I was at Mercer University with Wally Butts when he played end on the football team there. He was in some respects a small man in stature, but he had more determination and more power to win than any man that I have ever seen in my life. I would not stand before you in this case today arguing in his behalf if I thought that Wally Butts would not tell you the truth when he raises his hand on this stand and swears to Almighty God that what he is going to tell you is the truth. . . .

Somebody has got to stop them. There is no law against it, and the only way that type of, as I call it, yellow journalism can be stopped is to let the *Saturday Evening Post* know that it is not going to get away with it today, tomorrow, or anymore hereafter and the only way that lesson can be brought home to them, Gentleman, is to hit them where it hurts them, and the only thing they know is money. They write about human beings; they kill him, his wife, his three lovely daughters. What do they care? . . .

I say, Gentlemen, this is the time we have got to get them. A hundred million dollars in advertising, would ten per cent of that be fair to Wally Butts for what they have done to him. . . .

You know, one of these days, like everyone else must come to, Wallace Butts is going to pass on. No one can bother him then. The *Saturday Evening Post* can't get at him then. And unless I miss my guess, they will put Wallace Butts in a red coffin with a black lid, and he will have a football in his hands, and his epitaph will read something like this: "Glory, Glory to old Georgia."[68]

The jury of 12 men awarded plaintiff Butts $460,000, the equivalent of two cents for each of the 23 million issues in which the story appeared. Both a U. S. Circuit Court of Appeals and the U.S. Supreme Court upheld the jury's decision.

Judge's Instructions to the Jury

After the closing arguments have been delivered, the judge instructs the jury on the appropriate law to be applied in deciding the case. In most jurisdictions, including the federal system, the attorneys for both sides have the opportunity to submit to the judge specific instructions for the jury. Such requests have to be filed and the judge must rule on them *before* the closing arguments are made, but the instructions are not usually given to the jury by the judge until *after* the closing arguments. Under Rule 51 of the Federal Rules of Civil Procedure and most state rules, the judge can instruct the jury before or after the closing arguments or both, although judges rarely depart from the tradition of waiting until the arguments conclude. In complex cases, these instructions can be long, complicated and intensely boring for the jury, but they are important in the judicial process.

Jury Deliberations

Once the jury instructions have concluded, the members deliberate behind closed doors. After a foreperson is elected by the body, a tentative vote is first taken, usually by secret ballot. If a unanimous verdict is required (often it is not) and the vote is unanimous with no undecideds on the first ballot, the jury returns to the courtroom to announce its verdict. Generally, however, the first vote will not be unanimous and deliberations will last from a few hours to days and even weeks.

The Verdict

In a civil case, there are three major types of verdicts. The judge always determines which type of verdict is needed. The most frequent type is the *general verdict*. With a general verdict, the judge instructs the jury on the applicable law and requests that the members apply that law to the facts in the case and determine which side wins and the amount of damages or other relief if the plaintiff wins. Thus the jury is granted considerable flexibility in reaching its decision.

With a *special verdict*, the court requires the jury to render a verdict "in the form of a special written finding upon each issue of fact."[69] In other words, the jury is confined to making specific findings of fact, and the judge actually applies the appropriate law to the facts and renders the final verdict. The procedure is for the judge to submit to the jury a series of written questions, along with explanations and instructions, which the members answer in writing based on their findings during deliberations. Any party in a civil suit can request a special verdict, but the judge makes the final decision regarding the form of the verdict.

A third type of verdict, a sort of compromise between general and special verdicts, is the *general verdict accompanied by answer to interrogatories*.[70] This form of verdict, in which the judge requests a general verdict accompanied by written answers to one or more factual issues, has the advantage that the judge can compare the answers to the interrogatories to see if they are in line with the verdict. If they are consistent, all's right with the world, and the judgment is entered into the record. If the verdict and answers are at odds, the judge can either send the case back to the jury for further consideration or grant a new trial. This verdict form has the advantage that it allows the judge to head off the possibility of a successful appeal. Unfortunately, such a verdict can be very time consuming and potentially confusing to the jury.

Although its deliberations are secret, the jury verdict in both civil and criminal cases is announced in open court either by the jury foreperson or by the court clerk, depending on the tradition in that particular jurisdiction. If the jury has been unable to reach a verdict (for example, if it is unable to reach a unanimous verdict when required), there is a *hung jury*. If the judge is convinced that the jury could reach a verdict if given more time, the judge may order the jury to reconvene to try to reach a decision. Otherwise, the judge may declare a *mistrial*. Mistrials are relatively rare in civil cases, but they do occasionally occur in criminal cases.

Sixth Amendment Ban on Double Jeopardy

Can a defendant be tried again if there is a mistrial? The answer is yes in both civil and criminal cases. The Sixth Amendment ban on double jeopardy does not apply to civil cases, and there is no double jeopardy in a mistrial in a criminal case because no verdict has been rendered. However, if a defendant in a criminal suit is acquitted, the decision is final, and the defendant cannot be tried again for that same crime. However, if an individual has been acquitted of a federal crime but the same facts and circumstances support a trial on state charges, the person could face trial in state court. No double jeopardy arises because the two alleged crimes are not the same even though the facts surrounding them are similar or even identical. The same would be true if the acquittal was on state charges but the facts supported federal charges.

The judge always has the option in a criminal case of either granting an acquittal or a directed verdict, of course, before the case goes to the jury. In this case the judge must be convinced that a guilty verdict cannot be reasonably supported by the facts. The court can also order a new trial because of substantive procedural errors, but such decisions are relatively rare in both civil and criminal cases.

Impeachment of the Verdict

In very unusual situations, a jury verdict may be *impeached* based on juror testimony. The rule in most states, but *not* in the federal courts, is that juror testimony *cannot* be used to impeach a verdict. This rule, popularly known as the "Mansfield rule," does not prohibit other evidence, such as someone else's observations of jury misconduct, from being used for impeachment. A few states adhere to the "Iowa rule," under which jurors can testify regarding overt acts, but not opinions, of other members. For example, a juror could testify that another juror read newspaper stories about the trial even though the jurors had been instructed not to read such stories.

Federal Rule of Evidence 606 allows inquiry only into testimony by a juror only "on the question whether extraneous prejudicial information was improperly brought to the jury's attention or whether any outside influence was improperly brought to bear upon any juror."

Debriefing Jurors

While jurors may be prohibited from discussing a case while a trial is in progress, they are certainly free to talk once they have rendered a verdict and the trial is over or otherwise concluded. Thus a journalist or anyone else can "debrief" a juror with that person's consent. Many newspapers and radio and television stations now routinely interview jurors when the trial is over to ascertain how the decision was reached and what factors influenced the jurors. Jurors are sometimes reluctant to discuss cases, especially because they have been ordered not to do so while the trial was in session. However, a thoughtful and enterprising reporter can usually make such former jurors feel at ease and thus get an important "inside" story that helps the reader better understand the verdict.

Although the jury may have come and gone, its decision is not final until the judge enters a judgment on the decision, which may come a few or even several days later. Any specified deadlines for filing appeals and other motions do not begin to run until the judgment is entered.

Determining Damages

Unless there are applicable statutory limits, the jury has considerable discretion and leeway in setting damages in civil cases. In nearly all cases, however, the judge has the authority to increase or decrease the amount of damages awarded by the jury and even to modify the judgment in other ways before the final judgment is actually entered. For example, when actress and comedienne Carol Burnett was awarded $1.6 million in 1981 by a California jury for libel against the *National Enquirer*, as discussed in Chapter 7, the judge cut the total to $800,000.[71] In the same year when a former "Miss Wyoming" won a total of $26.5 million in damages in a jury trial for libel against *Penthouse* magazine, the federal court judge immediately halved the damages,[72] which the plaintiff never collected because she ultimately lost before a U.S. Court of Appeals.

Jury awards are typically small because the damages in most cases are not sizable; occasionally, however, juries do award large damages and such cases receive considerable publicity. In 1988, for example, the largest award was $30,256,768 in a case involving wrongful death in a truck collision. The remaining nine awards in the top 10 lineup ranged from $25 million for wrongful death and emotional distress in a truck-pedestrian collision to $14,013,655 for an aspiring male model who lost 14 teeth and three inches of jaw in a multiple car collision caused by New York City's failure to install a median barrier in spite of warning about the danger for eight years.[73] The largest verdict was settled shortly after the trial by all parties for an undisclosed amount of cash and at least four of the other judgments were appealed.[74] Several years ago, a Washington, DC, jury awarded an 8-year-old child $95 million against the manufacturer of Bendectin because he was born with deformed hands and arms after his mother took the prescription drug for morning sickness.[75] But by far the largest award to date was the $10.53 *billion* (that's billion, *not* million) verdict for Pennzoil in 1985 against Texaco.[76]

Most jury trials, whether civil or criminal, last no more than three or four days; however, some may go no longer than a few hours and others may continue for years. The record for the longest trial to date is the three-and-a-half-year *Kemner v. Monsato* dioxin trial. The trial over whether 65 plaintiffs were injured when a half teaspoon of extremely toxic dioxin leaked from a railroad tank-car during an accident began on February 22, 1984, and ended on October 22, 1987, with a jury verdict that ordered the defendant to pay $16.25 million in punitive damages.[77] The transcript in the trial was more than 100,000 pages, including testimony from 182 witnesses and some 6,000 exhibits. One report about the trial noted that one 27-year-old lawyer had worked on this single case since he graduated from law school,[78] and another article described how one juror was dismissed less than an hour before jury deliberations began after she had sat through all of the previous $3\frac{1}{2}$-years of trial proceedings.[79] The jurors awarded the 65 plaintiffs $1 each in compensatory damages.[80]

THE CRIMINAL TRIAL

The procedures and proceedings in a civil trial and a criminal trial are quite similar, but there are a few differences. First, the pretrial procedures in criminal cases are substantially different, primarily because various constitutional rights come into play, as discussed earlier, such as the Sixth Amendment right to a speedy and public trial and the Fifth Amendment right of due process. There are three major ways in which criminal charges are brought against an individual or legal entity such as a corporation. First, a grand jury can issue an *indictment*, which is **not** a finding of guilt. It is merely a finding that there is sufficient evidence, defined as *probable cause*, to warrant a trial.

Grand Jury Indictments

The grand jury system has both proponents and critics. The process has the advantage that it serves as a mechanism for filtering out criminal cases that have little merit. At the same time it can be argued that all too often grand juries have become mouthpieces for prosecutors. The truth is probably somewhere between these two stances.

Unlike trial juries (technically known as petit juries), grand juries sit for more than one case. Indeed, in the federal system, grand jurors serve for a year or more and can hear hundreds of potential cases during that time. The grand jury is also much larger than a trial jury—typically with 16 to 23 members in federal cases and a similar number in state cases. The role of a federal grand jury differs considerably from that of state grand juries. In fact, only about half of the states even use grand juries, and of those that do, many use them primarily as investigatory bodies to check on public fraud and corruption.

Two characteristics of the grand jury system that could be criticized as inherent weaknesses are (a) deliberations are always conducted in secret, away from the scrutiny of the press and the public, and (b) the prosecutor or, in the federal system, the U.S. Attorney for that district presents the evidence to the grand jury, without the opportunity for any potential defendant or actual defendant to present that side. According to the rationale for secrecy, witnesses will feel free to give their testimony without fear of revenge, but, by the same token, it could be argued that such a witness is more likely to exaggerate or even lie if that person knows the testimony will not be subject to public scrutiny. Interestingly, not only are the grand jurors restricted from publicly disclosing any information about the proceedings while the grand jury is in session but even the U.S. Attorney or prosecutor is gagged.

In the federal system and in most of the states that use the grand jury system, the press is usually allowed to watch witnesses as they enter and leave the grand jury room, but witnesses are not permitted to talk with anyone except authorized officials until after they have given their testimony. Ironically, once the witness has testified in secret, the individual can then talk freely about the testimony if willing. The enterprising reporter is always on the lookout for witnesses who volunteer to talk. But be careful! Witnesses can talk, if they wish, only **after** the testimony; the reporter who publishes information leaked by a grand juror or a prosecutor faces the real possibility of a subpoena to identify the source in court or face contempt of court charges, including a fine and/or a jail sentence.

There is a common perception, especially among attorneys and journalists who cover the courts, that grand jury leaks have increased considerably in recent years and that prosecutors are the biggest offenders. A report by the Committee on Criminal Law of the New York City Bar, however, concluded, with at least one strong dissenter, that many disclosures actually come from defense attorneys in the form of permissible (i.e., legal) communications.[81] The report also concluded that the press should adopt its own standards designed to prevent harmful grand jury leaks and, once the standards are adopted, the federal courts should order reporters to disclose the identities of government officials leaking grand jury secrets.[82]

If the grand jury determines that the evidence in the forms of testimony and materials and/or documents is sufficient to warrant a trial, the grand jury— upon the vote of a specified number of members (12 in the federal system)— will issue a *bill of indictment*, also known as a *true bill*, charging that individual with a particular crime or crimes. Unless the indictments have been ordered sealed, which occurs in rare circumstances, they are read and made available in open court and then filed as open records, usually in the court clerk's office. Seasoned reporters know that all defendant's names in an indictment are in all capital letters and that all charges are individually listed. Read names carefully because witnesses and other individuals may also be listed, but they are not defendants. (These names are **not** in all capital letters in the indictment.) For example, characterizing someone as a defendant who was merely a witness simply because you did not carefully read the indictment could bring you an unwanted suit for libel or false light, as discussed in later chapters.

Filing of an Information

The second method by which criminal charges can be brought is by *filing of an information* by a prosecutor such as a district or county attorney. This is simply a process by which the individual is formally accused without the use of a grand jury. Constitutional standards, including the Sixth and Fourteenth Amendments, require, just as in an indictment, that the exact (or approximate if exact cannot be determined) date, time and place of the alleged criminal act be specified. The information must also include the role the defendant played in the alleged crime and other known details. The idea is that defendants should be sufficiently informed so they can adequately defend themselves.

The filing of an information is often based on evidence obtained through a search warrant, which must conform to Fourth-Amendment standards as enunciated by the U.S. Supreme Court in a series of complicated decisions over the years. Basically, the Court has said that the warrant must be specific and narrowly drawn to insure that a constitutionally valid search is conducted. If a search warrant is improper, then the evidence garnered from the search generally cannot be used at trial, although in recent years the Supreme Court has carved out a series of "good faith exceptions" that some legal experts, especially criminal defense attorneys, find troubling.

One variation of the filing of information occurs when charges are initiated by one individual filing a criminal complaint against another—such as a wife filing charges against her husband for assault. The prosecutor has the discretion, however, on whether to act on the charges by a filing of information. In other words, the original criminal complaint basically serves as a request to the prosecutor to take further steps. The prosecutor can always choose not to proceed further, especially if there appears to be no probably cause to do so.

Citations

Finally, for certain misdemeanors, but **not** felonies, and other relatively minor crimes such as traffic violations, charges can be brought via a *citation* from a law enforcement or other designated officer. No grand jury or filing of information is required under these circumstances.

Arrest Warrant

Once the grand jury has returned the indictment or the prosecutor has filed an information, the court clerk issues an *arrest warrant* if the person is not already in custody. For example, the individual may already have been charged with another crime and thereby arrested or the person may have been detained at the time the alleged criminal act took place. Since a U.S. Supreme Court decision in 1966, known as *Miranda v. Arizona*,[83] police have been required, primarily under the Fifth Amendment ban on forced self-incrimination, to inform suspects in police custody of their constitutional rights **before** any questioning can begin.

Television shows and movies are fond of including the Miranda warnings, probably as a way of lending authenticity to their product. Almost any first-grader can utter, "Read me my rights." Television shows from "Hawaii Five-O" and "Dragnet" in the 1960s and 1970s to "Hooperman" and "Matlock" in the 1980s to "Murder, She Wrote" and "Law and Order" in the 1990s, have made the line "You have the right to remain silent . . ." as familiar as some of the theme songs that accompany the shows. One stipulation to the requirement that the Miranda Rule be followed is that the suspect must be in custody or be in a situation in which the ability to voluntarily leave is significantly restricted by police. If police fail to give the warnings when the rule is in effect, any confession or other incriminating evidence disclosed by that person can generally not be used to convict the person.

Preliminary Hearing

Unless defendants have been indicted by a grand jury, the next major step in the criminal procedure is an *initial* or *first appearance*, which is known in some jurisdictions as a *preliminary hearing* or *arraignment*. (Journalists should learn the proper terminology in their jurisdiction.) First, the judge will inform defendants of the specific charges brought against them and then inform defendants of their legal rights. At this stage, a judge must also decide if there is probable cause (i.e., sufficient evidence) to warrant bringing defendants to trial. If the judge believes the evidence is insufficient, the judge will dismiss the charge(s) and order that defendants be released.

If the judge finds there is probable cause to charge defendants, the judge will first determine if defendants need legal representation. If defendants cannot afford an attorney, the judge will make arrangements for a public defender to serve. Finally, the judge determines whether defendants will be allowed to post *bail* and, if so, how much must be posted prior to defendants' release from custody. The judge has several options, including allowing defendants to post a specified amount for bail, releasing defendants on their *own recognizance* (without having to post bond) and even denying bail in extreme circumstances, such as when a defendant has a history of "jumping" bail.

The fact that dangerous individuals are frequently released on bail has drawn much criticism from the public over the years, but judges are bound by the Eighth Amendment prohibition against excessive bail. The rationale in granting bail is to allow the defendant to prepare adequately for defense while a stick is held over the accused's head in the form of a posted bail bond that is forfeited if the defendant fails to appear at trial. The judge does have the option of imposing certain conditions on the bail—such as restricting the defendant's travel and personal contacts—so long as they are reasonable, and the judge can always set the amount of the bond sufficiently high to insure that the defendant does appear at trial.

Arraignment

If defendants have already been indicted, the first major step after indictment and arrest is *arraignment*. At this stage, individuals are read the indictment, the judge explains the legal rights and individuals enter a plea. If an initial appearance, as explained earlier, has already been made, the judge simply hears the plea. If defendants plead guilty, they will either be immediately sentenced, especially in the case of misdemeanors and minor offenses, or a date will be set for sentencing. If defendants plead not guilty, a tentative trial date is announced. It is not unusual for the trial date to be postponed one or more times before the actual trial.

In the case of federal crimes and in some states, the judge can also entertain a plea of *nolo contendere* (form the Latin meaning "I will not contest it"). Federal Rule of Criminal Procedure 11(b) permits this plea only with the consent of the judge, who must consider the rights of the parties and the public interest in effective administration of justice. Basically, the defendant is saying "I am neither admitting nor denying the charges but simply not fighting." Obviously, the judge in such a case can reject the plea or, if the judge accepts the plea, the judge can still fine and/or sentence the person. The major advantage for the defendant is that, unlike with a guilty plea, a plaintiff cannot use the plea as evidence against the defendant in a civil suit arising from the same actions as those associated with the criminal charges. In other words, a nolo contendere plea cannot be used as evidence in a civil suit.

Settlement Prior to Trial

The overwhelming majority of criminal and civil cases never come to trial because an agreement is reached between the two sides beforehand. For civil cases, this means an out-of-court settlement, but in criminal cases, the filtering process is called *plea bargaining*. Actually, plea bargaining can occur at any stage, but most agreements are made after the arraignment but before trial. One study[84] found that fewer than 5,000 (or less than 15 percent) of the 38,000 federal criminal defendants convicted in a fiscal year were convicted at trial. Obviously, the courts could not begin to handle the caseload if even just twice as many defendants insisted on having a trial to which they are constitutionally entitled. Plea bargaining has become **the** way of settling criminal cases. The public is often appalled when incorrigibles get a prosecutor to agree to ask the judge that they be charged with a lesser offense than in the original complaint and/or that they be granted leniency in sentencing in exchange for pleading guilty. Some people are particularly concerned because the plea bargaining process takes place out of the public limelight. The agreement usually becomes public only when the defendant appears in court. It is not well-known that the judge is not bound by any agreement between the prosecutor and the defendant. In other words, the judge can refuse to honor the agreement, although judges rarely override the recommendations of a prosecutor.

Discovery

If the case has not already been settled by a guilty plea or dismissal, the last major step in a criminal case before trial is *discovery*. The process is somewhat different in criminal than in civil suits. One of the most important differences is that depositions and interrogatories, which are almost essential in any civil case that goes to trial, are almost never conducted in criminal cases. They are usually unnecessary anyway because (a) the Fifth Amendment prevents a **criminal** defendant (but generally **not** a civil defendant) from being forced to give testimony, and (b) the federal system and most states have fairly strong disclosure provisions that require each side to keep the other side informed, including exchanging the list of witnesses that side expects to use at trial. The prosecutor is also required to reveal to the defense any evidence found during the investigation or discovery that would reflect on the defendant's guilt or innocence. This requirement is usually enforced in the form of a judge's order and can encompass the defendant's criminal records; documents, photos and other materials to be used at trial; medical reports and results of other tests such as a polygraph examination; and any recorded statements made by the defendant to police or other officials.

In the federal system and in most states, the prosecution also has the right of access to evidence to be used by the defense at trial, although, of course, the prosecution cannot get information that would be covered by attorney–client privilege or by some other exemption to the general rule of disclosure.

Much of the information exchanged by the two sides is public record, including discovery orders and responses. The astute reporter will frequently check with the court clerk to see if new documents have been added to the case file. It is particularly a good idea to establish rapport with the clerk because processing a document that has been filed may take awhile, especially if the clerk's office is overloaded at the time. Most court clerks are usually willing to allow the reporter to make a copy of a document as soon as it has been filed (i.e., officially received and stamped), but you should set up a cooperative arrangement with the clerk for doing this.

ALTERNATIVE DISPUTE RESOLUTION

As the workloads of most courts continue to increase, alternatives will get more attention and thereby begin to look more attractive. Clearly, the courts remain the best forum for many types of cases, but there are indeed some viable alternatives, many of which have long, distinguished histories. These options go by colorful names such as summary jury trials, minitrials, arbitration and mediation, but they all provide a way of resolving disputes outside the traditional trial. Some – such as summary jury trials – are more shortcuts than real alternatives, but they are becoming more popular as attorneys, judges and other legal experts discover their advantages and begin to feel comfortable in recommending them to clients and parties. A detailed discussion of each process is beyond the scope of this book, but we briefly explore the more popular alternatives so you will recognize their features and can learn, on your own if necessary, the inner workings of each one.

Summary Jury Trial

In 1980, a U.S. District Judge in Cleveland, Thomas Lambros, proposed a new process for encouraging negotiated settlements in civil cases. Several federal trial court judges have used the technique, known as a *summary jury trial*, usually with the consent of litigants on both sides. The idea of a summary jury trial is, at least intuitively, rather appealing. Instead of the usual drawn-out trial in which there are opening statements, direct examinations, cross-examinations, closing arguments, objections, motions and so on, the attorney for each side is granted a specific amount of time to **summarize** the case before a six-person jury, which then deliberates and renders a **nonbinding** verdict. Most summary jury trials take no more than a few hours to a day and they, theoretically at least, afford the parties the opportunity to see how an actual jury would weigh the evidence and decide.

In 1987, however, this procedure received a serious, although certainly not fatal, blow when the U.S. Court of Appeals for the Seventh Circuit held that federal judges lack the authority to **require** parties and attorneys to use summary jury trials.[85] Because the issue in the case was whether litigants could be forced to use the technique, the court did not rule on the legality of such trials in which both sides consent.[86]

The case arose when an attorney was cited for contempt and fined $500 by the trial court judge after he refused to participate in a summary jury trial even though ordered to do so. The trial court judge did **not** order that the case be settled with this process but merely that this alternative be used to attempt to induce a settlement. He used Rule 16 of the Federal Rules of Civil Procedure, which grants federal judges discretion in directing attorneys and parties to participate in a pretrial conference. The judge also cited a 1984 resolution by the Judicial Conference of the United States, endorsing summary jury trials.[87] Nevertheless, the court of appeals noted that although the rule "was intended to foster settlement through the use of extrajudicial procedures, it was not intended to require that an unwilling litigant be sidetracked from the normal course of litigation."[88]

According to one authority on alternative dispute resolution (ADR),[89] "the case begins to define how far courts can go when it comes to alternative dispute resolution. In the ADR movement, we have a ways to travel in terms of sorting out the rules of the court in imposing, stimulating, and encouraging ADR procedures."

One final note on summary jury trials: Terminology can be confusing. *Summary* is a fairly common legal term as in *summary* judgment and *summary* proceeding.

Arbitration

Certainly the oldest ADR mechanisms that are still used today are arbitration and mediation. These processes are often confused with one another, but they are quite different. The Council of Better Business Bureaus (BBB) defines *arbitration* as "a legal process in which two or more persons agree to let an impartial person or panel decide their dispute."[90] Except in very unusual circumstances, such as when an arbitrator or panel violates established rules or when the arbitrators clearly exceed their legal authority, a court will not even hear an appeal of an arbitration decision, let alone reverse it. Thus arbitration decisions are legally binding on all the parties involved, unlike court decisions, which can generally be appealed at least once. This is one of the major advantages of arbitration. The parties must agree to abide by the decision, regardless of whether it is favorable or unfavorable to a particular party, so both sides know from the beginning that the arbitrator's decision will settle the dispute once and for all. The savings in cost, time and attorneys' fees can be considerable. In fact, for most arbitrations, a party need not be represented by an attorney, although each side has the option of using legal counsel.

The Better Business Bureau is only one of several private organizations that conduct arbitration hearings. There are even some governmental agencies involved, such as the Federal Mediation and Conciliation Service (FMCS),[91] whose work includes resolving labor–management conflicts, and the Community Relations Service (CRS), whose primary concern is improving law enforcement-community interactions.[92] Both are little-known among the general public, but they provide services such as arbitration, mediation and conciliation that are becoming more prominent each day. The FMCS was established in 1947 to mediate labor-management disputes, whereas CRS was created with the Civil Rights Act of 1964 to provide help in resolving racial conflicts.[93] Many states now have public agencies for arbitrating and mediating disputes, usually connected with a state Consumer Protection Division.

Mediation

Mediation is the process by which a neutral party or parties intermediate between two or more parties in conflict, with their consent, in an attempt to get the opposing sides to settle the dispute on mutually satisfying terms. In other words, a mediator uses the power of persuasion, **not** coercion, to convince the two sides to reach an agreement. The mediator hears both sides, asks questions and works hard to get the parties to settle but does **not** make a binding decision, although the final agreement reached by the parties themselves, with the aid of the mediator, is usually legally binding. With arbitration, on the other hand, the arbitrator, after hearing both sides, will actually render a legally binding decision, which is usually in favor of one side.

ADR has become so popular that many major law firms and attorneys in private practice now offer arbitration, mediation and other forms of ADR as part of their service. In fact, the theme of the 1989 annual American Bar Association meeting in Honolulu was "Resolving disputes in Pacific Ways." Many prominent law schools such as Harvard University now offer seminars in mediation and negotiation.

American Arbitration Association

By far, the most widely known and prestigious private organization is the American Arbitration Association (AAA), founded in 1926. The AAA describes itself as "a public-service, not-for-profit organization offering a broad range of dispute resolution services to business executives, attorneys, individuals, trade associations, unions, management, consumers, families, communities, and all levels of government."[94] Its main offices are in New York, and their branch offices in 33 major cities serve most of the United States because hearings do not have to be held in an AAA office.

Each type of arbitration — commercial, construction industry, securities and so on — has its own set of rules, a copy of which is always available from the organization under whose auspices the process is conducted. If, as a reporter or writer, you are assigned to cover the business, labor or even the sports beat, it is likely that you will be assigned a story involving arbitration or mediation. Thus it would be well worth the effort to read and know the ADR rules governing a particular type of dispute.

For example, Cy Young Award recipient, pitcher Doug Drabek of the Pittsburgh Pirates, won a record $3.35 million salary through arbitration in 1990.[95] A year earlier, the dispute between George Steinbrenner, controversial owner of the New York Yankees, and Dave Winfield, the all-star outfielder, was arbitrated under AAA's Commercial Arbitration Rules, with a prominent New York attorney serving as arbitrator. One of the largest arbitration awards ever rendered was in 1988 when IBM won a $833.2 million package of past and future payments from Fujitsu, Ltd. after a long-standing software battle between the two computer giants.[96] Even foreign governments have used arbitration. For instance, a nine-year border dispute between Egypt and Israel was finally settled via arbitration several years ago with the assistance of the U.S. State Department.[97] According to the AAA, a record 60,808 cases were filed with the association in 1990 with the value of claims and counterclaims totalling more than $2.5 billion — another record.[98] One service offered by the AAA and other ADR organizations, of which many individuals including lawyers are not aware, is divorce mediation.

From a media perspective, it has the drawback that arbitration and mediation procedures are traditionally conducted in private, although parties will sometimes consent to opening them to the press and to the public, and a few states have statutes requiring that arbitration proceedings be public under specific conditions (such as when a governmental entity is an interested party). If you are doing a story about a dispute, do not hesitate to ask a party if the person is willing to talk about the conflict on the record. You can also ask the parties to consent to making the decision public. It is usually fruitless, on the other hand, to question arbitrators because they are bound to neutrality and fairness, and thus it is usually not appropriate for them to make any comments, no matter how objective such statements might be.

One development in ADR that seemed particularly promising for resolving libel cases was the Libel Dispute Resolution Program operated by the University of Iowa Libel Research Project. The program, which began in 1987 as a three-year experiment, used an adjudicator or neutral party to decide only whether a particular published statement (or statements) was (were) false and whether the complainant's reputation was thereby harmed.[99] Unlike a judge or jury, the adjudicator did not decide constitutional issues — such as whether the individual was a public figure or whether actual malice was involved. The adjudicator could order, when appropriate, that a media respondent publish the results of the decision or pay to have them published elsewhere. The goal was to have a decision within 60 to 75 days from the filing of the complaint.[100]

Unfortunately, the program failed to gain much interest from lawyers and ended in November 1991 after attracting only 5 of 128 libel cases to which it offered its services. Only one case was actually resolved through the process.[101] No doubt, there are various reasons for the failure of such a noteworthy project, but most ADR programs are successful.

SUMMARY AND CONCLUSIONS

Each jurisdiction, whether state or federal, has its own rules of civil procedure, criminal procedure and evidence that determine the specific steps involved in a civil or criminal case. Most states, however, conform fairly closely to the federal rules, with which any journalist who covers legal matters should become quite familiar. Whereas the trial process for a civil matter is quite similar to that of a criminal case, the pretrial procedures and evidentiary standards are rather different. For example, the typical civil case begins with the filing of a complaint; a criminal case can begin with an arrest, with the prosecutor's filing of an information or with a grand jury indictment. Both usually involve discovery, whereby the two sides disclose to one another the witnesses, documents, and other evidence expected to be used at trial. But in many jurisdictions, the prosecution has an affirmative duty to disclose to the defense any evidence uncovered during the investigation or otherwise found that would aid the defendant at trial. There is obviously no such duty on either attorney in a civil case, although a motion to discover is sometimes used to compel the other side to disclose books, records, and other documents relevant to the case.

The three most common evidentiary standards are preponderance of the evidence and clear and convincing evidence in civil cases and beyond a reasonable doubt in criminal cases. For example, in a libel suit by a public figure against a media defendant, the plaintiff must show by clear and convincing evidence that the false information was published with actual malice. In any criminal case, the jury must be convinced beyond a reasonable doubt that defendants committed the alleged crime before it can find them guilty.

Because both civil and criminal trials absorb considerable time and re-sources, including great strain on the courts, more judges and attorneys are using alternative ways of resolving disputes, popularly known as alternative dispute resolution (ADR). For criminal cases, the answer to the evergrowing backlog still remains plea bargaining, by which a defendant pleads guilty in return for the prosecutor's agreement to ask the judge to reduce the alleged crime to a lesser offense, that the judge be lenient in sentencing and so on. But, for civil matters, there are some viable alternatives that include minitrials, arbitration, mediation, summary jury trials and other forms of dispute resolution that are much faster, considerably less expensive and less burdensome on the participants and the court systems. Not all ADR programs survive, as demonstrated by the demise of the the University of Iowa Libel Dispute Resolution Program, but as courts continue to push for better alternatives to litigation, it will become essential to most journalists to be well-versed in ADR techniques.[102]

II Governmental Restraints

4 Prior Restraint

Freedom is not easy. Freedom is uncomfortable. The first Amendment is a tragic amendment in that it inflicts a great deal of pain on a lot of people.[1]

— writer Kurt Vonnegut

In determining the extent of the constitutional protection, it has been generally, if not universally, considered that it is the chief purpose of the guaranty to prevent previous restraints upon publication.[2]

— majority in *Near v. Minnesota* (1931)

Every freeman has an undoubted right to lay what sentiments he pleases before the public; to forbid this is to destroy the freedom of the press; but if he publishes what is improper, mischievous, or illegal, he must take the consequences of his own temerity.[3]

— British jurist Sir William Blackstone (1723–1780)

Sometimes the First Amendment drives me crazy. The only thing worse than all this clamor is silence. . . . We do not have to fear dissenting voices or even hostile voices. . . . What we have to fear is silence.[4]

— CBS newsman Charles Kuralt (1989)

In February 1989, the spiritual and religious leader of Iran, the Ayatollah Rhollah Khomeini, ordered his Moslem followers throughout the world to track down and murder Indian-born British author, Salman Rushdie, because he claimed that Rushdie's novel, *The Satanic Verses*, slandered Islam, a religion practiced by billions of individuals, especially in Asia and Africa. More specifically, the Ayatollah condemned certain passages in the book as blasphemous in the depiction of a relatively minor character, Mahound, whom Moslems contend is a thinly disguised representation of the prophet Mohammed. Almost immediately, the three largest bookstore chains in this country, Walden, B. Dalton and Barnes & Noble, announced they were pulling the book from their shelves, ostensibly out of fear that threats would be made against their stores and their employees. Eventually, all three chains changed their policy and displayed the books for sale. Even though Khomeini died four months after issuing his order, the religious leader's successors refused to commute the death order. Rushdie has periodically emerged from seclusion to make public appearances—to receive a First Amendment award from the Freedom Forum in Arlington, Virginia, and to speak at Columbia University in New York—but each time his visit was not announced in advance.

In late 1992 Warner Bros.-Sire Records, a division of media conglomerate Time Warner, Inc., rereleased rapper Ice-T's *Body Count* album at his request after police organizations called for a national boycott of the company.[5] Police groups were upset with a controversial song on the album, "Cop Killer," in which the rapper boasts that he's "'bout to dust some cops off" and proclaims "die, pig, die." The rerelease did not include the song. Several months earlier, Super Music, Inc., which owns 300 Turtles, Record Bar and Tracks shops, halted sales of the discs at its stores.

Earlier in the year, 275,000 federal employees insured by Blue Cross and Blue Shield finally got a chapter on contraceptives and teen sex that had been ordered deleted from a booklet entitled *Taking Care of Your Child*. A senior official with the government's personnel agency, the Office of Personnel Management, had found the material too controversial, and the insurer was told to drop the chapter. After the edited versions had already been distributed, Blue Cross succumbed to pressure from members of Congress and provided the missing chapter.[6]

Several years ago, a nursing student sued the publisher after she suffered injuries by treating herself for constipation using a hydrogen peroxide enema described in her textbook.[7]

A federal jury in Texas returned a $9.4 million verdict in 1988 against *Soldier of Fortune* magazine for running a classified ad that prompted a husband to hire a hitman to murder his wife. A year later, the Fifth Circuit U.S. Court of Appeals overturned the verdict, holding that the magazine had no duty to withhold publication of a "facially inocuous ad."[8] The classified ad read: "Ex-Marines—67-69 'Nam Vets, Ex-DI, weapons specialist—jungle warfare, pilot, M.E., high risk assignments, U.S. or overseas." The appellate court did say that the magazine owed a duty of reasonable care to the public and that the ad posed "a risk of serious harm," but it noted that such daily activities as interstate driving involved risks as well. "Given the pervasiveness of advertising in our society and the important role it plays, we decline to impose on publishers the obligation to reject all ambiguous advertisments for products or services that might pose a threat of harm," the court said.[9]

Two years after the federal circuit court ruled in its favor, *Soldier of Fortune* lost another round in a trial court when a U.S. District Court jury in Alabama awarded two brothers $2.375 million in compensatory damages and $10 million in punitive damages for the death of their father.[10] The judge in the case reduced the punitive damages to $2 million. Michael and Ian Braun's father was gunned down by a man hired by Braun's business partner after the following ad appeared in the magazine: "GUN FOR HIRE. 37-year-old professional mercenary desires jobs. Vietnam Veteran. Discreet and very private. Body guard, courier, and other special skills. All jobs considered." The classified then included an address and phone number. Citing the earlier Fifth Circuit decision, the Alabama federal judge ruled, in denying a motion for summary judgment, that this ad, unlike the earlier one, was not facially innocuous and that the magazine had breached its duty of reasonable care. The 11th Circuit U.S. Court of Appeals affirmed the district court decision in 1992, and the U.S. Supreme Court denied certiorari the next year.[11]

In the summer of 1987, British Prime Minister Margaret Thatcher successfully obtained injunctions in the British courts to prevent London newspapers from publishing excerpts from *Spycatcher*, the memoirs of former British intelligence officer, Peter Wright. In a symbolic protest, individuals opposed to the ban took turns reading the book, which offers inside details of dirty tricks executed by MI.5, Britain's domestic intelligence agency, in London's Hyde Park, which features the famous free speech "Speaker's Corner."[12] The ban was eventually overturned by the British courts after millions of copies of the book had been sold outside the country.

The movie *The Last Temptation of Christ* immediately spurred riots, arrests, lawsuits and condemnations around the country when it was released in 1988. One county adopted an ordinance, eventually declared unconstitutional by a federal district court judge, banning the movie. Numerous religious leaders called the film blasphemous and urged their congregations to boycott theaters showing the movie and even to picket theaters that featured the film. Indeed, in some major cities such as Cincinnati, Ohio, the film was never shown because theater owners did not want to be objects of protest. When the Martin Scorcese film, which includes a dream sequence in which Jesus, played by Willem Dafoe, imagines having sex with a woman, was released on video in June 1989, the overwhelming majority of video rental stores refused to stock it. In fact, the nation's largest video-store chain, Blockbuster Video, announced in advance that its company-owned stores would not make the movie available for sale or rental. However, several weeks after it was released to the home market in July 1989, enough video stores carried the movie to permit it to hit the top 10 several times on *Billboard* magazine's list of the most popular videocassettes rented.

In May 1989, a Green Bay, Wisconsin, Middle School lifted an earlier prohibition imposed by the school principal against students wearing T-shirts with the insignia of the rock bands Guns N' Roses and Black Sabbath. The principal imposed the ban after police linked the two bands' music to cult murders in Mexico. A month later, schools in Pasadena and Baytown, Texas, banned display of the peace symbol by students because the officials believed the symbol was used by devil worshippers.

Certainly the most insidious of all prior restraints in recent years was the bloody Chinese government crackdown against hundreds of thousands of pro-democracy demonstrators in May and June 1989. For several days in June 1989, U.S. media carried extensive coverage, including live television and radio broadcasts, from Tiananmen Square in China's capital, Beijing. CBS television news anchor Dan Rather, for example, reported the demonstrations live during the network's evening newscast, but eventually was prevented from broadcasting by Chinese authorities as the crackdown began. The United States and the rest of the world were very effectively blocked from seeing and even reading about the resulting massacre, but they at least were able to learn more about the tragic events than were most Chinese citizens, who were told only what government officials wanted them to know. In perhaps an ironic twist, many of the stories, especially those of the major television networks, newspapers and wire services focused on the mystery of how many Chinese demonstrators were actually killed in the uprising and later how many were executed for their participation, rather than on the democratic ideas for which these individuals had sacrificed their lives.

One unnamed Asian diplomat may have put the whole issue in perspective. "It doesn't matter if they killed 200 or 2,000," he is quoted as saying. "The fact is they fired machine guns at their own people and killed them. To save their own political lives, a handful of old men killed their own children. Whether it was 200 or 2,000, it was a massacre."[13]

All of the aforementioned examples involve some form of prior restraint, but not all of them meet the necessary criterion for First Amendment prior restraint — government action. However, as discussed later in this chapter, *government action* can be broadly interpreted within the context of prior restraint because prior restraint is such an abhorrent abridgement of freedom of expression. Although this chapter focuses on only a few major cases, prior restraint is not rare, as evidenced by the frequent news stories that appear about government censorship — federal, state and local.

CONTEMPT OF COURT

Contempt of court is, without doubt, one of the most serious, if not *the* most serious, prior restraint problem facing journalists in the 1990s. Ironically, most other types of prior restraint have become less of a threat than in the past, thanks to generally favorable rulings from the U.S. Supreme Court and other courts.

At first glance, contempt of court may appear to be unrelated to prior restraint. After all, contempt is generally either used as a coercion to attempt to force an individual to comply with a court order, such as to provide the identity of a confidential source, or as a means of punishing someone for demonstrating disrespect for the court or the judicial process. However, a fairly frequent use of what is known as **criminal contempt** (defined shortly) is to punish individuals for disobeying a court order—such as a gag order prohibiting attorneys and witnesses from discussing a case with reporters. Thus news sources are very effectively restrained from speaking out.

Contempt of court is generally defined as "any act which is calculated to embarrass, hinder, or obstruct court in administration of justice, or which is calculated to lessen its authority or its dignity."[14] There are two different ways of classifying contempt. First, contempt can be either *civil* or *criminal*. Unfortunately, this classification can be quite confusing because the distinction of civil versus criminal for purposes of contempt is not really parallel with the traditional criminal versus civil division in law. Instead, the categorization is a rather artificial one that has been known to confuse journalists and sometimes even judges and attorneys. *Civil contempt* involves the failure or refusal to obey a court order granted for the benefit of one of the litigants in a case. The offense, in other words, is *not* against the dignity of the court but against the party for whom the order was issued. The confusion is compounded by the fact that civil contempt can occur in both civil and criminal cases.

Criminal contempt, on the other hand, is indeed an affront to the court and the purpose of any fine and/or jail term imposed is to punish the offender.

Civil Contempt

The purpose of a fine or sentence for civil contempt is to coerce the individual into complying with the court order. Thus the penalty imposed must be lifted once the person obeys or once the judicial deliberations have ended. However, civil contempt orders can remain in effect indefinitely in some cases, as dramatically demonstrated in the case of Dr. Elizabeth Morgan, who served longer (25 months) than any other U.S. woman not convicted of a crime.[15] What was the former affluent plastic surgeon and medical writer's offense? She refused to obey District of Columbia Superior Court Judge Herbert Dixon's order to disclose the whereabouts of her young daughter in a contentious custody battle with the girl's father, whom Dr. Morgan accused of sexually abusing the child. He strongly denied the charges. A three-judge panel of the U.S. Court of Appeals for the District of Columbia Circuit ruled 2–1 that Morgan should be released because it appeared highly unlikely that she would disclose the location of her daughter and thus the efforts to force her to comply with the trial court judge's order served no further purpose. However, the Circuit Court meeting *en banc* (i.e., as the full court) soon overturned the appeal panel's decision so that Morgan was never released from jail. The full court did rule that she was entitled to a new hearing on her appeal of the civil contempt citation. She was freed on September 25, 1989, after the U.S. Congress passed a bill, specifically aimed to free her, limiting imprisonment for civil contempt in the District of Columbia to 12 months. President George Bush signed the bill on September 23, 1989, and the D.C. Court of Appeals ordered her released two days later. She still faced possible civil contempt charges again because the bill limits the maximum term on a *single citation*, and the judge could always issue a new contempt citation so long as she refused to obey the order. However, the judge chose not to do so in this case. Please note that this bill affected only *civil contempt citations* and only those in the *District of Columbia.* No court ever determined whether Morgan's spouse had abused the daughter. During the fall of 1992 ABC-TV broadcast a made-for-TV movie entitled *A Mother's Right: The Elizabeth Morgan Story* about the case.

Journalists are most often faced with civil contempt when they refuse to reveal confidential information or sources. Two well-publicized examples of how severe civil contempt sanctions can be are the separate cases of Myron Farber and and William Farr. Although most civil contempt citations against journalists usually result in incarceration of a few days, Farber and Farr each served more than 5 weeks.

While a *New York Times* reporter, Myron Farber was assigned to investigate mysterious deaths that had taken place several years earlier in a New Jersey hospital. The newspaper subsequently published a series of in-depth articles under Farber's byline that pointed to a possible link between at least some of the deaths and a Dr. "X." As a result, a physician was indicted by a grand jury on several counts of murder. During the subsequent trial, the doctor's defense attorney subpoenaed Farber and the *Times* to produce for trial various documents from the reporter's investigation, including transcripts and notes from interviews with witnesses.

The newspaper and Farber attempted to have the subpoenas quashed, but their efforts were unsuccessful both in appeals to the trial court judge and in the appellate courts, including the New Jersey Supreme Court.[16] The judge had offered to first conduct an *in camera inspection* (i.e., to look at them in his private chambers before ruling on whether the documents could be used at trial), but the *Times* and Farber rejected the arrangement.

The judge then cited the newspaper and Farber for both civil *and* criminal contempt and levied a single $1,000 fine against Farber and a $5,000 assessment *per day* against the newspaper for civil contempt. In addition, the *Times* faced a $100,000 penalty for criminal contempt, and Farber was fined

$1,000 and sentenced to 6 months in jail for criminal contempt. The civil penalties were designed, of course, to attempt to force the reporter and the newspaper to comply with the subpoenas; but why did they face criminal penalties? Both federal and state court judges have the authority to punish an individual or organization for criminal contempt for refusing to obey an order.

The conclusion to the Farber case came only after some strange twists and turns. Farber spent several days in jail after he was cited for contempt and was then released pending the decision by the New Jersey Supreme Court. After the state Supreme Court ruled 5–2 against him, Farber was sent back to jail, only to be released again once the case went to the jury. The jury ultimately acquitted the physician-defendant and the judge dismissed all pending contempt citations against Farber and the newspaper, including the criminal contempt citations. Farber had spend some 40 days in jail and the *Times* had paid $285,000 in fines for civil and criminal contempt. In 1982, four years after the case had begun, outgoing New Jersey Governor Brendan Byrne officially pardoned both Farber and the newspaper and ordered that more than $100,000 in criminal penalties be returned. The $185,000 in civil fines stood, however.

A somewhat less-publicized case involved, William Farr,[17] who actually spent 6 more days in jail for civil contempt than Myron Farber. The *Los Angeles Herald-Examiner* reporter was assigned to cover the trial of the notorious mass murderer, Charles Manson, in 1970. To ensure that Manson received a fair trial, the judge in the case issued a *restrictive* or *gag order* prohibiting out-of-court statements by attorneys and witnesses in the case. (*Gag order* is a pejorative term used primarily by the press to label what the courts usually call *restrictive orders*.) The judge had also ordered that the jury be sequestered. Although the gag order was not aimed specifically at journalists, Farr was ordered by the judge to identify his sources for a story based on pretrial statements by a witness whom Farr had promised confidentiality. The story had attracted considerable attention because it contained grisly details allegedly revealed by one defendant in the case, Susan Atkins, about the so-called Tate-Labianca murders and other murders planned by the Manson "family" against movie stars such as Elizabeth Taylor and Frank Sinatra. It was clear that some of the information reported by Farr in his stories could have been obtained only from sources whom the judge had ordered not to discuss the case publicly or with the media.

California Superior Court Judge Charles Older queried Farr about the source of his information, but Farr, claiming protection under a California shield law (shield laws are discussed in Chapter 9), steadfastly refused to disclose the name. Judge Older took no further action until after the trial was over when he ordered Farr again to reveal the name. By this time, Farr had obtained a new position as an assistant to a county district attorney. Farr still refused to provide the information, although he did indicate that he had received the information from two of the six attorneys involved. However, he would not identify the specific two, and thus the judge cited him for civil contempt with an indefinite jail sentence. The judge noted that the former reporter could no longer claim protection under the state's shield law because he now did not meet the definition of journalist under the statute. Some 46 days later, Farr was released when a state appellate court vacated the district court judge's contempt order, but only pending appeal. A cloud of doubt loomed over his fate, however, because if the judge were ultimately upheld by the appellate courts, Farr could have faced an indefinite jail term as long as he continued to refuse to obey the order to disclose. In late 1976, the California Court of Appeals permanently lifted the contempt order, 5 years after the case had begun and after the California Supreme Court[18] and the U.S. Supreme Court[19] had refused to hear Farr's appeals. In 1980, California residents, apparently largely in reaction to the Farr case, approved Proposition 5, which for the first time gave state constitutional protection for journalists in protecting confidential sources.[20]

The Farr case illustrates a Catch 22 for states that have chosen to grant protection for journalists against prior restraints imposed by restrictive orders and contempt citations — no matter how strong the protection the legislation or constitutional provision may have been designed to offer, the courts always have the authority to limit the protection or even strike the law down on the grounds that it violates the separation of powers provisions enunciated in Articles I, II, and III of the U.S. Constitution. Although, as one U.S. constitutional scholar has noted, "As an examination . . . readily reveals, separation was not intended to be total and airtight,"[21] both state and federal courts have been very reluctant to allow legislators to restrict their authority to regulate judicial proceedings, including the ability to cite individuals for contempt. Indeed, the California Court of Appeals in the Farr case no doubt reflected the reasoning of the vast majority of state and federal courts when it clung to the long-standing constitutional premise that courts have an inherent power to control judicial proceedings free from any interference from both the legislative and the executive branches of government. In sum, even when its use may mean serious prior restraint, contempt power is near and dear to the hearts of judges and justices, and thus courts will almost inevitably uphold its constitutionality except in extreme cases such as *Nebraska Press Association v. Judge Stuart*,[22] discussed *infra*.

Dickinson Rule

Probably the most serious Catch 22 situation facing journalists in the area of prior restraint is the so-called Dickinson rule formulated by the U.S. Court of Appeals for the Fifth Circuit in 1972.[23] The case began when two Louisiana newspaper reporters were covering a hearing in a U.S. District Court in which a black civil rights VISTA volunteer was challenging his indictment by a state grand jury for conspiracy to murder the local mayor. During the hearing, the judge issued a verbal order prohibiting publication of any information about the testimony given at the hearing even though the information had been disclosed in open court. The judge's order permitted the reporters to publish that the hearing had been held, but essentially nothing more.

In spite of the order, both reporters wrote news stories giving details of the hearing. For their defiance of his order, the judge in a summary hearing found them guilty of criminal contempt and fined both $300. Although the reporters were never jailed and the fines were relatively minimal, the newspaper, the *Baton Rouge Morning Advocate and State Times*, admirably chose to appeal the convictions. Most First Amendment experts would probably have concluded that the order was indeed unconstitutional, and, in fact, the U.S. Court of Appeals for the Fifth Circuit agreed and sent the case back to the District Court judge for further consideration. Not surprisingly, the judge reinstated the fines, and the newspaper filed another appeal. The Circuit Court then upheld the citations by reasoning that even constitutionally invalid restrictive orders must be complied with because (citing an earlier decision), "people simply cannot have the luxury of knowing that they have a right to contest the correctness of the judge's order in deciding whether to willfully disobey it."[24]

The court also reasoned that if individuals, including journalists, are permitted to disobey court orders, the judicial process would be seriously affected. After all, the court noted, such orders are to be used only "sparingly."[25] A journalist or anyone else can request an expedited review by the appeals court, but such reviews are relatively rare and unlikely to be granted in a case such as this one. The upshot is that journalists face the dilemma of disobeying an order risking fines and even jail sentences and getting the story published, or complying with the order by withholding the information from the public while waiting months or longer for the appeal to be heard. The Dickinson decision was appealed to the U.S. Supreme Court, but the court denied certiorari in 1973.[26]

DIRECT VERSUS INDIRECT CONTEMPT

Contempt can also be categorized into (a) *direct* and (b) *constructive* or *indirect*. Direct contempt is committed in or near the presence of the court ("so near thereto as to obstruct the administration of justice").[27] Indirect or constructive contempt, on the other hand, occurs or relates to matters outside the courtroom.

Although such a distinction may seem artificial or even contrived at first glance, there are major differences in the procedures followed in the two types of contempt and in the constitutional and statutory rights involved.

Suppose a judge issues a restrictive order forbidding all news media in the area from publishing or broadcasting the details of testimony given at the trial of a grandfather accused of sexually abusing his granddaughter and grandson. The judge exercises discretion under state statutes and the rules of criminal procedure by closing the testimony of the young victims to the public and the press. The judge had earlier issued an order barring all trial participants, including witnesses, jurors and attorneys from discussing the case with anyone else, including journalists.

Jane Enterprise, a reporter for the local television station, nevertheless, convinces one of the social workers who accompanied the children to the trial and sat in the courtroom while the children testified to disclose the details of the testimony. Enterprise then broadcasts a summary of the testimony on the six o'clock news. What is the judge likely to do?

First, there are two potential violations leading to contempt — the broadcast and the disclosure of information by the social worker. Assuming the reporter refuses to disclose the confidential source of her information, there is even a third possible contempt. Let's begin with this one first.

When Enterprise is called before the judge to explain why she violated the judge's order and is ordered to name her source but refuses, her refusal constitutes direct criminal contempt because (a) the contempt has occurred within the presence of the court and (b) her refusal can be considered an affront to the dignity of the court, that is, an interference with the orderly administration of justice. What can the judge do? The judge has the clear authority in this case to exercise **summary jurisdiction** in a **summary proceeding.** (As mentioned in the previous chapter, this proceeding is **not** the same as a summary judgment.) Quite simply, the judge can immediately cite Enterprise for contempt and immediately punish her within certain constitutional parameters. Within a matter of minutes or even seconds after she refuses to disclose her source, the judge can accuse her of contempt, determine that contempt has occurred and sentence her to jail. Journalists are often shocked by the swiftness of the summary proceeding, but state and federal rules of criminal and civil procedure grant this authority to judges and the courts have consistently upheld its constitutionality.

What are Enterprise's options? Obviously, she can plead with the judge not to find her in contempt, but, assuming that the judge does not accept the reporter's plea, Enterprise can then only appeal her conviction to a higher court or serve her time in jail. Can the judge also punish Enterprise for broadcasting the report in defiance of the order?

Yes, but the punishment would be for indirect criminal contempt because the broadcast interferes with the administration of justice (criminal contempt), and the action occurred outside the courtroom. With indirect contempt, unlike direct contempt, the accused is entitled to notice of the alleged offense and to a formal, separate hearing on the matter. Enterprise thus would have the opportunity to mount some type of defense, although the judge is still likely to ultimately punish her and probably even fine the station for defying the restrictive order. Ironically, Enterprise could also face civil contempt charges for failing to identify her source and thus be confined for an indefinite time in jail and be forced to pay fines as a means of coercing her to testify. Her confinement, as already indicated, could continue until the judge had determined it was fruitless to keep her in jail any longer, the name was disclosed by someone else, the trial ended or, of course, she relented and testified.

If Enterprise does disclose her source's identity or the judge somehow determines that the social worker has violated the earlier order, what are the possible consequences for the social worker? Although the social worker may have actually communicated the information to the reporter outside the courtroom, the worker would in all likelihood be cited for direct criminal contempt because "so near thereto" can be broadly interpreted to include such defiance. Because the purpose of citing the worker would be as punishment, criminal contempt has occurred. (There is nothing to coerce the worker to do.)

CONSTITUTIONAL LIMITS
ON CONTEMPT POWER

Bridges v. California
and *Times-Mirror Co. v. Superior Court*

Although judges have considerable power to cite and punish individuals, including journalists, for contempt, there have been some First Amendment limits recognized by the courts in the last several decades. The greatest protection, as one might expect, is for information disseminated outside the courtroom. In 1941, the U.S. Supreme Court held in *Bridges v. California* and *Times-Mirror Co. v. Superior Court* (the two appeals were decided together by the court)[28] that a judge may not cite journalists for contempt for publishing information about pending court cases unless there was a "clear and present danger" to the administration of justice. The Court noted that this clear and present danger standard was "a working principle that the substantive evil must be extremely serious and the degree of imminence extremely high before utterances can be punished."[29]

In *Bridges*, a union official had sent a telegram to the U.S. Secretary of Labor that was published in local newspapers in California. In the telegram, sent while the ruling on a motion for a new trial in a labor dispute was pending, Harry Bridges threatened to have his union strike if the judge's "outrageous" decision were enforced. The lower appellate courts upheld the leader's conviction for contempt as an interference with the "orderly administration of justice."

In *Times-Mirror*, while a decision was pending in the sentencing of two union members convicted of assaulting nonunion employees, the *Los Angeles Times* published a series of editorials in which it called the two "sluggers for pay" and "men who commit mayhem for wages" and contended that the judge would be committing a "serious mistake" if he granted probation. The paper was convicted of contempt and fined, and the conviction was upheld by the lower appellate courts, including the California Supreme Court. The U.S. Supreme Court, however, reversed the convictions of both Bridges and the *Times* on grounds that no clear and present danger had been shown.

Post *Bridges* Decisions

In three more major cases since *Bridges*, the Court has elaborated on the clear and present danger standard. First, in 1946 in *Pennekamp v. Florida*,[30] the Court reversed the contempt convictions of the *Miami Herald* and its associate editor for a series of editorials and an editorial cartoon accusing local judges of being more interested in assisting criminals than serving the public interest. The Court noted that the editorials had been based on false information, but it characterized the errors as relatively minor in light of the need for permissible commentary on the judiciary. No clear and present danger could be demonstrated, according to the majority opinion.

In the second case, *Craig v. Harney*,[31] the Court also acknowledged newspaper criticism aimed at a judge had been based on inaccuracies. "The fact that the discussion at this particular point in time was not in good taste falls far short of meeting the clear and present danger test," the majority asserted. The newspaper had severely criticized in an editorial and a series of articles the judge's handling of a civil case in which he directed a jury three times to find for a plaintiff in a landlord–tenant dispute. The first two times the jury found for the defendant; he was stationed overseas in the military and had failed to pay rent to the landlord, who was now seeking repossession of the building. But each time the Texas judge sent the jurors back to decide in favor of the plaintiff. Finally, they found for the plaintiff but made their objections known to the judge. Not surprisingly, the defendant's attorney filed a motion for a new trial. While the Court was deciding on whether to grant the motion, the newspaper published the articles and an accompanying editorial that Justice William O. Douglas, writing for the majority, characterized as "unfair" because of the inaccuracies, but that they, nevertheless, did not warrant the contempt citation and consequent three-day jail sentence imposed on the editor.

According to the Court, "the vehemence of the language used is not alone the measure of the power to punish for contempt. The fires which it kindles must constitute an **imminent**, not merely a likely, threat to the administration of justice. The danger must not be remote or even probable; it must immediately imperil" (emphasis added).[32] The majority pointed out, "Judges are supposed to be made of fortitude, able to thrive in a hardy climate." Thus the Court is saying that judges must be able to withstand press and public criticism, no matter how harsh or unfair. Justice Robert H. Jackson, in a strongly worded dissent, contended that the majority "appears to sponsor the myth that judges are not as other men are."

Finally, in the most recent case in which the Court has directly applied the clear and present danger test in a contempt case within a First Amendment context, Chief Justice Earl Warren, writing for the majority in *Wood v. Georgia*,[33] reversed the conviction for contempt of a Bibb County, Georgia, sheriff. The sheriff had issued a news release criticizing a judge's actions in a grand jury investigation of a voting scandal. Upset because the judge had ordered the grand jury to investigate rumors and accusations of "Negro bloc voting," Sheriff James I. Wood launched a news release calling the investigation "one of the most deplorable examples of race agitation to come out of Middle Georgia in recent years. . . . Negro people will find little difference in principle between attempted intimidation of their people by judicial summons and inquiry and attempted intimidation by physical demonstration such as used by the K.K.K."[34]

A month later, Wood was cited for contempt for creating a "clear, present and imminent danger" to the investigation and "to the proper administration of justice in Bibb Superior Court."[35] The defendant issued another press release the next day, essentially repeating his previous claims, and his contempt citation was amended to include this release as well. The U.S. Supreme Court noted that there were no witnesses at the contempt hearing and no evidence was presented to demonstrate that there was a clear and present danger to the administration of justice. The Court reversed the convictions, which had been affirmed by the Georgia Court of Appeals, except for a contempt charge based on an open letter the sheriff sent to the grand jury, which was set aside by the state appellate court. According to the U.S. Supreme Court:

> Men are entitled to speak as they please on matters vital to them; errors in judgment or unsubstantiated opinions may be exposed, of course, but not through punishment for contempt for the expression. [In] the absence of some other showing of substantive evil actually designed to impede the course of justice in justification of the exercise of the contempt power to silence the petitioner [Wood], his utterances are entitled to be protected.[36]

The *Bridges-Pennekamp-Craig-Wood* lineup offers strong but not absolute constitutional insulation for journalists and other individuals from contempt citations when they publish information about the judicial process, especially criticism of judges and information obtained in open court, even when such information is based on inaccurate data. Nevertheless, the contempt power of judges remains strong in most other circumstances, including coercion and punishment for refusing to reveal confidential information. In other words, the greatest protection appears to be when overt prior restraint, such as prohibiting someone from speaking out rather than when information is actually being sought for disclosure, is involved.

THE CLASSIC CASE: *NEAR V. MINNESOTA*

Certainly, the most significant prior restraint case ever decided by the U.S. Supreme Court is *J. M. Near v. Minnesota ex rel. Floyd B. Olson, County Attorney of Hennepin County, Minnesota*,[37] otherwise known as *Near v. Minnesota*. No other prior restraint case has been cited as often, and the Supreme Court consistently cites the holding in this case as controlling whenever it issues an opinion in any prior restraint case even though *Near* was decided six decades ago by a very slim 5–4 majority. Even the rather conservative current court headed by Chief Justice William H. Rehnquist has generally upheld the principles first enunciated in *Near*.

This case demonstrates how extreme cases are sometimes necessary to ascertain the outer limits of the First Amendment—the Larry Flynts, J. M. Nears, flag burners and cross burners of the world give the Supreme Court the opportunity to enunciate how far our constitutional rights extend. Larry Flynt, flag burners and cross burners are discussed in more detail later.

As Fred Friendly points out in his excellent account of the case, *Minnesota Rag*,[38] Minneapolis was a rather politically corrupt city in the 1920s and thus politicians had little tolerance for outspoken publications like J. M. Near's *The Saturday Press*. Near and his co-publisher, Howard Guilford, accused various local politicians and officials, including the police, of ignoring widespread racketeering, bootlegging and illegal gambling. According to the newspaper in a series of blatantly sensational, antisemitic articles, these activities were controlled by a "Jewish gangster." The Minnesota legislature had passed a statute in 1925 that allowed authorities to halt publication of any "obscene, lewd and lascivious . . . or malicious, scandalous, and defamatory newspaper, magazine, or other periodical" as a public nuisance. Anyone guilty of such a nuisance could be enjoined from further publication (except presumably with the approval of a judge). A quick look at old issues would probably convince most people even today that indeed the paper met all of the criteria of a scandalous and defamatory newspaper. For example, one of the editorials introduced into evidence at the trial referred to "Jew gangsters, practically ruling Minneapolis" and contended that "practically every vendor of vile hooch, every owner of moonshine still, every snake-faced gangster and embryonic yegg in the twin cities is a JEW" (capital letters in the original).[39]

Hennepin County Attorney Floyd Olson, who years later was elected state governor as a Populist, filed a criminal complaint against the paper and its publishers, charging that nine issues of the paper from September to November 1927 had contained "malicious, scandalous and defamatory articles" making false accusations against police and various public officials. After the prosecution presented its side and the defense immediately rested its case without presenting any evidence, the Minnesota trial court determined that Near and Guilford had violated the statute by creating a public nuisance. The judge then ordered that the paper be abated and that the defendants be "perpetually enjoined" from publishing "under the title of *The Saturday Evening Press* or any other name or title . . . any publication whatsoever which is a malicious, scandalous or defamatory newspaper." In other words, Near and Guilford were prevented not only from publishing any more issues of the *Press* but essentially any other newspapers of that type.

On appeal one year later, the Minnesota Supreme Court held the statute was constitutional under both the state and federal constitutions as a valid exercise of the broad police power of the state and that the order did not prevent them from "operating a newspaper in harmony with the public welfare." In a 5–4 decision that could have gone the other way had it not been for a few twists of fate, such as the death of an Associate Justice,[40] the U.S. Supreme Court reversed the order and struck down the statute as unconstitutional.

In delivering the majority opinion of the Court, Chief Justice Charles Evans Hughes characterized the statute as "unusual, if not unique." The decision, as fate would have it, was read as the last one on the last day of the Court's 1930-1931 term.[41] Drawing heavily on the ideas of the renown British legal scholar, Sir William Blackstone (1723-1780), the court noted (quoting the English jurist), "The liberty of the press is indeed essential to the nature of a free state; but this consists in laying no *previous* restraints upon publications, and not in freedom from censure for criminal matter when published."[42]

Justice Hughes' opinion then went on to reason that the First Amendment ban on prior restraint is "not absolutely unlimited" but that there are "exceptional cases" when prior restraint would be constitutional:

> When a nation is at war many things that may be said in time of peace are such a hindrance to its effort that their utterance will not be endured. . . . No one would question but that a government might prevent actual obstruction to its recruiting service or the publication of sailing dates of transports or the number and location of troops. On similar grounds, the primary requirements of decency might be enforced against obscene publications. The security of the community life may be protected against incitements to acts of violence and the overthrow by force of orderly government.[43] (cites omitted)

It should be noted that this decision offers the first hint of the later versions of reasonable time, place and manner restrictions that the Court has permitted on speech. These exceptions also point to more modern limitations usually grouped under the rubric of obscenity, national security and military secrets. Did any of the exceptions apply in this case? According to the Court, "These limitations are not applicable here". . . . We hold the statute, so far as it authorized the proceedings in this action . . . to be an infringement of the liberty of the press guaranteed by the Fourteenth Amendment."[44] Why did the Court invoke the Fourteenth Amendment?

As indicated in Chapter 1, the U.S. Supreme Court has over the decades selectively incorporated various rights under the Constitution's Bill of Rights, including those granted under the First Amendment. Until the *Near* decision, the Court had not specifically ruled whether First Amendment rights applied to the states. If this fact seems strange, closely examine the wording of the First Amendment, especially the reference to "Congress shall make no law." State and local governments are not mentioned. Theoretically, then, whereas one's First Amendment rights could not be trampled upon by the federal government, a state agency could infringe on those rights so long as it did not violate the state constitution or state or federal statutes.

However, the Supreme Court went beyond its traditional turf by asserting, "It is no longer open to doubt that the liberty of the press and of speech is within the liberty safeguarded by the due process clause of the Fourteenth Amendment from invasion by state action."[45] In other words, according to the Court, section 1 of the Fourteenth Amendment ("nor shall any State deprive any person of life, liberty, or property without due process of law") includes freedom of speech and of the press.[46]

A close reading of the majority opinion, especially the reasoning, provides a portentous glimpse at troubling decision's, such as the Pentagon Papers case[47] discussed *infra*, emerging decades later from the Court. Although *Near* was, fortunately, a strong affirmation of First Amendment rights, the Court reasoned (a) "Remedies for libel remain available and unaffected" (In other words, officials had the option of suing for libel, perhaps criminal as well as civil, **after** the publication had appeared); (b) the statute is too broad because it bans not only "scandalous and defamatory statements" aimed at private citizens but also charges against public officials of "corruption, malfeasance in office, or serious neglect of duty" (a preview of the *New York Times v. Sullivan* "actual malice" rule?);[48] (c) "the object of the statute is not punishment, in the ordinary sense, but suppression of the offending newspaper or periodical" (that is, prior restraint is the real evil); and (d) "the statute not only operates to suppress the offending newspaper or periodical, but to put the publisher under an effective censorship" (In essence, the kiss of death for the statute is that the prior restraint can be indefinite).[49]

The Court made two more major points that have stood the test of time. First, the Court indicated, "In determining the extent of the constitutional protection [of the First Amendment], it has generally, if not universally, considered that it is the chief purpose of the guaranty to prevent previous restraints upon publication."[50] The majority opinion then traced the historical background of freedom of the press, liberally quoting Blackstone and his progeny as well as his critics. The obvious purpose of the analysis was to attempt to delineate the primary meaning of the First Amendment. *Near* was a major step toward accomplishing this task, but, as indicated later, the Supreme Court continues to struggle with the boundaries of the freedom that undergirds all other constitutional rights.

Second, the Court effectively killed the idea that a prior restraint statute can be justified if it includes, as the Minnesota law did, a provision that permits the accused to use the defense that the information published was true and that it was "published with good motives and for justifiable ends." According to the Court, if this exception to the unconstitutionality of prior restraint were allowed, "it would be but a step to a complete system of censorship" because legislatures could thus arbitrarily determine what constituted justifiable ends. Clearly, if *Near* has any meaning, it is that legislatures cannot have unbridled discretion in determining permissible versus impermissible speech and publication. In actions involving prior restraint, the burden, as discussed shortly, is always going to rest on the government to show that the communication falls into one of the exceptions, **not** on the speaker or publisher to show that the communication is justified.

In analyzing *Near*, legal scholars usually include some discussion of the dissenting opinion of Associate Justice Pierce Butler, with which three of the other justices concurred. Although Justice Butler's view has yet to be shared by a majority of justices, it does represent a perspective that has some following among jurists and other legal scholars. Justice Butler contended that because the state clearly had the right to **punish** the "transgressions" that occurred as a result of the publication of the newspaper, there is no reason the state should not be permitted to prevent continuance of the harm. According to Justice Butler, "The Minnesota statute does not operate as a previous restraint on publication . . . [because] . . . [i]t does not authorize administrative control in advance . . . but prescribes a remedy to be enforced by a suit in equity."[51] He was particularly concerned that the doctrine espoused in the majority opinion in *Near* "exposes the peace and good order of every community and the business and private affairs of every individual to the constant and protracted false and malicious assaults" of ill-motivated publishers.[52]

Whereas Butler's reasoning may appear, at first reading, to expose a major weakness of the *Near* rationale, his reasoning begins to crumble under scrutiny when one realizes, as Chief Justice Hughes pointed out, that legislators and officials would have enormous power in silencing unpopular views, whether they be religious, political or whatever. All of this censorship would be accomplished with the blessing of courts beholden to the public that had elected them or to the officials who had appointed or hired them. The real evil of prior restraint arises when unpopular views, or views simply perceived by officials as unpopular or a threat their authority, are arbitrarily silenced with no opportunity for them to be accepted or rejected by society. In a democracy such as ours, we must take the risk that some individual or other entity may suffer harm from the publication of false information in order to ensure that all views have an opportunity to be heard. As Sir Blackstone believed, it is far better to allow the potentially harmful information to be disseminated and then punish the offender, if justified, than to permit the publication in the first place.

There is interesting footnote to the story of the *Saturday Press*. J. M. Near went virtually unmentioned in news accounts of the U.S. Supreme Court decision, but more than a year later, the newspaper reappeared under the editorship of Near with a front-page proclamation: "The only paper in the United States with a United States Supreme Court record of being right; the only paper that dared fight for freedom of the press and won."[53]

NEW YORK TIMES CO. V. U.S.

Some 40 years after the U.S. Supreme Court's decision in *Near*, the Court agreed to hear an appeal in a case that had the potential of answering many of the questions surrounding prior restraint that had not been answered in *Near*. From the beginning, the case had the makings of a landmark decision, although the pinnacle was never reached (discussed shortly).

In early 1969, President Richard M. Nixon's National Security Adviser, Henry Kissinger, commissioned the Rand Corporation, a Santa Monica, California, private consulting firm, to analyze the various military options available to the United States in the Vietnam War. Daniel Ellsberg, a military defense expert working at that time at Rand, was given the job of conducting the study. Ellsberg gained access to a 47-volume classified study entitled, *History of U.S. Decision-Making Process on Viet Nam Policy*, which became known as the "Pentagon Papers." Ellsberg spent several months reading the volumes and other documents he had carried from the Washington, DC, Rand field office to the headquarters in Santa Monica. According to one account, Ellsberg had access to all 47 volumes, thousands of pages, and even temporary, sole custody of 27 of the volumes.[54]

After Ellsberg had read the papers, he was convinced "beyond any doubt that the information in the Pentagon Papers, if widely available, would be explosive."[55] Ellsberg had been one of some 36 authors of the papers, which were the culmination of a 1967 study authorized by then-Secretary of Defense Robert McNamara to analyze the process by which the United States embroiled in Vietnam. After several unsuccessful attempts to get members of Congress, including U.S. Senator and Democratic presidential candidate George McGovern, to accept the papers and presumably make them public, in

March 1971 Ellsberg delivered photocopies of all but the last four volumes, which he apparently considered too sensitive to disclose,[56] to Neil Sheehan, a Washington correspondent for the *New York Times*. During the next two months, Sheehan and other *Times* journalists spent hundreds of hours reading and digesting the documents into article form, usually while they were squirreled away in a hotel suite away from the hubbub of the office. The ultimate decision was to publish the report in a comprehensive series of articles, with much of the writing completed on "Project X" (as the secret effort became known at the *Times*) headquarters at the New York Hilton, complete with security guards to keep an eye on the three-room suite when no one was there.[57]

On Monday, June 13, 1971, the *Times* published the first installment of what was intended to be a series of 10 articles summarizing and analyzing the Pentagon Papers. The next day, the second article appeared, and U.S. Attorney General John Mitchell (the same John Mitchell who served 19 months in a federal minimum security prison for his involvement in criminal activities in Watergate) asked the newspaper to voluntarily stop publication of the top secret documents. When the *Times* rebuffed him, Mitchell began a series of legal maneuvers to halt further publication of the documents. He claimed such prior restraint was justified under the Espionage Act of 1918 because publication would create an unwarranted infringement on national security. On Tuesday, the third article had appeared, but the government was able to convince federal Judge Murray Gurfein of the U.S. District Court for the Southern District of New York to issue a temporary restraining order (TRO) to prevent further publication of the articles in the *Times* until a hearing could be set on a permanent injunction. As indicated in Chapter 1, a TRO can be granted without hearing from the other side if it can be shown that irreparable harm will occur if such an order is not granted and that a reasonable effort was made to notify the other side. The TRO would be issued, of course, pending a hearing at which both sides would be permitted to appear before either a temporary or permanent injunction could be issued. Both sides did appear in this case, but the judge ruled in favor of the government. Thus for the first time in U.S. history, a judge had imposed prior restraint on a news medium to prevent it from publishing specific content. (In *Near* the judge prevented the editor from publishing any further issues of that or similar papers that constituted a public nuisance. Thus the injunction was not against a specific article.)

In the meantime, the *Washington Post* obtained photocopies of most of the Pentagon Papers report and after a protracted debate among its editors, reporters and even lawyers, on Friday, June 17, published the first of a planned series of articles, much along the lines of those in the *Times*. As expected, Attorney General Mitchell immediately requested the *Post* to voluntarily cease publication of the articles. The *Post* naturally refused his request, and he immediately sought a TRO in U.S. District Court for the District of Columbia. Judge Gerhard Gesell rejected Mitchell's request, and the government immediately filed an appeal with the U.S. Court of Appeals for the District of Columbia. After a hearing in which both sides participated, that appeals court upheld the lower court refusal.

During this same period, the federal trial court judge in New York, Judge Gurfein, denied the federal government's request for a permanent injunction. But when the government immediately appealed to the U.S. Court of Appeals for the Second Circuit, in a controversial 2-1 decision, that court reversed Judge Gurfein and reinstated the injunction. The court ruled that the ban should remain until a hearing could be conducted at which the government would have the opportunity to demonstrate why further publication would pose a serious threat to national security.

As a result of these decisions in two different appeals court circuits, the *Times* was legally prevented from any further publication of the Pentagon Papers and the *Post* effectively had the court's blessing to continue. Other newspapers, including the *Boston Globe*, the *St. Louis Post Dispatch*, the *Chicago Sun-Times* and the *Los Angeles Times*, entered the fray. In another illustration of how inconsistent federal courts and the government can be in prior restraint cases, the *Globe* and the *Post Dispatch* were enjoined by the courts, whereas the government chose not to seek injunctions against the other two newspapers.

On June 24, one day after the federal appeals court in New York ruled against the newspaper, the *Times* filed a motion for expedited review with a petition for a writ of certiorari with the U.S. Supreme Court. The next morning (Saturday), at the government's urging, in an unprecedented 5-4 decision the Supreme Court temporarily banned **all** further publication of the Pentagon Papers, not just in the *Times* and the *Post*, pending an expedited review. The Court very rarely deliberates on weekends, which proves this was no ordinary case. The Court's action was without precedent—never in history had the U.S. Supreme Court granted an injunction, temporary as it was, against a news medium.

In another unusual move, the Supreme Court heard oral arguments in the case on Sunday. The arguments were predictable. The U.S. Solicitor General, representing the government, contended that further publication of the documents would have a potentially serious adverse impact on the course of the Vietnam War and cause irreparable harm to national security. The newspaper lawyers asserted that the government had failed to show that such harm would occur and that such prior restraint violated the First Amendment. With surprising swiftness, the Supreme Court rendered its decision five days later on Thursday, June 30, 1971.[58] For those legal scholars and journalists who had awaited a strong reaffirmation of *Near* and a ringing victory for First

Amendment rights, the Court's decision was a hollow win and, to many, a major disappointment.

In a brief *per curiam* opinion (see discussion in Chapter 2), the Court merely held that the government had failed to meet the heavy burden required in justifying prior restraint against the press. The 6-3 decision in favor of the *Times* and the *Post* included separate opinions from each of the nine justices. In the unsigned opinion, the Court quoted a 1963 decision involving prior restraint, *Bantam Books, Inc. v. Sullivan*:[59] "Any system of prior restraints of expression comes to this Court bearing a heavy presumption against its constitutional validity." The opinion then went on to note that "the government 'thus carries a heavy burden of showing justification for the enforcement of such restraint'" (citing a decision earlier in the year, *Organization for a Better Austin v. Keefe*.[60] The citations, of course, also included *Near*, but none of the opinions, including the per curiam opinion for the court, sheds any real light on the limits of prior restraint. No consensus was reached regarding whether the injunctions had been constitutional, only that a heavy evidentiary burden had not been met.

Both the concurring justices and the dissenters looked to *Near*, but none of them went to great lengths to reaffirm the principles in *Near*. Instead they used the reasoning in *Near* to bolster their opinions. Associate Justice William O. Douglas, who had a long and distinguished record of defending First Amendment rights, was joined by Associate Justice Hugo Black (who was serving his last term on the Court and died three months later) in one concurring opinion, and Justice Black wrote another separate opinion that was joined by Justice Douglas.

Justice Black, joined by Justice Douglas, argued that "in seeking injunctions against these newspapers and its presentation to the Court, the executive branch seems to have forgotten the essential purpose and history of the First Amendment." According to Justice Black, "In revealing the workings of government that led to the Viet Nam war, the newspapers nobly did precisely that which the Founders hoped and trusted they would do." To hold that prior restraint may be imposed on news, as several of the justices advocated, "would make a shambles of the First Amendment," he claimed.[61]

Justice Douglas, joined by Justice Black, took essentially an absolutist view that "no law" means "no law." The First Amendment means there is "no room for governmental restraint on the press," according to Justice Douglas. Even though disclosures such as those made by the newspaper in this case "may have a serious impact . . . that is no basis for sanctioning a previous restraint on the press," he argued. "Secrecy in government is fundamentally anti-democratic, perpetuating bureaucratic errors. Open debate and discussion on public issues are vital to our national health."[62]

In a third concurring opinion, Justice William J. Brennan, Jr., also known for his unwavering support of a strong First Amendment, vociferously argued, "The error that has pervaded these cases from the outset was the granting of any injunctive relief whatsoever, interim or otherwise." He accurately noted that "never before has the United States sought to enjoin a newspaper from publishing information in its possession." Justice Brennan freely cited *Near* as affirming that prior restraint should be imposed in only the rarest of cases.[63]

Justices Potter Stewart and Byron R. White each wrote separate concurring opinions with which the other joined. Justice Stewart, joined by Justice White, made it clear that he did not share an absolutist view of the First Amendment on prior restraint. His opinion included a now famous quote, "For when everything is classified, then nothing is classified," which essentially argues that governmental secrecy must not be secrecy for secrecy's sake. "I am convinced that the executive is correct with respect to some of the documents involved," Justice Stewart concluded. "But I cannot say that disclosure of any of them will surely result in direct, immediate, and irreparable damage to our Nation or its people." Thus, in his view, the government had simply failed to overcome the heavy burden imposed by the Constitution to demonstrate that the prior restraint was justified under the circumstances.[64]

In his concurring opinion, Justice White, joined by Justice Stewart, went beyond the previous concurring opinion with Stewart to note that whereas the government had not been able to show the constitutionally mandated "unusually heavy justification" for prior restraint, "failure by the Government to justify prior restraints does not measure its constitutional entitlement to a conviction for criminal publication."[65] In other words, Justice White did not rule out the possibility that the government may have been able to seek criminal sanctions provided in the statutes **after** the publication even though it could not prevent the actual publication.

In the final concurring opinion, Justice Thurgood Marshall focused primarily on the doctrine of separation of powers and concluded that "this Court does not have authority to grant the requested relief [sought by the executive branch]. It is not for this Court to fling itself into every breach perceived by some government official."[66]

If read carefully, the dissenting opinions present a frightening view of First Amendment rights. In his dissent, Chief Justice Warren Burger noted, "The prompt setting of these cases reflects our universal abhorrence of prior restraint. But prompt judicial action does not mean unjudicial haste." The Chief Justice characterized the Pentagon Papers as "purloined documents" and pointed out that "it is not disputed that the *Times* has had unauthorized possession of the documents for three to four months." Chief Justice Burger severely criticized the newspaper for not submitting the materials to government officials so the parties could negotiate their possible declassification. "The consequence of all this melancholy series of events is that we literally do not know what we are acting on," according to the Chief Justice.

On the surface, Chief Justice Burger's arguments may seem reasonable; however, a closer look reveals that he is advocating that the newspaper impose self-censorship and submit the "stolen property" to governmental authorities so they could determine what, if anything, could be declassified. Barring such voluntary action by the *Times*, the Chief Justice would permit the trial court to continue the injunction until all of the facts were in and the case could be resolved at trial. Further, whereas he would have directed that "the district court on remand give priority to the *Times* case to the exclusion of all other business of that court . . . [he] would not set arbitrary deadlines." Throughout his opinion, the Chief Justice expresses his distaste for the speedy manner in which the case was granted certiorari and ultimately decided by the Court.[67]

Justice John M. Harlan, joined by Chief Justice Burger and Justice Harry A. Blackmun, also chided the majority for the swiftness with which the case was decided. He felt that the Court had been "almost irresponsibly feverish" in hearing and deciding the case. "This frenzied train of events took place in the name of the presumption against prior restraints created by the First Amendment," he complained. "Due regard for the extraordinarily important and difficult questions involved in these litigations should have led the Court to shun such a precipitate timetable." Justice Harlan then raised seven major questions that should be considered before deciding the case on its merits, including whether the newspapers were entitled to retain and use the "purloined" documents and "whether the unauthorized disclosure of any of these particular documents would seriously impair the national security."[68] Thus the three dissenters would have continued the injunctions at least until the lower courts could decide the cases on their merits. They make no mention of the fact that such deliberations, even if expedited, could take months or even years while the documents continued to be suppressed.

Finally, in a separate dissent not joined by any of the other justices, Justice Blackmun carefully avoided criticizing any judges or lawyers in the case but indicated he "would remand these cases to be developed expeditiously, of course, but on a schedule permitting the orderly presentation of evidence from both sides, with the use of discovery, if necessary." Justice Blackmun said he had studied the affidavits and some of the Pentagon Papers themselves and he believed that if the newspapers published the documents because of the majority opinion in the case, soldiers would be killed, alliances destroyed, negotiations with the enemy would be more difficult and the war would be prolonged, resulting in "further delay in the freeing of United States prisoners."[69]

Minus the four missing volumes that Daniel Ellsberg had considered initially too sensitive to disclose and that were never officially declassified, the Pentagon Papers were eventually published by newspapers throughout the United States, including the *Times* and the *Post*. Indeed, at least three versions of the 43 volumes were published in book form—the official version made available to the press and other interested parties by the Government Printing Office, a Bantam Books paperback edition based on the *New York Times* stories and a Beacon Press "Gavel" edition; the latter was named after Senator Mike Gavel (D-Alaska), who had managed, over the opposition of many of his colleagues, to have the documents officially entered into the record of a subcommittee hearing. Gavel was one of several members of Congress who had the opportunity to gain access to copies of the Pentagon Papers before they were eventually published, but he was the only one willing to publicly disclose them.[70]

By most, if not all, accounts, publication of the Pentagon Papers had virtually no impact on the Vietnam War. The Nixon administration chose to prosecute Ellsberg and Anthony J. Russo, Jr., who had helped Ellsberg photocopy the documents, charging them primarily with violating the U.S. Espionage Act[71] and for stealing government property. Both were indicted based on evidence presented by the U.S. Justice Department to a federal grand jury in Los Angeles. The first trial court jury impaneled in the case in July 1972 was dismissed after some complicated legal maneuverings, and all charges were dismissed on May 11, 1973, after it became known that the offices of Ellsberg's psychiatrist had been burglarized by President Nixon's Watergate "plumbers" (so-called because they had conducted illegal wiretaps against public officials and private individuals during 1969–1971 in an effort to plug government "leaks").

Although most newspapers and other media hailed the Court's decision as a triumph for the press, at least some First Amendment scholars saw the decision as a hollow victory at best. Prior restraint had been imposed on major news media for two weeks with the consent of the federal courts, including the U.S. Supreme Court, and the ultimate decision was merely that the U.S. government had failed to meet the heavy evidentiary burden in demonstrating that the prior restraint was constitutionally permissible. There is also little solace in the fact that each of the nine justices took somewhat different views of the meaning of the principles established in *Near v. Minnesota*.

Any impact on the Vietnam War was certainly minimal. There was no public clamor over the Court's ruling nor over the ultimate publication of the Pentagon Papers. Apparently, very few people, other than journalists, read the Papers in detail, although the *Times* book version sold more than a million copies.[72] Thousands of U.S. soldiers died in the Vietnam war which continued until a cease-fire agreement was signed in 1973 and U.S. troops made a relatively quick withdrawal. The war ended in 1975 when the North Vietnamese gained military control over the south with its final offensive against the South Vietnamese forces. Officially, 47,321 U.S. soldiers had died in combat; another 10,700 had died from other causes; and 153,303 had been wounded.[73] Thousands of others were missing in action and presumed dead.

ETHICAL CONCERNS
IN THE PENTAGON PAPERS CASE

The legal battle over the Pentagon Papers was certainly complex and even convoluted, but there are also serious ethical questions raised that make the case even more complicated. Putting the legalities aside (because they were never resolved), was it ethical for the newspapers to agree to accept stolen government property even if it was in the form of documents? Although it could be argued that Daniel Ellsberg had legal access to the classified materials, there is no doubt that he did not have authority to disclose the documents to the *Times* or others (such as members of Congress). Should a journalist agree to accept such documents knowing they are classified and illegally photocopied? When do the ends justify the means? Interestingly, the *Code of Ethics of the Society of Professional Journalists* and all of the other major media code of conduct are silent on this issue.

Most newspapers would probably not have been able to endure the agony and expense of the Pentagon Papers case. The *Times* spent $150,000 in legal fees in the two weeks between the time the injunction was sought and the U.S. Supreme Court issued its decision, and the *Post* faced a $70,000 bill.[74] Obviously, the expenses involved for the *Times* in researching the Papers and writing the articles were also high. Smaller newspapers and newspapers with weaker finances could ill afford to fight such a battle, and even the *Times* and the *Post* could not tackle many such matches with the government. Every media outlet should adopt a consistent policy for dealing with these ethical issues, including who has authority to review such materials and who will oversee their publication, if any. The Pentagon Papers were historical documents whose ultimate disclosure caused apparently no harm to U.S. security and diplomatic matters. What if there were a chance that such harm would occur but there was no way of determining at the time precisely what would happen? Should a newspaper or magazine go ahead and publish the materials?

These are thorny questions that were raised again, but never answered, in the strange and almost unbelievable story of *Progressive* magazine. It was inevitable that at some point a case would arise to test the constitutionality of prior restraint involving national security matters outside the historical context of the Pentagon Papers. An important issue in the Pentagon Papers case was, as one scholarly work has noted, "whether government ought to be able to imprison history,"[75] but *United States v. The Progressive, Inc.*[76] struck a contemporary note.

UNITED STATES V. THE PROGRESSIVE, INC.

Under the U.S. Atomic Energy Act of 1954:

> Whoever, lawfully or unlawfully, having possession of, access to, control over, or being entrusted with any document, writing, sketch, photograph, plan, model instrument, appliance, note, or information involving or incorporating Restricted Data— . . .
>
> (b) communicates, transmits, or discloses the same to any individual or person, or attempts or conspires to do any of the foregoing, with reason to believe such data will be used to injure the United States or to secure an advantage to any foreign nation, shall, upon conviction, be punished by a fine of not more than $10,000 or imprisonment for not more than ten years, or both.[77]

The act, which is still in effect, should be read by every aspiring or practicing journalist who plans to write about nuclear weapons and nuclear energy. The basic provisions of the act are quite broad, as witnessed by its definition of restricted data as "all data concerning (1) design, manufacture or utilization of atomic weapons; (2) the production of special nuclear material; or the use of special nuclear fuels in the production of nuclear energy."[78] The act also grants the U.S. Attorney General the authority to seek "a permanent or temporary injunction, restraining order, or other order" in court to prohibit "any acts or practices" that violate or would violate any provision of the act.[79]

In early 1979, *The Progressive*—a relatively small-circulation magazine founded in the early part of this century by Robert M. LaFollette as the official organ of the Progressive political party—hired a freelancer, Howard Morland, to write an article about the ease with which an H-bomb could be made. Morland and the magazine, including editor Erwin Knoll, claimed that all of the material for the article, "The H-Bomb Secret: How We Got It, Why We're Telling It," came from public documents and sources. The U.S. government, on the other hand, claimed the article revealed secret technical concepts whose dissemination would violate the Atomic Energy Act, although the government conceded during the trial that much of the information appeared in documents available to the public at the Los Alamos (New Mexico) Scientific Laboratory Library. When this fact become known, the government removed the documents from public circulation and had them classified as secret.

How did the government learn about the article in advance? Morland circulated a rough draft of the article among several scientists and other scholars for criticism on the technical accuracy of the article, and eventually the government learned of the article's existence. The U.S. Attorney General, citing the provisions of the Atomic Energy Act discussed earlier, moved immediately to stop publication of the article by seeking an injunction in federal court in Madison, Wisconsin, where the magazine is published. The federal government took this course of legal action after editor Knoll had refused to delete approximately one-tenth of the article that the government contended endangered national security. In March 1979, after hearing evidence presented by U.S. attorneys in a closed hearing in Milwaukee, U.S. District Court Judge Robert W. Warren granted the government's request for a temporary restraining order. The TRO was soon replaced by a preliminary injunction on March 26 after Judge Warren heard arguments on both sides of the case. He based his decision on grounds that the information, if published, would violate the Atomic Energy Act and that even though the article was not a " 'do-it-yourself' guide for the hydrogen bomb . . . [it] could possibly provide sufficient information to allow a medium size nation to move faster in developing a hydrogen weapon."[80]

Judge Warren seemed particularly concerned about the prospect that the article could start a nuclear war. While noting the First Amendment ramifications were quite serious (he cited the case as "the first instance of prior restraint against a publication in this fashion in the history of this country"), he nevertheless believed that a "mistake in ruling against the United States could pave the way for thermonuclear annihilation for us all. In that event, our right to life is extinguished and the right to publish becomes moot."[81]

What precedents did Judge Warren cite in his decision? As expected, *Near* set the standard, although the judge also reverted to the test proposed by Justice Stewart in the Pentagon Papers. Obviously, this test holds no precedential value because only Justice White joined the concurring opinion. Ironically, Justice Stewart found that in applying the test ("direct, immediate, and irreparable damage to our Nation or its people"), the *Times* and the *Post* should **not** have been enjoined because he was not convinced that publication would cause such harm. *The Progressive's* attorneys had contended that the purpose of the article was not to enable someone to build an H-bomb, but instead was to make the public aware of the dangers of nuclear war by demonstrating how easy it is to construct such weapons. Judge Warren called this goal a "laudable crusade" but still held that the portions of the article found objectionable by the U.S. government "fall within the narrow area recognized by the Court in *Near v. Minnesota* in which a prior restraint on publication is appropriate." *Near*, of course, makes no mention of hydrogen bombs, but Judge Warren drew a parallel between the troop movements exception ("the publication of the sailing dates of transports or the number and location of troops") and bomb information:

> Times have changed significantly since 1931 when *Near* was decided. Now war by foot soldiers has been replaced in large part by war by machines and bombs. No longer need there be any advanced warning or any preparation time before a nuclear war could be commenced. In light of these factors, this court concludes that publication of the technical information of the hydrogen bomb contained in

the article is analogous to publication of troop movements or locations in time of war and falls within the extremely narrow exception to the rule against prior restraint.[82]

How was this case different from the Pentagon Papers? Judge Warren contended that the Pentagon Papers were "historical data," whereas *The Progressive* article involved "the most destructive weapon in the history of mankind, information of sufficient destructive potential to nullify the right to free speech and to endanger the right to life itself."[83] The judge also noted that the U.S. government had simply failed to meet its heavy evidentiary burden in the earlier case. And, furthermore, although no federal statute applied in the Pentagon Papers, a specific federal statute (the Atomic Energy Act) granted the government authority to seek the injunction.

The preliminary injunction kept the article from being published, but the magazine appealed the judge's decision to the Seventh Circuit U.S. Court of Appeals in Chicago and sought a writ of mandamus from the U.S. Supreme Court to order the trial court to conduct an expedited review of the case. On July 2, the Supreme Court, in a 7–2 per curiam opinion that was a decision only on the request for expedited review, **not** a decision on the merits of the prior restraint, denied the motion. (Only Justices White and Brennan dissented.) The Court denied the motion primarily on the grounds that *The Progressive* had spent almost three months preparing the required briefs arguing the merits of the case and thus, in the eyes of the Court, negated any need for expedited review. Then on September 13, six months after the initial prior restraint had been imposed on the magazine, the U.S. Court of Appeals finally heard oral arguments on both sides, which essentially were the same as those made prior to the earlier decision.

Three days later on September 16, the case took a particularly bizarre turn. A small circulation newspaper, the *Madison* (Wisconsin) *Press Connection* — published by a group of employees then on strike against the two daily newspapers[84] — published a letter from a 32-year-old computer programmer and freelance writer who had developed a keen interest in the hydrogen bomb. The letter from Charles Hansen was addressed to liberal U.S. Republican Senator Charles Percy of Illinois, but copies were sent to various newspapers around the country. Hansen was miffed at what had happened to *The Progressive* and included essentially the same information — including a diagram of how the bomb works and a description of the process involved in manufacturing the device — in his letter that had been repressed from the magazine.

The U.S. government's reaction was immediate. But instead of hopping to court to seek another injunction or to criminally prosecute the magazine, the government dropped all efforts to seek a permanent injunction. Why? Officially, the U.S. Justice Department indicated that because the letter exposed most of the information the United States was seeking to prevent *The Progressive* from publishing, there was no longer any need for the injunction. The secrets were out and the damage was done. Would the government have ultimately prevailed had this case gone to the U.S. Supreme Court on its merits? No one knows for sure, of course, but, if the Court so chose, it could certainly have distinguished this case from the Pentagon Papers case, just as U.S. District Court Judge Warren had done. Once again, however, many questions were left unanswered; the Republic apparently was not harmed and life goes on. Several newspapers published the letter later, and *The Progressive* in its November 1979 issue finally published the original article under the title, "The H-Bomb Secret: To Know How Is To Ask Why." Judge Warren did not formally dismiss the case against the magazine until September 4, 1980, but the government's request that the case be dismissed effectively blocked any obstacles to publication.

Was this a victory for the press? Probably not, but it was certainly not a downright defeat. Press reaction to the case was rather mixed with the *New York Times* editorially supporting the magazine, and the *Washington Post* (yes, indeed, the same newspaper that had fought to publish the Pentagon Papers) criticized the magazine. Many journalists feared that if the U.S. Supreme Court had heard the case on its merits, an adverse ruling would emerge that could have dire consequences for First Amendment rights. Ignorance may very well be bliss, they reasoned.

JUDICIAL PRIOR RESTRAINTS

Most prior restraints occur when an agency of the executive branch of government, such as the U.S. Justice Department or a local prosecutor, seeks a court order to prohibit publication, but prior restraint can originate from any branch of government, including the judiciary. In 1976, for the first and, thus far, only time, the U.S. Supreme Court confronted the constitutionality of restrictive orders imposed on the press in attempting to preserve the constitutional rights of criminal defendants.[85]

NEBRASKA PRESS ASSOCIATION V. STEWART

On October 18, 1975, six members of the Henry Kellie family were viciously murdered in their home in Sutherland, a Nebraska hamlet of about 850 people. The state later charged that the murders had occurred in the course of a sexual assault, including that of a 10-year-old girl. The case naturally attracted immediate and widespread attention from the local, regional and national news media. Police released a description of a suspect, who was quickly

arrested and arraigned in Lincoln County Court the next day. Two days later
the suspect, Ervin Charles Simants, through his attorney and joined by the
county attorney, moved to close the judicial proceedings to the press and the
public. The county court judge heard oral arguments (probably a misnomer
here because both attorneys were in favor of a restrictive order and no attorney
for the news media was there to protest) and granted the motion for the
restrictive order on October 22.

As requested, the order strictly prohibited anyone at the hearing from
releasing or authorizing for public dissemination in any form or matter
whatsoever any testimony given or evidence adduced and required the press to
adhere to the Nebraska Bar-Press Guidelines. Bar-Press Guidelines (sometimes
also called Bench-Bar-Press Guidelines) have been drawn up in many states to
provide guidance to the news media on how criminal trials and other judicial
proceedings should be covered. Such guidelines are **always** voluntary, and thus
bear no sanctions or penalties for violation. The county court judge, however,
ordered the press to abide by the guidelines.

Surprisingly, the judge did not close the preliminary hearing for the
defendant even though he made the hearing subject to the restrictive order. In
other words, the news media was permitted to attend the hearing but was
prohibited from reporting virtually anything that had taken place. The judge's
justification for the extremely broad order was to preserve the Sixth Amendment right of the defendant to "a speedy and public trial, by an impartial
jury."

The county court bound Simants over to the district court for further
proceedings. On October 23, various members of the news media, including
the Nebraska Press Association, publishers and individual reporters, filed a
motion for leave to intervene in the district court, requesting that the restrictive
order be lifted. After a hearing, which included testimony from the county
court judge and admission into evidence of newspaper articles about the case,
District Court Judge Hugh Stuart granted the motion to intervene. On October
27, however, he issued his own restrictive order to be tentatively applied until
the trial court jury was selected, which could obviously be extended longer at
the judge's discretion. The order was quite broad because it prohibited the
news media from reporting:

(1) the existence or contents of a confession Simants had made to law enforcement officers, which had been introduced in open court arraignment; (2) the fact
or nature of statements Simants had made to other persons: (3) the contents of
a note he had written the night of the crime; (4) certain aspects of the medical
testimony at the preliminary hearing; (5) the identity of the victims of the alleged
sexual assault and the nature of the assault.[86]

As with the prior one, this order required the press to follow the Nebraska
Bar-Press Guidelines and even prohibited publication of the exact nature of

the order itself! In other words, the order prohibited public dissemination of virtually any information that could possibly prejudice potential jurors.

On October 31, the Nebraska Press Association and its supporters simultaneously asked the district court to vacate its order and filed a writ of mandamus, a stay and an expedited appeal with the Nebraska Supreme Court. Both the prosecuting attorney and Simants' attorney intervened and the state supreme court heard oral arguments on November 25. One week later the state supreme court issued a *per curiam* opinion that modified the district court order but still prohibited: "(a) the existence and nature of any confessions or admissions made by the defendant to law enforcement officers, (b) any confessions or admissions made to any third parties, except members of the press, and (c) other facts "strongly implicative" of the accused."[87]

Although this version of the order was not quite as restrictive as the original, the restraint on the press is still very broad. The Nebraska Supreme Court applied a balancing test that pitted the standard enunciated in the Pentagon Papers ("heavy presumption against . . . constitutionality validity" of any governmental prior restraint) against the Sixth Amendment rights of the defendant and found that Simants' right to trial by an impartial jury outweighed the First Amendment considerations. Interestingly, the state supreme court did not use the state Bar-Press Guidelines as justification, but instead referred to state statutory law permitting closure in certain circumstances. The Nebraska Supreme Court specifically rejected the "absolutist position" that prior restraint by the government against the press is never constitutionally permissible.

The Nebraska Press Association and the other petitioners quickly appealed the state supreme court decision to the U.S. Supreme Court, and in late 1975 the Court granted a writ of certiorari to hear the case. In the meantime, Simants was tried and convicted of first-degree murder and sentenced to death in January 1976. On April 19, 1976, the U.S. Supreme Court heard oral arguments in the appeal of the restrictive order and issued its decision on June 30. The Court had jurisdiction to hear the case despite the fact Simants was already convicted because the particular controversy was "capable of repetition." In other words, the Court felt this case was important enough to decide because of its implications for future cases even though the decision would have no impact on the case from which it originally arose.

The U.S. Supreme Court held that the restrictive order was unconstitutional. In the unanimous opinion written by Chief Justice Warren E. Burger, the Court contrasted the impact of prior restraint versus the after-the-fact impact on punishment on press freedom. "A prior restraint, by contrast and by definition, has an immediate and irreversible sanction," according to the Court. "If it can be said that a threat of criminal or civil sanctions after publication 'chills' speech, prior restraint 'freezes' it at least for the time."[88]

The Court saw three major issues that had to be addressed before the constitutionality of the order could be determined: "(a) the nature and extent of pretrial coverage, (b) whether other measures would be likely to mitigate the effects of unrestrained pretrial publicity; (c) how effectively a restraining order would operate to prevent the threatened danger."[89] Although the Court felt "that the trial judge was justified in concluding that there would be intense and pervasive pretrial publicity . . . [and] . . . that publicity might impair the defendant's right to a fair trial . . .," it characterized the judge's conclusions regarding the effect on potential jurors was "speculative, dealing as he was with factors unknown and unknowable."[90] The major problem, as the Court viewed the case, resulted because the judge did not demonstrate that measures short of the restrictive order would not have prevented or mitigated any potential violations of the defendant's Sixth Amendment rights. The Court listed several examples of measures that should have been attempted first by the judge before issuing the restrictive order. These included:

(a) change of trial venue to a place less exposed to the intense publicity that seemed imminent in Lincoln County [footnote omitted]; postponement of the trial to allow public attention to subside; (c) use of searching questions of prospective jurors . . . to screen out those with fixed opinions as to guilt or innocence; (d) the use of emphatic and clear instructions on the sworn duty of each juror to decide the issues only on evidence presented in open court.[91]

Other measures mentioned by the Court were sequestration of jurors and restricting what the lawyers, police and witnesses could say outside the courtroom. Most of these measures were first enunciated in a 1966 case, *Sheppard v. Maxwell*,[92] discussed in Chapter 9.

As in *Near* and the Pentagon Papers case, the Court made it clear that whereas the burden of overcoming the strong presumption against the constitutionality of prior restraint had not been met in the case at bar, "this Court has frequently denied that First Amendment rights are absolute and has consistently rejected the proposition that prior restraint can never be employed."[93] The Court also noted earlier in the opinion:

The extraordinary protections afforded by the First Amendment carry with them something in the nature of a fiduciary duty to exercise the protected rights responsibly – a duty widely acknowledged but not always observed by editors and publishers. It is not asking too much to suggest that those who exercise First Amendment rights in newspapers or broadcasting enterprises direct some effort to protect the rights of an accused to a fair trial by unbiased jurors.[94]

This theme of *rights incur responsibilities* permeates most of the Court's First Amendment decisions during the last decade, especially more recent decisions.

Although the Court's holding was unanimous, Justice William J. Brennan,

Jr. (joined by Justices Potter Stewart and John Paul Stevens), filed a separate concurring opinion, and Justices Byron R. White, Lewis F. Powell, Jr., and William H. Rehnquist wrote individual concurring opinions. Justice Brennan (with Justices Stewart and Marshall) characterized prior restraint as "a constitutionally impermissible method for enforcing" a defendant's right to a fair trial. Justice Brennan specifically rejected the "contention that speculative deprivation of an accused's Sixth Amendment right to an impartial jury is comparable to the damage to the Nation or its people that *Near* and *New York Times* would have found sufficient to justify a prior restraint on reporting." Thus he would never permit, apparently under any circumstances, a restrictive order to be issued against the press in a criminal proceeding. As he noted in his opinion: "The press may be arrogant, tyrannical, abusive, and sensationalist, just as it may be incisive, probing, and informative. But at least in the context of prior restraints on publication, the decision of what, when, and how to publish is for editors, not judges."[95]

In his brief concurring opinion, Justice White expressed "grave doubt in my mind whether such orders with respect to the press such as were entered in this case would ever be justifiable," but he was reluctant to announce a rule yet to cover all future cases of this type.[96] Justice Powell, in his brief concurring opinion, emphasized "the unique burden that rests upon the party, whether it be the state or a defendant, who undertakes to show the necessity for prior restraint on pretrial publicity" and contended that prior restraint in such cases is permissible "only when it is shown to be necessary to prevent the dissemination of prejudicial publicity that otherwise poses a high likelihood of preventing, directly and irreparably, the impaneling of a jury meeting the Sixth Amendment requirement of impartiality."[97]

Finally, Justice Stevens indicated in his brief concurring opinion that, although he had not yet made up his mind, "I do, however, subscribe to most of what Mr. Justice Brennan says and, if ever required to face the issue squarely, may well accept his ultimate conclusion [that prior restraint is never permissible to protect Sixth Amendment rights]."[98]

Because the composition of the Court has changed substantially since this case was decided in 1976, it is difficult to predict how the Court would decide other prior restraint cases involving restrictive orders imposed on the press, especially if such an order were narrowly tailored to protect the rights of a defendant when those rights were in very serious jeopardy and other measures would be highly unlikely to be effective. No such case has meandered to the Court yet. Justices Burger, Powell, Stewart, Marshall and Brennan no longer serve on the Court, but five new justices, considered by most legal scholars to be relatively conservative on First Amendment issues, sit in their stead — Justices Sandra Day O'Connor, Antonin Scalia, Anthony Kennedy (all three nominated by President Ronald Reagan) and David Souter and Clarence Thomas (nominated by President Bush). Justice Rehnquist, also generally considered a conservative on First Amendment rights, has served as Chief Justice since 1986. At the end of the 1992-1993 term, however, Justice Byron White resigned from the Court, offering President Clinton the opportunity to significantly alter the balance of the Court. As noted in Chapter 1, the U.S. Senate approved the president's nominee, Ruth Bader Ginsberg, whose votes on First Amendment issues were expected to be more in line with the moderate and liberal justices on the Court.

PRIOR RESTRAINT ON FREEDOM OF SPEECH

The First Amendment grants not only freedom of the press but freedom of speech and the right to peaceably assemble as well. Some of the most controversial cases to be decided by the U.S. Supreme Court have evolved from free speech/free assembly conflicts. Troublesome speech cases often produce inconsistent and confusing opinions. This section deals only with noncommercial speech because commercial speech is the focus of the next chapter.

One of the earliest U.S. Supreme Court decisions on free speech was *Jay Fox v. State of Washington* in 1915 in which a unanimous court ruled that a Washington State statute banning speech "having a tendency to encourage or incite the commission of any crime, breach of the peace, or act of violence" did not violate the First or Fourteenth Amendments. According to the decision, written by the infamous Justice Oliver Wendell Holmes, "In this present case the disrespect for law that was encouraged was disregard of it, an overt breach and technically criminal act."[99] The defendant had published an article encouraging a "boycott" of officials and others who were arresting members of a local nudist colony for indecent exposure. He was charged with inciting indecent exposure under the statute that made such an act a misdemeanor. This was an early indication of a distinction made many years later between **speech versus action** or **symbolic speech versus action speech**.

Schenck v. United States

One of the most famous of the early free speech cases was *Schenck v. U.S.* (combined with *Baer v. U.S.*)[100] in 1919 in which the U.S. Supreme Court for the first time applied the "clear and present danger" test in determining impermissible speech. Charles T. Schenck and Elizabeth Baer, members of the U.S. Socialist Party, were indicted and ultimately convicted by a federal jury of three counts of violating the federal Espionage Act of 1917. This act provided criminal penalties of up to a $10,000 fine and/or imprisonment for up to 20 years for conviction of various offenses during wartime, including "willfully obstruct[ing] the recruiting or enlistment service of the United States, to the injury of the service or of the United States." Both had been involved in sending brochures to potential draftees during World War I that characterized a conscript as little better than a convict and "in impassioned language . . . intimated that conscription was despotism in its worst form and a monstrous wrong against humanity in the interest of Wall Street's chosen few."[101]

According to Justice Holmes and the Court:

> We admit that in many places and in ordinary times the defendants in saying all that was said in the circular would have been within their constitutional rights. But the character of every act depends upon the circumstances in which it is done. The most stringent protection of free speech would not protect a man in falsely shouting fire in a theatre and causing a panic. The question in every case is whether the words are used in such circumstances and are such a nature as to create a clear and present danger that they will bring about the substantive evils that Congress has a right to prevent. It is a question of proximity and degree.[102]

The Court upheld the convictions on the grounds that the state was within its rights to punish Schenck and Baer because there was a possibility that the circulars could have obstructed recruiting even though no such obstruction was demonstrated by the state. According to the unanimous opinion, "If the act (speaking, or circulating a paper), its tendency and the intent with which it is done are the same, we perceive no ground for saying that success alone warrants making the act a crime."[103]

The clear and present danger test has had many advocates among the U.S. Supreme Court justices over the years, and the example of falsely shouting fire in a crowded theater has been frequently cited by the public and jurists alike in supporting restrictions on certain kinds of speech. But is it an appropriate test? Can it be fairly and consistently applied or does it become merely arbitrary? In *Schenck*, the Court emphasized that the country was at war and that Congress had specific authority under the federal statute to prohibit such actions. What if there had been no war at the time? What if no federal statute covered the speech?

Abrams v. United States

On May 16, 1918, Congress amended the 1917 Espionage Act to include a series of additional offenses such as promoting curtailment of the production of war materials. That same year Jacob Abrams and four other defendants, all Russian emigrants, were convicted in a federal court in New York of violating the act, including the 1918 amendments, for publishing information "intended to incite, provoke and encourage resistance to the United States" during the war and for conspiring "to urge, incite and advocate curtailment of production [of] ordnance and ammunition, necessary [to] the prosecution of the war."[104] What were their specific acts? They printed and distributed two different leaflets printed in English and Yiddish and threw copies out of the window of a building to passersby. One of the leaflets, as described in Justice Holmes' dissent (joined by Justice Louis D. Brandeis), said:

> The President's [Woodrow Wilson] cowardly silence about the intervention in Russia reveals the hypocrisy of the plutocratic gang in Washington. . . . The other leaflet, headed 'Workers – Wake Up,' with abusive language says that America together with the Allies will march for Russia to help the Czecko-Slovaks in their struggle against the Bolsheviki, and that this time the hypocrites shall not fool the Russian emigrants and friends of Russia in America.[105]

In a 7–2 decision, with Justices Holmes and Brandeis dissenting, the Court upheld the trial court convictions, noting, "All five of the defendants were born in Russia. They were intelligent, had considerable schooling, and at the time they were arrested they had lived in the United States terms varying from five to ten years, but none of them had applied for naturalization."[106]

In his dissent, Justice Holmes applied the clear and present test, which he had formulated in the majority opinion in *Schenck*, to the acts committed by Abrams and his co-defendants, but found a lack of proof of intent on the part of the defendants "to cripple or hinder the United States in the prosecution of the war." According to Justice Holmes: "I think that we should be eternally vigilant against attempts to check the expression of opinions that we loathe and believe to be fraught with death, unless they so imminently threaten immediate interference with the lawful and pressing purposes of the law that an immediate check is required to save the country."[107]

Does this case indicate the arbitrariness with which the clear and present danger test can be applied? The majority essentially applied the clear and present danger test but upheld the convictions anyway, whereas the architect of the test, Justice Holmes, applied the test but found no imminent danger.

In several other cases decided by the Court in 1919 and 1920, a majority of the justices consistently upheld convictions for speech, usually the distribution of pamphlets or for attempting to obstruct recruiting, under the Espionage Act of 1917.[108]

THE EXPANSION OF FREE SPEECH RIGHTS: *GITLOW V. NEW YORK* AND ITS PROGENY

In 1925 the U.S. Supreme Court tackled the first of a long series of cases that eventually broadened free speech rights and established much clearer guidelines on permissible versus impermissible speech. In the first case, *Gitlow v. New York*,[109] the Court upheld the conviction of Benjamin Gitlow for the distribution of 16,000 copies of *The Revolutionary Age*, the house organ of the radical left-wing section of the Socialist Party. Gitlow, an active member of the left wing who made speeches throughout New York State and who was on the board of managers of the paper and was its business manager, was indicted and later convicted under the state's criminal anarchy statute. The law, which had been enacted in 1902 after the assassination of President James McKinley in Buffalo by an anarchist a year earlier, made it a felony for anyone to advocate criminal anarchy in speech or in writing. Anarchy was defined as advocating, advising or teaching "the duty, necessity or propriety of overthrowing or overturning organized government by force or violence."[110]

There was no question regarding Gitlow's guilt. He freely admitted violating the statute, but he contended that (a) his conviction was a violation of the due process clause of the Fourteenth Amendment[111] and (b) "as there was no evidence of any concrete result flowing from the publication of the Manifesto or of the circumstances showing the likelihood of such a result, the statute . . . penalizes the mere utterance . . . of 'doctrine' having no quality of incitement, without regard either to the circumstances of its utterance or to the likelihood of unlawful consequences."[112] In a 7–2 decision with Justices Holmes and Brandeis dissenting, the Court held that even though there "was no evidence of any effect resulting from the publication and circulation of the Manifesto," the jury was "warranted in finding that the Manifesto advocated not merely the abstract doctrine of overthrowing organized government by force, violence and unlawful means, but action to that end."

According to the Court, Gitlow's First Amendment rights were not violated because the statute did not penalize communication of abstract doctrine or academic discussion but instead prohibited language that implied an urging to action, of which Gitlow was judged guilty by the trial court. This was the Court's first hint of a distinction that was to come many years later between advocacy to action versus mere abstract doctrine.

But what about the Fourteenth Amendment? The Court agreed that the Fourteenth Amendment applied in this case: "For present purposes, we may and do assume that freedom of speech and of the press — which are protected by the First Amendment from abridgement by Congress — are among the fundamental personal rights and 'liberties' protected by the due process clause of the Fourteenth Amendment from impairment by the States."[113]

Thus, as discussed earlier, the Court for the first time incorporated First Amendment rights into the Fourteenth Amendment so that citizens of all states have the same freedom of speech and of the press because the Fourteenth Amendment prohibits both federal and state abridgement of these rights as originally granted in the Constitution.

In effect, Gitlow won his argument that the First Amendment applied to the states (the statute was a New York law) through the Fourteenth, but he lost the argument that his First Amendment rights had been violated. Thus his convictions stood. The majority applied a so-called bad tendency test (implying an urging to action, as just mentioned), whereas Justices Holmes and

Brandeis applied the clear and present danger test, noting in their dissent that "there was no present danger of an attempt to overthrow the government by force. . . . The only difference between an expression of an opinion and an incitement in the narrower sense is the speaker's enthusiasm for the result."[114]

Gitlow served three years of his 5-to 10-year sentence. New York Governor Alfred E. Smith, who later ran unsuccessfully for the U.S. presidency, pardoned him. Gitlow became an anti-Communist informer during the 1940s and died in 1965.[115]

Two years after *Gitlow*, the U.S. Supreme Court had another opportunity to expand freedom of speech but chose once again not to do so. In *Whitney v. California* (1927),[116] the Court upheld the conviction of a Communist Labor Party member for violating California's 1919 Criminal Syndicalism Act. What was Anita Whitney's crime? She attended a 1919 Chicago convention of the Socialist Party at which a radical right wing of the party was formed—the Communist Labor Party. The state statute provided that any individual who "organizes or assists in organizing, or is or knowingly becomes a member of any organization, society, group or assemblage of persons organized or assembled to advocate, teach or aid and abet criminal syndicalism . . . [i]s guilty of a felony and punishable by imprisonment." Criminal syndicalism was defined "as any doctrine or precept advocating, teaching or aiding and abetting the commission of a crime, sabotage . . ., or unlawful acts of force and violence or unlawful methods of terrorism."

Whitney admitted that she had joined and helped organize the Communist Labor Party (CLP) of California but argued that "the character of the state organization could not be forecast when she attended the convention" and that she did not intend to create "an instrument of terrorism and violence." Furthermore, she contended that the CLP's endorsement of acts of criminal syndicalism took place over her protests. The majority opinion rejected Whitney's argument that her First and Fourth Amendment rights had been violated because "her mere presence in the convention, however violent the opinions expressed therein, could not truly become a crime."[117]

With Justice Louis D. Brandeis (joined by Justice Holmes) concurring in a separate opinion, the Court ruled that the jury had the authority to convict Whitney because the state statute, as applied, was not "repugnant to the due process clause." Citing *Gitlow*, the majority held that a state may punish those who abuse freedom of speech "by utterances inimical to the public welfare, tending to incite to crime, disturb the public peace, or endanger the foundations of organized government and threaten its overthrow by unlawful means."[118] What about the clear and present danger test? The majority refused to apply the test in this case, but Justice Brandeis strongly argued that the test should apply in such cases, and he greatly clarified the conditions necessary to meet the test. Why did Justices Brandeis and Holmes then concur with the majority? According to Justice Brandeis, Whitney had not adequately argued her case on constitutional grounds at the time of her trial:

> Whenever the fundamental rights of free speech and assembly are alleged to have been invaded, it must remain open to a defendant to present the issue whether there actually did exist at the time a clear danger; whether the danger, if any, was imminent, and whether the evil apprehended was one so substantial as to justify the stringent restriction interposed by the legislature . . . [Whitney] claimed below that the statute as applied to her violated the Federal Constitution; but she did not claim that it was void because there was no clear and present danger of serious evil.[119]

This concurring opinion illustrates a fatal flaw that even modern appeals of trial court decisions involving First Amendment issues sometimes suffer – the failure to attack a statute or state action on sufficient constitutional grounds. Although it is unlikely that Whitney's conviction would have been reversed if the arguments at trial had met the criteria enunciated in Justice Brandeis' opinion, in other cases meeting those standards may well have made the difference.

How should the clear and present danger test be applied? Justice Brandeis refined the test considerably:

> Fear of serious injury alone cannot alone justify suppression of free speech and assembly. . . . To justify suppression of free speech there must be reasonable ground to fear that serious evil will result if free speech is practiced. There must be reasonable ground to believe that the danger apprehended is imminent. There must be reasonable ground to believe that the evil to be prevented is a serious one. Every denunciation of existing law tends in some measure to increase the probability that there will be violation of it. Condonation of a breach enhances the probability. Expressions of approval add to the probability. Propagation of the criminal state of mind by teaching syndicalism increases it. Advocacy of lawbreaking heightens it further. But even advocacy of violation, however reprehensible morally, is not a justification for denying free speech where the advocacy falls short of incitement and there is nothing to indicate that the advocacy would be immediately acted on. The wide difference between advocacy and incitement, between preparation and attempt, between assembly and conspiracy, must be borne in mind. In order to support a finding of clear and present danger it must be shown either that immediate serious violence was to be expected or was advocated, or that the past conduct furnished reason to believe that such advocacy was then contemplated.[120]

Justice Brandeis' formulation was part of a concurring opinion rather than the majority opinion, which rejected the test; thus his opinion was apparently a major influence on a decision 42 years later in which the Court, in a per curiam decision, unanimously overruled *Whitney*. In *Brandenburg v. Ohio*,[121] the Court overturned the conviction of a Ku Klux Klan (KKK) leader who had been fined $1,000 and sentenced to 1 to 10 years in prison for violating Ohio's criminal syndicalism statute, quite similar to the statute in *Whitney*. Brandenburg had telephoned an announcer-reporter for a Cincinnati television station and invited him to attend a KKK rally at a nearby farm. With the cooperation of the KKK, the reporter and a cameraperson attended and filmed the events, which included a cross burning and speeches denouncing Jews and Blacks with such phrases as "Send the Jews back to Israel" and "Bury the Niggers." Portions of the film were broadcast on the station and on network television. The Court held that the statute under which the defendant was prosecuted was unconstitutional because it "by its own words and as applied, purports to punish mere advocacy and to forbid . . . assembly with others merely to advocate the prescribed type of action."[122]

There were several cases between *Whitney* and *Brandenburg* that should be briefly mentioned because they provide an indication of how free speech cases have evolved to the modern era. Ten years after *Whitney*, the U.S. Supreme Court, in an 8–0 decision, for the first time struck down a state criminal syndicalism statute, as applied, as a violation of the due process clause of the Fourteenth Amendment. In *DeJonge v. Oregon*,[123] the Court overturned the conviction of a member of the Communist Party for speaking at a peaceful meeting called by the party to protest police brutality and conditions at the county jail in Portland, Oregon, where longshoremen were being held after being arrested in a bitter strike against ship owners. Even the jury had difficulty in deciding Dirk DeJong's fate. After long deliberations, the jury at first deadlocked 6–6 but then ultimately voted 10–2 (Oregon permitted nonunanimous verdicts) for conviction after the judge promised the jury to give the defendant a light sentence. The jury and everyone else were apparently shocked when the sentence turned out to be seven years in prison.[124] The Oregon Supreme Court upheld DeJong's conviction even though it acknowledged that no criminal syndicalism or unlawful conduct had been advocated at the meeting and the defendant had simply conducted a meeting called by a party that advocated criminal syndicalism. Of the approximately 150 to 300 people who attended the meeting, very few were Communists, and none of the speakers, including DeJong, advocated violence.[125]

The concept of "fighting words" first emerged in 1942 in *Chaplinsky v. New Hampshire*[126] in which the Court unanimously held that such words have no First Amendment protection if, as the New Hampshire Supreme Court had ruled earlier in the case, they are "likely to cause an average addressee to fight." Thus the Court upheld the conviction of a Jehovah's Witness who had provoked a city marshal to fight with him on the sidewalk after he had called the official "a God damned racketeer" and "a damned Fascist" and had characterized the whole government of Rochester, New Hampshire, as "Fascists or agents of Fascists."[127] Fighting words, according to the opinion written by Justice Frank Murphy, are "those which by their very utterance inflict injury or tend to incite an immediate breach of the peace."[128]

In 1951 the U.S. Supreme Court tackled another free speech case involving Jehovah's Witnesses. Several members of the religious sect organization had held a meeting in a city park in Havre de Grace, Maryland, after they had been denied a permit by the park commissioner. Two speakers were immediately arrested, convicted and fined $25.00 each for violating a state "practice" (no statute was involved) or tradition for anyone to seek a permit before holding a meeting in a public park. In a unanimous opinion written by Chief Justice Fred M. Vinson, the Court held that such an arbitrary and discriminatory refusal to issue a permit was a clear violation of equal protection under the Fourteenth Amendment.[129]

In another case[130] decided on the same day as the one just mentioned, the U.S. Supreme Court upheld the disorderly conduct conviction of a college student who told a group of approximately 75 Blacks and whites that President Harry S Truman and the mayor of Syracuse, New York, were "bums" and that the American Legion was a "Nazi Gestapo." He also said, "The Negroes don't have equal rights; they should rise up in arms and fight them." Why was Irving Feiner arrested? A man in the crowd told a police officer, "If you don't get that son of a bitch off, I will go over and get him off there myself." At the trial, the police officer testified that he "stepped in to prevent it resulting in a fight." That was enough for the trial court to find that police "were motivated solely by a proper concern for the preservation of order and protection of the general welfare." The Supreme Court concluded that Feiner "was thus neither arrested nor convicted for the making of the content of his speech. Rather, it was the reaction which it actually engendered."[131]

It is unlikely today, even with the conservative Rehnquist court, that Feiner's conviction would be upheld, especially based on evidence that one person's reaction might cause an adverse impact on the public welfare, but the decision does illustrate how easily states can legally suppress freedom of speech. Indeed, 14 years after *Feiner*, the U.S. Supreme Court faced a similar set of circumstances. In two cases commonly known as *Cox I*[132] and *Cox II*,[133] the Court appeared to back substantially away from *Feiner*, although the majority opinion called the circumstances a "far cry" from that of *Feiner*. In *Cox I*, the Court held that a civil rights minister's conviction under a Louisiana "disturbing the peace" statute was an unconstitutional restraint on his freedom of speech and assembly. The minister, a field secretary for the Congress of Racial Equality (CORE), was arrested and convicted for breach of the peace and for obstructing a sidewalk after he gave a speech protesting the arrests of 23 Black college students after they picketed stores with segregated lunch counters. Reverend Cox encouraged a group of about 2,000 students to sit in at lunch counters, while a group of 100 to 300 Whites gathered on the opposite sidewalk. When some members of the crowd reacted with "muttering" and "grumbling," Reverend Cox was arrested and ultimately convicted. The defendant was also convicted of violating a state statute banning courthouse demonstrations, and this conviction was reversed in *Cox II* by the Supreme Court on the same grounds as *Cox I*.

One more case decided prior to *Brandenburg* that deserves attention is *Dennis v. United States*[134] in which the Court applied a variation of the clear and present danger test, ad hoc balancing, to uphold the convictions of 11 members of the U.S. Communist Party for violating the conspiracy provisions of the Smith Act of 1940, a peacetime sedition act enacted by Congress. The Court voted 6–2 to uphold the convictions, but only four justices could agree on the specific test to be applied. Party members were convicted for "wilfully and knowingly conspiring (1) to organize as the Communist Party . . . a society, group and assembly of persons who teach and advocate the overthrow and destruction of the Government . . . by force and violence, and (2) knowingly and wilfully to advocate and teach the duty and necessity of overthrowing and destroying the Government . . . by force and violence."[135] The plurality opinion, written by Chief Justice Fred M. Vinson, applied the test articulated by Chief Judge Learned Hand in the Second Circuit U.S. Court of Appeals decision in the case: "In each case [courts] must ask whether the gravity of the 'evil,' discounted by its improbability, justifies such invasion of free speech as is necessary to avoid the danger."[136]

The Court went on to note, "It is the existence of the conspiracy which creates the danger. . . . If the ingredients of the reaction are present, we cannot bind the Government to wait until the catalyst is added."[137]

In *Dennis* the trial court judge reserved the question of whether there was a clear and present danger for his own determination rather than submitting the issue to the jury. The defendants argued that the question should have been a jury issue because it was a question of fact. The U.S. Supreme Court, however, agreed with the trial judge that the presence or absence of such a danger is a question of law and thus for the judge to determine. The distinction may seem trivial to the layperson but it is extremely important because juries are often more lenient with defendants in free speech cases than judges. As discussed in the previous chapter, in a criminal case, such as *Dennis*, a jury verdict in favor of the defendant cannot be overruled by the judge, and a judge's decision can only be reversed by an appellate court.

Modern Free Speech Cases

The thesis, mentioned earlier, that extreme examples often provide the courts with the opportunity to delineate the outer boundaries of our First Amendment rights was well illustrated in a 1977 U.S. Supreme Court decision[138] involving the National Socialist Party, otherwise known as the American

Nazis. The Village of Skokie, Illinois, would seem on a map to be a fairly typical, small midwestern town, but appearances can be deceiving. Although the approximately 100,000 survivors of the Holocaust (the 1933–1945 persecution of European Jews by Nazi Germany in which more than 6 million individuals were systematically murdered while being held in concentration camps) are scattered around the world, about 600 live in the town.[139] Frank Collins, a leader of the National Socialist Party chose to march with his band of Nazi followers in Skokie after his request was strongly rebuffed by Skokie officials who told him he would have to purchase a $350,000 insurance bond to cover any damages. Shortly after the Nazis announced their plans to demonstrate in protest of the insurance requirement, the village council authorized the village attorney to file suit to obtain an injunction to prevent the march. An Illinois trial court judge granted the request and banned the party from conducting a number of actions from parading in uniform to distributing leaflets. The Nazis appealed the decision to Illinois Appellate Court, which refused to stay the injunction, and then to the state Supreme Court, which denied their petition for expedited review. Obviously, the party wanted a quick review so it could seek approval to demonstrate while the media attention was focused on its planned actions.

When the Illinois Supreme Court rendered its decision, the party filed a petition to stay the decision, pending expedited review, in the U.S. Supreme Court. In a 5–4 per curiam decision, the U.S. Supreme Court treated the stay petition as a petition for a writ of certiorari and summarily reversed the Illinois Supreme Court ruling. The Court said the injunction would deprive the Nazis of First Amendment rights during the appellate review process, which the Court noted could take at least a year to complete. The Court went on to hold, "If a State seeks to impose a restraint of this kind, it must provide strict procedural safeguards . . . including immediate appellate review. Absent such review, the State must instead allow a stay."[140] The Court, it should be noted, did **not** hold that the village could not ultimately have halted the march but instead that the Nazis must be granted an expedited decision rather than having to wait the usual lengthy period involved in appealing trial court decisions. By refusing to grant expedited review on a First Amendment matter as serious as this one, the Illinois appellate courts infringed on the party's freedom of speech and freedom of assembly.

The Illinois Appellate Court, following the dictates of the U.S. Supreme Court, set aside the original injunction, except for a provision banning the marchers from displaying the swastika.[141] On appeal, the state Supreme Court lifted the complete injunction on grounds that the ban was unconstitutional prior restraint.[142]

The battle was not over, however. While the case was on appeal, the Village of Skokie enacted several ordinances effectively banning demonstrations such as that proposed by the National Socialist Party. After fighting the ordinances in the federal courts—including the Seventh Circuit U.S. Court of Appeals, which ruled against the village, and the U.S. Supreme Court, which refused to stay the Court of Appeals decision—the march was presumably ready to begin. However, three days before the march was scheduled, Nazi leader Collins cancelled plans for the rally. Instead two demonstrations were held in downtown Chicago, one at the Federal Plaza on June 24, 1978, and the other in a public park more than two weeks later. Both marches involved a relatively small band of uniformed Nazis surrounded by thousands of police and counterdemonstrators. After short speeches, each was over almost as quickly as it had begun and the front-page stories and lead stories in television newscasts about the marches faded away.

The ability of the government to impose prior restraint on private citizens appears rather limited, but such censorship is routinely permitted against the government's own employees. A long line of cases in the Supreme Court has established the principle that the government can impose criminal penalties and recover civil damages when employees disclose classified information, but the Court had never determined until 1980 whether the government can punish or recover damages from ex-employees who disclose nonclassified information after signing a prepublication review agreement as condition for employment.

Frank Snepp, a former CIA intelligence expert during the Vietnam War, wrote a book entitled *Decent Interval*, which was sharply critical of U.S. involvement in Vietnam, especially during the interval in which U.S. troops were withdrawn. Snepp's book was published in 1977, four years after U.S. troops began withdrawing and two years after the Communists defeated the South Vietnamese Army. When he was hired by the agency in 1968 he signed a prepublication review agreement, typically signed by CIA workers, which specified he would submit to the agency for approval any materials to be published that were based on information he had acquired as an employee. Such agreements, which are now commonplace for federal employees with access to sensitive information, require prepublication review for the rest of the employee's life, even if the person is no longer employed by the government. This type of contract is obviously prior restraint because it involves governmental censorship of individuals; but is it unconstitutional?

It was undisputed in the case that Snepp did not seek CIA preclearance of his manuscript and he had knowingly signed the contract. Apparently, no classified information was published because the agency never asserted any claim that secrets were disclosed. Instead, the government argued that Snepp had intentionally breached his contract with the CIA and he was therefore obligated to pay all royalties to the agency. The CIA asserted that he should also be subject to punitive damages. The U.S. government successfully sought an injunction in U.S. District Court[143] to prohibit Snepp from committing any further violations of his agreement with the CIA. The injunction also imposed a *constructive trust* on all previous and future royalties from the book. A constructive trust is a legal mechanism created to force an individual or organization to convey property to another party on the ground that the property was wrongfully or improperly obtained.

The Fourth Circuit U.S. Court of Appeals[144] upheld the trial court's injunction but ruled there was no basis for a constructive trust, although the court did hold that punitive damages could be imposed. In a 6-3 curiam opinion[145] reflecting the views of Chief Justice Warren E. Burger and Associate Justices William H. Rehnquist, Potter Stewart, Harry A. Blackmun, Lewis F. Powell, Jr. and Byron R. White, the U.S. Supreme Court held that Snepp could not be forced to pay punitive damages but that a constructive trust was permissible because he had breached a *fiduciary duty* he owed to the government. Fiduciary duty simply means an individual or organization is acting as a trustee for another after having agreed to undertake such a duty. In other words, by signing the agreement, Snepp created a duty to act on behalf of the CIA in protecting and withholding information from public disclosure that he had acquired during the course of his work for the agency. By publishing the book, he breached that duty and could, therefore, be held accountable for the profits or gains from the book because he was not legally entitled to the proceeds.

Although Snepp argued that his First Amendment rights were being violated by this prior restraint, the Court mentioned First Amendment rights only once in its unsigned opinion—in a footnote, which said: "The Government has a compelling interest in protecting both the secrecy of information important to our national security and the appearance of confidentiality so effective to the effective operation of our foreign intelligence service. The agreement that Snepp signed is a reasonable means of protecting this vital interest."[146]

In a somewhat unusually strong dissent, Justice John Paul Stevens (joined by Justices William J. Brennan, Jr., and Thurgood Marshall) accused the majority of creating a "drastic new remedy to enforce a species of prior restraint on a citizen's right to criticize his government."[147] In a footnote, Justice Stevens also strongly criticized the majority for granting certiorari and then deciding the case **without a full briefing and oral arguments.** Although oral arguments are traditional in most Supreme Court cases heard under the grant of a writ of certiorari, the Court declined to hear oral arguments in this case.

SYMBOLIC SPEECH

Most of the cases discussed previously involved either the communication of verbal information, such as publishing classified materials, or some direct action, such as making an inflammatory speech or mounting a demonstration, but some of the most troublesome and controversial free speech decisions have involved so-called symbolic speech. Symbolic speech can range from wearing a black armband to desecration of the American flag.

One of the earliest U.S. Supreme Court cases[148] concerned a California statute that banned the display of any "red flag, banner, or badge . . . in any public place . . . as a sign, symbol or emblem of opposition to organized government." Violation of the law was a criminal offense. Yetta Stromberg, a member of the Young Communist League (an organization of the International Communist Party), was in charge of a children's camp where "a camp-made reproduction of the flag of Soviet Russia" was raised each morning. A jury convicted her of violating the statute, and the verdict was upheld by the state appellate court. However, in *Stromberg v. California* (1931),[149] the U.S. Supreme Court reversed her conviction in a 7–2 decision holding that the state statute was unconstitutional because it restricted "the opportunity for free political discussion." The majority opinion written by Chief Justice Charles E. Hughes, noted:

> The maintenance of the opportunity for free political discussion to the end that government may be responsive to the will of the people and that changes may be obtained by lawful means, an opportunity essential to the security of the Republic, is a fundamental principle of our constitutional system. A statute which upon its face . . . is so vague and indefinite as to permit the punishment of the fair use of this opportunity is repugnant to the guaranty of liberty contained in the 14th Amendment.[150]

Nine years after Stromberg, however, the Court upheld a public school regulation requiring students to salute the American flag, noting, "The mere possession of religious convictions which contradict the relevant concerns of a political society does not relieve the citizen from discharge of political responsibilities."[151] In 1943, though, the Court specifically overruled the earlier decision.[152] Both cases involved the children of Jehovah's Witnesses who refused to pledge allegiance to the flag as part of a daily ritual in their public schools. In the later decision, which is still precedent, the majority opinion written by Justice Robert Jackson held that the policy was a clear violation of the Fourteenth Amendment. The case involved seven children of a Jehovah's Witness family who were expelled for refusing to salute and whose parents had been prosecuted for causing delinquency. Furthermore, school board officials had indicated they would send the children to reformatory school![153] "If there is any fixed star in our constitutional constellation, it is that no official, high or petty, can prescribe what shall be orthodox in politics, nationalism, religion or other matters of opinion or force citizens to confess by word or act their faith therein," according to the Court.[154]

United States v. O'Brien

In the late 1960s, the free speech case that probably evoked more public controversy than any other was *United States v. O'Brien* (1968).[155] The decision came in the same year as the Tet offensive, in which the North Vietnamese Communists scored a major psychological victory over U.S. and South Vietnamese troops in the Vietnam War by demonstrating how easily they could invade urban areas of the south. Two years before the Tet offensive, at a time when the United States was becoming politically polarized by the war, David Paul O'Brien and three other war protesters burned their Selective Service registration certificates, or draft cards, on the steps of the South Boston Courthouse in clear and deliberate defiance of the Universal Military Training and Service Act of 1948. The act, as amended by Congress in 1965, required Selective Service registrants to have the certificates in their "personal possession at all times" and provided criminal penalties for any person "who forges, alters, knowingly destroys, knowingly mutilates, or in any manner changes any such certificate."[156]

O'Brien was indicted, tried, convicted and sentenced in the U.S. District Court for the District of Massachusetts. He did not deny burning the card, but instead argued that he was attempting to publicly influence other people to agree with his antiwar beliefs and his act was protected symbolic speech under the First Amendment.

The U.S. Court of Appeals essentially agreed with O'Brien by ruling that the 1965 amendment was unconstitutional because it singled out for special treatment individuals charged with protesting. In a majority opinion written by Chief Justice Earl Warren, the U.S. Supreme Court disagreed. The Court held:

> We cannot accept the view that an apparently limitless variety of conduct can be labelled "speech" whenever the person engaging in the conduct intends thereby to express an idea. . . . This Court has held that when "speech" and "nonspeech" elements are combined in the same course of conduct, a sufficiently important governmental interest in regulating the nonspeech element can justify incidental limitations on First Amendment freedoms. . . . We think it clear that a government regulation is sufficiently justified if it is within the constitutional power of the government; if it furthers an important or substantial government interest; if the governmental interest is unrelated to the suppression of free expression; and if the incidental restriction on alleged First Amendment freedom is no greater than is essential to the furtherance of that interest.[157]

There was considerable criticism of the Court's reasoning in this case, although the particular test enunciated has stood the test of time. What was the "substantial government interest" in this case? According to the Court, the country "has a vital interest in having a system for raising armies that functions with maximum efficiency and is capable of easily and quickly responding to continually changing circumstances."[158] The continuing availability of the draft certificates, the Court asserted, is essential to preserving this substantial interest, and destroying them frustrates this interest. Would burning a registration card today be punishable under the Constitution? O'Brien burned his card during the Vietnam War era when men were being drafted into the armed forces. The draft has since been eliminated, although all men are required to immediately register when they reach 18 years of age. Is there still a substantial government interest to be protected in preserving "nondraft" registration cards?

Tinker v. Des Moines Independent Community School District: Expanding the First Amendment Rights of High School Students

Opposition to the Vietnam War also formed the backdrop to a U.S. Supreme Court case one year after *O'Brien*. In *Tinker v. Des Moines Independent Community School District* (1969),[159] the Court held that students wearing black armbands in public school was a "symbolic act" protected by the First Amendment. With the support of their parents, two high school students and one junior high school student wore black armbands to class in December 1965 to protest the war. Two days prior to this act, local school principals met to issue a regulation specifically prohibiting the armbands after a high school student in a journalism class had asked his teacher for permission to write an article on Vietnam for the school newspaper. As the Court noted in its 7–2 opinion written by Associate Justice Abe Fortas, students in some of the schools in the district had been allowed to wear political campaign buttons and even the Iron Cross, the traditional Nazi symbol. A federal district court upheld the regulation as constitutional because school authorities reasonably believed that disturbances could result from the wearing of the armbands. Indeed, a few students were hostile toward the students outside the classroom, but according to the U.S. Supreme Court, "There is no indication that the work of the schools or any class was disrupted."[160] The official memorandum, prepared by the school officials after the students were suspended, was introduced at trial, and did not mention the possibility of disturbances.

   The test, the Court said, for justifying such prior restraint would be whether "the students' activities would materially and substantially disrupt the work and discipline of the school." The Court held:

> These petitioners [students] merely went about their ordained rounds in school. Their deviation consisted only in wearing on their sleeve, a band of black cloth, not more than two inches wide. They wore it to exhibit their disapproval of the Vietnam hostilities and their advocacy of a truce, to make their views known, and, by their example, to influence others to adopt them. They neither interrupted school activities nor sought to intrude in the school affairs or the lives of others. They caused discussion outside of the classrooms, but no interference with work and no disorder. In the circumstances, our Constitution does not permit officials of the state to deny their form of expression.[161]

In a sharp attack on the majority opinion, Justice Hugo L. Black appeared to compare the public classroom to a church or synagogue and settings such as the Congress and the Supreme Court: "It is a myth to say that any person has a constitutional right to say what he pleases, where he pleases, and when he pleases. Uncontrolled and uncontrollable liberty is an enemy of domestic peace. We cannot close our eyes to the fact that some of the country's greatest problems are crimes committed by the youth, too many of school age."[162]

Obviously, Justice Black placed little faith in school children's ability to responsibly exercise First Amendment rights, but his view was probably indicative of the mood of the majority in this country at the time and even today. Should public school children have the same free speech rights as adults? Would the Court have ruled differently if the school had been a private one such as a parochial school? Probably so, because no explicit governmental prior restraint would be involved.

Street v. New York: Flag Burning Protected

In the same year as *Tinker*, the Court tackled another thorny case involving prior restraint of symbolic speech. In *Street v. New York* (1969),[163] the Court split 5–4 in reversing the conviction of a Black man for protesting the sniper shooting in Mississippi of civil rights leader James Meredith, by burning a flag at a public intersection in Brooklyn, New York. After the defendant burned the American flag he owned, a police officer arrested him. The Court held that the provision in the state statute under which Street was punished was unconstitutionally applied in his case because it allowed the defendant to be punished simply for uttering defiant or contemptuous words about the American flag. The majority opinion contended that none of four potential governmental interests were furthered by the statute in this case, including (a) deterring the defendant from vocally inciting other individuals to do unlawful acts, (b) preventing him from uttering words so inflammatory as to provoke others into retaliating against him and thus causing a breach of the peace, (c) protecting the sensibilities of passers-by and (d) assuring that the defendant displayed proper respect for the flag. The four dissenting justices (including Chief Justice Earl Warren, Justice Abe Fortas, who wrote the majority opinion in *Tinker*, and Justice Byron White, who also dissented in two subsequent flag burning cases discussed *infra*) characterized Street's burning of the flag as action, not mere words.

Cohen v. California: Offensive Language on Clothing

As illustrated, the distinction between "action speech" and "pure speech" has proven very troublesome for the courts over the decades, despite the Supreme

Court's attempts to clarify the difference. How far does an individual have to proceed to transform words into deeds? Suppose an individual were to wear in public a jacket with an expression deemed obscene by some and at least indecent by most. Suppose women and children are present and can clearly read the expression. Can the individual be banned from wearing the jacket? Can he be convicted for maliciously and willfully disturbing the peace by offensive conduct?

In *Cohen v. California* (1971),[164] the U.S. Supreme Court reversed the conviction of a man for wearing a jacket with the clearly visible words, "Fuck the Draft," in the corridor outside the Los Angeles County Courthouse. The defendant testified at trial that he wore the jacket to protest the draft and the Vietnam War. He was convicted of violating Section 415 of the state penal code that bans maliciously and willfully disturbing the peace by offensive conduct and was sentenced to 30 days in jail. According to the Court, "There were women and children present in the corridor. . . . The defendant did not engage in, nor threaten to engage in, nor did anyone as the result of his conduct in fact commit or threaten to commit any act of violence."[165]

Once again, while the majority opinion characterized the situation as involving speech, the dissenters saw it differently. Writing for the majority, Justice John M. Harlan, said:

> The conviction quite clearly rests upon the asserted offensiveness of the words Cohen used to convey his message to the public. The only "conduct" which the State sought to punish is the fact of communication. Thus we deal here with a conviction resting solely upon "speech" . . . not upon any separately identifiable conduct which allegedly was intended by Cohen to be perceived by others as expressive of particular views. . . . Further the State certainly lacks power to punish Cohen for the underlying content of the message the inscription conveyed. At least so long as there is no showing of an intent to incite disobedience to or disruption of the draft, Cohen . . . [could not] . . . be punished for asserting the evident position on the inutility or immorality of the draft his jacket reflected.[166]

Citing *Chaplinsky*, discussed *supra*, the Court noted that states "are free to ban the simple use, without a demonstration of additional justifying circumstances, of so-called 'fighting words,' those personally abusive epithets which, when addresses to the ordinary citizen, are, as a matter of common knowledge, inherently likely to provoke violent reaction."[167] The Court also concluded that (a) the words were not obscene because they were in no way erotic, (b) no person would reasonably regard the words as a direct personal insult and thereby be provoked to violence and (c) the jacket was not akin "to the raucous emissions of sound trucks blaring outside . . . residences" because the people in the courthouse could simply turn their eyes to "effectively avoid bombardment of their sensibilities."[168]

Justice Harry A. Blackmun, joined by Chief Justice Warren Burger and Justice Hugo Black, called Cohen's effort an "absurd and immature antic" that "was mainly conduct and little speech."[169]

Flag Desecration Protection Continues

In 1974, the U.S. Supreme Court decided yet another flag desecration case. On May 10, 1970, a young man was arrested for violating a Washington State statute that banned the display of any American flag to which any word, figure, mark, picture, design, drawing or advertisement had been attached. Spence had put a large peace symbol made of removable tape on both sides of a flag he owned and displayed the altered flag out of the window of his apartment. At trial, he testified that he had done so to protest the invasion of Cambodia on April 30, 1970, by U.S. and South Vietnamese soldiers during the Vietnam War and the killing of four students by National Guardsmen at Kent State University in Ohio on May 4 during a war protest. "I felt there had been so much killing and that this was not what America stood for," he testified. "I felt that the flag stood for America and I wanted people to know that I thought America stood for peace." He also testified that he used removable tape to make the peace symbol so the flag would not be damaged.[170] Spence was convicted under a so-called improper use statute rather than the state's flag desecration statute because the desecration statute required a public mutilation, defacing, defiling, burning or trampling of the flag, and the other statute merely required placing a word, figure and so forth, on a flag that was publicly displayed.

In a 6–3 *per curiam* decision, the Court reversed the conviction on grounds that "there was no risk that appellant's acts would mislead viewers into assuming that the Government endorsed his viewpoint. To the contrary, he was plainly and peacefully [footnote omitted] protesting the fact that it did not. . . . Moreover, his message was direct, likely to be understood, and within the contours of the First Amendment."[171] The Court also noted that the flag was privately owned and displayed on private property. The dissenters, led by then-Associate Justice (now Chief Justice) William H. Rehnquist, contended that Washington State "has chosen to set the flag apart for a special purpose, and has directed that it not be turned into a common background for an endless variety of superimposed messages."[172]

Hazelwood School District v. Kuhlmeier: A Retreat from Tinker?

After *Spence*, relatively few prior restraint cases reached the U.S. Supreme Court until the late 1980s when the Court once again granted certiorari in a flag desecration case and a school censorship case. In 1988 the Court issued a decision in *Hazelwood School District v. Kuhlmeier*[173] that has probably generated more concern and comment among First Amendment scholars and journalists than any other prior restraint case in modern times. The case began innocently enough when the May 13, 1983, edition of the Hazelwood (St. Louis, Missouri) East High School student newspaper, *Spectrum*, was ready to go to press. The paper was produced by the Journalism II class under the supervision of a faculty adviser. This particular edition of the paper featured a special, two-page report with the headline, "Pressure Describes It All for Today's Teenagers." The two articles in the report touched on a variety of topics—such as teenage pregnancy, birth control, marriage, divorce and juvenile delinquency. On the day just before the paper was ready to be printed, the new faculty adviser, Howard Emerson, took the page proofs to the school principal, Robert E. Reynolds, who deleted the special report. Reynolds did not consult with the students and later said the article focusing on the pregnancies of three students was too sensitive for younger students and he was concerned the students quoted in the article would suffer from invasion of privacy even though pseudonyms were used. He killed the second article, which analyzed the effects of divorce on teenagers, because he said the father of one student, quoted as criticizing her father as abusive and inattentive, had not been given an opportunity to respond to the student's allegations.[174] Reynolds ordered the adviser, who had been appointed only 10 days earlier, to publish the paper without the special section. None of the articles contained sexually explicit language, although there was discussion of sex and contraception. Most of the information in the articles was garnered from questionnaires completed by the students at the school and personal interviews conducted by the newspaper staff. All of the respondents had given permission for their answers and comments to be published.

With assistance from the American Civil Liberties Union (ACLU), three of the students on the *Spectrum* staff—a layout editor and two reporters—filed suit against the school district and school officials in U.S. District Court (E.D. Mo.) three months after the incident. (The students had unsuccessfully tried to convince the principal to allow the articles to be published.) The complaint alleged that the students' First Amendment rights had been violated and requested declaratory and injunctive relief and monetary damages. ACLU attorneys argued in the federal trial court that the newspaper constituted a public forum and thus deserved full First Amendment protection and, as government officials, school authorities could impose prior restraint on the paper only if it were obscene or libelous or could cause a serious disruption of normal school operations, as the Court had held in *Tinker* in 1969.[175]

Attorneys for the school district argued, on the other hand, that because the newspaper staff was taking the journalism class for credit, just as any other course would be taken for credit, the newspaper was, therefore, not a public forum but instead merely part of the school curriculum.

In May 1985, the U.S. District Court decided in favor of the school and denied all relief requested. According to the court, school authorities may restrict student speech in those activities that are "an integral part of the school's educational function." The court also held that because publication of the paper was integral to the educational functions of the school, the principal was acting within his legitimate authority when he censored the article on divorce, which he believed violated traditional journalistic standards for fairness.[176] Monetary damages, the court noted, were not available because no First Amendment violations had occurred.

On appeal by the students, the Eighth Circuit U.S. Court of Appeals reversed the U.S. District Court ruling. The appeals court held in a 2-1 decision that the newspaper was a public forum even though the faculty adviser maintained considerable editorial control over the paper. According to the majority opinion, prior restraint was permitted, in line with *Tinker*, only if the school officials could demonstrate that such censorship was "necessary to avoid material and substantial interference with school work or discipline" (citing *Tinker*).[177] On the contention by the school board that the articles—especially the first one, which focused on teenage pregnancies—constituted a potential invasion of privacy, the federal appeals court held that because the way the articles were written did not expose the school to possible tort liability, prior restraint was not justified on these grounds either.[178]

In a move that surprised many First Amendment scholars, the U.S. Supreme granted certiorari on appeal of the decision by the school board. Oral arguments were heard on October 13, 1987, and exactly three months later on January 13, 1988, the Court handed down its decision, which has since provoked a torrent of criticism from professional journalism organizations—such as the Society of Professional Journalists, the Reporters Committee for Freedom of the Press, the Student Press Law Center and the Association for Education in Journalism and Mass Communication, all of whom had earlier either filed or joined *amicus curiae* ("friend of the court") briefs with the Supreme Court supporting the students and the federal appeals court decision.

Fate was not on the side of the students, however. In a 5-3 decision written by Justice Byron R. White and joined by Chief Justice William H. Rehnquist and Associate Justices John Paul Stevens, Sandra Day O'Connor and Antonin Scalia, the Court reversed the U.S. Court of Appeals and held that the First Amendment rights of the students had not been violated.[179] The Court began by reaffirming its 1969 principle in *Tinker* that it "can hardly be argued that either students or teachers shed their constitutional rights to freedom of speech or expression at the schoolhouse gate."[180] But, the Court went on to say that *Tinker* applies only to "educators' ability to silence a student's personal expression that happens to occur on the school premises" so that prior restraint is permitted when it is "reasonably related to pedagogical concerns." In other words, expression that occurs within the context of the school curriculum can be censored unless the restrictions have "no valid educational purpose."

The Court reasoned that the school was the publisher of the newspaper and it had not manifest an intention to make the *Spectrum* a public forum. As publisher, the school can impose greater restrictions so that students "learn whatever lessons the activity is designed to teach, that readers or listeners are not exposed to material that may be inappropriate for their level of maturity, and that the views of the school are not erroneously attributed to the school."[181] The majority went on to note:

> A school must be able to set high standards for the student speech that is disseminated under its auspices—standards that may be higher than those demanded by some newspaper publishers or theatrical producers in the "real" world—and may refuse to disseminate student speech that does not meet those standards. In addition, a school must be able to take into account the emotional maturity of the intended audience in determining whether to disseminate student speech on potentially sensitive topics.[182]

As expected, Justice William J. Brennan, Jr., wrote a very strong dissent to the majority decision. He was joined in his dissent by Justices Thurgood Marshall and Harry A. Blackmun. "In my view, the principal . . . violated the First Amendment's prohibition against censorship of any student expression that neither disrupts classwork nor invades the rights of others, and against any censorship that is not narrowly tailored to serve its purpose," Justice Brennan wrote. He reasoned, unlike the majority, that *Tinker* did apply to this case and thus the paper could be censored only if its content materially and substantially disrupted the educational process or interfered with the rights of others (such as the right of privacy). According to Justice Brennan, *Tinker* should apply to all student expression, not just to personal expression, as the majority had ruled.

One of the most surprising aspects of the majority opinion was the extension of its holding to include virtually all school-sponsored activities, not just laboratory newspapers. The U.S. Supreme Court, especially the Rehnquist Court, has usually limited its rulings on the First Amendment to the particular issue at hand, but in *Hazelwood* the Court chose to substantially broaden the scope of the activities affected by the decision. There was no direct indication from the Court as to why it had taken this unusual step in *Hazelwood*, but it is likely that the Court wanted to avoid having to tackle prior restraint on student expression on a situation-by-situation basis. In other words, the Court may have been attempting to forestall a flood of litigation on the issue that was quite likely to arise if it had narrowed the scope of the decision to include only laboratory newspapers.

What is covered by Hazelwood? According to the Court, any public school has a constitutional right to disassociate itself from all speech that others, including students, parents and the general public "might reasonably perceive to bear the imprimatur of the school."[183] The Court cited examples—such as theatrical productions—but it is apparent that other activities—such as art shows, science fairs, debates and research projects—come under the aegis of *Hazelwood*. As the Student Press Law Center indicates in its legal analysis of the case, "Any school-sponsored, non-forum student activity that involves student expression could be affected."[184]

The impact of *Hazelwood*, as might be expected, was immediate. Literally within hours, high school and even college newspapers felt the heavy hand of censorship. According to one report, a high school principal in California ordered the school newspaper not to publish a story based on an interview with an anonymous student who had tested positive for AIDS. Less than two hours after the Court's decision, the principal told the newspaper staff, "You won't run that story now."[185] In the months and years that followed, headlines such as "Concern Rises Over High School Journalism"[186] and "Censorship on Campus: Press Watchers Fear Rise"[187] were not unusual. A typical example of the use of *Hazelwood* by school officials was the principal's deletion of an editorial about teen intimacy in a March 1988 issue of *The Lafayette Times*, published by students at Lafayette High School in Lexington, Kentucky.[188] The editorial, which neither condemned nor condoned teenage sex, was written by the newspaper's co-editor. The editorial, which contained no explicit language, noted:

> No one should condone or condemn sex. The decision should be made for one's own self. Only the individual can decide when the time is right to become intimate with someone . . . Society has many unwritten laws by which we live— good and bad. You can change those by presenting yourself responsibly and with a caring attitude. Care about yourself and others in order to decide when sex is right for you.[189]

The school principal, was quoted as saying, "There were some implications that young people should make up their own mind about sex. I thought that in this community that was inappropriate." The Lexington (Kentucky) *Herald-Leader* reprinted the banned editorial in its entirety and noted in its own editorial the next day: "The U.S. Supreme Court's decision earlier this year [*Hazelwood*] affirmed a high school's right to censor articles such as Ms. Wohlstein's [the co-editor who wrote the editorial]. But in too many cases, school officials don't use that power wisely. Unfortunately, this is one such case."[190]

Although most newspapers and First Amendment scholars shared the sentiments of the *Herald-Leader* about *Hazelwood*, the Court was not without its supporters. A survey of high school principals in Missouri found that while 61.5 percent of them considered their student newspapers to be open forums and only 35.6 percent had kept something from being printed in a student publication, almost 90 percent of them said they might suppress "dirty language" in a student publication if they found it objectionable. More than 60 percent said they might suppress content dealing with sex. Articles on drugs might be censored by 56.8 percent of the principals, and almost 42 percent might restrain content dealing with student pregnancy.[191] A national survey completed in 1984–1985, before *Hazelwood*, found that nearly all principals and almost 90 percent of high school newspaper advisers believed that newspaper advisers should review all copy before publication. More than two-thirds of the principals and one-third of the advisers felt that school officials should ban articles considered harmful even if they are not libelous, obscene or disruptive.[192]

In a very thorough and thought-provoking analysis of *Hazelwood*, Louisiana State University Journalism Professors Louis A. Day and John M. Butler concluded:

> In summary, when viewed in the broad context of constitutional law, *Hazelwood* is not a significant retreat. It is predicated upon reasonable philosophical and educational theories and principles of sound public policy. It is time to disavow the alarmist attitudes represented by such publications as *Captive Voices* [a 1974 treatise promoting First Amendment rights for high school publications] and return to a rule of reason within the public academy.[193]

On the other hand, another thorough analysis of the case concluded, "The [Supreme] Court's view of the state's permissible role in restricting student expression has gone from expansive to narrow and back, culminating in its broad discretion to school authorities in *Hazelwood*."[194] The law review note suggests that school officials be required to conform to written regulations that would permit discretion while offering students the opportunity "to learn the full responsibilities of the first amendment through using it responsibly."[195]

As discussed in Chapter 1, states can always expand those rights recognized by the Court under the First Amendment. Although there has certainly been no mad dash by the states to enact legislation to expand high school student rights after *Hazelwood*, at least three states now offer broader protection. Section 48907 of the California Education Code provided extensive protection 10 years before *Hazelwood*. Under the code, public school students have the right to exercise an extensive array of speech and press activities regardless of whether such activities are financially supported by the school except "obscene, libelous, or slanderous" expression or "material which so incites students as to create a clear and present danger of the commission of unlawful acts on school premises or the violation of lawful school regulations, or the substantial disruption of the orderly operation of the school."[196]

Massachusetts had a statute even earlier than the California law, but the provision affecting school publications was optional until it became mandatory in July 1988.[197] On May 11, 1989, Iowa became the first state to enact legislation specifically geared to respond to the concerns of *Hazelwood*.[198] The statute is very similar to that of California, especially in its exceptions.[199]

What does *Hazelwood* really mean? University of Missouri School of Journalism Professor Dale Spencer, who died months after the Court's decision, eloquently noted:

> Few individuals have understood the dilemma the Court was handed. One commentator wrote that there is a difference between a government controlling its own communications and censorship of private speech. The argument ignores the fact that a high school journalism class is not government communications, but part of the educational process. . . .
>
> Yes the decision was bad. It will be used to censor student editors.
>
> But individuals who care about the future of journalism can use some of the language in the opinion in a positive way to help the journalism teacher and the student.[200]

Professor Spencer, who was also an attorney, spent much of his life fighting legal battles against censorship, including prior restraint of student publications.

Two more unrelated points need to be made before the *Hazelwood* discussion ends. First, the Court specifically avoided the question of whether its ruling would apply to college newspapers. In a footnote, the majority opinion stated, "We need not now decide whether the same degree of deference is appropriate with respect to school-sponsored activities at the college or university level."[201] Finally, a 1988 report jointly sponsored by the American Library Association and the American Association of School Administrators lists four major categories of motivation for school censorship—family values, political views, religion and minority rights,[202] all of which are common topics covered by school newspapers.

PRIOR RESTRAINT IN THE 1990S: THE STROKE BROADENS

Prior restraint gained even greater prominence in the 1990s, including a ban on press access to the war zone during the Persian Gulf Conflict in early 1991 and an injunction imposed on the Cable News Network (CNN) to bar the broadcast of an audio recording. The first real hint of a portentous rash of prior restraint cases can be traced to the mid-1980s. Until 1985 no one in this country had ever been convicted of a crime for leaking national security information to the press; in October of that year, Samuel Loring Morison was convicted in U.S. District Court in Baltimore[203] for providing three classified photographs to the British magazine, *Jane's Defence Weekly*, in 1984. The magazine published the photos and then made them available to various news agencies. One of the photos also appeared in the *Washington Post*.[204] Morison was not employed by the magazine at the time, although he worked for another magazine owned by the same company, *Jane's Fighting Ships*. He had gained access to the classified photos when he had been previously working for the U.S. Navy as an intelligence analyst. His prosecution came during a campaign under President Ronald Reagan to halt unauthorized leaks of sensitive government information.

Morison freely admitted to furnishing the pictures to the magazine, but he contended that he was not paid for the materials even though he had been paid by the magazine for his writing. His confession was ruled inadmissible at trial, and thus the government did not argue that he had been compensated for providing the materials. In his defense, Morison claimed that the statute under which he was prosecuted did not apply in his case but instead was intended to apply to the disclosure of classified information to foreign governments and thus not the press. Morison was sentenced to two years at a federal medium-security prison in Danbury, Connecticut, for violating two sections of the U.S. Espionage Act of 1917.[205] Morison appealed the decision to the Fourth Circuit U.S. Court of Appeals, but on April 1, 1988, a three-judge panel upheld the trial court decision, rejecting all of Morison's major contentions, including that he had not used the documents for personal gain, that he did not know the documents were classified, and that Congress had intended to restrict application of the law to traditional spying rather than disclosure to the press.[206]

On October 17, 1988, the U.S. Supreme Court denied *certiorari*,[207] effectively closing the case, while Morison continued to serve his prison term. As discussed in Chapter 2, denial of certiorari does **not** necessarily mean the Supreme Court agreed with the lower court's decision, but it does indicate that at least six justices did not feel the case deserved consideration because at least four justices must agree to hear a case before a writ of certiorari can be granted.

Texas v. Johnson and *United States v. Eichman*: Flag Burning Revisited

Clearly, the most controversial ruling issued by the U.S. Supreme Court during its 1988–1989 term was *Texas v. Johnson*,[208] in which the Court reversed the conviction of a Revolutionary Communist Youth Brigade member in Texas for burning the American flag at the 1984 Republican National Convention in Dallas. In a split 5–4 decision on June 21, 1989, which surprised many politicians and even legal scholars, the Court held that when Gregory Lee "Joey" Johnson burned an American flag in a nonviolent demonstration against President Reagan's administration, he was engaging in "symbolic" speech protected by the First Amendment. During the demonstration of approximately 100 protestors, the participants had chanted, "America, the red, white and blue, we spit on you." Johnson was the only individual charged with a criminal offense. He had been arrested and sentenced to a year in jail and fined $2,000 for violating a Texas flag-desecration statute, similar to a federal statute and laws in every state at that time except Alaska and Wyoming.[209] Such laws typically prohibit desecration of a "venerated object," such as a state or national flag, a public monument or a place of worship or burial. The Texas Court of Criminal Appeals overturned the trial court decision, holding that the First Amendment protected Johnson's flag burning as expressive conduct and the statute was not narrowly drawn enough to preserve the state's interest in preventing a breach of the peace.

The U.S. Supreme Court affirmed the Texas appeals court decision to overturn the conviction. The Court did **not** invalidate the Texas statute nor any of the federal and state statutes; it merely ruled that the Texas law, *as applied in this case*, was unconstitutional. Indeed, the majority opinion, written by Associate Justice William J. Brennan Jr., specifically pointed out that statutes banning flag desecration and similar acts when such acts provoke a breach of the peace and incitement to riot were not affected by the decision.

The lineup of the justices and the way in which the decision was delivered was somewhat surprising as well. Justice Brennan, the most senior member of the Court at 83 and the most liberal, wrote the majority opinion, but he was joined by two justices considered among the most conservative on the Court— Justices Anthony M. Kennedy and Antonin Scalia, both appointed by President Ronald Reagan. Also allied with the majority were, as expected, Justices Thurgood Marshall and Harry A. Blackmun. However, Justice John Paul Stevens, whom most First Amendment scholars expected to vote to reverse the conviction, sided with the dissenters, including Chief Justice William H. Rehnquist and Associate Justices Byron R. White and Sandra Day O'Connor. In a relatively rare move, two of the justices—Brennan and Stevens—read lengthy excerpts from their opinions. Justice Stevens delivered an impassioned plea on behalf of the dissenters:

[The American flag] is more than a proud symbol of the courage, the determination, and the gifts of nature that transformed 13 fledgling Colonies into a world power. It is a symbol of freedom, of equal opportunity, of religious tolerance, and of goodwill for other peoples who share our aspirations.

. . . The ideas of liberty and equality have been an irresistible force in motivating leaders like Patrick Henry, Susan B. Anthony and Abraham Lincoln, schoolteachers like Nathan Hale and Booker T. Washington, the Philippine Scouts who fought at Bataan, and the soldiers who scaled the bluff at Omaha Beach. If those ideas are worth fighting for—and our history demonstrates that they are—it cannot be true that the flag that uniquely symbolizes their power is not itself worthy of protection from unnecessary desecration.[210]

But the majority won the day:

> If there is a bedrock principle underlying the First Amendment, it is that the Government may not prohibit the expression of an idea simply because society finds the idea itself offensive or disagreeable. [citing *Hustler Magazine v. Falwell* and others].

> We have not recognized an exception to this principle even where our flag has been involved. . . . The way to preserve the flag's special role is not to punish those who feel differently about these matters. It is to persuade them that they are wrong. . . . We can imagine no more appropriate response to burning a flag than waving one's own, no better way to counter a flag-burner's message than by saluting the flag that burns. . . . We do not consecrate the flag by punishing its desecration, for in doing so we dilute the freedom that this cherished emblem represents.[211]

The majority reasoned that because there was no violence or disturbance of the peace at the demonstration, the state was banning "the expression of certain disagreeable ideas on the unsupported presumption that their very disagreeableness will provoke violence." The Court also contended that a government cannot legislate that the flag may be used only as a symbol of national unity so that other messages cannot be expressed using that symbol.

Justice Kennedy wrote a brief concurrence with the majority, noting, "The hard fact is that sometimes we must make decisions we do not like. We must make them because they are right, right in the sense that the law and the Constitution, as we see them, compel the result."[212] This contention prompted one expert to quip that, translated, Justice Kennedy is saying, "You hold your nose and follow the Constitution."[213] Justice Kennedy went on to assert, "It is poignant but fundamental that the flag protects those who hold it in contempt."

Certainly the most elaborate, eloquent and emotional plea came from Chief Justice Rehnquist in his dissent. The Chief Justice quoted extensively from Ralph Waldo Emerson's "Concord Hymn," Francis Scott Key's "The Star Spangled Banner" and John Greenleaf Whittier's poem, "Barbara Frietchie," which describes how the 90-year-old woman bravely flew the Union flag when Stonewall Jackson and his Confederate soldiers marched through Frederick town during the Civil War. According to Chief Justice Rehnquist:

> The American flag, then, throughout more than 200 years of our history, has come to be the visible symbol embodying our Nation. . . . The flag is not simply another "idea" or "point of view" competing for recognition in the marketplace of ideas. Millions and millions of Americans regard it with an almost mystical reverence regardless of what sort of social, political or philosophical beliefs they have. . . .

Far from being a case of "one picture being worth a thousand words," flag burning is the equivalent of an inarticulate grunt or roar that, it seems fair to say, is most likely to be indulged in not to express a particular idea, but to antagonize others.[214]

The U.S. Supreme Court decision in *Texas v. Johnson* by no means ended the controversy over flag desecration. President George Bush pushed strongly for a constitutional amendment to prohibit flag desecration in a variety of forms. President Bush had the strong support of most political conservatives and certainly the general public in his efforts to secure a constitutional amendment, but at least two traditionally conservative political writers, *Washington Post* syndicated columnist George F. Will[215] and syndicated Washington columnist James J. Kilpatrick,[216] oppose such an amendment. Will believes the case was wrongly decided by the Supreme Court, whereas Kilpatrick says, "given the undisputed facts, the Texas law and the high court precedents, the case was properly decided."[217]

A proposed amendment quickly garnered 51 votes in the U.S. Senate, but that was 15 short of the two-thirds necessary to pass it on to the states. Before becoming part of the U.S. Constitution, it would have to be ratified by at least 38 of the state legislatures. Congress then enacted the Flag Protection Act of 1989,[218] which became law without President Bush's signature. The President chose not to sign the bill because he believed it would eventually be struck down by the U.S. Supreme Court as unconstitutional, just as the Court had done the previous year in *Texas v. Johnson*. Thus for the President the remedy was a constitutional amendment. On June 11, 1990, President Bush was proven correct. In *United States v. Eichman* and *United States v. Haggerty*, Justice Brennan, joined by Justices Marshall, Blackmun, Scalia and Kennedy (the exact same lineup as *Texas v. Johnson*), struck down the federal statute on essentially the same grounds employed in the earlier decision. This time, though, Justice Stevens' dissent lacked much of his impassioned rhetoric of the *Johnson* decision, and he did not read it from the bench.

The case began when Shawn Eichman and two acquaintances deliberately set fire to several U.S. flags on the steps of the Capitol Building as a protest of U.S. domestic and foreign policy. They were arrested and charged with violating the criminal statute, which provided:

(a)(1) Whoever knowingly mutilates, defaces, physically defiles, burns, maintains on the floor or ground, or tramples upon any flag of the United States shall be fined under this title or imprisoned for not more than one year, or both.

(2) This subsection does not prohibit any conduct consisting of the disposal of a flag when it has become worn or soiled.

(b) As used in this section, the term "flag of the United States" means any flag of the United States, or any part thereof, made of any substance, of any size, in a form that is commonly displayed.[219]

Mark John Haggerty and three other individuals were also prosecuted by the federal government for setting fire to a U.S. flag to protest the passage of the federal Flag Protection Act. Both *Eichman* and *Haggerty* were dismissed by separate federal trial courts as unconstitutional. The U.S. District Court for the Western District of Washington and the U.S. District Court for the District of Columbia Circuit, respectively, cited *Johnson* as precedent. On appeal by the United States, the Supreme Court consolidated the two cases. The government bypassed the U.S. Court of Appeals by invoking a clause in the 1989 Federal Flag Protection Act that provided for a direct appeal to the Supreme Court and expedited review under certain conditions.

The Court expressly rejected the government's argument that U.S. statute, unlike the Texas law in *Johnson*, did not "target expressive conduct on the basis of the content of its message." According to the majority opinion, "The Act still suffers from the same fundamental flaw: it suppresses expression out of concern for its likely communicative impact."[220] The government also asserted that the statute should viewed as an expression of a "national consensus" supporting a ban on flag desecration. "Even assuming such a consensus exists, any suggestion that the government's interest in suppressing speech becomes more weighty as popular opposition to that speech grows is foreign to the First Amendment,"[221] according to the Court.

President Bush and a number of prominent politicians, principally Republicans, immediately called for a constitutional amendment to overturn *Texas v. Johnson* and *U.S. v. Eichman*, but the clamor gradually subsided after the measure appeared doomed. Most Democrats and some Republicans in Congress refused to back a provision that could lead to the first restriction on the Bill of Rights in its 200-year history, and public enthusiasm was not particularly strong either. By the time the 1992 presidential election had begun in earnest, the amendment was no longer a political issue. In fact, there was no mention of flag burning in any of the three presidential candidate debates.

United States v. Noriega
(In re Cable News Network, Inc.)

Five months after the justices struck a blow for the First Amendment, albeit in a 5–4 split, by invalidating the federal flag desecration statute, the Court refused to intervene in a situation that could bode even greater ill for freedom of the press and freedom of speech than the Flag Protection Act. The scenario began on November 7, 1990, when the Cable News Network aired an audiotape it had obtained through an anonymous source that included a conversation between former Panamanian dictator Manuel Noriega and one of his attorneys. At the time, General Noriega was in federal jail in Florida awaiting trial on various federal charges, including drug trafficking. He had been captured a year earlier in a U.S.-led invasion of Panama. The tape was one of several that had been made by prison officials, who indicated that the monitoring and recording of outgoing phone calls was in line with established policy and procedures. Noriega's lawyers denied the federal government's claim that their client had been aware of the taping. CNN included in the story about the tape an interview with one of the defendant's attorneys who indicated the tape was authentic.

Noriega's defense team immediately requested a temporary restraining order in U.S. District Court before the judge presiding over the criminal case, but CNN aired additional tapes before a hearing could be conducted the next day. At the hearing, the attorneys argued that further broadcasts of the tapes could jeopardize the deposed leader's Sixth Amendment right to a fair trial and would violate attorney-client privilege. Judge William Hoeveler granted the request at the hearing and later the same day issued an order that the network turn over all tapes in its possession so he could determine with an *in camera* inspection if broadcast of the tapes constituted "a clear, immediate and irreparable danger" to Noriega's Sixth Amendment rights.[222]

After conferring with its attorneys, CNN defied both the restraining order and the order to relinquish the tapes, claiming First Amendment protection. The network sought relief from the 11th Circuit Court of Appeals, but two days later, on November 10, the appellate court upheld the trial court's orders and, in a decision that severely criticized CNN, held that it must immediately produce the tapes for Judge Hoeveler.[223]

In an expedited review, the U.S. Supreme Court in a 7–2 vote on November 18, with Justices Marshall and O'Connor dissenting, denied certiorari,[224] thus allowing the 11th Circuit decision to stand. Two days later, CNN complied by delivering the tapes to the district court. One week later, after hearing arguments on both sides regarding Noriega's request for a permanent injunction and listening to the tapes, Judge Hoeveler ruled that further airing of the recorded conversations would not interfere with Noriega's right to a fair trial.[225] The tapes were then returned to CNN. Noriega was eventually tried and convicted.

Rust v. Sullivan and Gentile v. State Bar of Nevada: Prior Restraint on Speech in Professional Contexts

The U.S. Supreme Court handed down three major prior restraint decisions in 1991, two dealing with speech by professionals. The most controversial of the two was *Rust v. Sullivan*[226] in which a slim 5–4 majority upheld regulations promulgated in 1988 during President Reagan's administration by the Department of Health and Human Services (HHS). Under Title X of the Public Health Service Act passed by Congress in 1970, federal money may be used to support family planning services but not for programs in which abortions are an option. The 1988 rules went even further by barring Title X projects from providing abortion counseling, referral or advocacy, and requiring physicians, nurses and other health care workers to refer pregnant women only to agencies that provide prenatal care but not abortions. Under the rules, if a woman inquires about abortion, the health care provider had to respond that "the project does not consider abortion an appropriate method of family planning and therefore does not counsel or refer for abortion."[227]

Several physicians and Title X grantees banded together to challenge the regulations as unconstitutional prior restraint on freedom of speech because they impermissibly imposed "viewpoint-discriminatory conditions on government subsidies." The petitioners argued that the First and Fifth Amendment rights of their clients were being violated, as were the First Amendment rights of Title X-funded projects. They challenged the facial validity of the rules and sought a declaratory judgment and an injunction. A U.S. District Court judge initially granted a preliminary injunction but then reversed his decision and granted summary judgment for HHS. The Second Circuit U.S. Court of Appeals held the regulations were a permissible construction of the federal statute and did not encroach on First and Fifth Amendment liberties.

The Supreme Court agreed:

> The Government can, without violating the Constitution, selectively fund a program to encourage certain activities it believes to be in the public interest, without at the same time funding an alternate program which seeks to deal with the problem in another way. In so doing, the Government has not discriminated on the basis of viewpoint; it has merely chosen to fund one activity to the exclusion of another.[228]

Interestingly, the crucial vote in the split decision came from Associate Justice David Souter, who had been appointed to the Court at the beginning of the term to replace Justice William Brennan. In all likelihood, Brennan would have voted to invalidate the rule. Whether this decision poses a threat to free speech is still being debated,[229] but the rules remain in effect after President Bush's veto in late 1992 of a bill in Congress that would have killed the gag rule. In 1993 President Clinton reversed the rules by executive order, thus negating the impact of *Rust*.

The second decision by the Court concerned an attorney who held a press conference hours after his client had been indicted on criminal charges. The Nevada lawyer first read a prepared statement to the journalists and then outlined his client's defense while proclaiming the person's innocence. He claimed the prosecution was seeking to convict an innocent man as a "scapegoat" and that it had not "been honest enough to indict the people who did it; the police department, crooked cops." As he had predicted, his client was eventually acquitted on all counts. After the jury trail, the State Bar of Nevada filed a complaint against the lawyer, alleging that he had violated Rule 177 of the Nevada Supreme Court, which prohibits an attorney from making "an extrajudicial statement that a reasonable person would expect to be disseminated by means of public communication if the lawyer knows or reasonably should know that it will have a substantial likelihood of materially prejudicing an adjudicative proceeding." As the U.S. Supreme Court noted in its decision, this rule is almost identical to the American Bar Association Model Rule of Professional Conduct 3.6 (adopted in 1981), which has been adopted in some form by most states. The Nevada Supreme Court affirmed the decision of the bar association's disciplinary board that the attorney receive a private reprimand. In *Gentile v. State Bar of Nevada* (1991),[230] the Supreme Court held that the Nevada rule, as interpreted and applied in the case by the state, was unconstitutional because it contained a "safe harbor" provision that exempted a lawyer's unelaborated comments about the general nature of the defense. There was no evidence, the Court said, that Gentile "knew or reasonably should have known his remarks created a substantial likelihood of material prejudice, if the Rule's terms are given any meaningful content." Thus the rule was void for vagueness. "There is no support for the conclusion that petitioner's statement created a likelihood of material prejudice, or indeed of any harm of sufficient magnitude or imminence to support a punishment for speech," the Court held.[231] The majority made it clear, however, that it was not ruling on the constitutionality of the ABA Model Rule.

The Court noted that (a) Gentile had made his statements six months before the trial began; (b) only a "small fraction" of his comments were actually published; (c) the stories about the conference included the prosecution's response and details of a police press conference; and (d) during voir dire at the trial, not one juror indicated any memory of Gentile's press conference. In an usual twist to the Court's decision, five of the justices agreed with Chief Justice Rehnquist's contention in his dissent that the State could impose greater restrictions on speech by attorneys representing clients than on the general public because lawyers are officers of the court. Justice Stewart concurred in the result even though he favored a lower standard for determining constitutionality than that espoused by Justice Kennedy.

Given this complicated lineup of the justices, it is very unlikely that prior restraint rules such as the ABA model rule will be struck down by the Court.

Simon & Schuster
v. New York State Crime Victims Board

The U.S. Supreme Court of the 1990s has been largely unpredictable on decisions regarding the First Amendment, especially those involving prior restraint (as already illustrated), but both liberals and conservatives were surprised by the Court's holding in 1991 in *Simon & Schuster, Inc. v. Members of the New York State Crime Victims Board*.[232]

In 1977 the New York legislature enacted a statute that, as later amended, required that any income received by convicted or accused criminals for the sale of their stories be placed in an escrow account for five years during which a victim would have the right to sue in civil action for damages. The statute also mandated that any publisher contracting with the accused or convicted criminal must submit a copy of the contract to the Crime Victims Board. If a victim won a civil judgment against the criminal, the person would then be entitled to a share of the proceeds from the sale of the story or stories. The law also permitted a victim to obtain proceeds from the sale under certain circumstances for other uses such as legal fees and for creditors of the accused or convicted person. The statute was popularly know as the "Son of Sam" law because it was initiated in reaction to stories that David Berkowitz, convicted of killing six people in New York City after a highly publicized and sensationalized arrest and trial, planned to sell his story.

In an 8–0 decision with Justice Thomas abstaining, the Court held: "In the Son of Sam law, New York has singled out speech on a particular subject for a financial burden that it places on no other speech and no other income. The State's interest in compensating victims from the fruits of crime is a compelling one, but the Son of Sam law is not narrowly tailored to advance that objective."[233]

The justices noted that any statute that imposes a financial burden on a speaker because of the content of the speech "is presumptively inconsistent with the First Amendment." The law in this case was so broad, the Court said, that a person who had never been accused or convicted of a crime but who admitted in a book or other publication that she or he had committed a crime would be included. The case arose after the Board ordered publisher Simon & Schuster to turn over all money payable to admitted organized crime figure Henry Hill for his book *Wiseguy* (which later inspired a film called *Goodfellas* that won an award for best film in 1990. Hill was also ordered to turn over monies he had already received.

Simon & Schuster sued the board seeking a declaratory judgment that the law was unconstitutional. A U.S. District Court judge ruled against the publisher and the Second Circuit U.S. Court of Appeals affirmed. The Court reversed, pointing out that works such as *The Autobiography of Malcolm X*, Henry David Thoreau's *Disobedience* and even the *Confessions of St. Augustine* would have fallen under the shadow of the law if it had been on the books at the time they were written. There are other constitutional means of obtaining such proceeds, according to the Court, such as securing a judgment against the criminal's assets in civil suit.

R.A.V. v. City of St. Paul, Minnesota: Cross Burning and the First Amendment

In 1992 the U.S. Supreme Court handed down one of the most controversial free speech decisions in this decade. In *R.A.V. v. City of St. Paul,*

Minnesota[234] the justices unanimously ruled a city ordinance unconstitutional that provided criminal penalties for placing "on public or private property a symbol, object appellation, characterization or graffiti, including, but not limited to, a burning cross or Nazi swastika, which one knows or has reasonable grounds to know arouses anger, alarm or resentment in others on the basis of race, color, creed, religion or gender."[235]

The case originated on June 21, 1990, when several teenagers allegedly burned a cross, made by taping together broken chair legs, inside the fenced yard of a Black family in St. Paul, Minnesota. When charged with violating the ordinance as a result of the incident, one of the juveniles filed a motion to dismiss, claiming that the law was overbroad and impermissibly based on content and thus facially invalid under the First Amendment. A trial court judge granted the motion, but the Minnesota Supreme Court reversed on the ground that the provision simply regulated "fighting words," which can be punished, as previously affirmed by the U.S. Supreme Court. The state supreme court particularly cited *Chaplinsky v. New Hampshire* (1942),[236] in which the U.S. Supreme Court held that words "likely to provoke the average person to retaliation, and thereby cause a breach of the peace" (known as "fighting words") were not protected by the First Amendment.

Justice Scalia wrote the majority opinion, which was joined by Chief Justice Rehnquist and Associate Justices Kennedy, Souter and Thomas. The majority indicated it was bound by the construction given the ordinance by the Minnesota Supreme Court, including the interpretation that the law restricted only expressions that would be considered "fighting words." The opinion, however, skirted the issue of whether the ordinance was "substantially overbroad," as the petitioner (R.A.V.) had requested. Instead the Court said: We find it unnecessary to consider this issue. Assuming, *arguendo*, that all of the expression reached by the ordinance is proscribable under the "fighting words" doctrine, we nonetheless conclude that the ordinance is facially unconstitutional in that it prohibits otherwise permitted speech solely on the basis of the subjects the speech addresses."[237]

Thus the Court held:

> Applying these principles to the St. Paul ordinance, we conclude that even as narrowly construed by the Minnesota Supreme Court, the ordinance is facially unconstitutional. Although the phrase in the ordinance, "arouses anger, alarm or resentment in others," has been limited by the Minnesota Supreme Court's construction to reach only those words or displays that amount to "fighting words," the remaining unmodified terms make clear that the ordinance applies only to "fighting words" that insult or provoke violence, "on the basis of race, color, creed, religion or gender." Displays containing abusive invective, no matter how vicious or severe, are permissible unless they are addressed to one of the specified disfavored topics. Those who wish to use "fighting words" in connection with other ideas—to express hostility, for example, on the basis of

political affiliation, union membership, or homosexuality — are not covered. The First Amendment does not permit St. Paul to impose special prohibitions on those speakers who express views on disfavored subjects.[238]

The Court made it clear that "burning a cross on someone's front yard is reprehensible. But St. Paul has sufficient means at its disposal to prevent such behavior without adding the First Amendment to the fire." In a footnote earlier in the decision, the majority indicated that the conduct at issue in the case might have punished under statutes banning terroristic threats, arson or criminal damage to property.

In a concurring opinion joined by Justices Blackmun and O'Connor and Justice Stevens in part, Justice White strongly disagreed with the majority's standard for evaluating the ordinance. According to Justice White, the ordinance should have been struck down on overbreadth grounds. He characterized the decision as "an arid, doctrinaire interpretation, driven by the frequently irresistible impulse of judges to tinker with the First Amendment. The decision is mischievous at best and will surely confuse the lower courts."

The St. Paul ordinance was enacted at a time when there was considerable concern with so-called hate speech and what has become known as "politically correct" (PC) speech. There appears to have been a proliferation of incidents, including many on college and university campus, in which members of racial, ethnic and sexual preference minority groups have been targeted with epithets, anonymous hate letters, slogans painted on doors and walls and other forms of "hate speech." To counter this behavior, a number of cities and private and public universities have instituted codes of conduct that specifically ban this type of behavior. At the same time, political correctness has become a buzzword for the idea that both oral and written communication, including that in the mass media, should demonstrate greater sensitivity to race and gender bias, leading to guides such as *The Dictionary of Bias-Free Usage: A Guide to Nondiscriminatory Language, The Handbook of Non-Sexist Writing* and *The Elements of Non-Sexist Usage: A Guide to Inclusive Spoken and Written English*. Critics view the PC speech campaign with disdain because they believe it inhibits freedom of speech and freedom of the press, whereas PC supporters see the movement as a legitimate means of persuading writers and speakers to abhor sexist, racist and other biased speech.

In May 1990, for example, University of Northern Colorado President Robert Dickeson rescinded an invitation he had extended earlier to Linda Chavez, the highest ranking Hispanic in the Reagan administration at that time, to speak at commencement exercises. The president made his decision to back out of the invitation after various student and faculty groups — upset over her opposition to certain types of affirmative action policies, to comparable worth and to bilingual education — voiced considerable opposition to her appearance. One group, the faculty senate, voted unanimously to "disinvite" her. Initially, the president issued a paper to faculty and students that touted the value of freedom of speech. Two weeks later in a newspaper column, he called that step a "knee-jerk response" and explained his decision to invite Ms. Chavez to speak instead at "a more suitable forum than commencement, and for the same fee, so that both her right to speak and the rights of others could be more fully facilitated."[239]

"Hate speech" and "PC speech" are two sides of the coin, and the controversies they stir revolve around prior restraint. Can political and social hate groups be muzzled without denying their members their First Amendment rights? On the other hand, can policies and codes that either punish or strongly discourage sexist, racist or other biased language pass constitutional muster? What about a policy that simply strongly encourages bias-free speech as a means of consciousness raising? Eventually, the courts will have to tackle these issues, which will probably ultimately end up in the U.S. Supreme Court. Journalists appear to be splintered on these issues, as are civil rights and civil liberties groups. Some view the PC movement and the anti-hate speech campaign as unjustified attempts to restrict freedom of speech and freedom of the press, and others contend that the right of minorities to be free of hatred and bias directed toward them should take precedence over any First Amendment right that may exist in such contexts.

CONCLUSIONS

Although libel and privacy continue to be major concerns for the mass media and have a relatively long case history, the ground rules for these torts have been substantially clarified in the last few decades as the case law has matured and statutes have filled in the gaps left by the courts. Prior restraint is a different animal, however. Consistency and clarity are simply lacking. Although the government's burden in justifying prior restraint is indeed substantial, such simple questions as "What is symbolic speech?," "What is "government" for purposes of prior restraint?" and even "What is prior restraint?" have no definitive answers. Why is wearing a black armband in a public school protected speech, when burning a draft card is not symbolic speech and, therefore, can be punished? Why is it that burning an American flag and burning a cross on a Black family's lawn are protected expressions but publishing information obtained from publicly available sources (such as in the *Progressive* case) is apparently not covered by the First Amendment?

Some trends are discernible, however. Journalists and students, especially in elementary and secondary public schools, appear to have the least protection of all against prior restraint. *Hazelwood* made it clear that the high school press is perceived by the U.S. Supreme Court as essentially a training ground for budding journalists, not an opportunity for them to exercise First

Amendment rights enjoyed by adults. *Morison* and similar cases such as *Snepp* illustrated how easy the government can justify prior restraint, including criminal prosecution, in certain contexts such as national security matters, even though disclosure of such information probably would have limited, if any, impact on national security. Finally, speech within a public forum generally has the strongest protection of all against governmental censorship as *Skokie*, *Texas v. Johnson*, *U.S. v. Eichman* and *Tinker* demonstrate, but even this principle must be tempered by the Court's stand in *Rust v. Sullivan* that the government can selectively censor information about activities it does not wish to promote when it has subsidized another activity.

Some of the most interesting prior restraint cases receive little attention, probably because they do not affect millions of people, but they offer a taste of some of the thorny prior restraint issues we will face as the 21st century draws near. Schools in Pasadena and Bayton, Texas, have banned students from drawing the peace symbol in class because officials believe "devil worshippers" use it. One 12-year-old was quoted as responding, "If they ban peace symbols, they'll have to ban basic geometry because of all its lines."[240] A few years ago Eastfield Elementary School (Marion, N.C.) officials were faced with the problem of three children in the same family who continued to shout Bible verses and preach during classes. Duffey Strode (10) was suspended five times for his preaching, and his sister, Pepper (6), and his brother, Matthew (5), had been suspended four times each by the principal after hundreds of parents complained and signed petitions against the children's preaching. The children's parents claim their sons and daughter have a First Amendment right to sermonize in school, but other parents and school officials see it differently.[241]

After law student Tim Maguire claimed in 1991 in a story in the student paper, *Georgetown Law Weekly*, that the university's law center had lower admissions standards for Blacks than Whites, a free speech battle emerged during which the Black Law Students Association urged that Maguire be expelled. Charges that he had violated the student code were dropped after a settlement was reached in which he was allowed to graduate with a reprimand on his record.[242]

In a case that does not appear to involve any First Amendment rights but that illustrates how nongovernmental censorship can be just as effective as governmental prior restraint, Kroger and Wal-Mart stores nationwide removed all of the October 1989 issues of *Cosmopolitan*, *Ladies Home Journal*, *Glamour*, *Vogue*, *Mademoiselle* and *Redbook* from their magazine shelves. Other stores did the same or put them behind counters. What prompted this drastic action? An unspecified number of consumers complained about a Nivea Moisturizing Creme and Lotion advertisement featuring a nude woman posing against a cloudy sky, an ad very similar to those in many West European consumer magazines. One newspaper editorial criticizing the steps taken by the stores mused, "You've seen more explicit photographs in *National Geographic*. . . . The Nivea lady seems almost wholesome. Her image isn't half as offensive as numerous sexually exploitative ads on prime time television."[243] The U.S. subsidiary of the West German corporation that manufactures the cream and lotion quickly publicly apologized for the ad and cancelled that version of the ad for future issues of *Ladies Home Journal* and *Redbook*.

Finally, does an individual have a First Amendment right to speak out on her epitaph? When Shelia Shea, a 43-year-old mother of two, died of cancer in 1986, her executor honored a provision in her will that the epitaph on her tombstone say, "Who the hell is Shelia Shea?" Shea was buried in the Sleepy Hollow Cemetery in Concord, Massachusetts, where writers Ralph Waldo Emerson, Nathaniel Hawthorne, and Henry David Thoreau lie. Cemetery officials wanted the epitaph removed, but finally gave up after the executor refused to remove it and it appeared, at least to the officials, that the First Amendment would protect Shea's monument.[244] Her freedom of speech lives on.

5 Commercial Speech

Beginning in 1986 the annual expenditure on advertising in this country has exceeded $100 billion, ranging from $102.1 billion in 1986 to $132.13 billion in 1992 with $139.3 billion projected in 1993.[1] The average cost of a prime-time 30-second, network (ABC, CBS, Fox, and NBC) television commercial in 1991 was $104,500.[2] Political advertising on television is an example of how much the business has grown during the last two decades. In 1972, political candidates spent some $24.6 million on TV ads, but by 1988, the amount had grown to a whopping record $227.9 million, up 48 percent from 1984, the previous presidential election year.[3] In the 1992 U.S. presidential race, independent candidate H. Ross Perot spent more than $60 million on television advertising in his unsuccessful bid. President Bill Clinton and former President George Bush each spent more than $100 million. Advertising today is an enormous business in the United States and in many other countries.

In any big industry, there is always the possibility of abuse of the public trust, and advertising is no exception. Indeed, ever since the days of patent medicines and elixirs that promised cures for every ailment from indigestion to baldness in the late 19th and early 20th centuries, there has been concern about false, deceptive, and fraudulent ads. That concern on the part of the government and the public was never translated into affirmative regulations until the Federal Trade Commission was created by Congress in 1914. It was many years later before the FTC attempted to regulate advertising, but today the commission is clearly the prime regulator of advertising, although a myriad of other federal and state agencies are involved.

This chapter focuses on the regulation of commercial speech, primarily advertising, including the development of the "commercial speech doctrine" in

158

the U.S. Supreme Court. The analysis begins with Supreme Court decisions on commercial speech and then moves to state and federal restrictions on advertising.

THE DEVELOPMENT OF THE "COMMERCIAL SPEECH DOCTRINE" IN THE U.S. SUPREME COURT

The history of U.S. Supreme Court involvement in commercial speech issues is basically a patchwork of sometimes confusing and often contradictory decisions that strain even the most patient legal scholar's ability to discern trends and general principles. There has clearly been no evolution of constitutional law on commercial speech, but instead the Court has almost erratically switched from one principle to another, usually dependent on the individual facts in a particular case. The Court has established specific tests for determining whether a particular type of commercial speech has constitutional protection, but these tests have not proved definitive, as the case of *Board of Trustees of the State University of New York v. Fox*,[4] discussed later, illustrates.

The first major U.S. Supreme Court case on commercial speech did not emerge until 1942. The public and governmental concern with the massive anticompetitive trade practices and fraudulent marketing techniques, including false and deceptive advertising, during the start of the 20th century was channeled into federal legislation such as the Federal Trade Commission Act of 1914, the Clayton Act of 1914 (forbidding such practices as price-fixing and corporate mergers) and the Food, Drug and Cosmetic Act of 1938 (outlawing the interstate transportation of adulterated or mislabelled food, drugs and cosmetics), rather than specific legislation regulating advertising. The prevailing belief was that commercial speech had First Amendment protection and thus could not be severely restricted.

Valentine v. Chrestensen (1942)

In 1942, however, the U.S. Supreme Court tackled head-on the issue of whether commercial speech enjoys First Amendment protection. In *Valentine v. Chrestensen*,[5] the Court held that the First Amendment does **not** apply to "purely commercial advertising." In 1940 F. J. Chrestensen, a Florida resident, moored his submarine, formerly owned by the U.S. Navy, at a state pier in the East River near New York City. While he was distributing handbills advertising tours of the boat for an admission fee, the Police Commissioner of New York, Lewis J. Valentine, informed him that he was violating a state sanitary code prohibiting distribution of commercial and business advertising on public streets. Valentine, however, told Chrestensen that he could distribute handbills devoted solely to information or a public protest. The code effectively banned advertising but not political materials.

Chrestensen was not satisfied and cleverly printed a revision of the original on one side (omitting only the admission fee). The other side had no advertising but instead criticized the City Dock Department for banning the original version of the handbill. The entrepreneur dutifully submitted the new handbill to the Police Commissioner but was rebuffed once again. No problem, he was told, with handing out the protest information but no advertising. Chrestensen ignored the warnings, passed out the handbills and was expeditiously restrained by police. He then successfully sought an injunction in District Court for the Southern District of New York to prevent the Police from further restraining him. However, the judge granted only an *interlocutory injunction*, which is effective only until the controversy can be settled on appeal. In other words, the police could not prevent Chrestensen from distributing the handbills until a final decision could be made on whether the statute was unconstitutional by a higher appellate court. The New York Court of Appeals (Second Circuit), basically functioning as the highest appellate court in the state, upheld the district court decision.

On further appeal, though, the U.S. Supreme Court, in a decision written by Associate Justice Owen J. Roberts, unanimously reversed the lower court decree. According to the Court:

> This Court has unequivocally held that the streets are proper places for the exercise of the freedom of communicating information and disseminating opinion and that, though the states and municipalities may appropriately regulate the privilege in the public interest, they may not unduly burden or proscribe its employment in these public thoroughfares. We are equally clear that the Constitution imposes no such restraint on government as respects purely commercial advertising.[6]

This decision, which enunciates what became known later as the "commercial speech doctrine," was gradually chipped away over the decades, but it was accepted doctrine until the 1970s. Along the way, the Court attempted to distinguish commercial speech from noncommercial speech but generated more smoke than light.

From March through May 1943, the Court decided four cases involving door-to-door distribution of religious materials by Jehovah's Witnesses. Many First Amendment cases decided by the U.S. Supreme Court during this century have involved this religious sect, which has always been very fervent in its attempts to proselytize, much to the chagrin of more traditional religious denominations. Anyone who grew up in the rural South and Southwest during the 1950s and 1960s can well recall the numerous occasions on which Witnesses would canvass the neighborhood door-to-door seeking contributions in return for their religious tracts. The Witnesses persisted in their efforts despite many closed doors and verbal abuse from people who resented their intrusions.

Jamison v. Texas (1943)

Such persistence often met resistance not only from unsympathetic residents but also in the form of local ordinances and state statutes as well. *Jamison v. Texas* (1943)[7] is a prime example of the selective use of a city ordinance to restrict the activities of religious groups such as the Witnesses. Ella Jamison was convicted in a Texas court of violating a Dallas ordinance banning the distribution of handbills on public streets. She was fined $5 plus court costs for passing out literature about the Witnesses. Under Texas law at that time, Jamison could not appeal the decision to a higher state court and thus had to resort to appealing the case directly to the U.S. Supreme Court, which granted certiorari. In a unanimous opinion written by Justice Hugo L. Black, the Court reversed the conviction on the ground that it violated her First and Fourteenth Amendment rights of freedom of speech and freedom of religion. According to the Court, even though the handbills were *on the face* commercial, they were protected because of their religious content. The state had argued that *Valentine* should apply because the literature advertised religious books and other works, but the Court held that commercial religious materials of this type were not affected by the *Valentine* holding. "The mere presence of an advertisement of a religious work on a handbill of the sort distributed here may not subject the handbill to prohibition,"[8] the Court noted. The Court offered the rationale for this exception to the *Valentine* rule that the First Amendment was designed to protect this type of activity. The state simply cannot be permitted to ban such distribution "merely because the handbills invite the purchase of books for the improved understanding of the religion or because the handbills seek in a lawful fashion to promote the raising of funds for religious purposes."

Murdock v. Pennsylvania (1943)

On May 3, 1943, the U.S. Supreme Court issued three separate decisions, all of which dealt with "commercial" speech and involved Jehovah's Witnesses. Taken together, the majority opinions substantially define the extent to which the State can regulate religious speech within a presumably commercial context. In *Murdock v. Pennsylvania* (1943),[9] the Court reversed the convictions of eight Witnesses for violating a Jeannette, Pennsylvania, ordinance that permitted door-to-door sale of products only with a license, which could be obtained only upon payment of a specified fee. No exception was made in the law for religious literature. Although they were not jailed, the eight were ordered to pay fines after they were convicted for violating the ordinance by requesting contributions for religious literature they were peddling door-to-door. There was no question that they were guilty, but the defendants unsuccessfully argued before the trial court that the law violated their First Amendment rights of freedom of press, speech and religion. On appeal, both the Pennsylvania Superior Court and the Pennsylvania Supreme Court upheld the convictions.

The U.S. Supreme Court, however, ruled in favor of the Witnesses in a close 5–4 decision written by Associate Justice William O. Douglas. According to the majority, the Witnesses were involved in a religious, not a commercial, venture:

> The constitutional rights of those spreading their religious beliefs through the spoken and printed word are not to be gauged by standards governing retailers or wholesalers of books. . . . The taxes imposed by this ordinance can hardly help but be as severe and telling in their impact on the freedom of press and religion as the "taxes on knowledge" at which the First Amendment was partly aimed.[10]

Martin v. City of Struthers (1943)

The second decision involved a similar city ordinance being violated by a Jehovah's Witness, but the Supreme Court took a somewhat different tack in striking it down as unconstitutional. In *Martin v. City of Struthers* (1943),[11] the Court, in another 5–4 split, overturned the conviction of Thelma Martin for distributing leaflets door-to-door advertising a Jehovah's Witness service. She was fined $10 for violating a Struthers, Ohio, ordinance very similar to that in *Murdock*. There were two strange twists to this case that contrasted it with *Murdock*. First, Martin's case was initially rejected on appeal to the U.S. Supreme Court because the justices mistakenly assumed that no constitutional issue had been raised in the lower courts, but upon a motion for reconsideration, the Court granted a writ of certiorari on the ground that a constitutional question had arisen. The Ohio Supreme Court had turned down Martin's appeal because it concluded no constitutional issue was involved. Second, in striking down the ordinance as in violation of the First and Fourteenth Amendments, the Court also held that the ordinance infringed on not only the right of the disseminator of the information but also the right of the intended receivers, or area households, to receive the information. The Court realistically recognized the aggressiveness of sects such as the Witnesses in soliciting door-to-door. According to the Court, door-to-door solicitations **can** be regulated under certain conditions, but this law was too broad. The Court noted that an ordinance prohibiting solicitation of homes on which the owners had posted a sign or other notice asking not to be disturbed would be a possible way of overcoming the overbreadth of the law.

Douglas v. City of Jeannette (1943)

The third case, interestingly, garnered the unanimous opinion of the Supreme Court but the facts were somewhat different. In *Douglas v. City of Jeannette*,[12] the Court declared that a Jeannette, Pennsylvania, ordinance banning the solicitation of orders for merchandise unless the individual had already obtained a license and paid a fee was unconstitutional. Two distinctions marking this case were that the soliciting was not done door-to-door and the solicitation did not involve what is known today as "point of purchase sale" (i.e., soliciting for a product that is available on the spot).

New York Times v. Sullivan (1964)

Twenty-one years after these cases, the U.S. Supreme Court for the first time issued a major decision involving commercial "political" speech. In a landmark **libel** decision, indeed the most important libel decision ever rendered by the Court, *New York Times v. Sullivan* (1964),[13] the Court rejected the argument that First and Fourteenth Amendment freedoms of speech and press did not apply in the case because the allegedly libelous information appeared in a paid, commercial advertisement in the newspaper:

> The publication here was not a "commercial" advertisement in the sense in which the word was used in [Valentine v.] Chrestensen. It communicated information, expressed opinion, recited grievances, protested claimed abuses, and sought financial support on behalf of movement whose existence and objectives are matters of the highest public interest and concern. That the [*New York*] *Times* was paid for publishing the advertisement is as immaterial in this connection as is the fact that newspapers and books are sold.[14]

The Court went on to rationalize that if the Court had ruled otherwise, the effect would be to discourage newspapers from publishing this type of advertising, which the Court characterized as "editorial advertisements." The Court was particularly concerned that certain groups, such as civil rights organizations in this case, that do not have ready access to the press would be prevented from disseminating their ideas to a wide audience. As the majority noted, "The effect would be to shackle the First Amendment in its attempt to secure 'the widest possible dissemination of information from diverse and antagonistic sources.' "[15]

As already discussed, political communication has consistently been granted greater First Amendment protection than almost any other form of speech other than religious communication. Thus this decision that the *New York Times* did not lose its First Amendment protection because the communication was a paid advertisement fits handily into the Supreme Court's First Amendment mold. The question of whether the commercial speech doctrine would apply in this case was one of the most significant aspects of the *Sullivan* decision, although the new rule enunciated, known as the "actual malice" rule (as discussed in Chapter 7), overshadowed the "editorial advertisement" ruling. Indeed, it could be argued that *Sullivan* was the first major step taken by the Supreme Court toward eventually dismembering the commercial speech doctrine by the 1980s, even though *Sullivan* is generally not perceived as a commercial speech decision. An important question is whether the Court's reasoning on the commercial speech issue in *Sullivan* is supportable. Would struggling political groups be denied a public forum for their ideas if the press were faced with the possibility of having no First Amendment protection if it published their paid advertisements? Or, would the press still be willing to take the risk of no protection in order to obtain the advertising dollars that sustain the commercial media? No one has researched this question yet, but it is likely that if all commercial speech were treated the same for the purposes of the First Amendment, even under the expanded protection granted commercial speech in the last two decades, there would be a "chilling" effect; this could well work to the disadvantage of political and religious movements that garner little press attention and thus often resort to unconventional communication such as editorial commercials.

Until the early to mid-1970s, the U.S. Supreme Court generally avoided facing constitutional questions involving commercial speech by simply denying certiorari. But the so-called consumer movement beginning in the late 1960s and the polarization of public opinion on the issue of abortion that culminated with *Roe v. Wade*[16] in 1973 had an impact on the type of commercial speech cases reaching the Court. More specifically, the Court was faced with deciding the constitutionality of governmental restrictions on advertising that did not appear to fall neatly into either the religious or the political niche. Was such advertising *commercial speech* or was it a form of advertising that could be shielded by the First Amendment?

Pittsburgh Press v. Pittsburgh Commission on Human Relations (1973)

In 1973 the Court had the opportunity to pull back on the commercial speech doctrine by expanding the context in which commercial speech enjoys full First Amendment protection but chose instead to hold on to *Valentine v. Chrestensen*. The city of Pittsburgh enacted an ordinance in the late 1960s that banned sex discrimination by employers for a broad range of occupations. The *Pittsburgh Press* had long permitted employers placing help-wanted ads in the paper's classified section to list openings under "Jobs — Male Interest," "Jobs — Female Interest" and "Jobs — Male-Female." There was no doubt that these ads effectively permitted sex discrimination by allowing employers to screen out applications from members of the "unwanted" sex. The Court, however, was faced with the question of whether such ads were comparable to the ad in *Valentine v. Chrestensen* or the advertorial in *New York Times v. Sullivan*. Is it pure commercial speech or a hybrid that can be shielded by the First Amendment?

Pittsburgh Press v. Pittsburgh Commission on Human Relations (1973)[17] began when the Pittsburgh Commission on Human Relations, which had been granted the authority to enforce the city's antidiscrimination ordinance, charged the newspaper with violating the ordinance and, after a hearing, ordered the *Press* to comply with the law. On appeal by the paper, the Court of Common Pleas for Allegheny County affirmed the order. On further appeal, the Commonwealth Court of Pennsylvania modified the order to prohibit gender-designated classified ads only for those types of positions for which the ordinance forbade sex discrimination. Thus the newspaper was allowed to carry ads specifying gender for those occupations not covered by the law. The Pennsylvania Supreme Court declined to review the case, but the U.S. Supreme Court granted certiorari and heard oral arguments on March 20, 1973.

In a narrow 5–4 decision, the Court held that the ordinance did not violate the First and Fourteenth Amendments by banning illegal gender-specified advertising. The lineup of the justices was somewhat surprising but perhaps a harbinger of other commercial speech cases to come. Associate Justice Lewis F. Powell, Jr., wrote the 5–4 decision, and he was joined by staunch First Amendment advocates, Justices William J. Brennan, Jr., and Thurgood Marshall. The majority also included traditional conservatives, Justices Byron R. White and William H. Rehnquist. The four dissenters were Chief Justice Warren Burger and Associate Justices William O. Douglas, Harry A. Blackmun and Potter Stewart.

How could justices such as Brennan and Marshall justify what is clearly a prior restraint on the press. According to the majority, "No suggestion is made in this case that the Ordinance was passed with any purpose of muzzling or curbing the press."[18] Ironically, the Court quoted liberally from *New York Times v. Sullivan* to point to the importance of the First Amendment while, nevertheless, finding that the ads resembled those of *Valentine v. Chrestensen* rather than the ad in *New York Times v. Sullivan*. The majority opinion went even further, comparing the ad to one for narcotics or prostitution:

> Discrimination in employment is not only commercial activity, it is illegal commercial activity under the Ordinance. We have no doubt that a newspaper constitutionally could be forbidden to publish a want ad proposing a sale of narcotics or soliciting prostitutes. Nor would the result be different if the nature of the transaction were indicated by placement under columns captioned "Narcotics for Sale" and "Prostitutes Wanted" rather than stated within the four corners of the advertisement.

The illegality in this case may be less overt, but we see no difference in principle here.[19]

The majority simply did not see the state's action in this case as prior restraint even though the effect of the order was to prohibit the newspaper from publishing particular content. As Justice Stewart, joined by Justice Douglas, noted in a dissent: "So far as I know, this is the first case in this or any other American court that permits a government agency to enter a composing room of a newspaper and dictate to the publisher the layout and the makeup of the newspaper's pages. This is the first such case, but I fear it may not be the last. The camel's nose is in the tent."[20]

Justices Stewart and Douglas did acknowledge in the dissent that it was "within the police power of the city of Pittsburgh to prohibit discrimination in private employment on the basis of race, color, religion, ancestry, national origin, place of birth, or sex."[21] But they felt the government had no authority to tell a newspaper in advance what it could and could not publish.

Chief Justice Burger dissented on grounds that the decision was "a disturbing enlargement of the 'commercial speech' doctrine" and the ruling "also launches the courts on what I perceive to be a treacherous path of defining what layout and organizational decisions of newspapers are 'sufficiently associated' with the 'commercial' parts of the papers as to be constitutionally unprotected and subject to governmental regulation."[22]

Bigelow v. Virginia (1975)

Was the court headed down a "treacherous path"? Two years later in *Bigelow v. Virginia* (1975)[23] the Court issued another decision in another commercial speech case involving the mass media. Like *Pittsburgh Press*, this case had tones of prior restraint but with a new twist. This case also illustrates how the opinions in one case can spill over into other decisions on the same topic but on an issue involving much different principles. An apparent spillover in *Pittsburgh Press*, for example, can be surmised by the fact that Justices Brennan and Marshall consistently upheld the constitutionality of antidiscrimination laws and that the newspaper ads effectively promoted sex discrimination. In *Bigelow*, the apparent spillover was evidenced by the fact that Justices Byron R. White and William H. Rehnquist dissented both in *Roe V. Wade* (1973),[24] the controversial decision granting a woman the constitutional right to an abortion, and in *Bigelow*, which involved newspaper ads for abortions.

In 1971, two years before *Roe v. Wade*, abortion was illegal in Virginia, although it was permitted in some other states such as New York. Jeffrey C. Bigelow, a director and managing editor of *The Virginia Weekly* of Charlottesville, ran an advertisement in his newspaper for a New York City abortion referral service, the Women's Pavilion. (Abortion was legal in *New York* at the time the ad appeared but became illegal later.) The newspaper ad provided considerable information about abortions in New York, including the fact that residency was not required. There was no doubt that the ad was designed to encourage Virginia women to procure abortions in New York because it specifically mentioned that the Women's Pavilion could assist a woman in obtaining "immediate placement in accredited hospitals at low cost" and it would make all arrangements on a "strictly confidential" basis. It should be noted that the newspaper had a high circulation on the University of Virginia campus.

The statute under which Bigelow was prosecuted directly forbade anyone — including by publication, lecture or advertisement — from encouraging or promoting the procurement of an abortion or miscarriage. The editor was convicted of a misdemeanor (the statute made the crime a misdemeanor only) in Albemarle County Court. He appealed to the Albemarle Circuit Court and was granted a *trial de novo* (a new trial, as discussed in Chapter 2) but was convicted again. The Virginia Supreme Court affirmed the new conviction on the ground that the advertisement was purely commercial and therefore not shielded by the umbrella of the First Amendment. The U.S. Supreme Court granted certiorari and sent the case back to the Virginia Supreme Court for further consideration in light of *Roe v. Wade* (1973) and related abortion decisions. Once again, the state supreme court affirmed the conviction, and Bigelow filed another appeal with the U.S. Supreme Court. This time, fate was on his side. (This process is described to illustrate the sometimes enormous complexity of First Amendment cases and to review appellate court procedures.)

In a resounding 7-2 decision, the U.S. Supreme Court reversed Bigelow's conviction on June 16, 1975, near the end of its 1974-1975 term. In a majority opinion written by Associate Justice Harry A. Blackmun and joined by Chief Justice Warren Burger and Associate Justices William O. Douglas, Thurgood Marshall, William J. Brennan, Jr., Potter Stewart and Lewis F. Powell, Jr., the Court held that the ad did have full First Amendment protection, just as the ad enjoyed in *New York Times v. Sullivan*. According to the Court: "The fact that the particular advertisement in appellant's newspaper had commercial aspects or reflected the advertiser's commercial interests did not negate all First Amendment guarantees. . . . The advertisement . . . did more than simply propose a commercial transaction. It contained factual material of clear 'public interest.' "[25]

What material did the Court view as in the public interest? The Court cited the lines, "Abortions are now legal in New York. There are no residency requirements." The Court went on to note:

Viewed in its entirety, the advertisement conveyed information of potential interest and value to a diverse audience—not only to readers possibly in need of the services offered, but also those with a general curiosity about, or genuine interest in, the subject matter of the law of another State and its development, and to readers seeking reform in Virginia. The mere existence of the Women's Pavilion in New York City, with the possibility of its being typical of other organizations there, and the availability of the services offered, were not unnewsworthy.[26]

Notice the Court's reference to *newsworthiness*. In *New York Times v. Sullivan*, the Court did not refer to this factor and merely noted that the ad was not a commercial advertisement in the sense of *Chrestensen* but instead was an "editorial advertisement." How does an ad become newsworthy? Is newsworthiness alone sufficient to warrant full First Amendment protection for an ad or is it to be considered in light of other factors? Would the ad have been protected if had been nothing more than the name, address and telephone number of the Women's Pavilion under the heading "Abortion Referral"? In other words, does it enjoy constitutional protection primarily because of the "newsworthy" information it conveyed? The Court left these questions unanswered, but it was apparent that the Court was headed toward expansion of First Amendment rights for a variety of forms of advertising. No matter how hard one tries, it is impossible to fully reconcile *Chrestensen* with *Bigelow* and even with *New York Times v. Sullivan*. In his dissent, Justice William H. Rehnquist (joined by Justice Byron R. White) characterized the nature of the ad as an exchange of services rather than an exchange of ideas, but the handwriting was on the wall. (Both justices also dissented in the *Roe v. Wade* abortion decision.)

Virginia State Board of Pharmacy
v. Virginia Citizen's Consumer Council (1976)

Less than a year after *Bigelow*, *Chrestensen* began its slide toward oblivion. On May 24, 1976, the U.S. Supreme Court for the first time held that truthful commercial speech, even though purely commercial, is protected by the First Amendment. In *Virginia State Board of Pharmacy v. Virginia Citizen's Consumer Council* (1976),[27] the Court ruled 7-1 that a state statute under which licensed pharmacists could be punished for "unprofessional conduct" for advertising prescription drug prices was unconstitutional. The penalties ranged from small fines to license revocation. Interestingly, the statute was not attacked in the courts by pharmacists but instead by consumer groups who claimed "the First Amendment entitles the user of prescription drugs to receive information that pharmacists wish to communicate to them through advertising and other promotional means, concerning the prices of such drugs."[28]

The majority opinion, written by Associate Justice Harry A. Blackmun, noted, much to the surprise of many First Amendment scholars, that "in *Bigelow v. Virginia*, the notion of unprotected 'commercial speech' all but passed from the scene."[29] Even a close reading of the Court's opinion in *Bigelow* gives no clear indication that such is the case. The Court in *Virginia State Board* conceded that a "fragment of hope for the continuing validity of a 'commercial speech' exception arguably may have persisted because of the subject matter of the advertisement in *Bigelow*."[30] The Court then tackled the issue of whether "there is a First Amendment exception for 'commercial speech.' " The Court made it clear that *Virginia Pharmacy Board* did not involve cultural, philosophical or political speech, nor was the information newsworthy or generalized observations about commercial matters. Instead, the pharmacist, according to the Court, is attempting to communicate, "I will sell you the X prescription drug at the Y price."[31] Citing *New York Times v. Sullivan*, the Court then noted that it is well established that speech does not lose its First Amendment protection simply because money is spent to purchase it. According to the justices, "Those whom the suppression of prescription drug price information hits the hardest are the poor, the sick, and particularly the aged."[32] Thus a consumer's interest in such information could be as "keen, if not keener, than his interest in the day's most urgent political debate." The majority opinion strongly criticized Virginia's contention that price advertising would adversely effect the professionalism of pharmacists and ultimately harm consumers with low quality service and presumably inferior drugs. Keeping consumers ignorant is not the solution, according to the Court, but instead individuals should be permitted to make their own choices based on information freely available in the marketplace.

Although the justices held that Virginia's statute was unconstitutional, they did note that "some forms of commercial speech regulation are surely permissible." They specifically mentioned untruthful commercial speech such as false and misleading ads and false advertising that causes actual injury. Virginia, in the Court's view, was unconstitutionally suppressing truthful speech that could contribute "to the flow of accurate and reliable information relevant to public and private decisionmaking" for the sake of preventing the dissemination of falsehoods. In other words, the Court was warning the state not to throw the baby out with the bath water. The First Amendment warrants the risk that some false information may sneak into the marketplace so that the truth may prevail.

Justice William H. Rehnquist was the sole dissenter to the Court's decision. His opinion is worthy of note, not so much for its strange reasoning as for the fact that it represents a strong minority view shared by some professional associations. Justice Rehnquist was particularly concerned that the Court's opinion would open the way "not only for dissemination of price information but for active promotion of prescription drugs, liquor, cigarettes and other products the use of which it has previously been thought desirable to discourage."[33] To illustrate his point, he satirically penned some "representative" advertisements that a pharmacist might run in the local newspaper after the decision:

> Pain getting you down? Insist that your physician prescribe Demoral. You pay a little more than for aspirin, but you get a lot more relief.
>
> Can't shake the flu? Get a prescription for tetracycline from you doctor today.
>
> Don't spend another sleepless night. Ask your doctor to prescribe Seconal without delay.[34]

Of course, no such ads have appeared, and, in fact, the very prediction made by the majority—a free flow of commercial information in the marketplace—has occurred. Prescription prices have generally fallen and pharmacists are just as professional as they were before the decision. Any concern that the publication of prescription prices would somehow demean pharmacists has long since faded, but, as indicated in the decisions that follow, professional organizations, as a whole—whether they be of lawyers, physicians or other professionals—continue to harbor fears that advertising will spell the demise of the public respect for their particular profession.

One more point in Justice Rehnquist's dissent deserves attention because it represents a vocal, minority view that some scholars would say smacks of elitism. According to Justice Rehnquist, "The statute . . . only forbids pharmacists to publish this price information. There is no prohibition against a consumer group, such as appellees, collecting and publishing comparative price information as to various pharmacies in an area."[35] This view ignores the reality that consumer groups would have to expend considerable time and money to compile such information even though pharmacists are in a much better position because they have direct access to this information. Pharmacists also have a much more effective outlet for communication—newspaper advertising. Most consumer groups could probably not afford to place such advertising but would instead have to rely on alternative means such as pamphlets that would, in all likelihood, have very limited circulation, particularly among those groups—such as the poor and the elderly—who benefit the most from competition among pharmacies. This view has an aura of elitism because it assumes that consumers would not be able to effectively and efficiently discern accurate information from the deceptive and misleading.

Did *Virginia State Board of Pharmacy* settle the issue once and for all of whether commercial speech had First Amendment protection? Just as *Roe v. Wade* spurred more questions about abortion rights, the Virginia decision left a significant number of subissues to be resolved, which the Court continues to confront almost two decades later. Three major decisions on the issue were handed down by the next year, and there have been several subsequent rulings on the average of once every two years. Many of these have dealt with advertising of professional services, although other types of commercial speech have seen the spotlight as well.

The first two of the three 1977 decisions are only summarized here because they concern issues of relatively minor importance from a mass communication law perspective, but the third is discussed in detail because it deals with advertising by professionals.

Linmark Associates, Inc. v. Willingboro (1977)

In *Linmark Associates, Inc. v. Willingboro* (1977),[36] the Court held 8-0 (with Justice Rehnquist not participating) that a local ordinance banning the posting of "For Sale" and "Sold" signs on lawns violated the First Amendment. The opinion, written by Justice Thurgood Marshall, said that whereas the goal of the ordinance to prevent "block busting" (White flight from neighborhoods as they are being racially integrated) may have been noble, the town had not been able to show that such a restriction was necessary nor justified under the circumstances. "If dissemination of this information can be restricted, then every locality in the country can suppress any facts that reflect poorly on the locality, so long as a plausible claim can be made that disclosure would cause the recipients of the information to act 'irrationally,' " according to the Court.[37]

Hugh Carey v. Population Services International (1977)

In *Hugh Carey v. Population Services International* (1977),[38] a New York education law making it illegal for anyone to sell or distribute nonprescription contraceptives to minors under age 16 and for anyone to advertise or publicly display such contraceptives was declared unconstitutional by a divided court. Population Services International owned Population Planning Associates, a North Carolina corporation that advertised and sold contraceptives to customers of any age via mail order throughout the country, including in New York. (The ads appeared in New York magazines and newspapers.) In applying a "strict scrutiny" test to the statute because of an earlier decision by another divided court that appeared to recognize a limited constitutional right to privacy,[39] Justice William J. Brennan, Jr., writing for the majority held that the prohibition on the distribution of contraceptives violated the due process clause of the Fourteenth Amendment but the justices could not agree whether such a ban for minors under the age of 16 would be permissible. Furthermore, the Court held that the advertising restrictions violated the First Amendment, although the majority could not agree on whether such restrictions are inherently unconstitutional.

COMMERCIAL SPEECH FOR PROFESSIONALS AND CORPORATIONS: FROM *BATES* TO *SHAPERO*

Lawyer Advertising

Certainly, the most important decision regarding commercial speech in 1977 was *Bates v. State Bar of Arizona*,[40] the first of a series of cases involving lawyer advertising. In a split 5–4 decision written by Justice Harry A. Blackmun, the Court effectively broadened *Virginia Board of Pharmacy* to include the same type of advertising (i.e., prices) for lawyers. Attorney John R. Bates and his partner, Van O'Steen, started a legal services clinic in Phoenix that made extensive use of paralegals, standardized forms and other cost-cutting measures. In 1976, two years after they established the clinic that was designed to handle primarily routine services for lower income clients, the lawyers defied a state bar regulation that forbade advertising by placing an ad in the *Arizona Republican* that simply listed the services their firm offered and typical fees. The ad basically touted the availability of "routine services" for "very reasonable fees." No other claims were made.

At that time, Arizona, like most states, had strict regulations regarding advertising by certain professionals such as physicians and lawyers. These regulations were either in the form of codes of conduct that were enforced by the state licensing arm—such as the medical board or the state bar association—or of state statutes. Such regulations had the rationale that they would prevent deceptive and misleading advertising by these groups and that advertising demeans the profession. As Justice Rehnquist noted earlier in his dissent in *Virginia Board of Pharmacy*: "It is undoubtedly arguable that many people in the country regard the choice of shampoo as just as important as who may be elected to local, state, or national political office, but that does not automatically bring information about competing shampoos within the protection of the First Amendment."[41]

Although the Court ruled that the Arizona regulation was an unconstitutional infringement on freedom of speech and freedom of the press, the justices had a more difficult time dealing with this case than with the earlier pharmacy decision. As licensed attorneys themselves, the justices no doubt were concerned that a ruling that was too broad in granting lawyers the right to advertise could open a Pandora's Box that might ultimately undermine the standards and traditions of the profession. The close 5–4 vote certainly reflects that concern, as does the majority opinion itself. As Justice Blackmun indicated in the holding: "The constitutional issue in this case is only whether the State may prevent the publication in a newspaper of appellants' truthful advertisement concerning the availability and terms of routine legal services. We rule simply that the flow of such information may not be restrained."[42]

The Court not only made it clear that this holding was applicable only to the specific type of advertising involved, but it also went to unusual lengths to distinguish permissible versus impermissible forms of advertising. Whereas lawyers may advertise prices for such routine services as simple wills, uncontested bankruptcies, uncontested divorces and adoptions, the Court noted, advertising for more complex services such as contested divorces and estate settlements may be subject to regulation. The Court also indicated, as it had in earlier decisions, that false, deceptive and misleading advertising can be restrained. But the majority opinion also mentioned that advertising claims as to the quality of services and in-person solicitations might be justifiably suppressed or limited. The Court noted that a warning or disclaimer could be required for certain kinds of advertising. As might be expected, the justices made no judgment whether such restraints would be upheld because the case at hand did not involve any of this type of advertising: "In sum, we recognize that many of the problems in defining the boundary between the deceptive and nondeceptive advertising remain to be resolved, and we expect that the bar will have a special role to play in assuring that advertising by attorneys flows both freely and smoothly."[43]

Could the Court have broadened the decision to include advertising by other professionals? Over the decades, the Supreme Court has enunciated an *overbreadth doctrine* on First Amendment issues, which essentially permits individuals challenging a statute on First Amendment grounds to demonstrate that the statute could be applied unconstitutionally in circumstances beyond those at issue in the case. This doctrine flies in the face of the traditional rule in constitutional cases that a statute can be challenged only in relation to the conduct or circumstances at hand. However, in First Amendment cases the Court permits a broader challenge because "an overbroad statute might serve to chill protected speech. First Amendment interests are fragile interests, and a person who contemplates protected activity might be discouraged by the *in terrorem* effect of the statute."[44] Thus the justices could clearly have broadened the decision to include advertising by other professionals such as physicians and dentists. But the Court chose not to do so in *Bates* because "the justification for the application of overbreadth analysis applies weakly, if at all, in the ordinary commercial context."[45] According to the majority opinion, advertising is unlikely to be affected by a chilling effect because it is "linked to commercial well-being."

What is the importance of this case? Even with the 5–4 vote, *Bates* is definitely a broadening of the principles laid down in *Virginia Board of*

Pharmacy, but this extension of First Amendment protection to include advertising of routine legal services (*Virginia Board of Pharmacy* dealt only with advertising of prescription drug *prices*, not the availability of services) was not wide enough to put truthful advertising on par with other forms of speech. The Court chose deliberately from the beginning with *Bigelow* to follow the circuitous route of a case-by-case analysis rather than applying the overbreadth doctrine that would have protected truthful commercial speech to the same extent as political and religious speech. *Bates* raised far more questions than it answered, and many of those questions have yet to be resolved, although the Court wrestled with some of them in subsequent cases.

The dissenters included Chief Justice Warren Burger and Associate Justices Lewis F. Powell, Jr., Potter Stewart and William H. Rehnquist. Their basic argument was that the ruling was, as Justice Powell stated, "an invitation—by the public-spirited and the selfish lawyers alike—to engage in competitive advertising on an escalating basis."[46] Justice Rehnquist went even further in his dissent. Although Justice Powell indicated in his dissent that some forms of legal advertising might have First Amendment protection, Justice Rehnquist clung to *Valentine v. Chrestensen*: "The *Valentine* distinction was constitutionally sound and practically workable, and I am still unwilling to take even one step down the slippery slope away from it."[47] In subsequent decisions, Justice Rehnquist continued to hold that minority view even while serving as the Chief Justice, a role that has forced him to seek more consensus among the justices in forging more definite rulings.

Lawyer Solicitation: *Ohralik* and *In Re Primus*

Within a year after Bates, the Court began a series of decisions that set out the specific parameters of First Amendment protection for commercial speech of attorneys. In *Ohralik v. Ohio State Bar Association* (1978) and *In Re Primus* (1978),[48] the U.S. Supreme Court ruled on the extent to which states may regulate attorneys' solicitation of potential clients. In *Ohralik* the Court upheld the suspension of an attorney by the Ohio Bar Association for his in-person solicitation of two 18-year-old women shortly after they had been in a car accident. The lawyer's efforts resulted in both victims signing contingent fee agreements with him. The state bar association suspended Ohralik even though it was never able to demonstrate any harm to the women from the agreements. In his majority opinion, Justice Lewis F. Powell, Jr. distinguished this type of personal solicitation from the advertising in *Bates*. Ohio had a "legitimate and indeed 'compelling'" interest in "preventing those aspects of solicitation that involve fraud, undue influence, intimidation, overreaching, and other forms of 'vexatious conduct,' " according to Justice Powell.

In the second case, *In Re Primus*, a South Carolina volunteer American Civil Liberties Union attorney sent a letter to a former patient to solicit her as a potential plaintiff in a suit against the doctor. The lawyer believed the physician had sterilized pregnant women who were allegedly told they would no longer receive Medicaid care unless they agreed to the surgery. Justice Powell, again writing for the majority, set aside the public reprimand handed down to the attorney on grounds that the First Amendment right to freedom of speech protected this form of political expression because there was no demonstration of "undue influence, overreaching, misrepresentation, or invasion of privacy."[49] In other words, the Court viewed Primus' actions as political, not commercial, expression, while Ohralik was engaging in a commercial transaction. Some scholars would characterize such a distinction as hair splitting, but the Court saw a clear difference. Justice Rehnquist, as expected, dissented in *Primus* because he saw "no principled distinction" between the two cases in which " 'ambulance-chasers' suffer one fate and 'civil liberties lawyers' another? . . . I believe that constitutional inquiry must focus on the character of the conduct which the State seeks to regulate, and not on the motives of the individual lawyers or the nature of the particular litigation involved."[50]

First Amendment Rights of Nonmedia Corporations:
First National Bank of Boston v. Bellotti (1978)

Another 1978 Supreme Court decision on commercial speech went relatively unnoticed, probably because the case involved the First Amendment rights of nonmedia corporations. In *First National Bank of Boston v. Bellotti* (1978),[51] the Court struck down as unconstitutional a Massachusetts statute that banned banks and other businesses from attempting to exert direct influence on public opinion unless the issue involved directly and materially affected its business, property or other assets. The bank had tried to get voters to reject a proposed constitutional amendment granting the legislature the authority to enact a progressive (i.e., graduated) personal income tax. In striking down the statute, the Court for the first time held that nonmedia corporations have at least some First Amendment rights.

Advertising by Other Professionals:
Friedman v. Rogers (1979)

Just as the Court has been reluctant to grant full First Amendment rights to commercial speech of attorneys, it has also hesitated to broaden the constitutional protection for commercial speech of other professionals. Thus in 1979 in *Friedman v. Rogers*,[52] the justices held 7-2 that Texas could prevent optometrists from practicing under a trade name because the state had a "substantial and well-demonstrated" interest in protecting consumers from the deceptive and misleading use of optometrical trade names.

First Amendment Rights of Public Utilities: *Consolidated Edison* and *Central Hudson Gas and Electric*

One year later, the Supreme Court handed down two decisions on the same day dealing with commercial speech rights of public utilities. During the mid to late 1970s, many public utilities began speaking out on controversial issues such as nuclear energy and environmental regulations and discussing their views in "inserts" sent with the monthly bills. Both *Consolidated Edison Co. v. Public Service Commission of New York* (1980)[53] and *Central Hudson Gas & Electric Corp. v. Public Service Commission of New York* (1980)[54] involved attempts by a state regulatory agency (in fact, the same agency) to bar a utility from engaging in particular types of commercial speech. The content of the speech differed significantly between the two, but the First Amendment issues were quite similar.

In 1977, the New York Public Service Commission issued an order barring all public utilities from "using bill inserts to discuss political matters, including the desirability of future development of nuclear power." The order was sparked by a complaint filed by the Natural Resources Defense Council (NRDC), a consumer group opposed to nuclear power, after Consolidated Edison included an item entitled "Independence Is Still a Goal, and Nuclear Power Is Needed to Win the Battle" in its January 1976 monthly insert. The item specifically touted the benefits of nuclear energy and noted the benefits significantly outweighed any risks and that this form of energy was economical, clean and safe. The NRDC had asked the electric utility to include a rebuttal written by the NRDC in the next month's insert. When Cod Ed refused, the NRDC filed a complaint with the commission and requested that the commission order Con Ed to offer space in the monthly inserts to organizations and individuals holding views opposed to those expressed by the utility on public controversies. Instead of granting the NRDC's request, the commission adopted a policy of prohibiting public utilities from discussing any issues of public controversy. Although the ban was obviously aimed at the topic of nuclear energy, it nevertheless imposed prior restraint on all public controversies.

Consolidated Edison challenged the order in court. The New York Supreme Court (an intermediate state appellate court), Special Term, held that the order was an unconstitutional prior restraint, but the appellate division of the state supreme court reversed and the New York Court of Appeals, the highest appellate court in the state, affirmed. The state court of appeals held that the order was a reasonable time, place and manner restriction that was designed to protect a legitimate state interest—individual privacy (essentially the right not to be bombarded with utility propaganda). In a 7–2 decision written by Associate Justice Lewis F. Powell, Jr., the U.S. Supreme Court reversed the New York Court of Appeals. According to the Court, the ban was *not* "(i) a reasonable time, place and manner restriction, (ii) a permissible subject-matter regulation, or a narrowly tailored means of serving a compelling state interest."[55] The majority opinion specifically noted that "a constitutionally permissible time, place and manner restriction may not be based upon either the content or subject matter of the speech." This is a reiteration of a well-established principle that such prior restraint must be *content neutral.*

What about the consumer's right of privacy to not be exposed to such controversies when the monthly utility bill is opened? The Court strongly rejected this rationale and a number of other justifications the state had offered in its defense for imposing the ban. According to the Court:

> Passengers on public transportation or residents of a neighborhood disturbed by the raucous broadcasts from a passing soundtruck may well be unable to escape an unwanted message. But customers who encounter an objectionable billing insert may "effectively avoid further bombardment of their sensibilities simply by averting their eyes." . . . The customer of Consolidated Edison may escape exposure to objectionable material simply by transferring the bill insert from envelope to wastebasket.[56]

The Court also rejected the argument that the Court's decision in 1969 in *Red Lion Broadcasting v. Federal Communications Commission*[57] (discussed in the next chapter) upholding the Fairness Doctrine justified the ban, noting that the airwaves are a limited public resource while billing inserts are not. Even the argument that the ban would prevent consumers from subsidizing the expense of the utility's airing of its controversial views was rejected. Afterall, the Court stated, there was nothing to indicate that the regulatory agency "could not exclude the cost of these bill inserts from the utility's rate base."[58]

In *Central Hudson Gas & Electric v. Public Service Commission of New York* (1980),[59] the U.S. Supreme Court for the first time articulated a four-part analysis for determining whether a particular restriction on commercial speech is constitutional. In 1973, the United States suffered an "energy crisis" brought on by an Arab oil embargo imposed by the Arab cartel known as Organization of Petroleum Exporting Countries (OPEC) in October in retaliation for U.S. support of Israel during the Arab–Israeli War. The ban was lifted on March 18, 1974, after rather severe fuel shortages in this country. The federal government and most states adopted stringent energy conservation measures and launched a public relations effort to encourage Americans to adopt their own conservation methods.

During the energy crisis, the New York Public Service Commission (PSC) ordered the electric utilities in the state, including Central Hudson, not to advertise or promote the use of electricity. The electric companies dutifully complied with the order during the national energy crisis, but after the embargo was lifted in early 1974 and the effects of the shortage began to wear off, some public utilities slowly reverted to their traditional promotional advertising. In 1977 the New York PSC adopted a policy statement that continued its ban on promotional advertising even though the energy crisis had abated. The statement did not ban all advertising, only "promotional advertising," which the commission defined as that designed to promote the purchase of utility service. Institutional and informational advertising that was not aimed at increasing sales was not prohibited.

Central Hudson Gas & Electric challenged the ban on First and Fourteenth Amendment grounds in court, but the state trial court, intermediate appellate court and the New York Court of Appeals all held that the order was constitutional. However, in an 8–1 opinion written by Justice Lewis F. Powell, Jr., the U.S. Supreme Court ruled that the ban was unconstitutional. Although there were three separate concurring opinions, only Justice William H. Rehnquist dissented. According to Justice Powell:

> Our decisions have recognized "the 'commonsense' distinction between speech proposing a commercial transaction, which occurs in an area traditionally subject to government regulation, and other varieties of speech" [citing *Ohralik* and *Bates*]. The Constitution therefore accords a lesser protection to commercial speech than to other constitutionally guaranteed expression . . . the protection available for particular commercial expression turns on the nature both of the expression and of the governmental interests served by its regulation.

> The First Amendment's concern for commercial speech is based on the informational function of advertising. Consequently, there can be no constitutional objection to the suppression of commercial messages that do not accurately inform the public about lawful activity. The government may ban forms of communication more likely to deceive the public than to inform it . . . or commercial speech related to illegal activity.[60] (footnotes omitted)

The opinion went on to formulate a four-part analysis for courts to apply in commercial speech cases:

> At the outset, we must determine whether the expression is protected by the First Amendment. For commercial speech to come within that provision, it at least must concern lawful activity and not be misleading. Next, we ask whether the asserted governmental interest is substantial. If both inquiries yield positive answers, we must determine whether the regulation directly advances the governmental interest asserted, and whether it is more extensive than necessary to serve that interest.[61]

The Court then applied the analysis to the *Central Hudson* case and determined that the ban did indeed violate the First Amendment. The Court made several interesting points in its analysis. First, the opinion noted that unless there are extraordinary conditions, a monopoly position such as control over the supply of electricity in this case does *not* change the First Amendment protection accorded the business. Second, although the state's interest in imposing the ban (conserving energy and ensuring fair and efficient rates) was substantial, any negative impact of promotional advertising was "highly speculative." Finally, the Court contended that the State had not demonstrated that its goal of promoting energy conservation could not be accomplished by a less restrictive means than a total ban on promotional advertising.

As with any judicial analysis, the four-step *Central Hudson* test is probably not as clear and concise as some lower courts would prefer, but it has proven viable in subsequent commercial speech cases, as discussed later. The Court had effectively applied the test, or at least its basic premises, in more recent decisions leading up to *Central Hudson*, but this was the first time the justices had articulated a specific, step-by-step analysis. Not all of the justices agreed with the test. Indeed, Associate Justice Harry A. Blackmun, joined by Justice William J. Brennan, Jr., indicated in a concurring opinion that the test "is not consistent with our prior cases and does not provide adequate protection for truthful, nonmisleading, noncoercive commercial speech."[62] According to Justice Blackmun, "If the First Amendment guarantee means anything, it means that, absent clear and present danger, government has no power to restrict expression because of the effect its message is likely to have on the public."[63] Thus Justice Blackmun would extend the commercial speech doctrine to include a much broader range of expression than the *Central Hudson* formula. Justice John Paul Stevens, joined also by Justice Brennan, did not view *Central Hudson* as a commercial speech case at all because, as he saw it, the breadth of the ban exceeded the boundaries of the commercial speech concept: "This ban encompasses a great deal more than mere proposals to engage in certain kinds of commercial transactions."[64]

Finally, Justice Rehnquist, as would be expected based on his previous dissents in commercial speech cases, believed the state's ban was constitutional as a "permissible state regulation of an economic activity." He once again noted that "the Court unleashed a Pandora's box when it 'elevated' commercial speech to the level of traditional political speech by according it First Amendment protection."[65]

Could it be argued the promotional advertising was a form of political speech under the circumstances in *Central Hudson*? What if the utility had taken a direct stand against the PSC ban in its advertising? What if the company had indirectly promoted electricity by advertising new fuel-efficient appliances? Under Justice Rehnquist's analysis, could the commission have banned all utility company advertising, including "institutional and informational" ads?

Since *Central Hudson*, the U.S. Supreme Court has reviewed relatively few commercial speech cases, although two subsequent cases—one in 1988 and another in 1989—muddied the waters again on First Amendment protection for commercial speech. Three of the seven major Court decisions in this area since *Central Hudson* have concerned advertising by professionals.

Lawyer Advertising: Part II

Two years after *Central Hudson*, the Supreme Court ruled that a state may not restrict lawyer advertising to specific types of information. After the *Bates v. State Bar of Arizona* decision in 1977, the Missouri bar adopted some new rules of professional ethics that were believed to be permitted under the principles established in *Bates*. Most state bar associations, which traditionally determine the professional standards for attorneys in the state, have taken a rather conservative approach to advertising. Lawyers, in general, disapprove of most forms of promotion and advertising, and when a state or appellate court approves restrictions on advertising imposed by the bar association in one state, the bar associations in other states usually move quickly to adopt those tougher standards if they do not already have them. Lawyers are not the only professionals, of course, who abhor advertising. The same sentiment against professional advertising appears to prevail among physicians, pharmacists, nurses, accountants and so on.

The Missouri restrictions were rather severe, as the U.S. Supreme Court noted in *In the Matter of R____ M.J____* (1982),[66] in which the justices unanimously struck down a series of rules of professional ethics. "RMJ" was reprimanded for violating several of the rules, including restrictions on information about areas of practice, on announcements about office openings and on jurisdictions in which he was admitted to practice. The rules were so strict that only 23 specific terms could be used to describe areas of practice. "RMJ," for example, was reprimanded for using "real estate" instead of "property" in his ad and for listing "contracts" and "securities" as areas of practice. He also ran afoul of the rules by mailing out cards announcing the opening of his office to individuals who were not included in the categories to whom such information could be sent. "RMJ" was also cited for truthfully advertising that he was a member of the Missouri and Illinois bars and that he had been admitted to practice before the U.S. Supreme Court.

The majority opinion, written by Associate Justice Lewis F. Powell, Jr., pointed out that the Missouri bar made no assertions that the ads were in any way misleading or inaccurate and thus had demonstrated no substantial state interest in enacting the regulations. Indeed, about all the state had been able to show was that the ads may have approached being in bad taste. Although the Court held that all of the restrictions being challenged were unconstitutional, Justice Powell indicated that the line in the ad in large boldface type proclaiming that "RMJ" was a member of the U.S. Supreme Court bar may have been somewhat misleading and unfortunate. Rule 5 of the *Rules of the Supreme Court of the United States* allows admission to practice before the court if the attorney has been admitted to practice in the highest court of a state, territory, district, commonwealth or possession for a minimum of three years and if the person "appears to the Court to be of good moral and professional character." After an application is filed and an admission fee is paid, the attorney is then sworn in. Thus the vast majority of attorneys are eligible to become members of the Supreme Court bar. Nevertheless, the Court noted there was nothing in the record to indicate that even this information was actually misleading, although "this relatively uninformative fact . . . could be misleading to the general public unfamiliar with the requirements of admission to the bar" of the Supreme Court.

The Court found that the other violations, including the mailing of announcement cards to a larger audience than that permitted under the rules[67] and the listing of other jurisdictions to which "RMJ" had been admitted, were also not misleading and thus protected by the First Amendment.

The unanimous opinion in this case is not surprising in light of previous Court decisions, including *Bates*. Note that the rules in this case were very restrictive. Although the rationale of bar associations for imposing such regulations is ostensibly to preserve the public respect for and the dignity of the profession, one usual effect is to reduce competition among attorneys and thereby prevent legal fees from declining. No mention of such effects was made in the Court's decision, but consumer groups traditionally argue that advertising by professionals improves the marketplace for the consumer by increasing competition.

In the same year as *In the Matter of R ____ M.J ____* , the Court affirmed an opinion by the U.S. Court of Appeals for the Second Circuit[68] that upheld orders by the Federal Trade Commission (FTC) forbidding the American Medical Association and the American Dental Association from imposing total bans on advertising by members of their respective associations. In *American Medical Association v. Federal Trade Commission* (1982),[69] the Supreme Court upheld the appellate court decision without opinion. Thus we do not know specifically why the Court upheld the decision, although the rules did indeed bar truthful advertising by physicians and dentists. The FTC rules, by the way, appear to be in line with *Bates* because they permitted the regulation of deceptive and misleading advertising.

First Amendment Protection
for Unsolicited Mail Advertising:
Bolger v. Youngs Drug Products Corp. (1983)

During its next term, the U.S. Supreme Court faced what might initially appear to be a question with a complex answer: Is there a First Amendment right to mail *unsolicited* advertising for contraceptives? The answer provided by the Court in *Bolger v. Youngs Drug Products Corp.* (1983)[70] turned out to be rather simple: yes. Arriving at the answer was not a simple process, however. From the long line of cases discussed thus far in this book, it is clear that noncommercial unsolicited mailings have full First Amendment protection. Unsolicited commercial mail would also appear to have some First Amendment protection, thanks to *Bates* and *Central Hudson Gas & Electric.*

Youngs Drug Products, one of the largest manufacturers of condoms, planned to regularly send unsolicited advertising matter through the U.S. mail, including a drug store flyer and two pamphlets entitled "Condoms and Human Sexuality" and "Plain Talk about Venereal Disease." Upon hearing the company's plan, the U.S. Postal Service (USPS) notified the company that such mailings would violate a federal statute that provided "any unsolicited advertisement of matter which is designed, adapted, or intended for preventing conception is nonmailable matter."[71] The USPS rejected Youngs' contention that the law violated the First Amendment. When the manufacturer sought declaratory and injunctive relief from the USPS decision in U.S. District Court for the District of Columbia, the court granted the injunction and declared the statute unconstitutional. The USPS appealed, but the U.S. Supreme Court upheld the lower court ruling.

The threshold question was whether this type of speech was commercial or noncommercial. Surprisingly, the Court opted for the former even though the pamphlets were at least highly informational. One of the pamphlets made numerous references to condoms made by Youngs, whereas the other focused more on generic terms. Justice Thurgood Marshall wrote the majority opinion that agreed with the District Court that even the informational pamphlets constituted commercial speech:

> Most of appellee's mailings fall within the core notion of commercial speech — "speech which does no more than propose a commercial transaction." [citing *Virginia Pharmacy*] Youngs' informational pamphlets, however, cannot be characterized merely as proposals to engage in commercial transactions. Their proper classification as commercial or non-commercial speech thus presents a closer question. The mere fact that these pamphlets are conceded to be advertisements clearly does not compel the conclusion that they are commercial speech. [citing *New York Times v. Sullivan*, mentioned earlier in this chapter and discussed in detail in Chapter 7] Similarly the reference to a specific product does not by itself render the pamphlets commercial speech. Finally, the fact that Youngs has an economic motivation for mailing the pamphlets would clearly be insufficient by itself to turn these materials into commercial speech. [citing *Bigelow*]

> The combination of all these characteristics, however, provides strong support for the District Court's conclusion that the informational pamphlets are properly characterized as commercial speech.[72]

Finding that the proposed mailings were commercial speech, the Court then appropriately applied the *Central Hudson* four-part test for determining whether the specific governmental restrictions on this commercial speech were constitutional. Although the government in this case was federal rather than state, as it had been in earlier cases, the four-part test is still the same. First, the Supreme Court determined that the advertising was not misleading and was not concerned with illegal activities and that it promoted "substantial individual and societal interests," such as family planning and the prevention of venereal disease. The USPS had claimed the substantial government interest was in preventing interference with parents' attempts to discuss birth control matters with their children, but the majority reasoned that the particular statute lent "only the most incremental support for the interest asserted. We can reasonably assume that parents already exercise substantial control over the disposition of mail once it enters their mailbox."[73]

The Court then went on to conclude that the statute was overly broad in achieving its objective. Noting that the unsolicited mailings were "entirely suitable for adults," Justice Marshall's opinion evoked an interesting analogy: The "level of discourse reaching a mailbox cannot be limited to that which would be suitable for a sandbox."[74] This same reasoning has been applied in other contexts, including obscenity when the argument is made that sexually explicit materials could accidentally fall into the hands of children. (This is discussed in Chapter 11.)

Justice William H. Rehnquist (joined by Justice Sandra Day O'Connor) filed a separate but concurring opinion that foresaw the governmental interest as substantial, but Justice Rehnquist agreed with the majority that the statute was much too broad in light of the limited intrusion involved. Justice John Paul Stevens also filed a separate, concurring opinion in which he argued, "The statute . . . censors ideas, not style. It prohibits appellee from mailing any unsolicited advertisement of contraceptives, no matter how intrusive and tactful; yet it permits anyone to mail unsolicited advertisements of devices intended to facilitate conception, no matter how coarse or grotesque."[75]

The *Youngs Drug Products* decision is particularly apt as a new century approaches and the number of individuals with the Acquired Immune Deficiency Syndrome (AIDS) complex continues to escalate into a worldwide epidemic. Who would have predicted in 1983 that (a) the U.S. Surgeon General would six years later attempt to mail unsolicited to every household in the United States an information booklet on the disease, complete with prevention tips; (b) by the end of the decade radio and television public service announcements would appear regularly to warn of the dangers of "unsafe sex" in spreading AIDS and tout condoms as a means of preventing AIDS; and (c) some radio and television stations would eventually accept paid advertising for condoms, without even a whimper from the Federal Communications Commission? All three of the major commercial networks—ABC, CBS and NBC—

have continued to reject brand-name commercials for condoms, although they regularly air the free public service announcements.[76] But some over-the-air and cable TV stations have broadcast brand-name commercials, including two "whimsical" ones by condom manufacturer, Ansell-Americas. In the first, the Phantom of the Opera, complete with mask and cape, is told by a clerk in a drugstore that he does not need to wear a mask when purchasing condoms. In the second, Robin Hood asks the clerk for Lifestyle condoms for his Merry Men and is told, "You buy the same brand as the Sheriff of Nottingham."[77]

Lawyer Advertising Part III: *Zauderer, Shapero* and *Peel*

Unlike most professionals, such as physicians and pharmacists, lawyers have continued to test the First Amendment limits of advertising. Three cases in the last decade particularly stand out because lawyers in each went considerably beyond the guidelines or rules established by their bar associations and yet found constitutional protection in the U.S. Supreme Court. In the first case, *Zauderer v. Office of Disciplinary Counsel* (1985),[78] a Columbus, Ohio, attorney named Philip Q. Zauderer violated the Ohio Disciplinary Rules governing attorneys when he ran a newspaper advertisement that indicated he was willing to handle cases on a contingent fee basis involving women who had been injured by an intra-uterine contraceptive device known as the Dalkon Shield. The ad included an illustration of the device and claimed that no fees would be owed by the client unless she won damages. Both the illustration and the "no fees" assertion were in clear violation of the Ohio rules. The top part of the ad in bold type with all capital letters said: "DID YOU USE THIS IUD?" Along the side was the line-drawing of the Dalkon shield. The ad also noted, "Our law firm is presently representing women on such cases."

Zauderer was disciplined by the Ohio Office of Disciplinary Counsel for the ad on the grounds that he was soliciting business, had engaged in deceptive advertising and had included a drawing in the ad. The Ohio Supreme Court upheld the state's disciplinary action, but the U.S. Supreme Court in a 5–3 decision held that the Ohio rule regarding solicitation was a violation of the First Amendment. The majority opinion, written by Justice Byron R. White, said the rule was overly broad because it applied to all forms of such advertising — deceptive and nondeceptive. According to the Court: "were we to accept the State's argument in this case [that such solicitations are inherently misleading and therefore subject to the ban], we would have little basis for preventing the Government from suppressing other forms of truthful and nondeceptive advertising simply to spare itself the trouble of distinguishing such advertising from false or deceptive advertising."[79]

All eight of the justices voting found that the ban on illustrations was unconstitutional, although six of them agreed that Zauderer could be disciplined for his claim that "no fees would be owed by the client" because he failed to disclose that the client could be held responsible for court costs. While most states permit attorneys to represent clients at no charge and indeed encourage them to act *pro bono* for indigent individuals, courts and state codes of professional conduct generally do not permit attorneys to pay court costs for clients, although courts usually have the discretion of waiving such costs when warranted. Ohio rules required full disclosure of information regarding contingency fees, and this was constitutionally sound, according to the U.S. Supreme Court.

Zauderer basically stands for the principle that attorneys and, presumably, other professionals can engage in traditional forms of advertising and promotion so long as such commercial speech is neither misleading nor deceptive. The next case sent shock waves through some legal circles because it appears to have opened the door to a wide variety of advertising. The decision is particularly significant because it answered a major question that remained after *Ohralik*, *Bates*, and *Zauderer*: **Do attorneys have a First Amendment right to solicit clients via direct mail?**

A Kentucky attorney, Richard D. Shapero, requested the Attorneys Advertising Commission, a three-member body created by the Kentucky Supreme Court "to aid lawyers to ethically advertise and to protect the public,"[80] to approve a letter he wished to send to potential clients believed to be facing foreclosure on their home mortgages. The proposed letter urged the recipient to "call my office . . . for FREE information on how you can keep your home. Call NOW, don't wait. It may surprise you what I may be able to do for you" (capital letters in the original). Under the Kentucky Rules of the Supreme Court at that time, attorneys were banned from sending letters or advertisements to potential clients who might need legal assistance because of a change of circumstances such as a divorce, death in the family or foreclosure. Thus the commission rejected Shapero's letter as a direct solicitation in violation of the state supreme court rules. Shapero appealed the decision to the state supreme court, which ruled against him, but the U.S. Supreme Court ruled 6–3 in *Shapero v. Kentucky Bar Association*[81] that the Kentucky rule was a violation of the First and Fourteenth Amendments because it imposed a blanket ban on both deceptive and nondeceptive advertising through the mail. The state had argued that the prohibition was necessary to prevent lawyers from exerting undue influence or abusing individuals by taking advantage of potential clients facing serious legal problems. The majority opinion, written by Justice William H. Brennan, Jr., contended, as the Court did in *Youngs Drug Products*, that the potential for undue influence and fraud was significantly less than that of in-person solicitation, which the Court had held in *Ohralik* could be barred. The "File 13" proposition comes into play once again: If you don't like what you receive in the mail, throw it in the trash. Or, as Justice Brennan said, "Unlike the potential client with a badgering advocate breathing down his neck, the recipient of a letter and the reader of an advertisement can effectively avoid further bombardment of his sensibilities simply by averting his eyes."[82]

Attorney Shapero, by the way, continued to attract controversy. A year later he became the host of a 6–7 P.M., weekly call-in show on a Louisville, Kentucky AM radio station. "Shapero at Law" was criticized by the *Louisville Courier-Journal* for allegedly airing inaccurate information, but the president-elect of the Kentucky Bar Association (KBA) and the Chief Justice of the Kentucky Supreme Court refused to criticize Shapero's show even though the KBA and the Court were targets of the colorful lawyer's comments.[83]

At the time of the *Shapero* decision, about half of the states permitted solicitation by mail. Now such attorney advertising, so long as it is not deceptive nor misleading, is permitted in all states. The Kentucky Supreme Court, for example, revised its rules to delete this type of advertising as a violation, but still prohibits advertising that "contains a misrepresentation of fact or law . . . [i]s likely to create an unjustified expectation about results the attorney can achieve . . . [or] compares the attorney's services with another attorney's services, unless the comparison can be factually substantiated."[84] Most states, like Kentucky, permit attorneys to include a variety of types of information in an advertisement — including fields of practice, membership and offices in legal fraternities and legal societies, foreign language ability, names and addresses of bank references and contingent fee and hourly rates.[85]

In 1990 another barrier to certain types of lawyer advertising fell when the U.S. Supreme Court held in *Peel v. Attorney Registration and Disciplinary Commission of Illinois*[86] that attorneys have a First Amendment right to advertise specialties certified by private or nonbar organizations. The case began when attorney Gary Peel sent a letter to two clients. Peel's letterhead included the statement, "Certified Civil Trial Specialist by the National Board of Trial Advocacy." The information had appeared on his letterhead for three years with no complaints, but the administrative agency of the Illinois Supreme Court, the Attorney Registration and Disciplinary Commission (ARDC), filed a formal complaint against Peel for violating the state Code of Professional Responsibility. According to the code, "A lawyer shall not hold himself out publicly as a specialist, except as follows: patent lawyer, trademark lawyer, admiralty lawyer." After a hearing, the ARDC ruled that the attorney had acted improperly and recommended public censure. On appeal, the Illinois Supreme Court upheld the commission's findings, contending that the information on the letterhead was misleading to the public because of the similarity between "licensed" and "certified." The state supreme court also felt the public could wrongly believe that the attorney "may practice in the field of trial dvocacy solely because he is certified by the NBTA."

To be certified by the organization, a lawyer must have at least five years of civil trial practice and have been lead counsel in at least 15 civil cases. The lawyer must then pass a full-day exam. Approximately 1,200 attorneys have been certified by the group.[87]

In a 5–4 decision authored by Justice John Paul Stevens (joined by Justices Brennan, Blackmun and Kennedy, with Justices Marshall and Brennan concurring separately), the U.S. Supreme Court rejected the state's contention that the letterhead was deceptive. Citing *In Re R*____ M. J____ , discussed earlier, the majority said the claim of certification was information from which "a consumer may or may not draw an inference of the likely quality of an attorney's work in a given area of practice." Thus it was not automatically deceptive nor misleading. The Court chided the state for its "paternalistic" rule, noting that this information was essentially no different than the assertion "Practice before: the United States Supreme Court" approved in In Re R____ M. J____ . The majority compared the certification claim to that of a trademark, noting that "the strength of certification is measured by the quality of the organization for which it stands." Further, the justices said that the disclosure of **more** information, which was the case here, rather than withholding information, as the state wanted to do, best serves the public interest by educating consumers. Justice Marshall, joined by Justice Brennan, concurred with the Court's judgement that the Illinois regulation was unconstitutional but asserted that the letterhead could be misleading. According to these members of the Court, the total ban went too far because there were less restrictive ways of accomplishing the same result.

Many attorneys, judges and bar associations continue to oppose most forms of lawyer advertising, but anyone who regularly watches commercial television has no doubt noticed a proliferation of attorney ads, many of which are as crass and bold as those for new and used cars. Even the conservative American Bar Association (ABA), which for a long time opposed most forms of lawyer advertising, has relented. It should be noted that the particular rule struck down in *Shapero* had been adopted by Kentucky from the ABA's Model Rules of Professional Conduct. (Most state bar associations have adopted these rules, usually with revisions, for their own attorneys.) Now the *ABA Journal* frequently carries articles on topics such as successful marketing, including appropriate advertising techniques, "Hawking Legal Services" and "Improving Your Firm's Profitability." The ABA Model Rules of Professional Conduct now permit many forms of advertising, including direct mail solicitations of the type challenged in *Shapero*.

The amount attorneys spend on advertising has continued to climb during the years since *Bates*, but some states, such as Texas, still cling to rather stringent rules on ads. In 1988, the year *Shapero* was decided, the State Bar of Texas permitted an attorney to advertise only the law firm's address, the range of legal services offered and prices.[88] According to a publication of the Yellow Pages Publishers Association, one Texas law firm was cited by the State Bar of Texas for violating its rules when it failed to mention the specific names of lawyers responsible for the areas of specialization cited in a Yellow Pages ad. The same publication notes, on the other hand, that a Florida attorney was apparently not in violation of that state's bar association rules (a version of the ABA Rules of Professional Conduct) when his quarter-page spread in the local Yellow Pages proclaimed: "NATIONALLY KNOWN ATTORNEY WITH GUEST APPEARANCES ON 'GOOD MORNING AMERICA,' 'GERALDO,' 'ALAN BURKE' & OTHER SHOWS."[89]

According to the *ABA Journal* polls, one-third of all lawyers advertised in some form in 1987, compared to only 24 percent 2 years earlier.[90] No doubt, the percentage is substantially higher today, probably approaching the one-half mark. Obviously, most advertising is in the form a simple ad in the local newspaper or Yellow Pages, but there are the Joel Hyatts (Hyatt Legal Services) of the world who spend considerable sums on television and radio commercials to make themselves salient to large audiences of potential clients. Edward Burke, vice president of the management consulting firm of Hilde-brandt Inc., recommends that law firms marketing their services spend 1 to 3 percent of their gross revenues for marketing.[91]

In spite of *Shapero*, many prominent jurists such as former U.S. Supreme Court Justice Lewis F. Powell, Jr., current Justice Sandra Day O'Connor and Chief Justice William H. Rehnquist continue to oppose most types of lawyer advertising. One of the most articulate advocates of greater restraint in lawyer ads is former Iowa Supreme Court Chief Justice W. Ward Reynoldson, who contends that "marketplace lawyer advertising, using all the sights, color, sounds, subliminal messages and not-so-hidden persuaders of commercial television, adversely affects not only the public's perception of those court officers [lawyers], but also of the courts and the judicial system."[92]

Lawyers continue to test the bounds of their First Amendment rights and more cases involving attorney advertising will undoubtedly reach the U.S. Supreme Court for years to come, as answers are sought to the many questions still lingering after *Shapero* and *Peel*. Are testimonials by satisfied clients permissible in ads? Can a state bar association require that lawyers include their name and address in all advertising? (The Appellate Division of the New York Supreme Court held in 1988 that such a restriction is not a violation of the First Amendment.[93]) Can the use of dramatic music, catchy slogans, premium offers, slapstick routines or unusual backgrounds be prohibited? Stay tuned . . .

BANNING TRUTHFUL COMMERCIAL SPEECH: *POSADAS DE PUERTO RICO ASSOCIATES V. TOURISM COMPANY OF PUERTO RICO* (1986)

A 5–4 decision in 1986, written by Justice William H. Rehnquist, struck what some legal scholars believe to be a serious blow to the idea that truthful commercial speech concerned with a legal product or service has First Amendment protection. In *Posadas de Puerto Rico Associates v. Tourism Company of Puerto Rico* (1986),[94] the Court applied the four-part *Central Hudson* test for commercial speech to find that a government's restrictions on advertising for legal gambling were **not** in violation of the First Amendment. While the Court had indicated since *Bigelow v. Virginia* in 1975 and up through *Bolger v. Youngs Drug Products* in 1983 that advertising for legal products and services that was not misleading nor deceptive had constitutional protection, *Posadas* appears to have squelched much of the progress made in those cases toward putting commercial speech on an equal constitutional footing with noncommercial communication. No matter how much one scrutinizes the reasoning in *Posadas*, it is difficult to square it with the three Bs — *Bigelow, Bates* and *Bolger*.

In 1948 the Puerto Rican government legalized most types of casino gambling in an effort to beef up its tourism industry. The effort paid off as tourists flocked to the commonwealth. The 1948 legislation also banned all advertising by casinos to the residents of Puerto Rico, although such advertising was permitted to be directed at the tourists within the commonwealth and in the continental United States. Puerto Rican citizens were allowed to use the casinos. A governmental agency, known as the Tourism Company of Puerto Rico, was granted the authority to administer the statute, including the advertising provisions. The Condado Holiday Inn, which was owned by Posadas de Puerto Rico Associates, defied the ban on advertising directed to Puerto Ricans and was fined on several occasions. The hotel consequently filed suit against the government agency, asking for a declaratory judgment that the advertising prohibition was unconstitutional. After the case traveled through the Puerto Rican judicial system, including a dismissal by the Puerto Rican Supreme Court for lack of a substantive constitutional issue, the U.S. Supreme Court granted a petition for a writ of certiorari. On the threshold question of whether the particular speech in question was commercial or noncommercial, the Court determined that the case involved "the restriction of pure commercial speech which does no more than propose a commercial transaction." The Court thus applied the *Central Hudson* analysis to find (a) the restriction "concerns a lawful activity and is not misleading or fraudulent, at least in the abstract"; (b) the "reduction in demand for casino gambling by the residents of Puerto Rico" that the government claimed was the result of the ban constituted the necessary substantial government interest; (c) the statute directly advanced the government's substantial interest because the legislature could reasonably believe that "advertising of casino gambling aimed at the residents . . . would serve to increase the demand for the product advertised"; and (d) the restrictions were "no more extensive than necessary to serve the government's interest."

The casino had argued (a) the statute was too restrictive because it allowed advertising for other types of gambling such as lotteries, horse racing and cockfighting; (b) the government could more effectively reduce the demand for casino gambling by promulgating speech designed to discourage gambling rather than suppressing speech that promoted this activity; (c) the activity involved here was similar to that in *Bigelow* and, therefore deserved the protection offered by that case; and (d) once the government legalized gambling, the First Amendment granted protection for advertising related to such activity.

The Court handily rejected all of the appellant's arguments and concluded that the prior restraint had passed the *Central Hudson* test and thus the advertising could make no claim of First Amendment protection.

How can the Court justify such severe restrictions on the advertising of a perfectly legitimate activity? Compare gambling with alcohol and tobacco, and you have some indication of the rationale used by the Court. The casino had argued that because the government had legalized gambling for both tourists and residents, *Bigelow* and its progeny would dictate that the First Amendment would prevent the government from imposing advertising restrictions that were specifically designed to discourage citizens from legal gambling. In other words, once an activity, product or service is legalized, the First Amendment says, "Hands off any advertising, unless it is deceptive or misleading." In strongly rejecting that argument, the Court said the argument should be turned on its head:

> It is precisely because the government could have enacted a wholesale prohibition of the underlying conduct that it is permissible for the government to take the less intrusive step of allowing the conduct, but reducing the demand through restrictions on advertising . . . would . . . be a strange constitutional doctrine which would concede to the legislature the authority to totally ban a product or activity, but deny to the legislature the authority to forbid the stimulation of demand for the product or activity through advertising. . . . Legislative regulation of product or activities deemed harmful, such as cigarettes, alcoholic beverages, and prostitution on the one hand . . . to legalization of the product or activity with restrictions on stimulation of its demand on the other hand.[95]

Justice William J. Brennan, Jr. (joined by Justices Thurgood Marshall and Harry A. Blackmun), contended in his dissent that the distinctions between commercial and noncommercial speech did not "justify protecting commercial speech less extensively where, as here, the government seeks to manipulate behavior by depriving citizens of truthful information concerning lawful activities."[96] According to Justice Brennan, even if the government had been able to demonstrate that a substantial interest was involved, there was no evidence that this particular regulation would address those interests. The dissenting opinion also argued that the government could have attempted to control the particular harms asserted, such as organized crime and prostitution, by keeping a tighter rein on the casinos themselves: "It is incumbent upon the government to prove that more limited means are not sufficient to protect its interests, and for a court to decide whether or not the government has sustained this burden."[97]

A close reading of the holding in *Posadas de Puerto Rico Associates* could appear to justify similar restrictions on the advertising of products such as tobacco and alcoholic beverages, items that the courts have consistently permitted to be regulated. In fact, anyone looking for a legal precedent to justify a ban on all cigarette or alcohol advertising probably needs to look no further than *Posadas*.

The fourth prong of the *Central Hudson Gas & Electric* four-part test has caused considerable confusion among the lower courts in interpreting the meaning of "more extensive than necessary." As discussed earlier, a court must ascertain whether a regulation is more extensive than necessary in advancing the substantial government interest when commercial speech is at stake. Three years after *Posadas*, the U.S. Supreme Court attempted to pinpoint the applicable standard but appeared to create more smoke than light. In *Board of Trustees of State University of New York v. Fox* (1989),[98] a university regulation banning private companies from sponsoring parties in student dormitories when housewares are being promoted was challenged on First Amendment grounds. The Second Circuit U.S. Court of Appeals, in overturning the rule, held that the standard for determining whether the regulation was no more extensive than necessary was that the state must use the "least restrictive measure" that could protect the state's interest. This holding, at first analysis, may appear to be in line with *Hudson* and even *Posadas* but, on appeal, the U.S. Supreme Court, in a 6–3 decision authored by Associate Justice Antonin Scalia, disagreed with the U.S. Court of Appeals and remanded the case back to the lower court for further findings.

According to the majority opinion, the appropriate standard for determining whether the regulation is more extensive than necessary dictates that the restrictions must be "narrowly drawn" and "no more extensive than reasonably necessary" to further the substantial government interest. The Court noted that even for political speech, the "least restrictive measure" test had not been applied in determining the constitutionality of reasonable time, place and manner restrictions but instead the test has been whether the regulations are "narrowly tailored" to promote a significant state interest. The Court also noted that a similar test has been applied in determining the validity of restrictions on expressive conduct, including that in a political context. Thus, the Court reasoned, it would be inappropriate "to apply a more rigid standard" for commercial speech than for other forms of speech that presumably had greater protection. Or, as the Court said, "We think it would be incompatible," given the "subordinate position" of commercial speech "to apply a more rigid standard in the present context."

How should this test be applied? The state is not required to demonstrate that "the manner of restriction is absolutely the least severe that will achieve the desired end," but a balance, or "fit" as the Court called it, must be found between the asserted governmental interest and the approach taken to accomplish that interest —

> a fit that is not necessarily perfect, but reasonable; that represents not necessarily the single best disposition but one whose scope is in "proportion to the interest served" . . .; that employs not necessarily the least restrictive means but a means narrowly tailored to achieve the desired objective. Within those bounds we leave it to the governmental decisionmakers to judge what manner of regulation may be best employed.[99]

Whereas to the untrained observer, this case would appear to involve more semantics than real distinctions, the fact is that the holding represents a significant retreat from the standard that many courts, including the Second Circuit U.S. Court of Appeals, believed applied in commercial speech cases in light of *Central Hudson Gas & Electric*. No doubt it will be much more difficult for governmental restrictions on commercial speech, including advertising, to be struck down as unconstitutional, and thus we can expect a wave of new forms of restrictions that will have to be tested in the courts. History has shown that when a First Amendment standard is relaxed, as was the case here, the government is usually ready to step in and assert its broadened authority to regulate speech. We can expect to see renewed clashes between the commercial speech activists and legislators.

The Court did not rule on the constitutionality of the university regulation but instead remanded the case back to the trial court for a determination. Thus the restrictions could still be struck down but a balancing test would be performed, using the relaxed standard enunciated by the Court.

In mid-1993 the U.S. Supreme Court issued two commercial speech decisions — the first involving commercial handbills and the second concerning telephone sales. In *Cincinnati v. Discovery Network*,[100] the Court held 6–3 that the Ohio city's ordinance barring the distribution of commercial handbills in newsracks violated the First Amendment because it was content-based since the law imposed no such restrictions on traditional newspapers. In *Hall v. Minnesota*, however, the Court upheld a state ban on automatically dialed telephone sales calls. The majority ruled that such calls did not constitute protected commercial speech.

THE FEDERAL TRADE COMMISSION AND OTHER FEDERAL AGENCIES

The Federal Trade Commission (FTC) has had a controversial and colorful history, marred by battles with Congress, the executive branch, consumer advocates, advertisers and even within the commission itself, but it has survived, albeit in a substantially different form than when it was created by Congress in 1914. The Federal Trade Commission Act of 1914 specifically stated: "Unfair methods of competition in commerce are hereby declared unlawful. The commission [FTC] is hereby empowered and directed to prevent persons, partnerships, or corporations, except banks and common carriers subject to the Acts to regulate commerce, from using unfair methods of competition in commerce."[101]

Thus the mandate was for the commission to prevent unfair methods of competition, not to regulate practices that may harm consumers but would otherwise not affect competition. Most legislation in Congress involves compromises among various interests, and the FTC Act was no exception. Because the U.S Supreme Court had taken an active role in regulating business with several major decisions on business practices during the early 20th century, advocates on both sides of the regulation coin preferred that a quasi-legislative body or federal agency do the regulating. Both big business, which wanted the trend toward greater monopolization to continue, and antitrust advocates, who pushed for reforms to prevent trade restraint practices, were fearful of the consequences of the courts, most notably the Supreme Court, intervening in business. Businesses, of course, were concerned that certain traditional business practices would be restrained or prohibited, whereas antitrust supporters believed the Court would condone or at least refuse to ban anticompetitive trade actions. Thus both sides lobbied for a federal agency to administer antitrust laws. Unlike today, no consumer activist groups were involved in the lobbying efforts; it was decades later before any consumer movement made enough headway to attract the attention of the legislators in Washington, DC.

At the same time the FTC Act of 1914 was enacted, Congress also passed the Clayton Antitrust Act,[102] which banned price discrimination, exclusive sales contracts, corporate mergers, intercorporate stock and other practices whose effect was to significantly decrease competition or to create a monopoly. The Clayton Act was actually an amendment to the Sherman Antitrust Act of 1890,[103] which prohibited any unreasonable interference in interstate and foreign trade, whether by contract and/or conspiracy. The last major revision of the Clayton Act was the 1936 Robinson-Patman Act,[104] discussed later, which substantially strengthened the Clayton Act by providing severe criminal penalties for businesses that directly or indirectly discriminate in the pricing of similar goods when the impact is to harm competition. It is important to keep this historical background in mind while reviewing FTC regulations on advertising today because the commission's actions must be evaluated against the backdrop of the 1914 act that created the agency.

The FTC and Deceptive Advertising

The Federal Trade Commission wasted no time after it was created in attacking advertising it deemed deceptive. In 1916 the FTC issued cease and desist orders against two companies, both of which advertised clothing as made of silk when they were actually made of cotton and other materials.[105] Both companies were charged with engaging in deceptive advertising that resulted in harm either to silk manufacturers or to the silk trade in general. Even though the FTC Act makes no mention of deceptive advertising per se, the commission apparently assumed it had the authority to ban such advertising. How could the FTC subsume this power? The agency simply characterized deceptive advertising as unfair competition. It was inevitable, however, given the blatant abuses of advertising ethics in the early part of this century, that the commission would be forced to crack down on deceptive and fraudulent advertising without regard to its effect on the marketplace.

In 1922, the U.S. Supreme Court for the first time found that the FTC had the authority under the 1914 act to directly regulate deceptive ads as an unfair means of competition. In *FTC v. Winstead Hosiery*,[106] the Court upheld a commission ruling that marketing 10 percent wool underwear as "Natural Wool" and "Natural Worsted" constituted deceptive advertising. The majority opinion, written by Justice William Brandeis, reasoned that deceptive advertising is unfair competition because it wrongly attracts consumers who would otherwise purchase from manufacturers who do not use unethical advertising. There was an assumption that consumers cannot be expected to distinguish dishonest advertising from honest advertising and thereby may succumb to the wiles of the deceptive entrepreneur.

By 1930 regulating false and misleading advertising had become the major portion of the commission's work as advertising grew by leaps and bounds and the marketplace became more confusing for consumers. This was also a time when advertising agencies burgeoned to handle the marketing demand. In 1931, the FTC suffered what initially appeared to be a major setback in its regulatory efforts when the U.S. Supreme Court ruled unanimously in *FTC v. Raladam Co.*[107] that "unfair trade methods are not *per se* unfair methods of competition." Thus, the Court effectively held that false and deceptive advertising must be demonstrated to harm the marketplace (such as injuring a competitor). Raladam had advertised a cure for obesity that it claimed was safe, effective and convenient. The commission discounted those claims and sought to ban the advertising but made no assertion on appeal that the advertising had been anticompetitive.[108]

The Wheeler-Lea Amendments (1938): Regulating Unfair and Deceptive Practices

Any setback to the commission's ability to crack down on deceptive ads was only temporary—the FTC quickly began finding that such advertising was unfair competition and in 1938 Congress gave the agency a major boost with the passage of the so-called Wheeler-Lea Amendments.[109] These amendments to the 1914 FTC Act granted the commission broad authority over advertising by permitting it to ban "unfair or deceptive acts or practices in commerce." In 1975 the FTC Act was revised to include "unfair or deceptive acts or practices in or affecting commerce."[110] The 1938 amendments were enacted at a time when there was great public concern over abuses in the marketplace, including the tragic deaths that same year of 100 people who had taken a medication known as elixir sulfanilamide. The drug had been marketed by the Massengill Company without testing. In 1938 Congress also enacted the Food, Drug and Cosmetic Act that created the Food and Drug Administration (FDA), which still regulates much of the advertising for drugs, cosmetics and similar consumer products.

FTC Composition and Structure

Like other quasi-legislative, quasi-judicial federal agencies such as the Federal Communications Commission and the FDA, the Federal Trade Commission is an independent regulatory agency created by Congress under the authority granted in the Constitution under the federal preemption doctrine, discussed earlier. At the present time, there are five commissioners appointed by the President with consent of the Senate for staggered, renewable 7-year terms. The President also designates which member of the five will serve as chair. No more than three commissioners can serve from the same political party. The tradition has been that Presidents appoint the maximum (three) from their political party and then fill any other vacancies from the other political party with individuals whose views are similar to those of their own. The FTC, however, is much more than the commissioners who play the major role in policy- and rulemaking. There are three bureaus—Competition, Consumer Protection and Economics—staffed by some 1,200 employees. The Advertising Practices Division of the Bureau of Consumer Protection oversees:

1. Deceptive advertising in general for consumer products, especially claims about safety or performance.
2. Advertising for food and over-the-counter (OTC) drugs, particularly claims about nutritional benefits, safety and effectiveness.
3. Tobacco advertising, including enforcement of the federal cigarette and smokeless tobacco labeling statutes.

4. Performance and energy-saving claims for energy conservation products such as furnaces, room heaters and gas-saving products.
5. Environmental performance claims in ads for consumer products, such as assertions that they are environmentally safe, ozone-friendly or biodegradable.
6. Ads for diet products, including weight loss claims.
7. Program-length ads, popularly known as "infommercials."[111]

Informercials, which frequently appear on late-night cable television touting everything from cosmetics to miracle car polishes, are 30-minute to 60-minute commercials that can be easily be mistaken for talk shows because of their format, including a host and a live audience. Since the Federal Communications Commission lifted its limits in 1984 on the percentage of broadcast time that can be devoted to commercials, this form of advertising has flourished. A new twist to this format, which the FTC monitors to insure is not deceptive, is the "sitcommercial," launched in 1992 by Bell Atlantic Corporation on Baltimore, Maryland, television stations.[112] *The Ringers* is a half-hour situation comedy commercial featuring a family whose life focuses on the phone, including pitches for three-way calling, call waiting, speed calling, return calling and other services offered by Bell Atlantic.

Other FTC divisions in the Consumer Protection Bureau include *Credit Practices* (regulates unfair or deceptive acts or practices involving consumer credit and enforces various consumer protection statutes and rules), *Marketing Practices* (enforces laws against unfair or deceptive marketing and warranty practices from pyramid sales schemes to vacation timesharing), *Service Industry Practices* (regulates advertising of professional services such as eye care, legal services and health care and monitors investment schemes) and *Enforcement* (ensures compliance with FTC orders and enforces various trade regulation rules and statutes).[113]

FTC headquarters are at Pennsylvania Avenue in Washington, DC, but there are regional offices in Atlanta, Boston, Chicago, Cleveland, Dallas, Denver, Los Angeles, New York, San Francisco, and Seattle. The sizes of the staffs of these offices are relatively small compared to the main office, but each regional office usually handles thousands of complaints each year and can initiate investigations that can ultimately lead to a full-scale investigation by the national office.

FTC Modes of Regulation: Investigations

The Federal Trade Commission has a wide range of legal options in its regulation and enforcement activities. The most common are: *investigations, consent decrees, trade regulation rules, assurance of voluntary compliance, cease and desist order*, and *civil and criminal penalties*.

Investigations are a particularly important tool for FTC enforcement. Contrary to popular opinion, the FTC and other similar federal agencies do not need hundreds or thousands of complaints about a company or practice before the commission can take action. In fact, the FTC does not need even a single complaint but can instead begin an investigation based solely on information from a news story, a congressional inquiry or some other credible source. When the agency decides to conduct the investigation, it will first determine whether to publicly announce its intentions or to conduct its work in private. Typically, the FTC makes a public announcement when an entire industry is being investigated but keeps such efforts private when an individual company is involved.[114]

Most investigations are initiated by FTC regulatory staff members without formally seeking approval of the full commission, which concentrates its efforts on policy-making and major enforcement activities. Because of its rather limited resources, the FTC tends to follow the "Squeaky wheel gets the grease" principle—the most flagrant abuses get the most attention. Most investigations die at an early stage but those that survive often take considerable time. If an investigation reveals unfair and deceptive practices by an individual or industry, the staff can then recommend that the full commission take action. The most serious type of initial action is a formal hearing before an administrative law judge (ALJ), as discussed in Chapter 2. The ALJ conducts the hearing under formalized procedures similar to those in a court of law with each side given an opportunity to present its case following formal rules of evidence and rules of administrative procedure. The judge's decision can be appealed to the full commission, which can exercise its discretion in the matter by rejecting the appeal or ordering a hearing. If the defendant loses and does not appeal to the full commission, the FTC can take appropriate legal action such as a cease and desist order, fines or even criminal prosecution. The commission can always overrule the ALJ decision, of course. If a defendant's appeal is rejected by the full commission or if the full commission, after a hearing, rules against the defendant, the defendant can then appeal the decision to the U.S. Court of Appeals for the District of Columbia Circuit.

Cease and Desist Orders

A *cease and desist order* (CDO) issued by the FTC is legally enforceable and prohibits the individual or company from committing the particular act against which the order has been issued. A 1944 FTC case illustrates how this order works. From 1934 to 1939, Charles of the Ritz Distributing Corporation marketed a line of cosmetics, including a Rejuvenescence Cream with sales of about $1 million. In an extensive national advertising campaign, the company claimed the cream contained "a vital organic ingredient" and "essences and compounds" that "restores natural moisture necessary for a live, healthy skin."

The ad also said, "Your face need know no drought years" and that the cream gives the skin "a bloom which is wonderfully rejuvenating" and is "constantly active in keeping your skin clear, radiant, and young looking."[115] In light of some of the hype and puffery that bombards us today in advertising, these claims may seem mild by comparison. But the FTC ruled, after a hearing, that the advertising was false and deceptive. It issued a CDO prohibiting Charles of the Ritz from using the word *Rejuvenescence* or similar terms to describe its cosmetics in any advertising and from representing in any ads that the cream would rejuvenate the skin or restore youth or the appearance of youth to the skin. The company appealed the order, but the U.S. Circuit Court of Appeals upheld the FTC order.

A cease and desist order is clearly prior restraint, but the courts have consistently permitted the FTC and other federal agencies to issue such orders so long as a fair hearing is conducted. CDOs are powerful weapons in the FTC arsenal, but they are often time-consuming and expensive. Thus the commission usually attempts other forms of enforcement whenever feasible. Two common alternative approaches are *assurance of voluntary compliance* (AVC) and *consent decree*.

Assurance of Voluntary Compliance

An *assurance of voluntary compliance* is a relatively painless way of settling disputes over advertising in which the commission believes the company's claims have been deceptive or misleading. If the advertising appears to be fraudulent, it is highly unlikely that the FTC will seek an AVC because of the seriousness of the offense. The AVC process is quite simple. The agency staff conducts its usual investigation, which may be brief or protracted. If the evidence points toward deception but it appears that little or no harm has occurred to consumers or competitors, the FTC may opt to negotiate a settlement with the advertiser under which the company would agree to immediately halt further advertising of the type in dispute in return for the agreement by the FTC not to pursue the case further, assuming no other violations appear. If the advertiser agrees to the terms, the FTC presents an affidavit to its legal representative to sign that assures the ads will be halted voluntarily. The AVC is merely an agreement, not an order, so the company could not be cited for contempt for violating it, although a violation could be grounds for the FTC to reopen the investigation or to pursue other legal remedies such as a CDO.

Consent Decree

A stronger approach, but short of a CDO, is the *consent decree*. By far, the majority of cases decided by the FTC after an investigation result in a consent decree. The procedure is somewhat more complicated than an AVC but it is very effective. First, the FTC staff conducts its investigation. If the staff determines that the advertising is indeed deceptive or misleading, a recommendation is made that formal proceeding be initiated that could eventually lead to a CDO or even suit in federal court. A formal complaint is written and delivered to the alleged offender, along with the required notice that the FTC plans to conduct formal proceedings. The materials also include a CDO and a consent agreement that the advertiser has 10 days to sign or face a formal hearing. Most companies facing this dilemma sign on the dotted line because fighting such accusations can be extremely time consuming and expensive. In a consent decree, the company agrees to kill the particular ads but does **not** admit guilt of any type. It is not unusual, in fact, for the FTC and the company in their public relations releases and announcement to both emphasize that the consent decree does not imply or indicate that the advertiser has been guilty of any violations but merely that the parties have agreed that the advertising in question has ended.

The consent decree, however, differs substantially from an AVC in one regard: It has the same legal effect as an order and thus can be enforced under a threat of contempt. Failure to comply will almost certainly subject the company to a formal hearing and possible fines and other legal sanctions. Thus is it very rare when a company defies a consent decree. The risks of prosecution are simply too high.

As an administrative agency, the Federal Trade Commission has the authority to seek preliminary or permanent injunctions whenever it appears that a particular practice could cause immediate and irreparable harm to the public or to another business. In the latter case, however, the harmed business is more likely to seek the injunction in court on its own rather than indirectly through the FTC because the indirect route can take considerable time. Usually, the FTC will go the CDO or consent decree route rather than seek an injunction because the former techniques are quite effective in halting deceptive and misleading advertising.

Trade Regulation Rules

Although much of the enforcement by the FTC is conducted on a case-by-case basis, there are instances in which enforcement is better served by what are often called nonadjudicatory procedures. The most common of these is the *Trade Regulation Rule* (TRR). TRRs provide specific prohibitions on certain practices that are binding on all businesses for whom the rule was designed. Any violation of a TRR can be grounds for an unfair or deceptive act or practice that can subject the offender to civil and even criminal penalties. Although the commission first promulgated TRRs in 1962, its first major and certainly controversial TRR was a requirement in 1964 that all cigarette packaging carry a health warning. That TRR was followed 5 years later by a requirement that octane ratings be posted on all gasoline pumps. A number of other TRRs have been proposed by the FTC over the years, some of which were eventually promulgated but others died or were substantially weakened by the time the rule-making process, as described later, was complete.

In 1975 Congress considerably expanded the commission's authority to issue broad TRRs to prohibit unfair and deceptive practices. The Magnuson-Moss Warranty-Federal Trade Commission Improvement Act,[116] which was enacted in response to the active consumer movement of the late 1960s and early 1970s, also delegated authority to the FTC to even regulate local and state business activities "affecting interstate commerce." This power extends to the issuance of TRRs against local and state businesses.

The following are some of the surviving Trade Regulation Rules that have a direct or indirect impact on advertising:

1. *Appliance Labeling* — requires disclosure of energy costs of home appliances.
2. *Games of Chance in the Food Retailing and Gasoline Industries* — requires disclosure of the odds of winning prizes, the random distribution of the winning prize pieces and publication of the winners' names.
3. *The Retail Food Store Advertising and Marketing Practices Rule*, as amended — requires advertised items to be available for sale unless the store notes in the ad that supplies are limited or the store offers a rain check.
4. *R-value* — requires sellers to disclose the thermal efficiency of home insulation.[117]

Some proposed FTC Trade Regulation Rules have brought considerable fire from the industries to be affected and political pressures from Congress. The most notable of these is the commission's recommendation in the late 1970s that all television advertising directed toward children be prohibited. Although this proposal and the ensuing battle among the commercial TV executives, television critics and Congress are discussed in the next chapter, it should be noted that Congress responded to the flak it received from the industry by enacting the Federal Trade Commission Improvement Act in 1980,[118] which considerably expanded the sanctions available for violation of FTC rules and orders and broadened the civil remedies available to the courts in cases brought by the commission **but**, at the same time, specifically barred the FTC from enacting any TRRs directed at children's TV commercials. The act also limited the FTC's use of funding for consumer groups in FTC cases and required the commission to consider costs versus benefits before issuing rules.[119] The act now requires that the FTC enact TRRs only when there is a pattern of deceptiveness evident in the industry, not simply on the basis that the advertising may be unfair. Certainly the most telling provision of the act was that creating a legislative veto of any FTC rule if within 90 days of issuance of the rule, both houses of Congress vote against the rule. This legislative veto power was ruled unconstitutional by the U.S. Supreme Court in *Immigration and Naturalization Service v. Chadha* (1980)[120] and thus no longer affects the FTC nor other similar federal agencies.

The Issuance of Trade Regulation Rules

How are Trade Regulation Rules issued? First, the FTC conducts an investigation of trade practices within that particular industry. If the staff uncovers evidence of unfair or deceptive practices, such as misleading advertising, the commission can formally initiate the rule-making proceeding. Second, the staff writes a proposed trade regulation rule that is then reviewed by the full commission, which may accept it as is, modify it or kill it altogether. Third, if a proposed rule is approved for *further consideration* (**not for enactment**), a notice is published in the *Federal Register* indicating that a hearing is to be conducted on the proposal and giving the time and location of the hearing. The notice will also indicate the issues to be considered, provide instructions for groups and individual consumers on how to participate and reprint the text of the proposed rule. Fourth, a hearing or series of hearings is conducted. Not all of the hearings need to be held in Washington; some may take place at any of the FTC regional offices. All formal hearings are open to the public and the press representatives of consumer groups, as well as individual citizens, are typically permitted to testify at the hearings. Anyone may file written comments with the commission for consideration along with all of the evidence presented at the hearings, staff reports and the Presiding Officer's report (usually a member of the FTC staff versed in administrative procedures). Under the rules of the 1975 Federal Trade Commission Act, still in effect, if there are disputed issues of material fact, the commission must permit cross-examination of individuals whom the FTC believes to be appropriate and necessary for a full disclosure of the facts.[121]

As mentioned earlier, the full commission then votes on whether to implement the rule as is, to modify it or to reject it. If it chooses to modify or accept it as is, affected consumers and businesses have the right to appeal the commission's decision in any appropriate U.S. Court of Appeals, including the DC Circuit, but the appeal must be filed within 60 days from the time the rule takes effect.

Advisory Opinions

Other nonadjudicatory procedures used by the FTC are *advisory opinions*, *industry guides*, and *consumer education*. Whereas most state courts and all federal courts are prohibited from issuing advisory opinions, most state and federal agencies, including the FTC, routinely issue such opinions. One of the key limits on FTC advisory opinions is that they can be issued only for contemplated actions, not for actions already taken. For example, if a dog food manufacturer wanted to know if it could advertise and market a new line of dog food as "Premium Lite" that contains 15 percent fewer calories than its regular "Premium," it would ask for an advisory opinion so any potential litigation could be avoided. The company would file a written request with the commission describing the advertising under consideration. The FTC legal staff would then review the letter and issue an opinion based on current FTC policy, rules and regulations. All such advisory opinions become public record and can be used by other advertisers in similar situations. If the advertiser follows the advice in good faith, it cannot be sued by the the FTC unless the FTC enacts new rules, which would, of course, require public notice in the *Federal Register*, or the commission decides to rescind its approval, which requires written notification to the party.

The FTC will not issue advisory opinions when substantially similar action is already part of an official proceeding conducted by the FTC or other agency, when there is an ongoing investigation in that area or if issuing an opinion would necessitate lengthy investigation, research or testing.[122]

Industry Guides

While advisory opinions are geared primarily toward individual businesses and corporations, *industry guides* are intended to regulate practices of entire industries. For example, the FTC has issued industry guides for the advertising of gold and silver jewelry, watches and precious gems and for the labeling and advertising of feather and down products such as pillows, comforters and wearing apparel. Dozens of these often complex and detailed guides have been issued in recent years for products and services from eyeglasses to health care services. According to the FTC rules, industry guides are "administrative interpretations of laws administered by the commission for the guidance of the public in conducting its affairs in conformity with legal requirements."[123] Any business that violates an industry guide faces potential litigation because failure to comply is evidence of unfair or deceptive trade practices.

Consumer Education

Consumer education has been the least controversial of the FTC's non-administrative functions because these efforts rarely single out a particular business or industry for criticism except when very blatant violations are involved. The FTC publishes a wide variety of materials and makes use of press releases, interviews, press conferences and other public relations techniques to reach consumers. The commission regularly issues a two- to four-page leaflet entitled "Facts for Consumers" and dozens of free and inexpensive booklets for consumers and for business. Topics in "Facts for Consumers" have included program-length TV commercials, vehicle repossession and lawn service contracts. Other publications discuss "Car Ads: Low Interest Loans and Other Offers," "Using Ads to Shop for Home Financing" and "Health Claims: Separating Fact from Fiction." Those oriented toward business include "How to Advertise Consumer Credit" and "Offering Layaways." One booklet is directed at young adults — "Using Plastic: A Young Adult's Guide to Credit Cards."

The FTC is responsible not only for enforcing its own rules but for also enforcing specific consumer protection statutes through which Congress has delegated its authority to the FTC. These include a broad range of federal laws from the Hobby Protection Act (which requires imitation coins, medals and similar items be clearly marked "copy" and imitation political items be marked with the year of manufacture) to the Magnuson-Moss Warranty Act of 1975,[124] which requires manufacturers and sellers to disclose specific kinds of warranty information to potential purchasers before they buy consumer products included under the act.

Corrective Advertising

Prohibiting misleading and deceptive advertising is one important way of protecting consumers and presumably ensuring fair competition, but outright bans are not always effective or appropriate. Requiring affirmative disclosure can sometimes be a more effective remedy. Although the original FTC act and its subsequent revisions make no mention of affirmative disclosure, which usually comes in the form of *corrective advertising*, the federal courts have generally upheld the right of the FTC to impose such requirements on advertisers. As the cases attest, some of the largest corporations have been forced by the commission over the years to modify their advertising to include corrective statements. For example, the Warner-Lambert Company was ordered by the FTC in 1975 to clearly and conspicuously disclose in its next $10 million of advertising for Listerine Antiseptic mouthwash: "Contrary to prior advertising, Listerine will not help prevent colds or sore throats or lessen their severity." Listerine had claimed in its advertising that it could prevent, cure or alleviate the common cold. On appeal, the U.S. Court of Appeals for the DC Circuit held in 1977 in *Warner-Lambert v. FTC*[125] that the commission did "have the power to issue corrective advertising in appropriate cases" but that the preamble, "Contrary to prior advertising," was unwarranted, given the facts in the case. Thus for the next several years, all Listerine print ads and radio and television commercials carried the disclaimer, "Listerine will not help prevent colds or sore throats or lessen their severity." The FTC complaint against Warner-Lambert was initially filed in 1972 even though Listerine had advertised since 1921 that it would help colds. After 4 months of hearings at which some 4,000 pages of documents were produced and 46 witnesses testified before an administrative law judge, the ALJ ruled against Warner-Lambert. The company appealed to the full FTC, which basically affirmed the ALJ's decision in 1975. During the next 2 years, Listerine continued to make the claims until the U.S. Court of Appeals upheld the commission's decision with the modification just discussed and the U.S. Supreme Court denied certiorari in 1978.[126] Thus Listerine was able to make these presumably false assertions for 57 years, including 6 years after the complaint was filed.

The first successful attempt by the FTC to impose an order for corrective advertising came in 1971,[127] the year before the complaint against Listerine was filed. The ITT Continental Baking Company had advertised that Profile Bread could help reduce weight because it contained fewer calories than other similar brands of bread when, in fact, the bread was sliced somewhat thinner than normal and contained only seven fewer calories per slice than "ordinary" bread. ITT was ordered to spend at least 25 percent of its advertising budget for the following year indicating in its ads that Profile Bread contained only seven fewer calories than other breads and that this difference would not cause a significant weight reduction.

Other successful FTC efforts to require corrective advertising include Ocean Spray Cranberries, which agreed in 1972 after an FTC complaint to spend 25 percent of its ad budget for a year informing the public that the term *food energy*, which was used in previous ads, referred to calories rather than vitamins and minerals.[128] On rare occasions, the FTC is rebuffed in its push for corrective advertising; for example, in 1978 the U.S. Court of Appeals for the Seventh Circuit held that an egg industry group, the National Commission on Egg Nutrition (NCEN), could not be forced to carry in any future advertising or public statements that concerned the relationship between egg consumption and heart and circulatory disease that "many medical experts believe increased consumption of dietary cholesterol, including that in eggs, may increase the risk of heart disease."[129] The NCEN, in response to what the FTC described as "anticholesterol attacks on eggs which had resulted in steadily declining per capita egg consumption,"[130] mounted an advertising and public relations counterattack claiming that eggs are harmless and are necessary for human nutrition. For example, some of the advertising asserted that eating eggs does not increase blood cholesterol in a normal person and there is no scientific evidence that egg consumption increases the risk of heart and circulatory disease. The FTC ordered the NCEN to not only stop making such claims but to also make the corrective advertising, as noted.

The U.S. Court of Appeals held that the FTC could constitutionally prohibit the trade association from disseminating what the commission had determined to be false and misleading claims but that the group could be required to issue corrective advertising "only when NCEN chooses to make a representation as to the state of the available evidence or information concerning the controversy [over the connection between egg consumption and increased blood cholesterol and heart disease]."[131] The Court reasoned that because there had been no lengthy history of public deception, as there had been in *Warner-Lambert v. FTC* (1977), the original FTC order was broader than necessary to prevent future deception.

Affirmative Disclosure

The Federal Trade Commission has used two other major remedies for deceptive advertising—*affirmative disclosure* and *substantiation*. It is not unusual in a consent order or a cease and desist order for the commission to require that an advertiser not only refrain from making specific claims but also to require that all future advertising make certain disclosures designed to prevent deception—that is, *affirmative disclosure*. A classic case involving affirmative disclosure is the mid-1960s order by the FTC that the J. B. Williams Co., the distributor of Geritol, state in its commercials that "tiredness and that run-down feeling" were rarely caused by iron-poor blood, which the product claimed to cure. Geritol advertised rather heavily on network television, including the "Ted Mack Original Amateur Hour" on CBS, that its "iron rich formula" (primarily vitamins and iron) would cure "iron poor blood." The ads were particularly aimed at women, whom medical experts agree generally need more iron in their diets than men. As the FTC saw it, the ads, by failing to mention that Geritol may help only those rare individuals who suffer tiredness as a direct result of an iron deficiency. Geritol was simply a vitamin and iron supplement, not a cure for all tiredness. J. B. Williams appealed the FTC order, but the Sixth Circuit U.S. Court of Appeals in 1967 upheld the order as constitutional.[132] The Geritol story did not end in 1967, however. Six years later the commission fined the company more than $800,000 for allegedly violating the cease and desist order, but the Sixth Circuit U.S. Court of Appeals in 1974 ordered a jury trial, at which the company was ordered to pay $280,000 in fines.[133] An example of an affirmative disclosure requirement, by Congress rather than the FTC, is the set of federal statutes regarding cigarette and smokeless tobacco advertising.

Substantiation

Finally, the Federal Trade Commission uses *substantiation* as a mechanism to regulate advertising. Substantiation is a relatively new process for the commission, which began such a program in 1970 when it filed a complaint against Pfizer, Inc.,[134] manufacturer of Un-Burn, an over-the-counter, nonprescription medication for minor burns and sunburn. The product, which was advertised extensively on radio and television, claimed that it "actually anesthetizes nerves in sensitive sunburned skin" and that it "relieves pain fast." The FTC complaint alleged that these claims and similar claims for Un-Burn had not been substantiated by "adequate and well-controlled scientific studies or tests prior to the making of such statements."[135] The commission charged that Pfizer had engaged in unlawful deception and unlawful unfairness in violation of Section 5 of the FTC act.

Unlike other regulatory mechanisms, such as corrective advertising and affirmative disclosure, substantiation essentially places the burden of proof on the advertiser to show that there is scientific evidence to support the particular claim. In other words, the advertiser is forced to prove the truth of the assertions rather than the FTC being forced to prove they are false, as would be the case in a typical complaint for false and deceptive advertising. If a case were to go to trial, the FTC would have the burden of showing no scientific evidence existed to substantiate the claims, but this could be effectively accomplished with the testimony of expert witnesses and by showing that the advertiser had failed to provide any substantiation when it was requested. Ad substantiation cases at the FTC have been relatively rare since the program began more than 20 years ago, primarily because a complaint cannot be filed unless the advertiser makes an affirmative product claim without a reasonable basis for that claim, based on adequate and well-controlled scientific tests or studies. This standard, which continues today, does not require that the evidence be overwhelmingly in favor of the product or even that the *majority* of the evidence favor the claims. The advertiser simply has to demonstrate that there is a reasonable basis for making the claims. As the FTC noted in the Pfizer decision:

> The question of what constitutes a reasonable basis is essentially a factual issue which will be affected by the interplay of overlapping consideration such as (1) the type and specificity of the claim made—e.g.,safety, efficacy, dietary, health, medical; (2) the type of product—e.g., food, drug, potentially hazardous consumer product, other consumer product; (3) the possible consequences of a false claim—e.g., personal injury, property damage; (4) the degree of reliance by consumers on the claims; (5) the type, and accessibility, of evidence adequate to form a reasonable basis for making the particular claims.[136]

REGULATION
BY OTHER GOVERNMENT AGENCIES

Al though the Federal Trade Commission is the main federal agency responsible for regulating advertising, other federal agencies possess authority to regulate specific types of advertising under certain conditions and state and local government agencies are also involved in the process. The federal agencies include, but are not limited to, the Federal Communications Commission (FCC), the U.S. Postal Service (USPS), the Food and Drug Administration (FDA), the Department of the Treasury and the Securities and Exchange Commission (SEC).

The role of the FCC in regulating broadcast ads, such as its eventually successful attempt to restrict the amount and type of advertising in television programs oriented to children, is discussed in the next chapter.

The FDA, an agency with the Department of Health and Human Services (formerly the Department of Health, Education and Welfare until 1979 when a Department of Education was created), regulates the advertising of certain foods, prescription and nonprescription drugs and cosmetics, as provided under the Federal Food Drug and Cosmetic Act of 1938, as amended. The FDA advertising regulations are significantly stronger than those of the FTC. For example, prescription drugs are evaluated by the National Research Council Drug Efficacy Group of the National Academy of Sciences; if a drug is rated less than "effective," the rating must be included in any advertising. All claims in drug advertising regulated by the FDA must be backed by appropriate clinical studies or other tests conducted by recognized experts.[137] During President Ronald Reagan's administration and President George Bush's term, the FDA, yielding to pressure from prescription drug marketers, consumers (including groups representing AIDS sufferers) and politicians, eased the rules regarding the length of time a drug must be tested prior to mass marketing; the federal statutes and FDA rules regarding advertising were not eased, however. Much of the advertising for prescription drugs appears in professional publications such as medical and nursing journals, but the overwhelming proportion of over-the-counter drug advertising is found in consumer publications and on radio and television.

The other agencies mentioned play a fairly minor role in regulating advertising. The USPS regulates advertising sent via mail but, despite its rather broad authority of such advertising, tends to confine its efforts to blatantly unfair, misleading and fraudulent cases. Some of this reluctance may be attributed to privacy considerations, but limited resources and deference to the FTC may also explain its conservative approach. The USPS has always been aggressive in prosecuting certain con artist schemes that seem to never die, such as chain letters and "envelope stuffing" job "opportunities" ("make hundreds of thousands of dollars simply by stuffing envelopes in your own home"). The SEC regulates the advertising of stocks, bonds and other traded securities, whereas the Treasury Department is responsible for enforcing federal statutes regarding the reproduction of paper currency in ads.

Whereas the great bulk of advertising involves or affects interstate commerce and thus can be regulated by the FTC and other federal agencies, there are certainly exceptions that fall into the regulatory hands of state and local agencies. Because the FTC does not have exclusive control over advertising, even advertising that crosses state lines can under certain circumstances be regulated by the state or a local agency. For example, a mail order house based in State X advertising in newspapers, on network radio and television, on local stations and through the mail could find the FTC overlooking its national ads, the FCC reviewing the broadcast commercials, the state consumer protection agency regulating the ads in the local newspapers and the USPS keeping an eye on its mail advertising. If the company sells prescription drugs or securities, the picture would be even more complicated.

Most states have enacted what have become known as "little FTC Acts" or statutes creating a state consumer protection agency modeled after the FTC. Many of these statutes include provisions regarding advertising such as the "bait and switch" (deceptive ads in which a lower-priced model of a product is used to convince consumers to visit the store, where a salesperson will persuade them to purchase a much higher-priced model because the lower-priced one is "sold out" or "not worth purchasing").

SELF-REGULATION

In an ideal marketplace, consumers would regulate advertising by refusing to buy products that did not live up to their promises and expectations and thus make their distastes known to the manufacturers. Products and services that did not satisfy consumers would thus fade into oblivion. But consumer-regulation does not always work even though most advertisers are honest and make a concerted effort to please consumers. Government regulation is not always effective either. To fill the gap as well as to head off government intervention whenever possible, advertisers have established various self-regulatory boards over the years that review and evaluate ads either on a voluntary or, in some cases, nonvoluntary basis. The most powerful of these self-regulatory groups was not founded until 1971, but it has become an important broker in the world of advertising.

The National Advertising Division

The National Advertising Division (NAD) of the Council of Better Business Bureaus (CBBB) regularly monitors national ads appearing in all of the major media. If the NAD determines that an ad may be false, misleading or deceptive or makes unsubstantiated claims, an investigation is conducted. Investigations can also be initiated on the complaint of another advertiser, consumer group, individual or local Better Business Bureau. During the investigation, the advertiser is given the opportunity to respond to the allegations. If the NAD concludes that some action is warranted, it will request that the advertiser take the recommended steps, whether they be (a) to cease further advertising that may be misleading, deceptive or false, (b) to modify future advertising to delete certain claims or (c) to take some other action. An NAD decision is not necessarily final. The advertiser can always refuse to comply because the NAB has absolutely no governmental authority, or the advertiser can appeal to the National Advertising Review Board (NARB), a five-member board of the CBBB that oversees the NAD. Both the NAD and the NARB derive much of their persuasive power from the fact that their parent organization, the CBBB, has considerable clout in the marketplace. The NAD and NARB were jointly created by the American Advertising Foundation (AAF), the Council of Better Business Bureaus (CBBB), the American Association of Advertising Agencies (AAAA) and the Association of National Advertisers (ANA) in 1971. Decisions by the NARB cannot be appealed further, but, of course, the NARB has no punitive power. The NAD, however, makes very effective use of media publicity to inform consumers about companies that engage in false and misleading advertising. Should an advertiser decide to ignore an NAD/NARB decision, the NAD can always register a complaint with the FTC or other appropriate federal agency. Only rarely is this necessary because advertisers defy the NAD at their own peril.

Since 1974 the NAD/NARB has had a Children's Advertising Review Unit that focuses on advertising directed toward children. This unit operates in a manner similar to that of the NAD/NARB.

Each of the major commercial television networks, NBC, CBS, ABC and Fox, has its own network advertising standards. The networks, for example, refused to carry brand-name commercials for condoms because such advertising violated these codes. In addition, the AAAA requires all members to abide by its "Standards of Practice," which ban unfair, deceptive and misleading advertising.

ADVERTISING ETHICS AND OTHER PROFESSIONAL CONSIDERATIONS

Although some cynics might argue that *advertising ethics* is an oxymoron, this is an area of advertising that deserves more attention, especially in the current era of deregulation. Professional associations such as the AAF and AAAA have their own standards or codes that attempt to articulate the ethical standards of their members, and yet some questionable techniques and practices creep through in the ads of even some of the largest and most reputable corporations. No doubt some of these can be linked to the rigors of competition, but competition is only part of the equation.

A few years ago several major newspapers and a popular magazine inserted in Sunday newspapers around the country accepted an ad for an "Indoor TV

'Dish' Antenna" that contained some interesting claims, all of which would be very difficult to prove false but could easily confuse or mislead some consumers. According to the ad, "The [model] looks like an outdoor satellite 'dish,' but works *indoors* like ordinary 'rabbit ears.' " In other words, you get a set of rabbit ears shaped like a dish. The ad also noted, "Legal in all 50 states. *You pay no cable fees because you're NOT getting cable!!! You pay NO satellite fees because you're NOT using satellite technology or service!!!*" All of this is true. Rabbit ear antennas have never been illegal, and purchasers certainly will not get cable or satellite TV with this antenna and thus won't have to pay for something they don't get. Other claims in the ad are equally as silly: It works entirely with " 'RF' technology . . . to pull in all signals on VHF and UHF from 2 to 82." All receiving antennas use "RF technology." RF simply means radio frequency. Every antenna "pulls" signals right out of the air. Otherwise, it's not an antenna. The ad notes that the antenna "complies with all applicable federal regulations." Of course, there are no federal regulations governing an indoor TV antenna. The "sheer aesthetic superiority of its elegant parabolic design" make it a "*marketing breakthrough*," according to the company.

In other words, the advertiser thinks the dish looks good and makes a good marketing device. Even the advertised price for one antenna is actually 30 percent higher, thanks to an added $3.00 shipping and handling charge. Even the assertions that there is a limit of "three per address" and the company reserves "the right to extend above time and quantity guarantees" are dubious. Readers who order the antenna probably won't be surprised to get solicitations to order more. The clincher in the ad is the free "Basic Guide to Satellite TV" included with all orders, presumably so buyers can learn about all of the services "from Disney to XXX movies" that they won't get with the rabbit ears but could receive with a real satellite dish system. By the way, a nice set of rabbit ears (alas but without the parabolic design) can be purchased at Radio Shack and similar stores for $5 and up.

Puffery

This ad is an example of a common advertising technique known as *puffery* or evaluative advertising, which the FTC and other federal and state agencies permit so long as such exaggerations do not cross the line and become factual statements that could materially affect an individual's decision to purchase the product. These agencies assume that consumers do not take such claims seriously, and yet some of the most popular brands of products from toiletries to automobiles can trace their dominant market shares to extensive advertising using puffery. Examples include:

1. No one has a better chance of winning than you in our contest. *Translation*: Everyone who enters, including you, has the same chance of winning or losing.

2. The Hold That Loves to be Held. (Ad for hair spray)
3. No other skin lotion soothes, smooths, softens and saves you money like . . . (Ad for skin lotion)
4. . . . ends dry skin. (Ad for another skin lotion in same magazine)
5. . . . bleach makes your wash clean, fresh and wonderful.
6. Rich, satisfying taste. (Ad for cigarettes)
7. Exercise takes a lot out of you. Orange juice puts a lot back.
8. Introducing the freshest tomato taste. (Ad for pasta sauce)
9. Big discounts every day. (Ad for discount department store)
10. The best tasting dog food ever.

It is highly unlikely that any of the previous claims would be challenged by the FTC or any other regulatory agency even though these claims can indeed influence consumer decisions. Puffery, in its traditional form (best, number one, preferred, highest quality, best performer, most economical, lowest-priced, none better, freshest, best tasting, etc.), is an accepted marketing practice that probably causes little harm to consumers, although it conveys little, if any, useful information to a rational consumer.

Testimonials

Another persuasive technique that has become commonplace in advertising in the last few decades, especially in television commercials, is the *testimonial*, or paid endorsement by a well-known personality. Personalities such as Bill Cosby, Muhammed Ali, Alan Alda, Angela Lansbury, Whitney Houston and Mary Lou Retton receive substantial compensation for endorsing products. Clearly, they would not be hired if their endorsements did not improve sales. Until 1975, the FTC rules were rather lax regarding testimonials, although the commission has had guidelines for endorsements for many years. The industry guides adopted in 1975[138] focus on endorsers, not company spokespersons. The difference between a **spokesperson** and an **endorser** is quite significant — endorsers are well-known personalities such as professional athletes, TV and movie stars, and former politicians and **experts** or individuals who can claim expertise in a particular area because of experience, education or special training or a combination thereof.

The guidelines require that a personality or expert be a regular user of the product being endorsed and, indeed, that the advertising featuring the endorsement be discontinued if the product is no longer used by that individual. The guidelines also require that any financial interest by the endorser in the company be disclosed (such as in the disclaimers in the Colonial Life Insurance television commercials featuring Art Linkletter). The guidelines, however, do not require an advertiser to disclose that personalities or experts were paid for their testimonial. There is an assumption that consumers know such individuals are compensated and thus there is no need to repeat this fact in every ad. A spokesperson does not have to meet these standards. For example, TV or radio announcers for a headache remedy do not have to actually use the medication. They are simply serving as professional announcers, not endorsers or experts.

One trend in recent years is for company presidents to serve as spokespersons in advertising. Two salient examples of individuals who became household names by promoting their firms are Lee Iacocca of Chrysler and Victor Kiam of Remington. Both are identified by name and title in their ads even though most people can now readily identify each of them. Another trend, which has now been abruptly halted for all practical purposes, is the use of celebrity lookalikes and soundalikes (impersonators) in commercials. Chapter 8 discusses the tort in invasion of privacy known as *appropriation* or *misappropriation*, which involves the commercial use of a person's name, image or likeness without consent.

In the past, public figures, including entertainers, have generally been unsuccessful in stopping lookalikes and soundalikes. Among those who have won suits are Woody Allen, Jacqueline Kennedy Onassis and Tom Waits (who was awarded $4 million).[139] In 1989, a California jury in U.S. District Court awarded singer Bette Midler $400,000 against New York advertising agency Young & Rubicam for hiring Ula Hedwig, a member of the singer's backup group, to imitate Midler's voice in a Mercury Sable auto commercial.[140] Although the agency had obtained copyright permission to use the song, "Do You Wanna Dance?" made popular in 1971 by Midler, the singer had refused to sing the song in the commercial.[141] No mention was made of Midler and neither her picture nor her actual voice was used, but, according to testimony at trial, Hedwig was told to sing as much as possible like the popular singer. Midler sued for damages but lost initially in U.S. District Court when the judge ruled that no copyright infringement had occurred and the performer had no basis for a suit for appropriation. The Ninth Circuit U.S. Court of Appeals reversed the district court decision on the appropriation tort by holding that Midler had a cause of action under common law for appropriation.[142] On remand, the trial court judge dismissed Midler's claim for punitive damages, and the jury awarded Midler $400,000 in compensatory damages.[143] Interestingly, early in the trial, the judge dismissed the Ford Motor Co. as a defendant in the suit because he believed there was insufficient evidence to link the auto manufacturer to the tortious actions of the advertising agency. Thus only Young & Rubicam was ultimately held responsible.

The Midler case is not unique. Comic Rodney Dangerfield settled out-of-court for an undisclosed sum in 1989 from Parks Inn International for using an impersonator in ads. The son of singer Bobby Darin sued McDonald's and its ad agency for using an animated character shaped like a crescent moon to sing "Mac Tonight" similar to the late singer's 1959 "Mack the Knife." Singer Tom Waits sued Frito Lay and its ad agency and won $2.6 million in compensatory and punitive damages for a tortilla chip radio commercial featuring a soundalike singer, and the Ninth Circuit U.S. Court of Appeals affirmed the award in 1992.[144]

In the same year, the Ninth Circuit Court also held that Vanna White of "Wheel of Fortune" fame could sue Samsung Electronics for a futuristic ad featuring a robot with a blond wig, long gown and heavy jewelry turning big letters on a 2012 game show.[145] The electronics company did not deny that the ad had been inspired by "Wheel of Fortune," but argued that there was no cause of action since White's name, likeness and voice were not used. According to the appellate court, the determination to be made is whether Samsung has appropriated White's identity, not how. The U.S. Supreme Court denied certiorari.

Should mass media outlets refuse to carry questionable advertising and advertising in poor taste? Newspapers and other print media clearly have the right to refuse any and all advertising, thanks to the 1974 U.S. Supreme Court decision in *Miami Herald v. Tornillo*.[146] In this case the Court held that a Florida statute giving political candidates a right of access to editorial space in newspapers that had criticized them or endorsed an opposing candidate was unconstitutional. Now with the death of the Fairness Doctrine, broadcasters presumably can refuse any advertising, except political ads covered by the equal opportunities rule, which guarantees candidates for federal office the right to purchase broadcast advertising during certain times (discussed in the next chapter).

How often do the media refuse to carry ads that do not apparently violate the law? One study[147] of 75 daily newspapers' policies on rejection of advertising found that more than half (56 percent) have no set policy on advertising rejection but instead decide on a case-by-case basis. The survey found that only 8 percent of the papers refused more than 10 ads in an average month but there was considerable diversity in the types of ads refused with smaller circulation newspapers and southern papers, which tend to be more conservative as a whole and thus more likely to refuse ads for certain types of products and services.[148]

Washington Post syndicated financial columnist Jane Bryant Quinn has criticized the practice of some major newspapers that "stubbornly publish work-at-home schemes and offers of loans to bad credit risks, even though they are hardly ever legitimate. Get-rich-quick channels on some cable TV systems are especially bad."[149] Quinn noted in her column that the largest newspaper trade group, the American Newspapers Publishers Association, has no set of voluntary guidelines for advertising and sees no need for one. She also pointed out that the broadcast trade group, the National Association of Broadcasters, once had advertising standards (under the rubric of a "Code of

Good Practice") but they were killed in 1983 when the Justice Department filed an antitrust suit against some of the standards.[150]

Program-Length TV Commercials

In the last several years, three types of advertising have presented particularly thorny ethical problems—program-length TV commercials (or "infommercials," as discussed earlier), ads touting direct or implied health benefits for certain foods and lawn care ads. *Program-length commercials* (PLC) are a relatively newcomer to the advertising game but have created widespread criticism and confusion. In one of its fact sheets, the FTC describes the PLC:

> Seen increasingly on cable and independent television stations, many of these commercials have the look, feel, and duration of real TV programs, often imitating the format of genuine talk shows or investigative consumer news programs. The product being sold is often discussed as part of the program and touted by paid "experts," "moderators," or "reporters." These "shows" may last 15 minutes or longer and may even be interrupted by realistic-looking "advertisements" for the product with ordering information.[151]

However, there is a problem because even the most astute consumers sometimes have difficulty distinguishing a PLC from an independent consumer program. They are used to seeing a clear separation between program content and commercials, but the PLC makes that line blurry at best. Unfortunately, many cable networks, including several of the well-known national ones, routinely accept such advertising because it provides them with a ready source of income in a highly competitive advertising market. Even some local stations, especially independent stations not affiliated with one of the major commercial networks, carry PLCs. The two biggest areas for PLCs, according to the FTC, are health care and finances. Examples are weight loss plans, skin care products and "get-rich-quick" investment schemes.

Health-Oriented Advertising

With the "no cholesterol, low saturated fat, low salt, low calorie" focus of the 1980s and 1990s came a host of food products and brash advertising claims that have created apparent skepticism among consumers. A *Washington Post* nationwide, scientific poll[152] of more than 1,000 adults found that only 3 percent believed food manufacturers never make misleading claims about the health benefits of their products; one-third said such claims are made a "fair amount" of the time and another one-third indicated they believe these claims are made "a lot" of the time. Claims in food advertising have reached the point at which almost one-third of the $3.6 billion budget for food advertising goes for ads that have some type of health information.[153] Indeed the claims have reached the point at which much of the food advertising emphasizes "cholesterol-free" and "no cholesterol" when the product had no cholesterol to begin with, but may contain considerable fat. More than half of the people in the *Washington Post* poll characterized such claims as misleading even though the practice is rather commonplace.[154]

In mid-1993, the U.S. Food and Drug Administration began enforcing the Nutritional Labeling and Education Act, which requires detailed and specific information on most packaged food labels, including strict standards for claims such as "low cholesterol," "no cholesterol," "light" and "calorie free." This act has had a significant effect on nutritional claims, including those made in advertising. The long-term effect remains to be seen, however.

LAWN CARE ADS

Finally, from time to time particular products or services that are perfectly legal to own or use and thus to advertise nevertheless have serious problems that are not made readily apparent in the advertising and thus may mislead or misinform consumers. Cigarettes, even with the government mandated warnings, and alcoholic beverages are examples. One of the more recent examples is advertising for lawn care services. In 1988 the New York attorney general filed a civil suit against the largest lawn care company in the country, ChemLawn Services Corporation, to permanently bar it from engaging in any further allegedly false, misleading and deceptive advertising.[155] In particular, the attorney general sought to prevent the company from advertising that the chemicals used in its lawn care program do not harm humans or nontargeted plants or animals and its products are safe because they are registered by the U.S. Environmental Protection Agency.[156] If the past is any indication, most newspapers, magazines and radio and TV stations will continue to carry the advertising in dispute until the litigation is resolved rather than err on the side of safety. It should be mentioned that ChemLawn was also sued by several individuals for personal injuries.[157]

SUMMARY AND CONCLUSIONS

With advertising expenditures totalling more than $130 billion annually in this country, commercial speech has become a more important avenue for exercising First Amendment freedoms. Indeed, the mass media, as we know them today in the United States, could not survive without the continued influx of advertising revenues. Even traditionally noncommercial forms of mass communication, such as public radio and television, have come to rely on advertising, albeit in the form of brief spots and support acknowledgments. The protection granted commercial speech by the courts, particularly the U.S. Supreme Court, has expanded considerably since the unenlightened days of *Valentine v. Chrestensen* (1942), thanks to the advances forged in *New York Times v. Sullivan* (1964), *Bigelow v. Virginia* (1975) and *Virginia State Board of Pharmacy v. Virginia Citizens Consumer Council* (1976) and its progeny, and finally, *Central Hudson Gas and Electric Corp. v. Public Service Commission* (1980), which gave us the current four-part test for determining whether a particular type of commercial speech has First Amendment protection.

More recent Supreme Court decisions such as *Posadas de Puerto Rico Associates v. Tourism Company of Puerto Rico* (1986), *Shapero v. Kentucky Bar Association* (1988), *Board of Trustees of the State University of New York v. Fox* (1989) and *Peel v. Attorney Registration and Disciplinary Commission of Illinois* (1990) have both clarified Central Hudson's test and created confusion about its application. Like it or not, the Supreme Court will continue to face commercial speech cases in a variety of contexts until a strong majority on the Court is able to flesh out *Central Hudson* or create a new, clearer test for determining the scope of constitutional protection for commercial speech. The Court could always reverse itself and grant commercial speech the same protection as political and religious speech; but that scenario is still unlikely to occur soon, even though President Bill Clinton will almost certainly replace any retiring justices — liberal, moderate or conservative — with individuals who hold a more expansive view of First Amendment rights, as he did with Ruth Bader Ginsberg in 1993.

In 1993 the U.S. Supreme Court decided two cases that could have a substantial impact on the commercial speech doctrine. In *City of Cincinnati v. Discovery Network, Inc.* (1993), the U.S. Supreme Court upheld the Sixth U.S. Circuit Court of Appeals determination that Cincinnati's ban of all commercial handbills from newsracks on public streets was unconstitutional. The appellate court said that although the city's interest in aesthetics and safety may have been substantial, the means chosen (i.e., the ordinance) did not meet the "reasonable fit" test of *Board of Trustees of the State University of New York v. Fox* (1989). The U.S. Supreme Court agreed, noting that the city's policy was neither content-neutral nor narrowly tailored and thus could not be "justified as a legitimate time, place, or manner restriction on protected speech.[158]

In *Edenfield v. Fane* (1993),[159] the U.S. Court upheld a 11th Circuit U.S. Court of Appeals decision that while Florida's interest in maintaining public confidence in accountancy was substantial, an outright ban on in-person solicitation by certified public accountants nevertheless violated the First Amendment. The 11th Circuit Court justices felt this form of prior restraint did not meet the "reasonable fit" test of *Board of Trustees of S.U.N.Y.* The court distinguished the case from *Ohralik* (the lawyer solicitation case discussed in this chapter), noting that Florida had not shown strong enough link between solicitation by CPAs and "dishonest and oppressive" activities such as those in cases involving attorneys.

Because the U.S. Supreme Court upheld both of these lower appellate court decisions, commercial speech can undoubtedly claim much broader protection under the First Amendment.

Whereas the Supreme Court determines the scope of protection granted to the various forms of commercial speech, including advertising, federal and state agencies such as the Federal Trade Commission execute the day-to-day regulation of commercial speech. The FTC has, by far, the most direct impact on advertising regulation, but state and local agencies share in the regulation process. Congress and the state legislatures also play an important role by enacting specific statutes, usually to restrict or prohibit certain types of advertising. Finally, self-regulation such as the National Advertising Division and the National Advertising Review Board do work to eliminate false, misleading and deceptive advertising, even though they have no governmental authority and thus must rely on volunteer cooperation from advertisers and pressure from adverse media publicity to halt such advertising.

Unfortunately, such advertising continues to appear even in major newspapers and magazines and on radio and television. Self-regulation still typically weeds out only the most blatant and egregious abuses and government enforcement is usually only a few steps ahead of self-regulation. The media must impose stricter ethical standards for advertising or consumer confidence in advertising will continue to erode. Because the mass media are never required to accept any particular ads, except political ads by broadcasters, there is no rationale for publishing questionable ads even when they may avoid prosecution. Higher ethical standards for all forms of advertising would lead to more informed and rational consumers, which would, in the long run, benefit rather than harm the mass media.

6 Broadcasting

THE ORIGINS OF COMMERCIAL BROADCASTING

Although much of the electronic media is *privately* owned, the broadcast spectrum is considered a *public* resource or, more specifically, a **limited public resource.** The technical elements for broadcasting—electromagnetic radiation, air and space—have always existed, but a means of independently creating radio waves and then receiving them was not created until the late 19th century. Indeed, if the technology had existed a century or more ago to construct a radio receiver that even approached the capabilities of the early ones hand-built by amateur radio experimenters in the 1890s, radio "transmissions," not from humans but from the natural emanations from the environment—including magnetic radiation from "hot spots" on the sun, lightning and other weather phenomena—could have been picked up. Electromagnetic radiation is simply the end product of a charged particle (electric field) interacting with a magnetic field. Although radio, television and similar forms of electromagnetic radiation are characterized as media, primarily because they travel over the airwaves or a medium, radio waves (which would, of course, include television) can travel with no material medium, that is, in a vacuum. As early as 1865, a Scottish physicist, James Clerk Maxwell, had developed a mathematical theory of electromagnetic radiation that became the first of a series of steps taken by a whole cast of characters, generally without the knowledge of one another, toward the eventual development of broadcasting as we know it today. Although some of these odd characters were scientists, others were merely visionaries and even opportunists.

The Pioneers

Maxwell's 1873 *A Treatise on Electricity and Magnetism* theorized that electrical and magnetic energy move at the speed of light in transverse waves. Fourteen years later, another physicist—this time a German—conducted a series of experiments involving the reflection, refraction and polarization of magnetic waves. Heinrich Rudolf Hertz confirmed the existence of radio waves, providing the impetus for other experimenters to study how to harness, transmit and modify these waves so they would be capable of transmitting information over long distances.

In 1895, an Italian physicist whose name has become synonymous with the "wireless telegraph," Guglielmo Marchese Marconi sent what are known today as *long-wave* radio signals over more than a mile. This was a major accomplishment, on par with the Wright Brothers' first power-driven airplane flight in 1903. For the first time, a scientist had demonstrated that information could be transmitted and received over relatively long distances without benefit of a wire or cable, as had been required for the wired telegraph. Probably no one at the time, including Marconi himself, could have imagined a world less than a century later whose communication would be virtually controlled by radio waves. But Marconi and others continued their experimentation and made some remarkable achievements within a relatively short period of time. By 1901, Marconi had picked up the first transatlantic wireless transmissions and although the sounds were neither voice nor music but simply sparks and crackles, the world was on its way toward becoming a "global village," as the late Canadian communication theorist, Marshall McLuhan, would characterize it.

Historians are still divided over when the first voice broadcast occurred. Some claim that a Murray, Kentucky, farmer named Nathan B. Stubblefield broadcast "Hello Rainey" to his friend, Rainey T. Wells, in a demonstration in 1892, and other scholars attribute the first broadcast to Reginald A. Fessenden, who transmitted a short, impromptu program from Brant Rock, Massachusetts, in 1906 to nearby ships.[1] In 1991 officials of the Smithsonian Institute in Washington, DC, called Stubblefield's work "interesting and even important" to the development of radio but they rejected a petition by the farmer's grandson that Stubblefield be recognized as the inventor of radio. In 1904 the first telegraphic transmission of a photograph had been accomplished,[2] and although the reproduction was very crude by today's standards, it ushered in a new era of news—now news photos could be sent on a timely basis across considerable distances. In 1906 American Lee De Forest announced his invention of the triode, a vacuum tube that permitted the amplification of radio waves. Until the 1960s when the transistor was mass marketed, all radio receivers (and transmitters as well) required vacuum tubes to function. (The transistor was invented as early as 1948 but did not become commonplace in receivers until at least a dozen years later.) In 1910 De Forest made a live broadcast of the great Italian opera singer, Enrico Caruso, and 5 years later the Bell Telephone Company conducted a series of experiments involving voice transmissions across the Atlantic.[3] One year later on November 17, 1916, De Forest made what is generally recognized as the first newscast in the United States — using his experimental station at High Bridge, New York, he recited returns from the Wilson–Hughes presidential election to ham radio operators.[4] No one apparently faulted him for the fact that he ended the broadcast with the wrong result.[5]

THE ORIGINS OF GOVERNMENT REGULATION

In 1917 the United States entered World War I and the government subsequently prohibited all private broadcasting until the war ended 2 years later. By 1919 the groundwork was being laid for mass broadcasting with the creation of Radio Corporation of America (RCA) by the three communications giants — General Electric, Westinghouse and American Telephone and Telegraph. Although there was no indication at the time, the conditions were also being set for government regulation. First, newspapers became heavily involved in broadcasting, especially in establishing and owning stations. It would be decades later before strict federal rules were enacted regarding cross-media ownership, but newspaper companies early on established a strong foothold in the broadcast marketplace. Papers such as the *Atlanta Journal*, the *Louisville Courier-Journal*, the *Chicago Daily News* and the *Milwaukee Journal* had the financial finesse to keep the stations operating and the news gathering resources, including sports, to fill the airtime.

Second, radio proliferated and prospered, signaling potential problems with frequency spectrum allocation. In 1910 Congress passed the Wireless Ship Act, which required all ships leaving any U.S. port to have a wireless radio and skilled radio operator on board if they had 50 or more passengers.

Two years later Congress enacted the Radio Act of 1912, which for the first time required all radio stations to have a license from the Secretary of Commerce and Labor. The statute also set certain technical requirements and allocated certain radio bands for exclusive government use.[6] The act did not limit private broadcast stations to particular frequencies, but the Secretary of Commerce selected 750 kilohertz and 833 kilohertz on which they were to operate.[7] There was no requirement that the broadcasters operate in the public interest nor were there any real restrictions on content. Instead, broadcasters were permitted to operate as they wished without any substantial governmental interference. Unfortunately, the interest of private enterprise in radio grew so quickly that the Commerce Secretary was unable to prevent stations from interfering with one another even though many more channels were made available, limits on operating power and hours of operation were imposed and channels were separated by 10 kilohertz, as they still are today in the AM portion of the radio spectrum.[8]

The result was utter chaos as the number of stations escalated from a handful around 1920 to several hundred in 1923 to almost 600 toward the end of 1925, with a backlog of 175 applications for new stations, all broadcasting or wanting to broadcast in essentially the same space we call the AM band today. There are now almost 4,900 commercial AM stations on the air, but there is little interference because of strict limits on power, allocated channel space, operating hours and technical criteria.

Third, with the government giving its de facto or tacit approval of private ownership of broadcasting, it was becoming apparent that the role of government in broadcasting would be as a police officer, not as owner. The government did, of course, own and operate certain broadcast facilities for military and security purposes, but these were for private governmental use, not for public dissemination. Because broadcasting did not exist at the time the Constitution was enacted, there are no provisions specifically dealing with this type of commerce, but it is highly likely that the U.S. Supreme Court would have struck down any constitutional challenges to government ownership of broadcasting, just as it did to government regulation of radio and television. Thus, had the U.S. government or, more specifically, Congress chosen not to permit private ownership of the airwaves, our system of broadcasting may have evolved into a system in which there is a mix of private and government ownership — like that in Great Britain, Japan and West Germany — or even into a system in which ownership and operation were strictly in the hands of government. The private ownership that we have today was the direct result of a government policy to encourage development of the broadcast system by free enterprise. It was not the product of any laissez faire attitude by Congress. The First Amendment clearly prohibits government ownership of the press, which has been interpreted primarily to protect the print media, but no such prohibition applies to the broadcast media. The Supreme Court would probably never allow government takeover of broadcasting today, but the ban would likely be based on public policy and contractual grounds, not on purely constitutional grounds.

Just as there is debate among historians over who made the first voice broadcast, there are two conflicting claims as to which station was the first regular broadcasting station. The first station to be issued a regular (rather than experimental) broadcasting license, according to official records, was WBZ in Springfield, Massachusetts. The license was granted by the federal government on September 15, 1921.[9] Although KDKA in Pittsburgh, Pennsylvania, did not receive its license as a regular broadcasting station until several weeks later on November 7, 1921, mass communication historians generally credit KDKA as the "first fully licensed commercial broadcast station"[10] because it began transmitting news and music on a regular basis beginning in November 1920.

Newspapers and other owners such as the electronic giants of Westinghouse, General Electric and RCA realized rather early the enormous profit potential in broadcasting, although during the early years the income came primarily from the sale of crystal and later vacuum tube radio sets. Newspaper companies generally owned radio stations as a means of promoting the sale of their newspapers. It soon became apparent, however, that the sale of radio sets and newspapers was not the most profitable means of operating radio. Quite simply, the point would be reached at which everyone who could afford a radio receiver would have one and there would be no revenues except from the sales of second and replacement sets. Instead, broadcasters turned to advertising, which gave the new medium a substantial boost. This gold mine created such an enormous interest in broadcasting that by the end of 1925, almost 600 radio stations were already on the air and 175 applications for new stations were pending.[11] Chaos reigned on the airwaves with at least one station on every available channel and several stations on most channels.

The Passive Role of the Courts

The courts were of no assistance; a U.S. Court of Appeals ruled that the U.S. Secretary of Commerce could not deny a license to any legally qualified applicant even if the proposed radio station would interfere with the private and governmental stations already on the air.[12] Furthermore, an Illinois District Court held that the Secretary of Commerce could not institute frequency, power or operation hours restrictions, and a station operating on a different frequency than originally assigned was technically not in violation of the Radio Act of 1912.[13] Even the acting U.S. Attorney General got into the act by declaring that the Secretary of Commerce had no authority under the Radio Act of 1912 to regulate the power, frequency or hours of operation of radio stations.[14] An exasperated Secretary of Commerce, Herbert C. Hoover (who was inaugurated as the 31st President of the U.S. 3 years later), announced on July 9, 1926, the next day after the Attorney General's ruling, that he was giving up all attempts to regulate radio and urged stations to initiate self-regulation.[15]

The Intervention of Congress:
The Radio Act of 1927

Self-regulation never materialized, however, and on February 23, 1927, Congress stepped into the picture with the Radio Act of 1927 after President Calvin Coolidge had appealed to the legislative body for a solution. As a

Supreme Court Justice described the situation 16 years later in *National Broadcasting Co. v. the United States* (1943), "The result [of stations operating without regulations] was confusion and chaos. With everybody on the air, nobody could be heard."[16]

One could argue that radio was never given sufficient time to develop an effective system of self-regulation, but the fact remains that even the broadcasters themselves recognized that self-regulation probably would not work, at least for the immediate future. With airwaves in such a horrible mess, the potential for profits was substantially reduced because everyone wanted a piece of the spectrum without giving up any privileges.

THE FEDERAL RADIO COMMISSION

The Radio Act of 1927, the first of only two comprehensive broadcast regulatory schemes to be enacted by Congress, was designed to bring order to the chaos and set radio on a path to prosperity. The act created the five-member Federal Radio Commission (FRC) with broad and comprehensive licensing and regulatory authority. The body was granted specific power "to issue station licenses, allocate frequency bands to various services, assign specific frequencies to individual stations, and control station power."[17] Although he was not directly connected with the Federal Radio Commission, the Secretary of Commerce was assigned the responsibilities under the act of inspecting radio stations, formally testing and licensing station operators and assigning call signs.[18]

The commission took its tasks seriously and immediately began enforcing the rules created under the act. Some 150 of the 732 stations operating in 1927 eventually left the air. Today there are almost 4,900 commercial AM stations on the air operating in essentially the same frequency space as in 1927 but with strict technical limits on power and channel separation. This accomplishment can trace its origins to the Federal Radio Commission in 1927, which began the complicated and difficult task of reorganizing the broadcast spectrum. As the FRC progressed in its efforts to administer the act as "public convenience, interest, or necessity requires," it soon became apparent that the commission needed expanded regulatory powers and more than simply fine tuning was necessary to make the process effective. Soon after he became President in 1933, Franklin Delano Roosevelt asked his recently appointed Commerce Secretary, Daniel C. Roper, to establish an interdepartmental committee to study broadcasting and the Federal Radio Commission. The committee made several recommendations, including creating one federal administrative agency, similar to the FRC, to regulate all interstate and international communication by wire or broadcasting, not just commercial radio.

THE COMMUNICATIONS ACT OF 1934

Congress followed the committee's recommendation and enacted the Federal Communications Act of 1934, the second and last of the acts to deal comprehensively with electronic communications. The Communications Act continues to serve as primary statute under which the Federal Communications Commission functions today. Although there have been changes in the form of various amendments to the act, the primary provisions of 1934 have remained essentially intact.

The Federal Communications Commission

The 1934 act created a seven-member administrative agency similar to that of the FRC but renamed it the Federal Communications Commission (FCC). Under Public Law 97-253 (96 Stat. 763, 805) in 1982, nearly half a century after the FCC was created, Congress reduced the number of members to five, effective July 1, 1983. Each member is appointed by the President with the advice and consent of the Senate. The President designates one member to serve as Chair, who is responsible for organizing and coordinating the FCC's operations and, as would be expected, presides over commission deliberations. Commission members are appointed for 5-year terms, with the terms staggered so that one commissioner's term expires each year. If commissioners leave before their term has expired, the replacement serves only through the rest of the unexpired term. (Of course, the replacement could be reappointed for a regular five-year term at the end of the original term.) No more than three members can serve at the same time from the same political party. When terms expire or openings otherwise occur, Presidents typically appoint members of their own party until the maximum number of three has been reached. As is discussed later, Congress has enacted significant changes over the years – for example, the Communications Satellite Act of 1962, which granted broader authority to the commission, including the right to regulate satellite broadcasting.

An objective of the 1934 act was to unify the various statutes and rules and regulations affecting interstate communications and place the authority for enforcing them and setting policy under the umbrella of one independent, quasi-judicial, quasi-legislative federal agency. That objective has certainly been accomplished. Nearly every form of electronic communications is now affected by the FCC, including commercial and noncommercial broadcasting, satellite communications, amateur (ham) and citizen's band (CB) radio, cable television and new technologies such as teletext and direct broadcast satellite service (DBS). One major exception is governmental services, such as military communications and the Voice of America, the international service operated by the Department of State that broadcasts in more than 100 languages throughout the world.

Section 151 of the Communications Act of 1934 delegates to the FCC the authority to regulate

> interstate and foreign commerce in communication by wire and radio so as to make available to all the people of the United States a rapid, efficient, Nationwide and world-wide wire and radio communication service with adequate facilities at reasonable charges for the purpose of the national defense [and] for the purpose of promoting safety of life and property.[19]

Section 307 established the standard, which remains today, by which the FCC is to license stations—"public interest, convenience, or necessity."[20] This standard has been affirmed by the courts many times, such as by the U.S. Supreme Court in the 1943 landmark decision in *National Broadcasting Co. v. United States*.[21] The standard is rather vague, but it essentially grants the FCC very broad regulatory powers.

LIMITS ON FCC AUTHORITY

Even with such broad authority, certain limits have been placed on the commission by virtue of the fact that the agency can act only within those parameters enunciated by Congress in the Communications Act of 1934 and its subsequent revisions and amendments.

As mentioned earlier, the FCC has absolutely no authority over broadcast and related services owned and operated by the U.S. government.[22] Indeed a large chunk of the frequency spectrum has been specifically allocated to both civilian and military governmental services. Most of the authority for regulating these services has been delegated to the Department of Commerce, although the Department of State through the U.S. Information Agency (USIA) operates international broadcast services such as the Voice of America. Indeed, at least half of the broadcast frequency space allocated under various international treaties is **not** regulated by the FCC. As discussed shortly, however, the FCC does regulate far more than just the traditional over-the-air signals, including cable and satellites.

One area in which the commission has virtually no authority is advertising. The FCC cannot regulate individual commercials because this power falls under the aegis of the Federal Trade Commission. The agency does have the authority to issue guidelines regarding the amount of commercial time allowed in a given hour; but in the early 1980s it began a process of deregulating broadcasting which eliminated its guidelines on commercial limits that permitted up to 16 minutes of commercials per hour. Thus a station can theoretically carry as much advertising as it wishes; the recourse now to overcommercialization is for the consumer to tune out. It is not unusual now for radio and television stations and networks to carry as many as a dozen commercials in a row on popular programs whose viewers or listeners are willing to tolerate the clutter. Shorter commercials such as the newer 10- and 15-second spots add even more to the clutter. Indeed the situation has apparently become so bad that many radio stations now tout 30- to 60-minute blocks of uninterrupted music in an effort to solve the clutter problem ("10 songs in a row" or "one hour of commercial-free music").

Because the major commercial and noncommercial networks do not broadcast per se, the FCC neither licenses nor directly regulates them. That is not to say, however, that the FCC has no impact on the networks. The parent companies of the four major commercial networks—the American Broadcasting Co. (ABC), the Columbia Broadcasting System (CBS), the Fox Broadcasting Company (FOX) and the National Broadcasting Co. (NBC)—all own and operate radio and television stations that are licensed by the commission and thus must comply with FCC rules and regulations. In addition, the networks are beholden to their affiliates (i.e., those stations that contract with the network to carry its programming for a specified time, usually in exchange for compensation) because the affiliates are licensed. Thus a network that provided a program to its affiliates violating an FCC rule or regulation—such as the "Equal Opportunities Rule" (sometimes erroneously referred to at the "Equal Time" rule)—would create an uproar among the affiliates who faced the possibility of an FCC citation. Although the network--local affiliate relationship has changed dramatically over the years, the networks still scrupulously attempt to adhere to FCC rules and regulations to avoid causing trouble for their affiliates. With network revenues dropping, thanks to the loss of audience shares to the competition form cable, independent stations (stations with no major network affiliation), pay TV and even prerecorded videocassettes, the networks scramble to please their affiliates. In fact, until the Fox Broadcasting Network began competing in earnest in 1988 by offering its programming to "independent" television stations, there were only three major networks to split the audience shares.

Noncommercial networks, such as the Public Broadcasting System (PBS) for television and National Public Radio (NPR), are not licensed by the FCC, but PBS and NPR own no stations and thus are only indirectly regulated by the FCC. Nevertheless, the noncommercial networks must watch their steps, just as the commercial networks do, because their survival depends on their continued affiliation with local stations.

There are also constitutional limits on the FCC, just as there are for other federal agencies, and these are discussed at various points in the chapter. The First Amendment imposes some limits on the commission, but a trend throughout the history of broadcast regulation, from the 1930s until today, has been for the U.S. Supreme Court and other courts as well to defer to the FCC's perceived expert judgment in determining permissible versus impermissible authority over broadcasting. It is quite rare for the Supreme Court to slap the agency's wrist and even rarer for the Court to actually reverse an FCC decision. The rationales used to justify greater governmental control over broadcasting than the print media are now examined.

THE REGULATORY SCHEME

The concept of "limited public resource" has become synonymous with broadcast regulation and continues to remain the primary basis on which the courts justify considerably stricter government controls over the electronic media than would ever be permitted for the print media under the First Amendment. There is no doubt that the airwaves are limited, just as we have a limited supply of water, air and other resources. However, unlike water and air, the broadcast spectrum is not an exhaustible resource. The airwaves are not *consumed* but merely *occupied*. For example, if a new technology were developed that made it possible for radio stations to occupy only half of the usual frequency space, potentially twice as many stations could broadcast on the same portion of the spectrum. In other words, the real limits on broadcasting are technology, *not* consumption. The typical C-band commercial satellite has 24 transponders or television channels, whereas the newer Ku-band satellites have 36. There are already at least 18 active C-band and 15 Ku band satellites operating over North America. Dozens of new satellites designed to carry at least some commercial broadcasting are scheduled for launching in the next few years. Although most satellites have a least a few unoccupied channels, the satellites we have now are theoretically capable of delivering a total of almost 1,000 video signals and tens of thousands of audio signals if they were all operating at capacity. The typical cable television system converter now has a capacity for 100 or more channels and thanks to technologies such as fiber optics and integrated circuits, the capacity can be expanded to thousands of channels.

Why, then, do the courts, the FCC and Congress continue to cling to the scarcity concept? First, there are still more applicants for the typical broadcast frequency or channel than there are available frequencies. That is, the demand exceeds the supply, "forcing" the government to choose among competing applicants. Anyone or any organization can publish a newspaper or magazine without a license (other than the usual business license if the publication is operated as a business). There is no competition for existing space. Congress chose in 1934 with the Communications Act to adopt a policy of requiring the FCC to grant new and renewal licenses to specific applicants only "if the public convenience, interest, or necessity will be served thereby."[23] The fact remains that in spite of all the new technologies, there are certain technologies, media and frequencies that are substantially more coveted than others. For example, owning a television station in a major market such as New York or Atlanta can be extremely profitable, especially if the station is a VHF outlet and a major commercial network affiliate. Operating an independent UHF station in a smaller market such as Lexington, Kentucky, or Madison, Wisconsin, even though still profitable, would not garner nearly the revenues of the Atlanta or New York stations.

Although the courts have never seriously considered alternatives, there are certainly viable options to the current regulatory scheme of awarding licenses on a competing basis, applying the "public interest, convenience, or necessity" standard. In fact, beginning in the early 1980s, the FCC experimented with a lottery program for a relatively new technology[24] known as low-power television (LPTV). In 1982, the commission announced that it would begin accepting applications for a new class of LPTV stations that could operate with very few program or content restrictions so long as they met certain technical specifications such as no interference with existing full-power television stations (FPTV) and a primary signal of no more than approximately 10 miles in any direction. Under the lottery program, the FCC selected from among competing qualified applicants, if any, based on a random "drawing" for allotted frequencies. No attempt would be made to determine whether an applicant was better qualified than another or whether one would be more likely to serve the public interest, convenience or necessity better than another.

Unfortunately, the lottery program moved extremely slowly, primarily because the commission was overwhelmed with applications and had a relatively small staff to process them. However, by the early 1990s, dozens of new LPTV stations were on the air, but a huge backlog of applications had yet to be processed. LPTV stations can operate on either VHF or UHF channels with a maximum power of 10 watts on VHF or 1,000 watts on UHF. Under the 1982 FCC order, LPTV stations have the discretion of operating as full service channels or simply as translators so long as they have permission from the originating station. As part of its effort to deregulate broadcasting and promote competition in a free marketplace, the FCC imposed virtually no program restrictions on the stations, other than the usual rules against indecency, obscenity and so forth.

LPTV is a perfect illustration of how the commission typically confronts new technologies. During his administration (1977–1981), President Jimmy Carter established the National Telecommunications and Information Administration (NTIA) in one of many executive reorganization efforts. One of several functions assigned to the new NTIA was telecommunications applications, including the improvement of mass communication through the development of new technologies and the retreading of older ones. After a fairly comprehensive study of broadcast spectrum allocation, the NTIA concluded that one effective way of increasing the number of television stations on the air, especially for consumers in rural areas and other sites where cable access was low to nil, was to lift FCC restrictions that essentially permitted low-power TV stations to carry only retransmissions of programming from full-power stations. The FCC somewhat reluctantly accepted the NTIA recommendation in 1982 even though an economic projection from its own staff indicated that LPTV would have an uphill financial battle. By 1982 President Carter had been replaced by President Ronald Reagan, who pushed deregulation among all federal agencies. Thus the FCC (with the "King of Deregulation," Mark Fowler, at the helm) wisely chose not to impose programming and severe technical restrictions on LPTV. More than a decade later, low-power TV is still struggling, but every new technology from radio to satellites had to flounder before gaining a foothold in the mass communication scheme. Cable television, for example, began in the 1940s but did not become a truly mass medium until the 1970s as the nation became "wired." By 1990, it had become a $20 billion industry with more than 60 percent of all homes hooked to cable.[25]

A more recent illustration of the problems that any new technology faces is the ongoing saga of the portable wireless telephone. During the past few years, Larry McLernon, head of the Columbus, Ohio-based Litel Communications Corp. has been attempting to get approval for a system of wireless telecommunication involving lightweight, portable phones that operate similar to cellular phones except (a) they would cost only approximately $100, compared to the $1,500 tag for a typical portable cellular phone; (b) they would operate on radio waves, as cellular phones do, but within much smaller zones known as "micro-cells"; and (c) the system would apparently eventually make phone wiring obsolete.[26] In late 1993, the FCC issued technical standards and guidelines for personal communications services (PCS), a new form of wireless phones that work more effectively and are substantially less expensive than the traditional cellular phones now owned by 12 million Americans.

Licenses for cellular zones (known as "cells") are still being awarded by the FCC by periodic lotteries among qualified applicants, although nearly all of the major markets have been completed. Often these licenses are won in the special lotteries by speculators who then, in turn, sell them to phone companies such as the regional Bells. When he was President, George Bush proposed an auction system to replace the lotteries so that spectrum licenses would be awarded to the highest bidders, most likely large phone companies and communications conglomerates. Congress failed to approve the Bush administration's proposal, but it was estimated that if the system had been implemented, the cost for obtaining a national license would have been as much as $500 million.[27] Auctioning for PCS frequency space began in 1994.

McLernon estimates that his wireless phone could be mass marketed as early as 1995 if his system were approved, but he faces an uphill battle because the

FCC would have to find room in the already overcrowded frequency spectrum and the large phone companies appear poised to fight his plan. In the meantime, the NTIA, discussed later, undertook a broadcast spectrum allocation study completed in 1991. The United Kingdom is already well under way toward applying the technology with the first customers now on-line (on-wave?).[28]

FEDERAL COMMUNICATIONS COMMISSION GENERAL AUTHORITY

While the FCC, like all federal agencies, has limited authority over the industry it regulates, it clearly plays a major role in both the day-to-day operations and long-term development of broadcasting. Although the commission regulates a broad range of communications—including telephone, telegraph, two-way radio (such as citizen's band and amateur radio) and even cellular phones—this book focuses primarily on traditional forms of mass communication. Section 326 of the Communications Act of 1934 specifically says: "Nothing in this Act shall be understood or construed to give the Commission the power of censorship over the radio communications or signals transmitted by any radio station, and no regulation or condition shall be promulgated or fixed by the Commission which shall interfere with the right of free speech by means of radio communication."[29]

Just as a literal reading of the First Amendment could lead one to conclude that freedom of speech and freedom of the press were absolute ("Congress shall make no law . . ."), someone unfamiliar with the history of broadcast regulation could reasonably assume after reading Section 326 that the FCC played no role in regulating programming or, at the very least, that broadcasters enjoyed full First Amendment rights ("no regulation . . . shall interfere with the right of free speech . . ."). Nothing could be further from the truth. The commission is barred from engaging in direct censorship or prior restraint of specific programs, but a station that persistently flirts with violating FCC rules regarding political broadcasts (a la the Equal Opportunities rule discussed later) or indecent and obscene content risks reprimands, fines and even the serious possibility that its license will be revoked or not renewed.

This chapter focuses next on FCC policies affecting primarily the programming of traditional commercial and noncommercial radio and television stations, followed by a look at newer technologies such as cable and satellite broadcasting.

FCC POLICIES REGARDING POLITICAL BROADCASTING

While "indecent programming" appears to be the hot topic for the 1990s, as discussed in the next section, the one area of programming that has consistently created the most controversy has been political content. The Fairness Doctrine has also generated considerable heat, but it was dealt a fatal blow by the FCC itself in August 1987 (discussed later), and appears very unlikely to be resurrected anytime soon.

One of the common misperceptions, apparently even among some broadcasters, is that the so-called equal time requirement is a relatively new provision of the Federal Communications Act. One reason for this myth may be attributed to the considerable attention the provision received in 1960 when presidential candidates John F. Kennedy and Richard M. Nixon squared off in a live television debate before a national audience. Although it was unclear at the time whether Section 315 applied to presidential debates, Congress nevertheless chose to suspend the provision for the Nixon–Kennedy debates. Two years later, the commission indicated that such debates did fall under the rule. Another reason for the myth may be traced to the awareness that Congress has amended the Section several times over the years, usually to broaden its coverage.

The idea for a provision like Section 315 actually originated with the old Radio Act of 1927. Section 18 of the early act required all broadcasters to provide equal time (or more accurately, equal opportunities) to candidates for public office, once one legally qualified candidate had been granted airtime, whether paid or unpaid. Thus a broadcaster could effectively escape the requirement by simply denying access to all candidates for that particular office. Section 18 also prohibited a station from censoring any political candidate's broadcast.

Both ideas were adopted in essentially the same form when Congress enacted the Communications Act of 1934. Section 315 has been amended three times — in 1952, 1959 and 1972. As discussed shortly, the provision was significantly strengthened in 1972 with amendments to Section 312.

Section 315: Access for Political Candidates

Part (a) of Section 315 (as currently in force) provides:

FACILITIES FOR CANDIDATES FOR PUBLIC OFFICE

(a) If any licensee shall permit any person who is a legally qualified candidate for any public office to use a broadcasting station, he shall afford equal opportunities to all other such candidates for that office in the use of such broadcasting station; *Provided*, That such licensee shall have no power of censorship over the material broadcast under the provisions of this section. No obligation is imposed under this subsection upon any licensee to allow the use of its station by any such candidate. Appearance by any legally qualified candidate on any —

(1) Bona fide newscast,

(2) Bona fide news interview,

(3) Bona fide news documentary (if the appearance of the candidate is incidental to the presentation of the subject or subjects covered by the news documentary), or

(4) On-the-spot coverage of bona fide news events (including but not limited to political conventions and activities incidental thereto), shall not be deemed to be use of a broadcasting station within the meaning of this subsection. Nothing in the foregoing sentence shall be construed as relieving broadcasters, in connection with the presentation of newscasts, news interviews, news documentaries, and on-the-spot coverage of news events, from the obligation imposed upon them under this Act to operate in the public interest and to afford reasonable opportunity for the discussion of conflicting views of public importance.[30]

Laws are made to be applied as well as *interpreted*, and the Communications Act of 1934, including Section 315, is no exception. The federal courts, especially the U.S. Court of Appeals for the DC Circuit, have spent considerable time attempting to determine the legal meaning of terms such as "legally qualified candidate," "equal opportunities," "no power of censorship" and "public office." Sometimes the answers have not been to the FCC's liking, and, as a result, the commission has occasionally altered its rules. For example, in a 1975 case, *Flory v. FCC*,[31] the Seventh Circuit U.S. Court of Appeals ruled, much to the chagrin of the FCC, that a Communist Party member running as a U.S. Senate candidate in Illinois but who had not qualified for inclusion on the ballot was nevertheless a legally qualified candidate because there was the possibility he would be placed on the ballot and, further, that he had indicated he planned a write-in candidacy if he did not qualify to be on the ballot. As it turned out, Ishmael Flory did not gain access to the airwaves because the court held that he had not exercised his procedural rights before the commission, but the implications of the decision were quite serious—stations could be forced to grant equal opportunities to candidates based on the probability, or perhaps even just the possibility, that the candidates would run for public office. The commissioners lost little time in responding to the decision by adopting new "Rules Relating to Broadcasts by Legally Qualified Candidates."[32] The new rules define a legally qualified candidate as an individual who has publicly announced his candidacy *and* (not *or*) who "meets the qualifications prescribed by the applicable laws to hold the office for which he is a candidate" *and* either has qualified for a place on the ballot *or* "has publicly committed himself to seeking election by the write-in method *and* is eligible under the applicable law to be voted for by sticker, by writing in his name on the ballot, or other method, *and* makes a substantial showing that he is a bona fide candidate for nomination or office."[33]

The "ands" and "ors" in the rule can be confusing, but the 1984 FCC Political Primer makes it clear that a mere announcement by a candidate does not automatically make that person legally qualified. The person must also be eligible to hold the office and either have qualified to be on the ballot or have qualified, as detailed in the rule, as a write-in candidate.[34]

Section 315 has been the subject of substantial litigation over the years, probably because (a) it is such a sweeping rule and thus affects many political aspirants and all broadcast stations; (b) its language lacks the necessary precision to always make it crystal clear when it applies or does not apply; and (c) it does not stand alone but must instead be interpreted in light of other provisions of the FCC act, especially Section 312, and sometimes in conjunction with the Fairness Doctrine (when the doctrine was in effect). There have been battles in the courts over who is and is not a candidate, what is a public office and what is "use" by a station. A comprehensive review of FCC and federal court decisions in this area is beyond the scope of this text, but this chapter examines some basic principles and a few specific examples that illustrate these principles.

FCC Interpretation of Section 315

First, the FCC has clearly indicated that it takes the "publicly announced" requirement seriously. During the 1968 presidential campaign, Senator Eugene J. McCarthy, a publicly announced candidate for the Democratic nomination, requested "equal time" when President Lyndon B. Johnson conducted a December 7, 1967, interview with the major television networks. At the time, the President had not publicly announced whether he intended to run for reelection. (President Johnson eventually decided not to run.) The commercial networks refused to grant Senator McCarthy equal time, and he appealed to the commission. The FCC, contending that "to attempt to make finding on whether or when the incumbent has become a candidate during the usual, oft-repeated and varying preliminary period would render the statute unworkable," ruled against the senator and the U.S. Court of Appeals affirmed.[35]

Second, the commission has taken a conservative approach in its interpretation of "legally qualified candidate for public office." In 1972, for example, the FCC ruled that the presidential and vice presidential candidates on the Socialist Workers Party ticket were not legally qualified for purposes of Section 315 and Section 312—even though they had filed to be on the ballot in 15 states, had made it on six and collected almost a half-million signatures on petitions—because neither candidate was at least 35 years old, as required in Article II of the U.S. Constitution.[36]

Candidates have the burden of proof in demonstrating that they are legally qualified; they must even prove that their opponents are legally qualified candidates for the same office. Section 315 technically kicks in only when there are "opposing candidates."[37]

Third, "use" of a station has been very broadly construed by the FCC to include even broadcasts of old movies and television shows in which a candidate formerly appeared as well as appearances on radio and television that are part of the individual's regular responsibilities. Two examples show how this interpretation is applied. During the 1976 presidential Republican primary campaign, many TV stations were uncertain whether broadcasting old movies in which Ronald Reagan appeared would invite enforcement of Section 315. The FCC moved quickly to relieve the doubt by ruling that when an actor or actress becomes a legally qualified candidate for public office, such appearances constitute "use."[38] However, the equal time to which the opponent would be entitled would be *only* the amount of time during which the actor or actress actually appeared, not the entire time the movie or show was broadcast. Similarly, the opponent(s) of a candidate who was a radio or television personality, such as a host, anchorperson or disc jockey, would be eligible for time equal only to the amount of time during which the personality actually appeared.[39]

Fourth, the rules regarding broadcasting of debates have changed considerably over the years, beginning with a major overhaul in 1975. Prior to that year, the commission had generally held that debates and press conferences by candidates were not exempt from the equal opportunities rule. The four major exemptions (bona fide newscasts, news interviews, news documentaries and on-the-spot coverage of bona fide news events) were not added by Congress until 1959 and the FCC has generally taken a conservative (i.e., narrow) approach in determining what content was exempt from Section 315.

Aspen Institute Rulings on Political Debates

Until 1975 the commission had held that debates between political candidates and broadcasts of press conferences conducted by candidates did not fall within any of the exemptions under Section 315. In that year, however, the FCC made some surprising rulings that have become known as the *Aspen Institute* decisions. Federal administrative agencies such as the FCC traditionally rarely overrule previous decisions, especially relatively recent ones, but the commission actually did an about-face in *Aspen Institute*[40] when it held that under some conditions, coverage of debates among political candidates and press conferences of candidates would not invoke the equal "opportunities" provisions of Section 315 but instead would be exempt as on-the-spot coverage of bona fide news events. Indeed, the circumstances required for the exemption were essentially the same as those the FCC had ruled in 1962 precluded an exemption.

Why had the earlier decisions been erroneous? According to the FCC, the commissioners had simply misunderstood the legislative history that established Section 315 and Congress had actually intended for broadcasters to cover political news "to the fullest degree" rather than inhibit such coverage. The U.S. Court of Appeals affirmed this reasoning and concluded:

> In creating a broad exemption to the equal time requirements in order to facilitate broadcast coverage of political news, Congress knowingly faced risks of political favoritism by broadcasters, and opted in favor of broader coverage and increased broadcaster discretion. Rather than enumerate specific exempt and nonexempt "uses," Congress opted in favor of legislative generality, preferring to assign that task to the Commission.[41]

Thus a political debate could be considered on-the-spot coverage of a bona fide news event so long as (a) it was arranged by a third party (i.e., someone other than the broadcaster or network), (b) it did not occur in the broadcaster's facilities, (c) it was broadcast live and in its entirety and (d) the broadcaster's motive in carrying the debate was newsworthiness rather than as a political favor for a particular candidate. In sum, the commissioners gave their blessing for coverage of debates as news events but not as political fodder. Their reasoning was very much in line with the contentions in the petitions filed by the Aspen Institute Program on Communications and Society and CBS, Inc., that had triggered the FCC's reexamination of its earlier decisions.

Expansion of the Scope of the Aspen Decision

In 1983, the FCC considerably expanded the Aspen decision by ruling that even debates sponsored by broadcasters themselves are exempt under Section 315(a) (4) as on-the-spot news coverage.[42] The impact of this decision has been felt in almost every major national and state election since 1983 as more and more local and national broadcasters sponsor their own debates. In its 1983 ruling, the commission acknowledged that this greater flexibility granted to broadcasters could lead to bias, but opted nevertheless, to permit such sponsorship because "Congress intended to permit that risk in order to foster a more informed electorate."[43] According to the FCC, the "common denominator of all exempt programming is bona fide news value."[44] In the same decision, the commissioners killed a previous rule, known as the "one-day rule," which basically required contemporaneous or near contemporaneous broadcasting to trigger the 315(a) (4) exemption. The "one-day" label came from the fact that the commission generally expected the broadcast coverage of the particular political event to be aired no later than a day later.

In lieu of the one-day requirement, the FCC established a "rule of thumb" (the commission's characterization) that the broadcast simply "encompasses news reports of any reasonably recent event intended in good faith by the broadcaster to inform the public and not intended to favor or disfavor any candidate."[45]

Finally, the agency has spent considerable time during the last two decades defining "equal opportunities" under Section 315. Its 1984 political primer[46] lists numerous examples of lack of equal opportunities as well as cases where the FCC held that equal opportunities were provided. The former include (a) unequal audience potential of periods such as offering candidates the same amount of air time as their opponents but at a time when the audience is likely to be smaller, (b) allowing candidates to listen to a recording of an opponents' broadcast before it is aired while denying the opponent the same opportunity, (c) requiring one candidate but not another candidate to submit a script in advance, (d) charging unequal rates (a serious *faux pas*), (e) signing an advertising contract with one candidate that effectively excludes opponents from purchasing air time such as selling the candidate most of the available blocks of prime time, and (f) failing to abide by a preestablished interview format.[47] The last example arose in a case in which one candidate had less than 5 minutes of exposure, compared with 16 and 14 minutes for two other candidates because the television station strayed from the format the candidates had agreed to in advance.[48]

An Easing of the Burden of Section 315 by the FCC

Broadcasters generally consider the equal-opportunity requirements onerous, at best, and a violation of the First Amendment, at worst, but they have learned to live with them. To its favor, the commission has been rather lenient with broadcasters who make what it deems good faith efforts to comply with Section 315 and the rules themselves have become somewhat less burdensome over the decades, primarily because of more liberal interpretations of their meaning by the agency and actual rule modifications. Four points illustrate this trend. First, the FCC has made it clear that stations do **not** have to notify candidates of an opponent's time and that stations do **not** have to offer exactly the same time of day on the same day of the week nor to accept competing political ads on precisely the same program or series.[49] How will candidates know if a broadcaster has sold time to their opponent unless they see or hear the ads? Federal regulations require every station to maintain and provide regular public access to a file that contains complete information regarding all requests made for time by candidates or others on their behalf, the disposition of each request and the charges made, if any.[50] In a 1962 decision, the FCC held that candidates effectively have an affirmative duty to check the file if they want the information.[51] The station must promptly put the information in the file in an easily comprehensible form and retain the files for at least two years for public inspection, it has no obligation to automatically notify opponents when a candidate appears.

Second, the commission has enacted a requirement that is sometimes overlooked by candidates in exercising their equal-opportunity rights – the so-called seven-day rule.[52] According to the rule, political candidates must give timely notice to the licensee in order to qualify for air time when an opposing candidate has made "use" of the station. Timely notice is specified as "within one week of the day on which the first prior use, giving rise to the right of equal opportunities, occurred."[53] The rule applies strictly to individuals who are *legally qualified candidates at the time of the broadcasts.*[54] In adopting the rule, the FCC wanted to ensure that stations could make plans prior to the onslaught of the political campaign and to prevent a candidate from waiting until the election was almost over to obtain a large block of time.[55] The FCC has been quite strict in its enforcement of the rule.

Third, the commission has granted stations considerable leeway with news programs under Section 315(a). For example, if a political candidate appears in a bona fide newscast, opponents are *not* entitled to equal exposure in that newscast nor any other newscast. Technically, in fact, they would not be entitled to any news coverage, although public outrage would probably prevent a station from covering one candidate in its news to the exclusion of other candidates. Until August 4, 1987, when the FCC announced its decision to end enforcement of the fairness doctrine (reaffirmed on March 24, 1988),[56] a broadcaster who did not make a good faith effort to provide balanced election news could have faced repercussions from the commission. Now, however, with the death of the doctrine, its political communication provisions no longer apply.

Finally, whereas stations have an affirmative duty to provide reasonable access to legally qualified candidates for federal elective office, they always have the option of refusing to sell time in local, county and state elections. Indeed, Section 315 does not require broadcasters to provide access to candidates in every local, county and state election, although the FCC, courts and Congress have indicated that political broadcasting is a significant public service and that stations are expected to devote reasonable time to political races. The decision regarding which elections deserve attention and which can be ignored is left to the discretion of the station.[57]

Section 312: Political Candidates for Federal Offices

In 1972 Congress added Section 312(a) (7):

[(a) The Commission may revoke any station license or construction permit –

(7) for willful or repeated failure to allow reasonable access to or permit the purchase of reasonable amounts of time for the use of a broadcasting station by

a legally qualified candidate for Federal elective office on behalf of his candidacy.[58]

It should be emphasized that Section 315 and other provisions of the Communications Act of 1934 must generally be interpreted in light of Section 312, which codifies administrative sanctions available to the FCC.

Three examples illustrate the flexibility in nonfederal races. In 1976, the FCC ruled in *Rockefeller for Governor Campaign (WAJR)*[59] that in a state campaign a station is not required to sell air time at all so long as it has offered free reasonable time. In other cases, the commission has held that stations cannot be forced to sell a specific time period[60] and a broadcaster does not have to sell time several months in advance of an election or sell an ad of a specific length.[61]

AN EXCEPTION
TO THE EXCEPTIONS UNDER SECTION 315

Nothing is absolute, including Section 315 exceptions, as a rather novel case in 1988[62] illustrates. Although most of the First Amendment challenges to Section 315 have been launched by political candidates rather than journalists, a general assignment reporter for a Sacramento, California, television station became a candidate for a seat on the council of a nearby town. Because the station believed it would have to offer more than 30 hours of free time to comply with Section 315 to his opponents, William Branch was told to take a leave of absence if he wished to pursue politics. Branch requested a ruling from the FCC on whether the equal time provisions of Section 315 applied to him. Citing the legislative history of Congress' 1959 amendments to the FCC Act, the commissioners ruled against the reporter. On appeal, the U.S. Court of Appeals for the DC Circuit upheld the FCC decision:

> When a broadcaster's employees are sent out to cover a news story involving other persons, therefore the "bona fide news event" is the activity engaged in by those other persons, not the work done by the employees covering the event. The work done by the broadcaster's employees is not a part of the event, for the event would occur without them and they serve only to communicate it to the public. For example, when a broadcaster's employees are sent out to cover a fire, the fire is the "bona fide news event" and the reporter does not become a part of that event merely by reporting it. There is nothing at all "newsworthy" about the work being done by the broadcaster's own employees, regardless of whether any of those employees happens to be a candidate for public office.[63]

Branch also challenged Section 315 as a violation of his constitutional rights, including the First Amendment. However, the court struck down all three grounds, holding that the statute did not extinguish his right to seek political office because no individual has a right of access to the broadcast media; Section 315 does not violate the First Amendment because "the first amendment's protections for the press do not apply as powerfully to the broadcast media"; and the provision does not impermissibly limit "the discretion of broadcast stations to select the particular people who will present news on the air to the public."[64]

Two Hypotheticals

Suppose KOVR-TV had decided to keep Branch on the air despite his political ambitions but limited his exposure to no more than 10 minutes per week. Branch consents to the arrangement and the station dutifully offers free air time to his opponents. However, the station considers this election unworthy of news coverage and thus ignores it. Both Branch and his opponents complain that the station has written off the campaign simply because it wants to avoid the awkward situation of having a reporter appear as the subject of a story in the same newscast in which he covers a separate story. How would the FCC rule? In line with the previous discussion, the commission would probably not second-guess the station's news judgment so long as it could demonstrate its decision was based on news judgment, not political or other motives.

Or, what if the station keeps Branch on the air, complies with Section 315 by offering time to all candidates but also covers the campaign, including a press conference by Branch? Any 315 problems? Probably not, given the reasoning of the Court in *Branch v. FCC*. Afterall, if employees who are legally qualified candidates invoke 315 by covering a story, then would it not follow that employees who become *subjects* of bona fide news events do not trigger equal opportunities? Otherwise, they would be receiving discriminatory treatment under the law.

THE BIG BREAK FOR POLITICIANS: LOWEST UNIT CHARGE

Public awareness of the equal-opportunities rule is relatively weak, but one provision is virtually unknown among voters—the *lowest unit charge* obligation. The FCC routinely sends out reminders to over-the-air stations and cable companies (which also must comply with the equal-opportunities law) during each major election year. Section 315 (b) (1) and b (2) says:

(b) The charges made for use of any broadcasting station by any person who is a legally qualified candidate for public office in connection with his campaign for nomination for election, or election, to such office shall not exceed—

(1) during the forty-five days preceding the date of a primary or primary runoff election and during the sixty days preceding the date of a general or special election in which such person is a candidate, the lowest unit charge of the station for the same class and amount of time for the same period; and

(2) at any other time, the charges made for comparable use of such station by other users thereof.[65]

Thus under (b) (2), stations are not required to offer political candidates lowest unit rates outside the 45- to 60-day time frames, but candidates clearly receive very substantial discounts during the effective periods, compared to what they would pay if they were traditional advertisers. In enacting 315, Congress left the interpretation of *lowest unit charge* to the FCC, which has traditionally tracked industry sales practices. Periodically, the FCC sends public notices to broadcasters and cable companies to advise them of its current interpretation of *lowest unit charge*.[66] The computations can be fairly complicated and are beyond the scope of this book, but suffice it to say that candidates receive rates that compare quite well with those of high volume advertisers such as Procter and Gamble, General Motors and Coca Cola, even when their ads are low volume. Indeed, in its 1984 political primer, the FCC notes: "Briefly it means that candidates must be given all discounts, based on volume, frequency or any other factor, that are offered to the station's most favored commercial advertiser for the same class and amount of time for the same period, regardless of how few programs or spots the candidate buys. This includes discount rates given to commercial advertisers but not published on the rate card."[67]

In June 1992 the FCC released a Memorandum Opinion and Order that primarily codified its previous political programming policies. The Order also made some fairly significant changes in the commission's interpretation and enforcement of the lowest unit charge and reasonable access requirements of the 1972 Federal Election Campaign Act and the political broadcasting provisions of the Communications Act of 1934.[68] The commission still continues to leave interpretation of "reasonable access" essentially in the hands of the broadcasters, but it did not grant the industry full latitude.

First, the FCC made it clear that cable television does **not** fall under the reasonable access requirement. Second, the regulatory agency indicated that stations can adopt a policy of not selling federal political candidates advertising time **during** newscasts, but they **cannot** deny access to candidates during programming **adjacent** to newscasts unless they do not sell to other advertisers during that time. The time slots before and after news have been very popular periods for political ads, presumably because candidates like having their commercials associated with news and audience ratings tend to be high.

Third, the commission adopted a much more conservative definition of "use" by a political candidate. "Use" now means only those appearances that have the approval of the candidate. Thus it no longer includes spots by organizations and groups such as political action committees (PACs) unless they have the sponsorship or support of the candidate. Prior to this ruling, broadcasters presumably had to offer equal opportunity to opponents when an ad was aired for a candidate even when the person had no direct connection to the commercial. By effectively redefining "use," the FCC relieved stations of all of the other requirements when such ads appear, including the lowest unit charge and "no censorship" provisions, as discussed in the next section. Perhaps it is even more significant that the revised definition now means that showing a movie, television show or similar program in which a candidate had previously appeared as an entertainer, corporate head or whatever before becoming a candidate will no longer invoke Section 315. No doubt, many broadcasters wish this definition had applied in the 1980 and 1984 elections when former movie and TV star Ronald Reagan successfully ran for President.

There is still one potential trap for broadcasters. Because the "no censorship" provision no longer applies to ads not approved by the candidate, stations can be held liable for libel and other torts that stem from the airing of PAC and similar ads. Therefore, they should carefully screen these commercials for defamatory statements, obscenities and other unprotected content, or they can simply refuse to carry them at all.

Finally, in its 1992 order the commission finetuned the specifics of "lowest unit charge," but the details are rather complicated and beyond the scope of this book. According to the order, broadcasters must basically treat political advertising as they would their most favored advertisers. They do not have to offer special treatment, but they cannot restrict access or set rates for political commercials that are out-of-line with those of volume advertisers.

CENSORSHIP OF POLITICAL BROADCASTING

One of the more interesting provisions of Section 315 is its strong prohibition of censorship. Under Section 315 that prohibition is unequivocal ("such licensee shall have no power of censorship"), but there are no absolutes in government regulation. Two important FCC cases illustrate this point. The first arose in 1956 when A. C. Townley, a rather provocative and colorful candidate for the U.S. Senate in North Dakota, in a speech carried on WDAY-TV in Fargo, charged that his opponents and the Farmers' Educational and Cooperative Union had conspired to "establish a Communist Farmers' Union right here in North Dakota."[69] The station had told Townley before the program was aired that his statements could be defamatory, but he did not heed the warning. As a consequence, both the candidate and the station were slapped with a $100,000 libel suit in state district court. The trial court judge granted WDAY's motion to dismiss on the ground that Section 315 made the TV station immune from liability because the statute prohibited censorship so long as a valid "use" was made by a legally qualified candidate, as in the case at hand. In a 4–1 decision on appeal by the union, the North Dakota Supreme Court affirmed the lower court ruling. On further appeal, the U.S. Supreme Court for the first time confronted the question of whether a broadcaster can be held liable for libel when it was expressly forbidden by federal law from censoring the program that carried the statement(s). As discussed in the next chapter on defamation, in most states a journalist or media outlet can clearly be held liable for published statements of third parties, depending on the circumstances. But can a plaintiff who has been defamed under these circumstances recover damages from the station?

In a surprisingly close decision in *Farmers' Educational and Cooperative Union of America v. WDAY* (1959),[70] the U.S. Supreme Court affirmed the North Dakota Supreme Court holding. The majority opinion by Justice Hugo L. Black rejected arguments by the union that broadcasters do not need immunity because they can insure themselves or exercise the clause in Section 315 that effectively allows them to deny all political candidates the use of station facilities:

> We have no means of knowing to what extent insurance is available to broadcasting stations, or what it would cost them. Moreover, since 315 expressly prohibits stations from charging political candidates higher rates than they charge for comparable time used for other purposes, any cost of insurance would probably have to be absorbed by the stations themselves. . . . While denying all candidates use of stations would protect broadcasters from liability, it would also effectively withdraw political discussion from the air. . . . Certainly Congress knew the obvious—that if a licensee could protect himself from liability in no other way but by refusing to broadcast candidates' speeches, the necessary effect would be to hamper the congressional plan to develop broadcasting as a political outlet, rather than to foster it.[71]

The reasoning of the majority in this case was very much in line with the principle that the marketplace should determine which ideas are accepted and which are rejected. Because radio and television stations have a mandate from Congress to serve the public interest, including the dissemination of political content, they should not be saddled with unreasonable restrictions under this premise. The Court also felt it would be unfair to prohibit censorship while still holding the broadcaster liable for the consequences of compliance. In the dissenting opinion, Justice Felix Frankfurter (joined by three other justices) contended that while 315 barred censorship by stations, it did not relieve them of liability under *state* libel laws. According to Frankfurter, "Section 315 has left to the States the power to determine the nature and extent of the liability, if any, of broadcasters to third persons."[72]

Even though this decision answered one major question, a few questions remain. Would this holding apply to all types of content such as national security affairs, invasion of privacy, serious threats to civil or social order or obscenity? Does the holding apply in the same way to candidates for federal elective office because there is an affirmative duty to offer reasonable time for these candidates?

Given the usual campaign rhetoric and the increasing visibility of extremists in the political process, it was inevitable that the FCC would confront the issue of whether content that posed a potential threat to society enjoyed immunity from censorship. The WDAY case dealt with an allegedly civil offense against an organization — libel involves personal damages, not a social harm. On August 7, 1972, the perfect case fell into the commission's lap in the form of self-described "White racist" J. B. Stoner, the same individual who years later was convicted in the bombing of an Alabama church during the 1960s. During his unsuccessful campaign for the Democratic nomination to the U.S. Senate in Georgia, Stoner broadcast the following ad on radio and television:

> I am J. B. Stoner. I am the only candidate for U. S. Senator who is for the white people. I am the only candidate who is against integration. All of the other candidates are race mixers, to one degree or another. I say we must repeal Gambrell's civil rights law. Gambrell's law takes jobs from us whites and gives those jobs to the niggers. The main reason why niggers want integration is because the niggers want our white women. I am for law and order with the knowledge that you cannot have law and order and niggers too. Vote white. This time vote your convictions by voting white racist J. B. Stoner into the run-off election for U.S. Senator. Thank you.[73]

Various civil rights groups, including the National Association for the Advancement of Colored People (NAACP), petitioned the FCC to issue an order to permit stations to refuse to broadcast political ads that present an "imminent and immediate threat" to public safety and security such as creating racial tension or other social harm. Atlanta television and radio stations indicated they did not wish to carry the ads but that they were compelled by Section 315. Citing the *Brandenburg v. Ohio's* (1969)[74] standard that even the advocacy of force or of law violation may not be constitutionally prohibited unless it "is directed to inciting or producing imminent lawless action and is likely to incite or produce such action," the commission refused to grant the request:

> Despite your report of threats of bombing and violence, there does not appear to be that clear and present danger of imminent violence which might warrant interference with speech which does not contain any direct incitement to violence. A contrary conclusion here would permit anyone to prevent a candidate from exercising his rights under Section 315 by threatening a violent reaction. In view of the precise commands of Sections 315 and 326, we are constrained to deny your requests.[75]

The *Atlanta NAACP* FCC opinion did not make explicit the conditions under which a station could censor political broadcasts invoking the equal-opportunities rule because the agency merely cited *Brandenburg* without specifically adopting its precedent. However, "clear and present danger of imminent violence" remains the implicit standard, and the commission has not strayed from it since its invocation in 1972. Some relatively minor forms of censorship have been permitted, but these have had minimal impact on political broadcasting. For instance, although a station may *not* require candidates to submit a copy of their ad or program in advance so it can review the copy for inaccuracies, potential libel or other content problems, it *can* require an advance script or copy of a tape if done solely to verify whether the content is a "use" under the equal-opportunities rule, to determine it actual length for scheduling purposes or to ascertain that the show complies with sponsorship identification rules.[76]

POLITICAL EDITORIALS

While the equal-opportunity rules cover most situations involving political candidates, there are two areas that are handled by allied rules—political editorials and access by political parties. Under the *political editorial rules*, if a station editorially endorses or opposes a legally qualified candidate, it must contact the opponent(s) of the candidate who was endorsed or the candidate who was opposed within *24 hours* and offer a reasonable time for a response by the candidate or a spokesperson for the candidate. If the editorial is carried within 72 hours prior to the election, the candidate(s) must be notified "sufficiently far in advance of the broadcast to enable the candidate or candidates to have a reasonable opportunity to prepare a response and to present it in a timely fashion."[77]

A candidate is not entitled to respond in person because the station has the option of requiring a candidate to select a spokesperson to respond instead as a means of avoiding invocation of the equal opportunities provisions of 315. This keeps the station from having to offer opponents time to respond to the original response.

INDECENCY IN POLITICAL PROGRAMMING

Although indecent and obscene programming *in general* has received considerable attention recently, as discussed in the next section, very few allegations of indecent *political* programming have surfaced over the years. J. B. Stoner reemerged in the political arena during the 1978 Democratic primary for Georgia governor with ads containing his usual racial epithets. Once again, civil rights organizations asked the FCC to stop the ads, this time on grounds that they were indecent, as defined in *FCC v. Pacifica Foundation* (1978) (analyzed shortly).[78] But the Broadcast Bureau of the commission (which, as explained earlier, has initial jurisdiction over such cases) held that "nigger" did not qualify as language describing "sexual or excretory activities and organs, at times of the day when there is a reasonable risk that children may be in the audience" (the standard upheld in *Pacifica*).[79] By 1990 Stoner had been released from prison and ran unsuccessfully in the Democratic primary for lieutenant governor of Georgia without the usual rascist ads. Other alleged uses or threats of use of indecent or obscene political content have done little more than attract an occasional news story—for example, *Hustler* magazine publisher Larry Flynt's suggestion that he would use pornographic film clips in TV ads for his campaign for the presidency in 1983. The threats failed to materialize because Flynt never become a formal candidate. In 1992 television stations in Louisville, Kentucky, and Indianapolis, Indiana, were forced to carry Republican congressional candidate Michael E. Bailey's ads showing close-ups of dead fetuses.

INDECENCY AND OBSCENITY IN BROADCASTING

Government concern with obscene and indecent programming has heightened considerably during the 1990s and appears unlikely to die soon. Much of this focus can be attributed to increased pressures to ban all forms of indecency and obscenity from right-wing religious and political groups led by such conservative stalwarts as U.S. Senator Jessie Helms of North Carolina, television evangelists Pat Robertson (a Republican candidate for President in 1988) and Oral Roberts and, to some extent, President George Bush, until he lost reelection in 1992 to President Bill Clinton. This concern may be magnified now, but it is almost as old as broadcasting itself. In the congressional hearings that eventually led to the enactment of the Radio Act of 1927 and its successor, the Communications Act of 1934, there was discussion about the possibility that the radio waves could be used to carry obscene, indecent or profane programming. Section 29 of the 1927 Radio Act prohibited the airing of "any obscene, indecent, or profane language, by means of radio communication."[80] The same provision was carried over into Section 326 of the 1934 Communications Act, which also barred the FCC from engaging in censorship of radio communications or from interfering with the right of free speech.[81] While the provision regarding obscene and indecent programs was deleted by Congress in 1948 from Section 326 (the censorship provision was *not* repealed), it was recodified into 1464 of the Criminal Code:

> 1464. *Broadcasting Obscene Language.* Whoever utters any obscene, indecent, or profane language by means of radio communication shall be fined not more than $10,000 or imprisoned not more than two years, or both.[82]

Alongside 1980s shock radio and R-rated TV, programming in the early decades of radio/television was prude by comparison. However, that did not stop the Federal Radio Commission and its successor, the FCC, from repressing controversial content. Often, the questions raised by the commission were just as effective as legal actions. Even Congress occasionally investigated, at one point holding hearings about certain suggestive Spanish music carried on CBS and the NBC Blue Network during the mid-1930s.[83] The late, great actor Edward G. Robinson, Jr., owned a South Carolina radio station whose license was denied in the 1960s because the commission contended it had carried programs considered "coarse, vulgar, suggestive and of indecent double meaning" but not indecent or obscene.[84]

Shock or Topless Radio

By the 1970s, "topless radio" had become vogue, especially in larger markets such as New York and Los Angeles, as a viable format and, consequently, was the target of FCC and congressional inquiries. "Topless radio" derived its name from the fact that it consisted of talk shows with a male host discussing explicit sexual matters with listeners, usually females, who were encouraged to call in. For example, in 1973 WGLD-FM of Oak Park, Illinois, was fined $2,000 for discussions about such practices as oral sex during the daytime hours when young children could reasonably be expected in the audience. One excerpt of a WGLD broadcast went:

Female Caller: . . . I have a craving for peanut butter . . . so I spread this on my husband's privates and after awhile, I mean I didn't need the peanut butter anymore.

Male host: [*laughing*] Peanut butter, huh?

Caller: Right. Oh, we can try anything. . . . Any of these women that have called and . . . have hangups about this . . . they should try their favorite — you know like — uh . . .

Host: Whipped cream, marshmallow. . . .[85]

The FCC decided that this case and similar sessions violated both the indecency and obscenity standards of U.S. Criminal Code 1464, but the discussion of sex did not automatically risk punishment:

We are not emphatically saying that sex *per se* is a forbidden subject on the broadcast medium (sic). We are well aware that sex is a vital human relationship which has concerned humanity over the centuries, and that sex and obscenity are not the same thing. . . . We are . . . confronted . . . [here] with the talk or interview show where clearly the interviewer can readily moderate his handling of the subject matter so as to conform to the basic statutory standards which, as we point out, allow much leeway for provocative material.[86]

The radio station denied any wrongdoing in the case but paid the fine. That did not end the matter, however. Two public interest groups petitioned the commission for reconsideration on the ground that listeners had a right of access to such controversial programs and then appealed to the U.S. Court of Appeals for the DC Circuit when the FCC reaffirmed its decision. The appellate court, as expected, backed the agency: "We conclude that, where a radio call-in show during daytime hours broadcasts explicit discussions of ultimate sexual acts in a titillating context, the Commission does not unconstitutionally infringe upon the public's right to listening alternatives when it determines that the broadcast is obscene."[87]

About two weeks before the FCC notified WGLD-FM of an apparent violation, the Board of Directors of the National Association of Broadcasters (NAB), a powerful trade association of commercial and noncommercial television and radio stations, had unanimously adopted a resolution that "unequivocally deplored and condemned tasteless and vulgar program content, whether explicit or by sexually oriented innuendo."[88]

The debate over indecent programming probably owes much of its roots to an October 30, 1973, broadcast of comedian George Carlin's recorded monologue, "Filthy Words" on WBAI-FM in New York, owned by the Pacifica Foundation, whose alternative stations have been embroiled in various controversies over content with the FCC. Before the monologue was aired at 2:00 p.m., listeners were warned about its offensive language. Nevertheless, weeks later a listener filed a complaint with the FCC, indicating that he had heard the broadcast while driving with his young son. The commission issued a declaratory order granting the complaint but reserved judgment on whether to impose administrative sanctions while noting that its order would become part of the station's file. The FCC held that the language in Carlin's monologue was indecent within the meaning of 1464 of the U.S. Criminal Code (Title 18). The commission was particularly concerned with the time of the program, noting: "The concept of 'indecent' is intimately connected with the exposure of children to language that describes, in terms patently offensive as measured by contemporary community standards for the broadcast medium, sexual or excretory activities and organs, at times of the day when there is a reasonable risk that children may be in the audience."[89]

The commission's decision, which was not rendered until February 21, 1975, 17 months after the broadcast, implied that the program could have been played at a different time without incurring the FCC's wrath. "When the number of children is reduced to a minimum, for example during the late evening hours, a different standard might conceivably be used," according to the agency. No particular standard was enunciated nor did the FCC indicate directly that a presumably lower standard would apply.

Unlike WGLD-FM and Sonderling Broadcasting, Pacifica chose to fight. During the first round of the appeals process, Pacifica won when the U.S. Court of Appeals for the DC Circuit reversed the commission's decision, holding that its actions were tantamount to prior restraint and thus violated the First Amendment. The FCC appealed to the U.S. Supreme Court, which reversed the Court of Appeals decision in 1978, thus siding with the commission. In a 5–4 *plurality* opinion in *FCC v. Pacifica Foundation* (1978),[90] written by Justice John Paul Stevens, the Court held that the FCC could constitutionally prohibit language that was *indecent* even though not *obscene*. (The distinction between *indecency* and *obscenity* is analyzed in Chapter 11, but it should be pointed out for now that obscenity involves an appeal to prurient interests or eroticism, whereas indecency does not.)

Not surprisingly, the justices split on the decision, leading to the plurality opinion. According to Justice Stevens, whose opinion was supported only in part by four other justices, including Chief Justice Warren E. Burger:

> The prohibition against censorship [in §326, discussed earlier in this chapter] unequivocally denies the Commission any power to edit proposed broadcasts in advance and to excise material considered inappropriate for the airwaves. The prohibition, however, has never been construed to deny the Commission the power to review the content of completed broadcasts in the performance of its regulatory duties.[91] (footnote omitted)

The opinion also noted that "§326 does not limit the Commission's authority to impose sanctions on licensees who engage in obscene, indecent, or profane broadcasting" and that "of all forms of communication, it is broadcasting that has received the most limited First Amendment Protection." The Court's conclusion is especially troublesome in its rationale for individuals who advocate First Amendment rights for broadcasting on par with those of the print media:

> It is appropriate, in conclusion, to emphasize the narrowness of our holding. This case does not involve a two-way radio conversation between a cab driver and a dispatcher, or a telecast of an Elizabethan comedy. We have not decided that an occasional expletive in either setting would justify any sanction or, indeed, that this broadcast would justify a criminal prosecution. The Commission's decision rested entirely on a nuisance rationale under which context is all-important. The concept requires consideration of a host of variables. The time of day was emphasized by the Commission. The content of the program in which the language is used will also affect the composition of the audience, [footnote omitted] and differences between radio, television, and perhaps closed-circuit

transmissions, may also be relevant. As Mr. Justice Sutherland wrote, a "nuisance may be merely a right thing in the wrong place—like a pig in a parlor instead of the barnyard." [citing a 1926 case]. We simply hold that when the Commission finds that when a pig has entered the parlor, the exercise of its regulatory power does not depend on proof that the pig is obscene.[92]

Pacifica was only the beginning of a growing governmental and public concern with indecent programming, but its holding continues to be frequently invoked by the courts in spite of its plurality status. Indeed, the case has become popularly known as the "seven dirty words" decision because Carlin's 12-minute monologue revolved around the seven "words you couldn't say on the public . . . airwaves."[93] One of the misconceptions surrounding both the FCC and the Supreme Court's decisions is that the seven specific words have been banned from the air waves. Both the Court and the commission indicated it was the monologue, as a whole, broadcast in the specific context (early afternoon when children could be listening), that was indecent, not the individual profanities or vulgarities. Note that the commission did not take any criminal action or pose any sanctions; it simply warned the station that the offense would be in its administrative file.

SOME ETHICAL CONSIDERATIONS

It can be argued that *Pacifica* should have let sleeping dogs lie and thus not appeal the FCC decision because taking the case further could lead to an adverse decision and thus an erosion of First Amendment rights. No doubt the foundation felt it could win the case, as it did in the federal appellate court, only to be reversed by the Supreme Court. Should the station have appealed the decision?

At the time of the Court's decision in 1975, only about 10 million homes subscribed to cable television and Time Inc. had just begun to distribute its Home Box Office Service via satellite to cable systems. Now more than 80 percent of all U.S. homes have access to cable TV,[94] with more than 60 percent subscribing to at least basic service.[95] A substantial portion of the subscribers also pay for premium services such as HBO, Showtime, Cinemax, the Movie Channel and Playboy Television (formerly the Playboy Channel) and occasionally purchase pay-per-view movies and events that feature nudity, graphic violence, sex and strong language. The movies, for example, are typically unedited G, PG, PG-13, R and NC-17 rated versions as originally shown in theaters. These services carry appropriate warnings, usually in the forms of the MPAA rating and designated symbols in the printed program guides. All of these services, particularly Playboy at Night, carry movies and other programs that could be characterized as soft-core pornography. Although HBO and

Cinemax have a policy of showing R-rated and NC-17 movies only at night (usually no earlier than 8:00 p.m.), even PG-13 movies sometimes contain several of the words cited in the Carlin monologue. Occasionally, there are consumer complaints about offensive content in movies on these channels, but neither the FCC nor any other federal agency has given any warnings to cable companies that carry these services. Whereas the commission technically does not license HBO and similar networks, just as it does not license the commercial networks, it does have regulatory authority over cable. Should the FCC mandate that more effective measures – such as requiring a parental lock system on all cable converters – be taken to prevent children from gaining access to inappropriate content? At one time, a special effort had to be made to get access to cable channels outside the normal tuning range of the TV set; but now cable-originated (i.e., those fed from satellites) channels are interspersed with other over-the-air signals so that all signals are equally accessible. In other words, it is just as easy to tune to Playboy at Night (assuming you pay the monthly fee) as it is to get the local TV station. From a regulatory perspective, why should indecencies on cable be treated differently from those carried by standard broadcast stations?

INDECENCY AND OBSCENITY CONTINUED

The Carlin broadcast occurred during the tenure of Dean Burch as chairperson of the FCC (1969–1974), at a time when the commission was actively involved in the regulation process, and the Supreme Court decision was handed down just as an era of *deregulation* had begun. The deregulation process moved from moderation during 1978–1980 and then accelerated, with an emphasis on marketplace competition, beginning in 1981.[96]

Deregulation has never meant complete deregulation. Each commission has chosen its own areas of emphasis for enforcement, often in line with the dictates handed down by Congress in the form of statutes. In October 1977, President Jimmy Carter appointed Charles D. Ferris as chair of the FCC. Ferris, who served until February 1981, coined the term *reregulation* to characterize the tone of the commission during his tenure. The idea, according to the chair, was "to deregulate where markets would work effectively without regulation" while recognizing that "some markets are not competitive enough to be completely deregulated."[97] Robert E. Lee, who served the shortest term as chair of the FCC (February 5–May 18, 1981) even though he was a commissioner longer than any other individual in history, oversaw a continuation of the deregulation, which was substantially accelerated in 1981 when Mark Fowler took the helm. Indeed, the Fowler commission became known as the advocate of "unregulation" as it moved to eliminate as many regulations as possible, especially those involving programming. "Let the marketplace decide" soon became the buzz phrase of the Fowler administration as rules and regulations fell one by one, often with the rationale that the competitive marketplace was a more efficient and less expensive means of driving stations to serve in the public interest.

What was the impact of deregulation and unregulation on obscenity and indecency? During the next nine years after the *Pacifica* decision in the FCC essentially skirted the obscenity/indecency issue by announcing on several occasions that it was limiting application of *Pacifica* to repeated broadcasts of the "seven dirty words" earlier than 10:00 p.m.[98] During the entire 6-year reign of Mark Fowler — in fact during the entire period from the *Pacifica* decision in July 1978 until the end of the Fowler administration — not one broadcast station was cited for indecency in spite of numerous complaints by individuals and so-called morality groups. For example, soon after *Pacifica* the FCC turned to a petition from a group of citizens, Morality in Media of Massachusetts, to deny the renewal of the license of one of the top public television stations in the country, WGBH in Boston. The group complained that the Public Broadcasting Service (PBS) affiliate regularly carried programs with unacceptable language and themes as well as nudity. Among the programs cited were the acclaimed "Masterpiece Theatre," produced by WGBH and carried nationally over PBS, and the highly popular "Monty Python's Flying Circus," from the same team that later brought a string of irreverent film comedies such as *Monty Python and the Holy Grail*. In 1987, however, the picture changed dramatically. On April 16, the commission (a) cited three stations and an amateur ("ham") radio operator for broadcasting obscenities, and (b) announced that it would issue a public notice enunciating its position on indecency. Almost two weeks later, the FCC issued its public notice that it was no longer confining enforcement of 464 to the Carlin obscenities but instead indicated it would "apply the generic definition of indecency advanced in *Pacifica*. . . 'Language or material that depicts or describes, in terms patently offensive as measured by contemporary community standards for the broadcast medium, sexual or excretory activities or organs.' "[99]

Interestingly, even though the commission actually revoked the amateur radio operator's license,[100] it took a more lenient approach to the three broadcast licensees, referring one case to the U.S. Department of Justice (which declined to prosecute),[101] while taking no specific action against the other two.[102] The first broadcast station case involved another Pacifica station, KPFK-FM in Los Angeles, for airing excerpts from a play entitled "The Jerker" about two homosexuals with AIDS. The play, which had drawn critical acclaim when it ran in New York and at that time in Los Angeles, included rather explicit descriptions of the two men's sexual fantasies but advocated "safe sex" among homosexuals. A warning was given before the excerpts were aired after 10:00 p.m. In its later public notice, the commission explained that its previous assumption that children were not part of the audience at 10:00 p.m. had been proven wrong by recent research indicating that "there is still a reasonable risk that children may be in the . . . audience" after 10:00.

The second case involved a student-run station at the University of California, KCSB-FM, for broadcasting a rock song entitled "Makin' Bacon" after 10:00 p.m. According to the FCC, this song "contained a number of patently offensive references to sexual organs and activities." Finally, the third citation was the first of a series aimed at what is known as "shock radio." Infinity Broadcasting's station, WYSP-FM in Philadelphia, simulcast a morning drive-time program from WXRK-FM in New York City, "The Howard Stern Show" hosted by its namesake. (Only the Philadelphia station was cited, not the originating station in New York.) Stern is known in some circles as the "Daddy" of shock radio, also called "raunch radio" hosted by DJs or "shock jocks." The shock radio citation apparently caught many stations by surprise who were generally comfortable with the deregulatory— or as some critics characterized it, "unregulatory" or "nonregulatory"—stance of the FCC during Ronald Reagan's presidency under Chairs Mark Fowler (1981–1987) and Dennis Patrick (1987–1989).[103] But the move to stamp out indecency on the air was not abated even with one of industry's own at the helm, Alfred C. Sikes, who indicated on the day before he took over on August 8, 1989, "I hope as chairman of the FCC to help open markets, and I think the competition that results will help people."[104] He also said that the aggressive moves against obscenity begun by Chair Dennis Patrick would continue under his chairship: "I see carrying forward that vigorous enforcement."[105] During his confirmation hearings before the U.S. Senate Commerce Committee, much of the discussion centered on obscenity and violence (discussed later).[106]

In its citation against Philadelphia's WYSP-FM, which had moved in the audience ratings for that time slot from near the bottom of the heap to third place as a direct result of the "shock" show, the FCC included excerpts it considered indecent under its standards such as:

Howard Stern:	Have you ever had sex with an animal?
Caller:	No.
Stern:	Well, don't knock it. I was sodomized by Lambchop, you know that puppet Shari Lewis holds?
Stern:	Baaaaah. That's where I was thinking that Shari Lewis, instead of like sodomizing all the people at the Academy to get that shot on the Emmys she could've had lambchop do it.[107]

Shortly after the FCC cited WYSP-FM, Stern encouraged his listeners to voice their disagreement with the commission. "I am the last bastion of the First Amendment," he told them.[108] During 1992 and 1993 the FCC issued numerous notices of liability (NAL), including several against stations carrying Stern's show. With an NAL, the FCC cannot force a station to pay a fine unless the station decides not to fight the finding in court or the station loses in court.

Shock radio or derivations thereof continue on the airwaves, although such shows have toned down considerably since the FCC citations and their aftermath, which included a Reconsideration Order[109] in December 1987 in response to a flood of petitions on both sides of the issue; most were from broadcasters and their supporters requesting that the FCC rescind its order and provide clarification of standards of indecency being applied. Among the petitions was one from Morality in Media, asking that specific types of sexually explicit material be banned from the air even though they were not legally obscene. In its order the commission called the Morality in Media plan unconstitutional on the ground that the Supreme Court's holding in *Pacifica* clearly permitted only "reasonable time, place and manner restrictions" (see Chapter 4) on indecent content, not broad restrictions.

In a deft move but one certain to be appealed by public interest groups and broadcasters alike, the FCC refused to define *patently offensive* from its earlier order and particularly incensed First Amendment advocates by noting that it would not apply *Miller v. California's* (1973)[110] holding that *obscene* material must lack "serious literary, artistic, political or scientific value in evaluating whether broadcast content was *indecent*. "Merit is simply one of many variables, and it would give this particular variable undue importance if we were to single it out for greater weight or attention than we give other variables. . . . We must, therefore, reject an approach that would hold that if a work has merit, it is *per se* not indecent."[111]

The FCC emphasized that merit must be included among the variables and that the "ultimate determinative factor . . . is whether the material, when examined in context, is patently offensive." The order went on to announce that, for purposes of evaluating whether material was patently offensive, "contemporary community standards" (see *Miller*) would be defined as a national standard—an average broadcast viewer or listener: "In making the required determination of indecency, Commissioners draw on their knowledge of the views of the average viewer or listener, as well as their general expertise in broadcast matters. The determination reached is thus not one based on a local standard, but one based on a broader standard for broadcasting generally."[112]

In widely publicized footnote 47 in the reconsideration order, the Commission said, "We now indicate that 12:00 midnight is our current thinking as to when it is reasonable to expect that it is late enough to ensure that the risk of children in the audience is minimized and to rely on parents to exercise increased supervision over whatever children remain in the viewing and listening audience."[113] Thus the FCC was apparently establishing a so-called safe harbor beginning at midnight. Surprisingly, the decision made no mention of the hour at which this indecency window would end, although the general assumption was 6:00 A.M., as suggested by the FCC's General Counsel.

Action for Children's Television v. Federal Communications Commission (ACT I) (1988)

Further appeals were inevitable, given the potential impact of the original order and the reconsideration order. The culmination of those appeals arrived in the form of a U.S. Court of Appeals (DC Circuit) in 1988 in *Action for Children's Television v. Federal Communications Commission* (ACT I).[114] Before the decision arrived, however, a few skirmishes occurred. On January 12, 1988, the FCC initiated its first enforcement action against a TV station for broadcasting purportedly indecent material by announcing that KZKC-TV of Kansas City, Missouri, may have violated the new indecency standards established earlier in its reconsideration order.[115] The station, owned by Media Central Inc., had shown the R-rated movie *Private Lessons*, including scenes of a bare-breasted maid seducing a teenage boy, at 8:00 p.m. The owner claimed later the movie had been cut by an inexperienced editor and had violated the company's own standards but that the station should not be fined because the FCC standards were too vague and were being applied for the first time to a TV station.[116] (The earlier citations were against radio stations.) In June 1988, the FCC voted 2–1 (only three commissioners were on board at the time of the five maximum) to levy the maximum fine of $2,000 against the station but delayed assessing the fine because the U.S. Court of Appeals in *Action for Children's Television v. FCC*[117] ordered the commission to conduct a new hearing regarding the times at which indecent material may be aired.

Although there was hope at the time that *Action for Children's Television v. FCC* (1988)[118] would at least provide clearer guidelines regarding indecency, the decision of the court and the congressional action that followed muddied the waters even more. The Court of Appeals ruled that the FCC's definition of indecency was *not* substantially overbroad because "merit is properly treated as a factor in determining whether material is patently offensive, but it does not render such material *per se* not indecent"[119] The court also reiterated that indecent but not obscene material enjoys First Amendment protection, but the children's access to indecent material may be regulated through the use of channeling to protect unsupervised children.

The court was less than satisfied with the ratings data the FCC presented to show that large numbers of children were listening and watching during late hours, calling the evidence used in making channeling decisions "insubstantial . . . and more ritual than real." The midnight or "safe harbor" advice and the FCC's entire position on channeling "was not adequately thought through," the court said. Thus the judges instructed the commission to establish a safe harbor through a rulemaking proceeding so the FCC can "afford broadcasters clear notice of reasonably determined times at which indecent material may be safely aired"[120] and ordered a rehearing for two of the stations.

Within months after the court's decision, Congress, at the urging of conservatives such as Senator Jessie Helms (R-N.C.), passed an amendment to an appropriations bill that required the FCC to enforce its indecency policy 24 hours a day, effective January 27, 1989. The commission immediately complied and enacted such a rule. Upon petition, the U.S. Court of Appeals for the DC Circuit stayed the FCC rule, pending further review. In the meantime, the Court said, the FCC could gather evidence to support the ban. The Court order did *not* affect the commission's ability to enforce its "safe harbor" policy, and thus in September 1989 it fined Los Angeles talk radio KFI-AM more than $6,000 for airing indecent remarks during three afternoon programs hosted by shock jock Tom Leykis. Topics discussed with callers included penis size, "the grossest thing you ever put in your mouth" and "sexual secrets." The station chose not to appeal. Acting on public complaints, the FCC in August had cited WLUP-AM in Chicago, KSJO-FM in San Jose, California, and WFBQ-FM in Indianapolis, Indiana, for indecent programming. In October 1989, the agency fined two south Florida radio stations, WIOD and WZTA, for broadcasting song parodies the FCC considered indecent.[121] WIOD was slapped with a $10,000 fine ($2,000 for each of five offenses) and WZTA had to pay $2,000 for a single offense. The maximum fine permitted per offense is $2,000. All of the stations had been cited for daytime broadcasts. Finally, in mid-July 1990, the FCC felt it had gathered sufficient evidence to justify a 24-hour-a-day ban on indecent television and radio broadcasts and voted 5-0 to ask the U.S. Court of Appeals to lift its stay on enforcement of the rule. The purpose of the ban, according to the commission, is to protect children under 18, not just those under 12.

In voting to ask for reinstatement of the ban, the agency noted that it had received almost 90,000 complaints about indecent programming. TV Critic Ron Powers[122] of *GQ* magazine notes that the confrontation between programmers and the government has been building for decades as television in particular has pushed the permissible limits further and further. He points out that NBC-TV "Tonight Show" host Jack Paar was forced off the air in the

1950s for a reference to "WC" or water closet, a euphemism for bathroom, and the public was particularly concerned about "jiggly television" in the 1970s, which featured beautiful women bouncing around in skimpy clothes. Powers and other critics have denounced the FCC's actions as censorship, but Powers feels the broadcasters may very well have brought the suppression on themselves.[123]

Action for Children's Television
v. Federal Communications Commission
(ACT II) (1991)

In April 1991 the U.S. Court of Appeals for the DC Circuit held in *Action for Children's Television v. Federal Communications Commission* (ACT II) that the 24-hour ban was unconstitutional prior restraint because it totally barred indecent speech, which enjoyed First Amendment protection.[124] The appellate court, however, indicated the FCC should consider reinstituting a "safe harbor" period for indecent speech, but so far the commission and Congress have steered clear of the issue. Until the federal appeals court decision, Congress appeared determined to keep a 24-hour ban as did the FCC. As FCC General Counsel Robert L. Pettit noted before the court's ruling, "Under the Communications Act, the Commission is obliged to enforce an indecency standard; the Commission has consistently articulated a standard for indecency; it has been upheld by the Supreme Court."[125] Pettit also contends that indecency "is an area where the Commission has been given, by Congress, a statutory responsibility, and what we're doing is carrying out that congressionally mandated responsibility. It's no more and no less."[126]

In *ACT II*, the DC Circuit Court cited both *ACT I* and the 1989 U.S. Supreme Court decision in *Sable Communications v. FCC*[127] to justify its decision. While recognizing that Congress could prevent children from exposure to dial-a-porn messages (sexually oriented phone services), the Court ruled in *Sable Communications* that such restrictions must be strictly limited and thus the federal statute's outright ban on both indecent and obscene interstate commercial telephone messages was unconstitutional. The Court upheld a lower court's decision that the statute could not ban indecent messages but could prohibit obscene messages. In *Sable Communications*, the Supreme Court specifically rejected the 1978 *FCC v. Pacifica Foundation* decision, discussed earlier, as justification for the ban on indecent phone messages. The Court distinguished *Pacifica* by pointing to the narrowness of the *Pacifica* holding and the "uniquely pervasive" nature of broadcasting that "can intrude on the privacy of the home without prior warning as to program content." According to the court, "Placing a telephone call is not the same as turning on a radio and being taken by surprise by an indecent message." Thus the justices did not directly confront the 24-hour indecent broadcasting ban because this issue arose independent of the case at hand. However, in 1992 the U.S. Supreme Court denied *certiorari* on appeal, thus ending the indecency saga in the courts at least for awhile.

OTHER RESTRICTIONS ON CONTENT

Other forms of offensive programming, other than violence, have attracted virtually no attention from the commission. For example, there have been public complaints recently about racist, anti-Semitic and anti-homosexual comments from shock jocks. For example, WGST-AM (Atlanta) talk-show host Ed Tyll was suspended by station management for two weeks in July 1987 for comparing Georgia state representative, John Lewis, to the Buckwheat character in the old TV series, *"Little Rascals."*[128] In a March 10, 1989, show, shock jock Perry Stone of KSJO-FM in San Jose, California, encouraged two Brownies to steal Girl Scout cookie money and later insulted another girl on the air. As a result, he was suspended and then fired.[129]

The sizzle of competition on the airwaves is likely to drive stations to continue to test the limits of acceptability and to encourage the government to just as aggressively defend the limits. In 1992 Congress included a provision in its bill authorizing funding for public broadcasting that banned "indecent programming" on both radio and televisision between 6 a.m. and 10 p.m. on public stations and 6 a.m. and midnight for all other stations.[130] In 1993, the FCC issued rules implementing the provision.

Is there a solution to the confrontation? Former FCC Chair Al Sikes urged broadcasters to set their own standards by initiating a voluntary code. The National Association of Broadcasters, the nonprofit, nongovernmental organization mentioned earlier in this chapter, had a code of "good practice" from 1929 to 1983, which included standards for programming and advertising as well as regulations and procedures.[131] (Television and radio had separate but fairly similar codes). Both the family viewing and advertising provisions were challenged as illegal during the late 1970s, and the NAB, facing a likely long and expensive battle with writers groups over family viewing and the Justice Department over advertising restrictions, killed both the TV and the radio codes in 1983. The family viewing standards, which were adopted by the three commercial networks on April 21, 1975, included a provision that "entertainment programming inappropriate for viewing by a general family audience should not be broadcast during the first hour of network entertainment programming in prime time and in the immediately preceding hour."[132] This essentially restricted TV network programming to family entertainment from 8:00–9:00 p.m. during weekdays and 7:00–8:00 p.m. on weekends. The

Writers Guild of America challenged the provision as a violation of the First Amendment rights of television writers and fought the NAB in court until 1983 when the codes were abandoned by the NAB and thus the constitutional question was moot. The Justice Department attacked various restrictions imposed by the advertising standards — such as the limit on the number of products that could be featured in the same advertisement — as violating federal antitrust laws. The NAB reached an agreement with the Justice Department in 1982 to delete the code provisions in question in return for an end to the legal challenges.

During the fall 1993 season, the major commercial television networks began voluntarily labeling some shows such as the controversial ABC show, "NYPD Blue" with the advisory: "Due to some violent content, parental discretion is advised." In late 1993 Reed Hundt, a telecommunications lawyer, took over as FCC chair.

THE FAIRNESS DOCTRINE

Of all the issues in which the FCC has been embroiled, probably none has been more controversial than the Fairness Doctrine, first enunciated by the commission in 1949 in a "Report on Editorializing by Broadcasting Licensees" and clarified *ad infinitum* in numerous rulings since that time. The doctrine essentially explained that stations had an affirmative duty to devote a reasonable percentage of time to "consideration and discussion of public issues in the community." In 1959, Congress amended 315(a), which specifies exemptions under the equal opportunities rule, and *presumably* codified (i.e., systematically incorporated into statutory law) the fairness doctrine. Section 315 makes no direct mention of the doctrine but Public Law 86-274, which enacted the amendments stated, "Nothing in the foregoing shall be construed as relieving broadcasters from the obligation imposed upon them by this Act to operate in the public interest and to afford reasonable opportunity for the discussion of conflicting views on issues of public importance."[133]

In 1969 the U.S. Supreme Court for the first time chose to determine the constitutionality of the fairness doctrine. In *Red Lion Broadcasting v. FCC* (1969),[134] the Court held that the doctrine and its allied personal-attack rule were not unconstitutional and in a case decided at the same time, *U.S. v. Radio Television News Directors' Association* (RTNDA), upheld the political-editorializing rules. *Red Lion* was used for almost two decades by the commission to justify enforcement of the fairness doctrine. *Red Lion* arose when WGCB-AM, a small station in Red Lion, Pennsylvania, broadcast a 15-minute program by Rev. Billy James Hargis, as part of a "Christian Crusade" series. On the show, Hargis discussed a book by Fred J. Cook,

Goldwater—Extremist on the Right, and claimed that the author had been fired by a newspaper for making false charges against city officials. Hargis also said Cook had worked for a Communist-affiliated publication, had defended Alger Hiss and had attacked FBI Director J. Edgar Hoover and the Central Intelligence Agency. Cook's book, according to the minister, was "to smear and destroy Barry Goldwater."[135] The writer requested free air time to respond to the personal attack under the fairness doctrine, but the station refused. The FCC ruled in Cook's favor, and the U.S. Court of Appeals for the DC Circuit upheld the FCC decision. The RTNDA had challenged the doctrine and its political-editorializing rules, mentioned earlier in this chapter, which the seventh Circuit U.S. Court of Appeals declared unconstitutional. The U.S. Supreme Court upheld the DC Circuit decision and overturned the seventh Circuit ruling, thus upholding the constitutionality of the doctrine and its allied rules. "In light of the fact that the 'public interest' in broadcasting clearly encompasses the presentation of vigorous debate of controversial issues of importance and concern to the public . . . we think the fairness doctrine and its component personal attack and political editorializing regulations are a legitimate exercise of congressionally delegated authority."[136]

The 8–0 decision written by Justice Byron R. White emphasized the scarcity of broadcast frequencies and the "legitimate claims of those unable without governmental assistance to gain access to those frequencies for expression of their views" as justification for the doctrine.

During the chairship (1981–1987) of deregulation advocate Mark Fowler, only one station was ever cited by the full commission for violating the fairness doctrine. On October 26, 1984, the FCC ruled that WTVH-TV of Syracuse, New York, had violated the doctrine in airing a 1982 series of commercials arguing for construction of New York State's Nine Mile II nuclear power plant. According to the commission, the station had "failed to afford a reasonable opportunity for the presentation of viewpoints contrasting to those presented in the advertisements and, thus, has failed to assure that the public was not left uniformed."[137] In the same year, the FCC issued a Notice of Inquiry of the fairness doctrine, and the inquiry was completed on August 7, 1985, when the FCC issued its 1985 Fairness Report, which raised serious doubts about the constitutionality of the doctrine and concluded that it did not serve the public interest.[138] The agency, however, said it probably lacked authority to determine the doctrine's constitutionality and announced that it would continue to enforce the doctrine because Congress expected it to do so.

Two months after its Inquiry, the FCC denied the petition of Meredith Corp., owner of WTVH, for reconsideration, citing its decision in the 1985 Fairness Report that it would defer to Congress and the courts. Meredith subsequently appealed the decision to the U.S. Court of Appeals (DC Cir.).[139] In 1986 the Fairness Doctrine picture became even more confusing and complex when the U.S. Court of Appeals for the DC Circuit held in

Telecommunications Research and Action Center (TRAC) v. FCC[140] in a decision involving a new technology, teletext, that the doctrine had *not* been codified by the 1959 amendments. Instead, the court said, the amendment was an attempt by Congress to merely affirm that the commission had the *discretion* of enforcing or not enforcing the doctrine the commission had created. In the decision written by Judge Robert Bork (whose nomination by President Reagan to the Supreme Court was later rejected by the Senate), the Court also challenged the "scarcity" argument used to justify greater First Amendment restrictions on the broadcast media than the print media. This decision could very well be influential in convincing the U.S. Supreme Court in the near future to "eliminate the distinction between print and broadcast media."[141] Indeed, the Supreme Court has hinted on at least one occasion—in dicta in footnotes in *FCC v. League of Women Voters* (1984)[142] in which it held that a federal statute prohibiting editorials by federally funded public broadcast stations was unconstitutional—that the prevailing "spectrum scarcity" rationale for broadcast regulation may be worthy of reevaluation by the Court.

In January 1987, the battle lines began to be drawn with the FCC, the executive branch, broadcasters and strong First Amendment advocates on one side, with Congress and some public interest groups on the other side and the courts generally on the sidelines as referees. In *RTNDA v. FCC* and *Meredith Corp. v. FCC* (1987),[143] the U.S. Court of Appeals (DC Cir.) remanded *Meredith* to the commission for further determination of the constitutionality of the fairness doctrine and ordered additional briefs and oral arguments in *RTNDA* to determine whether the FCC had acted improperly when it refused earlier to initiate a rule-making proceeding at RTNDA's request on the doctrine. The handwriting was on the wall, and on August 4, 1987, the FCC announced that "the set of obligations known as the 'fairness doctrine' violated the First Amendment rights of broadcasters."[144] The action came in response to the remand order of the U.S. Court of Appeals in *Meredith*. The FCC went even further in urging the U.S. Supreme Court to reconsider the scarcity rationale on which it based the 1969 *Red Lion* decision, noting that the number of broadcast stations far exceeds the number of daily newspapers. The commission said the Court should, instead, apply a traditional First Amendment analysis to broadcasters.

Earlier, Congress had acted swiftly to enact the doctrine into federal law, and such a bill passed both the Senate (59–31) and the House (302–102), but President Reagan vetoed in on June 19, 1987. Congress then failed to get the necessary two-thirds majority to override the veto. On March 24, 1988, the FCC rejected petitions for consideration of its previous decision, but reaffirmed that it would no longer enforce the doctrine. The commission also reaffirmed that it was *not* abandoning the equal time and reasonable access provisions of the 1934 Communications Act, as amended, including §§312 and 315.[145]

Members of Congress have continued to attempt to have a measure codifying the fairness doctrine attached to various expenditure bills, but, thus far, their efforts have failed in one way or another. Former President Bush made it clear while he was in office that he would veto any bill to which such a measure was attached and any separate bills. The FCC gained further support for its position on February 10, 1989, when the DC Circuit of the U.S. Court of Appeals upheld the FCC's refusal to enforce the fairness doctrine against Meredith Corporation and WTVH-TV. The Court did not determine whether the doctrine was constitutional, but instead noted: "Although the Commission somewhat entangled its public interest and constitutional findings, we find that the Commission's public interest determination was an independent basis for its decision and was supported by the record. We upheld that determination without reaching the constitutional issue."[146]

As with indecency, this is an area whose ultimate fate has yet to be determined. As of this writing, the doctrine is dead, and its resurrection appears unlikely in spite of the fact that it has considerable support in Congress and in other circles. After decades of application, it may have met its demise. Nearly all media organizations including the NAB, RTNDA, the Society of Professional Journalists (SPJ), and the American Newspaper Publishers Association (ANPA) strongly support the FCC in its decision to kill the doctrine. During the life of the doctrine, the FCC reportedly received more than 137,000 letters, telephone calls, petitions and other forms of complaint about the doctrine.[147] Most members of Congress share the sentiments of Congressman Edward J. Markey (D-Mass.) who contends, "All the Fairness Doctrine requires broadcasters to do is what any good journalist would do anyway: address important issues in a fair and impartial manner."[148] Or, as journalism professor Jerry Dunklee notes, "Is fairness too much to ask of those who profit from the use of a commodity—the airwaves—which, unlike printing presses, belongs to all of us."[149] On the other hand, doctrine opponents such as SPJ's First Amendment Counsel Bruce Sanford argues, "Fairness Doctrine supporters should admit, however, that allowing . . . broadcasters the freedom to exercise good journalism is at the core of the First Amendment."[150]

CHILDREN'S PROGRAMMING

In late 1991 new FCC rules took effect to implement the Children's Television Act of 1990, passed by Congress and enacted without President George Bush's signature. The statute delegated to the commission the authority to interpret and enforce its provisions, which include a mandate that broadcasters serve the educational needs of children. Under the FCC rules, the maximum time allocated to commercials during programming directed primarily to children on both commercial and cable television is 10.5 minutes per hour on weekends and 12 minutes an hour on weekdays. The rules do not specify any minimum time that broadcasters must set aside for children's programming but instead left that decision in the hands of the networks and local stations. Broadcasters, however, must provide in their files for public inspection summaries of programming that they contend serves children.

The FCC decided not to clamp down on so-called 30-minute commercials, shows based on characters such as GI-Joe, He-Man, Thundercats and the Teenage Mutant Ninja Turtles. The commission said this type of program will be considered full commercial time only if the show includes paid advertising for the toy of the particular character. However, in March 1993 the FCC announced that these programs and others such as "The Jetsons" and "The Flintstones" could no longer count as "educational and informational" programming under the 1990 act. The Commission also adopted a Notice of Inquiry to identify TV programs that "serve the educational and informational needs of children" and that "further the positive development of children."

REGULATION OF NEWER TECHNOLOGIES

Cable Television

Although radio and television broadcasting preceded it, cable television is actually a relatively old technology, having been first developed in the 1940s as a means of hauling in signals from distant TV stations to rural communities that had no direct access to over-the-air broadcasts. According to the FCC, in 1950 there were only 70 communities in the whole country with cable systems.[151] By 1990, it had become a $15 billion industry with access to 80 million homes through more than 8,000 cable systems, of which only 32 had any direct competition. Whereas there were only 14 million subscribers in 1980, that had grown to 53.9 million or about 58 percent of all homes by 1990.[152] Unlike the early systems that usually offered no more than three or four VHF signals, the typical cable system now offers 50 or more channels that include local stations, public access channels, distant "superstations" and satellite-delivered general networks such as USA, Lifetime and Black Entertainment Television to specialized networks like the Weather Channel, The Nashville Network, Music Television, Comedy Central and even the Sci-Fi Channel and the Cartoon Network. A huge variety of pay or premium channels is available from HBO/Cinemax and Showtime/The Movie Channel to adult pay-per-view channels. Until March 25, 1990, there was even a

XXX-rated channel known as American Exxxtasy, which was available primarily to satellite dish owners, but the network left the air after a series of interesting circumstances, as described in Chapter 11.

Cable has been regulated by the FCC, although not exclusively, since 1965, but the 1984 Cable Communications Policy Act, with subsequent amendments, is the current regulatory scheme for cable, with the FCC having control over some aspects of the industry but with local franchising authorities having jurisdiction over other aspects. The basic scheme is that local governments (city, town or county) grant *franchises* to cable companies to operate local systems, although there are national standards for rate regulation, franchise renewals and franchise fees.[153] Cable systems are required to register with the commission, but they are not licensed *per se*, as are broadcast stations. The federal rules are primarily in the areas of cross-media ownership and technical specifications. Cable systems must also comply with §312 and §315. One of the most controversial provisions of the Cable Communications Policy Act of 1984 was §622, which kept local governments from charging more than 5 percent of gross revenues for franchising, and §623, which prohibited them in most instances from regulating rates for basic and premium services, effective January 1, 1987.[154] According to a General Accounting Office Report delivered to Congress in 1990, between November 30, 1986, and December 31, 1989, rates for the lowest-priced basic service increased 43 percent from an average per subscriber of $11.14 to $15.95. The public and organizations such as the NAB called for cable to be regulated again, and in October 1992 Congress passed a new cable regulation bill that was vetoed by President Bush. The Senate and the House, however, overrode the veto, and the legislation took effect. The statute was approved despite a multimillion dollar advertising campaign by the cable television industry to defeat the bill by trying to convince consumers that it would substantially increase cable fees. Under the statute, the Cable Television Consumer Protection and Competition Act of 1992,[155] (a) the Federal Communications Commission must establish regulations, which would be administered by local governments, to implement "reasonable" rates for basic cable subscriptions, installation fees and equipment; (b) the FCC would also set standards for reception quality and for customer service, including requests for service and complaints; (c) cable programmers such as Time-Warner, which owns Home Box Office and Cinemax, must license their programming to competitors such as microwave and satellite broadcasters; (d) cable companies are required to negotiate compensation agreements with over-the-air stations that have not previously been paid for the retransmission of their signals; and (e) cable companies must carry the signals of local affiliates of ABC, CBS, NBC, Fox and PBS as part of the basic package. The latter is known as the "must carry" rule.

Nearly all cable operators come under the statute because it exempts only those in a market in which there is a competing company available to at least half of the potential customers and in which a minimum of 15 percent of the households actually subscribe to the competing firm.

Less than 24 hours after Congress overrode the President's veto, the Turner Broadcasting System filed suit in U.S. District Court for the District of Columbia to challenge the "must carry" provision of the bill as a violation of the First Amendment. The TBS cable networks include superstation WTBS, the Cable News Networks (CNN and CNN Headline News), Turner Network Television and the Cartoon Network. In April 1993 the U.S. District Court for the District of Columbia ruled 2-1 that the must-carry provisions were not unconstitutional. According to the court, "[T]o the extent First Amendment speech is affected at all, it is simply a by-product of the fact that video signals have no other function than to convey information.[156]

Consumers have generally been pleased with the new cable law, but they were outraged by at least one other aspect of cable regulation, one not initiated by the industry, unlike the 1984 act, which had strong support from cable companies. In May 1988, the FCC adopted new syndicated exclusivity ("syndex") rules, similar to those in effect from 1972 to 1980 (when the FCC dropped them), which requires cable companies to black out syndicated programming available to local viewers from distant television stations such as "superstations" WTBS (Atlanta), WGN (Chicago) and WPIX (New York) when a local station has signed a contract with the syndicator for exclusive rights to the program. The syndex rules took effect January 1, 1990, after the DC Circuit U.S. Court of Appeals ruled the commission had the authority to enact and enforce them.[157] The rules do require that the local station request the blackout, but it is highly unlikely that a station with an exclusive contract with a supplier would not do so because the purpose of such a contract is to have exclusive control over the broadcasting of that program in that market, including cable signals. Consumers were initially upset because such popular syndicated shows as "Alf," "Cheers," and "Teenage Mutant Ninja Turtles" were excised. Network programs are not affected by the rules, although shows that have been on the networks in the past and that may still be running more recent episodes on the networks or have recently finished a network are affected. For example, older reruns of the "Cosby Show" were syndicated to local stations even though at one time NBC was showing original episodes and more recent reruns. The complaints appear to have abated as viewers adjust to the changes and some cable systems and superstations substitute alternative programming instead of a black screen.

There are a number of other FCC rules affecting cable television, but the basic approach of the commission and Congress until 1992 had been to maintain only minimum control over the industry, especially in the area of programming. Even the courts have occasionally handed the cable companies important victories—such as the rulings by the U.S. Court of Appeals (DC Cir.) in 1985[158] and in 1987[159] that the "must carry" rule was a violation of

MEDIA OWNERSHIP RULES   265

the First Amendment. In September 1993, however, a U.S. District Court judge upheld the provision in the 1992 Act known as the "retransmission" rule that required cable companies to negotiate compensation agreements with local affiliates.

MEDIA OWNERSHIP RULES

The FCC has adopted a series of regulations restricting ownership of stations, cable systems and cross-media ownership. These include:

1. **Radio-Television Cross Ownership.** Under this policy, known as the "one-to-a-market" rule, the same entity (corporation, individual or group) cannot own both a radio and a television station in the same market (primarily area of coverage) except in the top 25 markets in which at least 30 separately owned stations would remain or when one of the stations involved in the sale is bankrupt or has ceased broadcasting. A waiver must be sought for any such sale, but the commission has a flexible policy. The rule is under review and likely to change to allow more combinations.

2. **Duopoly Ownership.** This rule bars any entity from any ownership in two television stations whose Grade B service contours (i.e., secondary signals) overlap. This rule is also being reviewed.

3. **National Ownership Rules.** These include an ownership limit of 12 television stations in the country and 20 FM and 20 AM radio stations. The rules originally restricted ownership to 7 TV, 7 AM and 7 FM stations.

4. **Network-TV Cable Cross Ownership Rule.** In 1992 the FCC modified this rule to allow a national television network to own cable systems if the ownership does not exceed 10 percent of the homes in the country having access to cable or half of the homes with access within any area of dominant influence (ADI or primary area in which signals can be received over-the-air). An exception to the latter percentage can be made if there is a competing cable system.[160]

PROGRAM OWNERSHIP RIGHTS

The FCC not only has a hand in media ownership but also indirectly controls programming through two sets of rules—the **Financial Interest and Syndication Rules** ("fin-syn") and the **Prime Time Access Rule.** The fin-syn rules were first enacted by the commission in 1970 to keep the three major commercial networks at that time—CBS, NBC and ABC—from owning or having financial rights in syndicated programs. Contrary to popular belief, the networks do not own the copyright or other rights to most programs they carry. Instead they typically acquire from a production company the right to broadcast a program a specified number of times within a particular time, and then all rights revert back to the producer. The rules have been very heavily criticized over the years by many groups and broadcasters, but the FCC did not ease the rather strict rules until 1983. In 1991, the rules were relaxed even more to allow syndicated rights or financial interest by the networks in programs solely produced by the network, foreign co-productions by the network and certain kinds of domestic co-productions by the network and certain kinds of domestic co-productions. Such productions were, however, limited to no more than 40 percent of the network's prime time schedule.[161]

In November 1992 a three-judge panel of the Seventh Circuit U.S. Court of Appeals in Chicago vacated the fin-syn rules as modified a year earlier by the FCC and gave the commission the option of rewriting the rules.[162] With President Bill Clinton in office, a split Commission in April 1993 basically killed the fin-syn rules, including the 40 percent provision and the restrictions on network ownership of overseas syndication interests in both off-network and first-run programs. The FCC, however, voted to continue to bar the networks from owning *domestic* syndication rights of first-run programming.

With Reed Hunt on board as FCC Chair, the Commission was expected to be even tougher on cable television but allow more room for broadcasters.

The **Prime Time Access Rule** ("PTAR"),[163] also adopted in 1970, bars network-affiliated TV stations in the top 50 markets from broadcasting more than three hours of network programming during prime time (generally (7:00–11:00 p.m. Eastern and Pacific Time or 6:00–10:00 p.m. Central or Mountain Time) unless the program is a half-hour of network news either just before or just after a least an hour of local news or public affairs programming. There has been considerable pressure on the FCC to kill this rule, and it is likely to die in the next few years if not sooner.

There are also rules regarding simulcasting signals in the same market and multichannel services, but they are beyond the scope of this book. Telephone companies ("Telcos") until recently have been barred from cable ownership and from offering their own video services, known as "video dialtones." This restriction is being gradually lifted under the rationale that cable companies can now survive with competition and thus no longer deserve special protection.

RECENT TECHNOLOGICAL DEVELOPMENTS

The broadcast regulation picture is in a state of flux in many areas as new technologies are developed and new forms of content are introduced as well. For several years, Europe and Japan have been experimenting with high-definition television (HDTV), including over-the-air broadcasts; this revolutionary technology is not expected to be available in the United States for some time. According to the developers, HDTV is actually a new medium that will not only offer a picture and sound as good as or better than the movie theater, but it will also have an impact on the military, manufacturing and medicine.[164] Technical regulations are one matter, but content is another. For example, in April 1990 the FCC decided that HDTV broadcasts would be "simulcast" so that current television sets that use analog transmission would not become obsolete, or at least not immediately. Under this arrangement, stations would broadcast two signals — one analog and the other digital for consumers with HDTV receivers. Today's color TV sets have only 525 lines per inch rather than the 700-plus lines of systems in many other countries because the commission chose to restrict the color system to a technology that was compatible with existing black-and-white sets rather than choose a system with superior color and picture quality that would render the black-and-white sets obsolete. Thus this "two-channel" format would prevent the new HDTV technology from being held back by the older format. By 1994 the FCC was expected to decide which one of five HDTV systems would get the nod of approval.

In mid-1994 a new high-power direct broadcast service, DirecTV, was scheduled to begin offering 150 channels of digital television via satellite directly to consumers who purchased a $700 system that includes an 18-inch fixed dish that can be mounted on a window sill.

There are more new technologies on the horizon that may present regulatory problems for the commission, such as **Digital Audio Broadcasting** (DAB) that will make it possible to transmit radio signals directly to consumers in their cars, homes and offices via satellite, including subscription radio. The person would pay a monthly fee to receive a radio station or package of stations.

SUMMARY AND CONCLUSIONS

For more than 75 years, broadcasting has been regulated as a limited public resource, whose frequency space is occupied by licensees charged to serve the public interest, convenience and necessity. The primary governing body in this regulatory scheme has been the Federal Communications Commission since the Communications Act of 1934. During the last decade, the commission has taken a series of steps to deregulate many aspects of broadcasting, especially in programming, including abandonment of the fairness doctrine, which Congress continues to threaten to revive through codification but thus far to no avail. The one area of programming where the FCC has tightened the reins is indecency, whose regulation has support from Congress, the executive branch and the public. The 1992 Cable Act allows cable companies to establish a written policy that bans "programming that the cable operator reasonably believes describes or depicts sexual or excretory activities in a patently offensive manner as measured by contemporary community standards." It also appears that for the near future the agency will continue to enforce the equal opportunity rules and other political programming regulations unless the Supreme Court declares the scarcity rationale invalid for imposing greater First Amendment restrictions on broadcasting than print media. As new technologies such as Direct Broadcasting via Satellite (DBS), teletext and high-definition TV change the face of broadcasting, the regulatory scheme is likely to change as well, although it may be out of sync as the courts play catchup. It may well be that by the end of the century, broadcasting will have become a full-fledged member of the First Amendment fraternity.

In 1993, however, broadcasters suffered a major setback in seeking full First Amendment protection when the U.S. Supreme Court struck down a challenge to Title 18, §1304, of the U.S. Code. This section makes it illegal to broadcast lottery information if lotteries are illegal in the state in which the station transmits its signal. In *U.S. v. Edge Broadcasting*, the Court applied the *Central Hudson* test and held that Congress had the right to impose such prior restraint even though more than 90% of the radio station's audience was in Virginia where there is a state lottery. The station was headquartered in North Carolina, 3 miles from the Virginia border. (North Carolina did not have a lottery.)

7 Libel

They have committed false report; moreover, they have spoken untruths; secondarily, they are slanders; sixth and lastly, they have belied a lady; thirdly, they have verified unjust things; and to conclude, they are lying knaves.
—Dogberry in William Shakespeare's *Much Ado About Nothing*

And thus he bore without abuse
  The grand old name of gentleman,
  Defamed by every charlatan,
And soil'd with all ignoble use.
        —From Alfred Lord Tennyson's *In Memoriam A.H.H.*

Good name in man or woman, dear my lord,
Is the immediate jewel of their souls;
Who steals my purse steals trash; 'tis something nothing;
'Twas mine, 'tis his, and has been slave to thousands;
But he that filches from me my good name
Robs me of that which not enriches him,
And Makes me poor indeed.
              —Iago in William Shakespeare's *Othello*

A good name is more desirable than great riches;
to be esteemed is better than silver or gold.
                    —Proverbs 22:1 (NIV)

More than two decades ago when the late William L. Prosser, the country's foremost authority on the law of torts until his death, published his fourth edition of his hornbook, *Law of Torts*,[1] he noted from the outset:

It must be confessed at the beginning that there is a great deal of the law of defamation that makes no sense. It contains anomalies and absurdities for which no legal writer ever has a kind word, and it is a curious compound of a strict liability imposed upon innocent defendants, as rigid and extreme as anything found in the law, with a blind and almost perverse refusal to compensate the plaintiff for real and very serious harm.[2]

Little has changed in the decades since Prosser published these statements even though the U.S. Supreme Court alone has issued dozens of opinions on defamation and there have been thousands of libel trials and lower appellate court decisions. The law of defamation continues in many ways to defy logic and reasoning even with the constitutionalization of libel that arrived with the *New York Times v. Sullivan*[3] decision by the Supreme Court in 1964, as discussed *infra*. There are some basic rules that have been established, at least enough for the hornbooks, but the law of defamation is enormously complicated, confusing and cumbersome; but, most of all, it is downright frightening for journalists and the news media. The author of this textbook and another professor have been conducting research for the last several years on the chilling effect of libel suits on newspapers and other mass media. The studies have been rather consistent in their findings that (a) even the best newspapers and radio and television stations, as well as the networks, have lost some major libel suits, some to the tune of tens of millions of dollars; (b) both threatened and actual libel suits chill large and small media outlets into being less aggressive and overly cautious in their reporting and editing of news[4]; and (c) public perceptions about libel are appallingly inaccurate, especially in terms of understanding basic concepts such as actual malice and truth as a defense.[5]

Libel seminars appear regularly at professional association meetings, including those of the Newspaper Association of American (NAA), American Society of Newspaper Editors (ASNE), Investigative Reporters and Editors, Inc. (IRE), National Association of Broadcasters (NAB), Society of Professional Journalists (SPJ) and Women in Communications, Inc. (WICI). Inevitably, they are among the most widely attended sessions because journalists and publishers have seen the writing on the wall for some time as more and more plaintiffs win in libel trials and the stakes get higher and higher as megabuck awards become the norm. According to figures compiled by the Libel Defense Resource Center (LDRC), a nonprofit organization that monitors libel cases throughout the country, 72.4 percent of jury verdicts in libel cases during 1990–1991 were decided in favor of the plaintiff.[6] Those are great odds for a plaintiff in light of the fact that the percentage of successful suits for plaintiffs in other tort cases, such as those involving personal injuries and products liability, is substantially lower, typically less than 50 percent. Even on appeal, the odds are still unfavorable, although they have improved for media defendants. During 1987–1988, the chance of a defendant having a libel verdict in favor of the plaintiff overturned on appeal or having a verdict in favor of the defendant upheld was about 62 percent, a significant drop from the 75 percent of the past. During 1989–1990, the percentage fell further—to 52 percent, but it went up slightly in 1990–1991 to 53.1 percent. Only 58 of 167 libel awards, or slightly more than one-third, ended up with a check being written by the defendant to the plaintiff. Thus, if a case is heard by an appellate court, it is more likely to be decided in favor of the defendant than the plaintiff. The average libel award in 1990–1991 was $9 million, more than twice what it was the year before. The average punitive damages award jumped to $8.2 million, compared to $1.5 million the decade before.[7]

THE ORIGINS OF DEFAMATION

Defamation, which includes both libel and slander (as discussed in the next section), is clearly an old tort. But it is difficult to determine exactly how old, as evidenced by the different origins ascribed to each of these two causes of action by experts. Prosser traces modern-day defamation to 16- and 17-century England with the ecclesiastical and common law courts battling over jurisdiction in slander cases.[8] Later, political libel or sedition developed in the notorious Court of Star Chamber as mass printing became more prevalent, according to Prosser.[9] Gartner traces the word *libel* to the Latin *libellus*, meaning "little book"[10] to signify the pamphlets that were published to broadcast rumors and gossip about the famous to the masses or the not-so-famous during the Elizabethan era in England. Sanford notes that the Anglo-American libel suit can be traced to remedies provided to defamed individuals as early as pre-Norman times, with the church becoming the first major arbiter of Anglo-Saxon cases.[11]

Eventually four types of libel developed at common law in England—sedition, defamation, blasphemy and obscene libel.[12] *Sedition* or *seditious libel*, as discussed *infra*, was and still is criticism of the government and/or government officials. From the mid-15th century until its abolition by Parliament in 1641, the English Star Chamber secretly tried without a jury and ordered the torture of individuals who spoke ill of the monarchy. For some publishers, their fate for committing such an offense may have been worse than death. For example, in 1636, William Prynn was pilloried in stocks in the public square, had his ears cut off, was fined 10,000 pounds and then was imprisoned for life for denouncing plays and other activities in a book that was deemed to criticize the queen by inference.[13] John Twyn suffered an even more horrible demise in 1663 for advocating in his book that a ruler should be accountable to the people. He was sentenced by the judge to first be hanged by the neck and then, while he was still alive, to be cut down and castrated, after which his intestines were to be taken out and burned while he remained alive.

Finally, he was to be beheaded and quartered.[14] No mention was apparently made about what was to be done if he died before he had a chance to see his body parts removed!

Defamation, also known as *private libel* and handled at first by the ecclesiastical courts, gradually became a common law offense with requirements somewhat similar to those of libel and slander today. *Blasphemy* or *blasphemous libel* was principally criticism of God, Christ, the church or church leaders. It is nonexistent today in this country but is still alive and well in some countries and caught many individuals in its vise until the mid-19th century in England. In October 1992 when Irish singer Sinead O' Connor tore up a picture of Pope John Paul II on NBC-TV's "Saturday Night Live," many viewers reacted by characterizing her action as blasphemy, but no charges were ever brought against her. Even if she had been charged, she could never have been successfully prosecuted. This crime is, thankfully, dead. Finally, *obscenity* or *obscene libel* was not a major concern of the British until about the early 19th century with the spread of Methodism. But as *Regina v. Hicklin* (1868; discussed in Chapter 11) illustrates, obscenity was strongly suppressed by the mid-19th century in both England and the United States, which adopted the Hicklin rule until 1957.[15]

LIBEL VERSUS SLANDER

With the proliferation of mass printing, *defamation*, which is basically information that tends to subject an individual or other entity, such as a corporation, to public hatred, contempt or ridicule, involved a new factor — the multiplying of harm to one's reputation through widespread dissemination via publication. *Slander*, which is still oral defamation, and libel (printed defamation) became separate torts with somewhat different rules. The reasons for this distinction are mired in the complexity of history, but the distinction, nevertheless, continues, albeit with inconsistencies. Some states, for example, treat broadcast defamation as libel, although others follow the recommendation of the Restatement (Second) of Torts that print and electronic media be treated the same — that is, that both be considered libel.[16]

The distinction between libel and slander is very important because in most jurisdictions **special damages** must be demonstrated by plaintiffs before they can recover any damages unless the slander falls into one of four categories: (a) imputation of crime; (b) imputation of a loathsome disease such as leprosy or a venereal disease; (c) imputations affecting one's trade, business, profession or calling; and (d) imputation of unchastity to a woman (or man now in a few states). Special damages, as discussed *infra*, are specific pecuniary loss or what is commonly called "out-of-pocket" expenses. They are usually difficult to prove in slander cases, but, of course, they do not have to occur if the slander fits into one of the four traditional pegs. Except in broadcasting in a few jurisdictions, slander is not a major problem. Indeed, broadcasters generally do not object to falling into the slander category because they have much greater protection against slander than libel. Whereas slander requires special damages except for the four categories, harm to reputation without regard to special damages is all that needs to be proven in addition, of course, to the usual elements such as publication, identification and so on, that hold for all defamation.

A few jurisdictions differentiate slander and libel in other ways. Georgia, for example, characterizes broadcast defamation as "defamacast."[17] Kentucky[18] and some other states treat both print and broadcast defamation as libel but have somewhat different rules for defamation in the two types of media.[19] Most distinctions have no real practical effect unless it is a matter of categorizing one as slander and the other as libel.

LIBEL *PER SE* VERSUS LIBEL *PER QUOD*

Some courts have traditionally made a distinction between *libel per se* (statements defamatory on their face) and *libel per quod* (statements not defamatory on their face but defamatory with reference to extrinsic facts or circumstances). These distinctions have been less than clear at common law and in state statutes, although, according to the general rule, special harm must be shown for a plaintiff to recover for libel per se but this does not have to be demonstrated for libel per quod. Even this distinction has become blurred over the decades and centuries. Robert Sack points out, for instance, "In New York, the state of case law [on libel per se versus libel per quod] is so confusing and contradictory that it is impossible to be certain what the rule is."[20] New York is undoubtedly not alone. According to Sack, at least nine states[21] appear to have the rule that all libelous statements are treated as libel per se, thus not requiring proof of special harm.[22]

There have been literally hundreds of examples of libel per se cases in the last decade alone. Some of them resulted in awards for plaintiffs; others did not. "Supernaturalist" Uri Geller filed suit against James Randi for allegedly saying that Geller's feats "are the kind that used to be on the backs of cereal boxes when I was a kid."[23] In 1990 the ESPN sports TV network broadcast a retraction after one of its announcers said that a particular professional baseball pitcher transferred from a private university to a community college because he "failed his grades."[24] Ex-Beatle George Harrison asked for more than $200 million in a libel suit he filed against the *Globe* in Los Angeles Superior Court. The supermarket tabloid based in Boca Raton, Florida, had carried a story alleging that Harrison was a Nazi sympathizer and a devotee of Adolf Hitler.[25] In the early 1980s a jury in Austin, Texas, ruled that a book author's description of a woman as a "sex-bomb" was defamatory but true and therefore she was not entitled to any damages.

All of these are examples of how libel "on its face" can potentially get a publication or individual into trouble. First Amendment Attorney Bruce Sanford has compiled a list of what he calls "Red Flag" words that can lead to a suit if improperly handled: for example, *fascist, booze-hound, fawning sycophant* and *stool pigeon*.[26] Many of these are prime illustrations of libel per se.

Libel per quod can be quite troublesome for journalists because the words do not automatically throw up a red flag. For example, publishing the statement that a woman is pregnant is not defamatory on its face, but what if the woman is not married or 96-years-old? In December 1991 96-year-old Nellie Mitchell won $650,000 in compensatory damages and $850,000 in punitive damages from the *Sun* after a jury trial in U.S. District Court in Harrison, Arkansas.[27] The supermarket tabloid had published her picture with an article the year before in which it said a 101-year-old Australian newspaper carrier had quit her route because a millionaire customer had gotten her pregnant.

A *Sun* editor admitted during the trial that the story had been fabricated but that Mitchell's photo was used because he assumed she was dead. The *Sun's* attorney, Philip Anderson, argued at the trial that Mitchell was not libeled because "most reasonable people recognize that the stories [in the *Sun*] are essentially fiction."[28]

What about the discrepancy in her age or the false assertion that she lived in Australia? The last two facts, even though false, are probably not defamatory because they would probably not harm one's reputation unless some special circumstances existed—such as falsely indicating that a married man lived in Australia when his friends, acquaintances and family knew his spouse was still living in Cleveland, Ohio. At trial, these extrinsic facts and circumstances are relevant in showing the information was false and defamatory even though they were not widely known nor even known by the defendant. Of course, if the jurisdiction requires a showing of special damages, as some states do, before recovery by the plaintiff or if the libel per quod does not fall within one of the four special categories enunciated earlier under slander, a suit would be unsuccessful. But, in general, such damages need not be demonstrated.

THE TYPICAL LIBEL CASE

There is probably no real "typical" libel suit because every case has its own unique aspects, as even the big-name suits have demonstrated, but it may be useful to focus on a fairly typical case before a discussion of the elements of libel in the next section.

E. W. Scripps Co., The Kentucky Post and Al Salvato v. Louis A. Ball

E. W. Scripps Co., The Kentucky Post and Al Salvato v. Louis A. Ball[29] began on November 17, 1984, when the *Kentucky Post*, owned by the Scripps–Howard newspaper chain and the third largest daily in the state, published the first of a two-part series by reporter Al Salvato on the allegedly poor performance of Campbell County Commonwealth Attorney Louis A. Ball.[30] (The second part appeared two days later.) The articles dealt primarily with the prosecutor's allegedly lenient handling of repeat offenders and his strained relationships with local police. Both stories were the lead articles each day and were headed "Portrait of a Prosecutor." The major subhead in the November 17 article was "Lou Ball's Record Lags Behind Others," and the November 19 story's subhead was "Serious Gap with the Police." Both were accompanied with large graphs, photographs and other visual devices. An editorial entitled "Our Challenge to Lou Ball" appeared on November 26 and called on Ball to improve his record. The newspaper had also published an editorial critical of the prosecutor earlier in July. Although the series did not claim Ball was corrupt, it clearly implied that he was not doing a good job. A team of lawyers checked and rechecked the stories before they were published.[31]

One month later, the prosecutor filed a libel suit against the *Post*, claiming that the series and the two editorials were false and published with **actual malice**. Public officials, as discussed later in this chapter, must show "actual malice" before they can recover for libel. The U.S. Supreme Court defined *actual malice* as reckless disregard for the truth or knowledge of falsity in *New York Times v. Sullivan* in 1964. Slightly less than a year after the series had appeared and after months of discovery and the usual legal maneuverers, including the *Post* filing a motion to dismiss that was rejected by the judge, the trial began in Kentucky Circuit Court. The trial lasted for seven days and included testimony that Salvato, the reporter, bore a grudge against Ball because of an incident at a high school football game in 1982 in which a Bellevue (Ky.) police officer made the reporter leave the game. The officer had been called to investigate a report that Salvato was "trying to get some girls to take some dope with him," but he decided not to arrest the journalist after Salvato told him he was working on a story for the newspaper on drug use among young people. The grudge against Ball supposedly arose when the prosecutor failed to pursue Salvato's complaint against the police. During the trial, Salvato was persistently questioned about how he conducted his research that led to the series. He testified that he spent almost three months reviewing the records of nearly 3,000 Campbell County cases and that he interviewed more than 40 people, including Ball and his three assistants.

The plaintiff's attorney argued there was considerable evidence of actual malice, including the notation "good case" scribbled by the reporter on certain cases — such as when a felony charge was reduced to a misdemeanor — and that Salvato had used a statement by a former narcotics officer that criminals "couldn't have a better friend" than Ball even though a judge who knew the officer had told the reporter he was "a very poor police officer, totally unreliable." Ball's attorney claimed this statement and other allegations — such as that the prosecutor had lost about half of the cases he had taken to trial in the last 6 years and he had failed to assist a county attorney investigating misdemeanor obscenity charges involving an adult theater — were false and defamatory.[32]

The *Post's* attorneys countered that all of the allegations had been thoroughly checked and rechecked, that the reporter had no grudge against Ball and that most of the statements were opinions, not factual assertions and, therefore, protected by the First Amendment. The stories did contain some inaccuracies, which the newspaper's attorneys contended were minor and had no impact on the reader's perceptions of Ball. For instance, figures in one graph had been accidentally transposed so that Ball's record appeared worse than was the actual case. The defense noted that Ball did not point out the mistake when he was shown the graph before publication and asked for his comment.[33]

After deliberating only a few hours, the jury returned a verdict in favor of Ball and awarded him $175,000 in actual damages but opted for no punitive damages. The *Post* immediately appealed the decision, and on August 13, 1987, nearly 2 years after the jury decision and almost 3 years after the series appeared, the Kentucky Court of Appeals in a split (2–1) decision reversed the trial court, holding "there is no clear and convincing evidence that these articles were published with the requisite knowledge of falsity or reckless disregard for the truth necessary to remove them from constitutional protection." Ball then appealed the intermediate appellate court decision, and in June 1988 the Kentucky Supreme Court heard oral arguments. However, the state supreme court delayed its decision until a case it considered similar to this one, *Harte-Hanks Communications, Inc. v. Connaughton* (1989),[34] was handed down by the U.S. Supreme Court, as discussed *infra*.

On June 22, 1989, the U.S. Supreme Court issued its opinion in *Harte-Hanks*, upholding a jury finding of actual malice by the Hamilton (Ohio) *Journal News* in publishing a story and an editorial about a political candidate. Connaughton won $5,000 in compensatory damages and $195,000 in punitive damages in the trial court.

One year later in June 1990, the Kentucky Supreme Court heard rearguments in the case and then 5 months later on November 29, the state supreme court reversed the state court of appeals decision and reinstated the trial court award (with interest) to Ball. In a unanimous opinion (6–0), the Kentucky Supreme Court ruled:

Based on the law of libel in Kentucky, as constrained by the decisions of the United States Supreme Court regarding the First Amendment protection of freedom of the press, including the mandate that appellate judges in such cases "exercise independent judgment and determine whether the record establishes actual malice with convincing clarity" [citing *Bose v. Consumers Union of the United States* (1984),[35] discussed *infra*] we reverse the Court of Appeals and reinstate the judgment of the trial court.[36]

The state supreme court felt that the jury could reasonably infer that the *Post* reporter held a grudge against the prosecutor because of the incident at the high school game and from a statement made by Salvato to Ball in a phone conversation, presumably implying a threat that Ball would be "hearing from" him. The court also ruled that there was substantial evidence presented at trial that some six statements in the stories were false and defamatory, including the "they couldn't have a better friend" comment from the former narcotics officer and that Ball had lost about half of the cases he took to trial. Finally, the court rejected the paper's defense that the statements were opinions, not statements of fact and thus that they enjoyed First Amendment protection. The court also noted that the newspaper's refusal to publish a retraction could be evidence of actual malice as well.

On February 27, 1991, the *Kentucky Post* petitioned the U.S. Supreme Court to grant a *writ of certiorari*, but the Court turned down the appeal on April 22, 1991, $6\frac{1}{2}$ years after the series had appeared. The newspaper's insurance reportedly covered most of the several hundred thousands in legal fees incurred, but the *Post* probably paid from $50,000 to $100,000 as a deductible in the award payment to Ball plus a percentage (typically 20 percent) of the amount above the deductible.[37]

E. W. Scripps et al. v. Ball is rather typical of the libel suits newspapers and other media face today in at least four ways, even though some of the circumstances will certainly differ from case to case. First, the plaintiff was a public official and thus had to demonstrate with clear and convincing evidence or "convincing clarity" that the media defendant published the story with actual malice, as required under *New York Times v. Sullivan* (1964), discussed *infra*. Whereas public figures and public officials therefore have a much heavier evidentiary burden to meet in successfully suing for libel than do private individuals, they are far more likely to sue than nonpluses figures. There are three factors that probably explain this phenomenon. First, public officials/public figures garner considerably more media attention than private people, simply because they are supposedly more newsworthy. Second, public officials/public figures usually have greater financial resources and thus can persevere more than private citizens who may not be able to afford the expensive court costs and attorney fees. Finally, because they are in the public limelight, public officials/public figures are perceived to have broader and stronger reputations to defend from defamation. Often, their livelihood depends on a positive public image, and when that image is destroyed, the damages can mount.

A second way in which *E. W. Scripps v. Ball* typifies libel cases lies in the process by which it meandered through the courts. As indicated *supra*, plaintiffs are far more likely than the defendant to win a libel suit. Indeed, it is fairly unusual for a jury not to award damages these days. Far more libel suits are settled out of court than ever reach trial or they are dismissed before trial, but many of those settled are with some kind of payment to the plaintiff. Media defendants certainly cannot count juries among their friends. Juries are not only handing out more and more awards to libel plaintiffs, they are also upping the sizes of those awards, as indicated earlier.

Third, the treatment accorded the *Post* in the courts is very much in line with current trends. Whereas a lower appellate court may occasionally reverse a libel award, higher appellate courts, especially state supreme courts, are just as likely now to uphold an award as to reverse it and, as noted previously, the clear trend is toward siding with the plaintiff. As is indicated in the following discussion, state and federal appellate courts are simply following the lead of the U.S. Supreme Court. That's why the Kentucky Supreme Court delayed its decision on the appeal until *Harte-Hanks Communications v. Connaughton* could be decided. The facts in *Harte-Hanks*, contrary to the Kentucky Supreme Court's analysis, were much different from those in *E. W. Scripps*, as outlined later. Suffice it to say that the evidence of actual malice was substantially stronger in *Harte-Hanks*. In fact, the only evidence of actual malice that Kentucky's highest court could point to in *E. W. Scripps* was the "grudge" theory, the "good case" marks on the reporter's notes, that Salvato "selectively interviewed only a few persons hostile to Ball as background" while supposedly "deliberately choosing not to interview those who could contradict their claims" and the "[criminals] couldn't have a better friend" statement by the ex-police officer.

Finally, the case points out how attorneys on the other side can really harp away at seemingly innocent mistakes that even veteran journalists could easily commit, but that, nevertheless, can sway a jury toward the plaintiff's side. No story, no matter how much time is spent researching, writing, editing and checking it, will ever be perfect. There will always be one more source who should have been interviewed, a misspelled name, a wrong age or a transposed graph, but juries hold reporters and editors to high standards, so high, in fact, that they are sometimes impossible to meet. Juries are not a journalist's peers. They focus on the one story in dispute and fail to put the journalistic process into perspective by realizing that a reporter or editor usually cannot concentrate on one story to the exclusion of others but instead will usually be working on several stories at any given time. To the jury, mistakes may be unforgivable, no matter how minor. Or, in the eyes of the jurors, even if forgivable, minor mistakes point to sloppy reporting and editing that can lead to major errors.

In addition to the financial toll that libel suits exact from the news media, there is also a drain on personnel as staff members, especially the individual reporter or editor under fire, face hours and hours of depositions by opposing attorneys and briefings and pretrial preparations conducted by the media lawyers. Of course, all of the time spent in preparing for the case, appearing in court and so on, is time away from the newsroom. The toll can be enormous even when a media defendant wins.[38]

THE ELEMENTS OF LIBEL

As with any tort, libel requires that certain elements be demonstrated before a plaintiff can win the suit and then recover damages. This section examines each of these and cites examples as well as relevant case law, especially that promulgated by the U.S. Supreme Court. While there is agreement on the general nature of each of the requirements, there are significant differences among the courts and statutes in the role that each element plays in the whole libel picture. Inconsistencies and confusion abound.

The *Restatement (Second) of Torts*[39] enumerates four elements for demonstrating a *prima facie* cause of action for libel: (a) a false and defamatory statement of and concerning another (*identification*), (b) communication that is not privileged to a third party (*publication*), (c) negligence or greater *fault* on the part of the plaintiff, and (d) actual injury arising from publication of the statement (*harm*). The first element can actually be broken down into three requirements — *defamation*, *falsity* and *identification*.

Defamation

To be libelous, a statement must be defamatory. As indicated earlier, the words in and of themselves may be defamatory (*libel per se*) or they may be defamatory only when extrinsic facts and circumstances are known (*libel per quod*), but they nevertheless must be such that they would or could injure the reputation of a person or other recognized entity such as a business. A common definition of libel is information that tends to subject a person to public hatred, contempt or ridicule or tends to demean individuals in their profession or business. Statements that generally tend to enhance a person's reputation, even though they may be false, generally are not actionable in a suit for libel, although there may be instances in which such information could trigger a successful suit for invasion of privacy, as indicated in the next chapter. Characterizing a person as well-educated, intelligent or kind would not be libelous, even if false, simply because such information does not harm the individual's reputation, which is usually defined as the person's standing in the community—in other words, what others think about that person.

The question of whether a statement is defamatory is very crucial in many libel cases because it is usually relatively easy to establish most of the other elements, such as falsity, publication and identification. A few examples of information that the U.S. Supreme Court has either upheld as defamatory or sent back to a trial court or a lower appellate court for this determination include:

1. A magazine's false accusation that a college football coach had conspired with another coach to "fix" a game in *Curtis Publishing Co. v. Butts* (1967)[40]

2. A magazine's false claim that an attorney for a family in its suit against a police officer for killing their son had been an official of the "Marxist League for Industrial Democracy . . . which has advocated the violent seizure of our government" and that the attorney was a "Leninist" and a "Communist" in *Gertz v. Welch* (1974)[41]

3. A magazine's statement that the divorce of a multimillionaire from his wife was granted on grounds of adultery when it had actually been granted because of "a gross lack of domestication" on both sides in *Time v. Firestone* (1976)[42]

4. A credit reporting agency's circulation of a false statement that a contractor had filed for bankruptcy in *Dun & Bradstreet, Inc. v. Greenmoss Builders, Inc.* (1985)[43]

On the other hand, the following statements have been held as not defamatory under the particular circumstances:

1. Articles in a weekly newspaper that accurately reported on public debates over zoning, including the characterization by several citizens of a real estate developer's negotiating position as "blackmail" in *Greenbelt Cooperative Publishing Assoc. v. Charles S. Bresler* (1970).[44] The U.S. Supreme Court called the term *blackmail* merely rhetorical hyperbole that could not be reasonably understood in the context of a heated debate to be a criminal accusation.

2. A parody ad in *Hustler* magazine in which Rev. Jerry Falwell was depicted as having had sex with his mother in an outhouse in *Hustler Magazine and Larry C. Flynt v. Jerry Falwell* (1988).[45]

The U.S. Supreme Court reversed a jury decision awarding Falwell damages for intentional infliction of emotional distress even though the jurors found that no libel had occurred. There was no basis for a libel suit nor for an emotional distress suit, according to the Supreme Court, because the parody had not been touted as factual nor understood as such by readers.

Falsity

By virtue of its definition, libelous information must be false. Thus *truth*, as discussed later, is an absolute defense to libel. Truth, however, is not necessarily a defense to other torts — such as publicizing private matters, one of the four privacy torts — as indicated in the next chapter. Most state statutes make it clear that truth, if demonstrated, is a complete defense to libel. Truth is typically not an issue in libel cases, especially those involving the mass media, because defamation suits that survive a motion to dismiss almost inevitably involve false information. Inaccuracies, even those that may initially appear to be minor, traditionally trip up reporters and editors.

An important issue that sometimes does arise about the element of falsity is whether the plaintiff has the burden of proving the information is false or the defendant has the burden of showing the published statements are true. The assumption has been that public officials and public figures in libel suits have the burden of proving falsity because the U.S. Supreme Court's decision in *New York Times v. Sullivan* (1964)[46] requires public officials (and public figures, as enunciated later by the Court) to *show actual malice*, as discussed shortly; but, who has the burden in cases involving private figures? In 1977 in *Philadelphia Newspapers v. Hepps,*[47] the U.S. Supreme Court answered one-half of the question when it held that a private individual suing a media defendant for libel over a matter of public concern must demonstrate that the information published was false. In other words, the media defendant does not have the burden of proving truth. In its 5–4 decision written by Associate Justice Sandra Day O'Connor, the Court ruled unconstitutional the interpretation by some state courts, such as those in Pennsylvania, that *Gertz v. Welch* permitted a court to assume the information was false unless proven otherwise by the defendant. Instead, the Court said, the plaintiff must prove with **clear and convincing evidence** that the allegedly defamatory statements are false when they involve a matter of public concern. The Court appeared to leave the door open for state and lower federal courts to adopt the common law position that the burden is on the defendant to prove truth and even to apply the rule to situations involving public controversies but nonmedia defendants. Indeed, Associate Justices Brennan and Blackmun said the Court's rules were applicable to nonmedia defendants.

Identification

Before a person or other entity, such as a corporation, can be libeled, the information must be specifically linked with that individual. Otherwise, defamation cannot occur because no reputation is harmed if no one understands to whom the statements refer. Identification, however, does **not** have to be by name. Instead, the identification can be established with extrinsic facts. This latter process is known as *colloquium*.

Ordinarily, identification is not an issue in a libel case because the plaintiff is actually named or enough information is provided about the person in the story so there is little or no doubt about the individual's identity. There are three typical situations in which colloquium may be an issue: (a) stories in which no specific individual is named but in which allegations can be inferred to a particular person, (b) fictionalized stories and stories employing pseudonyms and (c) group libel.

The most famous libel decision of all time *New York Times v. Sullivan* (1964),[48] is an excellent illustration of the first situation. (The *actual malice rule* established in the case is far more important than the identification controversy and is discussed in considerable detail in the next section of this chapter.) On Tuesday, March 29, 1960, the *New York Times* published a full-page advertisement entitled "Heed Their Rising Voices."

Unfortunately, whereas the ad's descriptions of civil rights violations were faithful to real events throughout the South, the details of what had occurred in Montgomery, Alabama, at least, were somewhat inaccurate. As Law Professor Rodney A. Smolla pointed out in his book, *Suing the Press*, the Black students who demonstrated on the capitol steps in Montgomery sang the "The Star Spangled Banner" instead of "My Country 'Tis of Thee"; the nine Black students who were expelled from college were expelled for demanding service at a lunch counter in the Montgomery County Courthouse rather than for leading the demonstration; and the police had never "ringed" the Alabama State College campus, although they had been called to the campus three times in connection with civil rights protests.[49] Other errors included the assertion that Dr. Martin Luther King, Jr., had been arrested seven times (he had actually been arrested four times) and that the police ("Southern violators") had twice bombed his home (they were never implicated in the bombings and had, in fact, reportedly attempted to determine who had committed the violence).[50]

Soon after the ad appeared, the *New York Times* was sued by several Alabama politicians, including Governor John Patterson and L. B. Sullivan, a Montgomery city commissioner. The *Times* printed a retraction, as requested by the governor, but rejected the request for a retraction from Sullivan, who, as Commissioner of Public Affairs, was in charge of the police department. Nowhere in the ad is **any** mention made of Sullivan or of his position. Yet Sullivan successfully contended at the trial that the use of the term *police* in the third paragraph implicated him because his duties entailed supervising the police department and three other departments. He also claimed that he was implicated in the sixth paragraph's reference to "Southern violators," which he asserted meant the Montgomery County Police because any arrests would have been handled by police.

Sullivan's attorneys called a host of witnesses to indicate whether the ad was "of and concerning" the plaintiff, as required under Alabama libel law. All of them said they associated the allegedly defamatory statements with Sullivan or the police department.[51] Although the lawyers for the newspaper argued that Sullivan was not identified in the ad, the jury and the trial court judge, Walter Burgwyn Jones, were convinced otherwise and awarded the plaintiff $500,000, the largest libel judgment in the state's history at that time. (The newspaper's attorneys raised other defenses including lack of malice, privilege and truth, which are discussed *infra*.) In unanimously reversing the Alabama Supreme Court's decision to uphold the trial court decision, the U.S. Supreme Court did not buy Sullivan's contention. According to Justice Brennan's majority opinion:

> [The evidence] was incapable of supporting the jury's finding that the allegedly libelous statements were made "of and concerning" respondent [Sullivan]. Respondent relies upon the words of the advertisement and the testimony of six witnesses to establish a connection between it and himself. . . . There was no reference to respondent in the advertisement, either by name or official position.[52]

The Court noted that several of the allegedly libelous statements, such as the charge that the dining hall was padlocked and that Dr. King's home was bombed, did not even concern the police and the reference to "They" "could not reasonably be read as accusing [Sullivan] of personal involvement in the acts in question."[53] The Court went on to say, "Although the statements may be taken as referring to the police, they did not on their face make even an oblique reference to [Sullivan] as an individual."[54] The justices then reasoned that identification must thereby be established through the testimony of witnesses for the plaintiff, but "none of them suggested any basis for the belief that [Sullivan] himself was attacked in the advertisement beyond the bare fact that he was in overall charge of the Police Department and thus bore official responsibility for police conduct."[55] If identification or colloquium could be established on this basis, as the Alabama Supreme Court had indicated in upholding the verdict against the *Times*, then criticism of government (seditious libel) would rear its ugly head again because any criticism of government could easily become criticism of government officials and therefore punished. According to the U.S. Supreme Court:

> Raising as it does the possibility that a good-faith critic of government will be penalized for his criticism, the proposition relied on by the Alabama courts strikes at the very center of the constitutionally protected area of free expression. [footnote omitted] We hold that such a proposition may not constitutionally be utilized to establish that an otherwise impersonal attack on government opera-

tions was libel of an official responsible for those operations. Since it was relied on exclusively here, and there was no other evidence to connect the statements with [Sullivan], the evidence was constitutionally insufficient to support a finding that the statements referred to [Sullivan].[56]

The Court is **not** ruling out public officials being able to sue for libel for criticism in connection with their official duties. In fact, the Court established in this case the actual malice rule under which such officials could recover damages for libel from media defendants, but the Court was not willing to permit plaintiffs such as Sullivan to infer libel of them simply because government actions connected with them were attacked. This aspect of the *Sullivan* decision is often overlooked in discussions of the case even though lack of identification was clearly a major reason the U.S. Supreme Court reversed the Alabama Supreme Court's upholding of the trial court verdict against the *Times*.

The second category, *fictionalizations*, is illustrated in two cases: one involving a fictional "Miss Wyoming" and the other a fictional psychiatrist. In the first, *Pring v. Penthouse International, Ltd* (1982),[57] Kimerli Jayne Pring, the 1978 Miss Wyoming in the Miss America contest, won $25 million in punitive damages and $1.5 million in actual damages from *Penthouse* magazine in a jury trial in 1981. The trial court judge later reduced the punitive award to $12.5 million. The jury awarded Pring $10,000 actual and $25,000 punitive damages against the author, Philip Cioffari. The adult magazine had published a fictitious story about "Charlene," a fictional Miss Wyoming who was a champion baton twirler, as Pring had been, and also had another talent, or at least imagined she had another talent – she could make men levitate by performing fellatio on them. The article describes three incidents during which (2) Charlene levitates a football player from her school by performing oral sex; (b) she performs the same act on her football coach, Corky, while the audience applauds at the end of the pageant; and (c) she performs a "fellatio-like" act on her baton which stops the orchestra. The trial court jury and judge had no problem with associating the alleged libel with the real former Miss Wyoming, and, on appeal, the 10th Circuit U.S. Court of Appeals accepted that determination (i.e., that the article identified the plaintiff). However, the appeals court reversed the mega-award, ruling that the story was a "complete fantasy." According to the court, "It is impossible to believe that anyone could understand that levitation could be accomplished by oral sex before a national audience or anywhere else. The incidents charged were impossible. The setting was impossible." Thus the descriptions were "obviously a complete fantasy."[58] While the appellate court reversed the verdict on the ground that the story was too unbelievable to be libelous rather than for lack of identification, the judges did indicate that simply labeling a story as fiction is not enough: "The test is not whether the story is or is not characterized as 'fiction,' 'humor,' or anything else in the publication, but whether the charged portions in context could be reasonably understood as describing actual facts about the plaintiff or actual events in which she participated. If it could not be so understood, the charged portions could not be taken literally."[59]

The Court of Appeals did characterize the story as "a gross, unpleasant, crude, distorted attempt to ridicule the Miss America contest and contestants. It has no redeeming features whatsoever." The court still felt that it had First Amendment protection because the Constitution was intended to cover a "vast divergence in views and ideas," including those in the article.

Would the appellate court have decided differently if the story had concerned acts that were "physically possible?" What if the nonsexual talent for both beauty contestants had been something unusual, such as playing the piano while seated backward or speaking simultaneously in five languages? Would such details have been sufficient to constitute identification?

The second example of fictionalization, *Bindrim v. Mitchell* (1979),[60] may shed some light on these questions. Best-seller author Gwen Davis Mitchell decided to write a novel about leisure-class women. In an effort to gather background information for the book, she attended a nude therapy session offered by Paul Bindrim, a licensed clinical psychologist and author. Bindrim, who used a technique known as "Nude Marathon" in group therapy to get clients to shed their inhibitions, agreed to allow Mitchell to attend only if she agreed in writing not to take photos, write articles or in any way to disclose what happened at the workshop. Mitchell told the psychologist she had no intentions of writing about the marathon and that she was attending solely for therapeutic purposes.

Two months later, Mitchell contracted with Doubleday to write her novel and received $150,000 in advance royalties. The completed novel entitled *Touching* included an account of a nude encounter session in southern California led by a fictional "Dr. Simon Herford." Bindrim then sued for libel and breach of contract. A jury awarded the plaintiff $38,000 against the author for libel, $25,000 in punitive damages against the publisher for libel and $12,000 against the author on the contract claim. The total award was later reduced by the judge to $50,000. The Second Appellate District California Court of Appeal modified the amount of damages but otherwise affirmed the trial court decision. Both the California Supreme Court and the U.S. Supreme Court rejected further appeals.

The California Court of Appeals had no problem with the question of whether Bindrim was identified in the book: "There is overwhelming evidence that plaintiff and 'Herford' [the fictional doctor] were one." Both the trial court and the appellate court reached this conclusion in spite of the fact that there were major differences in the two's characteristics. The book character is described as a "fat Santa Claus type with long white hair, white sideburns, a cherubic rosy face and rosy forearms," whereas Bindrim had short hair and was clean shaven. The character was an M.D. but Bindrim held a Ph.D. Their names, of course, were completely different. The common links that convinced the court were the nude marathon technique and the similarity between an actual transcript of the weekend encounter the author attended and an encounter in the book. The court also relied on the identification by several witnesses of Herford, the fictional character, as Bindrim, the plaintiff.

While *Bindrim v. Mitchell* is binding only in California's Second Appellate District, it has nevertheless been an influential decision in other court cases, primarily because it invoked a common rule of identification employed in many other jurisdictions — whether a reasonable person exposed to the work would understand the fictional character as, in fact, referring to the real person. That is the key difference between *Bindrim* and *Pring*. While the appellate court ruling in *Pring* was handed down in a different jurisdiction and three years after *Bindrim*, the basic rule of identification was essentially the same. The *Penthouse* story was merely hype and fantasy, but *Touching* hit close to home — its descriptions of the therapy sessions were fairly close to what could have happened but did not.

What role did the contract Mitchell signed about nondisclosure play? Initially, the jury awarded Bindrim $12,000 in damages on the contract claim, but the trial court judge struck down the award. The appellate court upheld the judge's decision, noting that because Mitchell was a bonafide patient, she could write whatever she wished about what occurred in spite of the contract. Thus that contract clause was unenforceable. It is clear from the case, however, that even when fictional names are employed, authors must still be very careful about how close they come in their descriptions of fictional events based on factual situations. Changing names does not always "protect the innocent."

Group Libel

One situation in which identification is nearly always an issue is *group libel* or when defamatory comments are directed at a specific group of individuals. The general rule is the larger the group, the less likely a member of the group has been defamed. Group libel suits are fairly common but nearly always fail, usually by being dismissed, unless they involve a relatively small group. For example, former NBC-TV "Tonight" show host, Johnny Carson, was sued in 1987 for $5 million by a Long Island, New York, dentist for derogatory jokes that Carson told about dentists on his show in April 1986.[61] The jokes were directed at dentists in general and not at the dentist, Dr. Michael Mendelson, whose letter Carson read on the air before launching into a monologue about dentists. The suit was eventually dismissed. Dentists compose too large of a group for group libel. A similar suit was filed against Paramount Studios for $10 million in 1983 by a woman suing on behalf of all Polish-Americans for the harm caused by the "degrading and demeaning 'Pollack' jokes' " in the film, *Flashdance*.[62] It, too, was dismissed. A U.S. District Court judge in 1980 dismissed a class-action suit he characterized as bordering "on the frivolous" filed against the Public Broadcasting System (PBS) for carrying the film, *Death of a Princess*.[63] The plaintiffs sought $20 million in damages on behalf of all Muslims, who the plaintiffs assert were defamed by the film depicting the public execution of a Saudi Arabian princess for adultery. The total number of individuals alleged to have been defamed was 600 million. According to the court, "If the court were to permit an action to lie for the defamation of such as multitudinous group we would render meaningless the rights guaranteed by the First Amendment to explore issues of public import."[64]

Similarly, a specific chain of businesses would not be permitted to recover for group libel unless its size was relatively small. The late founder of the Kentucky Fried Chicken chain, Col. Harlan Sanders, was known for his outspokenness about the franchise long after he had sold it but for which he still served as a spokesperson in commercials. He told the Louisville *Courier-Journal* in a published story in the mid-1970s that the gravy on the mashed potatoes was "horrible" and that the potatoes had "no nutrition." He also said, "that new 'crispy' recipe is nothing in the world but a damn fried doughball stuck on some chicken." A franchise owner in Bowling Green, Kentucky, sued the colonel on behalf of the 5,000 franchised Kentucky Fried Chicken restaurants, but his suit was dismissed by the Kentucky Supreme Court on the ground that he could not demonstrate that the comments referred to him nor any of the other franchisees.[65]

The late Dean William Prosser noted in his *Law of Torts* that 25 persons had become a general rule in determining whether a group is small enough for individual members to have been defamed by libelous statements about the group as a whole,[66] and whereas some jurisdictions appear to apply such a rule of thumb, it is by no means universal. The U.S. Supreme Court has never dealt directly with the issue of whether group libel is even possible, although it may have the opportunity some day as the controversy over "politically correct" speech continues to grow. Several universities have enacted codes of conduct that bar students and faculty from uttering racial, sexual, ethnic and religious slurs in public on campus, including classrooms and school functions. Penalties for violations range from reprimands to expulsion from school or firing for faculty. The purpose of such codes is essentially to prevent libel of certain groups, and thus they could be challenged as unconstitutional prior restraint or as unenforceable because the size of the group makes it impossible to establish *colloquium* — that is, that the libelous statements individually harm the group's members. These codes could also be attacked as a form of seditious or criminal libel that the U.S. Supreme Court effectively struck down in *Garrison v. Louisiana* (1964).[67]

Racial and ethnic slurs are, of course, nothing new, but perhaps some progress has been made. During a flea market used book sale, the author of this textbook discovered a 1936 hardback book entitled *The World's Best Jokes* published by Garden City Books of Garden City, New York.[68] The editor of the book, Lewis Copeland, includes 28 categories of jokes. Tucked among the jokes about lawyers, doctors, drunks, preachers and Yankees are "Negro Jokes" (22 pages), "Jewish Jokes" (17 pages), and "Negro Dialect" (15 pages). The racial and ethnic jokes, suffice it to say, are rife with stereotypes and stereotypical dialects that must have been as insulting in the 1930s as they are now. Whereas such a publication would still have First Amendment protection against potential group libel suits, presumably no mainstream publisher would even consider publishing such defamatory information today.

There are at least two major points of view on group libel. On the one side are those individuals who believe that the press should be held accountable for group libel under certain circumstances—such as for racial, ethnic and religious slurs when they cause substantial harm to these groups. On the other hand, some scholars argue that there should be no control over the press in uttering whatever group slurs and defamations it wishes to air unless these comments would lead directly to violence. One writer has characterized these two perspectives as "communitarian" and "liberal," respectively.[69]

Publication

The second element that must be demonstrated in a libel case, **publication**, is typically the easiest for the plaintiff to prove because the allegedly libelous information has appeared in a news story, documentary, book or similar outlet. All that is required is simply that the information was communicated to a third party. Thus there is usually no dispute about whether publication has occurred. On rare occasions, though, publication may be in question. For example, suppose a television news director sends a confidential memo to one of the reporters falsely accusing him of doctoring his expense vouchers (i.e., inflating his mileage, meals costs, etc.). The director types the memo herself and sends it in a sealed envelope to the reporter. Has publication occurred? The answer is *absolutely not*. The information has not been transmitted to the necessary third party. What if the reporter then shares the memo with his friends and family? Publication has still failed because an individual cannot communicate a defamatory message about himself and then claim he has been libeled. In other words, "self-publication" will not work. Of course, if the alleged libeler publishes the defamatory remarks and then the person who is the object of the comments passes the information on to others, the libeler is certainly not off the hook. The key is that self-publication does not affect the outcome one way or another.

What if the director has his secretary type the memo, but the director still marks the envelope "confidential" and does not share the information with anyone else? Publication has been committed even if these three individuals are the only ones who actually see the memo. An equivalent situation happened in 1969 when two reporters, Joe Melosi and William Lhotka, at the *Alton* (Illinois) *Telegraph* sent a confidential memorandum to an attorney in the U.S. Department of Justice summarizing all of the information they had gathered in an investigation they had conducted about possible organized crime ties with a major local contractor and a local bank. The reporters had sent the information, much of which was unsubstantiated allegations, to fulfill a promise they had made to share the results of their investigations with the Justice Department in exchange for the department's cooperation. Each page of the memo was marked "confidential" and the reporters took pains to note that some of the charges were unsubstantiated.[70]

The attorney to whom the memo was directed left the Justice Department soon after the memo was delivered and the memo eventually fell into the hands of Federal Home Loan Bank Board (FHLBB) officials after Justice Department employees passed it on with a suggestion that the bank board review the files of a savings and loan (S&L) association to determine if loans to developer James Green had been proper. The memo from the reporters, which was never acted on by the Justice Department, had intimated that Green had some possible ties to organized crime, although these links were not substantiated. The review indicated that improper loans had been made and Green was denied any further loans. Consequently, Green and his company lost several construction projects. The lawyer for the S&L vice president who had facilitated the loans to Green discovered the existence of the confidential memo through a federal Freedom of Information Act request. By this time, the S&L was under the control of the FHLBB and Green's construction enterprise had fallen apart. Both the vice president and Green and his company sued the two reporters and the newspaper for libel even though the allegedly libelous information was never published in the *Alton Telegraph*. The two reporters had merely sent the memo in an effort to get help in verifying unsubstantiated allegations to which the Justice Department had never responded anyway.

In 1980, 11 years after the memo had been sent, an Illinois Circuit Court jury awarded Green and the other plaintiffs $6.7 million in compensatory damages and $2.5 million in punitive damages for a total of $9.2 million,[71] considerably more than the paper was worth.[72] At the time it was the largest libel award ever in this country.[73] An Illinois appellate court denied the newspaper's appeal of the decision on the ground that it lacked jurisdiction because the newspaper had failed to post the required $13.8 million bond.[74] The newspaper did not have the funds to post the bond and filed for bankruptcy. After the dust had settled in bankruptcy proceedings, the

Telegraph and its insurers agreed to pay $1.4 million to Green. The defense legal expenses alone were reportedly more than $600,000, which the paper had to pay itself rather than being reimbursed by its insurer.[75]

Privilege: Absolute, Qualified and Constitutional

The element of *publication* also involves the concept of privilege. If defamatory information is privileged, the defamed person cannot recover damages even though the statements may have been false and have caused harm. Thus privilege can act as a defense to a libel suit. There are two basic types of privilege — **absolute** (sometimes called "unconditional" or "constitutional") and **qualified** (also known as "conditional" and "limited"). There is a third type of privilege known as **constitutional privilege** that, as with absolute privilege, arises from the U.S. Constitution but, unlike absolute privilege, originates indirectly from the First Amendment rather than directly from a specific provision in the Constitution. Indeed, this third type of privilege did not exist until the *New York Times v. Sullivan* decision in 1964 when the U.S. Supreme Court announced that the press or media defendants could not be held liable for defaming public officials unless such plaintiffs could demonstrate actual malice, as discussed *infra*.

Except in one rare situation involving the broadcast media, as elaborated shortly, the press does **not** enjoy *absolute privilege*. Instead, this is a defense to libel that can generally be claimed only by participants, including public officials, in official proceedings.

The best example of absolute privilege, but one that is typically not connected with the media, lies in the "Speech or Debate" clause of the U.S. Constitution. Article I, Section 6, of the Constitution contains among other provisions the following clause: "They [Senators and Representatives] shall in all Cases, except Treason, Felony and Breach of the Peace, be privileged from Arrest during their attendance at the Session of their respective Houses, and in going to and returning from the same; and for any Speech or Debate in either House, they shall not be questioned in any other Place."

This clause ensures that any member of Congress cannot be held legally liable for any remarks made as part of an official proceeding in the Senate or the House, regardless of the harm they may cause, unless the remarks are tantamount to a criminal act. For example, a Senator would not be immune from prosecution for plotting the murder of a peer or committing criminal fraud even though it occurred during a Senate hearing. However, the Senator could certainly hurl false and defamatory remarks at a government official or even private citizens with impunity, as U.S. Senator Joseph Raymond McCarthy from Wisconsin did during the early 1950s when he launched vicious attacks on alleged Communists in a series of Senate hearings. None of the junior Senator's claims — that Communists were well-placed in government

positions and these persons were aided and abetted by "Communist sympa-
thizers"—were ever substantiated, but McCarthy remained immune in spite of
eventual condemnation by his fellow Senators in 1954. During the "McCarthy
era," there was widespread abuse of the absolute privilege, but this defense
remains alive and well, thanks to the Constitution. Since the 1930s, members
of the U.S. House of Representatives have invoked a ritual known as
"one-minute speeches," during the first 15 minutes of the legislative day in
which any member can speak out for 60 seconds on any issue. The speeches
require prior approval of the Speaker of the House, but the Speaker has always
granted the right. Sometimes these presentations become heated and controversial such as when Congressman Pat Williams (D-Mont.) called Vice
President Dan Quayle's visit in September 1988 to a federally funded job
training center "hypocrisy." Williams was verbally reprimanded by House
Speaker James Wright (D-Tex.) and then pressured to have the statement
stricken from the record. Williams may have violated House rules, which bar
personal attacks and ridicule, but he still had absolute immunity. (Ironically,
the attempt to get the "hypocrisy" comment stricken from the record resulted
in it being repeated as part of the exchange involving the comment.[76])

Hutchinson v. Proxmire (1979)

Another Wisconsin Senator, William Proxmire, discovered in 1979 that
absolute privilege has its limits. In March 1975, the Senator initiated a satirical
"Golden Fleece of the Month Award" to publicize examples of what he
considered wasteful government spending. Senator Proxmire cited the federal
agencies, including the National Science Foundation, the Office of Naval
Research and the National Aeronautics and Space Administration, which
funded research by Ronald R. Hutchinson, Director of Research at the
Kalamazoo, Michigan, State Mental Hospital. Hutchinson was granted more
than $500,000 over a seven-year period to conduct a study of emotional
behavior in certain animals in an attempt to devise an objective measure of
aggression. The tests included exposing animals, such as monkeys, to aggra-
vating stimuli to see how they clench their jaws under stress. Proxmire's
legislative assistant, Morton Schwartz, who had alerted the Senator to
Hutchinson's research, prepared a speech announcing the award to the
researcher, which Proxmire presented to the Senate, and an advance press
release almost identical to the speech that was sent to 275 members of the news
media in this country and abroad. Later, the Senator mentioned the research
and the award in a newsletter sent to about 100,000 constituents and others,
and he talked about the project on at least one television show. The next year
Proxmire listed all of the "Golden Fleece" awards for the previous year, among
which was Hutchinson's. Proxmire mentioned Hutchinson by name in his
speech and in his press release but not in the other publicity.

Among the comments by the Senator in the release and in the Senate speech were: "Dr. Hutchinson's studies should make the taxpayers as well as the monkeys grind their teeth. In fact, the good doctor has made a fortune from his monkeys and in the process made a monkey out of the American taxpayer."[77]

In April 1976 Hutchinson filed suit against Proxmire and Schwartz in U.S. District Court, claiming that as a result of the publicizing of the award, he "suffered a loss of respect in his profession . . . suffered injury to his feelings . . . [had] been humiliated, held up to public scorn, suffered extreme mental anguish and physical illness and pain." He also contended that he had lost income and the ability to earn future income.

The defendants in the libel suit made a two-prong attack on the plaintiff's claims. First, they moved for a change of venue from Wisconsin to the District of Columbia and for summary judgment on the ground that such criticism enjoyed absolute privilege under the Speech or Debate Clause as well as protection under the First Amendment. Second, Proxmire and Schwartz argued that the researcher was both a public figure and a public official and therefore must demonstrate *actual malice* under *New York Times v. Sullivan.* No actual malice existed, according to the defendants.

The federal District Court judge did not rule on the change of venue motion but did grant a summary judgment in favor of the defendants. The judge said the Speech or Debate Clause included investigative activities related to such research and thus afforded Schwartz and Proxmire absolute immunity. The trial court also held that the press release "was no different [from a Constitutional perspective] from a radio or television broadcast of his speech from the Senate floor."[78]

The District Court further held that Hutchinson was a public figure because of his "long involvement with publicly-funded research, his active solicitation of federal and state grants, the local press coverage of his research, and the public interest in the expenditure of public funds on the precise activities in which he voluntarily participated."[79]

The Seventh Circuit U.S. Court of Appeals affirmed the District Court ruling in 1978.[80] When Hutchinson appealed the decision to the U.S. Supreme Court, Proxmire and Schwartz offered a somewhat novel argument to support the appellate court ruling. They pointed out that the newsletters, press releases and media appearances were protected by the Speech or Debate Clause because they were necessary for communicating with other members of Congress; very little speech or debate now occurs on the floor of either House even though such activities were the impetus for originally including the clause in the Constitution. They also argued that an essential part of the duties of a member of Congress is to inform constituents and other members of the federal legislature of issues under consideration.

On further appeal, the U.S. Supreme Court, in an 8–1 decision written by

Chief Justice Burger, reversed and remanded to the U.S. Court of Appeals. The Court noted that a literal reading of the clause would confine its application strictly to speech or debate within the four walls of either House but that the Court had previously ruled that committee hearings had absolute protection even if held outside Chambers and that committee reports enjoyed the same status. However, the majority opinion held that the objective of the clause was to protect legislative activities. According to the Court: "A speech by Proxmire in the Senate would be wholly immune and would be available to other members of Congress and the public in the Congressional record. But neither the newsletters nor the press release was 'essential to the deliberations of the Senate' and neither was part of the deliberative process."[81]

The second issue the Court had to deal with was the status of Hutchinson. Although both the trial court and the lower appellate court ruled that the researcher was a "limited public figure" (this concept is discussed later in this chapter under *Gertz v. Welch*) for the purpose of comment on his receipt of federal funds, the Supreme Court held that he was not a public figure and thus did not have to demonstrate *actual malice*. His activities and public profile "are much like those of countless members of his profession. His published writings reach a relatively small category of professionals concerned with research in human behavior. To the extent his published writings became a matter of controversy it was a consequence of the Golden Fleece Award."[82] The Court also emphasized that "Hutchinson did not thrust himself or his views into public controversy to influence others" and that he did not have the requisite regular and continuing access to the news media to be classified as a public figure.

The lessons in *Hutchinson* are (a) absolute privilege has its limits even when public officials utter the defamatory statements as part of their perceived official duties, and (b) individuals do not become public figures or officials simply by virtue of their attraction of government funding nor can they be made public figures by the creation of a controversy by someone else. In other words, don't thrust individuals into the limelight and then claim that they are public figures.

State and Local Recognition of Privilege

There are other examples of absolute privilege, but litigation involving them is relatively rare. Most state constitutions, for instance, contain a provision that parallels the federal "Speech or Debate" clause so that state lawmakers can debate to their heart's delight without fear of libel or any other tort so long as they are participating in an official proceeding. Sometimes local governments enact ordinances granting such protection for their officials. In both federal and state courts, judges and trial participants can claim absolute privilege for remarks made during official proceedings. This does not mean that witnesses can lie, of course. They may be immune from libel and similar torts, such as invasion of privacy, but they can still be held in contempt for lying in the courtroom.

There has been only one modern-day instance in which the Supreme Court has recognized an absolute privilege for the media. In a split (5–4) decision in *Farmers' Educational and Cooperative Union of America v. WDAY* (1959),[83] the justices held that because the Federal Communications Act of 1934 bars censorship of political speech by radio and television stations, stations that carry these required broadcasts, including commercials under the Equal Opportunities Rule under Section 315 (as discussed in the previous chapter), can claim absolute immunity from libel suits that may arise from defamatory statements in the broadcasts. The ruling itself was not a great surprise because fairness would dictate that the government cannot require a station to carry a broadcast without any censorship and then subject it to potential liability for having complied with the law, but the narrow vote was somewhat surprising. The Court did indicate that the political opponent or whoever uttered the defamatory statements in the broadcast did not have absolute immunity and thus **could** face a libel suit.

Qualified Privilege

Qualified, conditional or *limited privilege* (a rose by any other name . . .) is the most common type of privilege available to the mass media. In proceedings such as legislative hearings and debates, the judicial process (grand jury deliberations, preliminary hearings, trials, etc.) and meetings of government agencies as well as for public records, the press has a qualified right to report information even though it may be defamatory. But there is an important condition: **The report must be fair and honest.** Different states employ somewhat different language in specifying the condition, but the gist of it is still the same—the report must be an accurate account of what transpired or what is in the record and it must not be biased so as to unfairly defame an individual or other entity. The requirement is **not** that the information be **truthful**; instead the report must be an accurate rendition. In most jurisdictions, if a plaintiff can prove that the publication was for an improper motive such as revenge or malice, the qualified privilege is defeated. The best tactic for journalists in demonstrating fairness is to show that they were acting to keep the readers or viewers informed about a matter of legitimate public interest. In other words, emphasize that citizens have a right to know what occurs in governmental proceedings and to know the content of official records, but make absolutely sure the information is accurate. Minor errors, such as a slightly misspelled name (unless someone else can claim the misspelled version) or slightly altering a quote for brevity (which is still an error and thus should not be done even though it may not prove fatal), are usually not enough to lose the privilege defense, but a seemingly minor oversight can sometimes lead to serious consequences. *Time* magazine learned this lesson in 1976 in *Time, Inc. v. Mary Alice Firestone.*[84]

Time, Inc. v. Mary Alice Firestone (1976)

In 1961 Mary Alice Firestone separated from her husband of three years, Russell Firestone, heir to the Firestone tire fortune. Russell Firestone subsequently filed for divorce on grounds of extreme cruelty and adultery. After a long trial in which there was considerable testimony from both sides regarding the other party's extramarital affairs, the Florida judge granted the divorce in a rather confusing judgment. He said, in part:

> According to certain testimony in behalf of the defendant [Russell Firestone], extramarital escapades of the plaintiff were bizarre and of an amatory nature which would have made Dr. Freud's hair curl. Other testimony, in plaintiff's [Mary Alice Firestone's] behalf, would indicate that the defendant was guilty of bounding from one bed partner to another with the erotic zest of a satyr. The court is inclined to discount much of this testimony as unreliable. Nevertheless, it is the conclusion and finding of the court that neither party is domesticated, within the meaning of that term as used by the Supreme Court of Florida. . . .
>
> In the present case, it is abundantly clear from the evidence of marital discord that neither of the parties has shown the least susceptibility to domestication, and that the marriage should be dissolved.[85]

Thus the judge was granting the divorce on the ground of lack of domesticity, not on the grounds of extreme cruelty and adultery, although his decision was not entirely clear on this point. The divorce proceedings had received extensive local and national publicity, and Mary Alice Firestone even held press conferences during the proceedings to discuss the matter with reporters.

Time was operating under a tight deadline in getting the story to the readers. The divorce decree was announced late on a Saturday afternoon, and the next deadline for the magazine was the following day. *Time*'s New York bureau first heard of the decision from an Associated Press wire story that indicated "Russell A. Firestone had been granted a divorce from his third wife, whom 'he had accused of adultery and extreme cruelty.' " In its evening edition on the same day, the *New York Daily News* published a similar report. *Time*'s New York staff got similar information from its Miami bureau and from a stringer in Palm Beach, Florida, where the trial took place. With the information in these four sources, the magazine's staff wrote the following item, which appeared in the "Milestones" section the following week:

> Divorced. By Russell A. Firestone Jr., 41, heir to the tire fortune: Mary Alice Sullivan Firestone, 32, his third wife; a one-time Palm Beach schoolteacher; on grounds of extreme cruelty and adultery; after six years of marriage, one son; in West Palm Beach, Fla. The 17-month intermittent trial produced enough testimony of extramarital adventures on both sides, said the judge, "to make Dr. Freud's hair curl."[86]

A few weeks later, Mary Alice Firestone requested a retraction of the article, claiming that a portion of it was "false, malicious and defamatory." (Florida law, similar to many states, requires that a demand for a retraction be made before a libel suit can be filed and allows the defendant to mitigate damages, as discussed later in this chapter, if it is published.) *Time* refused and a libel suit ensued. In a jury trial in which the plaintiff called witnesses to testify that she had suffered anxiety and concern over the inaccurate report, Firestone herself testified that she feared her young son would be adversely affected by the report when he grew older. Just prior to trial, she had withdrawn her claim for damages to reputation, asking instead for compensatory damages for harm other than to reputation, as permitted under Florida law. A sympathetic jury awarded her $100,000 in compensatory damages.

On appeal, Florida's Fourth Circuit Court of Appeals overturned the decision on, among others, the ground that the article was fair and no damages had been demonstrated. The Florida Supreme Court reinstated damages on the basis that the false information in the report constituted clear and convincing evidence of negligence. The U.S. Supreme Court in a 5–3 decision vacated the state supreme court decision for a determination of fault in line with *Gertz v. Welch*. The Court rejected the magazine's contentions that (a) the *New York Times v. Sullivan* privilege, discussed shortly, should be extended to include all reports of judicial proceedings, even when inaccurate and false, so long as there was no actual malice and (b) that Mary Alice Firestone was a public figure and thus under *New York Times* must show actual malice. The Court said that under *Gertz*, she was merely a private figure. According to the opinion: "Respondent did not assume any role of especial prominence in the affairs of society, other than perhaps Palm Beach society, and she did not thrust herself to the forefront of any particular public controversy in order to influence the resolution of the issues involved in it."[87]

The decision, written by Justice Rehnquist, went on to note, "Dissolution of a marriage through judicial proceedings is not the sort of 'public controversy' referred to in *Gertz*, even though the marital difficulties of extremely wealthy individuals may be of interest to some portion of the public."[88] The Court also rejected *Time*'s argument that the report was protected from libel because it was "factually correct" and "faithfully reproduced the precise meaning of the divorce judgment." According to the justices, for the report to have been accurate, "the divorce . . . must have been based on a finding . . . that

[Russell Firestone's] wife had committed extreme cruelty towards him *and* that she had been guilty of adultery," which was not the case, they said, in light of the trial court's findings.

Two years after the U.S. Supreme Court's decision, Mary Alice Firestone's attorneys announced that she was dropping the suit because the original jury's verdict had vindicated her.

One difficult problem faced by the media is determining precisely when qualified privilege can be invoked. State laws vary considerably with some statutes granting protection in a broad range of circumstances from pretrial proceedings and government subcommittee meetings to virtually all public records while others are more narrowly drawn. The key is to be accurate and fair regardless of deadline or other pressures. In footnote 5 of its *Time* decision, the Supreme Court indicated that it appeared that none of the magazine's employees had actually seen the Firestone divorce decree before the article appeared. *Time*'s attorneys indicated in their appeal that the weekly would have published an identical statement even if the staff had seen the actual judgment before the story was written. The fact remains, however, that a journalist well-versed in legal matters, as all journalists should be, might have spotted the potential error and thereby averted the lawsuit.

The third type of privilege, *constitutional privilege*, arose in the famed *New York Times v. Sullivan* (1964) decision, as discussed in the next section.

NEGLIGENCE OR GREATER FAULT

In 1964 the U.S. Supreme Court constitutionalized libel in a decision that the Court continues to affirm while still fleshing out its real meaning. As discussed earlier in this chapter, in *New York Times v. Sullivan* the Court established the so-called actual malice rule that the First and Fourteenth Amendments require public officials to show that defamatory material disseminated by a media defendant was published with knowledge of falsity or reckless disregard for truth.

Some of the facts of the *New York Times* case were outlined earlier and will not be repeated here, but there are some additional facts that bear on the impact of the case. Although only the bare bones of the case's history will be laid out in this section, there are some excellent reference sources that everyone should read to gain a fuller understanding of this landmark decision. These include Anthony Lewis' wonderful book, *Make No Law: The Sullivan Case and the First Amendment* (1991), and the fascinating chapters about the case in Peter E. Kane's *Errors, Lies, and Libel* (1992) and Rodney A. Smolla's *Suing the Press: Libel, The Media, and Power* (1986). Each offers its unique version of the case in a way that the reader will truly appreciate the importance of the 1964 decision that profoundly affected media law for decades to come.

Even today, more than a quarter of a century after *New York Times v. Sullivan* was handed down, most of the general public is unaware of the case and of the principle it established. A 1990 statewide random survey of Kentuckians by the author and another researcher found, for example, that almost seven out of ten respondents felt that if a newspaper accidentally used false information in an editorial criticizing a well-known person in that community, that individual would be justified in suing for libel.[89] Similar surveys in other states would likely find the same results even though the U.S. Supreme Court made it clear that public officials (later extended to public figures) would not be able to recover for the accidental disclosure of false information because that would constitute negligence, not the requisite *actual malice*.

At the time the *New York Times* decision originated, the climate for civil rights progress in the country, especially in deep southern states such as Alabama, was extremely hostile. The trial judge in the case, Walter B. Jones, announced before the trial began in earnest that the Fourteenth Amendment "has no standing whatever in this Court, it is a pariah and an outcast."[90] The judge also permitted several of the jurors in the trial to be seated in the jury box with Confederate uniforms because they had just participated in a re-enactment of the swearing-in of Confederate president, Jefferson B. Davis.[91] Seating at the trial was segregated by race. During the trial, one of Sullivan's attorneys, Calvin Whitesell, appeared to be saying "nigger" instead of "Negro" when he read the ad to the jury.[92] One of the defenses raised by the *New York Times* was lack of *in personam* jurisdiction by the Alabama court because only 394 copies out of a total circulation of 650,000 had been distributed in the state, but the trial court judge rejected the motion. The local lawyer for the newspaper, T. Eric Embry, made what is known as a *special appearance* (a procedure by which an attorney can challenge the jurisdiction of a court by making a one-time appearance strictly for that purpose without being subjected to jurisdiction). He followed the steps enunciated by Judge Jones (the same trial court judge) in a book the judge had written, entitled *Alabama Pleading and Practice*, only to have the judge overrule his own book and declare his appearance to be a *general appearance*, thus subjecting his client to the jurisdiction of the court.[93]

At the time of the *The New York Times* trial, Alabama, like a few other states, had a strict liability libel statute. Under this statute the judge instructs the jury that once the statements are determined to be *libelous per se* (as he had ruled) and are not privileged, to find the defendants liable the jury needs only to find that they had published the advertisement and the statements were "made of and concerning" the plaintiff. The jury was also told that because the statements were *libelous per se*, "the law . . . implies legal injury from the bare fact of publication itself," "falsity and malice are presumed." "General damages need not be alleged or proved but are presumed," and "punitive may be awarded by the jury even though the amount of actual damages is neither found nor shown."[94]

After a three-day trial, the jury deliberated for two hours and awarded the plaintiff the full amount he had sought — $500,000 — against the *Times* and the four ministers who were also defendants. The jury gave no indication of how much of the award was for actual damages and how much was punitive damages. The Alabama Supreme Court sprung no surprises in its decision on the appeal, sustaining the trial court verdict in its entirety. The U.S. Supreme Court granted *certiorari* and heard oral arguments on January 6, 1964. Two months later the Court handed down its historic unanimous opinion written by Justice Brennan.

New York Times v. Sullivan (1964): The Actual Malice Requirement

As discussed in Chapter 2, the federal courts, including the U.S. Supreme Court, are barred from hearing cases that do not involve federal question (or diversity if the case originates in U.S. District Court). Thus the Supreme Court had to find jurisdictional authority before it could hear the appeal from the *New York Times*. The Court readily disposed of both major arguments against its jurisdictional power over the case. First, the Court rejected the contention of the Alabama Supreme Court that the case involved private action, not state action, and that the Fourteenth Amendment, therefore, could not be invoked. The Court said the fact that the case involved a civil suit involving common law was irrelevant because the "test is not the form in which state power has been applied but, whatever the form, whether such power has in fact been exercised."[95] The Court had no problem finding state action in Alabama's attempt to impose restrictions on the constitutional rights of the defendants.

Second, the justices disagreed with the Alabama courts that First Amendment rights were inapplicable in the case because the libel involved a paid "commercial" advertisement. Noting that this argument relied on *Valentine v. Chrestensen*, as analyzed in Chapter 5, the Supreme Court said the *Times* ad was not a "commercial" ad in the sense of *Chrestensen*. The Court instead characterized it as an "editorial advertisement" that "communicated information, expressed opinion, recited grievances, protested claimed abuses, and sought financial support on behalf of a movement whose existence and objectives are matters of the highest public interest and concern."[96]

The Court clearly felt that public officials should be able to take the heat of criticism, even when false information is involved:

> Thus we consider this case against the background of a profound national commitment to the principle that debate on public issues should be uninhibited, robust, and wide-open, and that it may well include vehement, caustic, and

sometimes unpleasantly sharp attacks on government and public officials. [citations omitted] The present advertisement, as an expression of grievance and protest on one of the major public issues of our time, would seem clearly to qualify for the constitutional protection. The question is whether it forfeits that protection by the falsity of some of its factual statements and by its alleged defamation of respondent.[97]

Further, the Court rejected Sullivan's argument that the constitutional limitations against repression of freedom of speech and of the press under criminal statutes such as the Sedition Act applied to Congress, not to the states, and the Court made it clear that "what a State may not constitutionally bring about by means of a criminal statute is likewise beyond the reach of prosecution under a criminal statute." The justices then enunciated the now famous rule of law: "The constitutional guarantees require, we think, a federal rule that prohibits a public official from recovering damages for a defamatory falsehood relating to his official conduct unless he proves that the statement was made with actual malice — that is, with the knowledge that it was false or with reckless disregard of whether it was false or not."[98]

With this statement, the U.S. Supreme Court had set a new standard for determining when media defendants can be held liable for the publication of defamatory information about public officials. Thus the Court constitutionalized one dimension of libel by granting First Amendment protection for false, defamatory statements under certain conditions. As subsequent cases have demonstrated, proving actual malice with convincing clarity (as the Court said was necessary) is a tough but by no means impossible burden to carry for a libel plaintiff. When it applied this standard to the Sullivan case, the Court ruled in favor of the *New York Times* and the other four defendants.

New York Times v. Sullivan was handed down more than a quarter of a century ago, so none of the justices has remained on the Court and two Chief Justices have retired, but the decision continues to be reaffirmed, albeit with clarifications and, some critics would argue, revisions.

Garrison v. Louisiana (1964): The Death of Criminal Libel

Slightly more than seven months later, the U.S. Supreme Court expanded the *actual malice* rule to apply to criminal libel as well. In *Jim Garrison v. Louisiana* (1964),[99] the Court unanimously reversed the conviction of Orleans Parish (La.) District Attorney Jim Garrison[100] for criminal libel for attacking the conduct of eight judges of his parish's criminal district court at a press conference. Garrison attributed a large backlog of cases to "the inefficiency, laziness, and excessive vacations of the judges" and accused them of hampering his efforts to enforce state vice laws by refusing to approve disbursements for the expenses of undercover investigations of vice in New Orleans. He was tried without a jury by a judge in another parish and convicted of criminal libel under a Louisiana statute, which provided criminal penalties for the utterance of truthful statements with actual malice ("hatred, ill will or enmity or a wanton desire to injure") and for false statements about public officials unless made "in reasonable belief of truth." The Louisiana Supreme Court upheld his conviction, but the U.S. Supreme Court reversed.

The Louisiana statute was unconstitutional, according to the majority opinion written by Justice Brennan, because neither civil nor criminal liability can be imposed for false statements about official conduct unless such statements are made with knowledge of falsity or reckless disregard for the truth. In other words, the *actual malice* rule of *Sullivan* now applied to both civil and criminal libel for criticism of public officials. The Court also took the opportunity to clarify the meaning of *actual malice* by defining this term to include having "serious doubts" about the truth of the publication and uttering "false statements made with . . . [a] high degree of awareness of their probable falsity." The justices also indicated that the use of a "calculated falsehood" would not be immune from liability and that the *New York Times* rule "absolutely prohibits punishment of truthful criticism" of the official conduct of public officials. In effect, the decision effectively killed criminal defamation, which had presumably been destroyed anyway in the trial of John Peter Zenger for seditious libel, which is akin to criminal defamation.[101] The Court did not directly toll the death knell for criminal defamation, but this archaic relic of the Star Chamber was on its way to the graveyard. In fact, two years after *Garrison* the Supreme Court handed down another decision involving criminal libel—this time, common law rather than statutory law—without specifically referring to *Sullivan*'s actual malice rule. In *Steve Ashton v. Kentucky* (1966),[102] a unanimous court reversed the conviction of a man who had committed the common-law offense of criminal defamation by circulating a pamphlet in Hazard, Kentucky, in 1963 during a bitter labor battle. The pamphlet criticized the Hazard police chief, the local sheriff and one of the owners of a local newspaper, the *Hazard Herald*, for not supporting striking miners. He accused the sheriff of "probably" buying off the jury "for a few thousand dollars" and the state police of escorting "scabs into the mines and hold[ing] the pickets at gunpoint."[103] The trial judge, who fined Steve Ashton $3,000 and sentenced him to 6 months in prison, defined criminal libel as "any writing calculated to create disturbances of the peace, corrupt the public morals, or lead to any act, which, when done, is indictable."

In the majority opinion written by Justice Douglas, the Court held that such a law was much too vague to be constitutional because punishing someone for simply publishing a statement that tends to breach the peace makes that person "a criminal simply because his[or her] neighbors have no self-control and cannot refrain from violence."

Three months before *Ashton*, the Supreme Court took the opportunity to somewhat clarify the definition of a public official under *Sullivan*. In *Alfred D. Rosenblatt v. Frank P. Baer* (1966), six of the justices, in an opinion written by Justice Brennan, reversed a jury award of damages to the former supervisor of a county recreation area against a local unpaid newspaper columnist who alleged mismanagement by a ski resort after the plaintiff had been discharged. He claimed, "On any sort of comparative basis, the Area this year is doing literally hundreds of percent BETTER than last year." The column made no mention of the plaintiff, but the jury and trial court judge had no problem with this. The Supreme Court, however, said that "in the absence of sufficient evidence that the attack focused on the plaintiff, an otherwise impersonal attack on governmental operations cannot be utilized to establish a libel of those administering the operations."[104]

More importantly, the Court said that *public official* "applies at the very least to those among the hierarchy of government employees who have, or appear to the public to have, substantial responsibility for or control over the conduct of governmental affairs."[105]

New York Times' Progeny: Extending the Actual Malice Rule

Three years after *Sullivan*, the U.S. Supreme Court extended the application of the *actual malice* rule to public figures, which the Court defined as persons who thrust themselves "into the 'vortex' of an important public controversy." In *Curtis Publishing Co. v. Butts* and *Associated Press v. Walker* (1967),[106] the Court combined two cases whose trial court decisions had been made prior to *New York Times v. Sullivan*. University of Georgia Athletic Director Wallace Butts was awarded $60,000 in general damages and $3 million in punitive damages by a jury for an article in the *Saturday Evening Post* magazine that accused him and Alabama football coach, Paul "Bear" Bryant, of fixing a game between their two schools. The magazine had relied on information from an Atlanta insurance salesman who said he had accidentally overheard a phone conversation between the two men. The judge reduced the total award to $460,000, and upon appeal by the publisher, the Fifth Circuit U.S. Court of Appeals affirmed. The U.S. Supreme Court also upheld the verdict.

The second case involved an Associated Press story about retired army general Edwin Walker, which erroneously said he had led a violent crowd of protesters at the University of Mississippi to block federal marshals who were attempting to carry out a court order permitting James Meredith, a Black, to enroll at the segregated public university. Walker won $500,000 in compensatory damages and $300,000 in punitive damages in a jury trial, but the judge struck the award of punitive damages. The Supreme Court reversed the verdict.

In a plurality opinion written by Justice Harlan, the court distinguished the two cases. Both individuals were public figures, according to the Court, but the evidence indicated "the Butts story was in no sense 'hot news' and the editors of the magazine recognized the need for a thorough investigation of the serious charges. Elementary precautions were, nevertheless, ignored." The Court found the second case much different:

> There the trial court found the evidence insufficient to support more than a finding of even ordinary negligence and the Court of Civil Appeals supported the trial court's view of the evidence. . . .
>
> In contrast to the *Butts* article, the dispatch which concerns us in *Walker* was news which required immediate dissemination. The Associated Press received the information from a correspondent who was present at the scene of the events and gave every indication of being trustworthy and competent.[107]

The plurality opinion also advocated a somewhat different test for actual malice in the case of public figures than had been indicated for public officials in *New York Times*: "We consider and would hold that a 'public figure' who is not a public official may also recover damages for a defamatory falsehood whose substance makes substantial danger to reputation apparent, on a showing of highly unreasonable conduct constituting an extreme departure from the standards of investigation and reporting ordinarily adhered to by responsible publishers."[108]

Unfortunately, this test attracted the support of only three other justices besides Justice Harlan. Since then, some state courts and an occasional federal court has cited the test as appropriate, but the U.S. Supreme Court has never explicitly adopted this standard for public figures.

In the same year as *Curtis Publishing*, the Court ruled in a *per curiam* opinion that a clerk up for reelection for the Wyoming County (West Virginia) criminal and circuit courts had failed to demonstrate *actual malice* with the *convincing clarity* required under the *New York Times* standard when he was attacked in three editorials in a local newspaper. In *Beckley Newspapers Corp. v. C. Harold Hanks* (1967),[109] the Court reversed a $5,000 jury verdict because the evidence showed no "high degree of awareness of . . . probable falsity."

"Serious doubts" became the buzzword for actual malice in 1968 when the Court ruled 8-1 in *Phil A. St. Amant v. Herman A. Thompson* that a public official had failed to show defamatory statements about him in a televised political speech were made with actual malice. According to the opinion written by Justice White: "There must be sufficient evidence to permit the conclusion in fact entertained serious doubts as to the truth of his publication.

Publishing with such doubts shows reckless disregard for truth or falsity and demonstrates actual malice."[110]

Two years after *St. Amant*, the Supreme Court held in *Greenbelt Cooperative Publishing Assoc. v. Charles Bresler* (1970)[111] that the use of the term *blackmail* in referring to a real estate developer's negotiating stance could not be reasonably understood as a criminal accusation because it was merely rhetorical hyperbole. Thus the Court overturned a $17,500 jury verdict for the defendant. In a similar vein, the Court reversed the $20,000 jury verdict evenly split against a newspaper and the distributor of a syndicated column for referring to the criminal records of one of several candidates for the U.S. Senate primary in New Hampshire and for calling him a "former small-time bootlegger." The judge in *Monitor Patriot Co. v. Roselle A. Roy* (1971)[112] had erroneously instructed the jury, according to the Court, that actual malice had to be shown only if the libel concerned the plaintiff's fitness for office. The judge had allowed the jury to determine whether the alleged conduct was relevant, but the Supreme Court said that "a charge of criminal conduct, no matter how remote in time or place, can never be irrelevant to an official's or candidate's fitness for office for purposes of application" of the actual malice rule.[113]

On the same day as *Monitor Patriot Co.* the Court handed two other major libel decisions. In *Time, Inc. v. Pape* (1971)[114] the justices attempted to further clarify the actual malice rule in a very complex case beyond the scope of this discussion. The Court's analysis particularly focused on whether omission of the qualifier "alleged" by *Time* magazine in a story about an incident reported in a civil rights commission's report could be considered by a jury as evidence of actual malice. Characterizing the report as "extravagantly ambiguous," the Court's majority felt the failure on the magazine's part was "at most an error of judgment rather than reckless disregard of the truth" and thus could not be construed as actual malice, which the defendant in the case would have needed to demonstrate because he was considered a public figure.

In the last case decided on the same day, *Ocala Star-Banner Co. v. Leonard Damron* (1971),[115] the Supreme Court wrestled with an issue quite similar to that in *Monitor Patriot Company*—whether a false report of the alleged criminal misconduct of a public official is relevant to the person's qualifications. The case arose when a small daily newspaper accidentally used the name of the plaintiff instead of his brother who had been charged with perjury. The mistake was committed by an editor who had been at the paper for only about a month. Citing *Monitor Patriot*, the Court reversed a $22,000 verdict awarding compensatory damages.

The Court issued one other major libel decision in 1971, *George A. Rosenbloom v. Metromedia*,[116] a plurality opinion that the justices subsequently rejected. The essence of the ruling was that both public figures and private individuals who are involved in events of public concern must demonstrate actual malice. That view was never adopted by a majority of justices, although some state courts applied versions of it. Since then, the decision has been thoroughly discredited and thus will not be discussed here except to note that at this point the Court was obviously struggling to give greater meaning to the actual malice rule. In 1974, the 10th anniversary of *New York Times v. Sullivan*, the U.S. Supreme Court finally had the opportunity to effectively deal with questions that continued to surround its 1964 landmark decision.

Gertz v. Welch (1974: Handling the Standard of Care for Private Individuals Back to the States

In *Elmer Gertz v. Robert Welch, Inc.* (1974),[117] the Court for the first time dealt with the standard of care to be applied in the case of a private figure. In a 5–4 opinion second only to *New York Times v. Sullivan* in its stature among libel rulings, the justices held that each state may set its own standard so long as it does not impose liability without fault—that is, strict liability. The case began when Elmer Gertz, a well-known Chicago attorney, was severely criticized in *American Opinion*, a magazine published by the right-wing John Birch Society. Gertz had represented the Nelson family in a civil suit against a Chicago police officer, Richard Nuccio, who had been convicted of second degree murder in the death of their son. Although Gertz had played no role in the criminal proceeding against Nuccio, the magazine article, entitled "FRAME-UP: Richard Nuccio and the War on Police," accused the attorney of being an architect in a "frame-up" against the police. The story also said the police file on Gertz took "a big Irish cop to lift," that he had been an official of the "Marxist League for Industrial Democracy," and that he was a "Leninist," a "Communist-fronter" and had been an officer of the National Lawyers Guild, which it described as a Communist organization that "probably did more than any other outfit to plan the Communist attack on the Chicago police during the 1968 Democratic Convention."

The statements were blatantly false. Gertz had no criminal record, there was no evidence that he was a "Leninist" or "Communist-fronter," and he had never been a member of the Marxist League. He had been a member of the National Lawyers Guild 15 years earlier but there was no evidence that he or the organization had taken any part in the 1968 demonstrations. Robert Welch, the managing editor of the magazine, "made no effort to verify or substantiate the charges" against Gertz, according to the Court.

"The principal issue in this case is whether a newspaper or broadcaster that publishes defamatory falsehoods about an individual who is neither a public official nor a public figure may claim a constitutional privilege against the liability for the injury inflicted by those statements," the Court noted. The majority opinion, written by Justice Lewis F. Powell, Jr., rejected the test espoused by the plurality in *Rosenbloom* and instead granted "substantial latitude" to the states to determine the applicable standard: "We hold that, so long as they do not impose liability without fault, the States may define for themselves the appropriate standard of liability for a publisher or broadcaster of defamatory falsehood injurious to a private individual.[118]

Gertz had won $50,000 in damages in a jury trial against the magazine, but the judge in the case who had instructed the jury that the plaintiff was a private individual, not a public figure, concluded after the verdict that the actual malice standard of *New York Times v. Sullivan* should have been applied instead of the state's negligence standard and, therefore, issued a jnov overturning the jury's decision. The U.S. Supreme Court reversed the trial court decision and ordered a new trial.

At least 32 states now have a *negligence* standard. Alaska, Colorado, Indiana and New Jersey have adopted an actual malice standard for private figures. New York imposes a gross irresponsibility standard, and it is unclear from four states—Connecticut, Louisiana, Montana and New Hampshire— exactly what rule applies.[119]

The Court made two more significant points in *Gertz*. First, it determined that Gertz was not a public figure:

> He played a minimal role at the coroner's inquest, and his participation related solely to his representation of a private client. He took no part in the criminal prosecution of Officer Nuccio. Moreover, he never discussed either the civil or criminal litigation with the press and was never quoted as having done so. He plainly did not thrust himself into the vortex of this public issue, nor did he engage the public's attention in an attempt to influence its outcome.[120]

The Court further indicated there are two types of public figures. One type is a person who has achieved such "pervasive fame or notoriety that he [she] becomes a public figure for all purposes and in all contexts." This type of public figure is now generally called an **all-purpose public figure**. The second and more common type of public figure is "an individual [who] voluntarily injects [her] himself or is drawn into a particular public controversy and thereby becomes a public figure for a limited range of issues." This category is generally known as a **limited-purpose public figure**.

Under the *Gertz* rationale, both the all-purpose public figure and the public official must show actual malice before they can recover **any** damages for libel unless the libelous statements do not relate to their public performance. However, limited-purpose public figures need to demonstrate actual malice only if the libelous matter concerns the public issue or issues on which they have voluntarily thrust themselves into the vortex. The private individual need demonstrate only that the particular standard of care was violated, which is typically negligence, a much lower standard than actual malice. The Court did indicate that "hypothetically, it may be possible for someone to become a public figure through no purposeful action of his [her] own, but the instances of truly involuntary public figures must be exceedingly rare."[121] Indeed, the instances are so rare that in the almost two decades since *Gertz* was handed down, the U.S. Supreme Court has yet to uphold a libel decision in which a plaintiff was classified as an involuntary public figure. It is safe to assume when reporting about people who have somehow been involuntarily thrust into the public spotlight that they are private individuals, **not** public figures for libel purposes. Elmer Gertz, Mary Alice Firestone and Ronald R. Hutchinson were all private individuals, **not** public figures.

The Court emphasized that *self-help* is an important factor to consider in distinguishing categories of libel plaintiffs:

> The first remedy of any victim is self-help—using available opportunities to contradict the lie or correct the error and thereby to minimize its adverse impact on reputation. Public officials and public figures usually enjoy significantly greater access to the channels of effective communication and hence have a more realistic opportunity to counteract false statements than private individuals normally enjoy. [footnote omitted] Private individuals are therefore more vulnerable to injury, and the state interest in protecting them is correspondingly greater.[122]

The Court went on to note that private individuals usually lack "effective opportunities for rebuttal," whereas those who seek public office "must accept certain necessary consequences of that involvement in public affairs." This point was clearly a warning of what was to come.

Finally, the Court held that no libel plaintiffs—public or private—could recover punitive damages unless the person demonstrated actual malice. As the Court noted, "It is necessary to restrict defamation plaintiffs who do not prove knowledge of falsity or reckless disregard for the truth to compensation for actual injury."[123] The justices declined, however, to define "actual injury," deferring instead to the trial courts. They did indicate, though, that the term was not to be limited to "out-of-pocket loss" but could include "personal humiliation, and mental anguish and suffering."

Dun & Bradstreet, Inc. v. Greenmoss Builders, Inc. (1985): *Gertz* Clarified or Modified?

In a decision in 1985 that still has some scholars scratching their heads, the U.S. Supreme Court upheld, in a split 5–4 vote, a jury award of punitive damages in a case in which the trial court judge had not instructed the jury that a showing of actual malice is required under *Gertz*. On appeal of the trial court decision, the Vermont Supreme Court upheld the award on the ground that

Gertz is not applicable to nonmedia defendants. In *Dun & Bradstreet, Inc. v. Greenmoss Builders, Inc.*,[124] Justice Powell, joined by Justices Rehnquist and O'Connor, disagreed with the state supreme court's rationale. Justice Powell said that for matters of private concern, states can determine whether or not punitive and presumed damages require showing actual malice. Chief Justice Burger concurred separately, contending that *Gertz* should be overruled and restricted matters of public importance. In his concurring opinion, Justice White indicated he shared Burger's view.

The case began when Dun & Bradstreet, a credit reporting agency, sent a confidential report to five clients that falsely reported that Greenmoss Builders, a construction contractor, had gone bankrupt. Greenmoss won $50,000 in compensatory damages and $300,000 in punitive damages. Justice Powell noted that the report did not concern a matter of public interest but instead was "speech solely in the individual interest of the speaker" and its confidential subscribers. Some First Amendment experts viewed the decision as nothing more than a reaffirmation of *Gertz* because, as Justice Brennan indicated in his dissent, at least six justices appeared to agree that the press ("institutional media") has no greater nor no lesser protection against defamation suits than other defendants. On the other hand, other experts disagreed with that analysis, asserting that the Court was indeed granting states the opportunity to lower the Gertz standard for punitive damages below actual malice. The Supreme Court has yet to take the opportunity to clarify its confusing holding.

Harte-Hanks Communications, Inc. v. Connaughton (1989): A Public Official Recovers for Actual Malice

Only rarely has the Supreme Court permitted a public official to recover damages, but in 1989 the Court took the opportunity to do so in *Harte-Hanks Communications, Inc. v. Connaughton*.[125] This case involved a front-page story in the Hamilton, Ohio, *Journal-News*, which quoted Alice Thompson, a grand jury witness, as saying that municipal judge candidate Daniel Connaughton, had used "dirty tricks" in his campaign and had offered her and her sister jobs and vacation in Florida "in appreciation" for their help in an ongoing investigation of bribery charges against incumbent James Dolan's Director of Court Services. The gist of the story was that Connaughton had engaged in a smear campaign against Dolan. The story was published a month before the election in which the newspaper supported Dolan.

After he lost the election, Connaughton sued the *Journal-News* for libel and a jury awarded him $5,000 in compensatory damages and $195,000 in punitive damages. A court of appeals upheld the decision and the U.S. Supreme Court unanimously affirmed. In an opinion written by Justice Stevens, the Court pointed to strong evidence of actual malice, as determined by the trial court. First, the paper did not bother to interview the one witness that both the plaintiff and Thompson said could verify their conflicting accounts of the events surrounding the alleged bribery charges—Thompson's older sister, Patty Stephens: "It is utterly bewildering in light of the fact that the *Journal-News* committed substantial resources to investigating Thompson's claims, yet chose not to interview Stephens— while denials coming from Connaughton's supporters might be explained as motivated by a desire to assist Connaughton, a denial from Stephens would quickly put an end to the story."[126]

Second, the reporter for the story and the editors deliberately chose not to listen to the tape recordings of the original interview in which Thompson made her allegations of the "dirty tricks." Third, there was evidence that Thompson may not have been a credible witness. She had a criminal record, had been treated for mental instability and her version of events was disputed by at least six other witnesses to the conversation between her sister and Connaughton. Fourth, the newspaper printed an editorial before its investigative story appeared, indicating that damaging information would appear later about the candidates during the final days of the campaign. To the Court, this showed a lack of concern for unearthing the truth and potential bias against Connaughton. Finally, there was conflicting testimony at the trial from the newspaper's own staff about how the story was investigated.

Bose Corporation v. Consumers Union of the United States (1984): De Novo Review

The Supreme Court dealt with one other important issue in the *Harte-Hanks* case—whether the appellate court had conducted the required *de novo review* established in *Bose Corporation v. Consumers Union of the United States*[127] in 1984, the 20th anniversary of *New York Times v. Sullivan* and the 10th anniversary of *Gertz v. Welch*. Bose began with an article in the May 1970 *Consumer Reports* rating stereo speakers, which claimed that the Bose 901 speaker system reproduced the sound of individual musical instruments in such a way that they "tended to wander about the room." According to testimony at the trial, the sounds tended to wander "along the wall" between the speakers, not "about the room." The judge ruled that the company was a public figure but that there was clear and convincing evidence of actual malice. (This type of libel is known as **product disparagement** or **trade libel**.) A U.S. District Court judge at a second trial ordered Consumers Union to pay $115,296 in damages to compensate Dr. Amar G. Bose, who had invented the innovative speaker system, for $9,000 he had said he spent to counter the bad publicity and $106,296 in lost sales. On appeal, the First Circuit U.S. Court of Appeals agreed that the article was "disparaging" but reversed the district court decision after conducting a *de novo review*, or independent review of both the facts and the law in the case, that there was no evidence of actual malice. Bose appealed the appellate court's decision on the ground that Rule 52(a) of the *Federal Rules of Civil Procedure* (which bars federal appeals courts from determining facts in a case unless the trial court's decision was "clearly erroneous") should have been the standard of review, not a *de novo review*. The U.S. Supreme Court affirmed the Court of Appeals decision, holding that federal appellate courts **must** conduct a *de novo* review "in order to preserve the precious liberties established and ordained by the Constitution" in those cases related to First Amendment issues. Note that such a review is mandatory if an appeal involving the First Amendment is considered in the **federal** courts; it is not optional.

In *Harte-Hanks*, the Court found that the Court of appeals had conducted the independent review mandated in *Bose* and thus did not give undue weight to the jury's findings.

Michael Milkovich
v. Lorain Journal Company (1990):
Protection for Opinion

The majority opinion made one other point in *Gertz* that it eventually had to clarify, although it chose not to do so until 16 years later. In *dicta* in *Gertz*, the Court said, "Under the First Amendment there is no such thing as a false idea." To some courts and many media defendants in libel suits, this implied that ideas were libel proof, but *dicta* (officially known as *orbiter dicta*) are simply assertions without proof or force and thus are meant to represent the law. In *Michael Milkovich v. Lorain Journal Company* (1990),[128] in a 7–2 decision written by Chief Justice Rehnquist, the Court ruled that the First Amendment does not require a separate privilege for statements of "opinion." The justices held that the protection offered by *New York Times v. Sullivan, Curtis Publishing Co. v. Butts* and *Gertz v. Welch* is sufficient for both opinions and statements of fact:

> Thus, where a statement of "opinion" on a matter of public concern reasonably implies false and defamatory facts regarding public figures or officials, those individuals must show that such statements were made with knowledge of their false implications or with reckless disregard of their truth. Similarly, where such a statement involves a private figure on a matter of public concern, a plaintiff must show that the false connotations were made with some level of fault as required by *Gertz*. Finally, the enhanced appellate review required by *Bose Corp.*, provides assurance that the foregoing determinations will be made in a manner so as not to "constitute a forbidden intrusion of the field of free expression." [cites and footnotes omitted][129]

Milkovich concerned a sports column that said a high school wrestling coach "had beat the system with the big lie" and that "anyone who attended the meet . . . knows in his heart that [plaintiff] lied at the hearing after giving his solemn oath to tell the truth." The Supreme Court said that a "reasonable factfinder could conclude that the statements in the . . . column imply an assertion that Milkovich [the plaintiff] perjured himself in a judicial proceeding." According to the majority opinion, "The article did not use the sort of loose, figurative, or hyperbolic language that would negate the impression that [the columnist] was seriously maintaining Milkovich committed perjury."[130]

Thus the Court reversed the trial court's summary judgment in favor of the newspaper. Many journalists found the decision unsettling and even alarming, but at least one First Amendment attorney has characterized the decision in "purely legal terms" as "little more than judicial tinkering, unlikely to have more than a marginal impact, especially on mass media with the sophistication, resources and guts to do their jobs aggressively."[131]

Masson v. New Yorker Magazine (1991): Altered Quotes

In *Masson v. New Yorker Magazine*[132] in 1991 the U.S. Supreme Court reversed a Ninth Circuit Court of Appeals decision upholding a summary judgment by a California U.S. District Court judge in favor of a magazine, author and book publisher. The Supreme Court held that although a libel defendant's intentional alteration of direct quotes did not automatically equate with actual malice, such changes could constitute an issue of fact to be presented to a jury. The Court was particularly bothered by a passage in which the plaintiff, psychoanalyst Jeffrey Masson, was quoted as saying Sigmund Freud Archive officials had characterized him as an "intellectual gigolo" when a tape recording contained a much different statement. The opinion by Justice Kennedy also suggested that the term *actual malice* not be used in jury instructions because of the confusion surrounding the term. According to the Court, "it is better practice that the jury instructions refer to publication of a statement with knowledge of falsity or reckless disregard as to truth or falsity."

In 1993 a U.S. District Court jury in San Francisco in a retrial determined that the author, Janet Malcolm, had libeled Masson, but the case ended in a mistrial when the jury could not agree on damages.

INJURY

There is one final element for proof of libel: The plaintiff was injured. Damages fall into five major categories: (a) nominal, (b) special, (c) general, (d) actual, and (e) punitive. The U.S. Supreme Court has never dealt directly with nominal damages but there is some question whether such damages are still available after Gertz,[133] in which the Court said that compensation can be made only for actual injury. The Court broadly defined actual injury as previously indicated, unless actual malice is demonstrated. Nominal damages are merely a symbolic amount, such as $1, and a way of recognizing that a plaintiff has been defamed but that no real harm has occurred. For example, several years ago a federal trial court jury found that the controversial scientist/writer William F. Shockley had been libeled in an Atlanta newspaper column. The column compared his theory of genetic inferiority of Blacks to the genocide policies of Nazi Germany but awarded him only $1 in damages.

Special damages are awarded to libel plaintiffs to compensate them for out-of-pocket or pecuniary harm. For example, the judge in the Bose trial awarded the plaintiff special damages representing his actual loss of sales as a supposed result of the critical review. Ordinarily, plaintiffs do not seek special damages in libel cases because they are fairly difficult to demonstrate.

General damages are awarded to libel plaintiffs to compensate them for losses that cannot necessarily be measured. In 1986 a federal district court jury awarded Brown & Williamson Tobacco Corp. $3 million in general or compensatory damages and $2 million in punitive damages against CBS for a commentary on a network-owned television station, WBBM-TV in Chicago, which accused the company of advertising its Viceroy cigarettes so children would associate smoking with sex, alcohol and marijuana. The judge reduced the compensatory damages to $1 because he said the company had failed to show loss of sales. In 1987 the Seventh Circuit U.S. Court of Appeals upheld the punitive damages but restored the $1 million in compensatory damages. The U.S. Supreme Court denied certiorari.[134]

With *Gertz* and its requirement of actual injury for all plaintiffs, *actual damages* have become the norm. As the Court indicated in *Gertz*, these can be awarded for such injuries as harm to reputation, humiliation and mental anguish. In 1988 in *Hustler Magazine and Larry C. Flynt v. Jerry Falwell*,[135] the U.S. Supreme Court reversed a U.S. District Court jury verdict awarding the television evangelist $200,000 in damages, including $100,000 in compensatory damages and $50,000 each against the magazine and its publisher in punitive damages for intentional infliction of emotional distress. *Hustler* had published a parody of the Campari Liqueur ad in which Falwell talked about his "first time." The Campari ads refer to the "first time" the celebrity tasted the liqueur, but the magazine's parody included a picture of Falwell with the text of a fictional interview in which he describes his "first time" as incest with his mother in an outhouse.

The Supreme Court ruled that because the jury had determined Falwell had not been libeled, the minister was not entitled to damages for intentional infliction of emotional distress. The majority opinion written by Chief Justice Rehnquist said, "There is no doubt that the caricature of respondent and his mother published in *Hustler* is at best a distant cousin of the political cartoons . . . [of Thomas Nast] . . ., and a rather poor cousin at that."[136] To recover such damages, the plaintiff would have to show that the publication contained a false statement of fact which was made with actual malice, which Falwell had failed to do, according to the Court. According to the moral of this story, intentional infliction of emotional distress will be virtually impossible to demonstrate for libelous statements unless plaintiffs can demonstrate that they were also defamed and, for a public figure, that actual malice exists.

Finally, *punitive damages* are, of course, designed to send a message to defendants and to punish them for the libel. There is no real cap on such damages, although judges will often reduce huge awards. Entertainer Wayne Newton, as indicated earlier, initially won $19 million in compensatory and punitive damages from NBC for a television news report that he claimed falsely implied that the Mafia and mob sources helped him purchase the Aladdin in exchange for a hidden share of the hotel/casino and that he had lied under oath to Nevada gaming authorities about his relationship with the Mafia. The trial court judge reduced the amount to $225,000 for physical and mental injury, $50,000 as presumed damage to reputation and $5 million in punitive damages. Then the Ninth Circuit U.S. Court of Appeals overturned the entire verdict and the U.S. Supreme Court denied certiorari.[137]

DEFENSES TO LIBEL

There are five major defenses to a libel suit as well as three other ways for a defendant to attack a libel suit and either have the case dismissed or mitigate — that is, reduce — damages. The five hard-line defenses are **truth**, **privilege** (absolute and qualified), **fair comment and criticism**, **consent** and the **statute of limitations**. The other three methods of attack are **retraction or correction**, **libel-proof plaintiff** and **neutral reportage**.

Truth

Since the John Peter Zenger trial in 1735, presumably truth has been a defense to libel, or at least criminal libel, in this country. Every state permits truth as a defense in some form. Truth must be published with "justification" or "good motives" in about half of the states, but this requirement is merely theoretical and probably would not survive a constitutional challenge in light of *New York Times v. Sullivan*, which prominently mentioned the value of truth and, in some circumstances, even falsehoods in the uninhibited and robust debate that we cherish on controversial issues of public importance. Thus it can be safely assumed that truth is essentially an absolute bar to a successful libel suit. There are two problems, howevers that often interfere with the use of this otherwise great defense. First, most libel suits do not involve truthful information. In other words, plaintiffs generally do not sue for libel unless the information is false. Whether there are damages or whether the degree of falsity is sufficient to warrant a legitimate suit may be questionable in the case, but nearly always a suit that at least survives a motion to dismiss involves false information of some kind.

In 1986 in *Philadelphia Newspapers, Inc. v. Maurice S. Hepps*,[138] the U.S. Supreme Court ruled in a 5-4 opinion written by Justice Sandra Day O'Connor that when a private individual sues the media of libel and the information published is a matter of public concern, the plaintiff has the burden of demonstrating the allegedly defamatory statements were false. Thus a suit fails if the plaintiff fails to provide clear and convincing evidence that the information was false. The defendant does not have the burden of showing the information was true. Although the Court did not indicate directly in its ruling that this requirement would also prevail for public figures and public officials, there is little doubt that this would be the standard because it is highly unlikely that the Court would impose a tougher standard of proof on private individuals than it would on public figures and public officials. The Court also did not indicate what the rule would be in cases involving private individuals and nonpublic issues. It would be safe to assume from the split vote and the fact that the Court chose to specifically tie the rule to matters of "public concern" that states would make their own determinations of the burden of proof in nonpublic matters whether they involve private individuals or public figures, especially limited-purpose public figures, as defined in *Gertz*. The public issue in *Philadelphia Newspapers* was alleged ties of a franchised business to organized crime and the use of these supposed ties to allegedly influence the state's government.

Privilege

As discussed earlier in this chapter, there are three major types of privilege — **absolute**, **conditional** and **constitutional**. The latter two are by far the most useful as defenses. Each type has limited applicability, but all have proven useful in specific situations. Public figures and public officials occasionally win libel suits from sympathetic juries, but the vast majority of those verdicts have either the damages reduced or are tossed out altogether by an appellate court conducting a *de novo review*. The key is getting an individual declared a public official or public figure. A 1988 libel case[139] involving the *Lexington (Ky.) Herald-Leader*, in which the author of this text served the defense as an expert witness before the trial, is a good illustration of the importance of this classification. A former University of Pittsburgh assistant basketball coach sued the newspaper for information about him in a January 1986 reprint of an earlier article that alleged he made an improper recruiting offer to a high school player. Before the trial began, Fayette Circuit Court Judge James E. Keller ruled that Reggie Warford was not a public figure. But, as the suit neared trial, he reversed himself and ruled that the plaintiff was a public figure and thus would have to show actual malice by clear and convincing evidence.

After the plaintiff's attorney had presented his side at the trial itself, Judge Keller granted the defense's motion for a directed verdict on the ground that the plaintiff had not met his burden of proof. The plaintiff appealed the decision to the Kentucky Court of Appeals, which reversed the trial court decision, and ruled that Warford was not a public figure and the directed verdict was not warranted. The defendants then appealed the decision to the Kentucky Supreme Court, which affirmed the lower appellate court's holding and ordered a new trial. The U.S. Supreme Court denied certiorari in 1991 and the case was settled out-of-court for an undisclosed sum. This case illustrates the extreme importance of the constitutional privilege mandated by *New York Times v. Sullivan*. It is far easier to prove negligence, which was the standard of care for private individuals in the Kentucky case, than actual malice. *Conditional privilege* can also be excellent protection, but it is conditional — journalists must take steps, sometimes extraordinary ones, to ensure that their reporting is fair and honest. Otherwise, they can expect no protection from the statutes.

Fair Comment and Criticism

Fair comment and criticism is basically opinion in slightly different clothing. Both the common law and statutes have generally permitted criticism of matters of public concern and of public individuals in their public performance, whether political, artistic, literary or whatever. Contrary to what some doomsayers contend, *Milkovich* did not kill fair comment and criticism, nor did it kill opinion. Facts that are cloaked (in the eyes of the Court, at least) in the guise of opinions have no greater protection than any other factual statements. There have been a few isolated instances, and *Milkovich* is one of them, in which commentary has been considered libelous. The fact remains, however, that comment and criticism of public persons and public events so long as they are (a) based on facts the communicator genuinely believes to be true but not factual statements per se and (b) not published with malice are protected. Scathing reviews of movies, critical book reviews and slams at public officials are alive and well but they must be fair and must be opinions, not statements of fact. For example, a movie review that says the lead actor was "extremely convincing in his role as a hardened drug addict" is protected, but an assertion that he was such a "convincing actor that one would think he may have had experience with such drugs before taking on the role as an addict" probably steps over the line and could likely result in a successful lawsuit.

Consent

Consent, if it can be demonstrated, is a good defense, but it is rarely available simply because individuals and corporations rarely grant permission to a journalist to disseminate defamatory information about themselves. Such permission, when it is granted, must be done so voluntarily, intelligently and knowingly. As with torts, such as invasion of privacy, minors generally cannot grant informed consent.

Ethical Concerns with Consent

There is an ethical concern with consent anyway. When individuals, whether they are public figures or simply private figures, grant permission to communicate information about themselves that is potentially damaging, a red flag should go up in the reporter's head. The person may be mentally unstable or even setting up the journalist for a potential lawsuit. Obviously, there may be unusual occasions on which information that is potentially harmful to someone may be disclosed by that person and be newsworthy. For example, a political candidate responding to an attack by an opponent could, in a weak moment, say something like "I admit that I have had extramarital affairs in the past, but I haven't had an affair for the past two years. I've reformed." Such disclosures could be relevant and deadline pressures would dictate that only limited verification could be done. Consent would be a strong defense in the case if the politician knew he was revealing the information for public consumption. If he names his past liaisons, they should probably not be publicized for ethical reasons alone. There is nothing to be served by such information titillating as it may be.

Statute of Limitations

As with any other tort, causes of action for libel must be filed within a specified time, as delineated in the appropriate state statute. In the *Lexington Herald-Leader v. Warford* case mentioned earlier, the plaintiff had failed to file his libel complaint against the newspaper for the two original articles within one year required under the Kentucky statute of limitations but he met the deadline for filing a suit based on a reprint three months later. A 1984 U.S. Supreme Court decision, *Kathy Keeton v. Hustler Magazine*,[140] involved an interesting aspect of the statute of limitations defense. If a defendant can show that a defamation suit was filed even one day past the deadline under the statute of limitations, the suit must be dismissed, no matter how much harm has occurred. This defense, if successful is a complete bar.

Kathy Keeton, associate publisher of *Penthouse* magazine and the common-law wife of publisher Robert C. Guccione, filed a defamation suit against *Hustler* magazine for a series of items published between September 1975 and May 1976, including a cartoon in the May issue alleging Guccione had infected her with a venereal disease. Keeton first filed suit in Ohio against Larry Flynt, *Hustler*'s publisher, but the case was dismissed because the statute of limitations had tolled. Keeton then sued the defendant in New Hampshire because it was the only state of the 50 whose statute of limitations could be met. At that time New Hampshire's limit was six years, although the legislature has since reduced it to three years (still longer than the one-year limit in most states). Keeton was a resident of New York and had no contact with New Hampshire. *Hustler* had only the limited contact with the state of 10,000 to 15,000 copies distributed each month.

A U.S. District Court judge ruled that the state's **long-arm statute** (a statute under which a state under certain circumstances known as *minimum* contacts establish jurisdiction over an out-of-state resident) was too short to reach Flynt in Ohio. The U.S. Court of Appeals for the First Circuit affirmed the decision, but a unanimous U.S. Supreme Court held that the limited circulation of the magazine was sufficient to constitute the requisite minimum contacts. Keeton could take advantage of what is known as the **single publication rule**, the Court said, which exists in some states to permit a libel plaintiff to file one action in one jurisdiction for damages suffered in other jurisdictions. The Court rejected the defendant's argument that application of the single publication rule and the longer statute of limitations was unfair. As Chief Justice Rehnquist noted in the Court's opinion, "New Hampshire . . . has a substantial interest in cooperating with other States, through the 'single publication rule' to provide a forum for efficiently litigating all issues and damages arising out of a libel in a unitary proceeding."[141]

On the same day as *Keeton*, the Court held in *Iain Calder and John South v. Shirley Jones* (1984)[142] that actress Shirley Jones, who lived in southern California, could file suit in her home state and home county against the *National Enquirer* — a weekly tabloid published in Florida with a circulation of 4 million, of which 60,000 copies are sold each week in California. As with *Keeton*, the Court said the test of "minimum contacts" was met even though neither the reporter nor editor had visited the state during preparation for the story.

Thus a media defendant should assume that the statute of limitations in the state in which it does most of its business or has its home office may not necessarily be the statute that prevails in a libel suit. As both *Keeton* and *Calder* demonstrate, establishing the necessary minimum contacts for asserting long-arm jurisdiction over a defendant is not difficult.

OTHER DEFENSIVE MANEUVERS

There are several alternatives that defendants are sometimes forced to use or otherwise choose to assert in lieu of or in addition to the traditional defenses. Technically, these are **not** defenses, although they can sometimes serve to either mitigate or eliminate damages. The most common of these is **correction** or **retraction**. This incomplete defense is available in most states under a statute that permits a potential defendant to publish a bona fide correction of a previously published false statement, so long as it appears within a specified time after it is requested by the subject of the statement and is published in a position as prominent as the original item. These statutes are usually quite strict and operate only if the time limitation is met and the correction does indeed admit an error and provide correct information. Publishing or broadcasting the correction has the primary benefit it typically prevents the plaintiff from recovering punitive damages. The party is usually still allowed to seek actual, special and compensatory damages, however. The correction/retraction has the disadvantage that it is, in effect, an admission of negligence. It also brings attention to the media outlet's error, which can certainly have a negative impact on the audience. But if the journalist has goofed, this may be the best strategy for avoiding punitive damages and may, in fact, satisfy the aggrieved party. Studies on libel indicate that plaintiffs very often are not seeking monetary awards when they believe have been defamed but rather want an apology so their reputation can remain intact.[143] The decision on whether to issue a correction or retraction is often quite difficult because of the risk of having to pay damages other than punitive damages, but it may be made tougher by the fact that the defendant typically has little time—sometimes only 1 to 3 days for a newspaper or 24 hours for a broadcaster—to decide.

Libel-proof plaintiffs are very rare but there are individuals whose reputations are so damaged by their own actions they have no reputation to defend. Two possible examples are convicted mass murderers and former political leaders convicted of multiple felonies. The idea of this defensive maneuver is to claim that the person's reputation has been so lowered in the eyes of the public that the individual cannot be harmed with false, defamatory statements. Even when dealing with notorious criminals, a journalist should follow the same precautions to prevent a potential libel. Nearly everyone has some redeeming quality that could be infringed.

The most controversial of the alternative defense strategies is **neutral reportage**. In *Edwards v. National Audubon Society* (1977),[144] the Second Circuit U.S. Court of Appeals held that neutral reportage was a viable defense, but this ruling is limited to this federal circuit only, although a few state courts have recognized the defense and several others have specifically rejected it or narrowed its application to very limited circumstances.[145] The requirements for this defense are (a) the charges must be serious and newsworthy and create or concern an important public controversy, (b) they must be uttered by a responsible person or organization, (c) they must relate to a public figure or public official, and (d) they must be accurately and disinterestingly reported.

A possible example of a situation in which this defense might have been used occurred during the 1992 presidential campaign when Jennifer Flowers—a former beauty queen, broadcaster and Arkansas state worker—claimed she had a 12-year extramarital affair with Democratic presidential candidate Bill

Clinton while he was governor of Arkansas. Clinton denied he had such a relationship with Flowers, although he acknowledged that he knew her. All of the major media reported the story, which originally broke in the *National Enquirer*, even though they could not verify whether the claims were true— even after Flowers played a tape recording of telephone conversations she had with Clinton. Bill Clinton, of course, survived the allegations and went on to defeat President Bush.

Neutral reportage grants the media an opportunity to act responsibly when allegations about prominent individuals emerge that are hard to confirm, are made by a supposedly trustworthy source and are newsworthy. Important ethical concerns have to be considered before this kind of information is disseminated; occasionally such allegations turn out to be false and before the truth becomes known the harm is beyond repair. Prominent people and organizations sometimes make charges about other public figures and officials, especially during the heat of political campaigns and in the midst of pronounced controversies. Even where neutral reportage is available, it should be invoked only when strongly justified and thus not used as a shield to report sensational and unnewsworthy information.

SUMMARY AND CONCLUSIONS

Libel continues to be a serious threat to the news media, especially as the current Rehnquist court continues to make it much easier for both public figures/officials and private individuals to successfully sue for libel. Libel is defined as false and defamatory information that harms a person's reputation and subjects that person to public hatred, contempt or ridicule. Of all the defenses available, truth and constitutional privilege are the most effective. Truth is an absolute defense, whereas constitutional privilege under *New York Times v. Sullivan* and its progeny requires that a public official or public figure demonstrate clear and convincing evidence of actual malice (regardless of disregard for the truth or knowledge of falsity). Private individuals in most states need to show only negligence to win a libel suit, although they must also prove actual malice to obtain punitive damages, at least when the allegedly defamatory statements concern an issue of public importance. Other viable defenses include qualified privilege, statute of limitations and consent; the latter two are not typically applicable, however. Thus the hurdles to recovering punitive damages, which can be incredibly high because they are designed to punish the offender rather than to compensate the offended, continue to be rather strong.

The trend in both state and federal courts, though, is toward permitting more plaintiffs to succeed, especially when media defendants have clearly acted irresponsibly. To mitigate damages, the news media should consider publishing a correction/retraction. However, such action must be taken with extreme care because it effectively means an admission of negligence or guilt. Finally, neutral reportage is a very limited defense that must be used responsibly even in the few jurisdictions where it is recognized. It is quite possible that the shape of libel may change significantly in the years ahead as President Bill Clinton makes his imprint on the U.S. Supreme Court with several expected new appointments. These changes will almost certainly mean good news for the mass media with broader recognition of individual and press rights under the First Amendment, reversing the trends of the last two decades.

8 Right of Privacy

A 29-year-old man from Japan spent 6 weeks in the home of Stephen and Maritza French in Costa Mesa, California, during the summer of 1989. The family had assumed he was a Japanese exchange student who needed temporary housing while he worked at the nearby U.S. subsidiary of Nissan to improve his English. A few months later the Frenches sued Nissan for invasion of privacy, fraud, breach of contract, trespass and unfair business practices after a *Los Angeles Times* article claimed that Takashi Morimoto was sent as an "operative" who spent his time with the family, "observing, questioning and filling up pages of a notebook each night in his guest room."[1] Nissan Motor Corp. USA claimed Morimoto was not a spy but had told the family that he worked for Nissan and that he had come to this country "to better understand U.S. life-styles and attitudes about cars."[2] Invasion of privacy? The incident illustrates the high value Americans place on privacy in a day and age when privacy rights are being eaten away by court decisions, statutes and especially modern technologies that sometimes make a mockery of it. The suit also highlights the value corporations and other business entities attach to information about individual consumers. In the competitive marketplace, informed marketing is often a key to success. Acquiring the information, however, may require the use of techniques consumers view as obtrusive and unwarranted.

In May 1987 former Miami model Donna Rice suddenly became an unwanted celebrity when newspapers and radio and television stations around the country revealed that she had spent the night with Gary Hart in his Washington, DC, townhome. The *Miami Herald*, which first broke the story, had secretly stationed reporters outside Hart's residence (but not on his property) to watch him around the clock. More stories followed with specific details about the relationship between Rice and Hart, who dropped his campaign for the Democratic nomination for president as a result. Although the stories created considerable controversy over whether Hart, who was married at the time, and Rice had been the victims of an invasion of privacy, no lawsuits were ever filed. Both individuals heavily criticized the media. In a 1988 article she wrote for the publication of the Overseas Press Club of America, *Dateline*, Rice wrote:

> I felt like a piece of chum tossed as bait into shark-infested waters.
>
> It was impossible for me to resume my normal life, and I retreated into seclusion. Silence seemed to be my only alternative since I chose not to exploit the situation. . . . My silence was the result of shock, a natural discretion that led me to salvage whatever shreds of privacy I could and a sense of responsibility that I should not impede the political process.[3]

Ironically, several months later on November 18, 1988, Rice once again became an object of controversy when she literally fled the Cincinnati Convention Center where she had been scheduled to speak on media exploitation to the annual convention of the Society of Professional Journalists (SPJ). Rice became a "no show" for the panel after she saw that cameras and microphones were poised for the occasion. The pharmaceutical sales representative/actress issued a written statement that "it was my original understanding that this panel discussion was private and essentially off the record. But when I arrived a few minutes ago and saw the cameras, lights and tape recorders, I realized this wasn't the forum I had anticipated."[4] SPJ officials claimed that Rice had been told the press would be covering the session.

Every time you use a credit card, telephone an 800 or 900 number, write a check, rent a car, register at a hotel, join a social club, order merchandise from a catalog or through a TV shopping network, visit a physician, visit an emergency room or stay in a hospital or even notify the post office of a change of address, your personal privacy has been potentially invaded; but usually no law has been violated. Today's sophisticated computers make it possible for a wide range of government agencies, businesses and even private individuals to access an incredible amount of personal information, legally and without your consent. Credit reporting bureaus have drawn considerable flak in recent years because they are legally permitted to gather highly sensitive credit information about individuals and businesses and to sell that information under certain conditions for a profit to businesses and other enterprises. Optical scanners, combined with credit card and check transactions, can compile very detailed information about individual shopping patterns. Some of the largest corporations — such as Citicorp, IBM, Dun & Bradstreet and Procter & Gamble — sponsor "point-of-sale" data collection systems; the giant conglomerate, Citicorp, began compiling a "National Household Purchase Data Base" in

1987 that will eventually have information from 12,000 retail stores covering as many as half the households in the entire country.[5]

The largest collector of private information is clearly the U.S. government, with the Internal Revenue Service at the top. The Census Bureau, of course, has records on nearly everyone in the country but is prohibited by federal law from sharing any of this information, except for compiled statistics that do not identify specific individuals. The FBI alone has more than 20 million criminal files and had a reputation under Director J. Edgar Hoover for violating the very civil liberties it was established to protect, when politically expedient. For example, in one of many out-of-court settlements to various individuals over the years, the FBI paid the widow of American Communist Party leader William Albertson $170,000 in 1989 for forging and planting a report on him during the 1960s that falsely accused him of being an FBI informer.[6] Court documents in the case revealed that the agency had tracked Albertson for five years, wiretapped thousands of phone conversations, intercepted mail and monitored his bank account, all apparently without legal authority.[7] A University of Kentucky Survey Research Center Poll of 685 Kentucky residents selected at random in 1987 found:

1. Almost two-thirds (64.5 percent) either strongly agreed or agreed that there should be stronger laws to prevent credit bureaus from sharing private information.
2. Almost 8 of 10 (79.4 percent) strongly agreed or agreed that the Constitution should be amended to guarantee a right of privacy.
3. Nearly two-thirds (64.7 percent) **strongly disagreed** or **disagreed** that the government should be able to punish people who possess pornography in their own home.
4. More than 6 in 10 (60.1 percent) felt that government agencies should be able to share personal information about individuals.[8]

A UK Survey Research Center Poll four years later found that 80.8 percent of the 646 respondents felt the state should not regulate in-home sexual activity between consenting adults of the opposite sex and 62.2 percent indicated the state should not control such behavior between consenting homosexuals.

National polls reflect a similar concern with the erosion of privacy. A recent Louis Harris and Associates poll found that 71 percent of those surveyed agreed that "consumers have lost all control over how personal information about them is circulated and used by companies."[9] Less than 40 percent of Americans expressed such concerns in 1970, but the doubts have grown in each poll since then. The same Harris poll found that whereas 81 percent of consumers trust the Census Bureau to maintain confidentiality, only 67 percent trust the Internal Revenue Service, compared with 68 percent for life insurance companies, 61 percent for auto insurance companies, 59 percent for credit bureaus and only 34 percent for telemarketers.[10]

There is substantial evidence to support the belief that we are gradually giving up much of our personal privacy. From the proliferation of high-technology spying devices to the marketing of caller identification telephone services to the accumulation of massive governmental and private business data banks, the trend is as loud and clear as the conversations picked up on a supersensitive microphone. There are so-called spy shops popping up almost every day that offer a wide range of devices — including miniature video cameras hidden in TV sets, dolls, wristwatches (a la Dick Tracy) and attache cases; night-vision goggles; super-powerful telephoto lenses and electronic microphones capable of intercepting conversations through walls and other barriers.[11] Although Title 18 §2512 of the U.S. Criminal Code provides a fine of up to $10,000 and/or imprisonment for up to five years for anyone who mails or puts into interstate commerce "any electronic, mechanical, or other device, knowing or having reason to know that the design of such device renders it primarily useful for the purpose of the surreptitious interception of wire, oral, or electronic communications,"[12] such devices continue to be sold. Title 18 has similar provisions banning the manufacture, assembly, possession, advertising or sale of such apparatus.

Probably the most serious threat to personal and even corporate privacy is the proliferation of data banks whose information can be readily accessed with a few keystrokes on a computer linked through a modem. A private investigator (PI) in Austin, Texas, for example, now conducts all of his investigations electronically rather than working the streets to get information.[13] PI Ralph D. Thomas is only one among a growing fraternity of investigators who use the dozens of "super bureaus" around the country, which are little more than small, computerized offices that function as gatekeepers of information available for a fee from credit bureaus, lawyers, investigators, insurance companies and so on.[14] One such gateway is the National Credit Information Network created in 1987 by a Cincinnati, Ohio, businessman who has signed agreements with various credit firms that permit him to market credit records to employers, insurance companies, collection agencies and others who subscribe to his service.[15] Much of the information available about individuals and businesses can be obtained quickly and at no or low cost, as discussed in Chapter 9. The U.S. Postal Service, for instance, will provide you with a person's address, including forwarding addresses, if the individual has moved. Courthouses house a wealth of public information about personal transactions and ownership — listings of all real estate and personal property, including vehicles and large equipment registered to a person. You can even ascertain how much the property was sold for and its assessed value and the license plate number of all vehicles. Of course, any lawsuits or other civil or criminal actions taken against or on behalf of the person are also usually public record. In fact, many state, local and federal courthouses today have converted their records to computer data, which can be readily accessed through a modem on a personal computer or by simply using a computer placed in the courthouse itself. Thus the president of one Houston private detective agency for $500 offers to obtain within one week a person's age, businesses owned, tax liens, bankruptcy record, divorces and number of children.[16]

With more than a million computers and billions of personal files — an average of 15 files for every U.S. citizen when last tallied in 1982[17] and possibly twice as many today, the federal government is the largest repository. Over the years, various statutes have been enacted to prevent most agencies from sharing information with other agencies, but there have been a number of largely unsuccessful attempts over the years to permit a linking of computer files. In 1990, Director of National Drug Control Policy William Bennett proposed a Drug Intelligence Center that would compile an electronic data file of anyone *suspected* of drug violations, not simply those arrested or convicted.[18] Under the proposal, which has yet to be approved by Congress, the center would link 14 government agencies including the FBI, IRS, CIA, Drug Enforcement Administration; Departments of State, Defense, Treasury, Agriculture and Energy; National Security Agency, Federal Aviation Administration, the Coast Guard, Customs Service and Immigration and Naturalization Service.[19] The center would also link with banks, airlines, shipping companies and other commercial databases.[20] In late 1991 Equifax, one of the largest credit-reporting agencies in the country, announced that it would discontinue by the end of the year its sale of mailing lists to direct marketers even though this action would mean a loss of $11.5 million. The names and addresses had come from the 120 million files compiled by the company.

Some of the strongest criticism in recent years has been aimed at Caller Identification Service (CID), which is being offered for a monthly fee by many telephone companies around the country. To the phone companies who sell the service as a deterrent against obscene and other harassing calls, CID is another customer convenience for increasing company revenues. To civil libertarians, the service is an unwarranted invasion of privacy that promises the demise of the anonymous phone call.[21] Before a phone company can offer CID, it must obtain the approval of the state regulatory authority, usually the state public service commission. States such as Virginia, Maryland, California, Pennsylvania, New York, New Jersey, Kentucky and Florida have already approved the service, although often with restrictions, as discussed later. The push to get the service approved is likely to get stronger because phone companies stand to gain considerable profits, just as they have with other user services like call forwarding and call waiting, and because consumers generally appear unconcerned about the privacy issue and see CID as a convenient means of privately screening numbers and preventing harassment calls. Several companies have heavily advertised caller ID service.

As each of the aforementioned examples illustrates, privacy is a broad issue that actually encompasses a bundle of individual rights that derive from a myriad of sources from common law to statutes to the Constitution. Most Western societies have imposed various restrictions to ensure at least some semblance of individual privacy. The First, Fourth and Fifth Amendments to the Constitution specify certain conditions under which privacy must be reserved. The First Amendment provides for freedom of press, speech and religion as a means of ensuring that one's political beliefs and expressions may not be suppressed or adversely used by the government. The Fourth Amendment recognizes a right to be protected "against unreasonable searches and seizures," a right that has been considerably broadened over the years (discussed later), and the Fifth Amendment guarantees against self-incrimination, thus prohibiting the government from forcing persons to testify against themselves in a criminal action. Many Western constitutions make similar guarantees, but in some cultures, the concept of privacy has a much different meaning. In a study published in 1977, psychology Professor Irvin Altman examined privacy as a generic process and concluded it is present in all cultures but the means of regulating privacy differ considerably among them.[22] The differences can be quite dramatic. Among the Mehinacu Indians of central Brazil, for example, houses tend to be placed so that everyone can be seen as they move around and housing is communal with people entering dwellings without announcing themselves; yet there are secret paths and clearings in the surrounding woods that allow people to get away from others. In the Balinese culture, on the other hand, families live in homes surrounded by high walls. Entrances to doors are quite narrow, and only family and friends enter the yards without permission. The members of a Moslem sect in Northern Africa, known as the Tuaregs, wear sleeveless underrobes and long outer garments. The men wear a veil and headdress that permit only their eyes to be uncovered; the veil is worn even when the men sleep and eat.[23]

JUDICIAL ORIGINS OF A RIGHT
OF PRIVACY

Virtually every treatise or text on the origins of the tort of invasion of privacy in the United States traces its development to an 1890 Harvard Law Review article by Boston lawyers, Samuel D. Warren and Louis D. Brandeis.[24] Brandeis was appointed 26 years later as an Associate Justice of the Supreme Court, where he served until 1939. The article—which some legal scholar view as not only the most influential law review article ever written on invasion of privacy but even one of the most influential articles ever written in the history of law reviews in this country—appeared at the height of the era of "yellow journalism" or what some writers call "new journalism."[25] This was the heyday of editors and publishers such as Joseph Pulitzer, William Randolph Hearst and Edward W. Scripps, whose newspapers reflected the times to appeal to the masses. From the end of the Civil War (1865) to the end of the 19th century, "industrialization, mechanization, and urbanization brought extensive social, cultural, and political changes: the rise of the city, improved transportation and communication, educational advances, political unrest, and the rise of an extensive labor movement."[26] It was inevitable that a sense of a loss of privacy would develop, especially among the well-heeled such as prominent lawyers like Brandeis and Warren. They no doubt scorned the focus on sensationalism in the major newspapers of the time just as they probably mourned the extent to which a growing population density in the cities meant a decrease in physical privacy or what sociologists and anthropologists call "personal space." Some critics would say that Warren and Brandeis' description of the Boston newspapers of the time still rings true for some of the media today.

> When personal gossip attains the dignity of print, and crowds the space available for matters of real interest to the community, what wonder that the ignorant and thoughtless mistake its relative importance. Easy of comprehension, appealing to that weak side of human nature which is never wholly cast down by the misfortunes and frailties of our neighbors, no one can be surprised that it usurps the place of interest in brains capable of other things. Triviality destroys at once robustness of thought and delicacy of feelings. No enthusiasm can flourish, no generous impulse can survive under its blighting influence.[27]

Brandeis and Warren proposed in the article that a tort of invasion of privacy be developed that would today fall into the category of *unreasonable publication of embarrassing private matters*, as discussed shortly. They did not deal directly with the other three categories of invasion of privacy—*intrusion*, *appropriation* and *false light*. Libel was already a tort in most jurisdictions at that time, and their treatment of invasion of privacy as a tort drew considerably on the tort of libel. For example, words as well as pictures would be subject to liability and damages would be available for mental anguish and other harm to the individual. However, the two authors asserted that, unlike libel, truth would not be a valid defense to invasion of privacy. The focus of the article was more a concern that the private affairs of the prominent and well-heeled not become the subject of intense public scrutiny through the mass media. As you will see, to some extent this remains the concern today, although invasion of privacy has been broadened to include private individuals (i.e., nonpublic figures) and other situations, but much of the litigation can be traced to public figures who feel their privacy has been violated.

The ideas enunciated by Brandeis and Warren attracted some attention among legal scholars at the time, but no court was apparently prepared to recognize a common law right of privacy and no legislature was willing to take the initiative to enact a statute granting such a right. The New York courts had the first opportunity to acknowledge a common law right of privacy, but chose to punt instead. After a lithographed image of her appeared without her consent in an extensive advertising campaign for "The Flour of the Family," an attractive young girl named Abigail Roberson sued the flour company for invasion of privacy. The trial court and lower appellate court ruled Roberson was entitled to damages for the humiliation, embarrassment and emotional distress she had suffered because of the ads. But in a 4–3 decision in *Roberson v. Rochester Folding Box Company*,[28] the New York Court of Appeals (the highest appellate court in the state) rejected her claim on grounds that (a) no previous precedent had established a right of privacy; (b) if the trial court decision were permitted to prevail, a flood of litigation would inevitably follow; (c) it would be difficult to limit application of such a right, if recognized, to appropriate circumstances; and (d) such a right might unduly restrict freedom of speech and of the press. The court also implied that creation of such a right was more the province of the legislature than the courts. The court did cite the Brandeis/Warren article but rather coolly rejected its arguments. In their strongly worded dissent, the three dissenting judges attacked the majority for its failure to recognize privacy as an inherent right. Both the public and politicians assailed the decision. In fact, the N.Y. Court of Appeals decision sufficiently outraged the state legislature to enact the next year (1903) a statute that provided both civil and criminal liability for "a person, firm or corporation that uses for advertising purposes, or the purposes of trade, the name, portrait or picture of any living person without having first obtained the written consent of such person."[29] The law included minors such as Miss Roberson in its protection, requiring that consent be obtained from a parent or guardian. The statute did **not** protect the use of a dead person's name or image and consent was an absolute defense. Some states still do not recognize a right of privacy for the deceased, but the trend (discussed later) is toward granting a right of publicity even after death. The statute made the offense only a misdemeanor but it permitted compensatory and punitive damages in a civil suit. That statutory provision in slightly altered form still survives today, although New York statutes now include other privacy torts such as intrusion.

In 1905 Georgia became the first state to recognize a common law right of privacy. Once again, however, it was not a broad right of privacy but, similar to the right granted in the New York statute, it was limited to commercial use or appropriation. Paolo Pavesich, an Atlanta artist, awoke one morning to find his photograph and a testimonial in a newspaper advertisement for the

New England Life Insurance Company. The ad was quite complimentary of Pavesich; it portrayed him as a handsome, successful man touting the virtues of good life insurance. Unfortunately, Pavesich had never given his consent for his picture to appear in the ad and the testimonial had simply been made up by a copywriter. In *Pavesich v. New England Life Insurance Company* (1905),[30] the Georgia Supreme Court reversed the trial court decision dismissing Pavesich's claim for damages for invasion of privacy. The court specifically rejected the *Roberson* holding (which, of course, was not binding in Georgia nor any other state except New York) and generally bought the arguments advanced by Warren and Brandeis. It was some time before other courts jumped on the privacy bandwagon, but even when they hopped aboard, they limited the right to commercial use. Many courts refused to recognize the tort until the 1930s and 1940s when the commercial value of endorsements became more apparent with a boom in advertising.

Why did it take so long for courts and legislatures to act? The courts were probably reluctant because they generally tend to avoid establishing sweeping precedents. Instead they tend to defer to legislatures because precedents are difficult to overturn whereas statutes can be changed by simply enacting new legislation. Legislatures most likely did not get involved because there was no strong public pressure until an incident such as the *Roberson* case pointed to the need for privacy protection. Pulitzer, Hearst, Scripps and their colleagues gave the readers heavy doses of sensationalism, including facts about the private lives of public figures but they generally wrote about ordinary people in a positive light except when they were involved in alleged criminal activities. Indeed, the huge success of the "new journalism" newspapers demonstrated an insatiable public appetite for private information. Finally, the U.S. Constitution and most state constitutions do not enumerate any privacy rights other than that against unreasonable search and seizure and self-incrimination. There was simply no overriding concern with privacy at the time they were written.

Finally, why was this right restricted principally to appropriation for so long? Why not include other privacy rights? Physical intrusion was fairly difficult to accomplish because there were no phones to tap, no recording devices, no microphones to hide, and so on, and the tort of trespass was already available to prevent someone from intruding on another's land or physical solitude. The torts of false light, publicizing private matters and appropriation all involve publication. The New York Court of Appeals in *Roberson* pointed to a possible explanation for excluding these torts when it noted that any injury Miss Roberson may have suffered was purely mental, not physical, and that some targets of such publicity might actually be pleased to get such attention. In other words, Miss Roberson should be flattered that a company would want to use her image.

WHAT IS THE RIGHT OF PRIVACY?

Black's Law Dictionary defines right of privacy as:

> The right to be let alone; the right of a person to be free from unwarranted publicity. Term "right of privacy" is generic term encompassing various rights recognized to be inherent in concept of ordered liberty, and such right prevents governmental interference in intimate personal relationships or activities, freedoms of individuals to make fundamental choices involving himself, his family, and his relationship with others.[31]

The late William L. Prosser, the foremost authority on the law of torts until his death, delineated invasion of privacy into four separate torts:

1. *Appropriation* of one person's name or likeness for the benefit or advantage of another.
2. *Intrusion* upon an individual's physical solitude or seclusion.
3. *Public disclosure* of highly objectionable private facts.
4. Publicity which places an individual in a false *light* in the public eye.[32]

This chapter examines each of these four torts of invasion of privacy. Although each is distinct from the others, there is some overlap, as you will learn. It is also not unusual for two or more of the torts to arise from the same set of facts. Nevertheless, each tort is reviewed and overlapping characteristics are pointed out.

APPROPRIATION

Appropriation is by far the oldest form of invasion of privacy recognized at common law, as *Pavesich* demonstrates, but it is the one tort of the four that poses minimal problems for the mass media. The courts have generally held that even though newspapers, magazines and broadcasters make substantial profits form the dissemination of stories about people from the ordinary person to the millionaire movie star, they cannot be held liable for appropriation so long as the profit-making is incidental to the use. For example, CBS does not have to get the consent of or pay the rock group "New Kids on the Block," when "60 Minutes" does a feature on them and NBC need not seek permission of President Clinton when the "Nightly News with Tom Brokaw" covers a press conference with the President. The mass media, however, are not relieved of liability for strictly commercial use of a person's name, image or likeness.

There have been some interesting examples of alleged appropriation. In May

1984, Fred Rogers, host of "Mr. Rogers' Neighborhood" on the Public Broadcasting System, convinced Burger King Corporation to pull a 30-second commercial aired around the country. The commercial, which cost $150,000 to produce, featured a "Mr. Rodney" teaching viewers to say "McFrying" (taking a whack at Burger King's biggest competitor). According to news reports, the ad had appeared about two dozen times on the major commercial TV networks and 30 to 40 times in the typical major market.[33] Mr. Rogers never sued, but the commercials met a quick death after he complained to Burger King. About the same time, Eddie Murphy was doing his ghetto version of "Mr. Rogers' Neighborhood" on NBC's "Saturday Night Live." Murphy's skits were some of the most popular segments on the comedy show until he left to become a movie star.

In September 1986, Woody Allen received $425,000 in an out-of-court settlement with National Video, Inc., after the video rental franchise firm used look-alike Phil Boroff in an advertisement in 1984. As part of the settlement, Allen dropped suits against Boroff and his agency, Ron Smith Celebrity Look-Alikes. There was no disclaimer and Allen was not mentioned by name, although two of his movies, *Bananas* and *Annie Hall*, appear alongside two movies, *The Maltese Falcon* and *Casablanca*, featured prominently in past Allen films.[34]

In August 1988 a U.S. District Court judge in Manhattan dismissed a suit filed by dancer-actress Ginger Rogers against the producers of a film, *Federico Fellini's Ginger and Fred*. Judge Robert Sweet ruled the film was "protected artistic expression." Rogers co-starred with Fred Astaire in 10 movies during the 1930s and 1940s. She had claimed in the suit that the producers implied she had approved the film.

In November 1988, Vanna White of TV's "Wheel of Fortune" game show sued Samsung Electronics of California for $1 million for using what she claimed was her likeness to sell its brand of consumer electronics without her consent. In 1992 the Ninth Circuit U.S. Court of Appeals unanimously dismissed White's statutory claim of appropriation, ruling that her name and likeness had not been used, but a majority of the Court upheld her common law claim for misappropriation of her identity.[35] The U.S. Supreme Court denied *certiorari*. In 1989, a U.S. District Court judge in Los Angeles dismissed a claim by Vampira (real name: Maila Nurmi), a 1950s horror movie star, against Elvira (real name: Cassandra Peterson), the popular host of horror movies on TV stations around the country. The judge ruled in the $10 million suit that Elvira did not appropriate Vampira's image when Elvira made her TV debut in 1981. The courtroom audience laughed when Judge William M. Byrne, Jr., explained that the two women were "focusing on something other than the face," referring to their images as buxom vampires.

In 1989 actor-comedian Rodney Dangerfield of "I get no respect" fame settled out of court with a Florida car dealership that Dangerfield claimed used a sound-alike in a TV commercial. In June of the same year, Indiana Colts running back Eric Dickerson sued the National Football League Players Association, toy manufacturer Kenner Products and software firm Tecmo for using without his consent what Dickerson contended was his likeness in a figurine collection and in a video football game called "Tecmo Bowl."

Why do sports and entertainment celebrities and other public figures go to great lengths, such as protracted litigation, to protect their images from unauthorized commercial exploitation? The simple answer is economics. Whereas the amount of the out-of-court settlements and even jury awards is typically not high, as the previous examples illustrate, the long-term potential for earnings from authorized endorsements for some public figures can be very lucrative. A 1990 NBC-TV documentary, "Sex, Sell and Advertising," indicated just how much of a windfall celebrities, especially entertainment personalities, can expect when they sign their names on an endorsement contract. Singer/entertainer Michael Jackson reportedly received more than $1 million for his "New Generation" Pepsi commercial, according to the documentary. In 1990, Jackson added L.A. Gear clothing to his list of clients. One of the advertisers' concerns in 1993 when Jackson was accused of child sexual abuse was that Jackson's credibility as a product endorser would decline significantly.

The number of television and film stars and famous athletes who have made commercial endorsements over the years is large, with some figures becoming more famous for their commercials than their career feats. Karl Malden urged Americans to take along their American Express Travelers' Checks wherever they go ("Don't leave home without them"), and Bill Cosby hawks Coke, Kodak cameras and film and Jell-O. Alan Alda of "M*A*S*H" fame has touted the virtues of Apple computers, Elton John and Paula Abdul sing for Diet Coke, and Ray Charles says "Uh huh" for Diet Pepsi. Very few celebrities reject the opportunity to sell major brand products and services because the compensation can be quite attractive and the work involved in doing such ads is typically neither demanding nor time-consuming. A few stars refuse to sell rights in the United States out of concern that their images could be become tainted here, but nevertheless appear in ads in other countries where less stigma may be attached to endorsements. Much of the stigma or perceived loss of professional credibility connected with endorsements has actually disappeared even in the United States as more celebrities hop on the bandwagon, including such revered talents as the late actor John Houseman (of *Paper Chase* fame), the late Bing Crosby, June Allyson (for "Depends") and Kenny Rogers.

Forty-four states and the District of Columbia now recognize appropriation or misappropriation as a privacy tort. Only New Hampshire and Minnesota, have refused to recognize this cause of action; it is unclear in five states — Colorado, North Dakota, South Carolina, Washington and Wyoming — whether the tort exists because there have been no reported cases.

Although the previous examples are well-known public figures, private individuals can also recover for appropriation. It is quite rare for such persons to sue and even rarer for them to win an award, but some have prevailed. There are two major reasons for the lack of cases. First, private individuals appear in the media much less frequently than public officials and public figures. Second, private individuals have a rather tough task in demonstrating substantial damages, especially in establishing lost potential earnings. Although the plaintiff in an appropriation case theoretically need only demonstrate (a) commercial use and (b) identification (i.e., that a reasonable person could recognize the image or name used as that of the plaintiff), in reality, some commercial gain must usually be shown to recover significant damages. Because the market value of commercial use of a private figure's image, name or likeness is usually severely limited, damages are correspondingly low.

Whereas only living persons may secure damages for the other three types of invasion of privacy (discussed later), appropriation is different. In a number of states—including Georgia, New Jersey and Tennessee—legislatures have enacted statutes that permit the heirs of a deceased figure to assume and control the publicity rights during a specified time after the person's death. In other states, such as Illinois and Ohio, the courts have specifically rejected such protection in the absence of a statute. In June 1989, *U.S. News & World Report* readers were surprised when they opened their magazine to find theoretical physicist Albert Einstein gracing an ad for Olympic Wood Preservative. Although Einstein died in 1955, his image and name were licensed by his heirs to a Beverly Hills agency that also licenses Jimmy Durante, Marilyn Monroe (who died in 1962) and even Sigmund Freud (1856–1939).[36] Charlie Chaplin's (who died in 1977) Little Tramp has appeared in IBM commercials, and other deceased notables frequently appear in ads. The length of time during which the right of publicity is protected after death varies from state to state, with some extending protection as long as 50 years after death. No advertiser should ever assume that protection no longer exists for appropriation after an individual dies because the results of using such an image without consent could be an unnecessary expensive lesson.

Hugo Zacchini
v. Scripps-Howard Broadcasting Company (1977)

Only one appropriation case has been decided by the U.S. Supreme Court, although an apparently growing number of cases are meandering through the lower federal courts and state courts. In *Hugo Zacchini v. Scripps-Howard Broadcasting Company* (1977),[37] a case whose impact on appropriation is still not entirely clear, the Court ruled that a TV station could be held liable for invasion of privacy for broadcasting the entire act of a performer. What was the "entire act?" About 15 seconds of Hugo Zacchini being shot from a cannon to a net 200 feet away. An even stranger twist to the story is that the filmed performance was shown during a regular 11:00 P.M. newscast, not as part of an entertainment program. As discussed shortly, newsworthiness is a limited defense to three of the four types of invasion of privacy—but not intrusion. Thus, if newsworthiness could have been demonstrated in this case, the result would have been different.

A freelance reporter for WOWS-TV in Cleveland recorded the human cannonball at a local county fair despite the fact that on the previous day Zacchini had specifically denied the reporter's request. Reporters were granted free access to the fair, and the general public was charged an admission fee that included Zacchini's act. Moreover, the commentary by the anchors that accompanied the film clip on the TV station was quite favorable, encouraging viewers to attend the fair and to see the human cannonball's performance.

Zacchini claimed, however, that broadcast of his act without his consent violated his right of publicity and he was therefore entitled to $25,000 in damages for harm to his *professional* privacy. In his suit, the performer took an unusual tact—he contended that by showing the entire act, the station deprived him of potential revenue. As the U.S. Supreme Court noted in its narrow 5-4 decision:

> If . . . respondent [the TV station] had merely reported that petitioner was performing at the fair and described or commented on his act, with or without showing his picture on television, we would have a very different case. But petitioner is not contending that his appearance at the fair and his performance could not be reported by the press as newsworthy items. His complaint is that respondent filmed his entire act and displayed that film on television for the public to see and enjoy.[38]

The state trial court had granted the station summary judgment in the $25,000 suit, but an intermediate state appeals court reversed the decision. The Ohio Supreme Court reversed again, holding that the station had a First and a Fourteenth Amendment right to broadcast the act as a matter of public interest in the absence of an intent to injure the plaintiff or to appropriate his work for some other nonprivileged purpose. The U.S. Supreme Court disagreed strongly with the state supreme court. The Ohio Supreme Court had relied heavily on *Time Inc. v. Hill* (1967),[39] discussed in the "false light" section near the end of this chapter, but Justice Byron White, writing for the U.S. Supreme Court majority, noted that there were major differences in the two torts involved—false light and appropriation. Justice White and the other members of the majority argued that (a) the state's interest in providing a cause of action was different for the two, and (b) the two torts differ considerably in the extent to which they restrict the flow of information to the public. On the first point, the Court noted that false light involves reputation, parallel to that in libel, but right of publicity is linked to "the proprietary interest of the individual in his act in part to encourage such entertainment." The appropriate parallel for right of publicity is patent and copyright law, according to the

Court. For the second point, the majority asserted that false light victims want to minimize publicity, but the typical plaintiff in a right of publicity case usually wants extensive publicity as "long as he gets the commercial benefit of such publication."[40] In other words, false light plaintiffs want to stay out of the limelight whereas right of publicity plaintiffs want media attention on their terms—that is, with financial compensation.

No other appropriation case has ever been decided by the U.S. Supreme Court, and even *Zacchini* was not a full-blown or pure appropriation case because it dealt specifically with *right of publicity*, a tort that some states, including Ohio, treat somewhat differently from appropriation. Those dozen or so states that make a distinction generally do so by confining a right of publicity to celebrities who can demonstrate commercial value of their name, image or likeness and that the public figures have either sold some rights or could have sold such rights if they had chosen to do so. This illustrates, once again, why it is much easier for a public figure to recover for appropriation or right of publicity than a private individual. Obviously, the right of publicity plaintiff does not have to be a nationally prominent or even a regional celebrity. Zacchini may have been the last of a dying breed—human cannonballs—but he was certainly no major media star. In fact, although very few people then knew or now know of him and his act, the Supreme Court permitted him to pursue his appropriation claim.

Zacchini left many questions, some of which may never be answered. Is a right of publicity triggered only by the unauthorized dissemination of an entire work or could this right apply for *substantial portions* of a work, similar to the requirement in copyright infringement? Does this right survive the death of the person and thus become transferable to heirs? (Although some states, as noted earlier, recognize a right of publicity that survives the individual, this right has not been recognized by the Supreme Court.) Does the right extend to private individuals or is it restricted to public performers or public figures? For example, would the Court have ruled differently if Zacchini had been shot out of the cannon during a small company reception or if Zacchini had simply been a volunteer from the audience? Finally, what if his act had been filmed as part of a public celebration for which the human cannonball had been paid by the local government or a corporate sponsor, but for which the audience was not charged an admission fee?

Although appropriation is virtually unheard of in the U.S. Supreme Court, a plethora of cases have been decided in the lower federal courts and in the state courts. Interestingly, certain names have cropped up rather frequently, no doubt because they are among the most valuable from a publicity perspective. Not surprisingly, Elvis Presley's name has appeared in several cases. His name has become even more valuable since his death as his popularity has soared and copyright royalties, publicity revenues and income from other affiliated rights have poured into his estate.

The executors of Presley's estate have been aggressive in protecting these rights. As a result, they have been involved in almost a dozen suits against nonprofit and commercial enterprises that have attempted to cash in on the Elvis name. Three of those cases are reviewed here because they illustrate the complexity and range of application of the right of publicity.

The Elvis Cases

Three days after Elvis Presley died on August 16, 1977, a company known as Pro Arts marketed a poster entitled "In Memory." Above a photograph of Presley was the epithet "1935-1977." The copyright to the photograph had been purchased by Pro Arts from a staff photographer for the *Atlanta Journal*. Five days after it began distributing the poster, the company notified Boxcar Enterprises, the Tennessee Corporation established by Presley and his manager, Col. Tom Parker, for the sublicensing to other companies for the manufacture, distribution and sale of merchandise bearing the Elvis name and likeness. Two days after Presley's death, Boxcar Enterprises had granted another company, Factors Etc. the exclusive license to commercially exploit the Elvis image. When Factors learned of Pro Arts' poster, it told Pro Arts to immediately halt sale of the poster or risk a suit. Pro Arts ignored the warning and instead filed suit in a U.S. District Court in *Ohio* seeking a declaratory judgment that it had not infringed on the rights of Factors. Factors, in turn, successfully sought a preliminary injunction in U.S. District Court in *New York* to halt any further distribution or sale of the posters and any other Elvis merchandise offered by Pro Arts. On appeal to the U.S. Court of Appeals for the Second Circuit, the lower court injunction was upheld:

> In conclusion, we hold that the district court did not abuse its discretion in granting the injunction since Factors has demonstrated a strong likelihood of success on the merits at trial. Factors possesses the exclusive right to print and distribute Elvis Presley memorabilia. . . . Pro Arts infringed that right by printing and distributing the Elvis Presley poster, a poster whose publication was not privileged as a newsworthy event.[41]

The defendant, Pro Arts, had claimed in district court and in the appellate court that (a) the right of publicity did not survive the death of a celebrity and (b) it was privileged, as a matter of law, in printing and distributing the poster because it commemorated a newsworthy event. The U.S. Court of Appeals handily rejected both arguments. The court noted that the duration of any right of publicity was governed by state law—in this case, New York law— because this was a case involving diversity jurisdiction. (As indicated in Chapter 2, in diversity cases in federal court, *state* law prevails.) Even though the appellate court could find no New York state court cases directly addressing the issue, it cited two cases — *Memphis Development Foundation v. Factors, Etc., Inc.* (1977)[42] and *Price v. Hal Roach Studios, Inc.* (1975)[43] — that supported its position that the right of publicity did survive a celebrity's death.

In *Memphis Development Foundation*, a U.S. District Court in Tennessee held that Factors Etc. (the same company in the case at hand) had been legally granted exclusive rights to capitalize and publicize Presley's name and likeness, that the right of publicity survives a celebrity's death and that Factors was therefore entitled to a preliminary injunction to prevent the nonprofit Memphis Development Foundation from giving away eight-inch pewter replicas to anyone who contributed $25.00 or more toward a $200,000 fund to cast and erect a bronze statue of Presley in Memphis. Factors did not contest the right of the organization to commission and erect the statue but specifically the right to distribute the replicas. It is highly unlikely that erecting a statue under these conditions, especially for public display with no admission charge, would be considered a violation of the right of publicity. Why then would distribution of the replicas at no profit but solely for the purpose of financing the statue be a violation? As discussed in Chapter 10, nonprofit status does *not* automatically grant a corporation a license to essentially deprive an owner or authorized user of profits from a work. The nonprofit organization stands in essentially the same stead as a "for profit" enterprise — deprivation is deprivation, regardless of the worthiness of the cause.

What then is the underlying rationale for permitting states to extend a right of publicity beyond a person's death? Clearly harm to the individual's reputation is not at stake because courts have consistently ruled that other rights of privacy — where they are recognized, such as publication of private matters, intrusion and false light (discussed in the following sections of this chapter) — do *not* survive a person's death. As discussed in the previous chapter, nearly all state and federal courts that have been presented the question have held that an individual cannot be defamed once the person has died. The answer lies in a judicial doctrine known as **unjust enrichment**. This doctrine, grounded primarily in principles of equity and justice, holds that "one person should not be permitted unjustly to enrich himself at expense of another, but should be required to make restitution of or for property or benefits received, retained or appropriated."[44] The gist of this judicially created doctrine is that an individual or company should not receive a free windfall at the expense of another because of an event in which it played no role. Thus it is pure and simple economics. Why should Factors Etc. be forced to give up its legitimately purchased rights and thus, undoubtedly, highly lucrative profits for the undeserved and, presumably, unjust benefit of anyone who chose to cash in on Presley's fame after his death? It could be argued, on the other hand, that the death of a celebrity is just another market factor that a company should keep in mind when negotiating the terms of a licensing pact.

Why should only one or a limited number of individuals profit from the use of a celebrity's status after his or her death? Why not provide everyone the opportunity to compete equally in the marketplace? There has never been any constitutionally recognized right of publicity either before or after a person's death, whether a celebrity or not, but the decision of whether to grant a right of publicity that survives death is strictly a policy matter in the hands of legislators.

In *Price v. Hal Roach Studios, Inc.,* a U.S. District Court, applying New York law, held that the deaths of comic actors, Stanley Laurel and Oliver Hardy ("Laurel and Hardy"), did not extinguish any assigned rights of publicity. The court concluded that whereas death is a "logical conclusion" to a right of privacy, there "appears to be no logical reason to terminate" an assignable right of publicity.[45]

On appeal, the U.S. Court of Appeals for the Sixth Circuit in 1980 in a rather brief opinion reversed the U.S. District Court decision. In *Memphis Development v. Factors Etc.* (1980),[46] the federal appeals court held that Presley's right to publicity, even if exercised and exploited while he was alive, did not survive his death and thus was *not* inheritable. The U.S. Supreme Court refused to hear a further appeal, and four years later Tennessee enacted a statute that granted a right of publicity beyond the person's death.[47] In 1987 in *Elvis Presley Enterprises v. Elvisly Tours,*[48] the Sixth Circuit Court finally recognized a descendible right of publicity but under Tennessee *common law* in line with an earlier Tennessee Court of Appeals decision.[49]

One other case involving Elvis Presley deserves brief mention. In 1981 in *Estate of Presley v. Russen,*[50] a U.S. District Court in New Jersey ruled that Presley impersonator, Rob Russen, violated Presley's right of publicity with his "Big EL Show." Russen argued that he had a First Amendment right to impersonate the celebrity, but the court held that no such right existed because the show was designed to be entertaining rather than informative. Impersonators are rarely sued for infringement because they generally do not fare well anyway, given public fickleness with celebrities, but the courts are quick to side against impersonators who can be mistaken for the "real thing"—such as in the Woody Allen case, mentioned earlier—or when blatant commercial use is involved in advertising or similar contexts, even if the individual has died. But what about prominent figures who did not commercially exploit an image during their lifetime? A Georgia court tackled this question in 1982 in *Martin Luther King, Jr., Center for Social Change, Inc. v. American Heritage Products, Inc.*[51] The Georgia Supreme Court held that the King Center could be granted an injunction against American Heritage to prevent it from marketing plastic busts of the famed civil rights leader who was assassinated in 1968, even though King had clearly *not* commercially exploited his name or image during his life.

Thus far the cases we have considered involved the use of a person's name or act, but appropriation can occur with other attributes as well. In 1962, Johnny Carson became the host of "The Tonight Show" on NBC-TV. As the show's popularity grew over the years, the host became synonymous in the public's eye with "Here's Johnny," the introduction used on every show until he retired in 1992. (Various substitute co-hosts bellowed or blurted out the slogan, but permanent co-host Ed McMahon clearly had the edge.) Like many other celebrities, Carson licensed various adventures over the years from Here's Johnny Restaurants to Johnny Carson clothing for men. In 1976, Earl Braxton of Michigan founded a company known as Here's Johnny Portable Toilets, Inc. The toilets were marketed under the slogan, "The World's Foremost Commodian." Carson was not amused and filed suit against the company for unfair competition, federal and state trademark infringement and invasion of privacy and publicity rights. His requests for damages and an injunction to prohibit further use of the slogan, "Here's Johnny," were denied by the trial court on grounds that Carson had failed to demonstrate a likelihood of confusion between the toilets and products licensed by the talk-show host and that the right of privacy and right of publicity extended only to a name or likeness, not to a slogan.

Carson appealed the trial court decision and in 1983 in *Carson v. Here's Johnny Portable Toilets, Inc.*,[52] the U.S. Court of Appeals for the Sixth Circuit disagreed with the lower court, holding "that a celebrity's identity may be appropriated in various ways. It is our view that, under the existing authorities, a celebrity's legal right of publicity is invaded whenever his identity is intentionally appropriated for commercial purposes."[53] The court then noted that if the company had actually used Carson's name such as "J. William Carson Portable Toilet" or the "John William Carson Portable Toilet," there would have been no violation of Carson's right of publicity because his identity as a celebrity would not have been appropriated. Would "Johnny Carson Portable Toilets" have been an infringement? What about simply "Carson Portable Toilets?" What harm did Carson suffer from the marketing of the toilets? Was he deprived of potential revenues from licensed products under his name? Would the general public be so naive as to believe that Carson had endorsed the toilets? Evaluate *Estate of Elvis Presley v. Russen*, discussed earlier, in light of this case. How likely is it that someone would actually mistake impersonator Russen with the true "King of Rock 'n Roll"? Don't impersonators and toilet distributors usually increase interest in the particular celebrity and thus potentially stimulate greater sales of licensed products? The doctrine of unjust enrichment dictates that one person should not be unduly enriched at the expense of another.

Defenses to Appropriation

There are only two viable defenses to either appropriation or violation of the right of publicity—**consent** and **newsworthiness**. Consent is clearly the strongest defense, but newsworthiness is sometimes helpful, depending on the context. Consent, if knowingly offered in good faith, is usually an airtight defense, especially if it has been granted in writing. Oral agreements and even implied consent can be valid but their applicability varies from state to state and with the surrounding circumstances. It is not necessary that persons be compensated for commercial use of their name or persona, but very few celebrities or even private individuals are willing to grant consent *gratis*— money usually talks. Most newspapers, magazines, broadcast stations and advertising agencies have standardized release forms that assure informed consent, but there are traps for the unwary. For example, a person must have legal capacity to sign an agreement or otherwise grant consent. Thus a parent or guardian must usually sign for minors. Another pitfall is to assume that the consent is broad enough to cover all circumstances and all time.

In 1982 singer/actress Cher was awarded more than $663,000 in damages by a U.S. District Court judge in California in a suit against *Forum* and *Penthouse* magazines, the weekly tabloid *Star* and freelance author Fred Robbins for violation of Cher's right of publicity.[54] Cher had consented to an interview with Robbins under the assumption that it was to published in *US* magazine. *US* was not interested in the proposed article and simply paid Robbins a "kill fee" for his work. A "kill fee" is generally paid to a writer for a commissioned work that the publication decides not to use. The writer usually retains the right to submit the work for publication elsewhere. Robbins then sold the interview to the *Star*, a tabloid that competes with the *National Enquirer* at the supermarket checkout, and to *Forum*, a sexually oriented discussion magazine owned primarily by Penthouse International, which also owns *Penthouse* magazine.

Both publications carried the interview, but took somewhat different approaches in marketing and displaying the story. *Forum* placed ads in more than two dozen newspapers, aired radio commercials and printed subscription tearouts that touted, "There are certain things that Cher won't tell *People* and would never tell *US*. So join Cher and *Forum's* hundreds of thousands of other adventurous readers today." The promotions carried Cher's name and likeness. The front cover of the *Forum* March 1981 issue, which carried the interview, included "Exclusive: Cher Talks Straight" in large type. The *Forum* story briefly mentioned Robbins at the beginning, but the format implied that *Forum* had conducted the interview. The *Star* published the interview as a two-part series beginning on March 17, 1981, with the banner headline, "Exclusive Series: Cher, My Life, My Husband, and My Many, Many Men."

On appeal, in *Cher v. Forum International, Ltd.* (1982),[55] the Ninth Circuit U.S. Court of Appeals overturned the trial court award of $369,000 against the *Star* on grounds that Cher had not been able to demonstrate that the magazine acted with *actual malice*, as required for false light under *Time v. Hill*,[56] discussed later. The appellate court, however, upheld a $269,000 judgment against *Forum*. In 1983 the U.S. Supreme Court denied certiorari.

Another case illustrates how clear, written consent can work to the advantage of the creator of an intellectual property that is ultimately involved in commercial use. When she was 10 years old, actress-model Brooke Shields posed nude for photographer Gary Gross, who had paid $450 for the written consent of Shields' mother to virtually unlimited publication rights. The photographs were published but attracted little attention until several years later at which time Shields garnered considerable attention as a fashion model and actress, including appearing nude in the movie *Pretty Baby* about a New Orleans brothel. Shields sought an injunction to halt further publication of the photos, and the New York Supreme Court ruled in her favor on grounds that the signed agreement could later be revoked because she was a minor at the time.[57] The New York Court of Appeals, the state's highest court, reversed, holding that the New York privacy statute allowed a parent to grant consent on behalf of a minor, and the agreement was, therefore, valid.[58]

What if an individual signs a broad consent agreement, but major changes are made in the use of the person's name, image or likeness? For example, what if a professional model is paid to pose for a series of photographs but then the context is severely altered? Two cases illustrate how the courts generally treat such situations. In 1959, the New York Supreme Court ruled that even though Mary Jane Russell had signed a broad release form that ostensibly granted the Avedon Bookstore all rights to use her picture for advertising purposes, the model could recover damages for subsequent use of her image by another company.[59] Avedon had sold a photo of Russell to a bed sheet company that, in turn, considerably altered the photo and used the new version in a provocative series of ads. The state Supreme Court held that the extensive alteration negated the agreement because the resulting photo was not the same portrait to which Russell had originally granted broad consent for commercial use.

A later case illustrates a similar point. In the early 1980s, aspiring actress Robyn Douglass posed nude with another woman in suggestive poses for a photographer. Douglass signed a standard release form granting *Playboy* magazine the right to publish photos of her but only without the other woman. Later *Hustler* magazine publisher Larry Flynt purchased the photos and, according to court testimony, was verbally assured that the actress had consented to the use of the pictures. When the nude pictures appeared in *Hustler*, Douglass sued the magazine on grounds that her right of publicity had been violated, she had suffered intentional infliction of emotional distress (a rising tort, as discussed in the previous chapter, that is related to the right of privacy as well as libel) and she had been placed in a false light (a tort discussed later) because of the nature of the magazine. The Seventh Circuit U.S. Court of Appeals[60] reduced the damages awarded by the trial court to the extent to which they were based on emotional distress from appearing in *Hustler* because she had already voluntarily appeared in the buff in *Playboy*. The court also ruled against her on the false light claim, but still essentially upheld her right of publicity claim. The appeals court noted that being depicted as voluntarily associated with a magazine like *Hustler* "is unquestionably degrading."[61]

The only other defense to appropriation and right of publicity is **newsworthiness**, but this defense is rather difficult to evoke in a commercial context and rarely works for a media defendant. *Zacchini v. Scripps-Howard,*[62] discussed earlier, illustrates the dilemma of claiming newsworthiness even when the use is clearly in a traditional news context. Zacchini's act appeared in a regular newscast on the television station — it was apparently not shown in a promotional segment or used in a direct way to commercially exploit Zacchini's performance. The only pecuniary gain the station may have gained would have been potentially higher advertising revenues from increased ratings. Such a gain is highly unlikely, however, because ratings used to determine ad rates are generally measured over a period of a month, not one show for one night. The Court was concerned that the "broadcast of a film of petitioner's (Zacchini's) entire act poses a substantial threat to the economic value of the performance."[63] The Court also noted that the Ohio statute had "recognized what may be the strongest case for a 'right of publicity' — involving not the appropriation of an entertainer's reputation to enhance the attractiveness of a commercial product, but the appropriation of the very activity by which the entertainer acquired his reputation in the first place."[64]

In 1969 *Sports Illustrated,* (*SI*) magazine used a photograph of New York Jets quarterback and Super Bowl hero Joe Namath in its subscription promotion. The photo, which had been taken during the Super Bowl — in which the Jets had captured the title in spite of being the underdogs — was used extensively in ads in the magazine itself as well as in other periodicals. Namath sued the magazine for appropriation but a New York County Supreme Court held that because the New York statute allowed incidental but not direct use of newsworthy photographs even in a commercial context, Namath had no cause of action.[65] The court said that as "long as the reproduction was used to illustrate the quality and content of the periodical in which it originally appeared, the law accords an exempt status to incidental advertising of the news medium itself."[66] Note that the court clearly considered *Sports Illustrated* a news medium, not an entertainment medium, and the photo had been previously used in earlier stories in the same magazine. Thus it was unlikely that someone would see Namath's appearance as his endorsement of the periodical. What if *SI* had used a photo that one of its photographers had taken but had *not* been published in the magazine? What if *SI* had tried to entice subscribers with a photo it had purchased from a newspaper, which had previously published the picture, although the photo had never been in *SI*? The results may very well have been different because there could be an impression left on potential subscribers that Namath may have endorsed the magazine rather than the impression that the publication was merely offering a look at the type of stories that readers would find in its issues.

An earlier case illustrates this idea. In the late 1950s, *Holiday* magazine had published a photo of actress Shirley Booth while she was vacationing at a Jamaica resort. Both had granted consent for the photo but was outraged months later when the same picture appeared in promotional ads for *Holiday* in other periodicals. Booth sued the magazine for appropriation under the New York statute and won $17,500 in damages from the trial court. On appeal, a New York Supreme Court reversed, holding that such use was merely incidental and therefore permissible under the statute.[67] *Holiday* was certainly not a "news magazine" in the traditional sense, but the principle established here and reinforced in the later *Namath* case would appear to protect both "non-news" and news media in typical promotional campaigns that tout the kinds of stories the reader can expect to see in that outlet.

Throughout this discussion of appropriation and right of publicity, we have dealt only with commercialization of *human* names, images and likenesses. Today there are animals whose names and images clearly have commercial value and thus a potential right of publicity. Some of them have been prominent for a long time, and others are just gaining fame. The older cases include Lassie (actually several dogs) and Trigger, Roy Rogers' horse. Although animal names can usually be trademarked to protect use of the name, what prevents someone from marketing a painting or selling a photograph of a famous animal? Probably nothing at this point, although the picture may be changing. According to one law journal article,[68] the first big test case may arise in the horse industry because the owners of two of all-time winners, Secretariat and Easy Goer, have contributed publicity rights for the horses to a nonprofit foundation for equine medical research. To make commercial use of the horses' names, one supposedly must acquire a license and pay a 10 percent to 15 percent royalty.[69] Whereas some legal scholars argue that a horse is a horse, others contend that certain equine names are so valuable they deserve the same protection as a famous person's name. No doubt, the courts will soon face this issue as animal names and images become more valuable.

INTRUSION

The tort of intrusion bears many similarities to the tort of **trespass**, which at common law is basically unlawful interference with an individual's personal possessions (personalty) or real property (realty). Even accidental or unintentional interference can be the basis for a trespass claim because injury is generally considered to have occurred simply because the person has intruded on the property, even if there is no actual physical harm. In a similar vein, intrusion is the only one of the four torts of invasion of privacy that does *not* require publication. The fact that the intrusion occurred, regardless of any dissemination of information obtained as a result, is sufficient to constitute harm. Publication can, of course, substantially increase damages, but the tort then most likely becomes the publication of private matters, coupled with intrusion. For example, if a reporter eavesdrops on the private conversations of the local mayor by illegally bugging the mayor's phone and then publishes a story about the conversations he overheard in which the official conducted drug deals, the reporter could clearly be held liable for wiretapping (intrusion) but may very well be able to avoid any liability for the stories because they are newsworthy. In most circumstances, however, the reporter can even be held liable for invasion of privacy for disclosing illegally obtained information.

How does intrusion occur? Is there a difference in liability between wiretapping a phone and using a telephoto lens from a public street to catch two people making love on a couch in their own home or between a surreptitious recording by a reporter of interviews with her sources versus videotapes shot by a journalist while standing on private property without consent? Each situation is different, depending on a host of factors, including the particular jurisdiction in which the alleged intrusion occurred.

The rules regarding intrusion are intricate, complex and even downright inconsistent. Some basic rules are universal, but beyond these axioms, the road can be treacherous. It is clearly illegal to wiretap a phone, except one's own, without consent of the owner and usually of any and all parties to the conversation or without a court order (if you are a law enforcement official.) Even court orders can be granted only on a showing of *probable cause*, which requires that there be reasonable grounds to suspect that the individual was committing or is likely to commit a crime. The basic test under the Fourth Amendment, according to the courts, is whether the apparent facts and circumstances in the situation would lead a reasonably prudent person to believe that a crime had occurred or was about to occur. Mere suspicion, without some supporting evidence, is not sufficient to justify search and seizure or the issuance of a warrant. The courts have permitted warrantless searches and seizures under special circumstances—when a police officer witnesses a crime or when obtaining a warrant is highly impractical (e.g., when the officer is pursuing a fleeing felon). Traditional intrusion by the government—such as surreptitious recording, wiretapping and eavesdropping—always requires a court order or warrant, but, of course, there is no requirement that the government notify the individual until formally charged.

Dietemann v. Time, Inc. (1971)

Journalists on their own never have court authority to commit intrusion, no matter how justified the ends may be. If they are working with authorities, they may or may not be legally permitted to intrude on an individual's privacy. Clearly, the most cited case on journalistic intrusion is *Dietemann v. Time, Inc.* (1971).[70] The Ninth Circuit U.S. Court of Appeals reached its decision in the case on a narrow set of facts involving primarily California common law and the First Amendment. (The federal courts had jurisdiction because this was a diversity case.) In its November 1, 1963, edition, *Life* magazine carried an article entitled "Crackdown on Quackery," which characterized A. A. Dietemann as a quack doctor, along with two photographs taken secretly at Dietemann's home approximately five weeks earlier. The magazine editors had reached an agreement with the Los Angeles County District Attorney's office to send two reporters posing as husband and wife to the home armed with a hidden camera and microphone that transmitted conversations to a tape recorder in a parked car occupied by another magazine staff member, an assistant district attorney and a state Department of Public Health Investigator.

The purpose of the reporters' visit was to obtain information for use as evidence to prosecute Dietemann for practicing medicine without a license, but the investigators had agreed that the magazine could use the information to do a story as well. The district court described the plaintiff (Dietemann) as "a disabled veteran with little education . . . engaged in the practice of clay, minerals, and herbs—as practiced, simple quackery."[71] The two *Life* journalists did not identify themselves as reporters, but instead pretended to be potential clients. The female reporter asked the quack doctor to diagnose a lump in her breast. After examining her, Dietemann concluded that she had eaten some rancid butter 11 years, 9 months and 7 days before her visit. One of the secret photos published by the magazine was of the plaintiff with his hand on the upper portion of the reporter's breast. The trial court and the appeals court emphasized that Dietemann was a journeyman plumber who claimed to be a scientist, not a doctor, and that he "practiced" out of his private home. He did not advertise, had no telephone and did not charge a fee for his services, although he accepted "contributions." He was ultimately convicted for practicing medicine without a license after pleading *nolo contendere* to the charges. (The story was published in *Life* before his conviction.)

The U.S. District Court awarded the plaintiff $1,000 in general damages for invasion of privacy, and the U.S. Court of Appeals upheld that judgment. The appellate court rejected the magazine's argument that the First Amendment immunized it from liability for its secret recordings on grounds that tape recorders are "indispensable tools of investigative reporting." According to the majority opinion by Judge Hufstedler, "The First Amendment has never been construed to accord newsmen immunity from torts or crimes committed during the course of newsgathering."[72] But weren't the journalists acting, in effect, as agents of the police because they had consent of the district attorney's office and were cooperating with the D.A. and the health department investigator? The court cleverly skirted this issue by holding that because the plaintiff had proven a cause of action for invasion of privacy under California law and because the defendants could not shield their actions with the First Amendment, the latter issue was moot.

Legal scholars and courts have split among themselves on the importance of the *Dietemann* holding. Some courts have basically rejected the holding or diluted its impact by distinguishing the case as involving a narrow set of circumstances; other courts, probably the majority, cling to the principle that "the First Amendment is not a license to trespass, to steal, or to intrude by electronic means into the precincts of another's home or office. [footnote deleted] It does not become a license simply because the person subjected to the intrusion is reasonably suspected of committing a crime."[73] Although all courts and legal scholars would agree that the First Amendment is not a license to intrude, there are major differences over the definition of intrusion. This court was very careful to separate the physical act of intrusion from publication, which is definitely in line with the traditional meaning of intrusion. In other words, no publication is required for intrusion. However, publication can substantially enhance damages, as the appellate court held in permitting the plaintiff to seek damages for additional emotional distress as a result of the publication. This presents a "win-win" situation for the plaintiff but a "lose-lose" one for the defendant because the defendant is not allowed to claim a publication privilege for intrusion and the plaintiff can ask for additional damages from publication.

Pearson v. Dodd (1969)

Most likely, most courts would still rule as the Ninth Circuit Court did in 1971 that *Dietemann*'s holding has become more and more limited to the specific circumstances in the case, which included the private home setting, misrepresentation of identification by the journalists and the direct use of eavesdropping devices by the reporters. In fact, even this court circumscribed the case by footnoting that its facts were different from those of *Pearson v. Dodd*[74] decided two years earlier by the U.S. Court of Appeals for the DC Circuit.

In *Pearson*, the U.S. District Court for the District of Columbia granted a partial summary judgment for Senator Thomas Dodd of Connecticut for conversion against syndicated newspaper columnists Drew Pearson and Jack Anderson but denied a partial summary judgment for intrusion. The appeals court reversed the judgment for intrusion and affirmed the denial of the judgment for *conversion*. Conversion is an old tort that lies in the unauthorized control over another's property so the rightful owners are deprived of their rights of possession. Unlike theft, which is normally a criminal action, conversion is a civil action and the owner can be granted damages in addition to return of the property. Thus the higher court ruled there was no basis for Dodd's claims.

The facts of the case are quite similar to those that can occur in some investigative stories, especially those involving the misdeeds of prominent politicians. Two former employees of the U.S. senator secretly entered his office, removed various confidential documents from his files, made photocopies and then returned the originals without consulting with their ex-boss. The documents, which contained details of alleged misdeeds of the politician, were then turned over to Pearson and Anderson, who used the information to write six syndicated newspaper columns that offered their "version of . . . [Dodd's] relationship with certain lobbyists for foreign interests, and gave an interpretative biographical sketch of . . . [his] public career."[75]

The columnists admitted that they knew the documents were purloined, but claimed, in defense, that they had not actually participated in securing them. Two members of Dodd's current staff had gone with the ex-employees during some of the visits, but Anderson and Pearson had apparently played no role other than publishing the information. The journalists also argued that Dodd had no cause of action for invasion of privacy even for publication of the private information because it was in the public interest. The appellate court agreed, holding that the columnists could not be held liable for damages for invasion of privacy from the publication or for intrusion. In a majority opinion written by Circuit Judge J. Skelly Wright, the court said:

> If we were to hold appellants liable for invasion of privacy on these facts, we would establish the proposition that one who receives information from an intruder, knowing it has been obtained by improper intrusion, is guilty of a tort. In an untried and developing area of tort law, we are not prepared to go so far. A person approached by an eavesdropper with an offer to share in the information gathered through the eavesdropping would perhaps play the nobler part should he spurn the offer and shut his ears. However, it seems to us at this point it would place too great a strain on human weakness to hold one liable in damages who merely succumbs to temptation and listens.[76]

Of course, Pearson and Anderson did more than listen—they spread the information throughout the country, with resulting considerable harm to the senator's career and reputation. The information, however, "was of obvious public interest," according to the decision. The court also rejected Dodd's claim of conversion because the "documents were removed from the files at night, photocopied, and returned to the files undamaged before office operations resumed in the morning . . . [Dodd] was clearly not substantially deprived of his use of them."[77]

The key defense in this case was the lack of active participation by the defendants in intruding on the privacy of the plaintiff. Neither Pearson nor

Anderson nor anyone directly associated with them was involved in obtaining the documents from Dodd's office. There was, however, a difference in *Dietemann*: The reporters actually carried eavesdropping devices into the plaintiff's home.

Florida Publishing Company v. Fletcher (1976): Implied Consent

An often-cited Florida Supreme Court decision in 1976 added a new twist to the picture. In *Florida Publishing Company v. Fletcher*,[78] the state supreme court ruled that an "implied consent" based on the "doctrine of common custom and usage" prevented Mrs. Klenna Ann Fletcher from recovering damages for trespass, invasion of privacy and wrongful infliction of emotional distress. Mrs. Fletcher's 17-year-old daughter had died while alone in her home when a fire of unknown origin gutted the house. In Florida, as in many states, fire marshals and police traditionally permit reporters and news photographers to follow them as they conduct their investigation. A photographer for the *Florida Times-Union* took a picture of a "silhouette" that remained on the floor of the house after Cindy Fletcher's body had been taken away. The photo was taken at the request of a fire marshal who had run out of his own film and needed another picture. A copy of the photo was turned over to the investigators for their files, but the picture was also published with others from the fire in the newspaper. Unfortunately, Cindy Fletcher's mother, who was out of town at the time of the death, first learned of the tragedy and its suspicious circumstances (possible arson) when the photos and a story appeared in the paper. Her suit for invasion of privacy (intrusion) was dismissed by the trial court, which granted summary judgments for the defendants on two other counts—one for a combined trespass and invasion of privacy and another for wrongful infliction of emotional distress. An intermediate state appellate court held that Mrs. Fletcher should have been able to pursue the trespass claim at trial.

The Florida Supreme Court ruled against Mrs. Fletcher on all three counts, and the U.S. Supreme Court denied certiorari a year later.[79] The state supreme court reasoned, as did the trial court judge, that "it is common usage, custom and practice for the news media to enter private premises and homes to report on matters of public interest or a public event."[80] The court emphasized that the photographer's entry was at the express invitation of the investigators, but that "implied consent would, of course, vanish if one were informed not to enter at that time by the owner or possessor or by their direction."[81]

Thus the court was essentially imposing three requisite conditions before the media can be relieved of liability under such circumstances. First, there must be a standing agreement or at least general public acceptance that journalists are permitted to enter private premises in situations such as this one. Second, the matter covered must be of public interest or a public event. Finally, the owner or other person(s) entitled to possession of the property (such as a renter or lessee) must either not be present at the time to object or be present but not not object. This decision was by a state supreme court, thus it establishes no precedent in other jurisdictions; the holding has been favorably cited by many other courts, although never expressly upheld by the U.S. Supreme Court.

Some aspects of this decision are still unclear. For example, the Florida Supreme Court did not indicate whether all three of the conditions had to always be present. What if the owner objected but there was a strong public interest to be served and the authorities had granted consent? On the other hand, what if the owner granted consent but the investigators objected? Finally, could an event be so public or could the public interest be so strong as to override the objections of the owner and/or authorities?

Ethical Considerations

Beyond the legal questions, however, are a number of ethical concerns in such situations. Assuming the newspaper knew that Mrs. Fletcher had not been notified of her daughter's death (which was unclear from the court's decision), should it have gone ahead and published the pictures and the story? What if the pictures had included the actual body, not just the silhouette? Should they be published to show the tragedy of the event?

Newspaper and magazine reporters often draw the ire of the public and occasionally the courts when they are perceived to intrude on an individual's privacy. But the most intense criticism has been directed at photographers and electronic journalists, thanks largely to the images the public has seen of obtrusive microphones thrust into the faces of the families of victims of tragedies or the prying eye of the still photographer focused on the victim's body. Although the fact remains that sensationalized news constitutes a relatively small proportion of the typical newspaper or broadcaster's coverage, the courts and the public pay greater attention to the bizarre and unusual. Some of these potential intrusions lead to litigation, whereas others merely lead to irate phone calls and letters to the editor.

In 1985, the Associated Press distributed a photo obtained from a member newspaper in California that showed the parents and two brothers of a young boy's family in intense mourning just as the boy's body is pulled from the area where he had drowned. The picture is particularly shocking because the body appears very prominently in the foreground of the uncropped version. Public criticism of the paper's decision to run the shot was quite vehement, including a bomb threat and more than 500 irate phone calls.[82]

When a Pan American jet exploded in mid-air over Lockerbie, Scotland, on December 21, 1988, killing all 270 people aboard, the U.S. news media immediately converged on Syracuse, New York, because 35 of the passengers were students from Syracuse University. According to one account, the press coverage was quite intrusive. At a campus memorial service, "Photographers jammed the aisles and balconies with bulky TV equipment, and they triggered blinding strobe lights and noisy motor drives on still cameras. The service was more like a press conference than a prayer vigil."[83] Several reporters called friends and family members of the dead within hours after the tragedy; they resorted to interviewing students as they walked on campus and snapping their photos as they succumbed to grief. These scenes of supposedly private mourning appeared nationwide, countless times in the newspapers and on television.

Was there an invasion of privacy in the media obtrusiveness in either of these two unfortunate situations? From a legal perspective, the answer is *absolutely not*. Both were public events. The drowning occurred in a public area, apparently in plain view of anyone. The accident was also newsworthy, of course, and thus there was clearly no reasonable expectation of privacy. Similarly, the plane explosion was of legitimate public concern, but didn't the individuals attending the memorial service expect some privacy? Perhaps, but by permitting the media to cover the service, the university was effectively waiving the right to assert a claim of intrusion, including the presence of cameras. Interestingly, university public relations personnel reportedly provided journalists from around the globe with detailed information about when and where the first memorial service would be held, but by the second service, all reporters and photographers were confined to the balconies.[84]

There are two major codes of ethics connected with the mass media: (a) the *Society of Professional Journalists Code of Ethics*, and (b) the *Radio-Television News Directors Association Code of Broadcast News Ethics*. Both codes mention privacy, but neither code offers any clear guidance on the ethics of conduct that may occur in such situations. The SPJ text is the most explicit: "The news media must guard against invading a person's right to privacy."[85] But how is this right of privacy determined? Is it confined to the limits specified under the law, or are there limits defined by ethical standards that are broader than the legal standards and thus dictate that certain kinds of intrusion (or other forms of invasion of privacy) may be legal but nevertheless *unethical*? The RTNDA code merely says that members of the association will "respect the dignity, privacy and well-being of people with whom they deal."[86]

Public Places

One principle regarding expectation of privacy rings loud and clear from the courts — individuals who appear in public places, whether they are public or private figures, can expect substantially less privacy than when they are in private settings. The difficulty for the news media, however, is distinguishing between the public versus the private domain. Suppose a television reporter is assigned by the news director to cover alleged health code violations by local restaurants. The reporter is handed a list of establishments cited by the city health services administration. She selects one from the list and enters unannounced with cameras rolling and bright lights shining. The result is chaos: Waiting customers leave in anger, other patrons dash off without paying and still others hide behind napkins or under tables. Can she be held liable for intrusion under these circumstances?

An incident similar to this led to a jury verdict in favor of the restaurant to the tune of $1,200 in compensatory damages and a quarter of a million dollars in punitive damages. On appeal, the compensatory damages stood, but the case went back for retrial on the punitive award, which the judge ultimately dismissed.[87] In 1972, a reporter for Channel 2 TV (owned by CBS) in New York not only paid a surprise visit with cameras rolling and lights bright but continued to record the ensuing confusion after the manager asked the crew to immediately stop. Although the diner received only $2,500, probably less than court costs and attorneys' fees, the New York Supreme Court (Appellate Division) rejected CBS' claim of First Amendment protection. Citing *Dietemann v. Time*,[88] the court reiterated that the First Amendment has never been interpreted to grant journalistic immunity from crimes and torts committed during newsgathering.

It is interesting to note that the action was for trespass, not intrusion, because, in line with the Restatement (Second) of Torts,[89] most courts have held that corporations and businesses do not have a right of privacy. But the consequences of trespass can be just as severe as those intrusion, as this case illustrates.

Even when they appear in public places, individuals certainly do not give up all rights of privacy. The classic illustration of this is *Galella v. Onassis*,[90] in which Jacqueline Kennedy Onassis successfully sought an injunction restricting Ron Galella's attempts to photograph Onassis and her children. The celebrity photographer routinely staked out Onassis by keeping a constant watch on her movements and those of her children. Galella was usually careful to take his pictures only in public places such as sidewalks and schools, but, according to the court, he once came uncomfortably close to Onassis in a power boat while she was swimming, often jumped and postured while taking pictures of her at a theater opening, customarily bribed doorkeepers and even romanced a family servant so he would know the movements of the family. Galella was detained and arrested upon a criminal complaint by Secret Service agents in an incident involving John Kennedy while he was bicycling in Central Park. After his acquittal on the charges, Galella sued the agents and Onassis for false arrest and malicious prosecution. Onassis denied any role in the arrest and countersued Galella for invasion of privacy, assault and battery, harassment and intentional infliction of emotional distress.

A U. S. District Court granted a temporary restraining order that forbade Galella from "harassing, alarming, startling, tormenting, touching [Onassis] . . . or her children . . . and from blocking their movements in the public places and thoroughfares, invading their immediate zone of privacy by means of physical movements, gestures or with photographic equipment and from performing any act reasonably calculated to place the lives and safety of the defendant [Onassis] . . . and her children in jeopardy."[91] Within two months, the "paparazzo" (as Galella called himself, which literally meant "annoying insect," according to the Court of Appeals) was back in the District Court for violating the order. The U.S. District Court granted a new order, as a result, that required the photographer to keep 100 yards from the Onassis apartment in New York and 50 yards from her and her children.[92] The TRO also prohibited surveillance. After a six-week trial consolidating Galella's claims and Onassis' counterclaims, the U.S. District Court dismissed the celebrity photographer's claim and granted a broad injunction that included a provision keeping Galella from approaching within 100 yards of the Onassis home, within 100 yards of either child's school, within 75 yards of either child or within 50 yards of Onassis. The U. S. Court of Appeals for the Second Circuit modified the trial court's order by cutting the zone of protection to 25 *feet*, banning the photographer from touching Onassis, forbidding him from blocking her movement in public places and thoroughfares and engaging in "any conduct which would reasonably be foreseen to harass, alarm or frighten" Onassis. The appeals court also enjoined Galella from "(a) entering the children's schools or play areas; (b) engaging in action calculated or reasonably foreseen to place the children's safety or well-being in jeopardy, or which could threaten or create physical injury; (c) taking any action which could reasonably be foreseen to harass, alarm, or frighten the children; and (d) from approaching within thirty (30) feet of the children."[92] The Appeals Court applied a balancing test in reaching its decision:

> Of course legitimate countervailing social needs may warrant some intrusion despite an individual's reasonable expectation of privacy and freedom from harassment. However the interference allowed may be no greater than that necessary to protect the overriding public interest. Mrs. Onassis was found to be a public figure and thus subject to news coverage.[93]

It is important to realize that Galella's actions were quite extreme. It was very difficult for the family to go anywhere public without facing the photographer's flashing lights and clicking cameras. Indeed, the freelancer made considerable sums from his sale of the photos and continued to do so after the unfavorable decision. The Court of Appeals noted that, as modified, the order still fully allowed Galella the opportunity to photograph and report on Onassis' public activities and that "any prior restraint on news gathering is minuscule and fully supported by the findings."[94] Unfortunately, the court order did not halt Galella's surveillance. Nine years later he was found in contempt of court for repeated violations of the order and had to pay a $10,000 fine.[95] According to press reports, he finally relented and focused his efforts on other celebrities.

The Onassis case is still the exception. According to the general rule, at least as recognized by most courts, individuals have little, if any, claim to invasion of privacy on grounds of intrusion when they appear in public places. Obviously, a claim may exist on other grounds, such as false light (discussed later in this chapter) or appropriation.

A good illustration of how this general rule is applied is *Cefalu v. Globe Newspaper*,[96] in which a Massachusetts Court of Appeals upheld a trial court's summary judgment in favor of the *Boston Globe*. Angelo Cefalu claimed the newspaper had libeled him and invaded his privacy by publishing a photograph of individuals, including him,lined up to collect unemployment benefits in a state office building. The photographer obtained the consent of the public information officer who announced to the people standing in line that the photographer was taking a picture from the rear and that anyone who did not wish to be in the picture could face the front or step out of line. Unfortunately, Cefalu did not hear the announcement, and his face is one of the few in the picture that is recognizable. He was in the line, not to pick up a check for himself, but to serve as a translator for a non-English-speaking friend who was obtaining a check. The photo was published in April 1973 without complaint from Cefalu, who, according to the court, even showed the photo in his home. However, in September 1974, the paper selected the photo from its file for a feature story on unemployment. The captions for each photo were similar, essentially indicating that unemployed people were lining up for checks. No one's name or other identification was mentioned in the captions.

In upholding the trial court's summary judgment against the plaintiff, the appellate court noted that publication of the photo was not actionable:

> The notion of right of privacy is founded on the idea that individuals may hold close certain manuscripts, family photographs, or private conduct which is no business of the public and the publicizing of which is, therefore, offensive. *The appearance of a person in a public place necessarily involves doffing the cloak of privacy which the law protects.*[97] (emphasis added)

Private Places

Under the Fourth Amendment to the U.S. Constitution, "The rights of the people to be secure in their persons, houses, papers, and effects, against unreasonable searches and seizures, shall not be violated, and no Warrants shall issue, but upon probable cause, supported by Oath or affirmation, and particularly describing the place to be searched, and the persons or things to be seized."[98] In the last decade, but most notably in the last few years, the U.S. Supreme Court has broadened the authority of the government to conduct warrantless searches within the parameters of the Fourth Amendment. In 1991, for example, the Court ruled 6-3 that police who suspect contraband is being hidden in a car may legally search the vehicle and any closed container inside.[99] The decision effectively overturned a series of earlier rulings by the Court that held that police, under most circumstances, had to obtain a search warrant to open a closed container such as luggage or a bag. A week earlier, the Court had held that once a driver had given authorities consent to search a car, they could also open bags or containers in the vehicle. In both cases, the majority favorably cited the 1925 case of *Carroll v. United States*,[100] in which the Court had upheld a warrantless search of an automobile being driven on the highway so long as there was probable cause. The rationale was that any contraband (in this case, liquor) could be quickly moved during the interim in which a search warrant was sought.

The Fourth Amendment protects individuals only against governmental intrusion, *not* against intrusion by nongovernmental entities such as private corporations and the news media. The trend is clearly toward granting the government greater latitude in gaining access to what were formerly considered to be private places, but federal and state statutes have continued to bolster the rights of citizens to be free of intrusion from nongovernmental entities. It is ironic that the only U.S. Supreme Court decision apparently recognizing a general constitutional right of privacy involved governmental intrusion, and yet governmental intrusion has been granted greater legitimacy by the courts at the same time that nongovernmental intrusion has become more restricted.

Griswold v. Connecticut (1965)

In *Griswold v. Connecticut* (1965),[101] the Court ruled that a state statute forbidding the use of contraceptives and the dissemination of birth control information even to married couples was unconstitutional because it infringed on a right to marital privacy. The Connecticut law provided a fine of up to $50 and/or up to 60 days in prison for a violation. The test case arose after a member of the state Planned Parenthood League and a physician were arrested and fined $100 each for giving information about contraceptives to married couples. In striking down the statute, the majority opinion written by Justice Douglas found that "specific guarantees in the Bill of Rights have penumbras, formed by emanations from those guarantees that give them life and sub-stance. Various guarantees create zones of privacy."[102] The sources for these emanations, according to the Court, include the First Amendment right of association, the Third Amendment ban against the quartering of soldiers in a private home without consent during peacetime, the Fourth Amendment guarantee, just discussed, against unreasonable search and seizure, the Fifth Amendment self-incrimination clause, and, finally, the Ninth Amendment, which simply provides that "the enumeration in the Constitution, of certain rights, shall not be construed to deny or disparage others retained by the people."[103]

This constitutional right of privacy against governmental intrusion is by no means absolute, of course, as demonstrated in more recent decisions by the Court such as *Bowers v. Hardwick* (1986)[104] (upholding a state statute forbidding consensual homosexual activity even in a private home), *Webster v. Reproductive Health Services* (1989)[105] (5-4 decision upholding a Missouri statute placing restrictions on abortion that appeared to circumvent the Court's 1973 holding in *Roe v. Wade*[106] recognizing a Ninth and Fourteenth Amendment right of a woman to have an abortion under guidelines established by the Court), and *Planned Parenthood of Southeastern Pennsylvania v. Casey* (1992)[107] (5-4 decision in which a bitterly divided Court reaffirmed *Roe v. Wade* but with a new test and with new limitations). In *Planned Parenthood*, the plurality opinion of Justices O'Connor, Kennedy and Souter said that although a woman still has the constitutional right to decide whether or not to have an abortion, states could impose restrictions—such as requiring a woman to wait 24 hours before undergoing an abortion and to be informed about abortion risks and alternatives. The Court did strike down, however, the portion of the Pennsylvania statute being tested that required a woman to tell her husband of her intent to seek an abortion. Instead of the traditional strict scrutiny test, the test for determining the constitutionality of abortion restrictions should be whether they impose an "undue burden" on a woman's right of choice. Only two justices—Blackmun, who wrote the majority opinion in *Roe*, and Stevens—voted to apply the original "strict scrutiny" test of *Roe*. Indeed, the four remaining justices, including Chief Justice Rehnquist, said *Roe* should be overturned.

As privacy rights against governmental intrusion gradually erode, privacy parameters against intrusion by others are expanding. In 1986 Congress passed the Electronic Communications Privacy Act,[108] which provides:

(1) Except as otherwise specifically provided in this chapter any person who—

(a) intentionally intercepts, endeavors to intercept, or procures any other person to intercept or endeavor to intercept, any wire, oral or electronic communication . . . shall be punished . . . or shall be subject to suit.

An offense can be punished by a fine of up to $500 and/or imprisonment of up to five years.[109] Anyone found guilty of manufacturing, distributing, possessing or advertising such devices can be fined up to $10,000 and/or imprisoned for up to five years.[110] Most states have similar statutes because the federal statutes, under the Constitution, can regulate the transmission of interstate or foreign communications or communications affecting foreign commerce. That is, federal laws cannot regulate communication that is purely intrastate. There are numerous exceptions under the law, including law enforcement officials with a court order and monitoring by the Federal Communications Commission to enforce the Communications Act of 1934.

Participant Monitoring

One very important exception is consensual or participant monitoring, as specified in 2511:

> It shall not be unlawful under this chapter for a person not acting under color of law to intercept a wire, oral, or electronic communication where such person is a party to the communication or where one of the parties to the communication has given prior consent to such interception unless such communication is intercepted for the purpose of committing any criminal or tortious act in violation of the Constitution or laws of the United States or of any state.[111]

Prior to the 1986 Electronic Communications Privacy Act, this provision included "injurious purpose" with criminal and tortious acts. (The original act was passed in 1968 as the Omnibus Crime Control and Safe Streets Act.) These two words were deleted, however, in the 1986 act, primarily in response to a 1984 Sixth Circuit U.S. Court of Appeals decision in *Boddie v. the American Broadcasting Companies*.[112] That case arose on August 19, 1980, when ABC's "20/20" carried a story entitled "Injustice for All" by correspondent Geraldo Rivera, which investigated allegations that a Ohio judge granted leniency to women criminal defendants who had sex with him. Rivera interviewed Sandra Boddie, an unwed mother of four, who had received a lenient sentence from the judge, James Barbuto, although she claimed she had not had sex with him. The interview was recorded with a hidden video camera and microphone. When excerpts of the interview were broadcast, Rivera alleged that a friend of Boddie's had sex with the judge on behalf of Boddie. Boddie sued the network and Rivera 19 months later for libel, false light and civil violation of the federal statute. The trial court judge dismissed the eavesdropping claim and a jury ruled there had been no libel or an invasion of privacy. The U.S. Court of Appeals sent the case back to the trial court, ruling that the wiretapping claim had been improperly dismissed. Before the case was retried, Congress passed the 1986 act with revisions designed to permit surreptitious recording for news gathering under participant monitoring.

When the case was retried, the District Court judge dismissed Boddie's suit on the grounds that the 1986 revision simply clarified, rather than changed, the previous law and that Congress had not meant for "injurious purpose" to include newsgathering. Boddie appealed, and the U.S. Court of Appeals for the Sixth Circuit affirmed the dismissal on grounds that the "injurious purpose" language was unconstitutionally vague, holding that the trial court judge had erred when he dismissed Boddie's claims on the basis that the 1986 revisions had simply clarified the old law.[113] Although the Court of Appeals decision is technically binding only in the Sixth Circuit, it is a major recognition of the right of news organizations as well as the general public to secretly record conversations in person, via telephone or by other means when they are parties to the conversation or when they have consent of *one* of the parties. The appellate court made it clear that "even though the statute is not explicitly aimed at speech, uncertainty about its scope is likely to inhibit newsgathering and reporting."[114]

While the trial court and the appellate court agreed that the case should be dismissed, albeit on different grounds, both decisions reveal a potential undercurrent that should concern journalists. By erroneously ascribing the basis for the dismissal to clarification in the 1986 revision, the District Court was indicating that had Congress chosen to broaden the statute to include claims such as Boddie's, Congress would have been permitted to do so. In other words, Congress would not have violated the First Amendment. This situation is particularly troubling in light of the legislative history of the act, which shows that the Senate sponsors and other supporters of the revision expressed on the record that permitting civil damages under the wiretap statute would violate the First Amendment. Even the appellate court decision strikes a discordant note because the court also refused to dismiss the claim on grounds that the "injurious act" language specifically violated the First Amendment but instead clung to the notion of *constitutional vagueness*. The higher court gave no indication that an authorization of civil suits would violate the Constitution.

At the time of this writing, all but 10 states[115] allow participant recording, usually so long as the recording is not for the purpose of committing a crime or tort. Some of the most populous states, including California and Illinois, are in this group of 10. Journalists and others who secretly record any conversations by phone or other means risk criminal and civil penalties in those jurisdictions. *The rule in these states is that you must have consent of all parties before recording.* Even in the other 40 states and with interstate calls under the federal rules, there are other risks. While the Communications Act of 1934, in its current form, makes no mention of secret recordings by broadcasters, the Federal Communications Commission, which regulates broadcasting as well as common carriers such as telephone companies, still has rules that require telephone companies to cancel a customer's service when the person records phone conversations without notifying all parties with an audio tone or "beep" and that all radio and television stations must inform any participant if a *telephone* conversation is being recorded for broadcast. The later rule does not require that an audible tone be transmitted, as was the case many years ago, but instead that the participants be given reasonable notice at the time. This can be accomplished by simply telling the parties that a recording is being made. Written consent is not necessary.[116] Although no test case has arisen to challenge these rules as in violation of the 1986 Electronic Communications Privacy Act, it is quite likely that the federal courts would rule in such a case that the 1986 act preempted the FCC rules. Furthermore, the FCC rules do *not* affect face-to-face interactions, and phone companies generally do not enforce the rules anyway. Journalists should still be very careful recording in those 10 states, as illustrated in a Florida case, *Shevin v. Sunbeam Television.*[117] In 1969 Florida enacted a statute that permitted participant recording; five years later it revised the statute to require consent of all parties for intercepting wire and oral communication. A Miami television station and the *Miami Herald* challenged the 1974 law as a violation of the First Amendment because it impaired news gathering and constituted prior restraint. The Florida Supreme Court disagreed:

> News gathering is an integral part of news dissemination, but hidden mechanical contrivances are not indispensable tools of news gathering. The ancient art of investigative reporting was successfully practiced long before the invention of electronic devices, so they can not be said to be "indispensable tools of investigative reporting." The First Amendment is not a license to trespass or to intrude by electronic means into the sanctity of another's home or office. It does not become such a license simply because the person subjected to the intrusion is reasonably suspected of committing a crime.[118]

The U.S. Supreme Court refused to hear an appeal in the case on the ground there was no substantive federal question.

Illinois, as indicated earlier, is one of the 10 states that require consent of all parties, but a decision by the Illinois Appellate Court in the same year as *Shavin v. Sunbeam Television* illustrates an unusual way of invoking consent.[119] A Chicago massage parlor owner, who contended his business was being harassed by police, permitted a local television station to install video cameras so the actions of undercover police could be recorded. An undercover police officer paid an admission fee and was taken to a room in which cameras had been installed behind two-way mirrors to see a "de-luxe" lingerie modeling show. As he entered the room, he noticed camera lights and commented to the model that they made the room warm. He also made suggestive comments and physical advances toward her. When "sufficient" physical contact had been made, the police officer arrested the model for solicitation. After three other undercover agents arrived, they asked if anyone were present in the adjacent room. A member of the television news crew who had been watching and recording the scene behind the mirrors announced "Channel 7 News" and left. A trial court granted a summary judgment in favor of the station after the undercover police officer filed suit for eavesdropping and invasion of privacy. The Illinois Appellate Court affirmed, noting:

> We agree with the argument advanced by the defendants that the conduct of a policeman on duty is legitimately and necessarily an area upon which public interest may and should be focused. In the situation before us, we need not consider any theory of expressed consent. . . . In our opinion, the very status of the policeman as a public official . . . is tantamount to an implied consent to informing the general public by all legitimate means regarding his activities in discharge of his public duties.[120]

Note that although the plaintiff was in a private place of business and his activities were secretly recorded in a state that requires consent of all parties, his actions as a public official could be secretly recorded. Would the result have been the same if the police officer had granted permission but the owner had not? What if the police had not gone undercover, had identified themselves and permitted the station to secretly tape the encounter without the owner's knowledge? The answers probably depend on the jurisdiction.

The Impact of the Codes of Ethics

None of the major codes of ethics mentions surreptitious monitoring or recording, and the journalistic community remains divided on the propriety of common investigative reporting techniques that the public, by and large, considers improper—such as misrepresentation, sifting through individual's trash and accepting or using documents stolen by someone else without the cooperation of the media organization. Is it ethical for journalists to hound controversial figures wherever they go and to write about and photograph personal tragedies—that is, to engage in "herd journalism" with cameras, notepads and microphones always at hand. There were many tragic and telling moments captured on film and in print during the Vietnam War, some of which are said to have altered public support of the war; the picture of the naked Vietnamese girl screaming as she flees a napalm attack and the photo of the south Vietnamese soldier shooting the captured Viet Cong soldier through the head. In spite of severe restraints imposed by the military on the press during the Persian Gulf war in 1991, some of the stories and photos published were graphic and yet poignant. *Detroit Free Press* photographer David Turnley, for example, won accolades for what has been described as "the war's most memorable picture"—an American soldier sobbing a moment after he reaus the identification tag and discovers that the body in a bag in the helicopter ferrying him to a hospital is his friend.[121] In 1993 Cable News Network videos and photos of the desecration of an American soldier's body by Somali citizens intensified public pressure to remove U.S. troops from Somalia. *USA Today* carried a front-page photo of the scene.

Defenses to Intrusion

There is only one sure-fire defense to intrusion — **consent**. In those 40 states that permit participant monitoring, the consent needs to come from only one participant, which can include the individual actually making the recording. The same rule applies for interstate phone calls. Even in those 10 states that require consent of all parties, a form of implied consent can sometimes be invoked, as illustrated in *Florida Publishing Co. v. Fletcher and Cassidy v. ABC*. Because publication is not required for intrusion to occur, *newsworthiness* and *privilege* are not available as defenses for the intrusion itself, although they may provide protection for a defendant for publication of the information. For example, a reporter who illegally obtained documents indicating that the local police chief has been involved in drug trafficking would probably not face a suit for disclosing the information but might be charged with criminal offenses and possibly have to pay civil damages for the intrusion. Ethically, journalists should eschew secret recording and monitoring unless (a) the information is being obtained via a strictly legal means, (b) there is no other effective way of obtaining the information, and (c) publishing the information would definitely serve the public interest.

PUBLISHING PRIVATE MATTERS

This third tort of invasion of privacy goes by several names, but the basic elements are the same. These tags include publication of private matters and public disclosure of private facts. No one's life, even a person as prominent as the President of the United States, is entirely an open book, although, in general, the more prominent the individual, the less protection that person enjoys from unwanted publication of private affairs. This tort has three basic elements as indicated in the *Restatement (Second) of Torts*: "One who gives publicity to a matter concerning the private life of another is subject to liability to the other for invasion of his privacy, if the matter published is of a kind that (a) would be highly offensive to a reasonable person, and (b) is not of legitimate public interest."[122]

Publication

The first element, **publication**, is generally easy for a plaintiff to demonstrate and thus is usually not in dispute. Unlike libel, which requires that the defamatory information be communicated merely to a third party, public disclosure of private facts must be fairly widespread because this is a tort of publicity, not simply a tort of communication. Thus embarrassing facts jotted in a reporter's notebook would not be sufficient to meet the publication requirement nor would an internal memo about a worker that is circulated among supervisors. An in-house newsletter for employees and a gossip column in a small weekly newspaper would clearly satisfy the criterion.

Offensiveness

The second element, **offensiveness**, has been defined differently in different jurisdictions and is the subject of considerable litigation. A critical aspect is that the published facts must be *highly* offensive, not simply embarrassing, to the reasonable person. This determination is always a jury question (i.e., a question of fact) when there is a jury trial because jurors in a community are presumed to judge as reasonable people, just as they determine in obscenity cases (discussed in chap. 11), whether contemporary community standards have been violated. The courts, however, have been rather strict in applying the standard, much to the chagrin of the public, which tends to view much more of a person's private life as worthy of protection.

In 1987 when U.S. Court of Appeals Judge Robert Bork was unsuccessfully nominated as a U.S. Supreme Court justice, a small weekly newspaper in Washington, DC, *City Paper*, somehow obtained a list of movies that Judge Bork had rented from a local video store. The newspaper published the list along with a story that attempted to explore the "inner workings of Robert Bork's mind . . . revealed by the videos he rents." The Senate Judiciary Committee, which initially reviews Supreme Court nominees, was outraged, as was the majority of Congress, and enacted the Video Privacy Protection Act of 1988,[123] which is popularly known as the "Bork law." This statute provides civil damages but *no criminal penalties* against "video tape service providers" (presumably stores, although the wording is vague) that disclose "personally identifiable information concerning any consumer." Anyone "aggrieved" by the "wrongful disclosure of video tape rental or sale records" may recover actual damages of at least $2,500 and punitive damages for intentional disclosure. The law has had no adverse impact on the press thus far, and it is unclear whether any entity other than rental stores is covered. In fact, there have apparently been no suits yet against anyone for violating the statute. The law may very well be unconstitutional prior restraint, but it epitomizes the gap between judicial recognition of zones of privacy versus those dictated by legislation. It is highly unlikely that a court would consider public disclosure of one's video preferences highly offensive, but Congress was more than ready to carve out this area of privacy.

On September 14, 1989, a deranged and disgruntled former employee at Standard Gravure Corporation wounded 13 and killed 8 workers at the plant with a Chinese-made AK-47 assault rifle in a shooting spree before taking his own life with a pistol. The next day the *Louisville Courier-Journal* published a front-page photograph of one of the murder victims, press operator Richard Barger, sprawled on the floor. The photo did not identify Barger but part of his face was visible. The newspaper was besieged with public criticism for publishing the controversial picture, which it sold to *Newsweek* and other publications. Editor David Hawpe strongly defended his paper's use of the picture, noting that the decision came after extensive discussion with other editors. "We did think about the impact such a picture might have on the family and friends of the victim," according to Hawpe, "and we also thought about the need to confront readers in our community with the full consequences of gun violence. . . . The photo did what I wanted it to do by showing the reality of what assault weapons are capable of. A less graphic photograph would not have been as effective."[124]

The family of the victim sued the paper for invasion of privacy and intentional infliction of emotional distress, but a Kentucky Circuit Court judge dismissed the suit on grounds that the photo was newsworthy, that the family had no basis for a claim because dead individuals have no right of privacy under state law (other than appropriation) and that publication of the photo did not constitute extreme and outrageous conduct necessary for proving intentional infliction of emotional distress. A Kentucky Court of Appeals upheld the dismissal, the Kentucky Supreme Court declined to review and the U.S. Supreme Court denied certiorari.[125]

The public was similarly upset a month earlier when a video and still photos taken from it appeared in the media throughout the country, showing a man alleged to be U.S. hostage Lt. Col. William Richard Higgins dangling from a gallows. The tape was released to a Western news agency by pro-Iranian extremists who said they had tried and executed the U.S. officer, who was captured while serving in a U.N. observer group. Higgins' body has never been recovered.

Cox Broadcasting Corp. v. Martin Cohn (1975)

Most states have statutes prohibiting the publication of rape victims' names, but a decision by the U.S. Supreme Court in 1975 in *Cox Broadcasting Corp. v. Martin Cohn*[126] declared a Georgia statute unconstitutional that made it a misdemeanor to publish or broadcast the name or identity of any female who may have been raped or against whom a rape may have been attempted. The law violated the First and Fourteenth Amendments because it permitted civil liability against a television station that accurately reported the name of a rape victim it had obtained from a public record. In August 1971 17-year-old Cynthia Cohn was gang raped and murdered. Five of the six youths who had been indicted in the case pled guilty to rape or attempted rape after murder charges were dropped. The sixth defendant pled not guilty and was bound over for trial later. While he was covering the proceedings, a reporter for WSB-TV in Atlanta, where the crime occurred, obtained the victim's name from the indictments, which were available as public records. In the evening newscast, the reporter used Cynthia Cohn's name in a report about the proceedings, and the report was rebroadcast the next morning. Cohn's father filed suit against the station, claiming that his right to privacy had been invaded by disclosure of his deceased daughter's name. A state trial court granted summary judgment in favor of Martin Cohn and ordered a jury trial to determine damages. The Georgia Supreme Court ruled that the trial court had erred in construing a civil cause of action based on the criminal statute but that Cohn could sue under a common law right of privacy. On appeal, the U.S. Supreme Court reversed:

> In placing the information in the public domain on official court records, the State must be presumed to have concluded that the public interest was thereby being served. Public records by their very nature are of interest to those concerned with the administration of government, and a public benefit is performed by the reporting of the true contents of the records by the media. The freedom of the press to publish that information appears to us to be one of critical importance to our type of government in which the citizenry is the final judge of the proper conduct of public business. In preserving that form of government the First and Fourteenth Amendments command nothing less than that the States may not impose sanctions on the publication of truthful information contained in official court records open to public inspection.[127]

While the Georgia Supreme Court escaped the issue of the constitutionality of the state statute by holding that it did not provide a civil cause of action, the U.S. Supreme Court held, in effect, that the statute did create such a cause of action and was, therefore, a violation of the First and Fourth Amendments. To prevent the press from being punished either in a civil or criminal suit, the Court had to go further, however, by holding (as indicated earlier) that a constitutional privilege existed to give the media the right to publish truthful information obtained from public records. Thus this decision covers a broad range of information, not simply rape victim names. The Court did *not* say that rape victims' names could not be protected, but that such information could be published with impunity once it had become public record.

Florida Star v. B.J.F. (1989)

Fourteen years after *Cox Broadcasting v. Cohn*, the U.S. Supreme Court decided another case involving the publication of a rape victim's name. There are several parallels between the two cases but there were two major and interesting differences—the name in the 1989 case was accidentally published and was not in a court record. B.J.F. (the Court used only her initials to respect her privacy interests) reported to the Duval County, Florida, sheriff's department that she had been robbed and sexually assaulted by an unknown man. The department issued a report based on her information and placed the report, as it routinely did for reported crimes, in the press room, which was accessible to anyone. Unfortunately, the report included the victim's full name. A reporter-trainee for the *Florida Star*, a weekly newspaper that serves Jacksonville with a circulation of about 18,000, used the information in the report to write a police blotter story for the "Police Reports" section of the paper:

> [B.J.F.'s full name] reported on Thursday, October 20, she was crossing Brentwood Park, which is in the 500 block of Golfair Boulevard, enroute to her bus stop, when an unknown black man ran up behind the lady and placed a knife to her neck and told her not to yell. The suspect then undressed the lady and had sexual intercourse with her before fleeing the scene with her 60 cents, Timex watch and gold necklace. Patrol efforts have been suspended concerning this incident because of a lack of evidence.[128]

Like most newspapers, the *Florida Star* had a written internal policy against publishing the names of victims of sex offenses. B.J.F.'s name had simply been accidentally published; the report was one of 54 police reports that appeared that day in the paper. The victim sued both the *Star* and the Sheriff's Department for negligence. Prior to trial, the department settled out-of-court by agreeing to pay B.J.F. $2,500 in damages. After a day-long trial at which the woman testified that she had suffered emotional distress from threatening phone calls and other incidents as a result of the story, a jury awarded her $75,000 in compensatory damages and $25,000 in punitive damages. A state appeals court upheld the decision, and the U.S. Supreme Court granted certiorari. In *Florida Star v. B.J.F.* (1989), the Supreme Court ruled 5-4 in favor of the newspaper but disappointed most journalists by refusing to extend First Amendment protection to all truthful publications:

> Our holding today is limited. We do not hold that truthful publication is automatically constitutionally protected, or that there is no zone of personal privacy within which the State may protect the individual from intrusion by the press, or even that a State may never punish publication of the name of a victim of a sexual offense. We hold only that where a newspaper publishes truthful information which it has lawfully obtained, punishment may be imposed, if at all, only when narrowly tailored to a state interest of the highest order, and that no such interest is satisfactorily served by imposing liability under 794.03 [the Florida statute] to appellant [the *Star*] under the facts of the case.

The Court based its decision on *Cox v. Cohn* (1975) and two other cases—*Oklahoma Publishing Co. v. Oklahoma County District Court* (1977)[129] and *Smith v. Daily Mail Publishing Co.* (1979).[130] In *Oklahoma Publishing Co.* the Court held in a *per curiam* opinion that a trial court judge's order prohibiting the press from publishing the name and photo of an 11-year-old boy charged with murder was unconstitutional prior restraint because the hearing at which his name was revealed was open to the public. In *Smith*, a West Virginia statute was unanimously declared unconstitutional because it imposed criminal penalties for publishing, without permission from a juvenile court judge, the identity of a juvenile offender even when the information was lawfully obtained. *Smith* was a narrow decision, as the Court noted, because there was no question of unlawful access to court proceedings, privacy or of prejudicial publicity. In such a situation, the Court said "state officials may not constitutionally punish publication of the information absent a need to further a state interest of the highest order."[131] In neither *Smith* nor *Florida Star* had the state demonstrated such an interest. Nevertheless, in the latter decision the Court said it could "not rule out the possibility that, in a proper case, imposing civil sanctions for publication of a rape victim might be so overwhelmingly necessary to advance these interests [privacy of victims of sex offenses, physical safety of such victims and encouraging victims to report offenses without fear of exposure] as to satisfy the [*Smith v.*] *Daily Mail* standard."[132]

Two situations, both of which occurred in 1991, illustrate the complexity of the issue of whether rape victims' names should be made public. In the first, Palm Beach (Fla.) County Circuit Court Judge Mary Lupo issued a gag order in the trial of 30-year-old William Kennedy Smith, a nephew of Massachusetts' Senator Edward Kennedy. Smith was charged with second-degree sexual battery and misdemeanor battery in connection with the alleged rape of a young woman at his family's Palm Beach estate. The gag order itself was not highly unusual in such a case even though it barred all participants in the case, including all potential witnesses, from discussing the case outside the courtroom. What were unusual were the events that eventually led to the restrictive order. Before Smith was ever charged, several newspapers and NBC News identified the 29-year-old woman who had filed charges against him. The alleged victim was named first in a London tabloid newspaper and then in the U.S. tabloid, the *National Enquirer*. The newspapers also published her photograph, which was broadcast shortly thereafter by NBC television. Although most news organizations have either written or unwritten policies against publishing the names of victims of sexual assault, several newspapers—including the *New York Times*, the *San Francisco Chronicle*, the *Denver Post*, the *Fort Worth* (Tex.) *Star-Telegram* and the *Louisville Courier-Journal*,—identified the woman. The Associated Press and newspapers such as the *Miami Herald* and the *Lexington* (Ky.) *Herald-Leader* did not use the woman's name.[133] However, many of the news organizations that have such a policy do permit disclosure of the identity when individuals choose to make their name public. The *Des Moines* (Iowa) *Register*, which did identify the Palm Beach alleged rape victim, won a Pulitzer Prize a week earlier for a five-part series on the rape of Nancy Ziegenmeyer, who gave consent for her name to be published so people would understand how rape brutalizes its victims and thus should not be treated as just another crime. Ziegenmeyer decided to tell her story to the newspaper after the editor wrote a column arguing that withholding the names of rape victims added to the stigma of the crime.[134] After Smith was acquitted of the rape charge, his accuser went public to criticize the jury's verdict and gave interviews on several national talk shows. Nearly all of the news media in the country then revealed her name, although it has virtually faded into obscurity. Interestingly, the *Globe*, the Florida based tabloid that was among the first media outlets to publish the name of Smith's accuser, was charged with violating Florida's statute barring the publication of rape victims names. Palm Beach County Judge Robert Parker ultimately ruled that the law was unconstitutional on its face and as applied by prosecutors and dismissed the charge.[135]

The second occurrence attracted little media attention but may have been a significant development on this issue. In a highly unusual move, the U.S. Supreme Court identified a rape victim in a court decision. In a 7–2 opinion written by Justice Sandra Day O'Connor, the Court held in May 1991 that a defendant in a rape case may be barred under some circumstances from introducing evidence at trial of a previous sexual relationship with the victim. That decision, which had no direct bearing on First Amendment law, was nevertheless overshadowed by the identification. Justice O'Connor refused to indicate whether her action was intentional or an oversight, but no efforts were made to convince the news media to omit the name.

Even the media outlets who have policies against publishing names of victims of sex crimes are generally opposed to laws that prohibit such publicity. As mentioned previously, the *Lexington* (Ky.) *Herald-Leader* has such a policy, but in June 1991 when a local trial court judge issued an order to prohibit the news media and parties in a civil suit from disclosing the name of a teenager who had been sodomized when he was six, the newspaper challenged the gag order and the judge lifted it on the news media. The suit was filed by the mother of the boy against the man convicted of the sexual assault, in an attempt to obtain the man's $2 million lottery winnings. The boy's name was contained in several public records, including the complaint. According to the editor, "The Herald-Leader went to court to protect the principle that the decision to publish, or not to publish, material that has been lawfully gained should remain with the newspaper rather than being made by the judge."[136]

Three incidents in 1992 illustrated the dilemma the press faces in deciding whether to disclose the names of individuals involved in matters that are ordinarily considered private but which may be newsworthy. First, early in the year, the youngest boxer to win the world heavyweight championship, was tried and ultimately convicted by a jury in Indianapolis, Indiana, of rape and two counts of criminal deviant conduct. He was accused of assaulting Desiree Washington, a Miss Black America contestant, in a hotel during the pageant the summer before. Washington went public immediately after the trial and even appeared on the cover of the February 24 *People* magazine. Her name and face were shown around the country, but she had voluntarily disclosed her identity.

Second, in April 1992, the late tennis great Arthur Ashe held a press conference at which he announced that he had contracted AIDS, apparently through a blood transfusion during a cardiac-bypass operation in 1983. He did not know he had the fatal disease, however, until he took tests before brain surgery in 1988. Ashe made the announcement the day after a reporter for the newspaper *USA Today* contacted him to ask about the unpublished rumors that he had the disease. While indicating that he understood the role of the press, as a member of the corp himself (Ashe was a tennis commentator for HBO and ABC Sports and wrote for the *Washington Post*), he said he was "angry that [he] was put in the unenviable position of having to lie if [he] was to protect [his] privacy."[137] Ashe died on February 6, 1993, of AIDS-related pneumonia at the age of 49.

Finally, in July 1992, a school superintendent in Duncanville, Texas, resigned after a local television station videotaped him visiting adult book stores during school hours. The educator claimed he had made the visits as part of an official investigation, but he said he had "used poor judgment" in not consulting in advance with the school board.[138]

If the victims of sexual assaults should have their names kept confidential, how about the victims of other crimes? For example, should a man's name and address be given who fell into an investment scam? What about the name and address of a woman who was robbed in front of a local restaurant? Crime stories have been a staple of news since the penny press of the 1830s, but, except in sex offenses, victims of crimes have routinely been named in reports. In fact, many newspapers, such as the *Florida Star*, routinely carry a police blotter or summary log that is often one of the widest read sections, according to readership surveys. A survey of newspaper editors by Wolf, Thomason and LaRoeque[139] published in 1986 found a continuation of a trend toward less specific identification of crime victims. Almost half (46 percent) of the editors of the 110 papers responding indicated they decide whether to identify victims on a case-by-case basis, one-fourth said they have a general policy of publishing names and addresses of victims and another one-fourth use names but only general locations rather than specific addresses. In line with earlier surveys, this study found a definite trend toward deleting addresses and names of victims in stories about robbery and other crimes.

Briscoe v. Reader's Digest

Sometimes the individuals who commit crimes cry foul as well. A 1971 case, *Briscoe v. Reader's Digest*, is typical of the dilemma news media face in identifying people who have been convicted of crimes in the past. Marvin Briscoe, who with an accomplice had hijacked a truck in 1956, was convicted and thereafter rehabilitated. Eleven years later *Reader's Digest* published a story entitled "The Big Business of Hijacking," which included this sentence in its report on how truckers were fighting back against thieves: "Typical of many beginners, Marvin Briscoe and Garland Russell [his accomplice] stole a 'valuable-looking' truck in Danville, Ky., and then fought a gun battle with the local police, only to learn that they had hijacked four bowling pin spotters."[140]

No mention was made of when the incident took place. Briscoe sued for willful and malicious invasion of privacy as a result of this publication of what he contended were "embarrassing private facts about plaintiff's past life." A California Superior Court dismissed the case in favor of *Reader's Digest*, but on appeal, the Supreme Court of California reversed, holding that Briscoe could recover for damages if he could demonstrate that the magazine invaded his privacy with reckless disregard for fact and that a reasonable person would find the invasion highly offensive:

> First . . . a jury could reasonably find that plaintiff's identity in connection with incidents of his past life was in this case of minimal social value. . . .

> Second, a jury might find that revealing one's past for all to see is grossly offensive to most people in America. . . .

> Third, in no way can plaintiff be said to have voluntarily consented to the publicity accorded him here. He committed a crime. He was punished. He was rehabilitated. And he became for 11 years, an obscure and law abiding citizen. His every effort was to forget and have others forget that he had once hijacked a truck.[141]

Notice the court's intense concern with promoting rehabilitation by protecting the privacy of those who have become good citizens. The discordant note in this decision and those that followed in the U.S. Supreme Court (as discussed earlier) is that a news medium could be punished for publishing truthful information contained in a public record. *Florida Star v. B.J.F.* points in this direction, as does *Cox v. Cohn*.

Would the decision have been different if the magazine had given the year? Briscoe would still have suffered, as he pointed out in his complaint, because his eleven-year-old daughter and friends and acquaintances were not aware of his criminal history. Is it ethical to publish the name of someone who has been rehabilitated? At what point should a media outlet no longer identify a convicted criminal? One year? Five years? Immediately after release from incarceration? Should the period of time vary with the type of crime committed or the length of the sentence? It is not unusual for newspapers, magazines and the electronic media to cover the release of notorious criminals after they have served their terms. Does this serve the "compelling interest" of society, at least as perceived by this court, "in rehabilitating criminals and returning them as productive and law-abiding citizens"?[142] Does the public's need to know override this interest and the interest of individual's in protecting the privacy of their past?

When the *Briscoe* case went back to the trial court, it was removed to the U.S. District Court for the Central District of California. The federal trial court issued a summary judgment in 1972 in favor of the magazine, holding that the information was newsworthy, that it was published without malice or recklessness, that it was not an invasion of privacy and that it was thus protected by the First Amendment. Judge Lawrence T. Lydick pointed out in his opinion that Briscoe had actually been imprisoned in Kentucky until December 1961, that on his release he was placed on federal probation until December 1964 and on state parole until February 1969, almost a year **after** the article appeared. The judge also indicated that his name and exploits were clearly remembered by the people in his home town even at the time of the new trial.[143]

Virgil v. Time (1975)

A few years later the Ninth U.S. Circuit of Appeals dealt with another unusual invasion of privacy case arising in California. In *Virgil v. Time* (1975)[144] the court held that a 1971 story in *Sports Illustrated* containing embarrassing facts about a body surfer's private life could claim First Amendment protection only if the information was shown to be newsworthy and of legitimate public interest. The story focused on surfing at the "Wedge," a beach near Newport Beach, California, which was supposed to be the most dangerous place in the world for body surfing. Mike Virgil, who had a reputation for being the biggest daredevil of the surfers at the beach, was among the individuals described and was quoted in the 11-page article. Among the quotes attributed to Virgil are:

I quit my job, left home and moved to Mammoth Mountain. At the ski lodge there one night I dove headfirst down a flight of stairs — just because. Because why? Well, there were these chicks all around. I thought it would be groovy. Was I drunk? I think I might have been.

Every summer I'd work construction and dive off billboards to hurt myself or drop loads of lumber on myself to collect unemployment compensation so I could surf at the wedge. Would I fake injuries? No, I wouldn't fake them. I'd be damn injured. But I would recover. I guess I used to live a pretty reckless life. I think I might have been drunk most of the time. . . .

[in discussing his aggressiveness as a child] I bit off the cheek of a Negro in a six-against-30 gang fight. They had tire irons with them.[145]

The article quoted Virgil's wife as saying, "Mike also eats spiders and other insects and things." According to the story, "Perhaps because much of his time was spent engaged in such activity, Virgil never learned how to read." A photo caption read, "Mike Virgil, the wild man of the wedge, thinks it possible his brain is being slowly destroyed."[146]

While Virgil admitted in his complaint alleging invasion of privacy by the magazine that he had willingly talked with the reporter in the case, he claimed that he "revoked all consent" when he learned the article contained negative statements about him. He had learned about the references to "bizarre incidents in his life that were not directly related to surfing" from a staff member who had telephoned him and his wife to verify some of the information. At that time, Virgil told the checker that he did not want to be mentioned in the story and that he wanted the article stopped. Despite Virgil's opposition, *SI* published the story. The surfer then filed suit. At trial the U.S. District Court denied Time, Inc.'s motion for summary judgment, and the trial court's decision was upheld on appeal to the Ninth Circuit, which then remanded the case back to the trial court. The U.S. Supreme Court denied certiorari on further appeal.[147] Finally, the District Court ruled in favor of *Sports Illustrated* on grounds that the information in the story was newsworthy. The court did question whether the specific details about Virgil, such as diving down stairs and eating insects, were of legitimate public interest but ultimately concluded that this information helped the reader understand the frame of mind of people who are involved in high risk sports.[148]

Defenses to Publishing Private Matters

There are three basic defenses to publicizing private matters, none of which offer absolute protection: **consent, privilege** and **newsworthiness**. As *Virgil v. Time* illustrates, *consent* can be revoked if done so reasonably. Virgil had willingly talked with the *Sports Illustrated* reporter and indeed had disclosed embarrassing facts, but the court had no problem with his claim that he revoked his consent prior to publication by telling the checker that he wanted the story halted because he had discovered that the portrait would not be so flattering. As with the other torts of invasion of privacy, the consent must be voluntary and either explicit or implicit. The individual who is granting the consent must possess the legal and mental capacity to do so. Journalists should clearly identify themselves when interviewing potential sources and make it clear, whether on the phone or in person, that the information may be used in a story. They should **never** promise an interviewee that nothing negative will be used or that the story will take a particular approach. A practice in some news organizations is to have a copy editor check quotes and questionable facts with the sources to make sure the information is accurate. Unfortunately, this can lead to situations such as the one in *Virgil v. Time* in which an important source may have second thoughts and then attempt to revoke initial consent. On the other hand, this approach is an effective way of documenting consent. If it appears controversy may arise and lead to a possible suit, the reporter or editor should get consent in writing or, at the very least, have an independent witness or tape recorder at hand.

Privilege, whether constitutional or common law, is usually the strongest defense, as demonstrated in the *Florida Star* decision. *Constitutional privilege* simply means *First Amendment protection*, of course. *Florida Star v. B.J.F.* made it clear that truthful information from public records does not enjoy absolute privilege because a state could conceivably demonstrate that prohibiting disclosure would further a state interest of the highest order. The Florida statute has the fatal flaw that it applied only to an "instrument of mass communication," thus singling out the press for special punishment. The statute also failed constitutional muster because it imposed a negligence per se standard, which did not permit findings on a case-by-case basis to determine whether a reasonable person would find the information highly offensive. Because the government has the burden of demonstrating a state interest of the highest order, a media defendant remains relatively free to publish information from a public record but such dissemination should be made in good faith. A *common law privilege* exists in some jurisdictions for publishing public records, but *Cox Broadcasting* and *Florida Star* basically make such privilege unnecessary because the Court recognized a constitutional privilege in both cases that provides at least as much protection. Although some journalists and legal scholars are concerned that the Court did not broaden the sweep of the First Amendment to include all information in public records, the protection provided under *Florida Star* should be sufficient to permit anyone to publish truthful information lawfully obtained from a public record under almost any circumstances, including negligence, with impunity.

Newsworthiness is similar to common law privilege and indeed is recognized as common law but it extends beyond public records and public proceedings to include matters that are simply of public interest. The U.S. Supreme Court has avoided directly confronting the question of whether newsworthiness itself is a viable defense to the publication of private matters, but state and lower federal courts have tackled this issue and generally recognized this defense. One of the earliest cases involved a child prodigy who became famous in 1910. He lectured to distinguished mathematicians on "four-dimensional bodies" at age 11 and graduated from Harvard College when he was 16. William James Sidis subsequently avoided publicity, but was the unwilling subject of a brief biographical sketch and cartoon in 1937 in *The New Yorker*. Information was also published about him in a story in the magazine four months later, and an advertisement appeared in the publication to announce the first story.

According to the Second Circuit U.S. Court of Appeals in *Sidis v. F-R Publishing Corp.* (1940),[149] the initial article, which said Sidis had a "certain childlike charm," was "a ruthless exposure of a once public character, who has since sought and has now been deprived of the seclusion of private life."[150] The sketch was part of a regular feature in the magazine that described current and past personalities, with the latter appearing under the title, "Where are They Now?" The Sidis piece was subtitled "April Fool" (like the author of this book, Sidis was born on April 1) and described how the mathematical genius was now "an insignificant clerk" who collected streetcar transfers and lived in an untidy room. The Court of Appeals affirmed the District Court's dismissal of the invasion of privacy and malicious libel suit Sidis filed against the magazine, holding that even though the plaintiff had "cloaked himself in obscurity," his private life since he sought seclusion was nevertheless "a matter of public concern. The article in *The New Yorker* sketched the life of an usual personality, and it possessed considerable popular news interest."[151] The court noted, however, that it was not deciding whether newsworthiness was always a complete defense.

The approach taken by this court, although now more than 50 years old, is still being taken by other courts—newsworthiness is not a high and mighty concept that requires a demonstrated *need* for the public to know but instead can be framed in the context of what people want to know. The Sidis story served no noble cause—people were just curious about the status of an individual who had once enjoyed the limelight.

Many newspapers and magazines carry sidebars or vignettes recalling events from the past under such titles as "25 Years Ago Today" or "A Page from the Past" highlighting old news. Often, the individuals whose names appear in these stories are shocked when these appear, and some have sued for invasion of privacy. These items are different from the *Reader's Digest* story about Briscoe because they make clear the date of the event, and they are different from the Sidis article because they do not focus on one person and they do not indicate current status. Yet they can expose the individual to unwanted publicity. Fortunately, nearly all of cases involving this type of story have been decided in favor of the mass media. A typical example is *Roshto v. Hebert* (1983)[152] in which the Louisiana Supreme Court held that the *Iberville South*, a weekly newspaper, was not liable for publishing information about the conviction more than 20 years earlier of Carlysle Rosto and his two brothers for cattle theft in a "Page from Our Past" because the information was a truthful account of an event in the public record and was published without malice. The court overturned trial court verdicts of $35,000 for each brother.

In 1976, the *Des Moines* (Iowa) *Sunday Register* published a long investigative feature about alleged illegal activities at a county home, including deaths from scalding baths, sterilization of young women residents who were mentally disabled and improper shipments of prescription drugs. The article mentioned that an 18-year-old woman named Robin Woody had been sterilized in 1970 with the consent of her mother. It included quotes from an interview with the psychiatrist for the Jasper County Home, whom he characterized as an "impulsive, hair-triggered, young girl."[153] The feature gave other details of the sterilization and noted that Woody had been discharged from the home at the end of 1971 and her mother did not know where she was living. Although the newspaper did not know at the time the article was published, Robin Woody had become Robin Howard and, according to her petition to the court, had "led a quiet and respectable life and made friends and acquaintances who were not aware of her surgery."[154]

Robin Howard (the former Robin Woody) sued the newspaper and its reporter for disclosure of the information, but the Iowa District Court issued a summary judgment in favor of the defendants on the grounds that the article was "newsworthy and was not shockingly offensive or distasteful and was not a sensational prying into Plaintiff's private life for its own sake."[155] The trial court noted that newsworthiness was the most compelling reason for its decision. On appeal, the Iowa Supreme Court upheld the district court's summary judgment. The appellate court concluded that the plaintiff's name and the details of her sterilization had been obtained from public records (working files in the governor's office provided by an administrative assistant at the request of the reporter for the paper) and that the fact of the sterilization was a public rather than a private fact and a matter of legitimate public concern. According to the court:

> In the sense of serving an appropriate news function, the disclosure contributed constructively to the impact of the article. It offered a personalized frame of reference to which the reader could relate, fostering perception and understanding. Moreover, it lent specificity and credibility to the report.

> In this way the disclosure served as an effective means of accomplishing the intended news function. It had positive communicative value in attracting the reader's attention to the article's subject matter and in supporting expression of the underlying theme.[156]

The court was not willing to say that it was necessary for the newspaper to name names, but acknowledged that the *Register* had the right to treat the identities as a matter of legitimate public concern.

In 1975 ex-marine Oliver Sipple knocked a gun out of the hand of Sara Jane Moore just as she was attempting to fire a second shot at President Gerald Ford in San Francisco. His heroic act attracted extensive national media attention. The *San Francisco Chronicle* and other publications revealed that Sipple was homosexual, a fact he had not disclosed to family members in the Midwest, although he was well-known and active in the San Francisco's gay community, having marched in several gay parades. When Sipple sued for invasion of privacy, a California trial court judge granted summary judgment for the *Chronicle*. The California Court of Appeals upheld the lower court decision on grounds that Sipple's sexual orientation was public, not private, in this case and that this information was newsworthy.[157] According to the court, even though Sipple probably did not realize the consequences of his act at the time, his effort nevertheless attracted legitimate media attention that was "not limited to the event that itself arouses the public interest."[158] The court also contended that the coverage of his homosexuality arose from "legitimate political considerations, i.e., to dispel the false public opinions that gays were timid, weak and unheroic figures and to raise the equally important political question whether the President of the United States entertained a discriminatory attitude or bias against a minority group such as homosexuals."[159]

A few militant gay organizations and *The Advocate*, a Los Angeles magazine, employ a technique known as "outing," which involves publicizing the names of covert homosexuals as a means of forcing them to disclose their sexual preference. Most news organizations refuse to participate in the publicity, as illustrated in August 1991 when the magazine claimed that a prominent Defense Department official was gay and disclosed his name. Although the man's identity was well-known within the journalistic community, most newspapers, magazines and broadcast stations adamantly refused to reveal the name, primarily because they abhor the tactic and did not feel such information was newsworthy. One newspaper, the *Detroit News*, did publish the name because, according to its editor, "Unfortunately, once it's out of the bag in *The Advocate*, it becomes public knowledge,"[160]

Ethical Considerations

Has such information really become public? Do you think the court would have decided differently if the disclosure about Oliver Sipple had been that he had a history of mental illness or that he was an illegal alien? What if Sipple had not been homosexual but instead was married and having an affair at the time of the incident? What if Sipple had been charged with but never convicted of murder or child sexual abuse five years earlier? Should the facts about Sipple's private life have been published even if the newspaper editors knew this information had First Amendment protection? Was this information really relevant to the story? Is this a case in which the public is simply intensely curious rather than the information serving the public interest? Many newspapers and radio and television stations initially refused to publicize Sipple's sexual preference, but most did disclose the fact once a suit was filed.

FALSE LIGHT

In this age of docudramas and other fictionalized accounts of public and private events, from the sad story of actress Marilyn Monroe to the tragic shooting of James Brady (the presidential press secretary who was wounded along with President Ronald Reagan by John Hinckley), it may be surprising to some that the tort of false light is alive and well. The *Second Restatement of Torts* defines false light as:

> One who gives publicity to a matter concerning another that places the other before the public in a false light is subject to liability to the other for invasion of privacy, if
>
> (a) the false light in which the other was placed would be highly offensive to a reasonable person, and
>
> (b) the actor had knowledge of or acted in reckless disregard as to the falsity of the publicized matter and the false light in which the other would be placed.[161]

Thus false light shares elements of both publicizing private matters and libel but is still different from both. Whereas the information must be false and must be published with reckless disregard for the truth or knowing the information was false (what the U.S. Supreme Court characterized as "actual malice" from *New York Times v. Sullivan* until it retreated from this term in 1991; see chap. 7), it need not be defamatory. Only two false light cases have been decided by the U.S. Supreme Court, and although both were hailed as significant decisions by the Court, they only began to draw the boundaries of this amorphous and hybrid tort.

False light suits typically originate with individuals involuntarily attracting media attention that distorts or fictionalizes their lives or events in which they were involved. Generally, they are private people who want no media attention, even if sympathetic or positive. Each of the two Supreme Court decisions illustrate the false light trap.

Time Inc. v. Hill (1967): Extending the Actual Malice Rule to False Light

The first, *Time Inc. v. Hill* (1967),[162] arose when *Life* published an article in February 1955 entitled, "True Crime Inspires Tense Play," with the subtitle, "The ordeal of a family trapped by convicts gives Broadway a new thriller, 'The Desperate Hours.'" The feature described how three years earlier the James Hill family had been held prisoners in its home outside Philadelphia by three escaped convicts. It went on to note that Joseph Hayes' novel, *The Desperate Hours*, had been inspired by the family's ordeal and the story had been reenacted in a Broadway play based on the book and would be told in a movie.

The *Life* piece characterized the play as an "expertly acted . . . heartstopping account of how a family rose to heroism in a crisis." The magazine staff photographed the play while it was running in Philadelphia and took some of the actors and actresses to the house where the Hills lived at the time of the incident for pictures as well. (The Hills no longer lived in the house.) The two pages following the text included an enactment of the son being beaten by one of the convicts, entitled "brutish convict," and the daughter biting the hand of one of the convicts to force him to drop his gun, entitled "daring daughter." Another photo showed an actor portraying the father throwing a gun through the door after a "brave try" to save his family fails. Whereas it was true that James Hill and his wife and five children were held hostage in their Whitemarsh, Pennsylvania, home by three convicts for 19 hours, the family was released unharmed and members told reporters afterward that the convicts had treated them courteously, had not molested them and had not been violent. Two of the convicts were killed later in an encounter with police, and the Hills moved to Connecticut where they tried to avoid attention from the press.

Several months later, the novel appeared with a fictionalized account of the event in which a family of four is held hostage by three escaped convicts. The convicts in the novel beat the father and son and verbally assault the daughter with sexual insults. The play that followed was based on the book.

James Hill sued for invasion of privacy in New York, claiming that the magazine had used the family's name for trade purposes (i.e., appropriation), the article was a "fictionalization" as prohibited under New York's privacy statute and the article portrayed the family in a false light. A jury awarded him $50,000 in compensatory and $25,000 in punitive damages. On appeal, the Appellate Division of the New York Supreme Court ordered a new trial on damages but upheld the jury's verdict of liability. At the new trial on damages, the Appellate Division (a trial court despite the name) awarded Hill $30,000 in compensatory damages and no punitive damages. (In effect, the judge—a jury trial was waived—reduced the damages to $30,000.) The New York Court of Appeals, New York's highest court, affirmed.

The U.S. Supreme Court reversed the decision of the New York Court of Appeals in an opinion written by Justice Brennan: "We hold that the constitutional protections for speech and press preclude the application of the New York statute to redress false reports of matters of public interest in the absence of proof that the defendant published the report with knowledge of its falsity or in reckless disregard of the truth."[163]

Thus the Court extended the actual malice rule of *New York Times v. Sullivan* (1964)[164] (discussed in chap. 7) to include false light when the matter was one of public interest. In its 5–4 decision, the Court ruled that the content of the *Life* article was a matter of public interest and remanded the case back to the state appellate court. The Court also dismissed the claim that the article was published for trade purposes, noting that the mere publication of books, newspapers and magazines for profit does not constitute trade purposes. After 11 years of litigation, James Hill dropped his suit rather than pursue it further.

Cantrell v. Forest City Publishing Co. (1974)

Seven years after *Time v. Hill*, the U.S. Supreme Court decided the second and, thus far, last of the false light cases. *Cantrell v. Forest City Publishing Co.*[165] was the ideal case to clarify *Time v. Hill*.

Ten days before Christmas in 1967, 44 people, including Melvin Cantrell, were killed when the Silver Bridge spanning the Ohio River at Point Pleasant, West Virginia, collapsed. Joseph Eszterhas, a reporter for the *Cleveland (Ohio) Plain Dealer*, wrote a prize-winning feature about the funeral of Cantrell and the impact of his death on his wife and children. Five months later, the reporter and a photographer visited Point Pleasant for a follow-up feature. The two stopped by the Cantrell home and talked with the children for about an hour while Margaret Mae Cantrell, Melvin Cantrell's widow, was gone. The photographer, Richard Conway, took 50 pictures.

The result was the lead feature, "Legacy of the Silver Bridge," in the August 4, 1968, Sunday *Plain Dealer Magazine*. The story focused on "the family's abject poverty; the children's old, ill-fitting clothes and the deteriorating condition of their home."[166] The photos and text were used, as with the original piece, to demonstrate the effects of the disaster on the community.

Unfortunately, the article had several inaccuracies and false statements, including the following paragraph:

> Margaret Cantrell will talk neither about what happened nor about how they are doing. She wears the same mask of nonexpression she wore at the funeral. She is a proud woman. Her world has changed. She says that after it happened, the people in the town offered to help them out with money and they refused to take it.[167]

The reporter had never talked with Ms. Cantrell because she was not home at the time. Thus these statements were apparently fabrications. According to the Court, there were other misrepresentations in the descriptions of the family's poverty and "the dirty and dilapidated conditions of the Cantrell home."[168] Ms. Cantrell filed a diversity action against the reporter, photographer and newspaper in the U.S. District Court for the Northern District of Ohio, alleging that the story made the family the object of pity and ridicule and thereby caused "outrage, mental distress, shame and humiliation."[169] The federal trial court jury awarded Cantrell $60,000 in compensatory damages for false light. The District Court judge dismissed Cantrell's claim for punitive damages, supposedly on the ground that no common law malice had been demonstrated. The judge did rule, however, that Cantrell could recover actual or compensatory damages if she could convince the jury that the misrepresentations and false information had been published with "actual malice," as enunciated by the Supreme Court in *Time v. Hill.*

As mentioned in the previous chapter on libel, ever since the landmark *New York Times v. Sullivan* decision in 1964, there has been considerable confusion over the difference between *common-law malice* (evil intent arising from hatred, revenge or ill-will) and *actual malice* (reckless disregard for truth or knowledge of falsity). Indeed, as indicated in the previous chapter, in its 1991 decision in *Masson v. The New Yorker Magazine, Inc.* the Supreme Court suggested abandoning the term *actual malice* and said that the courts should instead refer to *knowing* or *reckless falsehood*. *Cantrell v. Forest City Publishing Co.* illustrates the wisdom of the Court's advice. On appeal, the Sixth Circuit U.S. Court of Appeals reversed the trial court decision because it interpreted the judge's finding that Mrs. Cantrell had not presented sufficient evidence that the publication "was done maliciously within the legal definition of that term" to mean that there was no actual malice. Thus the intermediate appellate court held that the defendants' motion for a directed verdict in their favor should have been granted under the *Time v. Hill* standard for false light actions.

But the Supreme Court noted: "Although the verbal record of the District Court proceedings is not entirely unambiguous, the conclusion is inescapable that the District Judge was referring to the common-law standard of malice rather than to the *New York Times* 'actual malice' standard when he dismissed the punitive damages claims."[170]

Therefore, the Supreme Court reversed the Court of Appeals, holding that:

> the District Judge was clearly correct in believing that the evidence introduced at trial was sufficient to support a jury finding that the respondents, Joseph Eszterhas and Forest City Publishing Co. had published knowing or reckless falsehoods about the Cantrells. [The Court indicated in a footnote here that "there was insufficient evidence to support the jury's verdict against the photographer Conway" because his testimony that his photos were fair and accurate depictions was not challenged and there was no evidence that he was responsible for the inaccuracies and misstatements in the article.] There was no dispute during the trial that Eszterhas who did not testify must have known that a number of the statements in the feature story were untrue.[171]

The Court characterized the reporter's implication that Ms. Cantrell had been at home during the visit and his description of her "mask of nonexpression" as "calculated falsehoods," thus justifying the jury decision that he had portrayed the family "in a false light through knowing or reckless untruth."[172]

A major question that remained unanswered at the time of the *Cantrell* decision was the impact of *Gertz v. Welch* (1974), discussed in the previous chapter, on the false light tort—specifically "whether a State may constitutionally apply a more relaxed standard of liability for a publisher or broadcaster of false statements injurious to a private individual under a false light theory of invasion of privacy, or whether the constitutional standard announced in *Time v. Hill* applies to all false light cases."[173]

The question is still unanswered because all of the parties accepted the *Time v. Hill* standard and thus the Supreme Court did not have to deal with this issue. One fact is clear, however: A solid 8–1 majority reaffirmed the position in *Time v. Hill*, which had been decided by a thin 5–4 margin. Only Justice William O. Douglas dissented: "It seems clear that in matters of public importance such as the present news reporting, there must be freedom from damages lest the press be frightened into playing a more ignoble role than the Framers visualized."[174] The message of *Cantrell* is equally clear: **Actual malice can be demonstrated in false light cases.**

It is instructive to compare the editorial decision making in the two false light cases. In *Time v. Hill* the *Life* article was prepared under the direction of its entertainment editor. The director of the play, which was based on the fictionalized account in the book, suggested that the editor do a story, and about the same time, the editor met a friend of the book's author, Joseph Hayes, who told the editor in a casual discussion that the book had been based on a real incident. The entertainment editor contacted Hayes, who confirmed the connection and arranged for the editor to see the former Hill's home. As the Court pointed out, "Neither then nor thereafter did Prideaux [the editor] question Hayes about the extent to which the play was based on the incident."[175] Prideaux's file for the story included news clippings with details about the incident, including the lack of violence, as well as a *New York Times* article by Hayes indicating that the book was a composite of news stories about incidents in New York, California, Detroit and Philadelphia. The first draft of the *Life* feature did not mention the Hills by name except in the caption for one of the photos. The draft mentioned that the play was a "somewhat fictionalized" account of the Hill incident, and a research assistant assigned to check the accuracy of the story put a question mark over the words, "somewhat fictionalized." When the draft was reviewed by a copy editor, he changed the first sentence to focus on the Hill incident, using the family's name, deleted "somewhat fictionalized," and added the statements that the novel was "inspired" by the incident and that the play was a "re-enactment."

In the *Cantrell* case, the Supreme Court offered little detail on the editorial review process other than that the story was the reporter's idea but was approved by the editor. But the justices obviously were convinced that the reporter had fabricated key points in the story and that these falsehoods and misrepresentations had escaped the scrutiny of the editorial review process. The Court agreed with the lower appellate court that the photographs did not cast the family in a false light, confirming the adage that pictures do not lie.

The circumstances under which the photographer and reporter entered the home to talk with the children while the mother was gone are unclear, but apparently no suit was filed for intrusion or publication of private matters. Could a case have also been built for these torts?

Defenses to False Light

As with the other torts of invasion of privacy, **consent** is a defense, but individuals rarely agree to have false information published about them. But if it can be demonstrated by preponderance of the evidence that the person had the legal capacity to grant consent and did so voluntarily and in good faith and did not revoke such consent, a suit for false light would theoretically fail. Jurors and judges, like anyone else, tend not to believe, however, that plaintiffs would consent to publication of falsehoods about themselves. Because journalists have an ethical and, sometimes, legal obligation to be accurate and truthful, jurors and judges are usually not sympathetic when a reporter or editor touts consent as a defense to publishing falsehoods. Thus consent can be a two-edged sword as a defense. By claiming consent, the journalist is admitting an abrogation of ethics.

Newsworthiness is also a weak, if not impossible, defense because, alone, it simply does not work. However, newsworthiness can be a very viable defense in conjunction with **constitutional privilege**. As the Court indicated in *Time v. Hill* and reiterated in *Cantrell v. Forest City Publishing Co.*, plaintiffs suing the mass media for publishing false information on matters of public interest must demonstrate actual malice (reckless or knowing falsehoods) before recovering for false light. In other words, if the subject matter is newsworthy, even if the information is false, actual malice must be shown. Unfortunately, the scope of this constitutional privilege remains unclear to this day because the Court has never determined whether a state could institute a lower standard such as negligence in a matter involving a private individual rather than a public figure or public official. The majority opinion raised this question without answering it, indicating that the Court may someday respond. With a solid coalition of conservative justices on First Amendment issues now on the Supreme Court, including Chief Justice William Rehnquist and Associate Justices Antonin Scalia, Anthony Kennedy, Sandra Day O'Connor, David Souter and Clarence Thomas, it is highly likely that the Court would apply the *Gertz* holding for libel to false light cases, thus permitting states to lower the standard to negligence for private individuals. In fact, when such a case arrives at the Court, the vote could be 9-0 with Associate Justices John Paul Stevens, Ruth Bader Ginsberg and even liberal

Harry Blackman joining the others. One question has never been tackled by the Supreme Court, but the Court's response could have a major impact on false light and even libel: Is there a constitutional privilege (albeit limited) to publish false information from the public record when such falsehoods are published without actual malice? *Florida Star v. B.J.F.* and *Cox v. Cohn* dealt only with truthful information in public records, and *Cantrell v. Forest City Publishing Co.* and *Time v. Hill* dealt with false information not in public records. It is very difficult to predict how the Court would deal with this issue nor even if the Court will consider such a case. In the meantime, journalists must be diligent and avoid publishing any false information even if the information is published in good faith; negligence is relatively easy to demonstrate and this may eventually become the point at which liability occurs in false light cases.

SUMMARY AND CONCLUSIONS

As the concern of citizens over governmental and corporate snooping intensifies and as communication technologies advance faster than legislation can respond with limits on their potential to invade individual privacy, journalists can expect more suits for invasion of privacy. Of the four torts of invasion of privacy—intrusion, appropriation, publicizing private matters, and false light—publicizing private matters and false light represent the greatest potential liability for the mass media. Statutory and constitutional laws regarding intrusion have been fairly well delineated by legislatures and the courts, although some of the newer technologies such as cellular phones present interesting dilemmas. For example, 1991 news stories, later confirmed by the senator himself, revealed that U.S. Senator Charles Robb (D-Va.) kept in his office a tape recording and transcript of a private cellular phone conversation between Virginia Governor Douglas Wilder and another individual. Wilder and Robb have been political rivals for some time, but many people were still shocked at the revelation. Robb suspended three of his staff members while an investigation was conducted, and said he believed that possessing the tapes and transcripts was not illegal, although he destroyed the tape. Title 18 of the U.S. Code §2511(4) (b) (ii) provides a fine of up to $500 on the first offense of intercepting and/or intentionally disclosing the contents of the radio portion of a cellular telephone communication (with certain specified exceptions).[176] Many general coverage radio receivers can pick up cellular phone conversations. Calls on cordless phones are even easier to intercept. Most news rooms at major newspapers and radio and television stations have scanners that legally receive police, fire and other public services, but listening to cellular conversations, other than for their own staff business, is still verboten. How much bite federal and state laws have on eavesdropping with the use of newer technologies remains to be seen, but reporters and editors rarely are involved in intrusion suits anyway.

Even when devices such as hidden cameras are used by the news media, the statutes protect them, as a few years ago when ABC-TV's "Prime-Time Live" sent staff members into 18 day-care centers in Louisiana and three other states where they posed as students studying day-care techniques. These undercover ABC employees had minature cameras on them that were not detected by day-care workers and owners. ABC installed some fixed position cameras that were also hidden. The three-and-a-half month investigation culminated in a shocking report that revealed horrible conditions and treatment of children at day-care centers that were licensed and regularly inspected by state agencies. Without the use of such hidden devices, eye-opening reports such as these would not be possible.

Appropriation is not a major problem either because the Bo Jacksons of the world are well-rewarded by Nike and Pepsi-Cola for the commercial use of their name, image or likeness. Unless the situation approaches that of *Zacchini v. Scripps-Howard Publishing Co.*, it is highly unlikely that a plaintiff will be successful in a suit for appropriation in a news context. Consent is always the best insurance when a potential commercial context appears because newsworthiness is not a defense to appropriation.

Publication of private matters and false light will continue to be troublesome for the press. The conservative Rehnquist court is unlikely to broaden the constitutional privilege for these two torts and indeed can be expected to further restrict that and other defenses such as newsworthiness and even consent, which is a weak shield anyway. When dealing with private matters, journalists should make sure there is a strong public interest to be served and, whenever possible, that they are dealing with public figures or public officials. Obviously, all news stories and features cannot or should they focus on public people, but reporters and editors must be wary of the traps when private individuals are involved because legislatures, the courts and the public (from which those "reasonable persons" — the jurors — are drawn) firmly believe that privacy for ordinary citizens is being quickly eroded and that the mass media are responsible for some of this erosion.

Finally, the boundaries of false light are obscure but likely to become clearer in the future, especially if this becomes the "new" area of privacy litigation, as some First Amendment scholars predict. Because false light requires no defamation but merely harm to an individual from the publication of false information, which can include fictionalization, a suit that might be unsuccessful for libel could strike gold under false light. If a flood of false light litigation hits the courts, which is possible, the U.S. Supreme Court may be faced with the task of defining the boundaries of this tort.

9

Press and Public Access to the Judicial Process, Records, Places, and Meetings

Whereas the First Amendment guarantees the press the right to be free from governmental prior restraint under most circumstances and the general right to publish without fear of criminal sanctions, the U.S. Supreme Court has never recognized a general constitutional right of the press to *gather* information. Indeed, in those rare instances in which the Court has enunciated a right of the media to have access to information and places, such as the right to attend criminal trials, the Court has done so on the ground that the press acts as a surrogate for the public. The Court clings to the principle that the press can claim no greater rights of access than those afforded the public under the U.S. Constitution. Even though the press is the only business granted special treatment in the Constitution, its privileges have basically been confined to a ban on governmental prior restraint and not to newsgathering. This creates an unfortunate dilemma for the press of having broad freedom to publish but considerably less freedom to ferret out the truth it is expected to publish. This situation may be due largely to the fact that the press at the time the Constitution was written consisted primarily of "party organs" financed by political and other special interest groups who had little concern with objectivity, fairness and truth. They were simply seeking to inform and influence their constituents and to make hay of their opponents, not necessarily to serve as a watchdog over the government.

In the 1970s, the doors to records, places and especially the judicial process began to open, thanks to a series of U.S. Supreme Court rulings and a flurry of state and federal freedom of information statutes that for the first time truly opened the government to the press and the public. This chapter reviews the progress as well as the limits journalists still face in seeking information. It also explores the parallel ethical problems that sometimes call for self-restraint even when the law permits access and disclosure.

ACCESS TO THE JUDICIAL PROCESS

Richmond Newspapers v. Virginia (1980): Criminal Trials

Since the adoption of the Bill of Rights in 1791, the Sixth Amendment has guaranteed, among other rights, the right of a criminal *defendant* "to a speedy and public trial, by an impartial jury of the State and district wherein the crime shall have been committed." The U.S. Supreme Court has wrestled for more than two centuries with issues such as the criteria for an impartial jury[1] and the meaning of "speedy," but the Court never directly acknowledged a constitutional right of *public access* to judicial proceedings until 1980 when the justices held 7-1 in *Richmond Newspapers v. Virginia*[2] that the First and Fourteenth Amendments guarantee the press and the public the right to attend **criminal trials**. The right was not absolute, according to the Court, but "absent an overriding interest articulated in findings, the trial of a criminal case must be open to the public."

One aspect of the decision that was troublesome for journalists was that, with six different opinions among the seven justices in the majority, there is no clear indication whether this is a First or a Sixth Amendment right. Chief Justice Warren Burger was joined by Justices Byron White and John Paul Stevens in the Court's holding that "the right to attend criminal trials is implicit in the guarantees of the First Amendment; without the freedom to attend such trials, which people have exercised for centuries, important aspects of speech and 'of the press could be eviscerated' " (citing *Branzburg v. Hayes*, 1972).[3] In separate opinions, Justices Byron White, John Paul Stevens and Harry Blackmun each concurred with the decision but not fully with the reasoning of the Court. Justice White criticized the Court for not having recognized this right under the Sixth Amendment one year earlier in *Gannett Co. v. DePasquale* (1979).[4] Justice Stevens characterized the case as a "watershed case," but chided the Court for not recognizing a right of access in *Houchins v. KQED*[5] two years earlier. In his concurring opinion, Justice Blackmun stuck to his view earlier in *Gannett Co. v. DePasquale* that the right to a public trial could be found explicitly in the Sixth Amendment but that "the First Amendment must provide some measure of protection for public access to the trial."[6]

The lone dissenter, Justice William Rehnquist, said he could find no prohibition against closing a trial to the public and the press anywhere in the Constitution, including the First, Sixth, Ninth, or any other Amendments.

Justice Rehnquist would instead defer to the states and to the people to make the judgment of whether trials should be open. He made no reference to the meaning of "public trial" under the Sixth Amendment, although he had joined the majority in *Gannett Co. v. DePasquale*, which held that "members of the public have no constitutional right under the Sixth and Fourteenth Amendments to attend criminal trials."[7]

The Court tackled three more major cases dealing with right of access to the judicial process after *Richmond Newspapers v. Virginia*, and in each case found a constitutional right, but continued to quibble over the origins of the right. The result was confusion that is unlikely to dissipate for some time. The determination of whether the right arises from the Sixth Amendment or the First Amendment could prove very significant in the long run. Four of the justices who decided *Gannett v. DePasquale* still sit on the Court — Chief Justice Rehnquist and Associate Justices Stevens, White and Blackmun. Justice Rehnquist found no constitutional right of access in either *Gannett* or *Richmond Newspapers*, whereas Stevens found no Sixth Amendment right in *Gannett* but appeared to recognize a First Amendment right in *Richmond Newspapers*. Justices Blackmun and White believed that the Sixth Amendment applied through the Fourteenth Amendment barred a state from closing the pretrial suppression hearing in *Gannett* even if approved by the defendant unless the Court strongly considered the public interest in open proceedings. Both justices believed the First Amendment guaranteed an open criminal trial in *Richmond Newspapers*.

The Court is not the only body ambivalent about opening the judicial process to press and public scrutiny. Lawyers, judges and the public seem split on the issue as well. Some judges have little hesitation in closing criminal trials and pretrial proceedings to the public and the press, whereas others take extraordinary measures to ensure public access while protecting the rights of the defendant. First Amendment attorneys generally favor open trials and open proceedings, and criminal defense lawyers are sometimes more comfortable with closed proceedings, especially in highly visible cases that are likely to attract media attention.

Why are courts so concerned with open proceedings? The most common fears are (a) a public trial can bias jurors and thus prevent a defendant from receiving a fair trial; (b) the presence of the news media will seriously affect the courtroom decorum and ultimately the judicial process; and (c) extensive publicity may adversely affect the defendant and other witnesses, including the victim.

Do public trials prevent jurors from rendering an impartial verdict, and, if so, would closing them ensure an unbiased decision? Some criminal trials attract so much pretrial media attention that the courts automatically assume that extraordinary measures must be taken even during voir dire. Typical examples are the William Kennedy Smith rape trial in Palm Beach, Florida, and the 1991 drug trafficking trial of former Panama leader Manuel Noriega in Miami, Florida. In both cases, thousands of news stories appeared about each defendant, and hundreds of potential jurors were questioned during voir dire before a final panel was selected. Most individuals were dismissed as potential jurors because they indicated they had seen and heard some of the massive publicity and thus were presumably biased.

Nebraska Press Association v. Judge Stuart (1976)

The principles laid down by the Court in *Near v. Minnesota* (1931)[8] and *Nebraska Press Association v. Judge Stuart* (1976),[9] however, effectively restrict judges from exercising control over pretrial and during-trial publicity, although they can certainly control what takes place in the courtroom. In *Near*, the Court said that the government could impose prior restraint against the press only in exceptional circumstances, such as obscene publications or a potential violation of national security, whereas in *Nebraska Press Association*, the Court unanimously held that a state trial court judge's restrictive order on the news media was unconstitutional because the judge had failed to exhaust other measures for ensuring a fair trial short of prior restraint. "We reaffirm that the guarantees of freedom of expression are not an absolute prohibition under all circumstances, but the barriers to prior restraint remain high and the presumption against its use continues intact.[10]

In a law review article entitled "Who Is an Impartial Juror in an Age of Mass Media?," Newton Minow and Fred Cate concluded:

> To think that jurors wholly unacquainted with the facts of a notorious case can be impaneled today is to dream. Anyone meeting that standard of ignorance should be suspect. The search for a jury is a chimera. It is also unnecessary. Knowledgeable jurors today, like 800 years ago, can form an impartial jury. In fact, the very diversity of views and experiences that they possess is the best guarantee of an impartial jury.[11]

The authors note that in 12th-century England, where the jury system was invented, an individual had to be familiar with the parties as well as the circumstances in the case before he was eligible. Strangers could not serve.[12]

In an indirect way, the U.S. Supreme Court has agreed with the premise that knowledgeable jurors can be impartial. In *Murphy v. Florida* (1975),[13] the Court held that Jack Roland Murphy, known as "Murph the Surf," was not denied a fair trial even though members of the jury that convicted him of the 1968 robbery of a Miami home had learned of the defendant's prior felony conviction and other facts from news stories. Murphy unsuccessfully argued that the extensive media coverage he received primarily because of his flamboyant life-style and his earlier conviction for stealing the Star of India sapphire prejudiced the jury. Murphy cited *Irvin v. Dowd*,[14] *Rideau v.*

Louisiana,[15] *Estes v. Texas*[16] and *Sheppard v. Maxwell*[17] to support his contention that "persons who have learned from news sources of a defendant's prior criminal record are presumed to be prejudiced."[18] In each of these cases, the Supreme Court reversed a criminal conviction in state court "obtained in a trial atmosphere that had been utterly corrupted by press coverage."[19]

Irvin v. Dowd (1961)

In *Irvin v. Dowd* (1961), the Court held unanimously that "Mad Dog Irvin" (as he was known in the press) had been denied Fourteenth Amendment due process and thus was entitled to a new trial. The Court pointed to the fact that 8 of the 12 jurors in the case had indicated during voir dire that they thought he was guilty of the murder for which he was being tried. All 8 said they were familiar with the facts and circumstances, including that Irvin had confessed to six other murders. They had acquired this information from the massive press coverage the story received, but all 12 told the judge they could still be impartial and fair. As the Court noted:

> No doubt each juror was sincere when he said that he would be fair and impartial to petitioner [Irvin], but the psychological impact requiring such a declaration before one's fellows is often its father. Where so many, so many times, admitted prejudice, such a statement of impartiality can be given little weight. As one of the jurors put it, "You can't forget what you hear and see." With his life at stake, it is not requiring too much that petitioner be tried in an atmosphere undisturbed that so huge a wave of public passion and by a jury other than one in which two-thirds of the members admit, before hearing any testimony, to possessing a belief in his guilt.[20] (citations omitted).

Rideau v. Louisiana (1963)

In *Rideau v. Louisiana* (1963), the Court reversed the death penalty of Wilbert Rideau, convicted of armed robbery, kidnapping and murder. The Court held that his right to due process had been violated because the state trial court refused to grant a change of venue even though most people in Calcasieu Parish, including the jurors, had seen a film broadcast three times on television in which the defendant confessed, without benefit of an attorney, to the sheriff that he had committed the alleged crimes. The Court was concerned because three members of the jury said during voir dire that they had seen the televised confession at least once. Further, two members of the jury were deputy sheriffs of the parish in which the trial occurred.

Estes v. Texas (1965)

The circumstances compelling the Supreme Court to overturn the swindling conviction of the petitioner in *Estes v. Texas* (1965) involved more than simply jury prejudice. The Court held that the Fourteenth Amendment due process rights of financier Billy Sol Estes had been violated primarily because of the publicity associated with the pretrial hearing, which had been carried live on both television and radio. Some portions of the trial were also broadcast,[21] and news photography was permitted throughout the trial. The Court was clearly unhappy with the massive pretrial and during-trial publicity, but its greatest concern was the presence of cameras at the two-day pretrial hearing, which included at least 12 camerapersons continually snapping still pictures or recording motion pictures, cables and wires "snaked across the courtroom floor," three microphones on the judge's bench and others aimed at the jury box and the attorney's table. By the time of the trial, the judge had imposed rather severe restriction on press coverage, and the trial was moved about 500 miles away. The Supreme Court did hint that cameras would return someday to the courtrooms:

> It is said that the ever-advancing techniques of public communication and the adjustment of the public to its presence may bring about a change in the effect of telecasting upon the fairness of criminal trials. But we are not dealing here with future developments in the field of electronics. Our judgment cannot be rested on the hypothesis of tomorrow but must take the facts as they are presented today.[22]

Chandler v. Florida (1981): Cameras in the Courtroom

The facts indeed did change as the technology changed, leading the court to rule in *Chandler v. Florida*[23] 16 years later that a state could permit broadcast and still photography coverage of criminal proceedings because cameras and microphones in the courtroom were no longer an inherent violation of a defendant's Fourteenth Amendment rights, contrary to the holding in *Estes v. Texas*. The majority opinion in *Estes* cited four major reasons for banning cameras from the courtroom: (a) the negative impact on jurors, especially in biasing the jury and in distracting its members; (b) impairment of the quality of the testimony of witnesses (the idea that witnesses may alter their testimony when cameras and mikes are present); (c) interference with judges in doing their job; and (d) potential negative impact on the defendant, including harassment. As the Court noted:

> Trial by television is . . . foreign to our systems. . . . Telecasting may also deprive an accused of effective counsel. The distractions, intrusions into confidential attorney-client relationships and the temptation offered by television to play to the public office might often have a direct effect not only upon the lawyers, but the judge, the jury and the witnesses.[24] (citation omitted)

With nearly all states and even the federal courts now permitting television and radio coverage in the courtroom with only limited restrictions, those words seem rather hollow, but the technology and public attitudes have changed considerably. When the cable network Court TV debuted in mid-1991, there were no outcries of sensationalism or complaints about lack of due process. Indeed, the network had a enormous variety of civil and criminal trials from which to choose to fill its 24-hour programming.

It is rather ironic that *Chandler v. Florida*, which recognized no constitutional right of access but merely held that the Constitution does not bar states from allowing radio, television and photographic coverage of criminal proceedings, has probably had a greater impact on opening up the judicial process than *Richmond Newspapers v. Virginia*, which did indeed recognize a constitutional right of access to criminal trials by the press and the public.

Are there situations in which criminal proceedings, including trials, can be closed without violating the First Amendment? *Richmond Newspapers v. Virginia* provides at least a partial answer. According to the Court, the trial of a criminal case that must be open to the public, "absent an overriding interest articulated in findings."[25] The Court, however, took no pains to explain "overriding interest," but did distinguish the case from *Gannett v. DePasquale* by noting that "both the majority [which upheld the closure of a criminal pretrial hearing as Constitutional] . . . and dissenting opinions . . . agreed that open trials were part of the common law tradition."[26] Unfortunately, the justices did not overrule *Gannett v. DePasquale*, which led Justice Byron White to argue in his concurring opinion in *Richmond Newspapers v. Virginia* that the latter case "would have been unnecessary had *Gannett* . . . construed the Sixth Amendment to forbid excluding the public from criminal proceedings except in narrowly defined circumstances."[27]

Richmond Newspapers was a particularly appropriate case for testing this implicit right of access in the Constitution because it involved a defendant who had been tried three times before and who had specifically requested closure with no objection from the prosecution. The defendant's first conviction of second degree murder was reversed because improper evidence was introduced at trial, and the second and third trials ended in mistrials. Because the defendant asked that the trial be closed, he effectively waived his right to a public trial. Thus a First Amendment rationale was necessary if the trial were to remain open. One of the more puzzling aspects of the decision is that the majority opinion (written by then-Chief Justice Warren Burger) felt it was "not crucial" to characterize the decision as "right of access" or a "right to gather information." The Court did not note that the "explicit, guaranteed rights to speak and to publish concerning what takes place at a trial would lose much meaning if access to observe the trial could, as it was here, be foreclosed arbitrarily.[28]

Sheppard v. Maxwell (1966): Prejudicial Publicity

Although it was technically not an access case, *Sheppard v. Maxwell* (1966)[29] was a watershed decision involving the Fourteenth Amendment rights of defendants, especially in highly publicized cases. It also played a major role in a movement by lower courts away from openness that began in the early 1990s. Indeed, the Court's decision served as a lightning rod for many state courts to close trials even though the justices clearly did not intend to send a message that press and public access should be restricted beyond the suggestions made for preventing a crowded courtroom.

The circumstances in the case are particularly important in understanding the Court's 8–1 decision. Samuel H. Sheppard, a prominent Ohio osteopath was tried and convicted by a jury of second degree murder after his wife, Marilyn, was bludgeoned to death in their Bay Village home in suburban Cleveland. The Supreme Court's opinion describes the case in considerable detail, but some highlights bear mentioning. Dr. Sheppard was a suspect in the murder from the beginning, especially because of contradictory information he and other witnesses provided about the circumstances in the matter. He claimed, for example, that he had fallen asleep on a couch the night his wife was murdered in her bedroom, but that he had heard her cry out in the early morning. When he ran upstairs to her bedroom, he saw a "form" standing over her bed and was then knocked unconscious when he struggled with the "form." When he regained consciousness, he checked his wife and believed she was dead after he could not get a pulse. He then checked on his son, found him unharmed and then chased the "form" out the door onto the lake shore, where he again lost consciousness.[30]

The publicity surrounding the case and the trial was unbelievable and on par with that in the 1934 trial of Bruno Hauptmann in the kidnap-murder of the 19-month-old son of famed aviator, Charles Lindberg. The indiscretions of the press in that case led the American Bar Association three years later to adopt Canon 35, which effectively forbade broadcast coverage and still photos in the courtroom for more than four decades. Of all the cases cited in this book, this is the one that must be read in full to be appreciated. Lack of space limits the details here, but a few examples will give a sense of why the Court denounced the "carnival atmosphere at trial." The headlines, stories and editorials in the Cleveland newspapers were relentless and merciless in their accusations against the defendant. Some typical examples among the dozens cited by the Court:

1. At the corner's request before the trial, Sheppard re-enacted the tragedy at his home, but he had to wait outside for the coroner to arrive because the house was placed in "protective custody" until after the trial. Because news reporters had apparently been invited on the tour by the coroner, they reported his performance in detail, complete with photographs.

2. When the defendant refused a lie detector test, front-page newspaper headlines screamed "Doctor Balks at Lie Test; Retells Story" and " 'Loved My Wife, She Loved Me,' Sheppard Tells News Reporter."

3. Later, front-page editorials claimed someone was "getting away with murder" and called on the coroner to do an inquest — "Why No Inquest? Do It Now, Dr. Gerber." When the hearing was conducted, it took place in a local school gymnasium, complete with live broadcast microphones, a swarm of photographers and reporters and several hundred spectators to witness Sheppard being questioned for five-and-a-half hours about his actions on the night of the murder, an illicit affair and his married life. His attorneys were present but were not allowed to participate.

4. Later stories and editorials focused on evidence that was never introduced at trial and on his alleged extramarital affairs with numerous women, even though the evidence at trial included an affair with only one woman, Susan Hayes, who was the subject of dozens of news stories.

5. Sheppard was not formally charged until more than a month after the murder, and during that time the editorials and headlines ranged from "Why Isn't Sam Sheppard in Jail?" to "New Murder Evidence Is Found, Police Say" and "Dr. Sam Faces Quiz at Jail on Marilyn's Fear of Him."

6. The trial occurred two weeks before the November general election in which the chief prosecutor was a candidate for common pleas judge and the trial judge was a candidate to succeed himself. All three Cleveland newspapers published the names and addresses of prospective jurors and during the trial the jurors became media celebrities themselves. During the trial, which was held in a small courtroom (26 × 48 feet), 20 newspaper and wire service reporters were seated within three feet of the jury box. A local radio station was even allowed to broadcast from a room next door to where the jurors recessed and later deliberated in the case. Each day, witnesses, the attorneys and the jurors were photographed as they entered and left the courtroom, and although photos were not permitted during the trial itself, they were permitted during the recesses. In fact, pictures of the jury appeared more than 40 times in the newspapers.

7. The jurors were never sequestered during the trial and were allowed to watch, hear and read all the massive publicity during the trial, which even included a national broadcast by the famous Walter Winchell in which he asserted that a woman under arrest for robbery in New York City said she was Sam Sheppard's mistress and had borne his child. The judge merely politely "admonished" the jurors not to allow such stories to affect their judgment.

As the Court noted, "bedlam reigned at the courthouse during the trial and newsmen took over practically the entire courtroom, hounding most of the participants in the trial, especially Sheppard."[31] As a result, Sheppard was denied a fair trial in violation of his Fourteenth Amendment due process rights, according to the Court, which ordered a new trial. At the second trial, 12 years after the first, the physician was acquitted.

In spite of the fact that Dr. Sheppard had been the subject of highly prejudicial, intense publicity, the Court recommended remedies short of prior restraint:

> Bearing in mind the massive pretrial publicity, the judge should have adopted stricter rules governing the use of the courtroom by newsmen. . . . The number of reporters in the courtroom itself could have been limited at the first sign that their presence would disrupt the trial. They should not have been placed inside the bar. Furthermore, the judge should have more closely regulated the conduct of newsmen in the courtroom. . . .

> Secondly, the court should have insulated the witnesses. All of the newspapers and radio stations apparently interviewed prospective witnesses at will, and in many instances disclosed their testimony. . . .

> Thirdly, the judge should have made some effort to control the release of leads, information, and gossip to the press by police officers, witnesses, and the counsel for both sides. Much of the information was inaccurate, leading to groundless rumors and confusion.[32]

The Court also suggested other remedies, including (a) continuance or postponing the case until prejudicial publicity subsides, (b) transferring to another county not permeated by the publicity, (c) sequestration of the jury to keep its members from being exposed to prejudicial publicity, and (d) ordering a new trial if publicity threatens a defendant's due process rights after the trial has begun. It is significant that the Court did not cite restrictive orders ("gag orders) on the press as a judicial remedy but instead favored restricting the parties, witnesses and attorneys. Unfortunately, many courts interpreted the *Sheppard* holding as a license to impose restrictive orders on the press anyway, prodding the Court to eventually rule out such censorship under most circumstances in a series of rulings that culminated in the decision in 1976 *Nebraska Press Association v. Stuart*, in which the Court held that restrictive orders against the press are "presumptively unconstitutional" and cannot be issued except in rare circumstances and then only after other measures less restrictive of the First Amendment such as those just discussed are exhausted.

Until *Richmond Newspapers*, the Supreme Court appeared to be moving toward severely restricting press access to the judicial process. While upholding closure of pretrial hearings, albeit in a 5–4 call, *Gannett v. DePasquale* represented only one part of the big picture. In *Pell v. Procunier* (1974)[33] and *William B. Saxbe v. The Washington Post Co.* (1974),[34] the Court decided 5–4 that journalists have no constitutional right of access to prisons or their inmates beyond those enjoyed by the public. *Pell* upheld a California Department of Corrections regulation barring the news media from interviewing "specific individual inmates." Four prisoners and three journalists had challenged the rule as a violation of their First and Fourteenth Amendment rights of free speech. According to the Court, "It is one thing to say that a journalist is free to seek out sources of information not available to members of the general public. It is quite another thing to suggest that the Constitution imposes upon government the affirmative duty to make available to journalists sources of information not available to members of the public generally."[35] The Court accepted the state's rationale that media interviews can turn certain inmates into celebrities and thus create disciplinary problems for these and other prisoners.

In *Saxbe*, issued on the same day as *Pell*, the Court upheld a federal rule similar to that of California that prohibited personal interviews by journalists with individually designated federal inmates in medium- and maximum-security prisons. The justices saw no major differences between the two regulations and noted that the federal rule "does not place the press in any less advantageous position than the public generally."[36] The *Washington Post* had filed suit after it was denied access to prisoners who had allegedly been punished for their involvement in strike negotiations at two federal facilities. In its reasoning, the Court relied heavily on *Branzburg v. Hayes* (1972),[37] which held 5-4 that the First Amendment grants no special privileges to journalists against revealing confidential sources or confidential information to grand juries.

Richard Nixon v. Warner Communications (1978): Right of Access to Public Recordings

In a 1978 decision that has had very limited impact on the press because of its rather unusual circumstances, the Court ruled 5-4 that no First Amendment rights were violated when the press was denied permission to copy, broadcast and sell to the public recordings of White House conversations that were played during one of the Watergate trials. *Richard Nixon v. Warner Communications*[38] was unusual in that Warner was requesting copies of tapes that had already been played at trial but were in the custody of the Administrator of General Services under authority granted by the Presidential Recordings Act approved by Congress.

Pell and *Saxbe* were basically reaffirmed four years later in a plurality opinion in *Houchins v. KQED* (1978),[39] in which the Court held that a broadcaster's First and Fourteenth Amendment rights were not violated when the station was denied access to the portion of a county jail where a suicide had occurred. According to the Court, "Neither the First Amendment nor Fourteenth Amendment mandates a right of access to government information or sources of information within the government's control. Under our holdings in [*Pell* and *Saxbe*], until the political branches decree otherwise, as they are free to do, the media has [sic] no special right of access to the Almedia County Jail [the facility in question] different from or greater than that accorded the public generally."[40] The station could use other sources, the Court noted, such as inmate letters, former inmates, public officials and prisoner's attorneys to gain the information it sought about conditions at the facility.

Robert K. Smith v. Daily Mail Publishing Co. (1979): Publishing Juvenile Offender Names

As if to illustrate this point but in a different setting, exactly one year later the Court unanimously struck down as unconstitutional a West Virginia statue that provided criminal penalties for publication, without the written permission of the juvenile court, of truthful information that had been lawfully acquired concerning the identity of a juvenile offender. In *Robert K. Smith v. Daily Mail Publishing Co.* (1979),[41] the justices said the asserted state interest of insuring the anonymity of juveniles involved in juvenile court proceedings was not sufficient to override the First Amendment's restrictions against prior restraint. The Charleston (West Virginia) *Daily Mail* and the Charleston *Gazette* published the name of a 14-year-old junior high student who had been charged with shooting a 15-year-old classmate to death at school. Reporters and photographers first heard about the shooting on a police radio and then were given the alleged assailant's name by several eyewitnesses, the police and an assistant prosecutor. After the name and photo of the teenage defendant appeared in the papers, a grand jury indicted both publications for violating the state statute, although no indictments were issued against three local radio stations who broadcast the name. (The statute applied only to newspapers, not to the electronic or other media, a deficiency duly noted by the Court in its decision.)

The holding in the case was narrow, as then-Chief Justice Warren Burger indicated, because "there is no issue before us of unlawful press access to confidential judicial proceedings [citations omitted]; there is no issue here of privacy or prejudicial pre-trial publicity."[42] Indeed, Justice Rehnquist, while concurring in the judgment of the Court, noted, "I think that a generally effective ban on publication that applied to all forms of mass communication, electronic and print media alike, would be constitutional."[43] The Court's opinion, representing the other seven justices voting in the case — Justice Powell took no part in the consideration or decision of the case — held that a state statute punishing the publication of the name of a juvenile defendant could never serve a "state interest of the highest order," as required to justify prior restraint. The majority opinion cited, among other decisions, *Landmark Communications Inc. v. Virginia* (1978),[44] *Cox Broadcasting Corp. v. Cohn* (1975),[45] and *Oklahoma Publishing Co. v. District Court* (1977).[46]

In *Landmark*, the Supreme Court ruled 7-0 that a Virginia statute subjecting individuals, including newspapers, to criminal sanctions for disclosing information regarding proceedings before a state judicial review commission was a violation of the First Amendment. The case arose when the *Virginian Pilot* published an article accurately reporting details of an investigation of a state judge by the Virginia Judicial Inquiry and Review Commission. One month later, a state grand jury indicted the company that owned the newspaper for violating the statute by "unlawfully divulg[ing] the identification of a Judge of a Court not of record, which said Judge was the subject of an investigation and hearing" by the commission. In a bench trial, Landmark was fined $500 and ordered to pay court costs. The company appealed and the Supreme Court held that the First Amendment does not allow "the criminal punishment of third persons who are strangers to the inquiry, including news media, for divulging or publishing truthful information regarding confidential proceedings" of the Judicial Inquiry and Review Commission.[47] The Court noted that the issue was narrow because the case was not concerned with application of the statute to someone who obtained the information illegally and then divulged it nor with the authority to keep such a commission's proceedings confidential. But it was, nevertheless, an important victory for newsgathering because it reinforced the principle that truthful information legally obtained enjoys First Amendment protection even when such information includes details of closed judicial proceedings. This protection is not absolute, of course, as the Court noted in both *Landmark* and *Smith*, but the state has a heavy burden in demonstrating that its interests outweigh those of the First Amendment. While admitting in *Landmark* that premature disclosure of the commission's proceedings could pose some risk of injury to the judge, judicial system or operation of the commission itself, the Court said "much of the risk can be eliminated through careful internal procedures to protect the confidentiality of Commission proceedings."[48]

In *Cox Broadcasting*, as discussed in Chapter 8, the U.S. Supreme Court declared a Georgia statute unconstitutional that made made the press criminally and civilly liable for publishing the name of a rape victim even when such information was obtained from public records.[49] Finally, the Court held in *Oklahoma Publishing Co.* that a state court injunction barring the press from publishing the identity or photograph of an 11-year-old boy on trial in juvenile court was unconstitutional prior restraint.[50] The Court struck down the judge's order because he had already allowed reporters and other members of the public to attend a hearing in the case in which the information was disclosed. Once truthful information is "publicly revealed" or "in the public domain," it cannot be banned, according to the Court.

Globe Newspaper Co.
v. Norfolk County Superior Court (1982):
Unconstitutionality of Mandatory Closures

In 1982 the U.S. Supreme Court issued the first of three rulings that appeared to significantly broaden the holding in *Richmond Newspapers* (1980) that criminal trials were under the Constitution presumptively open to the press and the public. While the first decision, *Globe Newspaper Co. v. Norfolk County Superior Court* (1982),[51] did not deal directly with the scope of *Richmond Newspapers*, it still paved the way for the two subsequent cases that confronted this issue. In *Globe Newspaper*, the Court in a 6–3 opinion struck down as unconstitutional a Massachusetts statute that the state Supreme Judicial Court construed to **require** judges to exclude the press and the public in trials for certain sexual offenses involving a victim under the age of 18 during the time the victim is testifying. The key factor in the case was *mandatory closure*—the judge had no discretion. Liberally quoting its decision in *Richmond Newspapers*, the Court rejected the state's contentions that the statute was necessary to protect "minor victims of sex crimes from further trauma and embarrassment" and to encourage "such victims to come forward and testify in a truthful and credible manner." According to the majority opinion:

> Although the right of access to criminal trials is of a constitutional stature, it is not absolute. But the circumstances under which the press and the public can be barred from a criminal trial are limited; the State's justification in denying access must be a weighty one. Where, as in the present case, the State attempts to deny the right of access in order to inhibit the disclosure of sensitive information, it must be shown that the denial is necessitated by a compelling governmental interest, and is narrowly tailored to serve that interest.[52]

The justices agreed that the first asserted state interest was compelling but that mandatory closure was not justified because "the circumstances of a particular case may affect the significance of the interest. A trial court can determine on a case-by-case basis whether closure is necessary to protect the welfare of a minor victim."[53] The Supreme Court was not convinced at all on the second asserted interest because the press and the public are allowed to see the transcript and to talk with court personnel and other individuals and thus ascertain the substance of victims' testimony and even their identity. Thus the Court left the door open for closure on a case-by-case basis, while clearly prohibiting mandatory closure as unconstitutional prior restraint.

Press Enterprise I (1984)
and *Press Enterprise II* (1986): Right of Access
to Voir Dire and Preliminary Hearings

Press Enterprise I (1984)[54] and *Press Enterprise II* (1986),[55] as they have become known, opened up voir dire and preliminary hearings, at least as they are conducted in California, respectively, to the press and the public. *Press Enterprise I* is particularly significant because the Court for the first time held that the jury selection process is part of the criminal trial itself and thus presumptively open under the First and Fourteenth Amendments. The unanimous decision reiterated that the "presumption of openness may be overcome only by an overriding interest based on findings that closure is essential to preserve higher values and is narrowly tailored to serve that interest."[56] In *Press Enterprise I*, the newspaper was denied access to most of the voir dire in a trial for the rape and murder of a teenage girl. The judge allowed the press to attend the "general voir dire" but closed the courtroom when the attorneys questioned individual jurors. In all, only three days of the six weeks of voir dire were open, and the judge refused to allow a transcript of the process to be released to the public. The jury selection process could under some circumstances invoke a compelling government interest, but no such interest had been demonstrated in this case, according to the Court. An example cited by the justices of such a justified closure might be to protect an individual's privacy when a prospective juror had privately told the judge that she or a member of her family had been raped but had not prosecuted the offender because of the trauma and embarrassment from disclosure.

Finally, two years later in *Press Enterprise II*, the Supreme Court held 7–2 that the press and the public enjoyed a limited First Amendment right of access in criminal cases to preliminary hearings. The holding was quite narrow because the Court emphasized that it applied only to such hearings "as they are conducted in California" where "because of its extensive scope, the preliminary hearing is often the most important in the criminal proceeding."[57] The case began when the newspaper was denied access to a 41-day preliminary hearing for a nurse charged in the murder of 12 patients. The defendant requested closure, and the magistrate in the case not only granted the motion but also sealed the record. The prosecution moved to have the transcript released and the trial court agreed to do so when the defendant waived the right to a jury trial, but the California Supreme Court reversed the trial court decision. The U.S. Supreme Court reversed, holding that "California preliminary hearings are sufficiently like a trial" to warrant a First Amendment right of access unless the state can demonstrate an overriding interest sufficient to overcome the presumption of openness.

Summary and Conclusions

Since *Press Enterprise II* the U.S. Supreme Court has not considered whether other portions of the criminal judicial process, including preliminary hearings in states that do not follow the California model, fall under the holding in *Richmond Newspapers*. The composition of the Court has changed substantially since 1986 with William H. Rehnquist assuming the position of Chief Justice, and new Associate Justices David Souter, Antonin Scalia, Anthony Kennedy, Clarence Thomas, and Ruth Bader Ginsberg. It appears likely that the Court will, if given the opportunity, continue to broaden, albeit in narrow increments, the scope of the limited First Amendment right of access to the criminal judicial process. The major question, however, is whether a majority of the justices will recognize a constitutional right of the press and the public to attend civil trials and related proceedings. Such a move would be a bold and unprecedented step toward truly opening the judicial system to the public, which it was designed to serve in the first place. Most civil trials are now routinely open in state and federal courts, but not necessarily to electronic media coverage, although even the federal courts are now permitting such access on an experimental basis, thanks to a 1990 decision by the U.S. Judicial Conference. The Conference authorized a 3-year test program that began July 1, 1991 and ends on June 30, 1994, under which specific appellate and district courts have discretion to allow audio and video recording and still photography in civil cases. The U.S. Supreme Court has always opened its formal proceedings, although not its deliberations, to the public—including oral arguments and the reading of decisions—but the justices have thus far banned cameras in the courtroom itself, except for ceremonial occasions.

As the Court has indicated in each of its decisions dealing with access to the judicial process, the right of access is not absolute but the burden on the state to justify closure must necessarily be heavy. The trials of Dr. Sam Sheppard and Bruno Hauptmann were aberrations and should be viewed as such by the courts. Openness clearly promotes fairness and justice because it subjects the judicial system to press and public scrutiny, which is essential in an age in which the public appears to have lost some of its faith in the process, thanks to revelations that have brought the demise of several state and federal court judges.

ACCESS TO PLACES

Introduction

Although access to the judicial process has significantly expanded in the last two decades (as indicated in the previous section), press and public access to places, especially government institutions, has actually become more restricted in recent years. The U.S. Supreme Court hinted at what was to come in 1972 in *Branzburg v. Hayes* (mentioned earlier in this chapter):

> Despite the fact that newsgathering may be hampered, the press is regularly excluded from grand jury proceedings, our own conferences, the meetings of other official bodies gathered in executive session, and the meetings of private organizations. Newsmen have no constitutional right of access to the scenes of crime or disaster when the general public is excluded, and they may be prohibited from attending or publishing information about trials if such restrictions are necessary to assure a defendant a fair trial before an impartial jury.[58]

Two years later the Court began drawing the boundaries with its decisions regarding access to prisons in *Pell v. Procunier* and *Saxbe v. the Washington*

Post. The task of defining the specific limitations, though, was left to other courts and legislators but the Supreme Court certainly set the tone—so long as the media are granted the same privileges as the general public in gaining access to places, no First Amendment rights are violated.

Access to public property is generally much easier than private property, especially where a "public forum" exists, but there are times and circumstances when it is reasonable, according to the courts, to limit access even to public places and public events. Disasters are a prime example of when authorities can severely restrict press and public access even though an event of great public interest may be involved. Two typical examples illustrate this principle. The first one developed in March 1977 when *Star-Ledger* photographer Harvey I. Lashinsky took pictures of a gory auto accident scene he noticed as he was driving on the New Jersey Garden State Parkway. Lashinsky got to the accident in which a seriously injured girl was pinned inside the car against the decapitated corpse of her mother about 20 minutes before a state police officer arrived. After calling for back-up units and an ambulance, the officer attempted to clear the area of spectators, including the photographer who was arrested after he allegedly argued with the officer and refused to leave when asked specifically to do so. In 1978, after a three-day trial, Lashinsky was convicted of violating New Jersey's disorderly conduct statute.[59] He was fined $25 and ordered to pay court costs, which was reduced in a trial de novo to a $15 fine and $5 in court costs.

On appeal, the New Jersey Supreme Court in *New Jersey v. Lashinsky* (1979)[60] upheld the defendant's conviction, rejecting his arguments that the statute was unconstitutional because it was too broad and too vague. The justices also disagreed with Lashinsky's contention that the statute did not apply to him as a member of the press because the state supreme court had in an earlier case decided that the right of the press to gather news was entitled to special constitutional protection:

> The Constitution does not serve to place the media or their representatives above the law. . . . In the present context, whether a newsperson's conduct is disorderly must turn on whether, from an objective standpoint and under all of the circumstances, the policeman's order to the newsman was reasonable, taking into account the special role performed by the press. . . . The officer, virtually working alone, could not, in his professional judgment, have permitted the defendant to remain, even as a member of the press, and still discharge his own paramount responsibilities for the safety and welfare of those who were his immediate concern.[61]

In a more recent situation, local police officers reportedly seized the film of a photographer for the *The Item*, a Sumter, South Carolina, newspaper, and then had him escorted off the premises by security guards at the site of an

Amtrak train accident near Camden, South Carolina, in August 1991.[62] Steve Bohnstedt said he had taken only three pictures before a Camden police officer told him he would be jailed if he did not give up his film and leave the property. A 16-year-old passenger said police also tried to handcuff him and take a videotape he had made of the accident in which 7 people were killed and 87 injured.[63]

No Special Right of Access to Public and Private Places by the Press

Typically, unless journalists can demonstrate either that (a) the government authorities acted unreasonably or in an arbitrary and capricious manner in blocking access or (b) the government discriminated against the press by blocking media access while allowing the public to enter the area, they will lose. Even when the public is given access, the media do not automatically have a right to full access by bringing cameras and other video and audio recording equipment. They simply have the right to treatment equal to that granted to the public. Most police departments, especially in larger metropolitan areas, have written guidelines for dealing with the press at accidents and disasters. Although these are usually not legally binding because they are merely guidelines rather than administrative regulations, journalists, including news photographers, should be familiar with them. Often such guidelines are drawn up after consultation with the press. When they prove unworkable or unreasonable, the media should pressure police department administrators to change them. The changes are more likely to occur when the press makes a concerted and organized effort through professional associations such as area press clubs and the local professional chapter of the Society of Professional Journalists.

Restrictions on press intrusion on private property are usually rather severe, as was illustrated in 1979 when several reporters and photographers were arrested and later convicted of criminal trespassing after they entered a nuclear power plant construction site in Rogers County, Oklahoma, known as "Black Fox Station." The plant was owned by the Public Service Co. of Oklahoma (PSO), which had a record of denying access to the plant to the news media and the public. The arrests occurred after the reporters followed a group of antinuclear protestors as they crossed a border fence to enter the privately owned nuclear power plant site. The Oklahoma District Court judge ruled that whereas "there is a First Amendment right of the news media to reasonable access to the news such as is available to the public generally," this right must be weighed against several opposing state interests.[64] (Although the power company was technically privately owned, the judge treated it as a governmental entity for purposes of the case because its operation was heavily regulated by the state and federal governments.) He then ruled that the reporters' First Amendment rights were not violated because the state had the duty to maintain public order and enforce criminal statutes and to protect property. The state Criminal Court of Appeals, in upholding the $25 fines imposed on each of the journalists by the trial court, held that the First Amendment does not guarantee the press access to property "simply because it is owned or controlled by the government."[65]

Restricted Access to the Military:
The Persian Gulf War

A more recent and very telling example of the restricted rights of access of the press is the treatment accorded the news media during the Persian Gulf War in early 1991. In June 1991 the Gannet Foundation (now known as the Freedom Forum) published a comprehensive report on the press and the Persian Gulf Conflict that is must reading for all journalists and future journalists.[66] Most of the findings in the report indicate that restraints were imposed on the press in ways that were unprecedented, even during World War II and the Vietnam War, for example. Nothing that although the invasions by U.S. military forces in Grenada in October 1983 and Panama in December 1989 foreshadowed the restraints the military would impose in future conflicts, the report concludes that "the media failed to take heed."[67] The report also criticizes the press for (a) its failure "to wage any significant battle against the military's press restrictions" (only three suits were filed challenging the military restrictions and none of them involved a major American news organization); (b) its acquiescence that "may have weakened [its] ability to challenge restrictions in any future conflict"; (c) losing the information war by extensively using military supplied briefings and videotapes so that the main source of gulf news, television, reflected the government's viewpoint; and (d) often lapsing "into cheerleading the war effort instead of striving for more balanced news and historical perspective."[68]

One reason the news media may have voluntarily agreed to abide by what one writer has described as a policy "to confine reporters to escorted pools that sharply curtailed when and how they could talk to troops"[69] is that the controls, in a document known as Annex Foxtrot, were implemented in increments that began months before the U.S. began attacking military targets in Iraq and Kuwait on January 16, 1991.[70] The result of this restricted access and military prior restraint of the press that both the media and the American public were deliberately deceived by the government in a concerted effort to deceive the Iraqi army. As one writer has noted, "The Pentagon and the White House used the media to shape public opinion — a time-honored practice in war and in peace — and to disarm potential opponents on the home front. Secrecy and deception are part of the nation's wartime tradition, and they helped bring American troops home to waving flags and banners."[71]

According to another journalist, "The Pentagon's primary effort at controlling the press — its system of keeping reporters in organized pools with military escorts — was designed not so much to deceive the press as to keep it away from the action."[72] By keeping the press at bay, the military was able to skillfully manipulate the information reaching the U.S. public, and when potentially damaging news got in the hands of journalists anyway because military censors had somehow failed, the Pentagon successfully convinced the news media to voluntarily withhold the information to protect national security. The plan worked so well that the Iraqis were duped into falsely believing that the Marines were going to launch an amphibious attack instead of attacking from the west as they successfully did.[73]

During the Vietnam War the press played a major role in reversing public opinion from strong support to doubts and opposition; the Persian Gulf War saw a return to "a patriotic press," the norm in wartime.[74] Media critic and columnist Richard Reeves, for example, suggested that the Cable News Network, which was the primary, source for news about the war for most Americans, according to opinion polls, should have been called PNN for the Pentagon News Network.[75]

Wars inevitably invoke different rules for access for both the press and the public, but, as you have seen, access can be restricted even when it means that significant news events will not be covered, both in peacetime and during war. The Persian Gulf War revealed one of the major ethical dilemmas facing journalists: *Should the press agree to "voluntary" restrictions by the government in covering an important event when the restraint would otherwise likely be unconstitutional?* It is significant, as the Gannett Center study pointed out, that not one major U.S. news organization joined the three unsuccessful lawsuits challenging the constitutionality of the Pentagon rules. Thus one of the five principal recommendations of the report indicates that "the American Media must learn to represent themselves collectively with one voice on matters of access to information and censorship in time of war without sacrificing the independence of individual media or their competitiveness."[76] One of the suggestions made for accomplishing this is developing a strategy to legally challenge, when necessary, "unacceptable restrictions on information as well as other policies and rules when appropriate."[77] It is also imperative that the news media continue to aggressively fight at all times for access to places and information on behalf of the public and the press when such access is essential to effectively gathering accurate data about events of public interest.

Voluntary restraint is justified under some circumstances, such a when national security would clearly be endangered, but the press must always be wary of agreeing to withhold information simply because the government has threatened to revoke a journalist's credentials or because the government has indicated it will deny access unless the news media exercise self-restraint.

Sometimes the press may need to challenge the government even when public sentiment is strongly against journalists, as was the case in the Gulf War. Indeed, one of the great ironies is that, according to polls, the public felt the major television networks (in particular, CNN, with 61 percent saying it did the best) did a good job covering the war, but people also agreed that the governmental restrictions were justified.[78]

One of the more controversial steps that some news organizations have taken is to work with governmental authorities, such as police and fire departments, to develop a system for issuing press passes. Such arrangements are becoming more and more common, but some journalists fear the result may be less rather than greater access.[79] Presumably, under this argument, the guidelines established for the use of the passes offer authorities the chance to prevent the media from going where they want to go at crime and disaster scenes under the guise of a formal agreement that the press has promised to respect.

ACCESS TO RECORDS

When it comes to gathering news, reporters and editors still rely most heavily on personal sources—experts, officials, politicians, eyewitnesses, ordinary individuals, lawyers and so on—for information, but records—written as well as computerized—usually provide much of the material as well that goes into a typical news story. These records can include birth, marriage and death certificates; divorce decrees; court documents; government agency materials; property deeds and even telephone books and city directories. Although the focus of this section is on obtaining public documents, private individuals should not be overlooked as sources of records, especially of nonpublic materials. In fact, when you are writing a story, it sometimes may be more expeditious to consult a nongovernmental source for a copy of a legal document than to wait for days or months for the government agency to release the information. However, you should make sure in such a case that your source is absolutely trustworthy and reliable (and thus will not give you an altered document) and that the person did not illegally acquire the document (such as by stealing it from an office).

This chapter can provide only a summary of the process for legally obtaining public documents, but there are several useful guides that you should consult for further information.[80]

Each of the 50 states has its own statutes regarding access to public government records, but there are two federal statutes that deal specifically with U.S. government documents—the 1966 Freedom of Information Act (FOIA)[81] and the 1974 Privacy Act.[82]

The 1966 Freedom of Information Act

The FOIA generally mandates that all federal executive and independent regulatory agencies (a) publish in the *Federal Register* descriptions of its central and field organizations and the employees from whom and the process by which the public can obtain records from the agency; (b) make available for public inspection all final opinions and orders made in the adjudication of cases as well as statements of policy and interpretation adopted by the agency, administrative manuals as well as current indexes providing identifying information to the public about any issued, adopted or promulgated by the agency after July 4, 1967 (the effective date of the act). Each agency is also required to publish at least quarterly and distribute copies of each index and to promulgate regulations regarding the schedule of fees for the processing of FOIA requests and the conditions under which fees will be reduced or waived. The upshot is that the agency must, on request, indicate the procedures and fees involved in obtaining records and make those documents readily available.

There are some limitations to the act, however. First, it applies only to federal agencies, not to state and local agencies, although, as previously noted, most state statutes make such records available at the state and local levels. Second, there are nine *exemptions*, discussed shortly, that prevent many documents from being accessible. Third, the statute does not apply to the courts or to Congress, which very conveniently exempted itself from the law. Finally, the information is not free, although agencies cannot charge for the first two hours of search time or for the first 100 pages of photocopies if the request is for noncommercial use. Even if fees are charged, a waiver or reduction can be granted "if disclosure of the information is in the public interest because it is likely to contribute significantly to public understanding of the operations or activities of the government and is not primarily in the commercial interest of the requester."[83] Journalists routinely ask for this waiver because news stories based on such documents generally do increase public awareness about the activities of government and newsgathering is one of the purposes Congress had in mind when the statute was written. Indeed, this is reflected by the fact that an agency can impose "reasonable standard charges for document search, duplication, and review, when records are requested for commercial use," but it can charge educational or noncommercial scientific institutions "whose purpose is scholarly or scientific research . . . or a representative of the news media" only fees for duplication, not for search and review.[84]

There are nine exemptions that permit an agency to withhold a record from the public. Matters that are:

1. specifically authorized under criteria established by an executive order to be kept secret in the interest of national defense or foreign policy and that is properly classified;

2. related solely to the internal personnel rules and practices of an agency;

3. exempted under another federal statute;

4. trade secrets and commercial or financial information obtained from a person and privileged or confidential;

5. inter-agency or intra-agency memoranda or letters;

6. "personnel and medical files and similar files the disclosure of which would constitute a clearly unwarranted invasion of privacy";

7. records or information compiled for law enforcement whose disclosure (a) could reasonably be expected to interfere with enforcement proceedings, (b) would deprive a person the right to a fair trial, (c) could reasonably be expected to be an unwarranted invasion of privacy, (d) could reasonably be expected to identify a confidential source, (e) would include law enforcement techniques, procedures or guidelines for investigations or prosecutions or (f) could reasonably be expected to endanger the life or physical safety of someone;

8. concerning the examination, operation or condition of a financial institution; and

9. geological and geophysical information and data, including maps, concerning wells.[85]

An agency cannot refuse to provide a record simply because some of the information in it would fall under one or more of the exemptions. Instead the FOIA provides that any "reasonably segregable portion of a record shall be provided to any person requesting such record after deletion of the portions which are exempt.[86]

Several of the exemptions have been tested in court and thus deserve some discussion. A loophole in Exemption 1 become apparent in 1973 when the U.S. Supreme Court held that the exemption (as then worded, without the reference to "properly classified") did not permit a U.S. District Court to conduct even an *in camera* inspection of records concerning an underground nuclear test, thus effectively granting the executive branch the sole discretion in determining what could be classified.[87] Congress rather quickly remedied that problem with a 1974 amendment that granted the courts the authority to conduct in camera inspections of documents whose disclosure is being sought to determine whether they have been properly classified.[88] Unfortunately, much of the impact of the new law was buffered by the fact that Congress instructed the courts to grant considerable deference to agencies in making the determination on matters of national security, and the federal courts have followed the directions well. The provision also has little teeth because the President determines by executive order the particular classification system. Currently, that system is one instituted by then-President Ronald Reagan, which President George Bush continued. Under Executive Order No. 12,356,[89] the test for classification is simply whether disclosure could reasonably be expected to endanger national security, and the classification can continue for as long as its disclosure could harm national security, theoretically forever (although the executive order does permit agencies to establish predetermined declassification dates at their discretion). The executive order even permits documents that have been declassified to be reclassified, including *after* an FOIA request has been filed. In other words, an agency could classify a document that was not already classified *after* it was requested under the FOIA.[90]

Department of Air Force v. Rose (1976): Exemption 2

Only one major U.S. Supreme Court decision has dealt directly with Exemption 2. In 1976 the Court ruled 5–3 in *Department of Air Force v. Rose*[91] that this exemption did not exempt from disclosure Air Force Academy case summaries, with identifying information excised, of Honors and Ethics Codes hearings because the purpose of the provision was to relieve federal agencies of the task of assembling and maintaining records that have no reasonable public interest value and thus are not applicable to matters of "genuine and significant public interest." The case arose when the *New York Law Review* was denied access to summaries of honors and ethics hearings even though the academy routinely posted this information and distributed it to faculty and administrators. The Air Force Academy also contended the records could be withheld under Exemption 6, but the Court rejected that argument as well, holding that "Exemption 6 does not protect against disclosure every incidental invasion of privacy—only such disclosures as constitute 'clearly unwarranted' invasions of personal privacy."[92] The majority opinion, written by Justice Brennan, noted the case summaries had no names, except Cadets determined to be guilty, and that they were widely disseminated within the academy.

Exemption 3

Only two Supreme Court cases have dealt specifically with the third exemption. Both have limited applicability, but shed some light on the exemption. First, in *Consumer Product Safety Commission v. GTE Sylvania* (1980),[93] the Court held that the Consumer Product Safety Commission (CPSC) was bound under the 1972 Consumer Product Safety Act rather than the FOIA in disclosing television-related accident reports. The purpose of Exemption 3 is to allow government agencies to withhold information even though it would otherwise have to be disclosed under the FOIA if there is a statute already permitting such withholding. In *CPSC v. GTE*, however, the safety commission released reports from television manufacturers to two consumer organizations, Consumers Union and the Public Citizen's Health Research Group, including reports—provided at the request of the commission—that the companies claimed were confidential. Under the 1972 act, the agency was required to notify the manufacturers at least 30 days before the information was released so they would have an opportunity to respond in advance. In a unanimous opinion written by Justice Rehnquist, the Court ruled that the CPSC Act took priority over the FOIA and thus the commission should not have released the report without the 30 days notice.

In the second case, *CIA v. Sims* (1985),[94] the Court unanimously held that the names of 185 researchers at more than 80 universities who had received funding from the Central Intelligence Agency to study the effects on humans of mind-altering drugs did not have to be disclosed under the FOIA. Even though two people had reportedly died and others suffered mental problems as a result of the MKULTRA experiments—including the powerful hallucinogen LSD, which in some cases had been administered without the knowledge of the individuals—the Court ruled the National Security Act of 1947 took precedence. Under the act, Congress granted the CIA director the authority to prevent unauthorized disclosure of intelligence sources. CIA files on the project were declassified in 1970, four years after the project ended.[95] The CIA made public all but 21 names of participating universities when a request was filed by the Public Citizen Health Research Group; they claimed these 21 schools had been promised confidentiality. The Court, in line with the intent of Congress, gave considerable deference to the agency, noting that Congress had granted the CIA director "very broad authority to protect from disclosure all sources of intelligence information."[96]

It is clear from this decision that the U.S. Supreme Court strongly defers to agency heads in determining the kinds of information that can be withheld under Exemption 3. Very often that authority lies in the enabling statute that created the agency.

Exemption 4

The first test of Exemption 4 came in 1979 in *Chrysler Corp. v. Brown*,[97] in which the Supreme Court ruled in what is known as a "reverse FOIA suit" that the FOIA gave federal agencies the authority to release certain kinds of information that private corporations and individuals had submitted to the agency, including trade secrets and other types of confidential information. The case arose when the Defense Logistics Agency (DLA) received a FOIA request for information about Chrysler's affirmative action policies. Chrysler had been required under federal statutes to provide the information to the Department of Labor because the company had several contracts with the federal government. (The DLA is the equal opportunity employment compliance agency for the Department of Defense.) Before the DLA could release the information, which it had decided should be publicly disclosed, Chrysler successfully sought an injunction in U.S. District Court for the District of Delaware to bar release of the data. The Third Circuit U.S. Court of Appeals overturned the trial court order, and the U.S. Supreme Court upheld the lower appellate court ruling and remanded the case back to the district court. The Court unanimously held that the FOIA did not grant the company any private right of action to stop such disclosures even when they involve possible trade secrets. The Court gave the message that the FOIA is a disclosure statute and thus the exemptions *permit but do not require* federal agencies to withhold the release of documents that fall within one or more of the exemptions.

The impact of the *Chrysler* decision was buffered somewhat by a 1986 executive order issued by President Reagan,[98] which required agencies to notify companies when an FOIA request has been filed for information they have submitted. The order, which is still in effect, also allows the corporation to comment on whether the data should be released and provides a 10-day period for the company to seek an injunction or other relief in court to stop the release if the agency decides to grant the FOIA request.

Exemption 5

Exemption 5 was designed to protect predecisional information, such as working drafts of documents, preliminary reports, tentative recommendations and similar materials that are part of the decision-making process. The idea is that agency personnel should be able to discuss matters under consideration without fear of disclosure before a final decision is made. Once the decision is final, of course, the agency is required to release the specific details, but administrators can engage in an freewheeling, confidential exchange while matters are under consideration. This exemption also includes agency–attorney communication as well as information obtained by the government in civil suits during the discovery phase when the agency is involved in the litigation. In *Federal Open Market Committee v. David R. Merrill*,[99] the Court ruled that the Federal Reserve Board could, as permitted by law, delay the release of certain monetary policy directives during the time they are in effect, usually a month, after which they appear in the *Federal Register*. According to the Court, this information met the definition of intra-agency memoranda "not available by law to a party other than another agency in litigation with the agency."[100]

Four years later in *Federal Trade Commission v. Grolier, Inc.* (1983),[101] the U.S. Supreme Court ruled that the work-product of government attorneys meets the criteria of Exemption 5, regardless of the status of the litigation involved. The effect of the decision was to make the working documents of federal agency attorneys privileged until the government chooses to make them public so long as such documents would traditionally be privileged under the Federal Rules of Civil Procedure. The case involved an FOIA request filed by Grolier, an encyclopedia publisher, with the Federal Trade Commission (FTC) for documents complied by FTC attorneys in a lawsuit against the company for deceptive sales practices. The suit was dismissed with prejudice (meaning the commission could not bring the same suit again against the publisher). According to its own testimony at trial, Grolier had sought the documents to determine how much the FTC had learned about its sales techniques through secret monitoring of door-to-door salespersons. The Court sided with the commission, however, contending that because it was silent about the status of litigation, Exemption 5 included work-product materials even when the litigation had presumably ended.

Exemption 6: *U.S. Department of State v. Washington Post Co.* (1982)

Exemption 6 has spurred considerable controversy and litigation. The first U.S. Supreme Court case involving the exemption was handed down in a unanimous decision in 1982. It held that "similar files" included information about the citizenship status of foreign nationals. *U.S. Department of State v. Washington Post Co.*[102] concerned an FOIA request filed by the *Washington Post* with the U.S. Department of State to determine whether two Iranian nationals living in Iran had valid U.S. passports. The Supreme Court ruled in favor of the State Department denial, agreeing that disclosure could constitute "a clearly unwarranted invasion of the personal privacy" of the two men since disclosure could threaten their safety in Iran because of intense anti-American feelings in the country. The justices remanded the case back to the District of Columbia U.S. Court of Appeals for a final determination.

The Supreme Court rejected the newspaper's claim that "similar files" was not intended to include all files with personal information but instead those with intimate details and highly personal information. According to the Court, Congress intended for the exemption to include detailed government documents on a person that "can be identified as applying to that individual," thus granting a broad definition to "similar files."

A rather unusual case involving Exemption 6 developed in 1986 when the *New York Times* sought the tape recording of the astronauts' voice communications just prior to the tragic explosion of the space shuttle *Challenger* on January 28 of that year. All seven crew members died as the space shuttle self-destructed 73 seconds after lift-off. In *New York Times v. NASA*,[103] the District of Columbia U.S. Circuit Court of Appeals affirmed a U.S. District Court decision ordering NASA to release the tape. The appellate court applied a two-prong test in determining whether the recording fell under the exemption: "The threshold question is whether the material at issue is contained in a personnel, medical, or similar file. If it is, the court must then balance the individual and governmental interests involved in order to determine whether disclosure would constitute a clearly unwarranted invasion of privacy" (citations omitted).[104]

The District Court ruled that the tape did not meet the threshold requirement and the Court of Appeals affirmed, concluding "that the information recorded on the tape is 'unrelated to any particular person' and therefore is not a similar file."[105] In 1990 the DC Circuit met en banc (with the full court participating rather than a panel of three) and reversed the earlier decision, holding that the tape was sufficiently similar to personnel and medical files so as to fall under Exemption 6. Upon remand, the District Court then ruled that releasing the tape would constitute a "clearly unwarranted" invasion of privacy and thus the tape was not made available.[106]

Exemption 7: *Department of Justice v. Reporters Committee for Freedom of the Press* (1989)

There has also been a great deal of litigation involving Exemption 7. It is clear in exemption 7 that the FOIA generally does not apply to records or information compiled for law enforcement purposes. However, such information is unavailable only to the extent that release of the information would meet one or more of the six standards listed in the exemption such as the disclosure would interfere with judicial proceedings, could reasonably be expected to disclose a confidential source or endanger the life or physical safety of a person. Probably the most important U.S. Supreme Court decision involving the exemption occurred in 1989 in *Department of Justice v. Reporters Committee for Freedom of the Press*[107] in which the Court unanimously ruled that reporters have no right under the FOIA to obtain computerized FBI criminal identification records, commonly known as "rap sheets." The Reporters Committee and CBS reporter Robert Schakne sought the FBI rap sheet on Charles Medico, whose company had allegedly won defense contracts with the U.S. government with the assistance of a member of the House of Representatives to whom the company had made substantial campaign contributions. The Justice Department refused to release the information on the ground that the disclosure "could reasonably be expected to be an unwarranted invasion of personal privacy," although it did release the records of Medico's three brothers—who were also allegedly involved in the scheme—after they died. The committee argued that much of the information in the rap sheets had already been made public anyway in state and local police and court records, but the Court disagreed: "Plainly there is a vast difference between the public records that might be found after a diligent search of courthouse files, county archives, and local police stations throughout the country and a computerized summary located in a single clearinghouse of information."[108] The Court also noted that the FBI maintains rap sheets on more than 24 million individuals and keeps the information on file until the person dies or attains age 80. The central purpose, according to the opinion written by Justice Stevens, "is to ensure that the government's activities be open to the sharp eye of public scrutiny, not that the information about private citizens that happens to be in the warehouse of government be so disclosed."[109]

In an earlier decision, the Court upheld the National Labor Relations Board's denial of potential witnesses' statements collected during a federal investigation of the labor practices of a tire company.[110] The majority opinion said that the information met the criteria of "investigatory records compiled for law enforcement purposes" that could reasonably be expected to interfere with enforcement proceedings. Finally, in 1982 the Court ruled 5–4 in *FBI v. Abramson*[111] that Exemption 7 was broad enough to include information originally compiled in the form of law enforcement records but that had been summarized as a new document not created for law enforcement. Howard Abramson, a freelance writer, was denied his FOIA request for a memo written by former FBI Director J. Edgar Hoover to Watergate conspirator John Erlichman. Abramason was also denied access to some 63 pages of "name check" summaries on various political targets of President Nixon's administration. According to the Court, once an agency has determined the information was compiled for a legitimate law enforcement purpose and that disclosure would cause one of the six types of harm, the information continued to be exempt even if recreated in a new form.

Exemption 8 and 9

The last two exemptions have stimulated little litigation, although Exemption 8 may be severely tested as more and more financial institutions fail; consider how the savings and loan scandals of the 1980s showed the underbelly of that segment of the financial industry.

Summary and Conclusions

The Federal Freedom of Information Act, which was strengthened by the Freedom of Information Reform Act of 1986, has generally granted much greater access of the press and the public to federal records. Unfortunately, the courts and the executive branch continue to place barriers to access. Occasionally, Congress knocks down the obstacles with mending legislation, but progress has been relatively slow. In 1992, for example, Congress passed a bill that was signed into law by President Bush to speed up the disclosure of federal documents about President John F. Kennedy's 1961 assassination. All information in the hands of the government will eventually have to be made available to the public, but a board of individuals appointed by the President would have the authority to delay disclosure when there would be a possible violation of national security or an invasion of individual privacy. In the same year, the U.S. Court of Appeals for the DC Circuit meeting *en banc* ruled 7–4 that the federal Nuclear Regulatory Commission (NRC) could deny a public interest group access to reports provided voluntarily to the NRC by the nuclear utilities industry.[112] The Court said such information would fall under Exemption 4 if it ordinarily would not have been released to the government without a promise of confidentiality, as was the case here. The U.S. Supreme Court was expected to have the final say.

ACCESS TO MEETINGS

Access to meetings of federal, state and local governmental agencies is no longer a major problem for the mass media. Since Congress passed the "Government in the Sunshine Act,"[113] which took effect on March 12, 1977, the meetings of all major federal agencies (such as the Federal Trade Commission and the Federal Communications Commission) have been open to the press and to the public. The exceptions are parallel to those of the FOIA, with two additions — (a) agencies responsible for regulating financial institutions, currencies, securities and commodities can close meetings that could lead to "significant financial speculation" or "significantly endanger the stability of a financial institution" and (b) meetings involving certain litigation matters such as issuing a subpoena or initiating a civil action. There have been few legal challenges to those meetings that have been closed, although some agencies are much more likely than others to broadly apply the exemptions. All 50 states and the District of Columbia have similar open meetings statutes, with some states offering greater access by having fewer exemptions and opening up more agencies.

10 Intellectual Property

Intellectual property is a relatively new term that describes three traditional areas of law: copyright, trademarks and patents. Most of this chapter is devoted to copyright because this is the area with the most substantial impact on mass communication, but we also deal briefly with the other two as well. The constitutional origins of intellectual property, at least for copyright and patents, can be traced to Article I, 8, of the U.S. Constitution, which provides, among other powers, that Congress shall have the authority "to promote the Progress of Science and useful Arts, by securing for limited Times to Authors and Inventors the exclusive Right to their respective Writings and Discoveries." Patents and copyrights are regulated almost exclusively by federal statutes (Title 35 and Title 17 of the U.S. Code, respectively) because Congress has chosen to invoke the preemption doctrine granted under Article VI of the U.S. Constitution (known as the "supremacy clause"), which provides in part: "This Constitution, and the Laws of the United States which shall be made in Pursuance thereof; and all Treaties made, or which shall be made, under the Authority of the United States, shall be the supreme law of the Land; and the Judges in every State shall be bound thereby, any Thing in the Constitution or Laws of any State to the Contrary notwithstanding."

Exclusive federal regulation of copyrights and patents is also justified under the "commerce clause" in Article I, 8 of the U.S. Constitution, which provides that Congress shall have the power "to regulate Commerce with foreign Nations, and among the several States, and with the Indian Tribes."

Trademarks, on the other hand, involve both state and federal law, although state laws are not permitted to conflict with federal law, which can be found primarily in Title 15 of the U.S. Code (known as the "Lanham Act"). Thus a trademark can be registered and have protection under either state or federal statutes.

PATENTS

Although the U.S. Copyright Office is an arm of the Library of Congress, the U.S. Patent and Trademark Office (which, as the name indicates, handles both patents and trademarks) is an agency in the Department of Commerce and is headed by the Commissioner of Patents and Trademarks, an Assistant Secretary of Commerce. Patents, trademarks and copyright are all forms of **exclusive** (i.e., monopolistic) **control** that owners, who can be individuals or companies, can exercise to insure that others generally cannot market, use or sell the work, invention or mark without consent of the owner. Patents usually have protection for one 17-year term, after which they pass to the public domain and can be used, marketed or sold to anyone without consent. In rare cases, the 17-year period can be extended for a maximum of 5 years when marketing time is lost because of regulatory delay.[1] When a patent expires for a popular drug or invention, the impact on the marketplace can be strong. For example, witness the proliferation of marketers of the artificial sweetener, aspartame, when the Monsato Co.'s patent expired in December 1992. Whereas the name NutraSweet continued to be protected as a trademark, any company could market aspartame under its own name or simply as a generic product with approval of the U.S. Food and Drug Administration (FDA), which regulates artificial sweeteners. By the way, securing a patent is typically only the first step in the process. Before the invention can be marketed, approval from other federal and state agencies may be needed. For example, a new food product or drug would probably require a green light from the FDA. Protecting a name under which the invention is to be sold would require compliance with provisions of trademark laws and probably trademark registration at some point.

Unlike the trademark and copyright laws, patent law is incredibly complex, and the process of obtaining a patent is expensive, time consuming and complicated. Even most attorneys have a limited knowledge of patent law. It is important, however, for journalists who may be covering stories dealing with patents to have at least an understanding of the fundamentals of patent law and especially the distinction among the three areas of intellectual property.

There are three basic types of patents: *utility*, *plant* and *design*. Patents on mechanical devices, electrical and electronic circuits, chemicals and similar items are known as *utility patents*.[2] *Plant patents* apply to the invention or asexual reproduction of a distinct new variety of a natural plant,[3] and design *patents* are issued for new, original and ornamental designs.[4] Under the federal statute, an invention **cannot** be patented if "the subject matter as a whole would have been obvious at the time the invention was made to a person having ordinary skill in the art."[5] Many patent applications have failed because the invention was too obvious.

The patent application process is beyond the scope of this book, but it should be noted that patents and patent applications are public records, although accessing them can be laborious, especially for the amateur. Many of the records of the patent and trademark office are now computerized, and several companies, including Mead Data Central and Dialog Information Services, offer databases that can be searched for specified fees. If you plan to do any serious research on patents for a news story, you may want to take a primer course on patents if you have time and one is offered nearby. Universities often offer these for laypersons. At the very least, you should read the basic literature available from the Patent and Trademark Office (PTO) in Washington, DC.[6] Occasionally, patent cases, especially those involving infringement, become news, and you should be prepared to cover them as you would any other specialized story. A good example of a patent case that attracted considerable media attention for years was the infringement suit over instant photography filed by Polaroid against Eastman Kodak.[7] When the dust had settled in 1986, Eastman Kodak was ordered to pay Polaroid more than $1 billion in damages and was prohibited from further sales of instant photo cameras, film and related products. The suit was based on patents granted to Polaroid in the 1970s. The stakes can be quite high, so patent holders for popular inventions rigorously defend their rights even against small-time entrepreneurs and companies. Patents are generally granted on a first-come, first-serve basis, and the race to the finish line can be intense when competitors battle. When two or more claimants apply separately for a patent on inventions that are essentially similar, the PTO will hold an *interference proceeding*, complete with motions and testimony, to ascertain the rightful inventor.

Finally, patent applications are processed by the PTO, but infringement suits and other legal wrangles occur in the federal courts. All trials are held in a U.S. District Court, as with any other federal matter, but appeals may be heard initially **only** in the U.S. Court of Appeals for the Federal Circuit. As October 1, 1982, appeals may not be filed in patent cases in any of the other 11 circuits. The PTO can issue patents **only** for the United States and its territories. An inventor typically must file separate applications to secure patent protection in other countries because there is no universal patent, although all of the major Western European countries belong to the European Patent Convention and the Paris Convention, which allow Europeanwide registration, and there is a Patent Cooperation Treaty that may someday provide universal patent registration.[8]

TRADEMARKS

The Patent and Trademark Office also handles trademark registration, but the process is much different and far less expensive than that for patents. In fact, copyright and trademark registration involve similar processes, even though each is administered by a different federal agency. However, the similarities between trademarks and copyright end there. Unlike copyright and patents, trademarks do not derive their origin from the U.S. Constitution, although the authority of Congress to regulate trademarks and service marks comes from the Constitution — more specifically, the infamous commerce clause mentioned earlier in this chapter. Trademarks and service marks are statutory creations of the states and the federal government. Trademark laws vary considerably from state to state, consequently state laws are not discussed here. However, some trademarks and service marks — those that are **not** used or intended to be used in interstate and/or international commerce between the United States and another country — can be registered and protected **only** under state law. Before a trademark or service mark can be registered under federal law (i.e., the Lanham Act), the owner must either (a) use the mark on goods that are shipped or sold in interstate or international commerce, or (b) have a bona fide intention to use the mark in such commerce.[9]

Until the Trademark Law Revision Act of 1988,[10] which became effective November 16, 1989, a trademark essentially had to actually have been used in some form of interstate commerce, but the new law permits registration so long as there is a bona fide *intent* to use it in interstate commerce. Nevertheless, trademarks that are strictly for intrastate use are registered with the Secretary of State in the state where they will be used.

The registration process and protection under federal law for trademarks and service marks are the same. Under the Lanham Act, a *trademark* is defined as "any word, name, symbol, or device, or any combination thereof adopted and used by a manufacturer or merchant to identify his or her goods or services."[11] Thus a trademark can be a slogan, design or even a distinctive sound so long as it identifies and distinguishes the goods or services from those of others. The key characteristics are **identification** and **distinction**. Trademarks and service marks differ in that the former is used to identify and distinguish goods, whereas the latter accomplishes this for services. To avoid repetition, we use the term *trademark* to refer to both trademarks and service marks throughout this chapter.

The Trademark Revision Act of 1988 also makes use prior to registration of the trademark unnecessary. Now, the trademark owner needs only to have a bona fide *intention* to use the mark. The new law also cut the term of registration in half — from 20 years to 10 years. Unlike copyrights and patents, which have limited duration, trademarks can last indefinitely if the owner takes appropriate steps to ensure that infringers are prosecuted and that the mark does not go on to the public domain. Protection can also be lost by abandonment.

Contrary to popular myth, registration is **not** necessary for a trademark to have protection. As with copyright (discussed shortly), there are some important advantages to registration, but it is not required. The following are some of these advantages:

1. It provides prima facie evidence of first use of the mark in interstate commerce and of the validity of the registration.

2. It permits the owner to sue in federal court (U.S. District Court) for infringement.

3. It allows lost profits, court costs, attorneys' fees, criminal penalties and treble damages, in some cases, to be sought.

4. It serves as constructive notice of an ownership claim, preventing someone from claiming that the trademark was used because of a good faith belief that no one else had claim to it. In other words, once the mark is registered, any potential user has an obligation to check the registry to ascertain that no one else owns the mark.

5. It establishes a basis for foreign registration.

Registration is a fairly simple process, although it is more complicated than copyright registration and much easier than securing a patent. First, owners or their attorney file (a) an application form (available from the Patent and Trademark Office), (b) a drawing of the mark, (c) a $175 filing fee for each class of goods or services for which the owner is applying, and (d) three specimens showing actual use of the mark on goods or services **if the mark has been used in commerce**. Once the PTO has received the application materials, a Trademark Examining Attorney must decide if the mark can actually be registered. This decision is then sent to the applicant about three months after the application is filed. A refusal can be appealed to the Trademark Trial and Appeal Board, an administrative tribunal in the PTO. Further refusal can then be appealed to a U.S. District Court and to the U.S. Court of Appeals for the Federal Circuit. The U.S. Supreme Court has jurisdiction to hear further appeals, but rarely does so. Once approval is granted, the mark is published in the Trademark Official Gazette, a weekly bulletin from the PTO. Anyone opposing the registration has 30 days after the publication to file a protest with the Trademark Trial and Appeal Board, which acts very much like a trial court. If there is no opposition, about 12 weeks after the mark is published, the registration then becomes official if the application was based on **actual use** in commerce. If the application is, instead, based on an **intention** to use the mark in commerce, the trademark owner then has 6 months to either use the mark in commerce, or request a 6 months extension. (Once the mark is used, a Statement of Use form must be filed.)

A journalist covering a trademark story should be very familiar with the registration process because it can play a major role in determining the outcome of an infringement suit or a suit over ownership of the mark. A good start is the PTO booklet, *Basic Facts About Trademarks*. The U.S. Trademark Association, a private organization in New York City, also publishes informative materials. Trademark battles can be intense and drawn-out because millions and sometimes even billions of dollars may be at stake. The basic purpose of a trademark is to enable the consumer, which can range from a private individual to a business conglomerate, to identify the source of a product or service, which may be a manufacturer, distributor, franchise or whatever. Through the effective marketing and communication of its trademark, an owner can build up invaluable market goodwill. Think about the value of trademarks such as Coca-Cola, McDonald's, IBM, Kodak, Xerox, Sony, Walt Disney and so forth. Coca-Cola, which has already celebrated its 100th anniversary, is such a valuable trademark that the corporation has licensed its own line of clothing. Walt Disney licenses or produces thousands of products, including toys, movies, clothes, games and, of course, its own entertainment complexes throughout the world. Famous service marks include Hertz, Avis, Home Box Office, The Movie Channel, Showtime, Citicorp, True Value and Minit-Lube.

Marks can be excluded from registration on the grounds that the mark:

1. Disparages or falsely suggests a connection with people, organizations, beliefs or national symbols or brings them into contempt or disrepute.
2. Consists of or simulates the flag, coat of arms or other insignia of the United States, a state, a city or any foreign country.
3. Is immoral, deceptive or scandalous.
4. Is the name, portrait or signature of a living person unless he or she has given permission.
5. Is the name, portrait or signature of a deceased U.S. President while his or her surviving spouse is alive unless the spouse has given consent.
6. Is so similar to a mark previously registered that it would be likely to confuse or deceive a reasonable person.
7. Is simply descriptive or deceptively misdescriptive of the goods or services.

If an applicant can demonstrate that a mark already being used in commerce has become distinctive enough that the public now identifies the goods or services with the mark, it can be registered even if it is merely descriptive. *World's Finest*, for example, is a registered trademark of World's Finest Chocolate, Inc.

Trademark registration is not restricted to commercial enterprises, of course. Nonprofit organizations, trade associations and other groups as well as individuals can register trademarks. For example, the Society of Professional Journalists (SPJ) registered its name and logo along with the name, Sigma Delta Chi, as trademarks in 1991. Trade names such as International Business Machines Corporation and Pepsi-Cola Bottling Company **cannot** be registered as trademarks under the federal statute, but the name associated with the product or service (i.e., International Business Machines, IBM, Pepsi-Cola, Pepsi, etc.) **can** be registered and the corporation name can be filed and registered with the appropriate official (usually the Secretary of State) in each state.

Some of the owners of very popular trademarks—such as Xerox, IBM, Kleenex and Kodak—sometimes purchase ads in professional publications such as *Editor & Publisher, Broadcasting* and the *Quill* (published by SPJ) informing journalists that their names are registered trademarks and should be identified as such. As a Xerox ad from *Quill* magazine indicates, many famous former trademarks—such as cornflakes, linoleum, mimeograph, escalator and raisin bran—went into public domain and thus lost their protection as trademarks because they were abandoned or the owners did not aggressively fight infringers. Thus Xerox places ads requesting that its trademark be used as a "proper adjective in conjunction with our products and services . . . and never as a verb." News stories can certainly mention trademarks without identifying them as such, but, as *The Associated Press Stylebook and Libel Manual* ("The Journalist's Bible") notes in its "trademark" entry, "In general, use a generic equivalent unless the trademark name is essential to the story."[12] The *Stylebook* also says that trademarks should be capitalized when they appear. Some companies have a reputation for notifying newspapers, magazines and radio and television stations when they believe their trademarks have been used inappropriately. Most likely, they feel this is one way of demonstrating a strong effort to protect the marks in case an infringement occurs and they have to counter the claim from a defendant that the mark has become generic and thus may no longer be worthy of protection. Although a company would have no real basis for claiming infringement simply because a news or feature story makes generic use of a trademark, good journalistic practice would dictate that the use of a trademark should be necessary to the story or, at least, enhance it. Why not say "He photocopied the paper" instead of "He Xeroxed the paper" or "She gulped a cola" rather than "She gulped a Dr. Pepper"? The second use may be perceived by the reader as a subtle form of advertising even though the writer may argue that the specific name lends color and detail to the story. When trademarks become news, of course, specific names have to be mentioned, and there are other situations in which the use of a trademark may be justified.

Thousands of court battles have been fought over trademarks over products from beer to cars. Even universities have entered the fray. In 1989 Toyota and Mead Data General fought in U.S. District Court over Toyota's use of *Lexus* as the trademark for its new line of luxury cars. Mead Data argued that the car line name was so similar to *Lexis*, the trademark for Mead's computerized information retrieval service, that consumers would be confused. Toyota argued that consumers did not confuse *Pulsar* cars by Nissan with *Pulsar* watches or *Lotus* computer software with *Lotus* autos. Ultimately, U.S. District Court Judge David N. Edelstein agreed with Toyota and permitted the registration; the Second Circuit U.S. Court of Appeals upheld the decision.[13] In 1990, Toyota also changed the logo for the cars under its own name to one with three ellipses.

In 1989 the PTO Trademark Trial and Appeal Board affirmed the decision of the Trademark Examining Attorney that Churchill Downs, Inc., in Louisville, Kentucky, be allowed to register *The Kentucky Derby* as a trademark for use on various consumer goods. The registration had been challenged by a gift shop operator who argued that the slogan was merely descriptive or generic. Products licensed include a *Derby Pie*, a great chocolate and pecan pie that has spawned numerous copycats, none of which can bear the *Derby Pie* trademark without consent.

In the same year, Harvard University became the last Ivy League school to register its name as a trademark. More than 100 colleges and universities have registered their names as trademarks. Usually the schools then license their products through one of the major licensing firms for a set fee and a percentage of the profits from the sale of products.

Some registration attempts have been unsuccessful—for example, the G. Anheuser-Busch Inc.'s failed effort with the mark, *LA*, for its low alcohol beer. The Seventh Circuit U.S. Court of Appeals upheld the decision of a U.S. District Court that *LA* was merely descriptive and thus had not acquired the requisite *secondary meaning*, or distinctiveness, as described previously. According to the court, the common sense view holds "that, as a practical matter, initials do not usually differ significantly in their trademark role from the description words that they represent . . . [and thus] . . . there is a heavy burden on a trademark claimant seeking to show an independent meaning of initials apart from the descriptive words which are their source."[14]

Once the federal registration is issued by the PTO (usually about six months after the application is filed if there is no opposition from another party and if the Trademark Examining Attorney gives the OK), the owner gives notice of registration by using the ® symbol, or the phrase, *Registered in U.S. Patent and Trademark Office*, or the abbreviation, *Reg. U.S. Pat. & Tm. Off.* These registration symbols cannot be used before registration, but owners are free to use TM or SM as symbols for trademark and service mark, respectively, although they are not required to do so. Recall that under the federal statute, registration is not required for trademark protection, although there are many advantages to registration (as enumerated earlier).

The Trademark Law Revision Act of 1988 made another important change that may have an impact on some nontraditional forms of mass media, especially some parodies. The act includes a provision that permits a trademark owner to recover damages and, under other provisions of the act, to get an injunction for product or service misrepresentation. The provision applies only to commercial use, not to political communication and not to editorial content, but it is apparently aimed at specific product disparagement, although some forms—such as that in *L. L. Bean, Inc. v. Drake Publishers, Inc.* (1987)[15]—may continue to be protected. When Drake published a sex catalog parodying L. L. Bean's famous clothing catalog, L. L. Bean filed suit, claiming that *L. L. Beam's Back-to-School-Sex-Catalog* violated Maine's antidilution statute. (Such statutes are aimed at protecting trademarks and similar names from suffering disparagement and thus having their commercial value chipped away through unauthorized use.) The First Circuit U.S. Court of Appeals ruled that because the sex catalog was noncommercial use, the antidilution statute could not be used under the First Amendment to prohibit its publication. (L. L. Bean had sought an injunction against the parody.)

If the sex catalog had been an attempt to actually market products rather than simply an artistic endeavor and had it been published after the new act took effect on November 16, 1989, the Court would probably have ruled in favor of L. L. Bean. Recall that Larry Flynt's notorious Campari parody with Jerry Falwell (discussed in chap. 7) had First Amendment protection, according to the U.S. Supreme Court. The manufacturer of Campari took no legal action against Flynt but would probably have been unsuccessful anyway because the ad was editorial content, not commercial speech.

Two common mistakes journalists make with trademarks are (a) confusing trademarks with other forms of intellectual property, especially copyright, and (b) failing to recognize trademarks. An example of the first type of error occurred in September 1990 in news stories about the new NC-17 rating instituted by the Motion Picture Association of America (MPAA). Several major newspapers and at least one wire service reported pornographic moviemakers started using the noncopyrighted X rating in the early 1970s, but the new NC-17 rating is copyrighted. We will protect the guilty here by omitting the names of the offenders, but, suffice it to say, none of the ratings are copyrighted—they are instead registered trademarks! As covered in the next section, names and titles cannot be copyrighted, but they can become trademarks. Open up the entertainment section of your favorite newspaper and you will clearly see the registered trademark symbol dutifully stationed after the rating of each movie, along with the MPAA symbol, which is also a trademark. The MPAA deliberately chose not to protect the X rating, but it did so by not registering it as a trademark rather than not copyrighting it (which it could not do anyway). The distinction between a *trademark* and a *copyright* is very important, and journalists should understand the difference before using the terms, just as they would make sure whether a complaint filed was for a civil assault or a criminal assault or both before filing a story about a violent incident.

The second type of mistake is certainly the most common. Whereas a news story is not required to indicate when a term, symbol or phrase is a trademark, the *Associated Press Stylebook* rule (mentioned earlier) is a good practice. In some cases you may wish to do more than capitalize the trademark—you may want to actually point out that a particular symbol is or is not a trademark. *Olympic* and the Olympic symbol (three intertwined circles) are registered trademarks of the International Olympic Committee. Indeed, many businesses, including the U.S. Postal Service, have paid fees for the use of the Olympic trademarks, and yet Olympic is often used in news stories as a generic term. In fact, in 1987 the U.S. Supreme Court, in a 5–4 decision, held that the U.S. Olympic Committee had the exclusive right to use the term and symbol and could therefore bar a homosexual group from using the trademark in a Gay Olympics.[16] Even *Star Wars* was registered as a trademark by Lucasfilm, Ltd., owned by George Lucas and others, during the height of Star Wars mania.

The BBB symbol of the Better Business Bureau is a registered trademark, but the walking fingers logo of yellow page fame is not a trademark. Although the famous *L'eggs* package for women's hosiery is now history because the Sara Lee Corp. phased out the containers in 1992 in favor of cardboard packaging that is less harmful to the environment, both the old and the new containers are registered trademarks. (Distinctive packaging can be trademarked.) Sometimes trademarks are changed or even taken off the market at the behest or urging of government, or sometimes because of consumer perceptions. In 1991 the Kellogg Co. changed the name of its "Heartwise" cereal to "Fiberwise" under pressure from the U.S. Food and Drug Administration, which has a policy of discouraging the use of *heart* in brand names.[17] In the same year the U.S. Federal Trade Commission rescinded its initial approval of "Powermaster" as a brand name for a beer with a higher than usual percentage of alcohol because the FTC has a policy of banning brand names of alcohol that promote the alcohol content. And, the Procter & Gamble Co. (P & G) redesigned its decade-old moon and stars trademark, including eliminating the curly hairs in the man's beard that look like the number "6." Since 1981 the company has filed lawsuits and repeatedly issued statements that attempted to dispel rumors that P & G supported Satan because of the sixes that appeared in the symbol's beard. (The number 666 is mentioned in the Book of Revelation in connection with the devil.) The company said that it planned to continue using the trademark in its revised form, but that it would also use two new symbols—a scriptlike *Procter &*

Gamble and *P & G*.[18] In 1985 P & G began omitting the moon-and-stars emblem from most of its products. The company said it would continue using the symbol (in revised form) on buildings, awards and some stationery.[19]

Even radio and television call letters and sounds can be trademarked. Many stations have registered their calls and distinctive sound identifications to differentiate them in a highly competitive market in which call letters readily alert listeners and viewers to their favorite channels and frequencies (for example, FOX '100, COZY '95, Double-Q and ROCK '105).

Journalists do not have to do an extensive search to determine whether a slogan, name or symbol is a trademark, but they should at least look for the registered trademark symbol or the TM designation. It may appear in small type, but it is there to alert the world to the trademark's status.

Two final notes about trademarks. First, they can last **indefinitely** so long as they are aggressively protected to avoid dilution and infringement and not abandoned. As noted earlier, registration lasts 10 years, but it can be renewed every 10 years by filing a renewal application during the 6 months before the registration ends. (A renewal request can be made only during the 6 months before the last registration expires — not before and not later.) Second, trademarks, like patents and copyrights, can be sold and transferred by a written agreement or contract just as with other types of property. When corporations merge and large companies acquire smaller ones, the trademarks are often among the most valuable assets. Consumers rely very heavily on brand names or trademarks in their decisions, which is why a company will pay hundreds of millions of dollars to acquire an already well-established trademark for a brand of candy bar, for instance, rather than market a similar candy bar under a new trademark. The existing brand is a sure-winner; a new name could be a huge risk.

COPYRIGHT: AN INTRODUCTION

On January 1, 1978, the law of copyright changed dramatically when the Copyright Act of 1976 took effect, and the pieces of what was once a colossal mess acquired some long-needed order. Prior to January 1, 1978, copyright was governed principally by a federal statute known as the Copyright Act of 1909, which had been revised on numerous occasions over a period of almost 70 years to try to accommodate new technologies and unresolved problems. In 1909 there were no computers, compact discs, photocopy machines, satellites or television broadcasts, and even radio had reached only an experimental stage. Copyright infringement was certainly possible, and authors definitely needed protection, but it was much more difficult then than it is today to make unauthorized use of a person's creative work. The idea of copyright, though, was not new even in 1909. Copyright laws arose as early as the 15th century in

Europe with the development of movable type and mass printing, but they were employed largely as a mechanism for prior restraint in the form of licensing and not as a means for protecting authors. The first federal copyright statute was enacted by Congress in 1790, one year after the U.S. Constitution was ratified and a year before the Bill of Rights took effect. A two-tiered system emerged with the federal statute protecting principally published works and state common law governing unpublished works. That system essentially continued with the 1909 law but was eviscerated by the 1976 statute in favor of a system that made common law copyright unnecessary and theoretically nonexistent.

Congress is often criticized for its laborious, cumbersome and time-consuming decision making, and some of that criticism may be in order for the deliberations involved in formulating a new copyright statute in the 1970s. But the end result was a well-crafted, albeit imperfect, federal law that differs substantially from the old 1909 scheme. Even the premises of the two are at odds. As Kitch and Perlman noted, "Under the old law the starting principle was: the owner shall have the exclusive right to copy his copies. Under the new law the principle is: the owner shall have the exclusive right to exploit his work."[20] The new law is clearly an author-oriented statute that offers tremendous protection to the creators of original works of authorship.

THE OLD VERSUS THE NEW LAW

There are some other major differences that need only brief mention here because most of them are discussed in more detail later in this chapter. First, the duration of copyright protection was considerably increased, even for works that began their protection under the old law. As discussed later, the present general term of protection for most works is the author's lifetime plus 50 years, compared to two 28-year terms under the old law. Second, under the old law works could generally claim federal copyright protection only if they were published, but under the new law publication is not required. Third, the scope of both "exclusive rights" (rights initially conferred solely on the creator of the work) and the types of works included was considerably expanded. Finally, registration is no longer necessary for protection. There are other differences, but they are not substantial enough to warrant discussion here.

THE NATURE OF COPYRIGHT
UNDER THE NEW LAW

Because the Copyright Act of 1976 effectively killed common law copyright, under which states offered perpetual protection for *unpublished* works, copyright is now strictly a **federal statutory** matter—more precisely, it arises from Title 17 of the U.S. Code §§101-180 and subsequent revisions. Under §102, copyright protection extends to "original works of authorship fixed in any tangible medium of expression now known or later developed, from which they can be perceived, reproduced, or otherwise communicated, either directly or with the aid of a machine or device."[21] This section enumerates seven categories of under works of authorship:

1. literary works;
2. musical works, including any accompanying words;
3. dramatic works, including any accompanying music;
4. pantomimes and choreographic works;
5. pictorial, graphic and sculptural works;
6. motion pictures and other audiovisual works; and
7. sound recordings.[22]

Section 102 (b) notes that copyright protection does *not* extend to "any idea, procedure, process, system, method of operation, concept, principle, or discovery, regardless of the form in which it is described, explained, illustrated, or embodied in such work."[23] As discussed earlier, some of these entities may enjoy protection as trademarks or patents, but they cannot be copyrighted even though works in which they appear can be copyrighted. More on this shortly. Section 103 specifies that compilations and derivative works have copyright protection, but this protection extends only to the material contributed to the author of a compilation or derivative work. Thus any preexisting material used in the derivative work or compilation does not gain additional protection but maintains the same protection it had originally. In other words, you cannot expand the protection a work originally enjoyed by using it, whether in whole or in part, in another work (such as a derivative work or compilation).

Section 101, which contains definitions of terms in the statute, defines a *compilation* as "a work formed by the collection and assembling of preexisting materials or of data that are selected, coordinated, or arranged in such a way that the resulting work as a whole constitutes an original work of authorship."[24] Compilations also include *collective* works, which are defined as "a work, such as a periodical issue, anthology, or encyclopedia, in which a number of contributions, constituting separate and independent works in themselves, are assembled into a collective whole."[25] A *derivative* work is

a work based upon one or more preexisting works, such as a translation, musical arrangement, dramatization, fictionalization, motion picture version, sound recording, art reproduction, abridgment, condensation, or any other form in which a work may be recast, transformed, or adapted. A work consisting of editorial revisions, annotations, elaborations, or other modifications, which, as a whole, represent an original work of authorship, is a "derivative work."[26]

A *compilation* and a *derivative* work differ in that (a) a compilation consists of a pulling together of separate **works or pieces of works** already created, whereas a derivative work can trace its origins to **one previous work**; and (b) the key creative element in a compilation is the way in which the preexisting works are **compiled** to create the whole—that is, the new work, but the creative dimensions of a derivative work are basically independent of the previous work. An example of a derivative is the film *Gone with the Wind*, which was based on Margaret Mitchell's book by the same name. An anthology of poems by Robert Frost, which consisted of poems previously published on their own or in even in other anthologies, is an illustration of a compilation that is also a collective work.

With certain exemptions, such as "fair use" and compulsory licensing for nondramatic musical works (both discussed later), the owner, who is usually the creator, of an original work of authorship acquires **exclusive rights** that only that person can exercise or authorize others to exercise. **Exclusivity** is a very important concept under the current copyright law because copyright owners are essentially granted a monopoly over the use of their works. No matter how valuable a work may be in terms of its scholarship, commercial value, artistic quality or contribution to society, its copyright owner has the exclusive right to control its use and dissemination during the duration of the copyright. For example, Margaret Mitchell's heirs, who inherited the rights to her novel when she was killed by an auto in 1949, nixed any sequels to the enormously popular book and movie until 1988; at this point Warner Books paid $4.5 million at an estate auction for the right to publish a sequel, although the estate retained the right to choose the author. A series of sequels, including books and movies, would probably have brought in millions of dollars in royalties, but *Gone with the Wind* devotees dying to learn the fate of Rhett and Scarlet had to wait until 1991 when Alexandra Ripley's *Scarlett: The Sequel to Margaret Mitchell's Gone with the Wind* was published. The 768-page sequel was published simultaneously in 40 countries, with excerpts appearing a month earlier in *Life* magazine.

Under §106 these exclusive rights are:

1. to reproduce the copyrighted work in copies or phonorecords;
2. to prepare derivative works based upon the copyrighted work;
3. to distribute copies or phonorecords of the copyrighted work to the public by sale or other transfer of ownership, or by rental, lease or lending;
4. in the case of literary, musical, dramatic, and choreographic works, pantomimes, and motion pictures and other audiovisual works, to perform the copyrighted work publicly; and

5. in the case of literary, musical, dramatic, and choreographic works, pantomimes, and pictorial, graphic, or sculptural works, including the individual images of a motion picture or other audiovisual work, to display the copyrighted work publicly.[27]

Actual ownership of a work, as opposed to ownership of the copyrights to a work, does **not** convey any copyrights. For example, if Jan Smurf purchases a videocassette of Walt Disney's (a registered trademark) *Cinderella* (a copyrighted work) at her local Wal-Mart (another registered trademark), she can play the tape to her heart's content in her own home and even invite her friends for an evening of magic on the big-screen Sony. However, she does not have the right to make a copy of the tape to play it at a neighborhood fundraiser for the homeless, no matter how worthy the cause. She does not even have the right to make her own edited version of the film. In other words, purchasing the cassette merely gave her the right to use it in the form in which it was intended to be used—nothing more. She could, of course, loan the movie to a neighbor or even sell her copy to a stranger, just as she could with a book or other physical object. Thus her rights are strictly tangible; that is, she has no intangible rights.

CREATION OF COPYRIGHT

Probably the most important difference between the old and the new copyright statute is the point at which copyright protection begins. Under the 1909 federal statute, federal copyright protection generally could not be invoked until a work had been published with notice of copyright. There were a few exceptions to this general rule, but unpublished works were basically protected only under state law or what was known as *common law copyright*, as mentioned earlier. Common law copyright certainly had some advantages, including perpetual protection for unpublished works, but, with each state having its own common law, there was no uniformity. The 1976 copyright law solved this problem very easily—copyright exists **automatically** "in original works of authorship fixed in any tangible medium of expression, now known or later developed, from which they can be perceived, reproduced, or otherwise communicated, either directly or with the aid of a machine or device."[28] No registration is necessary. No publication is required. Not even a copyright notice has to be placed on the work for it to be copyrighted. **Repeat: The copyright exists automatically upon creation.** This is one of the most difficult aspects of copyright for laypersons, including journalists, to understand. In the copyright workshops for laypersons taught by the author of this text, the most frequently asked question is, "What do I do to copyright my book (or other creative work)?" The answer is simply "nothing," because the work was copyrighted the very second it was created in a tangible medium. Nothing could be simpler: There is no hocus-pocus, smoking mirrors or other magic; there's not even a government form to complete.

The person actually wants to know: How do I *register* the copyright for my work? As discussed shortly, there are some major advantages to registration, but this step is **absolutely not** essential to secure copyright protection, only creation and fixation in a tangible medium.

A work is *created* under the statute "when it is fixed in a copy of phonorecord for the first time."[29] Thus a work cannot be copyrighted if it exists only in the mind of the creator, but once it is fixed in a tangible medium, the protection begins. When a work is developed over time, the portion that is fixed at a particular time is considered the work at that time. For instance, the copyrighted portion of this textbook at the time these words are being written on the author's word processor is everything written thus far to the end of this sentence. If a work is prepared in different versions, each version is a separate work for purposes of copyright.[30] Thus the first edition of this book is considered a separate work from the second edition and so on.

When is a worked actually *fixed* in a medium? According to §101:

> A Work is "fixed" in a tangible medium of expression when its embodiment in a copy or phonorecord, by or under authority of the author, is sufficiently permanent or stable to permit it to be perceived, reproduced, or otherwise communicated for a period of more than transitory duration. A work consisting of sounds, images, or both, that are being transmitted, is "fixed" for purposes of this title if a fixation of the work is being made simultaneously with its transmission.[31]

Suppose an enterprising skywriter composes a love poem in the sky to her fiance during half-time in the final game of the World Series. A few miles away another romantic scribbles in the ocean sand the opening of a modernized version of the film *Beach Blanket Bingo*. How can these two original works of authorship be copyrighted? Both face a major obstacle: They are not yet fixed in a tangible medium of expression. Almost as soon as the love poem is written in the sky, it evaporates into thin air. Thus its transitory nature prevents it from being "fixed" for purposes of copyright. The same holds true for the film's opening sequence because it ends up blowing in the wind. How *do* we "fix" them? An easy way would be to write them on a piece of paper or perhaps photograph or videotape them before they fade. But won't paper eventually deteriorate? (The yellowed and tattered newspaper clippings from our glory days in high school are testament to this.) Fixation does **not** require permanency—only, as indicated earlier, that the medium be sufficiently permanent or stable to allow it to be perceived, copied or otherwise communicated for more than a transitory duration. (By the way, the film sequence has another problem – potential copyright infringement as an unauthorized derivative work, if published, to which we return later.

THE COPYRIGHT OWNER

There is a world of difference between the treatment of copyright ownership under the 1909 statute and co-existing common law versus the treatment under the Copyright Act of 1976. Prior to January 1, 1978 (the effective date of the new statute, as mentioned earlier), when authors, artists or other creators sold their copyright, the presumption was that all rights had been transferred unless rights were specifically reserved, usually in writing. For instance, an artist who sold a original painting to someone effectively transferred copyright ownership as well because the common law recognized that the sale of certain types of creative works invoked transfer of the copyright to the purchaser as well. Now, the presumption works in the opposite direction. None of the exclusive rights enumerated here or any subdivision of those rights can be legally transferred by the copyright owner **unless the transfer is in writing and signed by the copyright owner or the owner's legal representative.**

Under the new statute, unless a work is a "work made for hire," the copyright is immediately vested in the creator. If there is more than one creator (i.e., there is joint authorship), the copyright belongs to all of them – *no ifs, ands or buts.* The creator or creators can, of course, transfer their rights, but the transfer of any exclusive rights must be in writing. Oral agreements are sufficient for the transfer of nonexclusive rights. To illustrate, a writer could have a valid oral agreement with a magazine editor to publish the latest installment in a series of short stories about the demise of the Yuppie generation. At the same time, the author could have an agreement with a newspaper syndicate to distribute the story around the country. On the other hand, if the author chose to transfer an exclusive right, such as the sole right to reproduce the work, or even a subdivided right, such as the right to reproduce the work in paperback form or the right to produce a derivative work such as a play, he would need to make the transfer in writing for it to be binding.

The sole exception to this rule is a *work made for hire*, which exists in two situations, as defined in §101:

1. a work prepared by an employee within the scope of his or her employment; or
2. a work specially ordered or commissioned for use as a contribution to a collective work, as part of a motion picture or other audiovisual work, as a translation, as a supplementary work, as a compilation, as an instructional text, as a test, as answer material for a test, or as an atlas, if the parties

expressly agree in a written instrument signed by them that the work shall be considered a work made for hire.[32]

In the case of a work made for hire, the employer is considered the author for purposes of copyright and automatically acquires all rights, exclusive and nonexclusive *unless* the parties have signed an agreement to the contrary. Thus the employer effectively attains the status of creator of the work. A regular reporter for the *New York Times*, for instance, would have no rights to the stories he wrote for the newspaper, which would instead own the copyright. On the other hand, a feature by a freelance writer for *USA Today* normally would not be a work made for hire unless the writer and the paper had signed a contract specifically stating that the story would be a work made for hire. Ordinarily, the newspaper would acquire only first North American serial rights (the right to publish the story first in North America) from the freelancer, who is contractually an **independent contractor**. Suppose the *Wall Street Journal* copy editor writes a novel about a fictional investigative reporter for his newspaper. The book is written at home on his own time, but much of his inspiration comes from his observations at work. Is the novel a work made for hire? Clearly not, because the writing was completed outside the scope of his employment even though he may have gotten some ideas from interaction with his colleagues. Serving as a source of inspiration alone is not enough for an employer of an individual to claim copyright. An employer–employee relationship must have existed in the context in which the work is created.

What about a syndicated columnist? Many columnists have contracts with the local paper that serves as their base and with the national or regional syndicate that distributes the columns to other newspapers. Such a contract specifies that they retain all rights to their musings except for the right to publish the columns a specified number of times. In other words, whereas they would ordinarily be considered employees of the publication or the syndicated service and thus their output would be considered work made for hire, a signed contract to the contrary overcomes the initial presumption.

WORK MADE FOR HIRE: COMMUNITY FOR CREATIVE NON-VIOLENCE V. REID

Freelancers create much of the copyrighted material today, and work made for hire principles play a major role in the copyright status of their creative output. Unfortunately, the 1976 law left a gaping hole on this issue because even though the statute defines dozens of terms from an "anonymous work" to a "work made for hire," there is no definition of either "employer," "employee" or "scope of his or her employment." In 1989, however, the U.S. Supreme

Court settled some perplexing questions regarding work made for hire by enunciating a clear principle for determining whether an individual is an "employee." In *Community for Creative Non-Violence v. Reid* (1989),[33] in an opinion written by Justice Thurgood Marshall, the Court unanimously held: "To determine whether a work is for hire under the Act [Copyright Act of 1976], a court must first ascertain, using principles of general common law of agency, whether the work was prepared by an employer or an independent contractor. After making this determination, the court can apply the appropriate subsection of §101."[34]

The Court then indicated those factors under the general common law of agency to be applied in determining whether the hired party is an employee or an independent contractor, including:

> the hiring party's right to control the manner and means by which the product is accomplished. Among the other factors relevant to this inquiry are the skill required; the source of the instrumentalities and tools; the location of the work; the duration of the relationship between the parties; whether the hiring party has the right to assign additional projects to the hired party; the extent of the hired party's discretion over when and how long to work; the method of payment; the hired party's role in hiring and paying assistants; whether the work is part of the regular business of the hiring party; whether the hiring party is in business; the provision of employee benefits; and the tax treatment of the hired party. . . . No one of these factors is determinative.[35] (footnotes omitted)

Agency law deals with the relationship between two individuals or between an individual and a corporation or other entity in which the person performs a task for the other within the context of master–servant, employer–employee, employer–independent contractor or other similar relationships. The factors mentioned by the Court are among those cited by other courts in determining the relationship. Note the Court's holding that no one of these is determinative; instead the factors are considered as a whole in the analysis.

The facts of *CCNV v. Reid* are rather interesting and provide insight into the Court's reasoning and its conclusion that sculptor James Earl Reid was an independent contractor. They also reinforce the need for written agreements in such situations, as discussed shortly.

In 1985 Community for Creative Non-violence (CCNV), a Washington, DC, nonprofit organization for eliminating homelessness in America, reached an oral agreement with Reid to produce a statue with life-size figures for display in the annual Christmas season Pageant of Peace in Washington, DC. The original idea for the display came from association members. After negotiations over price and the materials used to make the statue, Reid and CCNV agreed to limit the cost to no more than $15,000, excluding Reid's donated services. The sculpture was made from a synthetic material to keep costs to a minimum. Reid was given a $3,000 advance. At the suggestion of Mitch Snyder, a member and trustee of the organization, Reid observed homeless people both at CCNV's Washington shelter and on the streets for ideas on how to portray the figures in the statue, entitled "Third World America." Throughout November and the first half of December, he worked exclusively on the statue in his Baltimore, Maryland, studio, where several members of the agency visited to check on his progress and to coordinate construction of the statue's base, which CCNV built on its own. CCNV paid Reid in installments, and he used the funds to pay a dozen or so assistants during the process. During their visits, CCNV representatives made suggestions about the design and construction of the sculpture, and the artist accepted most of them — such as depicting the family (a man, woman and infant) with personal belongings in a shopping cart rather than in a suitcase, as Reid had wanted. When Reid delivered the completed work on December 24, 1985, he received the final installment of the agreed price of $15,000. CCNV then placed the statue on its base (a steam grate) and displayed it for a month near the pageant, after which it was returned to Reid for minor repairs. Several weeks later when CCNV's Snyder devised plans to take the work on a fund-raising tour of several cities, the creator objected because he felt the statue would not withstand the tour. When Snyder asked that the sculpture be returned, Reid refused, registered the work in his name with the copyright office and announced his intentions to take the sculpture on a less ambitious tour than CCNV had planned. Snyder immediately filed copyright registration in the agency's name. Snyder and CCNV then sued Reid and his photographer (who never appeared in court and claimed no interest in the work) for return of the sculpture and a decision on copyright ownership.

A U.S. District Court judge granted a preliminary injunction, ordering that the piece be returned to CCNV. (Injunctions are among the remedies available to copyright owners against infringers, as discussed later in this chapter.) At the end of a two-day bench trial, the court decided that CCNV exclusively owned the copyright to the sculpture because it was a work made for hire under §101 of the Copyright Act. According to the district court, the agency was "the motivating force" in the creation of "Third World America" and Reid was an employee for purposes of copyright. The U.S. Court of Appeals for the District of Columbia held that Reid owned the copyright because the sculpture was not a work made for hire and thus reversed the trial court ruling and remanded the case.

According to the appellate court, "Third World America" was **not** a work made for hire under any of the provisions of the Copyright Act, including §101. Applying agency law principles, the court thus held that Reid was an independent contractor, not an employee, although the court did remand the case back to the trial court to determine whether Reid and CCNV may have been **joint authors**. The U.S. Supreme Court affirmed the decision of the U.S.

Court of Appeals and remanded the case back to the trial court to determine whether CCNV and Reid are joint authors of the work.

CCNV v. Reid will, undoubtedly, have a major impact on the issue of work made for hire. Indeed it is one of the most important copyright cases decided thus far by the Court since the new law took effect. At the time the case was decided, there were several conflicting lower appellate court holdings on the issue. Now it is clear that the presumption will be that a work is not a work made for hire unless there is a written agreement stating there is the traditional employer–employee relationship. As the justices noted in their reasoning, the legislative history of the 1976 act provides strong evidence that Congress meant to establish two mutually exclusive ways for a work to acquire work-made-for hire status, as indicated in § 101. The Court also pointed out that "only enumerated categories of commissioned works may be accorded work for hire status . . [and that the] . . . hiring party's right to control the product simply is not determinative."[36] The Court specifically rejected an "actual control test" that CCNV argued should be determinative. Under such a test, the hiring party could claim the copyright if it closely monitored the production of the work, but the Supreme Court said this approach "would impede Congress' paramount goal in revising the 1976 Act of enhancing predictability and certainty of copyright ownership."[37] The Court went on to note that "because that test hinges on whether the hiring party has closely monitored the production process, the parties would not know until late in the process, if not until the work is completed, whether a work will ultimately fall within §101(1)."[38]

The idea, as the Court believed Congress intended it in 1976, then, indicates that *it must be clear at the time a work is created who owns the copyright.*

JOINT AUTHORSHIP:
AN ALTERNATIVE TO WORK FOR HIRE?

Section 101 of the Copyright Act defines a "joint work" as "a work prepared by two or more authors with the intention that their contributions be merged into inseparable or independent parts of a unitary whole."[39] Unless there is a written agreement stating otherwise, joint authors are considered co-owners of the copyright in a work. While the Supreme Court held that Reid was an independent contractor, not an employee, it agreed with the appellate court that he and the organization might be joint authors, with this matter to be determined by the U.S. District Court.[40]

Although it is difficult to detect any trend yet because *CCNV v. Reid* is only a few years old, it is quite likely that more individuals and organizations hiring authors and artists will attempt to contribute enough to production of a work to meet the criteria for joint authorship. Joint authorship is certainly advantageous to the hiring party because a joint author has an undivided interest in the work and can make use of the work without seeking permission from the other joint owner or owners unless the owners expressly agree in writing how the copyright ownership in the work is to be divided. Thus, although *CCNV v. Reid* was a major victory for freelancers, it created a problem one First Amendment expert characterizes as "gratuitous joint-authorship claims of commissioning parties," which he believes could be remedied if Congress enacted a statute proposed by Senator Thad Cochran (R-Miss.). The law would ban commissioning parties from asserting joint authorship based primarily on supervision of the production of the copyrighted work.[41] Under the bill, freelancers would not inadvertently become joint authors because the parties would have to agree in advance in writing if the work were to be considered jointly authored.[42]

WORKS NOT PROTECTED BY COPYRIGHT

People unfamiliar with the law wrongly assume that any creative work can be protected by copyright. While the 1976 statute is broad, certain types of works do not fall under its wings. The most obvious example is a work that has not been fixed in a tangible medium, but the Copyright Act also excludes "any idea, procedure, process, system, method of operation, concept, principle, or discovery."[43] Whereas such works have no protection in and of themselves, expressions of them can be copyrighted. A university professor who writes a textbook based on his ideas about mass communication law and ethics, for example, cannot protect his ideas per se, but the expression of those ideas — this book — is copyrighted the moment it is created and put in a tangible medium. Titles, names, short phrases, slogans, familiar symbols and designs and mere listings of ingredients and contents have no copyright protection,[44] although these may enjoy other forms of legal protection such as trademarks (as indicated earlier in this chapter). Any attorney practicing copyright law can verify that the most common question clients ask is: "What do I need to do to copyright my great idea?" The "shocking" answer: "Sorry. You can't copyright an idea." After a discussion about original works of authorship, tangible media and automatic copyright, the client usually recovers from the shock.

A 1980 Second Circuit U.S. Court of Appeals decision illustrates how the courts, at least, divide the line between an idea and the expression of an idea. In *Hoehling v. Universal City Studios, Inc.* (1980),[45] the federal appellate court ruled that Universal had not infringed on the copyright of A. A. Hoehling's book, *Who Destroyed the Hindenburg?*, in a movie about the explosion of the German dirigible at Lakehurst, New Jersey, in 1937. The film was based on Michael Mooney's book published in 1972, 10 years after Hoehling's work. Both books theorized that Eric Spehl, a disgruntled crew member who was among the 36 people killed in the disaster, had planted a bomb in one of the gas cells. The 1975 movie, which was a fictionalized account of the event, used a pseudonym for Spehl, but its thesis about the cause of the tragedy was similar to that in Hoehling's book. (Investigators had concluded that the airship blew up after static electricity ignited the hydrogen fuel, but speculation has always abounded about the actual cause.)

A U.S. District Court judge issued a summary judgment in favor of Universal City Studios and the U.S. Circuit Court of Appeals upheld the decision. According to the court:

> A grant of copyright in a published work secures for its author a limited monopoly over the expression it contains. The copyright provides a financial incentive to those who would add to the corpus of existing knowledge by creating original works. Nevertheless, the protection afforded the copyright holder has never extended to history, be it documentary fact or explanatory hypothesis. The rationale for this doctrine is that the cause of knowledge is best served when history is the common property of all, and each generation remains free to draw upon the discoveries and insights of the past. Accordingly, the scope of copyright in historical accounts in narrow indeed, embracing no more than the author's original expression of particular facts and theories already in the public domain.[46]

Hoehling claimed there were other similarities, including random duplication of phrases and the chronology of the story, although the court saw no problem with such overlap.

> For example, all three works [Hoehling had sued the author of a second work with a similar thesis as well] contain a scene in a German beer hall, in which the airship's crew engages in revelry prior to the voyage. Other claimed similarities concern common German greetings of the period such as "Heil Hitler," or songs such as the German National anthem. These elements, however, are merely *scenes a faire*, that is, "incidents, characters or settings which are as a practical matter indispensable, or at least standard, in the treatment of a given topic." [footnote omitted] Because it is virtually impossible to write about a particular era or fictional theme without employing certain "stock" or standard literary devices, we have held that *scenes a faire* are not copyrightable as a matter of law.[47] (citing earlier decision)

Four more categories of work also lack copyright protection:

1. Any work of the U.S. government, although the government can have copyrights transferred to it by assignment, bequest or other means.[48] State and local governments are **not** precluded from copyright works; only the federal government comes under this rule.

2. Works consisting wholly of common information having no original authorship such as standard calendars, weight and measure charts, rulers, and so forth. Works that contain such information can be copyrighted even though the information itself cannot be. For instance, a calendar with illustrations of herbs for each month could be copyrighted but the copyright would extend only to the illustrations and any other original work on the calendar, not the standard calendar itself.

3. Public domain works—that is, works that were never copyrighted or whose copyright duration has expired.

4. Facts.

The Copyright Act of 1976 prohibits the federal government from copyrighting works it creates, but the government can **acquire** copyright for works it did not create. U.S. Postage stamp designs are copyrighted, as witnessed by the copyright notice in the margins of sheets and booklets, in spite of the fact that the U.S. Postal Service (USPS) is a semiautonomous federal agency. Typically, the Postal Service contracts with freelance artists, who design the stamps and then transfer the copyrights to the agency. In 1991, for example, USPS commissioned the famous Broadway caricaturist, Albert Hirschfeld, to design a series of five different copyrighted stamps featuring U.S. comedians.

Although most government works—such as Federal Trade Commission pamphlets on fraudulent telephone schemes and U.S. Public Health Service studies on AIDS—are not copyrighted, until March 1, 1989 (when the United States joined the Berne Convention; discussed later), publications incorporating noncopyrighted U.S. government works or portions of such works were **required** to carry a notice indicating that such use had been made and specifying either (a) the portion or portions of the work that are federal government material, or (b) the portion or portions of the work for which the author is asserting copyright. Such a notice is no longer mandatory, but the U.S. Copyright Office still strongly recommends that such a notice be posted to prevent innocent infringement,[49] a topic discussed later in the section on infringement.

Remember that under the 1909 law, copyright protection lasted for a maximum of two terms of 28 years each for a total of 56 years. As indicated in the next section, even works copyrighted before the new law took effect had the period of protection extended, but any work that was copyrighted prior to 1903 or any work whose copyright was not timely renewed no longer has protection. Thus some works copyrighted as late as 1949 went into the public domain because no copyright renewal application was filed. That's the reason you can find such great prices on some old, classic movies and television shows at your local Wal-Mart or K-Mart. Copyright owners simply did not bother to renew the copyright. Once a work becomes public domain property, no royalties have to be paid and no permission needs to be sought from any owner. Usually, the copyright owners felt there was no viable market for the works. No videocassette recorders (VCR) were around and television viewers had lost interest in old films and vintage television shows. However, copyright owners who had foresight filed applications for renewal and were amply rewarded when the VCR and cable television created a new market for nostalgia.

Even under the 1909 statute, facts alone could not be copyrighted. The expression of facts does enjoy protection, of course. Thus whereas news cannot be copyrighted, newscasts can be. In *Miller v. Universal City Studios* (1981),[50] the Second U.S. Circuit Court of Appeals overturned a U.S. District Court decision that Universal had infringed the copyright of Gene Miller, a Pulitzer Prize-winning reporter for the *Miami Herald*, in a book entitled *83 Hours Till Dawn* about Barbara Mackle. Mackle was rescued after being kidnapped and buried underground for five days in a box in which she could have survived for only a week. The trial court was impressed by the approximately 2,500 hours Miller said he had spent researching and writing the book: "To this court it doesn't square with reason or common sense to believe that Gene Miller would have undertaken the research required . . . if the author thought that upon completion of the book a movie producer or television network could simply come along and take the profits of the books and his research from him.[51]

Although there were several similarities between Miller's book and the script for Universal's docudrama, *The Longest Night* (including some of the same factual errors), the appellate court ordered a new trial on the ground that "the case was presented and argued to the jury on a false premise: that the labor of research by an author is protected by copyright."[52] The court indicated that Miller had presented sufficient evidence that an infringement may have occurred but on other theories of copyright law, not on the basis of research alone. "The valuable distinction in copyright law between facts and expression of facts cannot be maintained if research is held to be copyrightable. There is no rational basis for distinguishing between facts and the research involved in obtaining the facts,"[53] according to the Court of Appeals. This decision, in line with those of other federal courts, points to a very important differentiation under copyright law. All of the major television and radio networks appear now to register the copyright for their newscasts with the Copyright Office, as indicated by the prominent display of their copyright notice at the beginning and end of each newscast. Many local stations are doing the same. In fact, networks such as CBS and C-SPAN, the public affairs cable service, continuously or or at frequent intervals display their logos at the bottom right corner of the television screen as a means of discouraging and perhaps tracing unauthorized use of their programs. Entertainment networks such as "Arts and Entertainment," "Showtime" and "USA" also flash their insignia at selected intervals during programs, probably for the same purpose. (The logos also serve as identifiers to viewers completing logs for rating services such as A. C. Nielsen and Arbitron.)

In one of the few copyright cases decided by the U.S. Supreme Court since the new law took effect, the justices in 1991 attempted to clarify the concept of "originality," which is closely linked to the facts/compilation of facts distinction. In *Feist Publications v. Rural Telephone Service Co., Inc.,*[53] the Court, in a decision written by Justice O'Connor, unanimously held that the white pages of a telephone directory could not be copyrighted. The case revolved around a telephone book publisher's use of the names and telephone numbers from a telephone company's directory to compile its own areawide telephone directories. The Court noted that whereas the phone company could claim copyright ownership to its directory as a whole, it could not prevent a competitor from using its compilation of names, towns and phone numbers to create its own directory. Facts are not copyrightable, the justices said, but compilations of facts generally can be copyrighted.

The decision stressed that hard work or "sweat of the brow" is not enough; there must also be originality, which the Court characterized as the *sine qua non* of copyright. "To be sure, the requisite level of creativity is extremely low; even a slight amount will suffice," Justice O'Connor wrote. She went on to note that originality and novelty are not the same for purposes of copyright and cited the example of two poets who independently create the same poem: "Neither work is novel, yet both are original and, hence, copyrightable."

Misappropriation and Unfair Competition

If the daily *Bugle* publishes a story by one of its reporters at the city desk about the indictment of the local police chief on drug trafficking charges, the newspaper cannot claim a copyright monopoly on the coverage of the event, although it can certainly copyright its own story. A reporter for a rival paper could write a copyrighted story using some of the same direct quotes from the chief at his press conference and include similar facts. There likely will be no copyright infringement under the circumstances. But, other reporters simply took the *Bugle's* story and rewrote it for their own paper, they might be able to avoid a successful copyright infringement suit by sticking strictly to the facts and avoiding use of any of the expressions in the original story, but they could face a possible suit for **misappropriation.**

Misappropriation is a broad tort that covers a variety of situations, including the commercial use of a person's name, image or likeness (discussed in chap. 8). This common law creature, also known as **unfair competition,** has been incorporated into most state statutes and in the federal Lanham Act,[54] the same statute that in 1947 revised trademark law. It is occasionally invoked in addition to or in lieu of a copyright infringement suit. The idea of the tort, as illustrated in the classic U.S. supreme Court decision in *International News*

Service v. Associated Press (1918),[55] maintains that one should not be permitted to compete unfairly through the misappropriation of the toils of another, especially by palming off another's work as one's own. Like copyright infringement, misappropriation is a form of intellectual theft that usually does not quite approach the standards for copyright infringement.

In *INS v. AP*, the International News Service[56] owned by the infamous "yellow journalism" publisher, William Randolph Hearst, admitted pirating AP stories from early editions of AP member newspapers and from AP bulletin boards. AP claimed that INS also bribed AP employees to get stories before they were actually sent to AP newspapers. INS editors rewrote some of the stories and sent others verbatim to its own subscribers. In its defense, INS claimed that because the AP did not copyright its stories, the information was therefore in the public domain. INS also claimed that it could not get information about World War I because INS reporters had been denied access to the Allied countries, thanks to Hearst's pro-German stance.

In a 7–1 decision, the U.S. Supreme Court upheld a Second Circuit Court of Appeals decision granting AP an injunction against INS's use of AP stories. The Court reasoned that although the Constitution does not grant a monopoly, even for a limited period, to the first person to communicate a news event, INS's methods were "an unauthorized interference with the normal operation [of AP's business] . . . precisely at the point where the profit is to be reaped."[57] The justices concluded that INS's misappropriation of AP's stories created unfair competition that could therefore be prohibited.

What is the harm in one news service disseminating information obtained without consent from a competitor? After all, INS did not stop the flow of AP news; it merely copied it to distribute to its own subscribers. What about a small radio station that "rips and reads" stories from the local daily newspaper because it has no budget for its own reporters or for joining a wire service? If the station simply takes the facts from the stories and rewrites them without expressions from the originals (a time-consuming feat, to say the least!), there will probably be no copyright infringement because news cannot be copyrighted — only the expression of news. There could be the basis for an unfair competition suit, however, depending on the circumstances. The harm that occurs is two-fold. First, such activities could in the long haul discourage the newspaper from engaging in comprehensive newsgathering because the competitor draws away advertising by scooping the paper or offering the same information for free. Second, a competitive media marketplace presumably serves the public better by ensuring a broader dissemination of news from a variety of sources. When two media outlets rely on the same source for news, there is no diversity. Thus, according to the premise, competition results in a better product — news, in this case.

Although *AP v. INS* was decided almost 75 years ago, it remains the basis of most of the court decisions today regarding misappropriation of news. The scenario in *INS v. AP* is an extreme example, even by today's standards, but rivals do sometimes pirate one another's copy. The rumors about smaller newspapers and radio stations using rewritten copy from larger newspapers occasionally prove true when one of small outlets is hauled into court and ordered to pay damages to the larger one. Courts are rarely sympathetic to excuses such as low profits and tight budgets. Competition must be fair, with the greater rewards going to those who work the most. There are also some serious ethical problems in such situations, not the least of which is professional malpractice. Legitimate newsgathering is an active process by which journalists use their professional skills and knowledge to acquire as much information as necessary to write a balanced, complete and objective story; it is not a passive process of simply rewriting someone else's work. (Editors, of course, legitimately rewrite stories of their own reporters to improve the writing in the stories.) When an individual, rather than an organization, engages in misappropriation, it is usually considered **plagiarism** (discussed near the end of this chapter), and the consequences can be quite serious. It is unlikely, however, that the individual's employer will face a lawsuit for misappropriation, although the media outlet may lose some of its credibility and prestige in the eyes of the public and professional journalist. None of the major codes of journalism ethics specifically mentions misappropriation or unfair competition, although the Society of Professional Journalists Code says, "Plagiarism is dishonest and unacceptable."[58]

COPYRIGHT DURATION

The term of copyright was fairly simple prior to enactment of the Copyright Act of 1976. Under the 1909 statute, copyright protection began on the day the work was published or on the date it was registered if unpublished and continued for 28 years. If the copyright were renewed by filing the appropriate form and fee with the Copyright Office during the 28th year, the protection continued for another 28-year term and then went into the public domain. The new statute is much more generous, but the precise term of protection depends on a number of factors: whether the work was created before, on or after January 1, 1978; whether the work is a work made or hire and the identifying status of the work. Table 10.1 is an attempt to simplify duration.

For works that had already secured federal copyright protection before January 1, 1978, an additional 19 years of protection was tacked on to the previous maximum of 56 years, assuming the copyright owner filed or files a renewal application during the last year of the first term of 28 years. In effect, this provision created a relatively easy way of equalizing duration of copyright under the 1909 law with duration under the 1976 statute. Congress could have chosen to make the periods precisely the same, but this would have made the

TABLE 10.1
Copyright Duration in Years

	Identifying Status			
	Author Named	Pseudonym	Anonymous	Work for Hire
Created Before 1/1/78	75*	75*	75*	75*
Created After 1/1/78	life of author +50**	75/100***	75/100****	75/100****

*If renewal is filed during last (28th) year of first term
**If more than one author, life of last surviving author + 50 years
***75 years from publication or 100 years from creation, whichever comes first unless the author's real name is indicated on the copyright registration form, in which case the term is the same as an "author named" work
****75 years from publication or 100 years from creation, whichever comes first

calculations extremely difficult because the old law was not tied to an author's life and copyright protection did not begin until registration or publication.

Beginning in 1962, while Congress was debating the provisions of a long-overdue new statute to replace the 1909 one, a series of congressional enactments extended the second term of all renewed copyrights that would have expired between September 19, 1962, and December 31, 1976.[59] Then a provision of the 1976 Act extended the period further by granting an automatic maximum of 75 years protection for copyrighted works that had already been renewed and began their second term anytime during December 31, 1976 to December 31, 1977. The extension was automatic because no additional forms had to be filed for the extension (only the renewal form for the second term).[60]

Taken as a whole, the prior extensions and the provisions of the new statute effectively granted a maximum of 75 years of protection for all **copyrighted** works that had **not** lost copyright protection before September 19, 1962. Protection was lost, of course, if the copyrighted work had fallen into the public domain prior to that date either because of a lack of renewal or expiration of both copyright terms. Thus the only way one can safely assume that a work is not copyrighted is to check the copyright notice on the work or the date on the registration form in the copyright office and determine that it was copyrighted more than 75 years ago. The present law contains no provision for reviving the copyright for any works that had gone into the public domain.

Works Created But Neither Published Nor Copyrighted Before January 1, 1978

Under the present law, neither publication nor registration is required for copyright but, as already noted, one of these conditions must have been met under the old statute. But what about those works that were never copyrighted but instead were filed away in a drawer or framed on Aunt Sally's wall? Because there was no effective way of establishing a date of creation for these works, Congress had to devise a different scheme for determining how long they were to be protected or even if they could be copyrighted at all. The solution was simple, although the calculations are a bit complicated. The legislators opted to automatically protect these works, which had enjoyed common law protection in individual states but were no longer shielded by the common law because the new law explicitly nixed common law copyright. The duration of protection for such works is computed the same way as works created on or after January 1, 1978—life of the author (or last surviving author if more than one) plus 50 years for works whose author is identified, or if pseudonymous and the author's actual name is indicated on the registration form. For anonymous works and works made for hire, the protection is 75 years from publication or 100 years from creation, whichever is shorter.[61] **However,** Congress provided that the term for such a work would expire no earlier than December 31, 2002, or if the work is published on or before that date, the term will not expire until December 31, 2027. The key to extending protection is to publish a work by the end of 2002 so it can enjoy an additional 25 years of protection. (The criteria for **publication** are specified later in this chapter.) Even if an author has been dead for 50 years, the work is automatically copyrighted and thus protected at least until the end of 2002 so long as it was **not** previously copyrighted **and** did not fall into the public domain. As you can see, by publishing the work on or before the end of 2002, the copyright owner has protection automatically extended another 25 years! This provision was designed to incorporate some of the protection previously afforded by common law copyright but without recognizing common law protection. The new law obviously makes common law protection unnecessary anyway for works created after January 1, 1978, because copyright automatically exists from the moment of creation.

A journalist attempting to use works created prior to January 1, 1978, that were not previously copyrighted through registration or publication must be very cautious because even very old works may still have copyright protection. This provision in the law is not widely known among media professionals. The same defenses, such as fair use, apply to these works as to newer works, but communication practitioners are sometimes lulled into making extensive use of old, unpublished and unregistered materials on the assumption that they are in the public domain when, in fact, they may still be copyrighted.

Sooner or later even the great classics fall into the public domain, as in the case of Willa Cather's novel *O Pioneers!*, published in 1913. When Cather died in 1947, her will provided that the novel could not be adapted for film,[62] but the copyright finally expired in 1988 and a 1992 movie version appeared on

CBS-TV starring Jessica Lange. No permission had to be sought from the former copyright owners of the novel.

COPYRIGHT RENEWAL

For works created on or after January 1, 1978, there is **no** renewal. When the author has been dead 50 years or for some pseudonymous and all anonymous works and works made for hire after 75 or 100 years, the death bell tolls for copyright and anyone can make use of the work in any way. The copyright can also expire if the owner of a work copyrighted prior to the magic date fails to a file a renewal application during the last year of the first 28-year copyright term. Thus renewals are essential for works copyrighted before the new law took effect that did not go into the public domain. The present statute specifically requires that all renewals must be filed between December 31 of the 27th year and December 31 of the 28th year of the first term. If renewal is not done during this one-year time frame, the work will **permanently** lose protection. For example, the author of this book completed his doctoral dissertation in August 1974 and registered the copyright at that time. The renewal has to be filed between December 31, 2001, and December 31, 2002. If the renewal is made, the work will have an additional 47 years of protection until December 31, 2049. A final note on renewal: *All copyright terms run to the end of the calendar year in which the copyright would otherwise expire,*[63] thus granting as much as a year of additional protection for some works. For example, a painting by an artist who died on January 1, 1995, would be copyrighted automatically until December 31, 2045.

COPYRIGHT NOTICE

One of the most persistent myths about copyright, perhaps due to the fact that 1909 statutory requirements were so rigid, is that a copyright notice cannot be placed on a work unless it has been registered. Nothing could be further from the truth. The new law not only permits posting of the copyright notice on all works — registered and unregistered — but actually encourages this practice. Under the 1909 law, **published works** that did not bear a copyright notice were lost forever in the twilight zone of public domain. Unless they were registered, **unpublished works** had no federal protection anyway and thus a copyright notice was irrelevant. Until March 1, 1989, when the United States joined the Berne Convention for the Protection of Literary and Artistic Works,[64] published works were required to post a correct copyright notice or risk losing protection. Even an incorrect notice subjected the work to possible loss of protection. **Copyright notice is now optional for all works published on or after March 1, 1989,** although it is still highly recommended that the notice be posted anyway, as discussed shortly.

Copyright notice is still mandatory for works published before March 1, 1989, although failure to include the notice or giving an incorrect notice does not automatically negate the copyright, as it did under the 1909 law. Instead, the copyright owner is permitted to take certain steps, as provided in §§405 and 406 of the statute, to preserve the copyright. These steps include (a) registering the work before it is published or before the omission took place or within **five years** after the error occurs, **and** (b) making a reasonable effort to post a correct notice on all subsequent copies.[65] **If these steps are not followed, the work will automatically go into the public domain in the United States five years after publication.** The work may continue to have protection in some other countries, depending on their copyright provisions. Some omissions are not considered serious enough to require correction—such as failing to place the notice on only a few copies, dating a notice more than a year later after the first publication and leaving off the © symbol or the word "Copyright" or the abbreviation "Copr."[66]

Although not mandatory for works first published on or after March 1, 1989, a copyright notice is highly recommended because it gives the world notice that the work is protected and provides useful information, including the copyright owner and year of publication, to anyone who may wish to seek permission to use the work. Providing the notice also prevents an individual or organization from claiming *innocent infringement* as a defense to unauthorized use. Under §405(b) of the Copyright Act, a person who infringes on a copyrighted work by relying innocently on the omission of a copyright notice on a work published before March 1, 1989, cannot be held liable for actual or statutory damages before being notified by the owner of the infringement.[67] "Innocent infringers" must demonstrate that they were misled by the omission of notice and can still be sued for any profits from the infringement, if the court allows.

Similar provisions in the statute[68] provide an innocent infringement defense for works first published without notice on or after March 1, 1989. Under §401(d) (dealing with "visually perceptible copies") and §402(d) ("phonorecords of sound recordings"), if the correct copyright notice appears on the copies of the work to which an infringer had access, the defendant cannot claim innocent infringement in mitigation of actual or statutory damages (except for employees of nonprofit educational institutions, libraries and archives and employees of public broadcasting entities under certain conditions). **Thus it is very important that all published works carry a proper copyright notice, even though it is no longer required.**

Under the 1976 statute, copyright notice has never been required for unpublished works, but unpublished works have always been permitted to carry the notice. An individual or organization cannot use the defense of innocent infringement for unauthorized use of an unpublished work. This defense is available for published works that omit the notice. Freelancers, in particular, are often hesitant about posting a notice on unpublished materials, especially those submitted for review because they believe publishers will be offended. This is, unfortunately, a misconception. The 1976 Copyright Act was designed to offer strong protection to original works of authorship, and the creators of those works should not be reluctant to exercise their rights and to notify others of their intentions. They have nothing to lose by posting a copyright notice on all works—published and unpublished.

Proper Notice

For purposes of notice, the copyright law divides works into two categories: (a) visually perceptible copies ("copies from which the work can be visually perceived, either directly or with the aid of a machine or device"[69]), and (b) phonorecords of sound recordings.[70] The first category includes all copyrighted works except phonorecords of sound recordings. The distinction is important because the notices are different for the two. For visually perceptible copies, the key three elements of notice are:

1. The **symbol** © or the word "Copyright" or the abbreviation "Copr."
2. **The year of first publication.**
3. **The name of the copyright owner.**[71]

Examples of a proper notice are:

1. © 1994 Roy L. Moore
2. Copyright 1994 Roy L. Moore
3. Copr. 1994 Roy L. Moore

The first example is the one most recommended because it is the only form acceptable under the Universal Copyright Convention, of which the United States is a member. The UCC was founded in Geneva, Switzerland, in 1952 to attempt to bring international uniformity to copyright and revised its rules at a meeting in Paris in 1971 (which the United States implemented on July 10, 1974).

For phonorecords of sound recordings, the notice is the same except the symbol ℗ is used instead of ©, "copyright" or "copr." An example is:

℗ 1994 Roy L. Moore

If a work is unpublished, there is no mandatory form for notice because notice is not required anyway, but a recommended form is:

Unpublished work © 1994 Roy L. Moore

For works that incorporate U.S. government materials, the notice must include a statement distinguishing the author's work from the U.S. government work, if published before March 1, 1989. Two examples are:

1. © 1994 Roy L. Moore. Copyright claimed in all information, except information from U.S. government documents on pages 100–110.
2. © 1994 Roy L. Moore. Chapter 10 and photo on page 11 are U.S. government works.

Similar notices should be placed on works published after March 1, 1989, although no longer required. They are particularly useful for informing readers and potential users which portions you are copyrighting.

Placement of Notice

The copyright statute itself is fairly vague about where a copyright notice should be placed, but the Copyright Office has issued regulations that are quite specific, but flexible.[72] The statute says simply that for visually perceptible copies, "The notice shall be affixed to copies in such manner and location as to give reasonable notice of the claim of copyright."[73] Congress delegated authority to prescribe regulations regarding notice to the Copyright Office in the same provision.[74] A similar provision governs phonorecords: "The notice shall be placed on the surface of the phonorecord, or on the phonorecord label or container, in such a manner and location as to give reasonable notice of the claim of copyright."[75]

Examples of conforming positions of notice in the Copyright Office regulations for books are (a) title page, (b) page immediately following the title page, (c) either side of front or back cover and (d) first or last page of the main body of the work.[76] For "collective works" (defined earlier in this chapter), only one copyright notice needs to be given—that is, it is not necessary (although permissible) for each separate and independent work to carry its own notice. Collective works include magazines, journals, encyclopedias, newspapers and anthologies. The exception to this rule is advertising. If an advertiser wishes to comply with notice requirements, it must include a separate notice such as to defeat a defense for innocent infringement or to comply with international regulations. Some freelancers insist that their contracts with publishers include a provision requiring a separate notice, a practice that more writers should follow to avoid any notice problems. A separate notice identifies the copyright owner for readers and is good insurance. Even though they already register each issue as a collective work, some major newspapers and television stations have a policy of including a separate notice on stories by their own reporters that other publications are likely to want to use, such as multipart investigative reports. Thus other readers and viewers see or hear a nice plug for the media outlet that originated the story such as "In a copyrighted story in *The Daily Bugle* today, . . ." As you will learn in the next section, the other outlets must still obtain permission before using the story or portions of it. Simply giving credit is not sufficient.

COPYRIGHT INFRINGEMENT

The Copyright Act of 1976 has considerable teeth for punishing infringers. Chapter 5 of the act provides a wide variety of remedies, including civil and criminal penalties and injunctions. The 1989 revision implementing the Berne Convention treaty increased the penalties even more. The statute sends a clear message that copyright infringement does not pay. An *infringer* is defined as "anyone who violates any of the exclusive rights of the copyright owner . . . or who imports copies or phonorecords into the United States in violation of section 602" ("Infringing importation of copies or phonorecords").[77] The list of individuals and organizations who have been sued (many successfully) for copyright infringement reads like a *Who's Who*. In 1984, the Roman Catholic Archdiocese of Chicago was found guilty of copyright infringement by a U.S. District Court jury and ordered to pay $3.2 million in damages for using copyrighted hymns without permission. The rights were owned by Dennis Fitzpatrick, a composer and president of F.E.L. Publications Ltd. of Los Angeles. The archdiocese unsuccessfully claimed that it had made an honest mistake and had not intentionally avoided paying royalties.[78] In 1988 reggae musician Patrick Alley of the Bronx sued rock artist Mick Jagger in U.S. District Court in New York, claiming that Jagger's 1985 hit, "Just Another Night," contained the chorus of Alley's 1979 song by the same name. After hearing testimony from experts on both sides and from Jagger himself that included singing of some of the lyrics, the federal jury ruled there was no infringement.[79] In 1989 Walt Disney Productions ordered the Very Important Babies Daycare Center in Hallandale, Florida, to remove paintings of Mickey and Minnie Mouse, Donald Duck and Goofy from its walls because of copyright infringement.[80] (While the characters themselves are trademarks, their depictions, such as drawings, are copyrighted.) Even legal research firms have entered the fray. After three years of litigation, West Publishing Co. and Mead Data Central, the two largest computerized legal research companies in the country, agreed to a settlement in 1988 under which Mead now pays license fees to use West's case report scheme known as "star pagination" from West's copyrighted National Reporter System.[81] Mead, which (as indicated earlier) owns the Lexis computer research service, claimed that West's system could not be copyrighted because it lacked originality and was therefore tantamount to public property. Garrison Keillor, the star of National Public Radio's (NPR) "A Prairie Home Companion," sued the noncommercial network in 1988 for copyright infringement after NPR included a Keillor speech in its catalog of cassettes offered for sale to the public. The tape contained Keillor's presentation to the National Press Club the year before, which was carried live on NPR. Keillor claimed he owned the rights to the recording and that he had never granted NPR permission to tape and distribute it in its catalog. The two parties reached an out-of-court settlement in which the radio network agreed to make available 400 cassettes of the speech free to anyone who requested one.[82]

Although infringement suits usually attract little, if any, attention in the mass media — except in cases involving major figures — the stakes can be quite high, especially with videotaped movies and computer software. For example, it is estimated that there are from one to four bootlegged copies in circulation for each legal copy of computer software sold,[83] and the Software Publishers Association claims the industry loses $2 billion annually to pirates.[84] One company, Xyquest, found in one year alone more than $400,000 worth of pirated copies of its XyWrite software, and its president acknowledged, "we know that the real figure is many times greater."[85]

The motion picture industry probably loses even more in piracy, with one estimate for *international* piracy alone at $1 billion each year, most of it in video piracy.[86] The Motion Picture Association of America (MPAA) believes that video piracy in the United States deprives the industry of more than $100 million annually and that video shop retailers lose from $150 million to $200 million each year from piracy.[87] In some countries there is especially a high rate of bootlegging such as in Turkey, where the estimate is that almost all videotapes sold are pirated copies, and Japan, where the figure is an estimated 70 percent.[88] Two motion picture industry executives, John D. Maatta of N.I.W.S. Productions (a subsidiary of Lorimar Telepictures) and Lorin Brennan of Carolco Pictures, indicate that video piracy takes two basic forms: (a) unauthorized duplication and sale in which pirates acquire a master, make duplicates and then sell them, and (b) "second generation" video piracy in which pirates forge copyright documents so it appears they are the legitimate owner and then go to another country and force the rightful owner to prove claim of title.[89]

According to one source, the three leading nations in piracy in Asia are now Thailand, Singapore and Taiwan, where anyone can buy illegal audiotapes, videotapes and software at very low prices.[90] For example, a copy of any of the *Rocky* or *Rambo* movies can be purchased at Bangkok street stalls for the U.S. equivalent of 38 cents.[91] Walt Disney began a crackdown on copyright pirates in Asia in the late 1980s after estimating it was losing $10 million to $20 million a year in royalties from pirating in the region. Thailand was targeted first because of its leniency toward infringers, and in 1989 the entertainment conglomerate worked with local police to conduct a series of raids against violators[92] that appear to have been successful in reducing piracy.

The motion picture industry has taken some significant steps in recent years to combat piracy, both within and outside the country. Before Warner Brothers released the movie *Batman* in 1989, the studio marked each of the 4,000 prints distributed to theaters with a unique electronic code that appears on any video copies so investigators can trace pirated copies to a specific source.[93] Warner Brothers, in coordination with the MPAA, announced a reward of $15,000 to anyone providing information that led to the arrest and conviction of anyone for pirating the movie and a $200 reward for the first 15 pirated copies turned in.[94]

International Protection for Copyright Infringement

U.S. companies are able to take criminal and civil action against infringers in other countries because of various international agreements the United States has signed and conventions treaties we have joined. However, it should be noted that there is **no** universal international copyright, but instead the treatment afforded works copyrighted in the United States differs considerably from country to country. One of the earliest international copyright agreements was the 1910 Buenos Aires Convention, which the United States joined in 1911 with several Latin American states, including Argentina, Bolivia and Panama, but there are even earlier bilateral agreements, such as the one made with Cuba in 1903, that is still in effect. The two most important international copyright conventions are the Universal Copyright Convention (UCC) and the Berne Union for the Protection of Literary and Artistic Property (Berne Convention). Both have substantially simplified international copyright by bringing some consistency in international protection. The United States joined the UCC in 1955 and revisions made at a subsequent UCC in 1971 became effective here in 1974. The most sweeping changes in international copyright were wrought by the Berne Convention, which met first in Berlin in 1908 and most recently in Paris in 1971. The United States, however, did not join the convention until March 1, 1989, after 78 other nations were already members. Some of the changes effected by the federal act implementing Berne membership have been discussed previously and others are mentioned later, but suffice it to point out that at least a few of the revisions were fairly substantial.[95] The most important impact was that the United States must now treat the copyrighted works of nationals of other Berne Convention countries the same as it treats works of its own citizens, and member countries must offer at least the same protection for U.S. works as they do for those of their own citizens.[96] You can expect to see more moves by U.S. firms to haul more and more international pirates into courts in their own countries so they can be punished. For the first time, the United States can really hit the infringers where it hurts—the pocketbook.

Finally, all works created on or after March 1, 1989, by citizens of Berne Convention countries and all works first published in a Berne Convention country enjoy automatic protection in the United States. No registration or other formality is necessary.

DEFENSES TO INFRINGEMENT

There are seven major defenses to copyright infringement, although the first one is technically not a defense but a mitigation of damages: (a) innocent infringement, (b) consent, (c) compulsory license (for certain types of works), (d) public property, (e) statute of limitations, (f) expiration of copyright or public domain and (g) fair use.

Innocent Infringement

Innocent infringement, as indicated earlier, occurs when a person uses a copyrighted work without consent on the good faith assumption that the work is not copyrighted because the work has been publicly distributed without a copyright notice. Innocent infringers must prove that they were misled by the omission of such notice and can still be liable, at the court's discretion, for profits made from the infringement, although actual or statutory damages would have to be paid. Thus this claim, if proven, merely mitigates damages; the innocent infringer can still have to fork over any profits. There are two major limitations to this "defense." **First, an individual cannot claim innocent infringement in the case of works published after March 1, 1989**, the effective date of the Berne Convention Implementation Act of 1988. (The Berne Convention does not require a copyright notice on any works—published or unpublished—and thus effectively prohibits a claim of innocent infringement.) **Second, innocent infringement can be claimed only for published works, not for unpublished works** because a copyright notice was not required for unpublished works even before March 1, 1989.

Consent

As noted earlier, the transfer of any of the exclusive rights and any subdivision of those rights must be in writing to be effective. This means, quite simply, that **consent** in most cases must be **written**. The typical way in which a right is transferred is through a contract. The Copyright Office does not publish a model contract, but there are dozens of copyright and intellectual property handbooks—some geared to attorneys and others aimed at laypersons—that provide sample agreements. Section 205 of the 1976 Copyright Act allows, but does **not** require, parties to record transfer agreements in the Copyright Office.[97] With such a recording, the individual to whom a right or rights have been transferred gains some important legal advantages, including serving as *constructive notice*[98] of the terms of the agreement to other parties if certain conditions have been met.[99] Recordation also provides a public record of the terms of the agreement and, if certain conditions are met, establishes priorities between conflicting transfers.[100] It is extremely important that recordations of transfers comply completely with the provisions in § 205 and rules of the Copyright Office. A $20 fee must also be paid for each document.

All transfer documents are first checked by the Copyright Office to make sure they comply with the requirements and then cataloged and microfilmed for the public record.[101] Anyone can gain access to copies of the documents through the Copyright Office's on-line computer file, known as COHD, or by using the microfilm readers/printers in the Copyright Card Catalog in the Library of Congress in Washington, DC.[102]

Another provision in the statute deals with terminations of transfers. Under §203, a copyright owner can terminate a grant of any exclusive or nonexclusive right after 35 years by notifying the individual or organization to whom the right was transferred.[103] This is an often overlooked provision that can certainly work to the advantage of a copyright owner. It applies to both works that were created on and after January 1, 1978, as well as those created before that date *so long as the transfer of rights was executed on or after the date.* (Of course, the work must not have already lost copyright protection.) The owner can make the termination effective anytime during a five-year period beginning at the end of 35 years from the date of execution of the transfer or from date of publication, if the transfer involves publication, to the end of 40 years from the day the transfer was effective, whichever term ends first.[104] **This special termination of transfers provision does not apply to works made for hire or to a grant to prepare a specific derivative work.**[105] This is another reason freelance writers should not sign work-made-for-hire contracts. Termination of transfers is another fringe benefit of the new copyright law that can be very us useful, especially when a work is slow gaining popularity, but writers who commit themselves to a work-made-for-hire agreement are out of luck. The exception regarding derivative works simply provides that where an author has granted someone the right to do a particular derivative work, that right cannot be terminated if the specific derivative work has been completed before the five-year termination window. The author can, however, terminate the right of the person to any other derivative works.

Compulsory License

One of the most controversial and complicated provisions of the Copyright Act of 1976 was §111, which provides a mechanism by which the "secondary transmission of a primary transmission embodying a performance or display of a work is not an infringement of copyright"[106] if certain conditions are met. For example, the management of a hotel, apartment complex or similar type of housing can retransmit the signals of local television and radio stations to the private lodgings of guests or residents if no direct charge is made so long as the secondary transmission is not done by a cable system.[107] Whereas this aspect of the provision has attracted virtually no controversy, §111(c), which deals with secondary transmissions by cable systems, continues to pit various powerful groups against one another in a battle over royalties provided by a scheme known as *compulsory licensing*. The groups include commercial broadcasters (represented by their trade organization, the National Association of Broadcasters), cable television companies (in the form of the National Cable Television Association), program syndicators, noncommercial broadcasters and the music industry. Under compulsory licensing, a copyrighted work can be used without obtaining consent from the copyright owner under certain conditions by following procedures specified in the statute, including the payment of royalty fees to the Copyright Office. The Copyright Office then turns the fees over to a Copyright Royal Tribunal (CRT), which has the authority to establish royalty rates charged to users as well as the distribution of the fees.[108] The fees are **not** a tax because the federal government collects and distributes them to others rather than retaining them for governmental use. The CRT deducts only an administrative fee to pay the salaries of the three CRT Commissioners and other overhead.[109]

Compulsory licensing was a good faith but rather unsuccessful attempt by Congress to correct an inequity in the 1909 law. Until the 1976 act, the U.S. Supreme Court had consistently ruled that cable television operators could not be held liable for copyright infringement under the 1909 statute for retransmitting either local signals or distant network signals[110] called "superstations"—such as Ted Turner's WTBS-TV from Atlanta. WTBS began offering its signal to cable systems via satellite in 1976 and now has the largest audience of any cable channel in the country in spite of competition from other independent (i.e., nonnetwork affiliated) superstations—such as WGN in Chicago (the second largest), WOR (New York), WPIX (New York) and KTVT (Dallas-Fort Worth). Cable systems have an option of either obtaining a compulsory license or negotiating directly with the stations or with common carriers, third parties that uplink station signals. Most have opted to obtain the compulsory license, which can be acquired by paying set fees established by the Copyright Royal Tribunal. The fee schedule and distribution formula are incredibly complex and continue to be controversial. The different interests fight to increase their share of royalties, which have risen substantially as the CRT has responded to changes in Federal Communication Communication rules that have helped the cable television industry increase its revenue by taking advantage of greater deregulation. The FCC has advocated elimination of compulsory licensing for the last decade or so.[111] The commission feels cable television has outgrown the need for a royalty collection system that is an enormous financial windfall for the cable industry because the royalty percentages set by the CRT are no doubt considerably lower than they would be if cable firms had to negotiate directly with stations. Under compulsory licensing, cable companies now pay a fee to carry local as well as distant signals but the fees are computed based on "the gross receipts from subscribers . . . for the basic service of providing secondary transmissions of primary broadcast transmitters."[112] The fees vary depending on the size of the system and the distance of a station's signal from the primary coverage area served by the cable firm. Small cable systems particularly enjoy a low rate—one-half of 1 percent if gross revenues do not exceed $80,000. Compulsory licensing deals only with broadcast signals and thus does not directly affect services carried strictly by satellite—such as the USA network, Cable News Network (owned by Turner Broadcasting, which also owns WTBS) and the Weather Channel. Instead cable owners pay a fee, which is typically a few cents per subscriber per month. For so-called premium services, such as Home Box Office and Showtime, the cable system charges the subscriber an add-on monthly fee of several dollars and then splits the income with the service owner. In 1988 the U.S. Court of Appeals for the DC Circuit overturned a U.S. District Court decision that "gross receipts" included only income from the retransmission of broadcast signals, not income from satellite originated programming such as the Arts and Entertainment network and ESPN or from premium channels.[113] The appellate court said the trial court should have deferred to the CRT, which had included in gross receipts all fees for any tier of programming that included at least one broadcast signal. Thus many cable services group broadcast signals into the basic tier, which usually includes a few but not all of the nonbroadcast signals, to lower the compulsory fee.

Satellite carriers who transmit signals of nonnetwork broadcast signals (superstations) to private owners of satellite dish receivers (known as TVROs for "Television Receive Only") are also allowed to obtain a compulsory license.[114] They are also permitted to make secondary transmissions of network stations to private satellite dish receiver owners in "unserved households,"[115] which the statute defines as a household that "cannot receive through the use of a conventional outdoor rooftop antenna, an over-the-air signal of grade B intensity (as defined by the Federal Communications Commission) of a primary network station affiliated with that network" and has not subscribed within the previous 90 days to a cable system that carries such a network signal.[116]

The primary beneficiary of the royalties generated by compulsory licensing has been program syndicators, represented principally by the MPAA. This group has typically gotten more than two-thirds of the licensing revenue each year, but there are several other recipients, including the music industry (represented by the American Society of Composers, Authors & Publishers, ASCAP, and Broadcast Music Inc., BMI), professional and college sports associations and even National Public Radio (NPR).

It is possible that Congress will eliminate compulsory licensing for cable systems in light of the continued problems with the system and the fact that the cable industry no longer needs this protective umbrella. One communications law expert has characterized the compulsory license system as "fundamentally flawed" because it "interferes with market operation without apparent benefit to either the industries involved or the public."[117] Fred H. Cate and many others believe the compulsory license should be replaced by a system that imposes full copyright liability for all public performances of copyrighted works.[118]

Finally, operators of coin-operated phonorecord players, or "jukeboxes," as they are affectionately known, may obtain a compulsory license for the public performance of nondramatic musical works (in other words, for playing recorded songs in their jukeboxes).[119] The fee collection mechanism is much simpler than that for cable television; the jukebox owner simply files an application, pays an $8 annual fee for each player and affixes a Copyright Office certificate to the machine. The royalties are then distributed to the owners of copyrighted music under a formula established by the Copyright Royal Tribunal.

Other Types of Licensing

There is one other mechanism for licensing that enables a potential user of a copyrighted work to avoid having to negotiate with individual copyright owners—the *blanket license*. Blanket licenses, which are purchased for a fee based on a percentage of a radio or television station's revenue, allow a broadcaster to publicly perform any of the music for which the licensing agency has acquired a nonexclusive right. The two primary licensing agencies in the United States are the American Society of Composers, Authors and Publishers (ASCAP) and Broadcast Music, Inc. (BMI).[120] Both organizations serve similar functions. ASCAP, a membership association of approximately 30,000 composers, authors and publishers founded in 1914, has nonexclusive rights to more than 3 million musical compositions.[121] BMI, a nonprofit corporation formed in 1939, has about 50,000 writer and publisher affiliates and holds nonexclusive rights to the public performance of more than one million musical compositions.[122] Both agencies grant blanket licenses to broadcast stations so they can use any of the music licensed to the agency without having to obtain the permission of individual copyright owners. Unlike the old law, the 1976 statute makes it clear that playing a recorded copyrighted song without consent or a license is infringement. Thus whereas for many years radio stations paid no royalties when they played recorded music (which they usually obtained free from recording industry promoters anyway), they must now pay royalties even if they actually purchased the record. At one time record companies and performers were happy to have airtime and therefore did not object to the scheme under which they provided free copies in return for airplay. However, many copyright owners realized they were losing considerable sums in royalties with the arrangement and successfully pushed Congress to include broadcast use under public performances protected by the new statute. Blanket licensing is an efficient mechanism for collecting the millions of dollars in royalties because individual copyright owners are not faced with the onerous task of monitoring broadcast stations around the country to catch copyright violators and then prosecute them. Instead the licensing agency can handle this. The income from the fees garnered by each agency is distributed, after a deduction for administrative expenses, to the copyright owners with whom the agency has an agreement. Typically the composer of a licensed song gets the same share of royalties as the publisher.

A blanket license normally grants a TV station two types of rights: *synchronization rights* and *performance rights*. A *"sync" right* allows the licensee to copy a musical recording onto the soundtrack of a film or videotape in synchronization with action so a single work is produced. A *performance right* allows the station to transmit the work to the public, either live or recorded. Both ASCAP and BMI also offer a *program license* that grants the broadcaster the right to as many of the compositions licensed by the agency that the stations wishes on a specific program. The fee for this license is a set percent of the advertising revenue from the program.[123]

Over the years, blanket licensing has survived a number of legal challenges, most recently in 1984 in *Buffalo Broadcasting Co. v. American Society of Composers, Authors and Publishers*,[124] in which the Second Circuit U.S. Court of Appeals overturned a U.S. District Court decision that blanket licensing constituted an unlawful restraint of trade. The District Court's injunction against ASCAP and BMI to prevent them from licensing nondramatic music performance rights to local stations for syndicated programming was also lifted by the Court of Appeals. On further appeal, the U.S. Supreme Court denied certiorari.[125]

Broadcasters are not the only ones affected by licensing. In 1982, the Second Circuit U.S. Court of Appeals held that Gap clothing stores could be enjoined for copyright infringement for playing copyrighted music without a license.[126] The company retransmitted a radio station's signal over a speaker system to customers in its stores. There are dozens of music services such as Muzak,

Super Radio and the Instore Satellite Network that offer stores and other public facilities audio services. Most are delivered via satellite and are unscrambled but they cannot be broadcast without consent, which involves paying a monthly fee with the proceeds shared with owners of the copyrighted music, including composers and publishers. An office, store or other business (whether for-profit or nonprofit) does not have the right to rebroadcast radio signals even if they are from a local commercial or noncommercial station because the station's blanket license covers only the original broadcast, not any other "public performance." Secretarys who listen to their favorite country/ western station at the office each day are not engaging in copyright infringement, but a metropolitan newspaper that retransmits the local top 40 station to its 50 individual offices in the building without consent is likely in violation.

Finally, it is no secret that ASCAP, BMI and other licensing agencies routinely monitor radio and television stations and visit restaurants, bars, department stores and other public facilities to spot potential copyright infringers who are usually warned and threatened with a lawsuit if they do not halt infringement or obtain a blanket or other appropriate license. Millions of dollars are at stake, and the copyright law provides writers, artists, performers, composers and publishers with powerful tools of enforcement (as indicated later). Licensing agencies are merely acting on behalf of their members or affiliates in aggressively pursuing infringers.

Public Property

Certain kinds of works are considered *public property* because they have no original authorship and, as such, cannot be copyrighted. These include "standard calendars, height and weight charts, tape measures and rulers, and lists or tables taken from public documents or other common sources."[127] Public property also includes works created by the federal government, as noted earlier, but bear in mind that the U.S. government can have copyrights transferred to it by individuals who are not regular government employees. Although not required because of the Berne Convention, a copyright notice will usually be posted on those works for which the government is claiming copyright under a transfer, but the government usually does **not** include a notice on noncopyrighted works to inform the reader that the work is in the public domain. Instead, the idea of the government appears to be that it is not necessary to inform the public that a particular government work can be used without consent. U.S. government bookstores, such as the main office in Washington, DC, carry thousands of noncopyrighted government works for sale ranging from congressional reports to wildlife posters that can be reproduced without consent. Most of the materials are printed by the U.S. Government Printing Office.

Statute of Limitations

The *statute of limitations* for both criminal and civil violations of copyright is **three years**. According to §507, "No criminal proceeding shall be maintained . . . unless it is commenced within three years after the cause of action arose"[128] and "no civil action shall be maintained . . . unless it is commenced within three years after the claim accrued."[129] Thus a plaintiff has a fairly lengthy period in which to file an infringement suit against an alleged offender, and the federal government (usually the Federal Bureau of Investigation) must file any criminal charges against an alleged infringer within the three years. If such actions are not initiated within that time, the statute of limitations imposes a complete bar, no matter how serious or extensive the infringement. For example, an unscrupulous writer who uses another writer's chapter without consent in his book published in January 1991 could be sued anytime until January 1994 for the initial publication. However, if he continues to publish the book with the pirated chapter, he can still be held liable in February 1994 for a book he permitted to be sold in March 1991 even though the initial infringement occurred more than three years ago. Thus each publication, sale, and so on, constitutes a separate and new infringement. Because the statute of limitations is relatively long, it is rarely used as a defense to either criminal or civil infringement.

Expiration of Copyright

In 1893 Patty Smith Hill and her sister, Mildred J. Hill, two kindergarten and Sunday school teachers from Louisville, Kentucky, composed a melody whose lyrics later become the famous song, "Happy Birthday to You."[130] The song was not published and copyrighted, however, until 1935. In 1988 the Sengstack family of Princeton, New Jersey—which for 50 years had owned Birchtree Ltd., the company that owned the copyright to the song[131]—sold the company along with the rights to "Happy Birthday to You" to Warner Chappell (a division of Warner Communications, Inc. and the largest music publisher in the world) for a reported $25 million.[132] Why did Warner want the copyright to the song? According to the *Guinness Book of World Records*, it is the one of the three most popular songs in the English language, along with "Auld Lang Syne" and "For He's a Jolly Good Fellow."[133] The good news is that the song garners royalties of about $1 million a year, but the bad news is that it becomes a public domain work in 2010 when its 75-year-old copyright expires. The other two popular songs are already in the public domain because their copyrights have long expired. "Happy Birthday to You" lives on. Interestingly, the Sengstack family sold the copyright reportedly because Birchtree did not have the resources to aggressively protect the copyright and market the song.[134]

Until the song attracted attention with its sale in 1988, most people assumed it was not copyrighted. Every day the song is sung at thousands of birthday parties and no royalty is paid because it would be difficult to enforce the copyright in those situations. However, when the song is sung on television or radio or its lyrics appear in an advertisement, a royalty is due; chances are very good that it is paid because Warner rightfully protects the songs for which it owns the copyright. It is essential that anyone, including journalists, make absolutely sure that a work's copyright has expired before assuming it is public domain and making use of the work without consent. As indicated in the "Duration" section, once the copyright expires the work remains in the public domain forever. But copyright duration under the new law is quite extensive, both for works that were copyrighted before the statute took effect and for works created on or after January 1, 1978.

Fair Use

Fair use is the one defense to copyright infringement with which most people are familiar. Unfortunately, it is also the most misunderstood concept. Consider some of the myths about fair use. **Myth 1**: If less than 10 percent of a work is used, that's fair use. **The truth**: There is no specified amount, either in the statute or in case law. **Myth 2**: If you acknowledge (i.e., give credit) when you include excerpts from another's work, that's fair use and no consent needs to be obtained. **The truth**: Fair use has nothing to do with whether you give credit. In fact, when you acknowledge using the other person's work, you are, in a sense, admitting possible infringement if you do not have a legitimate defense otherwise. **Myth 3**: If the use would seem fair to a reasonable person, then it's fair use. **The truth**: If you have a "gut feeling that what you are doing is "unfair" or "wrong," you are probably treading on dangerous ground and committing infringement. But, on the other hand, if you feel comfortable, your actions still may not be fair use. For example, many people see nothing wrong with dubbing a compact disc album onto an audio tape if they already own the disk. Under the statute, this is not permissible as fair use, and even though one's chances of being sued in such a case are virtually nil when it is for home use, the act is, nevertheless, infringement. **Myth 4**: Fair use is a First Amendment right. **The truth**: Nothing could be further from the truth. Fair use has always been a common law creature that was given federal statutory life only in 1978 when the new law took effect. Interestingly, the courts, including the U.S. Supreme Court, in recent years have either ignored or dismissed claims of First Amendment or other constitutional protection by defendants in fair use cases. **The moral**: Throw up the statute as a "fair use" shield, but do not expect the First Amendment to save you when you have used copyrighted material without consent.

What Is Fair Use?

Congress included dozens of definitions in the Copyright Act of 1976 from "anonymous work" to "widow" and "widower," but fair use is deliberately not among them because the legislators had difficulty defining the concept, as indicated in a 1976 report of the House of Representatives Judiciary Committee:

> The judicial doctrine of fair use, one of the most important and well-established limitations on the exclusive right of copyright owners, would be given express statutory recognition for the first time in section 107. The claim that a defendant's acts constituted a fair use rather than an infringement has been raised as a defense in innumerable copyright actions over the years, and there is ample case law recognizing the existence of the doctrine and applying it. . . .
>
> Although the courts have considered and ruled upon the fair use doctrine over and over again, no real definition of the concept has ever emerged. Indeed, since the doctrine is an equitable rule of reason, no generally applicable definition is possible, and each case raising the question must be decided on its own facts.[135]

Thus Congress chose instead to incorporate into §107 four criteria that had evolved from the courts in determining fair use:

> In determining whether the use made of a work in particular case is fair use the factors to be considered shall include—
>
> (1) the purpose and character of the use, including whether such use is of a commercial nature or is for nonprofit educational purposes;
>
> (2) the nature of the copyrighted work;
>
> (3) the amount and substantiality of the portion used in relation to the copyrighted work as a whole; and
>
> (4) the effect of the use upon the potential market for or value of the copyrighted work.[136]

Section 107 mentions specific examples of purposes that can involve fair use, including "criticism, comment, news reporting, teaching (including multiple copies for classroom use), scholarship, or research."[137] While it is not part of the statute and it cannot be used to definitively determine the intent of Congress in enacting the Copyright Act, the House Report gives an indication of the law's purpose:

> The statement of the fair use doctrine in section 107 offers some guidance to users in determining when the principles of the doctrine apply. However, the endless variety of situations and combinations of circumstances that can rise in

particular cases precludes the formulation of exact rules in the statute. The bill endorses the purpose and general scope of the judicial doctrine of fair use, but there is no disposition to freeze the doctrine in the statute, especially during a period of rapid technological change. Beyond a very broad statutory explanation of what fair use is and some of the criteria applicable to it, the courts must be free to adapt the doctrine to particular situations on a case-by-case basis. Section 107 is intended to restate the present judicial doctrine of fair use, not to change, narrow, or enlarge it in any way.[138]

Thus Congress chose to establish broad guidelines and trust the courts to determine on a case-by-case basis what is and is not fair use, and that is exactly what the courts have done, occasionally even revealing gaps in the statute. There have been hundreds of court decisions dealing with fair use, both under the 1909 statute and the 1976 one. This section focuses on those that have had a major impact and/or illustrate important aspects of the concept. Each of the four factors is important, but none is, by itself, determinative. Instead, the courts evaluate each situation in light of all four and attempt to strike a balance among them, as illustrated in a 1968 decision by a U.S. District Court in New York. In *Time, Inc. v. Bernard Geis Associates*,[139] the federal trial court ruled that the author and publisher of a book containing charcoal sketches of frames from the famous Zapruder copyrighted film of President John F. Kennedy's assassination constituted fair use. When Kennedy was killed on November 22, 1963, amateur photographer Abraham Zapruder took color, 8 mm moving pictures of the shooting. Zapruder had three copies made, of which two were given to the U.S. Secret Service with the understanding that they would not be made public but used only for the government's investigation. He then signed a contract with *Life* under which the magazine acquired ownership of all three copies for $150,000. *Life* subsequently published individual frames of the film in various issues but did not register its copyright until 1967, although the magazine issues in which the frames appeared had already been registered.

Bernard Geis Associates negotiated unsuccessfully with Time, Inc. (the publisher of *Life*) for the right to publish several frames from the Zapruder film in a book, *Six Seconds in Dallas*, by Josiah Thomas.[140] After being denied the right, Thomas and the publisher hired a professional artist to draw charcoal sketches of the frames, 22 of which appeared in the book when it was published in late 1967. Time, Inc. sued for copyright infringement, and Bernard Geis claimed fair use as a defense and that *Life* had no valid copyright in the film. A U.S. District Court judge balanced each of the four factors (listed earlier) and issued a summary judgment in favor of Bernard Geis Associates. Judge Wyatt determined that Time, Inc. had a valid copyright, but the book had made fair use of the film and therefore had not infringed:

There is a public interest in having the fullest information available on the murder of President Kennedy. Thompson did serious work on the subject and has a theory entitled to public consideration. While doubtless the theory could be explained with sketches of the type used at page 87 of the Book and in *The Saturday Evening Post*, the explanation actually made in the Book with copies is easier to understand. The Book is not bought because it contained the Zapruder pictures; the Book is bought because of the theory of Thompson and its explanation, supported by Zapruder pictures.

There seems little, if any, injury to plaintiff, the copyright owner. There is no competition between plaintiff and defendants. Plaintiff does not sell the Zapruder pictures as such and no market for the copyrighted work appears to be affected. defendants do not publish a magazine. There are projects for use by plaintiff of the film in the future as a motion picture or in books, but the effect of the use of certain frames in the Book on such projects is speculative. It seems more reasonable to speculate that the Book would, if anything, enhance the value of the copyrighted work; it is difficult to see any decrease in its value.[141]

Although this case was decided prior to the 1976 statute, it is a good illustration of how courts balance the factors. Notice that the court was particularly concerned about factor four — the effect of the use on the potential market for or value of the copyrighted work. The judge made it clear that the two parties were not in competition; indeed the book could even *increase* the value of the film. He also weighed the public interest served in line with factor one. In another part of the decision, the Court noted that whereas Thompson had made "deliberate appropriation in the Book, in defiance of the copyright owner . . . it was not the nighttime activities of Thompson which enabled defendants to reproduce Zapruder frames in the Book. They could have secured such frames from the National Archives, or they could have used the reproductions in the Warren Report or in the issues of Life itself."[142]

In 1985 the U.S. Supreme Court issued the most important fair use decision thus far. In *Harper & Row v. Nation Enterprises*[143] held in a 6–3 decision written by Justice Sandra Day O'Connor that *Nation* magazine had infringed the copyright jointly owned by Harper & Row and Reader's Digest Association to the unpublished memoirs of former President Gerald Ford. In early 1977 shortly after he stepped down as President, Gerald Ford signed a contract with Harper & Row and Reader's Digest to publish his then-unwritten autobiography. Ford granted the two publishers the right to publish the manuscript in book form and as a serial ("first serial rights"). In 1979 they sold *Time* magazine the exclusive right to excerpt 7,500 words from Ford's account of his pardon of former President Richard M. Nixon for any crimes connected with the 1972 attempted burglary by Nixon operatives of the Democratic campaign headquarters at the Watergate office building in Washington, DC. (Nixon was forced to resign from the presidency as a result of his involvement in the cover-up of the burglary.) The contract with *Time* included provisions that the magazine would be allowed to publish the excerpt approximately one week before the book would be shipped to bookstores and that *Time* retained the right to renegotiate part of its payment if the material in the book were published before the excerpt.

In March 1979 an unidentified source furnished Victor Navasky, editor of the *Nation*, a monthly political commentary magazine, with a copy of the unpublished manuscript, *A Time to Heal: The Autobiography of Gerald R. Ford*. Before *Time* could publish its excerpt, in April *Nation* carried a 2,250-word feature that included verbatim quotes of 300 to 400 words from the original manuscript. According to the Court, these quotes composed about 13 percent of the *Nation* article, and the editor made no independent commentary nor did any independent research because, as he admitted at trial, he wanted to scoop *Time*. *Time* thus decided not to publish its excerpt and refused to pay Harper & Row and Reader's Digest Association the remaining $12,500 of the $25,000 it had agreed to pay for the prepublication rights. Harper & Row and Reader's Digest then filed suit against *Nation* for copyright infringement.

The U.S. District Court for the Southern District of New York ruled against *Nation* in its defense of fair use and awarded the plaintiffs $12,500 in actual damages for copyright infringement. However, the Second Circuit U.S. Court of appeals reversed, holding that although the memoirs were copyrighted, the *Nation* disclosure of the information was "politically significant" and newsworthy and thus fair use. The U.S. Supreme Court disagreed with the lower appellate court. The Court analyzed the case in light of each of the four factors but paid particular attention to the fourth factor:

> In evaluating character and purpose [factor one] we cannot ignore the Nation's stated purpose of scooping the forthcoming hardcover and Time abstracts. The Nation's use had not merely the incidental effect but the intended purpose of supplanting the copyright holder's commercially valuable right of first publication. . . .
>
> The fact that a work is unpublished is a critical element of its "nature." [citations omitted] Our prior discussion establishes that the scope of fair use is narrower with respect to unpublished works. While even substantial quotations might qualify as fair use in a review of a published work or a news account of a speech that had been delivered to the public or disseminated to the press, . . . the author's right to control the first public appearance of his expression weighs against such use of the work before its release. The right of first publication encompasses not only the choice whether to publish at all, but also the choices when, where and in what form first to publish a work.[144]

On the third factor (amount and substantiality), the Court noted that whereas "the words actually quoted were an insubstantial portion" of the book, *Nation*, as the District Court said, "took what was essentially the heart of the book."[145] The Court cited the *Nation* editor's own testimony at trial as evidence that he selected the passages he ultimately published "precisely because they qualitatively embodied Ford's distinctive expression."[146]

On the last factor (effect of the use on the potential market), the Court was particularly critical of the *Nation's* action and its impact. Noting that this factor "is undoubtedly the single most important element of fair use," the majority pointed to the trial court's finding of an actual effect on the market, not simply a potential effect:

> Time's cancellation of its projected serialization and its refusal to pay the $12,500 were the direct result of the infringement. . . . Rarely will a case of copyright infringement present such clear cut evidence of actual damage. Petitioners [Harper & Row and Reader's Digest] assured Time that there would be no other authorized publication of any portion of the unpublished manuscript prior to April 23, 1979.[147]

The justices went on to contend, "Placed in a broader perspective, a fair use doctrine that permits extensive prepublication quotations from an unreleased manuscript without the copyright owner's consent poses substantial potential for damage to the marketability of first serialization rights in general."[148] Thus *Harper & Row v. Nation Enterprises* has typically been classified as a "unpublished works" case, but at least one copyright expert views the decision differently. Kenneth M. Vittor, Vice President and Associate General Counsel of McGraw-Hill, Inc., believes the holding "is more properly understood as an attempt by the Court to protect the right of authors to choose the timing of the first publication of their soon-to-be-published works."[149]

Three major points emerge from this decision. First, a defense of fair use is less likely to succeed in the case of an unpublished work than with a published work. Would *Nation* have won if all the circumstances had been the same except that the extensive excerpt from Ford's memoirs had already appeared in *Time*? What if the both the book and the *Time* excerpt had already been published? The Court apparently assumed that the manuscript had been purloined, even though the *Nation* magazine editor himself had apparently not been directly involved. This allegation hurt the magazine's claim that the information was in the public interest. As the Court iterated, the book took two years to produce, including hundreds of taped interviews, which then had to be distilled into a single work. If one were allowed to profit from taking another's work under these circumstances, the Court felt authors would be discouraged from creating original works, thereby depriving the public of important historical information. In other words, if researchers/authors face the risk that their work will garner no rewards or royalties, they are unlikely to be interested in conducting the extensive research and making the other efforts necessary to produce the work that might ultimately add to public knowledge.

The Court was also concerned that offering protection for *Nation* in this case would establish a precedent in which the defense of fair use would be broadened so much that it would "effectively destroy any expectation in the work of a public figure."[150] Was it unethical for *Nation* magazine to scoop *Time* magazine with a story based on information that was possibly improperly obtained? Can public interest justify the use of tainted information under any circumstances? Some First Amendment scholars are becoming increasingly concerned, especially in light of recent U.S. Supreme Court decisions in libel and privacy, that the Courts are no longer hesitant to dictate ethical standards to journalists, especially to those who step into the gray area between legal and illegal conduct. As discussed elsewhere, two of the major media law decisions issued by the U.S. Supreme Court during its 1990–1991 term alone involved matters that could have been resolved with stronger ethical standards — *Cohen v. Cowles*[151] (which developed when two newspapers editors deliberately disclosed the names of sources to whom their own reporters had promised confidentiality) and *Masson v. New Yorker*[152] (involving fabricated quotes). Copyright is certainly not immune from ethical dilemmas, as *Harper & Row v. Nation Enterprises* illustrates.

The principles established in *Harper & Row v. Nation Enterprises* played a major role two years later in an important copyright decision by the Second Circuit U.S. Court of Appeals. In *Salinger v. Random House* (1987),[153] the federal appellate court granted an injunction sought by reclusive writer J. D. Salinger (author of the classic and popular 1951 novel, *The Catcher in the Rye*) against publication of Ian Hamilton's unauthorized biography, *J. D. Salinger: A Writing Life*. Hamilton made extensive use of information, including direct quotes, he had obtained from some 70 copyrighted letters Salinger had sent to various individuals who had, in turn, donated them to several university libraries. Although the biographer had substantially altered the book before it went to press after complaints from Salinger, the writer was not satisfied and filed suit for copyright infringement. The U.S. District Court sided with Hamilton and refused to issue the injunction (one of the remedies available for infringement, as indicated shortly); it felt most of the material used from the letters was protected by fair use because it consisted primarily of Salinger's ideas expressed in Hamilton's own words rather than Salinger's specific expressions. The U.S. Court of Appeals reversed, holding that Hamilton was not protected by fair use and that, under *Harper & Row v. Nation*, unpublished works "normally enjoy complete protection against copying any protected expression."[154] According to the appellate court, "Public awareness of the expressive content of the letters will have to await either Salinger's decision to publish or the expiration of his copyright."[155] Interestingly, Salinger indicated that he had no intentions of publishing the letters, but because he wrote them, the copyright belonged to him, not the recipients. Thus he had every right to halt publication of their content, in the eyes of the court. The U.S. Supreme Court denied certiorari in the case.

Two years later, the Second Circuit tackled the fair use issue once again in a case that has particularly troubled many First Amendment experts, not because of its outcome but because of the court's opinion. In *New Era Publications International v. Henry Holt & Co.*,[156] the Court of Appeals affirmed a U.S. District Court decision **not** to grant an injunction against publication of a highly critical and unauthorized biography of the controversial L. Ron Hubbard, founder of the Church of Scientology. Applying the principles established in *Salinger v. Random House*, District Court Judge Pierre N. Leval had ruled that Russell Miller's *Bare-Faced Messiah: The True Story of L. Ron Hubbard* had infringed on the copyrights held by New Era Publications to Hubbard's writings because "there is a body of material of small, but more than negligible size, which, given the strong presumption against fair use of unpublished material, cannot be held to pass the fair use test."[157] However, Judge Leval ruled an injunction was not appropriate because of First Amendment concerns over prior restraint that outweighed the copyright owner's interests in the case and because New Era could still seek damages (another remedy for infringement discussed shortly).

The Second Circuit Court upheld the trial court decision but on the ground of *laches*, not fair use. *Laches* is the equitable doctrine that when a party unreasonably delays asserting a right or a claim to the detriment of the other party, its request will be dismissed. According to the court, New Era had failed to make any efforts to protect its copyrights until the biography was actually published, even though it had clearly been aware for several years that Miller's work was underway: "The prejudice suffered by Holt as a result of New Era's unreasonable and inexcusable delay in bringing action invokes the bar of laches."[158] Miller had gathered most of his information about Hubbard from court documents, interviews with Hubbard's acquaintances, news stories and Hubbard's own writings, including letters and diaries.

The appellate court particularly noted its displeasure with U.S. District Court Judge Leval's analysis, especially his First Amendment concerns: "We are not persuaded . . . that any first amendment concerns not accommodated by the Copyright Act are implicated in this action." The U.S. Court of Appeals felt that the biography was a much more serious infringement than the trial court had claimed. Henry Holt filed a request for rehearing on the issue of fair use in the case even though it had won on the laches ground, but the appellate court rejected the request in a sharply divided 7–5 opinion.[159]

One year later, the same appellate court in another fair use case involving another unauthorized biography of L. Ron Hubbard overturned a U.S. District Court injunction against publication of Jonathan Caven-Atack's *A Piece of Blue Sky: Scientology, Dianetics and L. Ron Hubbard Exposed*. In *New Era Publications International v. Carol Publishing Group*,[160] the Second Circuit U.S. Court of Appeals ruled in favor of Carol Publishing (which had published the biography) on all four of the fair use factors. The appellate court felt the materials used in the work were particularly protected because they had been taken from dozens of published works rather than Hubbard's unpublished writings. The court noted that the works were factual and that the scope of fair use is greater for factual than nonfactual writings and that the amount of the materials used in the biography were neither qualitatively nor quantitatively substantial. Finally, the court said that although the book was intended to make profits and it might "discourage potential purchasers of the authorized biography [which New Era planned to publish], this is not necessarily actionable under the copyright laws. . . . Harm to the market for a copyrighted work or its derivatives caused by a 'devastating critique' that 'diminished sales by convincing the public that the original work was of poor quality' is not 'within the scope of copyright protection' "(citations omitted)."[161]

Whereas the last decision provided some comfort for biographers and other writers who use primarily published materials in their works, the earlier decisions continue to haunt those who want to use unpublished documents.

The aftermath of the *Salinger v. Random House* and *New Era Publications v. Holt* decisions, according to one news account, has been self-censorship by book publishers with "the authors themselves try[ing] to figure our history in a straitjacket."[162] A spate of lawsuits has ensued in the wake of the holdings, and no end appears in sight. Although the Second Circuit's opinions are binding only on federal courts in Vermont, Connecticut and New York, its opinions have traditionally been very influential on courts in other circuits. The U.S. Supreme Court denied certiorari in both cases, and there is no indication that the Court is likely to tackle this issue anytime soon. In the meantime, historians and other researchers can be expected to exercise extreme care in using unpublished materials, including those of public figures even when the information is readily accessible to the public already in libraries and other depositories.

Harper & Row v. Nation may have opened a can of worms that will haunt or at least chill the dissemination of information based on unpublished materials used without the consent of the author or other copyright owner. One fair use loophole has now been closed, however. In October 1992 President Bush signed legislation that amends §107 of the Copyright Act to include the following: "The fact that such a work is unpublished shall not itself bar a finding of fair use if such finding is made upon consideration of the above factors."[163] Had this provision been effective at the time the Copyright Act took effect in 1978, *Salinger* and similar cases may very well have been decided differently.

In 1992, U.S. District Court Judge Pierre N. Leval (S.D. N.Y.) issued a decision in a case centering on fair use that is expected to have a major impact on interpretation of the doctrine. The decision is legally binding only in the Southern District of New York, but its holding is likely to be followed in many other federal district courts. In *American Geophysical Union v. Texaco,*

Inc.,[164] the judge held that a Texaco scientist's making of single copies of journal articles was not fair use under §107 of the Copyright Act of 1976 and therefore an infringement. The "test case" (under which the parties agreed to stipulate certain facts to avoid high discovery expenses and to expeditiously settle the issue) involved a Texaco scientist (whose name was drawn at random for the case from among those who worked for the oil company.) From Dr. Donald Chickering II's files, eight copies of complete articles that appeared in the *Journal of Catalysis* were selected. According to the opinion, Texaco scientists such as Chickering routinely have the company library make single photocopies of articles from journals to which the library subscribes. The advantages of this procedure include permitting the workers to keep easily referenced files in their desks or on their office shelves, eliminating the risk of errors when data are transcribed from articles and then taken back to the lab for research, and making it possible for them to take articles home to read. Nevertheless, the Court ruled that this was not fair use because (a) Texaco's use was for commercial gain, (b) substantial portions of the works were copied, and (c) Texaco's use deprived the copyright holder of potential royalties. One solution suggested by the judge was for the company to obtain clearance from the nonprofit Copyright Clearance Center, which grants blanket advance permission for a specified fee to photocopy (usually noted on the copyrighted material itself).

Two major court decisions in recent years have had a particularly important impact on the use of copyrighted materials in higher education. The most recent one, in fact, probably played a role in the supplemental materials your instructor selected for this course. On March 28, 1991, U.S. District Court Judge Constance Baker Motley of the Southern District of New York issued a decision that will continue to affect how colleges and universities use copyrighted materials in the classroom for years to come. In *Basic Books, Inc. v. Kinko's Graphics Corp.*,[165] the federal trial court judge soundly rejected Kinko's claim that the fair use doctrine permitted it to photocopy without consent anthologies of copyrighted materials as part of its "Professor Publishing" program. Under the program, the firm photocopied journal articles, book chapters and other copyrighted materials selected by college and university instructors as readings for their classes. These anthologies were then sold for profit to students. The suit was filed in April 1989 by eight publishers who said two of the stores owned by the graphics company had engaged in copyright infringement by photocopying substantial portions of 12 books for use in anthologies used at New York University, Columbia University and the New School for Social Research. Neither the schools nor the professors involved were named as defendants.[166]

In her 57-page opinion, Judge Motley held that Kinko's had intentionally violated the copyright statute and ordered the chain to pay $510,000 in actual damages as well as the plaintiffs' court costs and attorneys' fees. She also issued an injunction barring the company from photocopying and selling copies of copyrighted materials without obtaining the consent of copyright owners and paying any royalties requested. As a result, Kinko's changed its Professor Publishing Program policies to comply with the court order, including obtaining permission for the photocopying of any copyrighted material from the copyright owner or requiring professors to obtain such permission even when they believe the photocopying would be protected under the fair use doctrine.[167]

In 1986, a U.S. District Court judge in California granted summary judgment for the University of California, Los Angeles, in a copyright infringement suit filed against the university by BV Engineering, a computer software company based in California. The company had asked for $70,000 in damages from UCLA for allegedly making unauthorized copies of seven computer programs and user manuals for which BV Engineering owned the copyright. The federal trial court judge ruled that the 11th Amendment to the U.S. Constitution barred state-supported institutions from being successfully sued under federal laws, including the Copyright Act of 1976, unless Congress specifically allows such litigation or the state has explicitly waived its immunity.[168] In *BV Engineering v. University of California at Los Angeles* (1988),[169] the Ninth Circuit U.S. Court of Appeals upheld the lower court decision, and in 1989, the U.S. Supreme Court denied certiorari.[170] Because the case simply pointed to a gap in the 1976 statute, Congress quickly revised the federal copyright statute with very little opposition. Even colleges and universities generally supported the bill because they, too, own copyrights they prefer to protect from infringement by state agencies. The impact of the case was rather minimal even before the new law because the court's holding did not exempt individual professors from being held liable nor did it prevent a copyright owner from seeking an injunction against a state agency for infringement. The decision merely barred BV Engineering from obtaining damages, thanks to an oversight by Congress. Under the revision, effective November 15, 1990,[171] the definition of "anyone" for purposes of infringement now includes "any State, any instrumentality of a State, and any officer or employee of a State or instrumentality of a State acting in his or her official capacity."[172] The act also makes it clear that any "State, any instrumentality of a State, and any officer or employee of a State acting in his or her official capacity, shall not be immune, under the Eleventh Amendment of the Constitution of the United States or under any other doctrine of sovereign immunity, from suit in Federal court" for copyright infringement.[173] The revised statute also preserves the same remedies — including actual damages, profits, statutory damages and so on — for infringement that are available for nongovernmental entities.[174] The net effect of the new law is to put state governments in the same position as everyone else (except the federal government) for purposes of copyright infringement.

Section 107 of the 1976 statute specifically mentions *criticism, comment,* and *news reporting* as purposes that can be considered fair use, but, as the courts have made clear, these uses do not always enjoy protection in an infringement suit. In May 1991 a U.S. District Court Judge in Atlanta awarded WSB-TV $108,000 plus attorneys' fees and courts costs against TV News Clips for videotaping portions of the station's local newscasts and selling them to the public.[175] The court also issued a permanent injunction barring the company from making any further copies of newscasts or offering them for sale. The news clips service charges clients $65 for the first program and $30 each for additional program. In October 1983 the same company was ordered to pay $35 in damages to another Atlanta station, WXIA-TV,[176] which eventually obtained an injunction prohibiting the service from making any copies of the station's newscasts.[177]

In 1991 several Los Angeles police were indicted for assault and other charges for allegedly beating or failing to stop the beating of an area motorist pulled over for speeding. George Holiday, an amateur photographer, videotaped the beating from his apartment window. The videotape was shown hundreds of times on television stations around the country and on the major networks after it was allegedly distributed by a Los Angeles TV station without consent of Holiday, who owned the copyright to the tape, which had also been registered with the Copyright Office. Holiday's attorney reportedly mailed a letter to more than 900 television stations around the country demanding payment for use of the film. Whether the stations are protected under the fair use doctrine has yet to be determined, but it is likely that the stations could be held liable because the tape is copyrighted and will probably not be considered a public document or in the public domain. In 1992 in *Lish v. Harper's Magazine Foundation*,[178] Gordon Lish won a $2,000 judgment for copyright infringement against *Harper's*, which had published more than half of the fiction writer-editor-teacher's unpublished letter to his students. U.S. District Court Judge Morris E. Lasker's ruling rejected the magazine's claim of fair use. The New York judge indicated that the evidence supported Lish on each of the first three factors associated with fair use (as discussed earlier), although the publication had little or no impact on the market for the work (the fourth factor).

In a case that could have a major impact on the entertainment industry, the U.S. Supreme Court agreed to rule during its 1993–94 term whether a 2 Live Crew parody of Roy Orbison's song, "Oh Pretty Woman" was a copyright infringement. The Sixth Circuit U.S. Court of Appeals said in 1992 that the parody was not fair use.[179]

REMEDIES FOR INFRINGEMENT

Under §501(a) of the current copyright statute, anyone (including state agencies and officials, as just discussed) who violates any of the exclusive rights of the copyright owner is an infringer. The statute provides a wide range of remedies from injunctions to criminal penalties, although it does not codify common law infringement. To prove infringement, plaintiffs must demonstrate that (a) they own the copyright to the infringed work, and (b) the defendant(s) copied the work. The latter involves proving the defendant(s) had access to the work and that the two works are substantially similar. Proving ownership is usually not difficult because owners simply have to produce sufficient evidence that they created the work or that the rights to the work were transferred to them. Registration is one way of establishing this because it constitutes prima facie evidence in court of the validity of the copyright if it is made prior to or within five years after publication. Sometimes ownership may be in dispute, however, as illustrated in a 1990 decision by the U.S. Supreme Court involving the 1954 Alfred Hitchcock movie, *Rear Window*. In *Stewart v. Abend*,[180] the U.S. Supreme court ruled 6–3 that actor James Stewart and the late film director Alfred Hitchcock had violated the copyright of Sheldon Abend to *Rear Window* when they released the film in 1981 for television and in 1983 put it on videocassette and videodisc.

The complicated story began in 1942 when a short story entitled "It Had to Be Murder" by Cornell Woolrich appeared in *Dime Detective* magazine. In 1945 Woolrich sold the movie rights only, **not** the copyright itself, to the story to B. G. De Sylva Productions for $9,250, with an agreement that De Sylva would have the same rights for the renewal period (which under the statute at that time was an additional 28 years). De Sylva then sold the movie rights in 1953 to a production company owned by Stewart and Hitchcock, which made the story into the still highly popular classic film, *Rear Window*.[181] When Woolrich died in 1968, he left his estate, including copyrights to his works to Columbia University. Chase Manhattan Bank, the executor for Woolrich's estate, renewed the copyright and in 1971 sold the renewed movie rights to "It Had to Be Murder" to literary agent Sheldon Abend for $650. In that same year, the movie was made available for television, and Abend informed Stewart, Hitchcock's estate and MCA, Inc. (which had released the film) that he would file suit for copyright infringement if the movie were distributed further. When MCA ignored the warning and allowed the ABC Television Network to broadcast *Rear Window*, Abend made good on his threat and sued, but the parties eventually settled out of court, with Abend getting $25,000. The saga continued, however.

In 1977, the Second Circuit U.S. Court of Appeals held that a company that had acquired derivative rights to a work still retained those rights even if the transfer of rights from the original work had expired.[182] MCA relied on that holding because *Rear Window* was a derivative work and re-released the film in 1983 on videocassette and for cable television. Abend filed suit once again, and it was dismissed by a U.S. District Court judge. On appeal, the Ninth Circuit U.S. Court of Appeals reversed, and the U.S. Supreme Court upheld the decision, 6–3. Abend stood to make millions of dollars in profits because the the re-release had generated more than $12 million worldwide by the time of the Supreme Court decision plus another $5 million in profits from release on home video.[183] Writing for the majority, Justice Sandra Day O'Connor said the 1977 Second Circuit decision was wrong because the 1909 statute in effect at the time of the ruling provides that the original copyright to a work continues, if renewed, even if derivative rights have been granted. Thus derivative rights expire when the original copyright expires, and the owner of the original rights can prevent the owner of the derivative rights from continuing to use the work. The Court was not sympathetic to the complaint by MCA, Stewart and Hitchcock's heirs that "they will have to pay more for the use of works that they have employed in creating their own works. . . . Such a result was contemplated by Congress and is consistent with the goals of the Copyright Act."[184] The decision affected hundreds of films and was estimated to cost the movie industry millions of dollars.[185]

Demonstrating *access* is usually a relatively simple matter, especially when a work has been widely distributed, but occasionally a defendant is able to prove lack of access. A typical example occurred in 1988 when singer Mick Jagger successfully fought a copyright infringement suit against him for his hit song, "Just Another Night."[186] Reggae musician, Patrick Alley, claimed the chorus from Jagger's song had been lifted from his 1979 recording, "Just Another Night." Alley claimed that Jagger had access to his song through a drummer who had played on both records and that Jagger probably heard Alley's song when it was played on several smaller New York radio stations. Jagger denied he had heard the song, and a U.S. District Court jury in New York ruled in his favor after hearing testimony from the defendant which included Jagger singing some of his lyrics.[187]

Substantial similarity is typically the key in deciding an infringement case. Although it was rendered prior to enactment of the current copyright statute, a 1977 ruling by the Ninth Circuit U.S. Court of Appeals has become a leading case of the criteria for evaluating substantial similarity. In cases of direct copying (such as a chapter, extensive excerpts and appropriation of exact wording), proof of copying is usually cut and dried, but indirect proof is typically all that can be shown and this can be done with evidence of substantial similarity. In *Sid and Marty Krofft Television Productions, Inc. v. McDonald's Corp.* (1977),[188] the creators of the show,"H.R. Pufnstuf" successfully claimed that McDonald's television commercials infringed on their copyright because the McDonaldland setting in the hamburger chain's ads and the characters portrayed in them were substantially similar to those in "H.R. Pufnstuf." The U.S. Court of Appeals applied a two-prong test in reaching its conclusion. First, *is there substantial similarity between the underlying general ideas of the two works*? If the answer is "no," there is no infringement. If "yes," the second question is: *Is there substantial similarity in the manner of expression of the two works*? If "yes," there is infringement. If no, the lawsuit fails. Both of these are questions of fact for a jury to determine or for the judge in a bench trial. Substantial similarity is often difficult for a plaintiff to prove on the two questions, but as the Krofft case illustrates, this can be done. The court found that McDonaldland and "H.R. Pufnstuf's" Living Island had substantially similar characters, scenery, dialogue and other features. Some of the most damming evidence presented at trial was that former Krofft employees had helped design and build McDonaldland.

A classic case of substantial similarity involved the highly popular movie, *Jaws*. In 1982 a U.S. District Court in California found that the movie, *Great White*, was substantially similar to *Jaws* and, therefore, an infringement.[189] The similarities were quite striking, as the court noted, including very similar characters (an English sea captain and a shark hunter who together track down a vicious shark, a similar plot, and even opening and closing sequences that were virtually identical). The judge in the case felt it was obvious that "the creators of *Great White* wished to be as closely connected with the plaintiff's motion picture *Jaws* as possible."[190] The producers of the infringement movie were ordered to pay damages, and an injunction was issued to ban further distribution of the film. *Great White* was dead with no sequels in sight.

The similarities were also striking in a 1989 Seventh Circuit U.S. Court of Appeals decision involving greeting cards.[191] For two years, Ruolo designed distinctive greeting cards for Russ Berrie & Co. under a contract granting the latter the exclusive right to produce and sell them under the "Feeling Sensitive" line. When the contract expired and Ruolo notified the company that it would not be renewed, Russ Berrie marketed a similar line of cards known as "Touching You." The appeals court upheld a jury decision that Russ Berrie had infringed because the cards were substantially similar, including being designed for similar occasions and identical in size and layout. Both cards featured two colored stripes on the left side on which a foil butterfly is superimposed and one colored stripe on the right side. Both series of cards were printed on cream-colored paper with handwritten messages in brown ink. The Court of Appeals characterized the action as *trade dress infringement* in which the substantial similarities lie in the overall image or "look and feel" of the works, as evidenced in size, shape, color, graphics, packaging and other visual aspects. The appellate court upheld the jury award of $4.3 million.

This same "look and feel test" is often applied in determining infringement in computer software cases, although a recent article on the issue concluded that "while broad protection may be given by some courts to the structure, sequence and organization of a program, copyright law provides no general protection for the overall 'look and feel' of a computer program."[192] The author predicts that instead patent law will emerge to grant the necessary protection that copyright law does not provide for computer software.[193]

Injunctions, Impoundment and Disposition

Under §502 of the Copyright Act, federal courts can grant both temporary and permanent ("final") injunctions to prevent infringement once infringement has been proven. The permanent injunction against *Great White* (as mentioned earlier), is an example of how this form of equitable relief can be effective. With the injunction, the movie could no longer be distributed, shown or sold anywhere in the United States. Although injunctions are clearly a form of prior restraint, the courts have indicated they are constitutionally permissible to prevent further infringement of intellectual property rights. A mere threatened infringement is usually not sufficient to warrant an injunction, but once infringement is proven, an injunction becomes a potent weapon available for the copyright owner. As with all injunctions, violations can subject a defendant to citation for contempt and fines as determined by the court.

Section 503 provides two other effective remedies—impoundment and disposition. *Impoundment* involves the government seizing potentially infringing materials or forcing a defendant to turn them over to the custody of the court until the case is decided. In its final decision, the court can also "order the destruction or other reasonable disposition of all copies or phonorecords" determined to violate copyright.[194] The federal courts rarely have to resort to these remedies, but they clearly have the authority to use them.

Damages and Profits

The most common remedy for infringement is an award of damages. Copyright owners who file suit against an alleged infringer can opt at any time before the court issues its decision (before "final judgement") for either actual damages along with any additional profits **or** statutory damages, but they cannot recover both. Under §504 an infringer can be liable for actual damages caused by the infringement plus any profits attributable to the infringement. All the copyright owner needs to show at trial to establish the amount of profit is the infringer's gross revenue.[195] A defendant can offset the profits awarded the plaintiff by providing deductible expenses and any portion of the profits that did not come from the infringement. Otherwise, he or she may have to fork over all profits. There is no limit on the amount of actual damages the copyright owner can recover so long as there is sufficient evidence to demonstrate the extent of the harm suffered. As with all civil suits in federal courts, judges have a responsibility to ensure that awards are not excessive in light of the evidence presented at trial. However, the judge and jury have considerable discretion in determining what is reasonable.

The 1988 revision of the Copyright Act[196] substantially increased the amount of *statutory damages* available. If copyright owners of an infringed work choose statutory damages instead of actual damages and profits, they obtain an award from $500 (minimum) to $20,000 (maximum) for each work infringed, depending on what the court considers an appropriate amount.[197]

If copyright owners can prove the infringement was willful, they can recover, at the court's discretion, up to $100,000 for each work.[198] On the other hand, if infringers can convince the court that they were not aware and had no reason to believe that they were infringing (i.e., innocent infringement), the court can reduce the statutory damages to as low as $200.[199] There is a "fair use" provision tucked away in § 504 under which "an employer or agent of a nonprofit educational institution, library, or archives acting within the scope of his or her employment" cannot be held liable for statutory damages for infringement in reproducing a work if the person believed and had reasonable grounds for believing that the use was a fair use.[200] A similar exception is made for public broadcasting employees who infringe by performing or reproducing a published nondramatic literary work.[201]

Other Remedies

Under § 505, the court can award court costs (i.e., the full cost of litigation for that side) and reasonable attorney's fees to whichever side wins.[202] These remedies are at the discretion of the judge. Finally, under certain circumstances, anyone who willfully infringes for commercial or private financial gain can be fined up to $250,000 and/or imprisoned for a maximum of five years. These offenses include such actions as reproducing or distributing during any 180-day period at least 10 copies or phonorecords of one or more copyrighted works, with a retail value of more than $2,500.[203] A second or subsequent offense can increase imprisonment to a maximum of 10 years.[204] Most videotape recordings now carry the standard Federal Bureau of Investigation warning, complete with seal, at the beginning of the tape. The FBI is indeed the primary police authority for enforcing the criminal provisions of the copyright statutes. The statutes also include a provision making it a federal crime to traffic in counterfeit labels for phonorecords and copies of motion pictures and other audiovisual works.[205]

In spite of its best efforts, Congress left some gaps in the copyright law, many of which have been closed with the nearly 20 amendments enacted since the legislation originally passed in 1976. One gap has yet to be resolved, although an unusual accord recently reached between the music and electronics industries may provide direction for federal lawmakers. The most prominent gap, at least from the consumer perspective, was revealed in the one U.S. Supreme Court copyright decision with which the public is familiar — *Sony Corporation of America v. Universal City Studios, Inc.* (1984).[206] The "Sony decision" or "Betamax case," as it is popularly known, is probably the most misinterpreted and misunderstood case involving copyright in the years since the new statute took effect. Some of the misunderstanding can be traced to inaccuracies in news stories about the decision and to the apparent general attitude among the public that home videotaping is a fair use and should not be regulated.

The case developed when Universal Studios, Walt Disney Productions and other television production companies sued the Sony Corporation, the largest manufacturer of videocassette recorders (VCRs)[207] sold in the United States at that time, for contributory copyright infringement. The production companies claimed the Japanese firm marketed to the public the technology to infringe on copyrighted works they owned. This infringement occurred, according to the plaintiffs, when consumers used Sony's Betamax VCRs[208] to record copyrighted programs broadcast on local stations, including "time-shifting," or recording for later use programs not viewed at the time they were broadcast. (The Court characterized this practice as the principal use of a VCR by the average owner.)

A U.S. District Court judge for the Central District of California ruled that recording of broadcasts carried on the public airwaves was a fair use of copyrighted works and thus Sony could not be held liable as a contributory infringer even if such home recording were infringement. The Ninth Circuit U.S. Court of Appeals reversed the trial court's decision, but the U.S. Supreme Court reversed the appellate court ruling. In a very narrow decision that dealt only with Sony's liability for manufacturing and marketing the recorders, the Court agreed with the district court that the company was not guilty of contributory infringement. In a 5-4 opinion written by Justice John Paul Stevens, the Court concluded that home time-shifting was fair use:

> In summary, the record and findings of the District Court lead us to two conclusions. First, Sony demonstrated a significant likelihood that substantial numbers of copyright holders who license their works for broadcast on free television would not object to having their broadcasts time-shifted by private viewers. And second, respondents failed to demonstrate that time-shifting would cause any likelihood of nonmimimal harm to the potential market for, or the value of, their copyrighted works. The Betamax is, therefore, capable of substantial noninfringing uses. Sony's sale of such equipment to the general public does not constitute contributory infringement of respondents' rights.[209]

The Court went on to note that there is no indication in the Copyright Act that Congress intended to make it unlawful for consumers to record programs for later viewing in the home or to prohibit the sale of recorders. "It may well be that Congress will take a fresh look at this new technology, just as it so often has examined other innovations in the past. But it is not our job to apply laws that have not yet been written."[210]

After the decision, several bills were proposed in Congress to respond to the Court's holding — such as taxing recorders and blank tape — but most legislators apparently felt the political fallout from such legislation would be too great. Federal lawmakers have yet to act to fill the perceived loophole. In the meantime, VCR ownership has expanded to an estimated 90 percent of homes, with the majority of families owning more than one recorder. Ninety percent of U.S. homes are now wired for cable television, with 60 percent actually subscribing.[211]

The *Sony* decision, which barely attracted a majority of the justices (two of whom are no longer on the Court), left many unanswered questions. Is videotaping at home an infringement? The Court said that the record supported the trial court's decision that home time-shifting was fair use, but the fair use doctrine does not mention such use as permissible. In fact, a literal application of the four criteria for fair use would appear not to protect this practice. For example, hometaping typically involves recording the entire program (more than a substantial portion under the third factor), its purpose is entertainment rather than nonprofit educational use (factor one) and, contrary to the Court's musings, such taping very likely negatively affects the potential market for the work (factor four). Is it fair use to record cable television programs, including pay channels? Is it fair use to edit programs as they are recorded such as deleting commercials? Do recorded programs have to be erased as soon as they are viewed or is it fair use to archive them for future multiple viewings?

The solution to this dilemma may lie in an agreement carved out between the music industry and electronics manufacturers in July 1991 on audio digital recording. In an unprecedented accord, the two industries struck a compromise for dealing with the new technology known as digital audio tape (DAT), which enables nearly perfect copying of audio recordings. They successfully lobbied Congress to enact legislation in 1992 under which a tax or "royalty," as the music industry calls it, is now imposed on the sale of all home digital recorders and blank tapes. The royalties all go to the music industry for distribution to copyright owners of songs recorded on digital tape.[212] Because digital equipment records in distortion-free computer data, the recordings are nearly flawless, lacking the usual "hiss" and other distortions of conventional or "analog" recordings. Several manufacturers are already marketing moderately priced digital tape recording systems called digital compact cassette (DCC) for consumers. Interestingly, Sony is marketing a somewhat different digital system that records on small discs rather than tape. In 1992 Congress amended the Copyright Act to create a royalty payment system and a serial copy management system for digital audio recording.[213]

The federal statute has no direct impact on other technologies such as VCRs. However, the private accord established by the two industries that have often clashed in the past over copyright issues paves the way for agreements on other technologies. Such compromises are a win-win situation for all sides. Consumers get the latest technology at reasonable prices and acquire the right to make legal copies of recordings under certain circumstances. Manufacturers (some of whom, such as Sony and its acquisition of CBS Records, now also own the copyrights to musical works and movies) can market their wares without fear of copyright infringement suits. And, finally, the music industry and its writers and artists reap a windfall of royalties that would have been virtually impossible to collect otherwise, even though they may have been rightfully entitled to the fees.

REGISTRATION

Even though registration is no longer required for copyright protection except in two specific situations,[214] there are some major advantages and the process is relatively simple. The advantages include:

1. Public record of the copyright.
2. Standing in court to file suit for infringement.
3. If made within five years of publication, prima facie evidence in court of the copyright's validity.
4. If made within three months after publication or prior to infringement, the availability of statutory damages and attorney's fees.

Registration may be made anytime during the duration of the copyright by simply sending the following in the same envelope or package to the Copyright Office:

1. A completed application form (different types of works have different forms, as indicated later).
2. A $20 filing fee (for most works).
3. One copy or phonorecord if the work is unpublished or was first published outside the United States, or two copies or phonorecords if the work was first published in the United States.

For copyright renewal, no copies have to be sent, but a completed "RE" form and a $20 fee must be filed. Copyright renewals are made only for those works that were published or registered before January 1, 1978. There are 10 different registration forms, and it is essential that the correct form be filed. There is even a form CA to correct or amplify information given on an earlier form. Form TX is used to register published and unpublished nondramatic literary works, and Form SE is for serials such as newspapers, periodicals, magazines, newsletters and similar publications. Motion pictures and other audiovisual works use Form PA, and Form VA handles works of the visual arts such as sculptures and architecture. Form SR is for sound recordings, and there are forms for certain types of group registrations such as Form G/DN for daily newspapers. Registration is effective the day the Copyright Office receives the properly completed application, fee and materials. Certificates can take as long as four months, but most are mailed within one to two months. The certificates are simply copies of the form signed and dated by the Copyright Office.

COPYRIGHT PROTECTION
FOR NEWER TECHNOLOGIES

Copyright protection exists for a wide range of technologies, including computer programs, automated databases and semiconductor chips (also known as *mask works*). Computer programs have been the subject of considerable litigation even with the new statute, but the courts have made it clear that computer software enjoys copyright protection. In June 1988 the Copyright Office announced, after public hearings and a review of public comments, that it would "require that all copyrightable expression embodied in a computer program owned by the same claimant, including computer screen displays, be registered on a single application form" (Form TX or PA).[215] Until that time, conflicting court opinions had muddled the issue of whether a single form could be used. Now the question appears resolved, although other new technologies will undoubtedly raise other questions. The courts have also made it clear that copyright protection covers object codes, source codes and microcodes in software as well as the overall structure of the program or the "look and feel," as it is commonly known.

The copyright statute does not specifically mention automated data bases, but the Copyright Office and the courts interpret the legislative history of the act to include automated data bases, as complications of facts and thus literary works.[216] Such data bases, as with all copyrightable works, must involve originality and not simply be a mere mechanical collection of information.[217]

Finally, semiconductor chips (sometimes called "integrated circuits) were added to the list of copyrightable works with the Semiconductor Chip Protection Act of 1984.[218] The provisions regarding these mask works differ some from those of other works. For example, to secure copyright protection, the owner must register a work within two years after it is first "commercially exploited" or the protection is lost.[219] Protection is good only for 10 years, and the form of notice is Ⓜ followed by the owner's name. The year of first publication is not required.[220]

MORAL RIGHTS

The most controversial issue in the debate over whether the United States should join the Berne Convention was Article 6bis, which requires Convention members to protect the *moral rights* or *droit moral* of authors.[221] These rights are entirely independent of copyright, but by agreeing to adhere to the Convention the United States is obligated to abide by all of the provisions, including those involving moral rights. Moral rights fall into two categories under the Convention: *paternity rights* and *integrity rights*, both of which have been formally recognized in many other countries for some time. *Paternity rights* involve the right to be credited as the author of a work and to prevent others from attributing a work to you that is essentially not your work. For example, a publisher who, without consent, omitted the name of the primary author from a book or a magazine editor, who, without consent, falsely attributed an article to a well-known author to sell more copies or lend credibility to the magazine would be violating paternity rights. (Even if famous author contributed a small amount to the work, the name cannot be used without that person's consent.) *Integrity rights* basically involve "the right to object to distortion, other alteration of a work, or derogatory action prejudicial to the author's honor or reputation in relation to the work."[222] A classic example of the latter was the 1976 Second Circuit U.S. Court of Appeals decision that the copyright of the British comedy troupe known as Monty Python of "Monty Python's Flying Circus" fame was violated when the ABC Television Network extensively edited the programs primarily to make room for commercials.[223] The court held that the changes significantly impaired the integrity of the works and that Monty Python had the right to prevent "distortion or truncation" of its creations. The court cited the common law, copyright law and §43(a) of the Lanham Act dealing with unfair competition for its authority. Thus even though the comedy team had granted the British Broadcasting Corp. the right to license the programs overseas, that right did not include allowing licensees to significantly distort them.

PLAGIARISM

Space precludes an extensive discussion of *plagiarism*, or the misappropriation of another's intellectual or creative works, but it should be noted, at least, that this is a recurrent problem among journalists. It is often difficult to demonstrate, however. Accusations of plagiarism or some form of it plague journalists and others from time to time. During the 1988 presidential election, one of the primary candidates admitted to quoting a British statesman without attribution, and a few years ago a prominent syndicated advice columnist was accused of recycling some of her earlier columns without informing readers of the fact (a form of self-plagiarism, perhaps?). More recently, talk-show host Phil Donahue said he had used false names in a syndicated essay entitled, "Confessions of a Fallen Schoolboy," about the role nuns played in his Catholic childhood.[224] The revelation came after a Catholic News Service reporter called Donahue's old school and discovered that at the time the TV star attended, there were no nuns with the names used in the story. Donahue said he believed he had committed no sin because everything in the story was true except "I changed the names of the nuns to protect the innocent."[225] Finally, H. Joachim Maitre, Dean of Boston University's College of Communications resigned a week after he was accused of plagiarism for using several passages that were identical or nearly identical to those in an article by Public Broadcasting System film critic, Michael Medved.[226] His alleged plagiarism was uncovered by the *Boston Globe*. Most actions of this type do not result in a lawsuit for copyright infringement, but the resultant negative publicity is often punishing. In these two instances, journalists brought the alleged offenses to light, but sometimes journalists became the objects of such accusations. When there is any doubt about whether a reader, listener or viewer would be misled into thinking that a work is entirely original when it is not, the journalist or other individual should always clearly attribute ideas and expressions. Attribution will not necessarily prevent a successful lawsuit for copyright infringement, but it can at least alleviate perceptions of plagiarism.

SUMMARY AND CONCLUSIONS

The Copyright Act of 1976 made substantial changes in copyright law, not the least of which was significantly increasing the amount and duration of copyright protection for original works of authorship. Public perceptions and even those of journalists still consist of myths and distortions that bear little relationship to the real world of copyright. Many writers and artists still find it difficult to believe that copyright protection exists automatically upon creation of a work in a tangible without benefit of registration and that attribution alone does not protect one from a successful infringement suit. The concept of "fair use" is even more difficult to comprehend, and the courts as well as Congress have added to the confusion.

Nevertheless, the new federal copyright statute is a powerful arsenal for the creators of original works of authorship. The fact that copyrighted works, other than works made for hire and anonymous works, are protected for 50 years beyond the last surviving author's death reflects the tone of law. It is an authors' law, plain and simple, but that means the writers and artists must be cautious in using the expressions of others. The law is not very forgiving, as attested by its provisions granting remedies from injunctions and damages to criminal penalties.

11 Indecency, Obscenity, and Pornography

On the evening of March 26, 1990, satellite dish owners who tuned to Spacenet 1, transponder 18, saw the following message roll continuously on the television screen:

> CUSTOMERS, WE ARE EXTREMELY SORRY. AN UNFORTUNATE CHAIN OF EVENTS HAS REMOVED AMERICAN EXXXTASY FROM THE AIR PERMANENTLY. IT IS TRULY A SAD DAY. IN CONSIDER-ATION, WE HAVE AUTOMATICALLY ADDED FOUR EXTRA MONTHS OF OUR EDITED ADULT CHANNEL, TUXXEDO NETWORK (GALAXY 2 CHANNEL 4) FOR EVERY MONTH REMAINING ON YOUR AMEXXX SUBSCRIPTION. ALTHOUGH WE ARE WORKING ON OTHER RESOLU-TIONS, THIS IS THE BEST WE CAN DO AT THE PRESENT TIME. THIS WILL BE DONE AUTOMATICALLY SO, PLEASE DO NOT CALL THE OFFICE. IF NECESSARY, WRITE
> HOME DISH
> 419 PARK AVENUE, SOUTH #4
> NEW YORK, NY 10016
> THANK YOU FOR YOUR SUPPORT OVER THE PAST FOUR YEARS.

The demise of American Exxxtasy, an X-rated subscription service, is an interesting and instructive illustration of the ongoing clash between purveyors of sexually explicit materials, or pornography, and local, state and federal government officials. It is also an unusual example of the gap that occasionally emerges between a new communications technology and the law. The public and customers of obscene materials generally play a minor role in the inevitable battle between the two powerful adversaries. Public opinion polls

481

consistently find that most citizens consider the proliferation of sexually explicit materials a problem but they generally do not favor the types of actions taken by police against book stores, theaters and other distributors because they overwhelmingly feel that adults should be able to judge for themselves which books, magazines or films to consume even when such works explicitly depict sexual conduct unless such depictions include minors, violence or deviant sex.[1] (Federal and state statutes imposing strict bans on child pornography, as discussed later, enjoy widespread public support.)

Less than eight months later, officials of Home Dish Only (HDO) Satellite Network, the parent corporation of American Exxxtasy, had pleaded guilty to two misdemeanor charges of distributing obscene material in Montgomery, Alabama, and by the end of the year had pleaded guilty to federal charges of broadcasting obscenity via satellite to Buffalo, New York, and Salt Lake City, Utah. HDO was fined $5,000 and ordered to pay $75,000 each to two children's homes as penalties for the Alabama violations and fined $150,000 on the federal charges. HDO also agreed as part of the consent decree with the U.S. Attorney General's Office to erase all taped movies and not to promote or distribute sexually explicit films.

HDO transmitted its signal around the country from New York for four years via satellite space leased from GTE, a major satellite owner. The X-rated movies were carried only after 8:00 P.M. and were scrambled so that only the 30,000 paying subscribers could legally view them. The service was not available to cable customers, only to satellite dish owners. For a fee of $150 for six months or $240 a year, subscribers received an alternating stable of movies and other sexually explicit programs of the type available in most video rental stores that carry X-rated titles. Except for promotional announcements that included nudity in R-rated rather than X-rated excerpts from its films and except for an occasional commercial program offering adult videos and sexually related products such as condoms and vibrators, Amexxx was scrambled. These announcements were broadcast unscrambled ("in the clear") an hour or so prior to the scrambled X-rated (or as HDO called the, "triple X-rated") programs.

How was HDO indicted and ultimately forced to plead guilty to obscenity charges or face likely conviction by juries in the Alabama and federal courts? Amexxx is an example of how the law eventually caught up with technology. HDO was able to carry its XXX-rated channel nationwide and even bypass cable systems, thanks to the same technology that transformed a small UHF television station owned by entrepreneur Ted Turner into Superstation TBS — gestations satellites that spin with the earth's orbit. Section 639 (added with the Cable Communications Policy Act of 1984) of the Federal Communications Act of 1934 provides: "Whoever transmits over any cable system any matter which is obscene or otherwise unprotected by the Constitution of the United

States shall be fined not more than $10,000 or imprisoned not more than 2 years, or both.[2]

Notice that the provision makes no mention of satellite transmission or of subscription television. That omission was remedied with Public Law 100-690 in 1988, which added the following section to the FCC Act:

1468. Distributing Obscene Material by cable or subscription television

(a) Whoever knowingly utters any obscene language or distributes any obscene matter by means of cable television or subscription services on television, shall be punished by imprisonment for not more than 2 years or by a fine in accordance with this title or both.

(b) As used in this section, the term "distribute" means to send, transmit, retransmit, telecast, broadcast, or cablecast, including by wire, microwave, or satellite, or to produce or provide material for such distribution.

(c) Nothing in this chapter, or the Cable Communications Policy Act of 1984, or any other provision of Federal law, is intended to interfere with or preempt the power of the States, including political subdivisions thereof, to regulate the uttering of language that is otherwise obscene or otherwise unprotected by the Constitution or the distribution of matter that is obscene or otherwise unprotected by the Constitution, of any sort, by means of cable television or subscription services on television.[3]

By including satellite in the definition of "distribute," Congress granted the FBI the authority to prosecute Amexxx. Note that the section includes a clause (item c) that makes it clear the states still retained the authority to conduct their own prosecutions. In fact, Montgomery County, Alabama, District Attorney Jimmy Evans, who was a candidate for state attorney general at the time, was the first official to prosecute HDO. He convinced an Alabama grand jury to indict four executives of the network for allegedly violating state obscenity statutes. In October 1990, HDO pleaded guilty to two misdemeanor charges of distributing obscene material and was fined $5,000 and forced to pay $75,000 each to two children's homes.[4]

According to rumors in the satellite industry trade press, Alabama authorities were alerted to Amexxx after school officials discovered that high school students were distributing among their peers tapes of the network's programming, some of which may have been recorded with pirated or illegal descramblers. FBI agents filed their charges after an agent purchased a decoder and paid a subscription fee to watch the programming. The agency began its 13-month investigation after several dish owners complained about Amexxx's unscrambled commercials. HDO pled guilty to an information before it could be indicted by a federal grand jury. HDO was then fined

$150,000 on a single count of broadcasting an obscene fine via satellite and agreed to a consent decree under which it erased all of its X-rated movie inventory.[5]

In addition to American Exxxtasy, HDO offered a premium movie service known as "Stardust" and an R-rated adult service called "Tuxxedo," both of which folded shortly after the Alabama indictments, apparently because the revenues from Amexxx were subsidizing the other two services. All three services were available only to dish owners.

FROM *HICKLIN* TO *ROTH*:
AN EMERGING DEFINITION OF OBSCENITY

It took a new federal statute for the federal government and the state of Alabama to successfully prosecute HDO for transmitting obscenity via satellite, but a U.S. Supreme Court decision 17 years earlier provided the real foundation for the demise of the X-rated programmer.

Obscenity has been suppressed and prosecuted throughout history, always somehow managing to survive even when it was forced to go underground, and it has actually thrived during some eras. Until 1957 the U.S. Supreme Court avoided getting embroiled in defining obscenity, relying instead on lower courts to enunciate the boundaries between acceptable and unacceptable sexually oriented speech.

The two major influences on obscenity prosecutions from approximately the mid-19th century to the mid-20th century were American Anthony Comstock and an 1868 British court decision known as *Regina v. Hicklin*.[6] Comstock, who lived from 1844 to 1915, founded and directed the New York Society for the Suppression of Vice, which was instrumental in lobbying state and federal legislators to enact statutes strictly regulating obscenity. According to one source, Comstock himself helped destroy 160 tons of literature and pictures.[7] In fact, the statutes whose passage he spearheaded were popularly known as "Comstock laws." The federal law was enforced primarily by the U.S. Post Office, which had the authority to bar the mailing of obscene materials and to prosecute violators. During much of the time he was involved in the suppression, Comstock was a paid special agent of the Post Office and reportedly received a share of the proceeds from the fines imposed on offenders. The current federal statute and many state statutes today still reflect the cries of the antiobscenity crusades of Anthony Comstock.

Regina v. Hicklin

Regina v. Hicklin began when British trial court Judge Hicklin enforced a recently enacted antiobscenity law by ordering the confiscation and destruction of copies of a pamphlet entitled *The Confessional Unmasked*, which included depictions of sexual acts. The trial court's decision was upheld on appeal to the Queen's Bench in an opinion by Lord Chief Justice Cockburn, who formulated what become known as the Hicklin test for determining obscenity: "whether the tendency of the matter charged as obscene is to deprave and corrupt those whose minds are open to such immoral influences and into whose hands a publication of this sort might fall."[8]

The test essentially barred all sexually oriented materials because (a) an entire publication could considered obscene if *any* portion, no matter how small, could "deprave and corrupt"; and (b) the work was obscene if it would deprave and corrupt the minds of even the most sensitive and easily influenced individuals, including children. In fact, successful prosecution did not require that the crown demonstrate that the materials actually fell into the hands of susceptible people but merely that they *could* end up there. By taking isolated passages out of context and convincing judges and juries that these passages could stimulate immoral thoughts within children and other sensitive individuals, the state could successfully censor almost any publication referring to sexual conduct of any type.

Until the Civil War (1861–1865), public concern in the United States over obscenity was not high. But when stories appeared about soldiers reading and viewing allegedly pornographic materials, the stage was set for severe suppression of such works after the war. With Anthony Comstock at the helm, legislators and judges responded by enforcing statutes already on the books and enacting new laws where needed. Because the U.S. Supreme Court had never dealt with the issue head-on, the lower courts, both state and federal, generally adopted the handy *Hicklin* definition, complete with isolated passage and sensitive individual provisions.

U.S. v. Ulysses

The tide against this oppressive rule began to turn in 1934 when U.S. District Court Judge John M. Woolsey in New York held that James Joyce's *Ulysses* was not obscene and, therefore, could be imported into the United States.[9] (Custom officers had prohibited the book's entry into this country.) Judge Woolsey rejected the *Hicklin* rule and instead offered a new test that nevertheless kept some elements of the old rule. According to Judge Woolsey, a work is obscene if it "tends to stir the sex impulses or to lead to sexually impure and lustful thoughts. Whether a particular book would tend to excite such impulses must be the test by the court's opinion as to its effect [judged as a whole] on a person with average sex instincts."[10]

Thus the isolated passages provision of *Hicklin* was replaced by a requirement that the work must be judged in its entirety, and the court must look at the effect of the material on the average person ("a person with average sex instincts"), not on sensitive individuals. Another significant change was the substitution of "lead to sexually impure and lustful thoughts" for "deprave and corrupt," which essentially meant that the work must be sexually exciting, not merely corrupting, or at later court decisions, including those of the U.S. Supreme Court, the material must appeal to prurient interests. There is still debate among scholars over how much influence the *Ulysses* holding had no modern obscenity tests, but it is clear that *Hicklin* was crumbling away by the time of *Ulysses* and the U.S. Supreme Court would eventually have to intervene to bring some consistency to obscenity prosecutions. One year later, the Second Circuit U.S. Court of Appeals affirmed the lower court decision, and the federal government chose not to appeal the ruling, thus denying the U.S. Supreme Court the opportunity to consider the case. *Ulysses* miraculously survived the *Hicklin* sword, primarily because of an enlightened jurist who realized that the book deserved First Amendment protection, but other literary works were not so fortunate and were at least temporarily banned thanks to *Hicklin*. These have included Henry Miller's *Tropic of Cancer*, Ernest Hemingway's *For Whom the Bell Tolls*, Erskine Caldwell's *Tobacco Road*, William Faulkner's *Mosquitoes* and Dr. Alan Guttmacher's *Complete Book of Birth Control*.[11]

Butler V. Michigan: Rejecting the Hicklin Standard

Except for a few isolated decisions involving matters that were more procedural than substantive, the U.S. Supreme Court chose not to tackle the issue of obscenity by specifically defining it until 1957. The Court took the first step in this direction in *Butler v. Michigan* (1957)[12] when it struck down as unconstitutional a provision in the Michigan Penal Code that banned any material "tending to incite minors to violent or depraved or immoral acts manifestly tending to the corruption of the morals of youth." According to the unanimous opinion by Justice Felix Frankfurter:

> The State insists that, by thus quarantining the general reading public against books not too rugged for grown men and women in order to shield juvenile innocence. It is exercising its power to promote the general welfare. Surely this is to burn the house to roast the pig. . . . We have before us legislation not reasonably restricted to the evil with which it is said to deal. The incidence of this enactment is to reduce the adult population of Michigan to reading only what is fit for children.[13]

Roth v. U.S. and *Alberts v. California* (1957): A New Obscenity Standard

The *Butler* decision was especially significant because it specifically rejected the *Hicklin* standard on which the Michigan statute had been patterned and thus paved the way for the Court's landmark ruling exactly four months later in *Roth v. U.S.* and *Alberts v. California* (1957).[14] Samuel Roth was convicted by a jury in the U.S. District Court of the Southern District of New York for violating *federal* obscenity statutes—more specifically, the Comstock Act—barring the mailing of obscene materials. He had sent allegedly obscene circulars, ads and a book, *American Aphrodite.* His conviction was affirmed by the Second Circuit U.S. Court of Appeals. David S. Alberts, a mail-order entrepreneur, was sentenced by a California municipal court for violating the obscenity provisions of the California Penal Code. His conviction in a bench trial was upheld by the Appellate Department of the California Superior Court.

The Court itself struggled with the case, as evidenced by the 5–4 majority opinion, which included a 7–2 vote upholding the conviction of Alberts and a 6–3 vote affirming Roth's conviction. The majority decision, written by Associate Justice William Brennan, who had been nominated only a few months earlier by President Dwight David Eisenhower, offered considerably broader protection for sexual expression than had been previously granted. Nevertheless, the Court made it clear that obscene speech did not fall under the umbrella of the First Amendment.

Indeed, the Court began by settling issue once and for all:

> The dispositive question is whether obscenity is utterance within the area of protected speech and press. Although this is the first time the question has been squarely presented to this Court, either under the First Amendment or the Fourteenth Amendment, expressions found in numerous opinions indicate that this Court has always assumed that obscenity is not protected by the freedoms of speech and press.[15]

The significance of this point is that once material has been properly deemed obscene by a court, prior restraint can be imposed within the limitations of *Near v. Minnesota* (1931)[16] (discussed in chap. 4). Justice Brennan went on to note:

> All ideas having even the slightest redeeming social importance—unorthodox ideas, controversial ideas, even ideas hateful to the prevailing climate of opinion—have the full protection of the guaranties [of the First and Fourteenth Amendments], unless excludable because they encroach upon the limited area of more important interests. But implicit in the history of the First Amendment is the rejection of obscenity as utterly without redeeming social importance. . . . We hold that obscenity is not within the area of constitutionally protected speech or press.[17]

The latter statement has led to this test being characterized as the "utter" standard for judging obscenity, although there are actually four prongs to the test: (a) whether to the average person, (b) applying contemporary community standards, (c) the dominant theme of the material taken as a whole (d) appeals to prurient interest. The Supreme Court has spent the years since this decision attempting to define such vague terms as *average person*, *contemporary community standards* and *prurient interest*. The Court did make a good faith, although somewhat unsuccessful, effort to distinguish sex from obscenity:

> Sex and obscenity are not synonymous. Obscene material is material which deals with sex in a manner appealing to prurient interest. The portrayal of sex, e.g., in art, literature and scientific works, is not itself sufficient reason to deny material the constitutional protection of freedom of speech and press. Sex, a great and mysterious motive force in human life, has indisputably been a subject of absorbing interest to mankind through the ages; it is one of the vital problems of human interest and public concern.[18]

Only four other members of the Court signed on with Justice Brennan, but Chief Justice Earl Warren filed a brief separate concurring opinion in which he argued, "The conduct of the defendant is the central issue, not the obscenity of a book or picture." The Chief Justice felt that the defendants "were plainly engaged in the commercial exploitation of the morbid and shameful craving for materials with prurient effect [one of the common definitions of obscenity]. That is all these cases present to us, and that is all we need to decide."[19] Years later, the Court would pick up on this theme after it became clear that the *Roth* standards were unworkable. Justices Douglas and Black strongly dissented from the majority decision, contending that the "government should be concerned with antisocial conduct, not with utterances. Freedom of expression can be suppressed if, and to the extent that, it is so closely brigaded with illegal action as to be an inseparable part of it. . . . I have the same confidence in the ability of our people to reject noxious literature as I have in their capacity to sort out the true from the false in theology, economics, politics, or any other field."[20] This minority view has never commanded a majority of the members of the Supreme Court.

Smith v. California (1959): The Requirement of Scienter

The next piece in the perplexing obscenity puzzle emerged two years later in *Smith v. California* (1959)[21] in which the U.S. Supreme Court unanimously reversed the conviction of a Los Angeles bookstore owner for violating a municipal ordinance barring the possession of any obscene or indecent writings, including books, in any place of business. Justice Brennan was able to garner the agreement of four other justices (although they were not the exact same four who had joined him in *Roth*) in holding that the ordinance was unconstitutional because the city law made booksellers liable even if they were unaware of the contents of the book. The other four justices concurred in the result but with different reasoning. According to the majority, in order to pass constitutional muster, such an ordinance must require the government to prove *scienter*—that is, the individual had knowledge of the contents of the allegedly obscene materials. Otherwise, the Court reasoned a chilling effect will prevail:

> If the bookseller is criminally liable without knowledge of the contents and the [ordinance] fulfills its purpose, he [she] will tend to restrict the books he [she] sells to those he [she] has inspected; and thus the State will have imposed a restriction upon the distribution of constitutionally protected as well as obscene literature. . . . And the bookseller's burden would become the public's burden, for by restricting him [her] the public's access to reading matter would be restricted. If the contents of bookshops and periodical stands were restricted to material of which their proprietors had made an inspection, they might be depleted indeed.[22]

State statutes now typically include this element of *scienter* as essential for an obscenity conviction. Kentucky's penal code dealing with the distribution of obscene matter, for example, reads: "A person is guilty of distribution of obscene matter when, *having knowledge of its content and character* . . ." (emphasis added)[23] Georgia's parallel statute stipulates that the offense of distributing materials occurs when the person sells, lends, and so forth, or otherwise disseminates obscene material "knowing the obscene nature thereof" and defines "knowing" as "either actual or constructive knowledge of the obscene contents of the subject matter, and a person has constructive knowledge . . . if he has knowledge of the facts which would put a reasonable and prudent person on notice as to the suspect nature of the material."[24]

Manual Enterprises v. Day (1962): Patent Offensiveness

In 1962 the U.S. Supreme Court considered a new aspect of the definition of obscenity—sexual explicitness or what has become known as *patent offensiveness*. In *Manual Enterprises v. Day*,[25] a majority of the justices, led by Justice John M. Harlan, overturned a U.S. Post Office Department ban against the mailing of several homosexually oriented magazines with titles such as *MANual*, *Grecian Pictorial* and *Trim* that the court characterized as "dismally unpleasant, uncouth and tawdry." Why were the magazines protected? They merely featured male nudity and were not patently offensive. As Justice Harlan noted, the Post Office had not been able to ban materials simply featuring female nudity and male nudes were no more objectionable than female nudes even though the former was directed to homosexuals. *Patently offensive* was thus added as a new requirement to the definition of obscene. What is *patently offensive*? Material that "affronts community standards," according to the Court.

But what *community* is used to determine community standards? This question has become one of the most troublesome for the Court. Two years after *Manual Enterprises*, the U.S. Supreme Court attempted to define this important concept when it reversed the conviction of the manager of a movie theater in Cleveland Heights, Ohio, on two counts of possessing and showing *Les Amants* ("The Lovers"), which includes a fairly explicit but brief love scene. The defendant was found guilty in a bench trial and fined a total of $2,500. His convictions were upheld by an intermediate state appellate court and by the Ohio Supreme Court. The effort of the Court to define the concept added to the confusion and signaled further trouble ahead. Although six justices agreed in *Jacobellis v. Ohio* (1964)[26] that Nico Jacobellis had been wrongly convicted, they splintered in their reasoning, thus preventing a majority opinion. Pieced together, however, the various opinions of the justices supporting a reversal appeared to point to a national standard, in line with what the Court had enunciated earlier in *Roth-Alberts*. As discussed shortly, however, defining *community* has become a far more complex and difficult task than the Court probably ever imagined in *Roth-Alberts*. Perhaps the most memorable aspect of *Jacobellis* was a now-famous statement in Justice Potter Stewart's concurring opinion attempting to define obscenity: "I know it when I see it, and the motion picture involved in this case is not that." Justice Stewart's statement has been ridiculed and satirized for its obtuseness, but he was, nevertheless, making the important point that obscenity convictions should be limited to what is typically characterized as hardcore pornography, not a works that merely deal with sexual matters.

On the same day as *Jacobellis*, the justices struggled with another obscenity controversy—whether an adversary hearing is required to determine whether materials are obscene prior to the issuance of a search warrant. Once again, the justices splintered. Seven justices agreed in *A Quantity of Copies of Books v. Kansas* (1964)[27] that a state statute permitting prosecutors to obtain warrants for the seizure of allegedly obscene materials before an adversary hearing was unconstitutional, but they disagreed on the reasoning. Under the statute, once the materials had been seized and then been determined obscene, they could then be destroyed. The flaw was, of course, not in the destruction of the materials once they had been declared obscene by the appropriate court because an adversary hearing was held before the destruction but in the issuance of the seizure order without an adversarial hearing before the warrant was executed. As Justice Brennan noted in a plurality opinion joined by three other justices, including Chief Justice Warren, the statute posed the danger that public would thereby be denied access to nonobscene or constitutionally protected works.

Freedman v. Maryland (1965):
The Constitutionality of Censorship Boards

A similar sticky issue was involved in 1965 in *Freedman v. Maryland*,[28] although by then the justices began to reach some agreement at least on procedural points even though other important matters continued to elude them. In *Freedman* the Court unanimously struck down a Maryland motion picture statute that mandated that movie exhibitors submit their films to a state board of censors for approval prior to showing. Justice Brennan once again wrote the majority opinion that declared the law in clear violation of the First Amendment because it placed the burden of proof on the exhibitor and failed to provide a means for prompt judicial scrutiny of an adverse decision by the board, which granted licenses only for those films that it approved as not being obscene. Ronald Freeman was convicted for showing a film, *Revenge at Daybreak*, prior to submitting it to the censorship body. Interestingly, the board indicated in its arguments against Freedman's appeal of his conviction that the film was not obscene and thus would have been approved if it had been reviewed. The Court saw this as unconstitutional prior restraint because the law "fails to provide adequate safeguards against undue inhibition of protected expression."[29]

The Court held that to escape the First Amendment axe, "a noncriminal process which requires the prior submission of a film to a censor" must have three procedural safeguards:

> First, the burden of proving that the film is unprotected expression must rest on the censor. . . . Second, while the State may require advance submission of all films, in order to proceed effectively to bar all showings of unprotected films, the requirement cannot be administered in a matter which would lend an effect of finality to the censor's determination whether a film constitutes protected expression. . . . [Third] the procedure must also assure a prompt final judicial decision, to minimize the deterrent effect of an interim and possibly erroneous denial of a license.[30]

The *Fanny Hill* Case: Applying the "Utter" Test

On March 21, 1966 the U.S. Supreme Court announced three decisions focusing on obscenity, each of which touched on a different aspect of the controversy that refused to go away. In *A Book Named "John Cleland's Memoirs of a Woman of Pleasure" v. Attorney General of Massachusetts*,[31] the Court reversed an equity decision that the famous 1750 British novel popularly known as *Fanny Hill* was obscene. The book had been widely available in this country since the early 19th century but Massachusetts was determined to ban the book that had been reissued in 1963 by G. P. Putnam's Sons Publishers. The commonwealth indeed proceeded with its prior restraint in spite of the fact that the publisher had orders from many universities and libraries, including the Library of Congress, which had asked for permission to translate the classic into Braille.

Fanny Hill is clearly not a book for the faint of heart even though its language by modern standards is rather reserved. As the prosecuting attorney noted at the hearing that led to the book's ban, the work describes several acts of heterosexual intercourse, male and four female homosexuality, flagellation and female masturbation. But various expert witnesses at the proceeding testified that the book had literary, cultural and educational value.

Once again, the court struggled with the nature of obscenity, with a fractured result. Six members of the Court voted to reverse the equity court ruling and thus declare that *Fanny Hill* was not obscene, but no majority opinion surfaced. Instead, Justice Brennan forged a plurality opinion with Chief Justice Warren and Associate Justice Abe Fortas that strongly reaffirmed the three-pronged *Roth* test. The opinion noted that the Supreme Judicial Court of Massachusetts was wrong in asserting that the jury was not required to find the work was "utterly without redeeming social value" to declare it obscene. According to Justice Brennan, any redeeming social value, no matter how minimal, is sufficient to save a work from the obscenity censors:

> We defined obscenity in Roth in the following terms: "whether to the average person, applying contemporary community standards, the dominant theme of the material taken as a whole appeals to prurient interest." [citation omitted] Under this definition, as elaborated in subsequent cases, three elements must coalesce: it must be established that (a) the dominant theme of the material taken as a whole appeals to a prurient interest in sex; (b) the material is patently offensive because it affronts contemporary community standards relating to the description or representation of sexual matters; and (c) the material is utterly without redeeming social value.[32]

Ginzburg v. U.S. (1966): Pandering

The central issue of the second case decided on March 21, 1966, was the role of *pandering*, or the way in which a work is promoted and advertised, in determining whether material is obscene. In *Ginzburg v. U.S.* (1966),[33] Justice Brennan was able to attract four other justices, including the Chief Justice, for a majority opinion affirming the 28-count conviction of Ralph Ginzburg for engaging in "the business of purveying textual or graphic matter openly advertised to appeal to the erotic interest of customers." But the dissenting voices of the remaining four justices were unusually strong in condemning the majority holding.

Ginzburg was convicted, fined $28,000 and sentenced to five years in prison for violating federal obscenity statutes by mailing *Eros*, an expensive hard-cover magazine dealing with sex; *Liaison*, a biweekly sex-oriented newsletter; and a short book entitled *The Housewife's Handbook on Selective Promiscuity*.

Where did Ginzburg go wrong? The materials he distributed were probably not even obscene, a point conceded by the prosecution. As Justice Brennan noted in his opinion, the prosecutor "charged the offense in the context of the circumstances of production, sale, and publicity and assumed that, standing alone, the publications themselves might not be obscene." Yet Justice Brennan and four of his colleagues upheld the conviction because, as Justice Brennan said, Ginzburg had shown the "leer of the sensualist." The Court extended the message that if distributors promote their works in a manner that emphasizes the nonredeeming social value or sexual provocativeness, the materials can be assumed to be obscene—even if considered without the promotion or pandering, they would not necessarily pass the test for obscenity! Thus, according to the plurality opinion:

> We agree that the question of obscenity may include consideration of the setting in which the publications were presented. . . . Each of the accused publications was originated or sold as stock in trade of the sordid business of pandering. . . . Where the purveyor's sole emphasis is on the sexually provocative aspects of his publications, that fact may be decisive in the determination of obscenity. . . . In close cases evidence of pandering may be probative with respect to the nature of the material in question and thus satisfy the Roth test.[34]

The dissenters were as fractured in their reasoning as the majority but they shared a conviction that the Court had made a serious error in its decision to uphold Ginzburg's sentence. Justice Hugo L. Black took his usual stand that the federal government had no authority under the Constitution to censor any speech or expression of ideas: "As bad and obnoxious as I believe governmental censorship is in a Nation that has accepted the First Amendment as its basic ideal for freedom, I am compelled to say that censorship that would stamp certain books and literature as illegal in advance of publication or conviction would in some ways be preferable to the unpredictable book-by-book censorship into which we have now drifted."[35]

Justice William O. Douglas continued with his consistent theme that he had expressed in *Memoirs* the same day in which he contended that "the First Amendment does not permit the censorship of expression not brigaded with illegal action," a relatively absolutist view that he clung to until he retired from the Court in 1975. Justice John M. Harlan concurred with Justice Douglas and the other dissenters but on the ground that the government could only ban only hard-core pornography, a category into which he felt these materials did not fall. Finally, Justice Potter Stewart dissented because he believed that censorship "is the hallmark of an authoritarian regime. In upholding and enforcing the Bill of Rights, this Court has no power to pick or to choose."

Mishkin v. New York (1966): Obscenity Directed to Deviants

The third and final decision handed down on that same day involved an intriguing argument by an obscenity defendant. Edward Mishkin was sentenced to three years in prison and fined $12,500 for selling obscene books that Justice Brennan said in his majority opinion "depict such deviations as sado-masochism, fetishism and homosexuality." Typical titles were *Dance with the Dominant Whip* and *Mrs. Tyrant's Finishing School*. These materials were clearly hard-core pornography because they featured explicit sexual depictions, but Mishkin argued on appeal that they did not meet the *Roth* test for prurient interest because the average person would find them unappealing rather than sexually stimulating. However, the Court called his bluff and in a 6-3 decision upheld his conviction in *Mishkin v. New York* (1966): "Where the material is designed for and primarily disseminated to a clearly defined sexual group, rather than the public at large, the prurient-appeal requirement of the *Roth* test is satisfied if the dominant theme of the material taken as a whole appeals to the prurient interest in sex of the members of that group."[36]

Although *Roth* is no longer the test for determining obscenity (as discussed later), *Mishkin* has never been overturned and thus presumably still dictates the rule of determining the reference group for prurient appeal—**go to the group to which the work is directed.** As Mishkin soon learned, there is no loophole for evading the prurient appeal requirement.

In *Mishkin*, the Court simply said that the materials were aimed at those individuals interested in the particular "deviant sexual practices" depicted. Does this mean that magazines depicting gay men and lesbian women will pass the prurient appeal test if they sexually excite or stimulate members of these particular groups? The Court in *Mishkin* apparently assumed that the specific type of sex shown determined the prurient-appeal reference group—that is, that books focusing on sadomasochism will be judged by their prurient appeal to the average sadomasochist and so on. Yet, studies have shown that the vast majority of pornography is geared to heterosexual males, although there is also a flourishing market for gay material. Virtually none of the material is geared to lesbians and female heterosexuals, even though the vast majority of books, magazines, videos and so on, available from aboveground sources—

such as adult bookstores and the adult sections of local video rental outlets —
portray heterosexual and purported "lesbian" couplings. In other words, the
reference group cannot always be determined by simply reviewing the types of
sex depicted, as illustrated by the fact that the primary audience for sexually
explicit works portraying lesbians is male heterosexuals, not female homosexuals, whereas the predominant consumers of gay materials are homosexual
men. Which specific reference group is to be used then in determining the
average person for the *Roth* prurient interest test? The Court has simply
avoided this issue, leaving the lower courts to make this crucial determination
with the expected resulting inconsistencies.

Ginsberg v. New York (1968): Variable Obscenity Laws

After its 1966 triple holdings, the U.S. Supreme Court apparently became so
frustrated that it effectively abandoned its efforts to define obscenity until the
seven-year itch hit in *Miller v. California* (1973),[37] (discussed in the next
section). By 1967 the august body was ready to freely admit it had reached a
deadlock; there was no agreement among its members as to the meaning of
obscenity even for those who had generally stuck together both in reversing
and confirming lower court obscenity convictions. In a *per curiam* decision in
Redrup v. New York (1967),[38] a majority of the justices outlined their
individual tests and reversed the conviction in a city trial court of a clerk at a
New York City newsstand for selling two paperbacks, *Lust Pool* and *Shame
Agent*, to plainclothes police. As part of the same decision, the Court also
reversed the conviction of a Paducah, Kentucky, bookstore owner for allowing
a female clerk to sell two magazines, *High Heels* and *Spree*. The majority also
overturned a civil decision by a prosecuting attorney in Arkansas who declared
several magazines obscene — including *Gent, Swank, Bachelor, Modern Man,
Cavalcade, Gentleman, Ace* and *Sir*, most of which are still being published.
In its brief, unsigned opinion, the Court acknowledged that the reversals were
in order regardless of the test employed. For the next two years, the Supreme
Court handled obscenity cases, which continued to climb in number, by just
denying certiorari or by reversing convictions whenever at least five justices,
applying their own individual tests, could agree that the particular materials in
question were not obscene. Dozens of cases were handled in this manner,
typically without the benefit of oral arguments or written opinions. The iron
was not hot enough yet to be struck, but that would eventually change.

The next year the Court upheld the constitutionality of a New York statute
known as a *variable obscenity law*. In *Ginsberg v. New York* (1968),[39] [not to
be confused with *Ginzburg v. United States* two years earlier] a 6-3 majority
ruled that the statute, which prohibited the knowing sale to individuals under
17 years old of "materials harmful to minors" regardless of whether the works

would be obscene to adults. The decision was not a major surprise because even the most liberal courts have approved good-faith efforts to protect children from materials and products that are readily available to adults such as alcohol and cigarettes. That trend has continued (discussed later in this chapter) with the Court consistently upholding child pornography or "kiddie porn" laws that apply substantially stronger standards for children than for adults.

The case arose when Sam Ginsberg at "Sam's Stationery and Luncheonette," operated on Long Island by Ginsberg and his wife, sold two "girlie" magazines to a 16-year-old boy. The particular magazines had already been declared not to be obscene by the U.S. Supreme Court the year before in *Redrup v. New York*. But the judge convicted Ginsberg anyway for violating the state statute, which established minors as the group used to determine whether the materials were harmful, appealed to prurient interest and so on, when such materials were knowingly distributed to minors. Thus the general purpose of the law was to keep works out of the hands of minors that were perfectly permissible for sale to adults. Although the judge suspended Ginsberg's conviction, the defendant appealed the decision anyway. Ginsberg also attacked the statute as void for vagueness because of its use of the concept "harmful to minors" and other terminology, but the Court refused to accept this argument as well.

On the same day as *Ginsberg*, the Court did strike down a Dallas, Texas, ordinance in *Interstate Circuit v. Dallas* (1968),[40] which banned showing a film to persons under age 16 if it portrayed "sexual promiscuity" that would "create the impression on young persons that such conduct is profitable, desirable, acceptable, respectable, praiseworthy or commonly accepted . . . [or] . . . its calculated or dominant effect on young persons is substantially to arouse sexual desire." The fatal flaw in the ordinance, according to Justice Thurgood Marshall and five other justices, was that it was unconstitutionally vague in failing to enunciate appropriately narrow standards and definitions. Two other members of the Court concurred with the result on the ground that obscene materials enjoyed First Amendment protection. In his dissent, Justice Harlan maintained, "The current approach has required us to spend an inordinate amount of time in the absurd business of perusing and viewing the miserable stuff that pours into the Court, all to no better end than second-guessing judges."[41] (Justice Harlan consistently noted in his opinions — both concurring and dissenting — that no significant First Amendment concerns were involved in obscenity cases but instead individual states should be permitted to determine what sexually oriented materials should be censored and what should flourish.)

Stanley v. Georgia (1969): Privacy and Obscenity

The road from *Roth* to *Miller* took a surprising turn in 1969 when the U.S. Supreme Court unanimously held that individuals could not be punished for the mere possession of obscene materials in their own home. In *Stanley v. Georgia* (1969),[42] the justices reversed the conviction of a suspected book-maker for violating a state statute that barred the knowing possession of obscene works, even in one's personal residence. In an opinion, joined by five of his colleagues, Justice Marshall reversed Stanley's conviction on First and Fourth Amendment grounds, although the focus in the decision was on privacy concerns, as the Court emphasized in later cases. The police had discovered three sexually explicit 8-mm films in a desk drawer in the defendant's bedroom during the execution of a search warrant for evidence of illegal gambling. The police used a projector, which they found nearby, to view the movies and then promptly charged Stanley for possession of obscene materials. (No bookmaking evidence was found.)

For purposes of the case, the defendant stipulated that the films were obscene, and thus the issue became primarily one of right of privacy. All nine justices agreed that Stanley's conviction should be overturned but for different reasons (as the Court usually did in obscenity cases). According to Justice Marshall's majority opinion:

> Fundamental is the right to be free, except in very limited circumstances, from unwanted government intrusion into one's privacy. . . . Mere categorization of these films as "obscene" is insufficient justification for such a drastic invasion of personal liberties guaranteed by the First and Fourteenth Amendments. Whatever may be the justifications for other statutes regulating obscenity, we do not think they reach into the privacy of one's own home. If the First Amendment means anything, it means that a State has no business telling a man, sitting alone in his own house, what books he may read or what films he may watch.[43]

The Court particularly rejected Georgia's argument that the State has a right to punish individuals for possession of such materials even in their own home because exposure to obscenity leads to deviant sexual conduct and violent sexual crimes. Instead, the Court said that just as the State cannot prohibit possession of chemistry books on the ground that it may lead to the manufacture of homemade spirits, it cannot prohibit the mere possession of obscenity on the basis that it may cause antisocial conduct.

1970 PRESIDENTIAL COMMISSION ON OBSCENITY AND PORNOGRAPHY

There were two major developments in 1970, neither of which had any major immediate impact on the regulation of obscenity but both of which signaled the beginning of a new era in obscenity law, albeit not necessarily in line with what had been expected. First, the 1970 Presidential Commission on Obscenity and Pornography issued its report. The commission, chaired by the former dean of the University of Minnesota Law School, William B. Lockhart, had been appointed in 1967 by President Lyndon B. Johnson. The 18-member group was charged with the mission of studying the obscenity and pornography trade to determine its nature and scope, including its impact on adults and minors, and to make recommendations for restricting obscenity within constitutional parameters. After spending thousands of hours and more than $2 million studying the problem, the body filed a report in 1970 whose content reflects the same ambiguity that was so evident on the U.S. Supreme Court. Only 12 of the 18 members joined the majority report that made the following surprising recommendations:

1. An end to all local, state and federal censorship of materials directed to consenting adults, but a continuation of strong obscenity laws governing minors, including their depiction in sexually explicit works. The commission cautiously noted that after a thorough and extensive review of studies on the effects of obscenity, it found scant evidence that reading or viewing of sexually explicit materials leads to any antisocial conduct such as criminal activities or sexual deviance.

2. Enactment of strong statutes to protect children from exposure to obscene materials, primarily photos, films and other visual representations.

3. Enactment of legislation to restrict pandering and other techniques directed at unwilling individuals, including unsolicited mail and public displays.

4. A comprehensive sex education curriculum in public schools, for both elementary and secondary school students.

By the time the commission had finished its work in 1970, Richard M. Nixon had become President and the country was clearly headed in a rather conservative direction. The President publicly rejected the commission's report, characterizing its report as "morally bankrupt." Even the Senate moved into the picture with a resolution supported by 60 and opposed by only 5 members. Public criticism was also rather intense, leading President Nixon to vow to appoint to the Supreme Court only justices who opposed relaxed regulations on obscenity. The President had already successfully nominated conservative Associate Justice Warren Burger to replace liberal Chief Justice Earl Warren, who had stepped down in 1969. Harry A. Blackmun was then appointed in 1970 to fill the slot opened by the resignation of Associate Justice Abe Fortas after the Senate rejected his nomination as Chief Justice.

MILLER V. CALIFORNIA (1973): A CONJUNCTIVE TEST OF OBSCENITY

For the next three years, the U.S. Supreme Court issued no major decisions dealing directly with obscenity. It began a relatively short wait for a new majority coalition to emerge; President Nixon got the opportunity to see his wish come true as the liberal majority was replaced by a new conservative majority, including two more Nixon nominees — Lewis F. Powell and William H. Rehnquist, both of whom joined the Court in 1972. (Fourteen years later Justice Rehnquist became the current Chief Justice.) The new majority also consisted of Chief Justice Burger and Associate Justice Byron R. White (a conservative, at least on obscenity issues, who had been nominated by President Kennedy in 1962). Indeed, Justice Burger deftly used the authority granted him as Chief Justice to avoid scheduling any oral arguments in cases involving obscenity except for two fairly minor decisions in 1971, *United States v. Reidel*,[44] and *United States v. Thirty-Seven Photographs.*[45] In *Reidel*, the usual majority rejected the reasoning of a U.S. District Court Judge indicating that because *Stanley* permitted the possession of obscene materials in a private home, the federal statute banning the mailing of obscene works to private residences, including those of consenting adults, was unconstitutional. Led by Justice White, the majority found the trial court's decision much broader than that intended in *Roth* and *Stanley*: "*Roth* has squarely placed obscenity and its distribution outside the reach of the First Amendment and they remain there today. *Stanley* did not overrule *Roth* and we decline to do so now."

The second decision concerned whether *Stanley* extended to the luggage of a tourist arriving from overseas. The same majority refused to broaden *Stanley*, ruling that no zone of privacy existed for purposes of obscenity carried in one's luggage and thus the federal statute permitting prosecution for such possession was constitutional.

By 1973 the necessary five-person majority had coalesced and the Court was in a position to utter the final word on obscenity by once and for all defining this elusive concept. On June 21, 1973, just before its 1972–1973 term ended, the Court issued *five* separate opinions that established the current test for obscenity. In fact, since that time the justices have steered clear of obscenity cases except to refine and fine tune the *Miller* test, as it has become known. In each of the five cases, the 5–4 vote lineup was the same, with the thin but nevertheless effective majority of Chief Justice Burger and Associate Justices Powell, Rehnquist, White and Blackmun and the outnumbered but adamant minority of Associate Justices Douglas, Stewart, Marshall and Brennan. Justice Brennan, as indicated earlier, was the architect of several of the majority opinions (including *Roth*) that rejected First Amendment protection for obscenity, but in the second of the five cases, *Paris Adult Theatre I v. Slaton*,[46] Justice Brennan explained his conversion in a strongly worded, lengthy dissent:

> Our experience with the *Roth* [case] has certainly taught us that the outright suppression of obscenity cannot be reconciled with the fundamental principles of the First and Fourteenth Amendments. For we have failed to formulate a

standard that sharply distinguishes protected from unprotected speech, and out of necessity, we have resorted to the *Redrup* approach, which resolves cases as between the parties, but offers only the most obscure guidance to legislation, adjudication by other courts, and primary conduct. By disposing of cases through summary reversal or denial of certiorari we have deliberately and effectively obscured the rationale underlying the decisions. It comes as no surprise that judicial attempts to follow our lead conscientiously have often ended in hopeless confusion.[47]

This section focuses only on the first two cases — *Miller v. California*[48] and *Paris Adult Theatre* I — because they are the most important and established the modern test for obscenity. Both decisions were written by Chief Justice Burger who formulated a new three-prong test for determining obscenity.

In *Miller* the Court remanded the conviction of Marvin Miller back to the state appellate court to determine the outcome of his appeal in light of the new test enunciated by the Supreme Court. Miller had been convicted of a misdemeanor for violating the California Penal Code by conducting a mass mailing campaign advertising the sale of illustrated sexually explicit books. Five copies of the brochures were sent unsolicited to a restaurant and were opened by the owner and his mother. Inside were ads for four books — *Intercourse, Man-Woman, Sex Orgies Illustrated* and *An Illustrated History of Pornography* — and one film, *Marital Intercourse*. As the Court noted, "While the brochures contain some descriptive printed material, primarily they consist of pictures and drawings very explicitly depicting men and women in groups of two or more engaging in a variety of sexual activities, with genitals often prominently displayed."[49]

After summarizing the background of the case, Chief Justice Burger's majority opinion quickly framed the issue:

This case involves the application of a State's criminal obscenity statute to a situation in which sexually explicit materials have been thrust by aggressive sales action upon unwilling recipients who had in no way indicated any desire to receive such materials. This Court has recognized that the States have a legitimate interest in prohibiting dissemination or exhibition of obscene material when the mode of dissemination carries with it a significant danger of offending the sensibilities of unwilling recipients or of exposure to juveniles. . . . It is in this context that we are called on to define the standards which must be used to identify obscene material that a State may regulate without infringing on the First Amendment as applicable to the States through the Fourteenth Amendment.[50] (footnote and citations omitted)

The Court used the "unwilling recipient" principle (which even the 1970 President's Commission on obscenity endorsed] as a diving board to plunge into a new definition of obscenity. The justices could very easily have upheld

Miller's conviction using almost any of its previous decisions, but the majority was obviously determined to establish a new test. Indeed *Paris Adult Theatre I* presented the perfect opportunity for the Supreme Court to apply the new test in a much broader context—a public setting in which only consenting adults are involved with minors and unwilling recipients are specifically excluded.

In *Miller*, the Court:

1. **Reaffirmed the holding in *Roth* and subsequent cases that "obscene material is unprotected by the First Amendment."**

2. **Strongly criticized the plurality opinion in *Memoirs*, especially the "utterly without redeeming social importance" prong**: "Thus, even as they repeated the words of *Roth*, the *Memoirs* plurality produced a drastically altered test that called on the prosecution to prove a negative, i.e., that the material was 'utterly without redeeming social value'—a burden virtually impossible to discharge under our criminal standards of proof."

3. **Formulated a new three-prong conjunctive test for obscenity**: "The basic guidelines for the trier of fact must be: (a) whether 'the average person, applying contemporary community standards' would find that the work taken as a whole appeals to the prurient interest . . .; (b) whether the work depicts or describes, in a patently offensive way, sexual conduct specifically defined by the applicable state law; and (c) whether the work, taken as a whole, lacks serious literary, artistic, political, or scientific value."

4. **Cited examples of what a state could define under the second prong**. These included "(a) [P]atently offensive representations or descriptions of ultimate sex acts, normal or perverted, actual or simulated. (b) Patently offensive representations or descriptions of masturbation, excretory functions, and lewd exhibition of the genitals."

5. **Indicated that only hardcore sexual conduct was to be punished under the new test**: "Under the holdings announced today, no one will be subject to prosecution for the sale or exposure of obscene materials unless these materials depict or describe patently offensive 'hard core' sexual conduct specifically defined by the regulating state law, as written or construed."

6. **Held that "obscenity is to be determined by applying 'contemporary community standards,"' . . . not 'national standards.' "** In fact, the Court held that the requirement under California's statute that the jury evaluate the materials with reference to the "contemporary community standards of the State of California" was constitutional. As the Court had indicated earlier in the opinion, "It is neither realistic nor constitutionally sound to read the First Amendment as requiring that the people of Main or Mississippi accept public depiction of conduct found tolerable in Las Vegas, or New York."

In his bitter dissent, Justice Douglas lambasted the majority for, in effect, making a criminal law *ex post facto* (which is impermissible under the U.S.

Constitution) by devising a new test that "would put a publisher behind bars under a new law improvised by the courts after the publication." He also repeated his contention from previous obscenity cases that judges were never given the constitutional authority to define obscenity.

Justice Brennan, joined by Justices Stewart and Marshall, referred in a one-paragraph dissent, to his dissenting opinion in *Paris Adult Theatre I* (discussed next), noting that his view in the latter substantially departed from his prior opinions.

In *Paris Adult Theatre I*, two Atlanta "adult" theatres and their owners and managers were sued in civil procedure by the local district attorney to enjoin them from showing two movies, *Magic Mirror* and *It All Comes Out in the End*, which the Georgia Supreme Court characterized in its decision on appeal as "hard core pornography" leaving "little to the imagination," although by today's standards the movies would probably fall into either the "R" or NC-17 ratings of the Motion Picture Association of America (MPAA). The films did feature, as the Court noted, scenes of simulated fellatio, cunnilingus and group sex, but according to photographs presented to the trial court, which dismissed the prosecutor's complaint, the theatres entrance (there were two theatres but they shared a common entrance) was conventional and inoffensive with no pictures; there were simply two signs proclaiming: "Atlanta's Finest Mature Feature Films" and "Adult Theatre — You must be 21 and able to prove it. If viewing the nude body offends you, Please Do Not Enter." The Georgia Supreme Court reversed the trial court decision and the U.S. Supreme Court in a 5–4 vote vacated and remanded the case back to the state supreme court for reconsideration in light of *Miller*.

The majority opinion by the Chief Justice agreed with the Georgia Supreme Court that the movie houses did not enjoy constitutional protection even though the state appellate court assumed that they showed the films only to consenting, paying adults and minors were never permitted to enter. The justices made it clear that whereas it had consistently recognized a state's legitimate interest in regulating the exposure of obscenity to juveniles and nonconsenting adults, these were by no means the only legitimate state interests permitting regulation of obscene works:

> In particular, we hold that there are legitimate state interests at stake in stemming the tide of commercialized obscenity, even assuming it is feasible to enforce effective safeguards against exposure to juveniles and passersby. Rights and interests "other than those of the advocates are involved." . . . These include the interest of the public in the quality of life and the total community environment, the tone of commerce in the great city centers, and, possibly, the public safety itself.[51] (footnotes and citations omitted).

The opinion then cited the Hill-Link Minority Report of the Commission on Obscenity and Pornography (the 1970 Presidential Commission discussed *supra*). Interestingly, both the majority and the dissenting opinions in *Paris Adult Theatre I* and *Miller* make little reference to the commission's report in spite of the fact that it was the most comprehensive study ever made of the obscenity problem. In *Paris Adult Theatre I* the majority cited a passage from the main presidential commission report acknowledging that there was a split among medical experts over whether there is link between exposure to pornography and antisocial conduct. The opinion also cited the commission's minority report's claim that female and male juveniles are among the "heavy users and most highly exposed people to pornography." In his dissenting opinion, which was joined by Justices Stewart and Marshall, Justice Brennan included one footnoted reference to the commission's report, which claimed that no empirical research had found any evidence to date "that exposure to explicit sexual materials plays a significant role in the causation of delinquent or criminal behavior [in] youth or adults."

Thus the presidential commission report apparently received little attention from the Court in its deliberations. Media and public attention was also fairly minimal except for the initial flurry over President Nixon's and the Senate's rejection of the report.

In his fairly brief separate dissenting opinion, Justice Douglas commended Justice Brennan in his effort to "forsake the low road" and join the side of the dissenters. According to Justice Douglas, there is "no constitutional basis for fashioning a rule that makes a publisher, producer, bookseller, librarian, or movie house operator criminally responsible, when he fails to take affirmative steps to protect the consumer against literature, books, or movies offensive to those who temporarily occupy the seats of the mighty" (footnote omitted).[52]

Justice Brennan's dissent is well worth reading in its entirety, even by those who vehemently disagree with him. Substantially longer than the majority opinion, it traces the 16-year history of the Supreme Court's attempts to define obscenity and eloquently describes what many jurists consider to be the four main options in dealing with obscenity:

1. **Draw a new line between protected and unprotected speech while still allowing states to suppress all unprotected materials.** (This would essentially take the issue of obscenity out of federal hands and put it exclusively in the regulatory hands of the states.)

2. **Accept the new test enunciated by the Court.**

3. **Leave enforcement primarily in the hands of juries with the Supreme Court and other appellate courts intervening only "in cases of extreme departure from prevailing standards."**

4. **Adopt the view that the First Amendment bars the suppression of any sexually oriented expression, as advocated by Justices Black and Douglas.**

Justice Brennan then went on to advocate a fifth option:

Allow sexually oriented materials to be controlled under the First and Fourteenth Amendments only in the manner of their distribution and only when there are strong and legitimate state interests such as the protection of juveniles and nonconsenting adults. In other words, consenting adults would make their own choices about what to see and read without interference from government.

Justice Brennan opted for the last approach; he felt it had flaws but that they were less serious and obtrusive than those of the other options.

THE AFTERMATH OF *MILLER* AND *PARIS ADULT THEATRE I*

There have been relatively few obscenity cases to be granted certiorari since *Miller et al.*, and among the limited number of decisions that have been handed down, there have been no major surprises. In the year following *Miller*, the Court issued two obscenity decisions on the same day. *Hamling v. U.S.* (1974)[53] tied a couple of the many loose ends left in *Miller*. The Court affirmed the federal obscenity convictions of four individuals and two corporations for mailing approximately 55,000 copies of a brochure throughout the country advertising *The Illustrated Presidential Report of the Commission on Obscenity and Pornography*. The jury was unable to reach a verdict on charges that the illustrated report itself was obscene. The single-sheet brochure (printed on both sides) included:

a full page splash of pictures portraying heterosexual and homosexual intercourse, sodomy and a variety of deviate sex acts. Specifically, a group picture of nine persons, one male engaged in masturbation, a female masturbating two males, two couples engaged in intercourse in reverse fashion while one female participant engages in fellatio of a male; a second group picture of six persons, two males masturbating, two fellatrices practicing the act, each bearing a clear depiction of ejaculated seminal fluid on their faces; two persons with the female engaged in the act of fellatio and the male in female masturbation by hand; two separate pictures of males engaged in cunnilinction; a film strip of six frames depicting lesbian love scenes including a cunnilinguist in action and female masturbation with another's hand and a vibrator, and two frames, one depicting a woman mouthing the penis of a horse, and a second poising the same for entrance into her vagina.[54]

The reverse side of the brochure contained an order form and several paragraphs touting the "research" value of the book and chiding "Mr. President" for suppressing the report. Obviously, the Ninth Circuit U.S. Court of Appeals had no difficulty affirming the convictions nor did the U.S. Supreme Court. The primary issue in the case was what rules of law would govern obscenity convictions, like this one, that had been decided in the trial and lower appellate courts before *Miller* was handed down. The 5–4 majority opinion authored by Justice Rehnquist held (a) that jurors in federal obscenity cases can draw on the knowledge of the local community in determining contemporary community standards; (b) that jurors can, if they wish, ignore the testimony of experts because they are themselves the experts ("average person"); and (c) that the prosecution is required to show only that a defendant had actual knowledge of the contents in order to prove *scienter*, not that the defendant knew the materials were obscene.

Billy Jenkins v. Georgia (1974): Mere Nudity Is Not Enough

In the second case, *Billy Jenkins v. Georgia* (1974),[55] the Court reversed the conviction of a theatre operator manager of distributing obscene materials by showing the film *Carnal Knowledge* at an Albany, Georgia, drive-in theatre. In January 1972 (before *Miller* was delivered), law enforcement officers seized the film while Jenkins was showing it and charged him with violation of state obscenity statutes. Two months later, a jury convicted him and he was fined $750 and given 12 months probation. The state supreme court in a split decision affirmed the conviction while acknowledging that the definition of obscenity in the state statute was "considerably more restrictive" than the new test set forth in *Miller*, which had been recently handed down. In an opinion written by Justice Rehnquist, the Court unanimously overturned the trial court decision. The Court considered it relevant that the film had received very favorable reviews from critics and was on many "Ten Best" lists for 1971. Its stars include Ann Margret, Candice Bergen (now on "Murphy Brown" on CBS Television) and Art Garfunkel (of the former "Simon and Garfunkel" duo). According to the majority opinion:

> Our own viewing of the film satisfies us that "Carnal Knowledge" could not be found under the *Miller* standards to depict sexual conduct in a patently offensive way. . . . While the subject matter of the picture is, in a broader sense, sex, and there are scenes in which sexual conduct including "ultimate sex acts" is to be understood to be taking place, the camera does not focus on the bodies of the actors at such times. There is no exhibition of the actors' genitals, lewd or otherwise, during these scenes. There are occasional scenes of nudity, but nudity alone is not enough to make material legally obscene under the *Miller* standards.[56]

These two cases provide appropriate examples of what the Court had in mind for protected versus unprotected works when it fashioned the *Miller* test.

The *Hamling* brochure was clearly hard core sexual content, whereas *Carnal Knowledge* was far from patently offensive. The *Jenkins* case is a frightening illustration of how suppressive prosecutors and juries can be in judging works that they deem offensive. No doubt, there are many more examples of censorship of constitutionally protected materials but which never sought redemption from what some critics have donned "the High Court of Obscenity."

In 1982 the U.S. Supreme Court exercised the opportunity to have its say in a serious problem facing the country—child pornography or "Kiddie Porn," as it is popularly known. During the mid-1970s several states and the U.S. Congress responded to public outrage over the perceived proliferation of child pornography as detailed in various media reports. New York enacted one of the toughest statutes[57] in the country in 1977, the same year a new federal statutes took effect—the "Protection of Children Against Sexual Exploitation Act of 1977."[58] Both statutes provided stiff fines and prison sentences for individuals convicted of using minors to engage in sexually explicit acts for still and moving image cameras of any type.

Paul Ira Ferber, the owner of a Manhattan store, was convicted in a New York trial court on two counts of violating child pornography laws for selling to an undercover police officer two films showing young boys under the age of 16 masturbating. The state's highest court, the New York Court of Appeals, reversed the conviction on the ground that the state statute was underinclusive and overbroad. In *New York v. Ferber*,[59] the U.S. Supreme Court reversed and remanded to the state Court of Appeals. In the 6–3 decision written by Justice White, the Court said that the constitutional standards for child pornography are not the same as those for adult materials. According to the justices, states could impose stricter bans on materials involving the sexual depiction and conduct of minors and ban such materials even if they did not meet the legal definition of obscenity in *Miller*. The Court noted that 47 states already had such laws and that the regulations could go beyond *Miller* because "the prevention of sexual exploitation and abuse of children constitutes a government objective of surpassing importance." The Court did, however, say that criminal liability may not be imposed unless *scienter* is shown on the part of the defendant.

The U.S. Supreme Court handed down two decisions in 1986, and neither outcome was a surprise. In *City of Renton v. Playtime Theatres*,[60] the Court held that a Renton, Washington, zoning ordinance restricting so-called adult theaters from operating within 1,000 feet of any residential zone, single or multiple family housing, school, park or church was constitutional. According to the 7–2 opinion by Justice Rehnquist, the law represented a legitimate State response to the problems generated by these establishments and did not infringe on First Amendment and Fourteenth Amendment freedoms even though it restricted the showing of nonobscene plays, films and printed works.

Ten years earlier, the Court had upheld a similar zoning ordinance in Detroit,noting that the ordinance did not totally ban such businesses but merely restricted them to certain areas of the city. Both ordinances, the Court said, were reasonable time, place and manner restrictions permissible under the Constitution.

In the second 1986 case, *Arcara v. Cloud Books*,[61] the U.S. Supreme Court gave the constitutional nod of approval to a New York state statute under which an adult bookstore was prosecuted and then shut down. An undercover investigation by the local county sheriff's department allegedly revealed illegal sexual activities, including prostitution and lewdness, taking place in the store. One sheriff's deputy testified that he witnessed customers masturbating, fondling one another and performing fellatio as well as prostitutes soliciting sex. A 6–3 opinion by Chief Justice Burger compared the situation to the draft card burning in *U.S. v. O'Brien* (1968) (discussed in chap. 4), which the Court asserted is a form of expressive conduct. Furthermore, the majority contended, sexual activities such as these have even less protection than draft card burning: "Unlike . . . symbolic draft card burning . . . the sexual conduct carried on in this case manifests absolutely no element of protected expression." Of course, as dissenting Justices Blackmun, Brennan and Marshall, pointed out, the store itself was closed to prevent the activities by imposing liability on the owners rather than simply punishing the conduct itself.

THE 1986 ATTORNEY GENERAL'S COMMISSION ON PORNOGRAPHY REPORT

No doubt, the one event calling the most attention to the pornography issue in 1986 was the July 9 release, amid much political fanfare, of the 1,960-page report of a $500,000 study entitled *The Attorney General Commission on Pornography Report*.[62] The 11-person commission—which had been appointed by President Reagan's Attorney General, Edwin Meese—a year earlier made 92 recommendations, many of which were opposite to those of the 1970 presidential commission. With two members dissenting, the commission recommended or endorsed:

1. Stronger state and federal obscenity statutes
2. A ban of all obscene shows on cable television
3. A ban on "dial-a-porn" (explained later) telephone services
4. Increased involvement of citizen groups against businessess that sell, distribute or produce sexually explicit materials, including picketing and boycotting
5. Creation of a high-level U.S. Department of Justice task force on obscenity

6. New laws permitting the federal government to confiscate the assets of businesses that violate obscenity laws
7. Prosecution of producers and actors and actresses involved in pornographic films under prostitution laws
8. Enactment of legislation making a second-offense arrest under obscenity laws a felony rather than a misdemeanor.[63]

Many criticisms were levelled at the group from organizations such as the American Civil Liberties Union, First Amendment societies and professional journalism associations. These groups contended that most of the recommendations would be unconstitutional if carried out and the commission produced little scientific evidence to support its conclusion that "substantial exposure to sexually violent materials can cause "antisocial acts of sexual violence and possibly to unlawful acts of sexual violence."[64] Indeed, Commission Chair Henry Hudson acknowledged at a press conference on the day the report was released that the committee had relied heavily on common sense and the testimony of expert witnesses and citizen groups rather than scientific studies. The two dissenting members also accused the commission of bias and distortion, noting that most of the more than 200 witnesses were individuals and groups opposed to pornography such as police and antiporn leaders.[65]

Some of the recommendations of the commission have been implemented such as tougher obscenity statutes, but others have not enjoyed widespread public support. For example, the commission recommended that federal and state governments step up obscenity prosecutions through the use of what are known as "RICO" (Racketeer Influenced and Corrupt Organizations) statutes. In 1970 Congress passed the RICO provision as part of the Organized Crime Control Act.[66] It was amended in 1984 to include obscenity convictions, which gave the federal government the chance to seek stiffer fines and prison sentences against distributors and sellers of pornography as well as a forfeiture of assets when a pattern of racketeering can be demonstrated in court.[67] The federal statute has been used rather successfully to crack down on interstate trafficking in pornography, and many states have now adopted similar statutes. In 1989 in *Fort Wayne Books v. Indiana*,[68] the Court ruled that a state RICO-type statute was not unconstitutionally vague in its language permitting the prosecution of obscenity as a form of racketeering or organized crime, but the Court held that a pretrial seizure of, allegedly obscene materials was a violation of the First Amendment because it was effectively prior restraint. The case arose when two adult bookstore owners were separately charged with violating Indiana's RICO statute. One of the defendants challenged the statute as unconstitutional on the ground that it permitted seizure of his entire store inventory. The Court agreed that his assets could not be seized unless rigorous safeguards laid out in *Freedman v. Maryland* (discussed earlier in this chapter) and a long line of other cases were employed, but it did not strike down the statute. According to the Court, "While a single copy of a book or film may be seized and retained for evidentiary purposes based on a finding of probable cause, books or films may not be taken out of circulation completely until there has been a determination of obscenity after an adversary hearing."[69] The message of the Court is clearly that books, films, magazines and other forms of expression must be treated as though they have First Amendment protection until a determination has been made by a court that they are obscene. Thus prosecutors cannot seize these materials in the same manner in which they confiscate presumably illegal drugs, weapons and other items.

One other important recommendation of the commission that eventually saw the light of day was the establishment of federal obscenity task force. In March 1987 Attorney General Meese set up a National Obscenity Enforcement Unit within the Department of Justice, and it has been involved in a number of prosecutions against alleged pornographers.

Probably the only U.S. Supreme Court decision since *Miller* that raised a few eyebrows of surprise came in 1987 in *Pope v. Illinois*.[70] The case involved the prosecution of two adult bookstore clerks who sold magazines to Rockford, Illinois, detectives which the prosecution claimed were in violation of the state obscenity statute. When the judge at the trial instructed the jury, he faithfully reviewed the Miller three-prong conjunctive test but told the jurors that in applying the "laps" prong (Does the material in question lack serious literary, artistic, political or scientific value?), they should do so "by determining how it would be viewed by ordinary adults in the whole state of Illinois." In other words, they were to apply a state standard in determining the "laps" value. After separate trials, the defendants challenged their convictions on the ground that the Illinois statute was a violation of the First Amendment because it invoked a local or state standard in determining "laps" value rather than a national basis.

In a 5–4 decision written by Justice White, with Justice Scalia concurring separately, the Court agreed with the challengers and remanded the cases back to the state appellate court for consideration. The Court held that the "laps" determination should be made based on a "reasonable person" and thus invoke a national or objective standard:

> Just as the ideas a work represents need not obtain majority approval to merit protection, neither, insofar as the First Amendment is concerned, does the value of the work vary from community to community based on the degree of local acceptance it has won. The proper inquiry is not whether an ordinary member of any given community would find serious literary, artistic, political, or scientific value in allegedly obscene material, but whether a reasonable person would find such value in the material taken as a whole.[71]

The justices emphasized that *Miller* was never intended to protect only those works in which the majority would find value but to provide a First Amendment shield as well for materials for which merely a minority would ascribe value. With application of the reasonable person standard, the Court felt minority views would be better protected than with the use of local community standards.

It should be noted that the defendants in *Pope* were not entirely off the hook even though the Court agreed with them. The Court indicated that the state appellate court must review the case and determine beyond a reasonable doubt whether the erroneous instruction by the judge affected the outcomes in the two trials. If the mistake was simply a "harmless error," the convictions should stand upon remand, according to the majority opinion.[72]

In 1990 the U.S. Supreme Court answered a question left in the air after the *Ferber* (see discussion *supra*) decision—*Does the* Stanley *bar against prosecution for possession of obscene materials in the privacy of one's home cover child pornography?* Recall that in *Ferber* the Court held that the same standards did not apply for child pornography as for adult materials because children are a protected class and "the use of children as subjects of pornographic materials is harmful to the physiological, emotional and mental health of the child."[73]

In *Osborne v. Ohio* (1990),[74] the Court upheld 6–3 a state "kiddie porn" statute that included penalties for the private possession of child pornography. In the decision written by Justice White, who was joined by Chief Justice Rehnquist and Associate Justices Blackmun, O'Connor, Scalia and Kennedy, the Court said:

> The threshold question in this case is whether Ohio may constitutionally proscribe the possession and viewing of child pornography, or whether as Osborne argues, our decision in *Stanley v. Georgia* . . . compels the contrary result. . . . We find this case distinct from *Stanley* because the interests underlying child pornography prohibitions far exceed the interests justifying the Georgia law at issue in *Stanley*. (citation omitted).[75]

The majority opinion went on to note, "Given the importance of the State's interest in protecting the victims of child pornography, we cannot fault Ohio for attempting to stamp out this vice at all levels of the distribution chain."[76]

The case began when 61-year-old Clyde Osborne was prosecuted after police searched his home on a tip and found in an album four sexually explicit photos of a boy believed to be 13 or 14. The state statute, which the Court upheld, specifically banned the possession of lewd material or material that focused on the genitals of a minor. The law also forbade the possession or viewing of "any material or performance that shows a minor" nude. There were exceptions in the statute for photos taken by parents and for photos with an artistic, medical or scientific purpose. Osborne was sentenced to six months in prison and fined $100. Ironically, he was granted a new trial by the U.S. Supreme Court on the ground that the jury that had convicted him had not been properly instructed. Ohio's statute, however, stood intact because it met constitutional muster, according to the Court.

A concern related to child pornography has been how to keep sexually oriented materials out of the hands of minors. A few state and local governments have enacted statutes or ordinances requiring all businesses that sell such magazines, books, videos and other works to place them where children can not see or peruse them. Virginia has such a statute, and it was challenged as unconstitutional by the American Booksellers Association. In *Virginia v. American Booksellers Association* (1988),[77] the U.S. Supreme Court remanded a ruling by the Fourth U.S. Circuit Court of Appeals that the state statute was unconstitutionally over broad back to the court on the ground that the lower appellate court's decision was not supported by the record.[78] On remand,[79] the circuit court ruled the statute did not violate the First and Fourteen Amendments because, as construed by the state supreme court, it penalized only businesses that knowingly permitted or failed to act reasonably to prevent minors from gaining access to such materials and only when the works lacked serious literary, artistic, political or scientific value "for a legitimate minority of normal, older adolescents." Thus, according to the federal appellate court, the statute gave establishments adequate notice of what was prohibited. The U.S. Supreme Court denied *certiorari* on the American Booksellers Association's appeal of the Fourth Circuit decision.[80]

RECENT EXAMPLES
OF OBSCENITY PROSECUTIONS

The long-term impact of the *Miller* decision has been exactly what the U.S. Supreme Court clearly intended with its three-prong test — a myriad formed by the different ways in which communities have approached the issue. In other words, different jurisdictions have shown different degrees of tolerance of sexually explicit materials: Some cities and towns use selective prosecution to rid themselves of adult bookstores and theaters whereas other communities tolerate the availability of such works with local video stores, for example, renting and selling both Walt Disney's *Cinderella* and (in another section accessible only to adults) "XXX-rated" *Nancy Nurse* and *Turn up the Heat* (the films being shown at the adult theater in Sarasota, Florida, on July 26, 1991, when actor Paul Reubens aka "Pee-wee Herman" was arrested and later pleaded no contest to a charge of indecent exposure for masturbating during nighttime showings).[81]

Two examples, both of which occurred in 1990, illustrate the complexity and inconsistencies of obscenity prosecutions. In the first case, U.S. District Court Judge Jose Gonzalez of the Southern District of Florida ruled in a 62-page decision that an album entitled "As Nasty as They Wanna Be" by the controversial rap group, 2 Live Crew, was obscene under Florida law, applying the standards established in *Miller*.[82] The civil suit was prompted by a county circuit court judge's ruling that there was probable cause to believe the album was obscene. The county judge was acting on a request from Broward County Sheriff Nick Navarro that he be granted authority to arrest shopkeepers who continued to sell the album. More than 1.7 million copies had been purchased nationwide before the court's decision. The sheriff was acting, he said, based on complaints from local citizens. After the county judge's probable cause ruling, the Sheriff and his deputies distributed copies of the ruling to record stores throughout the county and threatened to arrest anyone who sold the album. Attorneys for 2 Live Crew promptly filed suit against the sheriff after sales of the record in the area were effectively stopped. The rap group sought a declaratory judgment that the album was not obscene and a restraining order to prevent further actions from the sheriff to stop the sales.

U.S. District Court Judge Gonzalez agreed after a trial in *Skyywalker Records, Inc. v. Navarro*[83] that both the *ex parte* application from the sheriff and the county judge's order itself violated the due process standards for prior restraint established in *Freedman v. Maryland*, discussed *supra*, but he nevertheless went on to declare the album obscene because it appealed to prurient interests, was patently offensive as defined by state law and lacked any serious literary, artistic, political or scientific value. Judge Gonzalez specifically did not prohibit sale of the album nor did he find there was any criminal liability because the decision was based on a civil suit. According to the district court judge:

> It [the album] is an appeal to "dirty" thoughts and the loins, not to the intellect and the mind. . . . The recording depicts sexual conduct in graphic detail. The specificity of the descriptions makes the audio message analogous to a camera with a zoom lens, focusing on the sights and sounds of various . . . sex acts. It cannot be reasonably argued that the violence, perversion, abuse of women, graphic descriptions of all forms of sexual conduct, and microscopic descriptions of human genitalia contained in this recording are comedic art.[84]

The decision was the first time a federal judge had declared a record album obscene. Although the main impact of the decision, as might be expected, was a substantial increase in sales of the album around the country, at least one record shop owner was arrested the next day after the judge's decision. E-C Records proprietor Charles Freeman was arrested by six deputies of the Broward County Sheriff's Department after he sold a copy of the album to an undercover officer. He was handcuffed and taken to the county jail, where he was charged with the misdemeanor of distributing obscene material.[85] Four days after the ruling, Broward County Sheriff's deputies arrested, as they had promised after the judge's ruling, two members of 2 Live Crew after the band performed its "adults-only" show to a packed audience at a Hollywood, Florida, nightclub.[86] Like Charles Freeman, the band members faced a maximum penalty of $1,000 and/or a year in jail. A third member of the four-person band was arrested and charged later. The band members went on trial in October 1990, and a jury acquitted all three members after a two-week trial in which much of the evidence consisted of a poor videotape recording of the performance. The jury deliberated only about two hours before reaching its verdict.[87] Since that time, the controversy has essentially died down, and there have been no arrests reported. Ironically, a band known as Too Much Joy was arrested in August of the same year by Broward County deputies after they played songs from the 2 Live Crew Album to 350 people in a Hollywood, Florida, nightclub as a protest of the federal district court decision declaring the "As Nasty as They Wanna Be" album obscene.[88] In May 1992 the Eleventh Circuit U.S. Court of Appeals overturned the District Court ruling. A three-judge panel of the appellate court ruled that Sheriff Navarro had not proven that the "As Nasty As They Wanna Be" recording met the legal definition of obscenity, as established in *Miller*.[89]

Interestingly, the 2 Live Crew carried a warning label as part of a voluntary uniform label system unveiled by the Recording Industry Association of America (RIAA), whose members produce more than 90 percent of the records, tapes and compact discs sold in this country.[90] The system is strictly voluntary, although most record companies are apparently placing the black-and-white label that reads: PARENTAL ADVISORY — EXPLICIT LYRICS. The labels are placed in the lower right-hand corner of any album that contains material believed objectionable to children such as lyrics dealing with sex, violence, drugs and bigotry. Incidentally, neither the RIAA nor the National Association of Recording Merchandisers (NARM) publicly supported 2 Live Crew in its civil suit that ultimately led to the obscenity determination.[91] Before the rap group's acquittal on the obscenity charges relating to its live performance, many record stores and Wax Works, the nation's eighth largest retail-store chain announced they were pulling the latest album of another rap group, N.W.A., off the shelves.

Two weeks before the 2 Live Crew acquittals, the Contemporary Arts Center of Cincinnati, Ohio, and its director, Dennis Barrie, were found not guilty of charges that they pandered obscenity when the gallery featured a controversial exhibit of photographs by the late Robert Mapplethorpe.[92] The jury also cleared the defendants of two charges of exhibiting nude photos of children. The center and its director were indicted by a Hamilton County grand jury the same day the exhibit opened. The 20-year retrospective of the acclaimed photographer's work, entitled "The Perfect Moment," consisted of 175 photographs, including five homosexual pictures and two of children. One of the five homosexual pictures includes a male urinating into the mouth of another male, and the others are of various sexual acts. One of the photos is of a very young girl sitting on a porch with her skirt up to reveal her genitals, and the other is of a young boy standing nude on a couch. Most of the other photos in the display were of flowers and nude male and female figures.

According to press reports, the gallery spent $350,000 in legal expenses to defend itself at the two-week jury trial, and the city spent $14,550 in the prosecution.[93] More than 40,000 paid to see the show during its first three weeks and another 40,000 reportedly saw it before it ended its run. In contrast to the 2 Live Crew case, First Amendment groups from around the country supported the defendants in the Cincinnati trial.[94] The exhibit was able to continue because the center successfully sought an injunction from a U.S. District Court judge to bar city and county law enforcement officers from confiscating or otherwise interfering with the exhibit until a judicial determination had been made that the photographs were obscene.[95]

OBSCENITY VERSUS INDECENCY

The U.S. Supreme Court and other appellate and trial courts have not confined their deliberations to obscene speech when it comes to sexually oriented or other offensive materials. They have also tackled *indecency*. From a legal perspective, there one major difference between *indecency* and *obscenity*. The latter must appeal to prurient interests, but the former need not do so. Both usually involve nudity and sex in some form, although their impact on the average person is different according to the courts. There is also one other major difference: Indecent speech enjoys constitutional protection in some contexts, whereas obscenity can never count on the First Amendment shield. Here are some examples of speech that could be considered indecent but are very likely not obscene. Madonna's 1991 documentary film *Truth or Dare*, includes Madonna exposing her breasts, Madonna simulating oral sex with a bottle, two male dancers kissing one another, a friend of the singer discussing a lesbian relationship, the star simulating orgasm from masturbation during a concert and a strong dose of profanity. Yet the R-rated movie would never pass the *Miller* conjunctive test because it probably holds some literary and artistic value and does not appeal to prurient interest.

In the fall of 1990, several central Kentucky stores and other stores elsewhere in the country pulled copies of *Vogue* and other fashion magazines that included an ad for Nivea skin care products because it featured the bare breasts of a female model. A 32-year-old Smyrna, Georgia, man was convicted in 1990 by a state trial court judge for having a "Shit Happens" sticker on the bumper of his 1976 Dodge van. The charge—violating a Georgia statute that states: "No person owning, operating, or using a motor vehicle in this state shall knowingly affix or attach to any part of such vehicle any sticker, decal, emblem or other device containing profane or lewd words concerning sexual acts, excretory functions or parts of the human body."[96] James Cunningham was fined $100 for his offense.

INDECENCY IN BROADCASTING

The U.S. Supreme Court has been most heavily involved in indecency in the broadcast media. While generally shying away from dealing with indecency in the print media, the Court has been very active in establishing the parameters for regulating indecency on radio and television. The Court became entangled in this issue initially in 1978 in the so-called seven dirty words case of *FCC v. Pacifica Foundation*,[97] one of the least publicly understood decisions ever made by the justices. *Pacifica* began at 2:00 P.M. on October 30, 1973, when New York radio station, WBAI, licensed to and owned by the Pacifica Foundation, broadcast George Carlin's now-famous "Filthy Words" monologue. The comedian's 12-minute monologue had been recorded before a live audience in a California theater. The gist of the presentation is that there are seven words you cannot say on the public airwaves—shit, piss, fuck, cunt, cocksucker, mother-fucker and tits. According to Carlin in the monologue, "those are the ones that will curve your spine, grow hair on you hands and maybe, even bring us, God help us, peace without honor and a bourbon." He then spends the next several minutes discussing the different meanings and contexts of the first and third words, amidst considerable laughter.

After hearing the broadcast in the car with his 15-year-old son, a Florida man visiting New York City, the home of WBAI, filed a complaint with the Federal Communications Commission. A year and a half later, the commission issued a declaratory order, after hearing from the station, holding that the language as broadcast was indecent and prohibited under title 18, section 1464 of the U.S. Code, which forbids the use of "any obscene, indecent, or profane language by means of radio communications." The FCC did not take any administrative action against the station, other than indicating that its order would become part of the station's FCC file. The commission characterized the monologue as "patently offensive" but not necessarily obscene. Upon appeal by the station, the FCC decision was reversed by the U.S. Circuit Court of Appeals for the DC Circuit. In a 5-4 plurality opinion written by Justice John Paul Stevens, the U.S. Supreme Court held that the FCC was justified in finding the broadcast indecent even though it might not be obscene. The Court reasoned that "of all forms of communication, it is broadcasting that has received the most limited First Amendment protection." The opinion also pointed out the "uniquely pervasive presence" of broadcasting and that the electronic media are "uniquely accessible to children, even those too young to read." The Court made it clear that although the commission was barred under the FCC Act of 1934 from engaging in censorship or prior restraint, it can act on a nuisance rationale to take sanctions against and impose reasonable restrictions on such content, taking into account the time of day, the composition of the audience and other relevant factors. The Court emphasized the narrowness of the decision: "We simply hold that when the Commission finds that a pig has entered the parlor, the exercise of its regulatory power does not depend on proof that the pig is obscene."

Until the mid-1980s the commission took little action against broadcast stations for indecency, but by 1987 the picture had changed after organized complaints from various groups and individuals arrived at the commission's door. Using the rationale provided for it in the *Pacifica* ruling, the FCC issued warnings to three broadcast stations, including the Pacifica Foundation again for allowing one of its radio stations, KPFK-FM in Los Angeles, to broadcast excepts from a play about homosexuals and AIDS called *Jerker*. The commission also filed a complaint against University of California-Santa Barbara campus radio station KCFB for playing a song that contained what the commission considered "patently offensive references to sexual organs and activities." Finally, the agency determined that WYSP-FM in Philadelphia and WXRK-FM in New York City had violated its standards for indecency, which the commission defined as "material that depicts or describes, in terms patently offensive as measured by contemporary community standards for the broadcast medium, sexual or excretory activities or organs."[98]

The FCC was acting against what had become known as "shock radio," led by the "shock jock" Howard Stern, who was carried on the two stations. In its 1987 order, the FCC cited excerpts from Stern's broadcasts, such as the following:

Excerpt 1

Stern: God my testicles are like down to the floor. Boy, Susan you could really have a party with these. I'm telling you honey.

Ray: Use them like Bocci balls.

Excerpt 2

Stern: Let me tell you something, honey. Those homos you are with are all limp.

Ray: Yeah. You've never even had a real man.

Stern: You've probably never been with a man with a full erection.

Excerpt 5 (as part of a discussion on lesbians)
Stern: I mean to go around porking other girls with vibrating rubber
products and they want the whole world to come to a
standstill.[99]

Notice that Stern does not use any of the "seven dirty words," which, contrary
to popular opinion, the FCC never said were specifically banned from the
airwaves. Instead, as the FCC noted in its decision, Stern used off-color and
offensive comments with occasionally explicit references to "masturbation,
ejaculation, breast size, penis size, sexual intercourse, nudity, urination, oral-
genital contact, erections, sodomy, bestiality, menstruation and testicles."[100]

In November 1987, the FCC in a 4–0 decision enacted a ban on indecent
broadcasts between 6:00 A.M. and midnight when, according to the commission, a sizable portion of children were likely to be in the audience. Thus the
FCC established a de facto "safe harbor" period during which presumably
indecent, but not obscene, programming could be aired. Broadcasters and
media interest groups, such as Action for Children's Television, challenged the
FCC's definition of indecency and the decision to restrict such programming to
6-hour time frame. In *Action for Children's Television v. FCC* (ACT I)
(1988),[101] the U.S. Court of Appeals for the D.C. Circuit upheld the FCC's
definition of indecency but said that under the First Amendment any safe
harbor rule must be reasonable. The appellate court then remanded the case
back to the commission with instructions to review its 1987 decision with an
eye to voluntary control rather than government restraints.

Two months later, Congress approved on an amendment to an appropriations bill authored by North Carolina Senator Jesse Helms that enacted a
24-hour ban on indecency. This law was then challenged by the same public
interest organizations as unconstitutional, and in *Action for Children's
Television* (ACT II)[102] (1991), the same circuit court held that indecent
broadcasts enjoy some First Amendment protection so long as they are not
obscene and that a 24-hour ban was unconstitutional. The appellate court
ordered the commission to determine the period during which such broadcasts
could be aired and to provide appropriate definitions of *children* and
reasonable risk.

During the period of April 1987 when the FCC issued its original order until
the ACT II decision, the commission had fined 14 broadcast stations for
indecent programming, with six stations alone fined from $2,000 to $10,000
during July 1990 to May 1991.[103]

Another area of obscenity and indecency in which the FCC has become
involved is the so-called Dial-A-Porn telephone services, which use 976 call
prefixes to offer sexually explicit recordings and, in some cases, two-way
conversations on sex with the caller, who is charged a fee ranging from $2 to

$5 per minute or more. Dial-A-Porn had become big business by the time Congress acted in 1988 to amend §223(b) of the 1934 Federal Communications Act to ban both indecent and obscene interstate telephone messages. The purpose of the amendment was clearly to crack down on the Dial-A-Porn services. Sable Communications, one of the services, which had been operating for five years, filed suit against the FCC, seeking a declaratory judgment that the indecency and obscenity portions of the amendment violated the First and Fourteenth Amendments to the Constitution. In *Sable Communications of California v. FCC* (1988),[104] the U.S. Supreme Court upheld a U.S. District Court decision that the amendment's indecency provision but not the obscenity provision violated the Constitution. The Court ruled 6–3 in an opinion written by Justice White that, in its present form, the law "has the invalid effect of limiting the content of adult conversations to that which is suitable for children to hear. It is another case of 'burning up the house to roast the pig.'" The justices felt that the legislation had not been drawn narrow enough to promote the government's legitimate interest in protecting children from exposure to indecent telephone messages.

In response to the *Sable* decision, in 1989 Congress passed a new amendment sponsored by Senator Helms again that revised §223 of the Federal Communications Act of 1934 to ban the use of a telephone for "any indecent communication for commercial purposes which is available to any person under 18 years of age or to any other person without that person's consent, regardless of whether the maker of such communication placed the call." The law requires phone companies to block access to Dial-A-Porn services unless the customer requests access in writing. In June 1990 the FCC issued rules that defined telephone indecency as descriptions of "sexual or excretory activities or organs in a patently offensive manner as measured by contemporary community standards for the telephone medium" (essentially the same as its definition for indecency for broadcasting except that standards, of course, would be for the broadcast media). The FCC also promulgated new rules that established a defense for such telephone services if they gave written notice to the telephone company that they provided such communications or if they required an identification code before transmitting the messages or scrambled the messages so they could only be deciphered by someone with a descrambler.

One of the providers of Dial-A-Porn, Dial Information Services of New York and three other similar companies sought an injunction in U.S. District Court in Manhattan to prevent the commission from implementing the Helms amendment.[105] On August 29, 1990, just two days before the law was to take effect, U.S. District Judge Robert P. Paterson granted the request on the grounds that the law was likely unconstitutional because it required common carriers (telephone companies) to make a prior determination of whether particular speech was or was not indecent and the term *indecency* was too vague. Judge Paterson also said the law did not, as required, use the least restrictive means of imposing prior restraint to keep minors from obtaining access to the messages. The FCC appealed the decision. In a 3–0 ruling in *Dial Information Services of New York Corp. v. Thornburgh*[106] in July 1991, the Second Circuit U.S. Court of Appeals reversed the trial court decision. It held that the statute's definition of indecency was adequately defined and the regulations were not unconstitutional prior restraint because the services merely had to classify their messages, not halt them, and any adults attempting access to the services could still do so by simply stating their intent in advance. According to the Court of Appeals, "It always is more effective to lock the barn before the horse is stolen."[107] On January 27, 1992, the U.S. Supreme denied certiorari.[108]

LIVE NUDITY AND THE FIRST AMENDMENT

Finally, the U.S. Supreme Court has become the final arbiter in deciding whether nude dancing has constitutional protection. Obviously, live performances that are deemed obscene can be banned, but what about nonobscene nude performances? Until recently, the Court kept its views on the issue undercover, but it was inevitable that the justices would some day have to give either a green or a red light to state statutes around the country that bar or severely restrict nude public performances.

The Court first became involved in the constitutional aspects of nude dancing in 1956 when it upheld an obscenity conviction of a stripper on the ground that the statute was a valid exercise of the State's police authority.[109] For the next 16 years, the justices simply denied certiorari when such cases were appealed to the Court, but in 1972 the Supreme Court upheld a California statute that prohibited acts of "gross sexuality," which included sexually explicit live entertainment where alcohol was served.[110] Several similar decisions followed in which the Court essentially held that both nude and topless dancing in businesses where alcohol was served could be prohibited.[111] Only one Supreme Court decision gave any reprieve to nude dancing and that occurred in 1975 when the Court unanimously overturned a preliminary injunction issued by a New York trial court judge against three North Hampstead bars that featured topless dancing.[112] The U.S. Supreme Court said the state statute involved was too broad and therefore unconstitutional because it applied to all live entertainment, including artistic works. This decision was cited for many years as granting First Amendment protection to nude dancing, but that was a serious misinterpretation because it was clear that the Court was not trying to protect traditional nude barroom dancing but instead to protect plays and other socially redeeming works that might include some nudity.

In 1991, however, the Court wrestled with the issue of whether nude dancing enjoyed First Amendment protection as speech or expression or whether it was really conduct. In *Barnes v. Glen Theatre* (1991),[113] the justices lined up 5–4 against the dancers by upholding an Indiana public indecency statute that required female strip-tease dancers to wear at least G-strings and pasties in their performances. The Supreme Court overturned a Seventh Circuit U.S. Court of Appeals ruling involving dancers at the Kitty Kat Lounge in South Bend, Indiana, that "non-obscene nude dancing performed as entertainment is expression and as such is entitled to limited" First Amendment protection. The plurality opinion written by Chief Justice Rehnquist who was joined by Justices O'Connor and Kennedy said "nude dancing of the kind sought to be performed here is expressive conduct within the outer perimeters of the First Amendment, though we view it as only marginally so." That protection, however, is overridden by the State's interest in protecting morals and public order. "The requirement that the dancers don pasties and G-strings, Rehnquist said, "does not deprive the dance of whatever erotic message it conveys; it simply makes the message slightly less erotic."

Associate Justice David Souter concurred only with the result of the case, asserting that the statute was a valid exercise of the State's interest in preventing prostitution, sexual assault and other crimes. Justice Scalia also concurred with the Court's judgment but on the ground that the statute involved no First Amendment issues. Justices Marshall (who resigned at the end of the Court's term and was replaced by Clarence Thomas), Blackmun, Stevens and White dissented on the ground that the dancing was protected expression.

ETHICAL DILEMMAS FACING THE MEDIA
IN OBSCENITY AND INDECENCY CASES

Obscenity cases such as police raids on adult bookstores and indecency cases like *Barnes* generally attract considerable media attention, although their impact to the First Amendment may arguably not be as strong as other less "sexy" restraints on free expression. Public officials inevitably damn the evils of pornography and indecency, often confusing the two and, thereby, add to public misunderstanding. Taken out of context, even the mildest forms of depiction of sex and nudity can appear offensive, as the Georgia prosecutors demonstrated in the dispute over the movie *Carnal Knowledge* in *Jenkins v. Georgia*. But, as the Court said in the decision led by the conservative Justice Rehnquist, *Miller* requires that hard-core depictions be involved. Nudity itself is not enough. Yet a close reading of the plurality opinion in *Barnes* and the concurring opinions reveals a rather different attitude of the Court—one that sees virtually no protection in nude expression. Whereas there may be a difference between live nude performances and nude photographs or film, the fact remains that each form involves expression. The only real difference is that one is live and, therefore, ephemeral, and the other is recorded and thus more permanent. Yet the less permanent form enjoys virtually no protection, and the more permanent can count on substantially greater protection. Thus a dancer at the Kitty Kat must wear panties and G-strings, but if she becomes the *Playboy* centerfold, she can bare all.

This situation touches on the first of five major ethical dilemma facing the news media in covering obscenity and indecency stories: **How far should journalists go in defending individuals and organizations that test the First Amendment to its limits?** Neither the Kitty Kat dancers nor 2 Live Crew attracted much support from the news media and even the Cincinnati Contemporary Center for the Arts gained only limited editorial favor from the news media in fighting prosecution over the Mapplethorpe photo exhibit. As former U.S. Supreme Court Justices William O. Douglas, William Brennan and Thurgood Marshall have so eloquently argued over the years, the First Amendment must be strong in order for it to have any meaning. Protecting thoughts alone is not enough; we must protect the expression of those thoughts as well. Most of the major news media such as the *New York Times* and major chains such as Gannett, Knight-Ridder and Scripps-Howard continue to fight in editorials and in other ways against restrictions on freedom of speech and freedom of the press even when the situations and individuals involved have no popular support, especially from politicians. Perhaps erotic dancers do not deserve First Amendment protection; but where is the line drawn beyond nude dancing? What about plays that include nudity? Why should the latter be considered First Amendment expression when the former, as Justice Rehnquist said in *Barnes*, is "within the outer perimeters . . . only marginally so"? Is it because the audience for one is a group of blue-collar, middle-age males, whereas the other attracts people with an interest in art and culture?

A second dilemma facing journalists in dealing with obscenity and indecency is **deciding how graphic or detailed descriptions of cases should be.** During the November 1991 final Senate Judiciary hearing on President Bush's nomination of Judge Clarence Thomas as associate justice of the Supreme Court, some of the testimony from University of Oklahoma Law Professor Anita Hill and other individuals about Thomas' alleged sexual harassment of her was quite graphic; there were references to a pubic hair on a Coke can and a porn star named "Long Dong Silver." The Cable News Network and other networks carried all or some of the testimony live to one of the largest television audiences ever of a Senate hearing. Some people were angered that this content was aired without editing, but most simply were surprised that the sexually explicit references were aired and published. During the December 1991 Palm Beach, Florida trial in which William Kennedy Smith was acquitted of the alleged rape of Patricia Bowman, there was some rather explicit testimony about semen, ejaculation, the lack of a condom and so on. This was also carried live on cable by Court TV and some portions of the trial were broadcast by CNN and the other networks. (Incidentally, Bowman's name was revealed by only some of the news media until her interview on ABC-TV's "PrimeTime Live" after Smith was acquitted.) Both the Smith trial and the Thomas confirmation hearings significantly boosted CNN's ratings, although they had little impact on the numbers for NBC, CBS and ABC.[114] Once again, there was considerable criticism from the very public that bolstered the ratings, and President Bush indicated that he felt the two events should not have been televised because of the offensive language. Media critics generally split on whether the intense attention by the press was warranted and whether the language should have been edited, but certainly a strong argument can be made that the public must be exposed to the grit in such situations in order to understand and evaluate. Anita Hill's explicit references clearly were relevant in understanding her charges, and the Smith rape trial was handled in the courtroom the way almost any other rape trial would be, including explicit testimony that the jury had to hear as evidence.

A third and related dilemma is **whether the print and electronic media should include the specific words in indecency cases and specific pictures, items, and so on, in obscenity prosecutions.** Obviously, it would be highly irresponsible for a TV or radio newscast, especially in primetime, to broadcast words such as those in *Pacifica Foundation* even though they may be integral to understanding a story, for example, about a local campus radio station that had drawn the ire of some members of the community for its music lyrics. But, is there a context in which those words can be repeated so the reader does not have to rely on rumors to know the language involved? What about in a sidebar inside the newspaper? In the late night newscast? Or, is it better to simply use euphemisms such as "explicit sexual references," "bodily functions," and "offensive language?" How about using the omitted letters technique — f — k, s — t and p — s or simply f — , s — and p — ?

Different news organizations handle these situations in different ways, but every station, newspaper or magazine should have a written, clear policy about how these kinds of stories are to be covered. Regardless of how it is done, readers will complain, and so news organizations need to be able to easily explain why the specific language did or did not appear. A similar sensitive problem sometimes arises when police conduct raids of adult theaters and bookstores. How do you convey to the reader or viewer exactly the kinds of materials confiscated or the specific act that Pee-wee Herman allegedly committed at the adult theater in Sarasota, Florida? Some of the news stories about the incident simply said that Paul Reubens had been charged with indecent exposure; others stated that he was arrested for masturbating. There seemed to be much greater concern about how parents should explain to children what had happened to "Pee-wee Herman" than with the legal fate of Paul Reubens. In fact, there was substantially more space devoted in the news media to the reactions of parents and children than to resolution of the case. When Reubens pleaded "no contest" and paid a $50 fine, the decision warranted little more than a 15-second blip on the TV screen and a few column inches in the daily newspaper.

Typically, newspapers and television newscasts will show police loading marked boxes and cartons when they conduct a search of an adult bookstore, and the public is invariably left with no idea of the exact materials seized. Were the books and videos the same as these available in more "proper" establishments, such as chain drug stores, convenient marts (behind the counter, of course) or the local video rental store (in that special "adult" section)? Or, are the works truly hard-core? It is certainly not necessary for reporters to hold up copies of the actual pages or to show excerpts from the X-rated movies, but shouldn't they at least be more specific about the kinds of sex featured? The consumer is usually quite interested in knowing whether there is "deviant conduct," such as bestiality and child pornography depicted or if the works are typical heterosexual and homosexual depictions familiar to most adults. Why should members of the public know less about the nature of such materials than the jury and judge that will be deciding the owner's fate? In murder and other criminal trials, the public usually has more information available to it than the jury, which is restricted from seeing and hearing certain kinds of information? Why should the reverse be true in obscenity and indecency cases?

With stories about nudity and sex, some newspapers and magazines as well as television—shows such as "A Current Affair," "Inside Edition" and "Entertainment Tonight"—carry edited versions of recordings, pictures, and so on, with the nudity blurred out or the profanities bleeped just enough to offer the public a good idea of the subject matter but not enough to incur outrage from government officials. Are these techniques more ethical than exposing the consumer to the actual nudity or words, or are they simply a means of avoiding the wrath of the FCC and angry viewers or readers? On the other hand, it certainly could be argued that providing even the edited versions is really just a convenient cover for attracting a larger audience with titillations and tasteless promos. Where should the line be drawn?

A fourth dilemma involves **whether the print and electronic media should accept (a) advertising for adult bookstores, theatres and movies (with or without provocative titles and visuals) and/or (b) advertising for ordinary products that contain offensive language or full or partial nudity.** The broadcast industry has been far more conservative than newspapers on this issue, probably because of concerns about possible FCC actions, but all of the mass media, except some magazines, have traditionally rejected both types of advertising even though there is virtually no fear they would ever be prosecuted, even in the most conservative communities; They probably fear public pressure. Some news media, especially major daily newspapers, compromise by permitting adult establishments to advertise but not to mention specific titles (whether or not highly offensive) or to use terms such as *X-rated*, *explicit material*, and so forth. Some news media even carry ads from "adult escort" firms and Dial-a-Porn services, usually under the rationale that they cannot make judgments about acceptability of businesses so long as they are offering a legitimate product or service.

Broadcasters, magazines and newspapers can never be required to carry any particular ad or form of advertising, but at least one newspaper has been caught in a bind over legal notices. In 1991, the *Boston Globe* reluctantly published a 2½″ × 15½″ legal notice listing titles of 355 allegedly pornographic books and magazines seized by police.[115] Under a 1945 Massachusetts statute, publications cannot be officially prosecuted as obscene until a legal notice has been published in a Boston newspaper and in a newspaper in the county where the materials are seized. Many of the titles were quite graphic and used profanities. Examples included *Mother's into Bondage* and *Sextraverts*.[116] The other Boston daily, the *Boston Herald*, refused the ad, as it had the right to do, because newspapers cannot be required to publish legal notices unless they have a contract as the official organ of state. Both the *Globe* and the the *Times-Union* in Springfield, Massachusettes, where the publications were confiscated from the Video Expo and Magazine center, published the ad twice, as stipulated in the statute. The *Globe* included a notice with the ad indicating that it was being published to comply with state law, whereas the *Times-Union* ran no disclaimer but did run an editorial saying that the legal notice was not an endorsement of the prosecutor's actions.[117]

The final dilemma is one that the news media rarely face, but one that, nevertheless, can be rather difficult to resolve: *How specific should a story be about an incident involving indecency or pornography when there is no major concern about offending language or nudity but instead about the possibility of copycats*? A prime example of this problem is illustrated in a Fifth Circuit U.S. Court of Appeals decision in 1987, *Herceg v. Hustler*.[118] The appellate court held that *Hustler* could not be held liable for the death of a 17-year-old boy who died after he attempted a technique he had read described in the magazine. The article offered detailed information on *auto-erotic asphyxia*, in which a person affixes a rope around his neck to stop his breathing at the peak of sexual stimulation. When the case originally arose, it received little press attention, probably because editors feared attracting more individuals to read the article and possibly attempt the same act. The article, according to the Court decision, did stress the "often-fatal dangers" of the practice and recommended "readers seeking unique forms of sexual release DO NOT ATTEMPT this method" and indicated that the information was "presented here solely for an educational purpose." Even when the decision was handed down by the appellate court, most newspapers and TV and radio newscasts either overlooked or ignored it, even though it had considerable public interest. Generally, there is no liability even for the publication that originally carried the story and certainly no fear of liability for news coverage about such cases, no matter how detailed they may be. But, is it ethical to carry these stories? If they deserve attention, how far do you go? Should the technique be outlined with a warning and the hope that it will educate the individuals who might be tempted and possibly save a life? On the other hand, should the specific magazine and issue be mentioned when it would provide ready access to someone who might model the incident? What are the ethical responsibilities in these situations, which invoke the same concerns as "copycat suicides"?

SUMMARY AND CONCLUSIONS

Obscenity, pornography and *indecency* are terms, often used interchangeably by the public and sometimes even by journalists, that are not the same. Whereas pornography is simply a layperson's term for obscenity, the term used by the courts, there are major differences between obscenity and indecency in the eye of the law. **Obscenity**, as defined by the U.S. Supreme Court in *Miller v. California* in 1973 requires (a) that the average person, applying contemporary community standards, find the work as a whole appeals to prurient interests, (b) that the work depict or describe in a patently offensive way sexual conduct specifically defined by state law, and (c) that the work, taken as a whole, lacks serious literary, artistic, political or scientific value. This standard is conjunctive, which means that all three prongs of the test must be met before a work can be declared legally obscene. Contrary to popular opinion, featuring explicit sex alone or nudity alone is not enough. As the Supreme Court said in *Jenkins v. Georgia*, the conduct depicted must be hard-core sexual activities, not simply nudity or offensive conduct. Even explicit sex is not enough, however, as illustrated by an advisory jury's decision in 1981 in a case involving the movie *Caligula*.[119] Penthouse International, the owner of the film, filed a request in equity court for a declaration that the film was not obscene and an injunction to enjoin the Solicitor General of Fulton County (Atlanta), Georgia, to enjoin him from arresting or prosecuting anyone connected with the film's distribution—as he had threatened to do if the film were shown in his jurisdiction. An advisory jury determined that the film was patently offensive and its sexual depictions an affront to community standards, but, viewed as a whole, the film did not appeal to the average person's prurient interest in sex (applying contemporary community standards). The judge in the case also found that, based on expert testimony, the movie had both serious and artistic value. Thus the film was not obscene even though it contained "a prolonged and explicit lesbian love scene" and "is a dizzying display of bodies, genitals, orgies, heterosexual and homosexual activity, masturbation, bodily functions, and sexual conduct and excesses of all varieties."[120] To be obscene, a work must pass all *three* prongs of the *Miller* test, not just one or two.

It is extremely rare for a newspaper or radio or television station to be prosecuted for obscenity, although magazines, books and films occasionally face such charges. Indecency is generally not a major problem for the print media, but broadcasters still have to worry about offending the FCC and Congress even though the DC Circuit U.S. Court of Appeals has determined that an around-the-clock ban is unconstitutional. Indecency, unlike obscenity, need not appeal to prurient interest, and thus is easier to demonstrate, especially when explicit sexual expressions and terms are used. The U.S. Supreme Court has generally eschewed indecency cases, except the most recent case involving nude dancing, *Barnes v. Glen Theatre* (1991). A majority held that the State could bar such activities, although no majority rationale emerged, indicating that the Court could at some point rule that some forms of nude dancing may have First Amendment protection, just not the kind displayed at the Kitty Kat Lounge.

Both obscenity and indecency continue to draw inordinate attention from politicians and police, but the U.S. Supreme Court appears to be steering away from becoming the high court of obscenity again. Any future decisions in this area are likely to be little more than fine tuning, as the Court did in *Pope v. Illinois* (1987), the last step determining the level of authority involved in each of the three prongs of the *Miller* standard. We now know that prong one relates to *local community standards*, prong two to *state standards* and the third prong (the "laps" test) must look to *national standards*.

In September 1990, the Motion Picture Association of America—the industry association that rates movies voluntarily submitted from G to X based on their level of violence, sex and offensive language—abolished the X-rating. It replaced the X-rating with NC-17 (No children under 17 admitted) in response to public criticism of its rating system, complaints of unwarranted censorship from filmmakers and critics and the extensive use of the X-rating by the pornographic film business of the X-rating, which the MPAA had not trademarked. The first movie to get the NC-17 rating was 1990's *Henry and June*. Very few MPAA films ever received a final X-rating anyway, although some acclaimed productions—such as *Midnight Cowboy, Last Tango in Paris* and *Clockwork Orange*—were released with the tag. Now, however, X is left for the "adult movies" that have become primarily a video industry.

One final note: The next technology likely to face a crackdown from authorities over alleged indecency and pornography is the home computer. Many of the software catalogs, including those selling public domain programs and shareware, already sell sexually explicit disks containing adult sex games or actual computer images of explicit sex, for example. The *Houston Chronicle* conducted a four-month study in 1990 of Internet computer network established for the electronic exchange of scientific information and found a variety of sexually explicit stories and pictures available for retrieval by members through the use of a personal computer.[121] More recently, there have been serious predictions of computer-simulated sex with the next wave of video technology known as *virtual reality*,[122] which makes three-dimensional images possible with a personal computer. Perfection of this technology is a decade or so away, but it will be interesting to see how the courts struggle with the inevitable prosecutions once it becomes possible to intercept their transmission. *Computerized search warrants, anyone?*

Endnotes

CHAPTER 1

[1]*Survey Says Too Few Understand Constitution*, Lexington (Ky.) Herald-Leader (Associated Press), February 15, 1987, at A6, col. 1.

[2]More than 1,000 people were interviewed via telephone in October and November 1986. The margin of error was plus or minus 3.2 percent.

[3]Unpublished poll provided to author by the center director.

[4]DeBenedictis, *27th Amendment Ratified*, 78 A.B.A. J. 26 (August 1992).

[5]Preemption is a U.S. Supreme Court doctrine derived from the supremacy clause of Article VI of the U.S. Constitution, which reads: "This Constitution and the Laws of the United States which shall be made in Pursuance thereof; and all Treaties made, or which shall be made, under the authority of the United States, shall be the supreme Law of the Land; and the Judges in every State shall be bound thereby, any Thing in the Constitution or Laws of any State to the Contrary notwithstanding."

[6]5 U.S. (1 Cranch.) 137, 2 L.Ed. 60.

[7]BLACK'S LAW DICTIONARY 43 (5th ed. 1979).

[8]An excellent resource on how to conduct legal research is Christopher G. and Jill Robinson Wren's second edition of THE LEGAL RESEARCH MANUAL: A GAME PLAN FOR LEGAL RESEARCH AND ANALYSIS (2nd ed.) (Madison, Wisc.: Adams & Ambrose Publishing, 1986). This very comprehensive text covers in clear detail how to gather and analyze facts, identify and organize legal issues, find the law, update the law and even conduct computerized legal research.

[9]BLACK'S LAW DICTIONARY, 484–485.

[10]610 F.2d 1353.

[11]In *Ross v. Bernhard*, 396 U.S. 531 (1970), the U.S. Supreme Court held that a jury trial is required under the Seventh Amendment when the underlying nature of the issue at hand is one of law. Earlier (1959) the court ruled in *Beacon Theatres, Inc. v. Westover* that when there is a legal issue that involves both relief at law and in equity, the legal issue must be tried first with a jury before the judge can decide the equitable issue.

[12]Foundation Press (2nd ed. 1974).

[13]Foundation Press (1989).

[14]BLACK'S LAW DICTIONARY 1335.

[15]An *ombud* or *ombudsperson* is an individual hired by the newspaper or other media organization to investigate consumer complaints against it and take action, when appropriate, such as writing a report or an apology or correction.

[16]*See* Appendix A.

[17]28 U.S.C.A. § 1251 *et seq.* specifies the scope and extent of federal court jurisdiction. Under the U.S. Constitution, Congress possesses the authority to define and limit the jurisdiction of the federal courts, except those matters specifically mentioned in the Constitution as within either the original or appellate jurisdiction of the U.S. Supreme Court. *See* Article III, § 2.

[18]*See* Pritchard and Morgan, *Impact of Ethics Codes on Judgments by Journalists: A Natural Experiment*, 66 JOURNALISM Q. 934 (1989).

CHAPTER 2

[1]These and other specialized courts are nicely diagrammed and described in a chart of the U.S. judicial system distributed by West Publishing Company and often displayed in law libraries.

[2]AMERICAN BAR ASSOCIATION, LAW AND THE COURTS (15 Chicago: ABA, 1987).

[3]Reske, Record State Caseloads in 1990, 78 A.B.A. J. 23 (August 1992) and ADMINISTRATIVE OFFICE OF THE UNITED STATES COURTS, UNDERSTANDING THE FEDERAL COURTS (1992) at 8, 10.

[4]*Sheppard v. Maxwell*, 384 U.S. 333 (1966).

[5]BLACK'S LAW DICTIONARY 1343.

[6]326 U.S. 310 (1945).

[7]*See* especially *Shaffer v. Heitner*, 433 U.S. 186 (1977) and *Kulko v. Superior Court of California*, 436 U.S. 84 (1978).

[8]LAW AND THE COURTS, p. 21.

[9]112 S.Ct. 2791, 60 U.S.L.W. 4795 (1992).

[10]Wohl, *The Dry Docket* (Supreme Court Report), 77 A.B.A. J. 44 (January 1991).

[11]Associate Justice Kennedy was selected after U.S. Appeals Court Judge Robert H. Bork failed in October 1987 to garner the required two-thirds approval of the U.S. Senate and law professor Douglas Ginsberg withdrew his nomination after publicly admitting he had smoked marijuana while a law student and later as a law professor.

[12]Justice Souter's confirmation had relatively smooth sailing, but Justice Thomas rode on troubled waters, as discussed later in this chapter.

[13]Gunther, Gerald, CONSTITUTIONAL LAW: CASES AND MATERIALS (10th ed.), 1980 (Mineola, N.Y.: Foundation Press), p. 1670.

[14]*See* Marcotte, *Some Relief for Supreme Court*, 74 A.B.A. J. 33 (September 1988).

[15]*See* Stern, Gressman & Shapiro, *Epitaph for Mandatory Jurisdiction*, 74 A.B.A. J. 68 (December 1988).

[16]*Id.*

[17]*Id.*

[18]403 U.S. 29.

[19]376 U.S. 254 (1964).

[20]*New York Times Company v. the United States*, 403 U.S. 713 (1971).

[21]Technically, all federal judges serve during "good behavior," which has been interpreted to mean for life unless impeached.

[22]Ford, of course, became President in 1974 when President Richard Nixon was forced to resign by revelations of a conspiracy to cover-up the Watergate break-in.

[23]These and other interesting facts about the Court can be found in a booklet, *The Supreme Court of the United States*, updated each term and available from the main office of the court.
[24]BLACK'S LAW DICTIONARY 1260.
[25]Choice of law principles go by such colorful names as lex fori, center of gravity, renvoi and grouping of contracts. This topic has been the subject of numerous books, articles and treatises and, in fact, is regularly taught as an elective course at most law schools.

CHAPTER 3

[1]There is at least one notable exception to the general rule that television shows with law themes do not reflect reality. "On Trial," a daily show syndicated by Republic Pictures and seen in more than 100 markets, uses videotaped footage from actual trials, not reenactments. According to a December 13, 1988, report on National Public Radio's news show, "Morning Edition," the program was canceled by a Boston television station after one segment included what a station spokesperson called "explicit" excerpts from an actual rape trial. The series is able to use videotapes from real trials because most state courts and a few federal courts now permit television and still cameras in the courtroom, as discussed in Chapter 9. Cable network Court TV, which was launched in 1991, has carried live court proceedings such as the rape trial of William Kennedy Smith, the Jeffrey Dahmer murder trial, the parole hearing of Charles Manson and the trial of Los Angeles police in the beating of Rodney King, all in 1992.
[2]Reske, *Record State Caseloads in 1990*, 78 A.B.A. J. 23 (August 1992).
[3]*See* FED. R. CIV. P. 4(b).
[4]*Id.* 4(d).
[5]*Id.* 4(c).
[6]*Id.* 4(d).
[7]*Id.*
[8]*Id.*
[9]*Id.*
[10]*Id.*
[11]*Id.* 8(b).
[12]*Id.* 8(d).
[13]*Id.* 8(b).
[14]*Id.* 13(a)-(f)
[15]*Id.* 7(a).
[16]*Id.* 12(b)(6).
[17]See *Anderson v. Liberty Lobby, Inc.*, 477 U.S. 242, 106 S.Ct. 2505, 91 L.Ed.2d. 202 (1986).
[18]*See* FED. R. CIV. P. 12(b)(6) and 56.
[19]*Id.* 12(c).
[20]*Id.* 12(e).
[21]*Id.* 12(t).
[22]*See* Marcotte, *High-Tech Depositions*, 73 A.B.A. J. 26 (December 1987) for an interesting discussion of a legal reporting service in Pennsylvania that offers satellite depositions.
[23]*See* FED. R. CIV. P. 33(a).
[24]*Id.* 45.
[25]*Id.* d(1).
[26]*Id.* 26(c).
[27]*Id.* 26(b)(1).
[28]*Id.* 26(b)(3).
[29]*Id.*

[30]*Id.*

[31]*See id.* 16(b).

[32]*See* FED. R. CIV. P. 16(c).

[33]FED. R. CIV. P. 16(e).

[34]*Ross v. Bernhard*, 396 U.S. 531 (1970).

[35]*Beacon Theatres, Inc. v. Westover*, 359 U.S. 500 (1959).

[36]*Apodaca v. Oregon*, 400 U.S. 901 (1970).

[37]*Colgrove v. Battin*, 413 U.S. 149 (1973).

[38]AMERICAN BAR ASSOCIATION, LAW AND THE COURTS 46 (Chicago: ABA, 1987).

[39]U.S. District Court Judge Jim Carrigen of Denver, quoted in Moss, *Voluntary Increase in Voir Dire*, 74 A.B.A. J. 22 (September 1988). *See also* Moss, *A Right to Voir Dire?*, 73 A.B.A. J. 31 (November 1987).

[40]Frederick, 24 TRIAL 66 (1988).

[41]Vinson, 24 TRIAL 58 (1988).

[42]Frederick, *supra.*

[43]Vinson at 58–59, 61–62.

[44]Susan Crittenden of the *Indianapolis* (Ind.) *Star. See* Fitzgerald, *Reporter Serves as Juror in Case She Reported*, 118 Editor & Publisher 12 (1985).

[45]*Id.*

[46]476 U.S. 79 (1986), 106 S.Ct. 1712.

[47]§ 1 states "nor shall any State deprive any person of life, liberty, or property without due process of law; nor deny to any person within its jurisdiction the equal protection of the laws."

[48]*Batson.*

[49]Judge Daniel F. Breck of the Sixth Cir. Court, Oakland County, Mich.

[50]Breck, *Peremptory Strikes After Batson v. Kentucky*, 74 A.B.A. J. 54 (April 1988).

[51]*See id.* at 56, 58.

[52]*Press-Enterprise v. Superior Court*, 464 U.S. 501, 104 S.Ct. 819, 78 L.Ed.2d 629, 10 Med.L.Rptr. 1161 (1984).

[53]Vinson, *supra*, at 61.

[54]BLACK'S LAW DICTIONARY 414 (5th ed. 1979).

[55]*Id.* at 221.

[56]FED. R. EVID. 611(c).

[57]*Id.* 611(b).

[58]McElhaney, *Cross-Examination*, 74 A.B.A. J. 117 (March 1988).

[59]*Id.*

[60]FED. R. EVID. 803(1)-(24).

[61]*Id.* 804(b)(1)-(5).

[62]*Id.* 805.

[63]*Id.* 801(d)(2).

[64]FED. R. CIV. P. 50(b).

[65]Marcotte, *The Jury Will Disregard . . .*, 73 A.B.A. J. 34 (November 1987).

[66]*Id.* at 35.

[67]FED. R. CIV. P. 61 and FED. R. CRIM. P. 61.

[68]*Curtis Publishing Company v. Butts*, 351 F.2d. 702 (5th Cir. 1965); 388 U.S. 130 (1965).

[69]FED. R. CIV. P. 49(a).

[70]FED. R. CIV. P. 49(b).

[71]*Burnett v. National Enquirer*, 9 Med.L.Rptr. 1921 (Cal. App. 1983).

[72]*Pring v. Penthouse*, 695 F.2d. 438 (10th Cir. 1983), 8 Med.L.Rptr, 2409.

[73]Sella, *The 10 Largest Jury Verdicts of 1988*, 75 A.B.A. J. 45–51 (March 1989).

[74]*Id.*

[75]*Sekou Ealy v. Richardson Merrell Dow, Inc.*, Civ. Act. No. 83-3504 (D. D.C. 1987).

[76]One of the jurors in that case, James Shannon, has written a book about his experiences, TEXACO AND THE $10 BILLION JURY, (Englewood Cliffs, N.J.: Prentice Hall, 1988).

[77]*See* Blodgett, *Longest Trial is Over*, 73 A.B.A. J. 22 (November 1987) and Blodgett, *Longest Trial Verdict In*, 73 A.B.A. J. 34 (December 1987).

[78]Dadisman, *What Did You Do in Trial Today, Daddy?*, 14 BARRISTER 23–26 (Fall 1987).

[79]Blodgett, *Juror Dismissed After 3 $\frac{1}{2}$ Years*, 73 A.B.A. J. 23 (November 1987).

[80]Marcotte, *The Longest Trial, Cont.*, 74 A.B.A. J. 30 (September 1988).

[81]Moss, *Grand Jury Leaks? Not so Fast*, 74 A.B.A. J. 32 (September 1988).

[82]*Id.*

[83]384 U.S. 436, 86 S.Ct. 1602, 16 L.Ed.2d 694 (1966).

[84]Cited in AMERICAN BAR ASSOCIATION, *supra*, at 44.

[85]*In Re Strandell v. Jackson County*, 838 F.2d 884 (1987).

[86]Marcotte, *No Forced Summary Jury Trials*, 74 A.B.A. J. 32 (April 1988).

[87]Postell, *Summary Jury Trials: How Far Can Federal Judges Go?*, 24 TRIAL 91 (May 1988).

[88]*In Re Strandell, supra.*

[89]James Henry of the Center for Public Resources in New York City, quoted in Postell, *supra.*

[90]BETTER BUSINESS BUREAU, UNIFORM RULES FOR BETTER BUSINESS BUREAU ARBITRATION (1984).

[91]*See* Schweber, *You're in Good Company: An Overview of Dispute Resolution Providers*, CONSUMER ARBITRATION 6–9 (Fall 1988) for an excellent description of major ADR providers.

[92]*See* 29 U.S.C.A. § 172 *et seq.*

[93]Schweber, *supra*, 6.

[94]AMERICAN ARBITRATION ASSOCIATION, COMMERCIAL ARBITRATION RULES (1992), 3. For more information, contact AAA at 140 West 51st St., New York, N.Y. 10020-1203, (212) 484–4000.

[95]AMERICAN ARBITRATION ASSOCIATION, ARBITRATION TIMES 1 (Spring 1991).

[96]ARBITRATION TIMES 1 (Winter 1989).

[97]*Id.* at 3.

[98]ARBITRATION TIMES 1 (Spring 1991).

[99]Moss, *New Remedy for Libel Claims*, 73 A.B.A. J. 42 (August 1987).

[100]Id.

[101]DeBenedictis, *Little Interest in Libel ADR*, 78 A.B.A. J. (January 1992).

[102]The American Bar Association and the Society of Professional Journalists began a joint project in 1988 to produce a series of primers, accompanied by a videotape and seminar planning guide, on a wide variety of legal topics. The first in the series is *A Journalist's Primer on Federal Criminal Procedure* (a 52-page booklet with a glossary of selected legal terms) and a videotape on federal criminal procedure. The ABA has also produced a booklet and videotape on *A Journalist's Primer on Locating Legal Documents* (1990). Both are very well-written and informative and should be consulted by any journalists covering criminal cases. For more information, write the ABA's Public Education Division at 750 N. Lake Shore Drive, Chicago, Ill., 60611, (312) 988–5725.

CHAPTER 4

[1]Shenck, *Duty to One's Country (Conversation with Kurt Vonnegut)*, 1 CV 58 (April 1989).

[2]*Near v. Minnesota*, 283 U.S. 697, 51 S.Ct. 625, 75 L.Ed. 1357, 1 Med.L.Rptr. 1001 (1931).

[3]4 W. BLACKSTONE, COMMENTARIES ON THE LAWS OF ENGLAND 151–52 (1820).

[4]C. Kuralt, *Annual Joe Creason Lecture at the University of Kentucky Honors Day* (April 28, 1989) (reprinted in booklet published by the University of Kentucky School of Journalism First Amendment Center).

[5]*See Police Group Seeks Boycott on Rap Song "Cop Killer,"* Lexington (Ky.) Herald-Leader (Associated Press), June 18, 1992, at A-12, col. 1 and *Minus "Cop Killer," Ice-T Album Races Up Charts after 17 Weeks,* Lexington (Ky.) Herald-Leader (wire services), August 7, 1992, at A-20, col. 1.

[6]*See Sex Chapter Is Restored to Child-Car Handbook,* Lexington (Ky.) Herald-Leader (New York Times Service), April 6, 1992, at A-22, col. 1.

[7]*Jones v. J. B. Lippincott Co.,* 694 F.Supp. 1216, 15 Med.L.Rptr. 2155 (D.C. Md. 1988).

[8]*Eimann v. Soldier of Fortune Magazine Inc.,* 880 F.2d 830 (5th Cir.), 16 Med.L.Rptr. 2148 (1989), *cert. denied,* 493 U.S. 1024 (1990).

[9]*Id.*

[10]*Braun v. Soldier of Fortune Magazine Inc.,* 757 F.Supp. 1325, 18 Med.L.Rptr. 1732 (M.D. Ala. 1991).

[11]*Id.,* 968 F.2d 1110, 20 Med.L.Rptr. 1777 (11th Cir. 1992), *cert. denied,* 113 S.Ct. (1993).

[12]Baker and Clifton, *Britain: Tinker, Tailor, Censor, Spy,* NEWSWEEK 32 (August 17, 1987).

[13]Simons, Lexington (Ky.) Herald-Leader (Knight-Ridder News Service), June 25, 1989, at A-1 col. 1.

[14]BLACK'S LAW DICTIONARY 288-289 (5th ed. 1979).

[15]The American record for incarceration for civil contempt is supposedly the five years served by a man who refused to testify before the N.J. Crime Commission about his knowledge of organized crime.

[16]*In re Farber,* 78 N.J. 259, 394 A.2d 330, 4 Med.L.Rptr. 1360 (1978).

[17]*Farr v. Superior Court of Los Angeles County,* 22 Cal.App.3d 60, 99 Cal.Rptr. 342, 1 Med.L.Rptr. 2545 (1971).

[18]22 Cal.app.3d. 60 (1971)

[19]*Cert. denied,* 409 U.S. 1011.

[20]Cal. CONST. 2, subd. (b). Farr's troubles did not end with the California Court of Appeals decision. Two of the six lawyers Farr had named when he refused to identify specific sources sued him for libel but were unsuccessful because they had failed to file suit within California's five-year statute of limitations.

[21]G. GUNTHER, CONSTITUTIONAL LAW 384 (5th ed. 1980).

[22]427 U.S. 539, 96 S.Ct. 2791, 1 Med.L.Rpt. 1064 (1976).

[23]*United States v. Dickinson,* 465 F.2d 496 (5th Cir. 1972, *cert. denied,* 414 U.S. 979, 94 S.Ct. 270, 38 L.Ed.2d 223 (1973).

[24]*Id.*

[25]*Id.*

[26]*Cert. denied,* 414 U.S. 979 (1973).

[27]18 U.S.C.A. 401.

[28]*Bridges v. California,* 314 U.S. 252, 625 S.Ct. 190. 86 L.Ed. 192 (1941).

[29]*Id.*

[30]*Pennekamp v. Florida,* 328 U.S. 331, 66 S.Ct. 1029, 90 L.Ed.2d 1295 (1946).

[31]*Craig v. Harney,* 331 U.S. 367, 67 S.Ct. 1249, 91 L.Ed. 1546 (1947).

[32]*Id.*

[33]*Wood v. Georgia,* 370 U.S. 375, 82 S.Ct. 1364, 8 L.Ed.2d 568 (1962).

[34]*Id.*

[35]*Id.*

[36]*Id.*

[37]*Near v. Minnesota.*

[38]F. FRIENDLY, MINNESOTA RAG (1981). *See also* chapter 3 in F. FRIENDLY & M. J. ELLIOTT, THE CONSTITUTION: THAT DELICATE BALANCE (1984).

[39]*See* n. 1 of Associate Justice Pierce Butler's dissent.

[40]*See* FRIENDLY & ELLIOTT, *supra,* for an interesting account of the circumstances surrounding the decision.

[41]Id. at 46.

[42]*Near v. Minnesota.*

[43]*Id.*

[44]*Id.*

[45]*Id.*

[46]The Fourteenth Amendment also says, "No State shall make or enforce any law which shall abridge the privileges or immunities of citizens of the United States; [known as the "privileges and immunities" clause] nor shall any State deprive any person of life, liberty, or property, without due process of law; ["due process clause"] nor deny to any person within its jurisdiction the equal protection of the laws." ["due protection" clause]. § 5 grants Congress the authority to enforce the amendment.

[47]*New York Times Co. v. U.S.* and *U.S. v. The Washington Post Co.*, 403 U.S. 713, 91 S.Ct. 2140, 29 L.Ed.2d 822, 1 Med.L.Rptr. 1031 (1971).

[48]*New York Times v. Sullivan*, 376 U.S. 254, 84 S.Ct. 110, 11 L.Ed.2d 686 (1964). *See* chapter 7.

[49]*Near v. Minnesota.*

[50]*Id.*

[51]*Id.*

[52]*Id.*

[53]FRIENDLY & ELLIOTT, *supra*, at 49.

[54]S. UNGAR, THE PAPERS & THE PAPERS 69 (1989). This is an extremely interesting and informative account of the legal and political battles in the Pentagon Papers case.

[55]*Id.* at 65.

[56]*Id.* at 83.

[57]*Id.* at 95.

[58]*New York Times Co. v. United States* and *United States v. The Washington Post.*

[59]372 U.S. 58, 70 (1963).

[60]402 U.S. 415, 91 S.Ct. 1575, 29 L.Ed.2d. 1, Med.L.Rptr. 1021 (1971).

[61]*New York Times Co. v. United States* and *United States v. The Washington Post.*

[62]*Id.*

[63]*Id.*

[64]*Id.*

[65]*Id.*

[66]*Id.*

[67]*Id.*

[68]*Id.*

[69]*Id.*

[70]*See* chapter 3 in S. UNGAR, *supra*, for an insightful and highly interesting account of Gavel's efforts, including a filibuster that was cut short after he began crying while he was trying to read "a section of the Papers describing the severing of arms and legs in battle" (p. 262).

[71]18 U.S.C.A. 641.

[72]UNGAR, *supra* at 301-02.

[73]THE WORLD ALMANAC AND BOOK OF FACTS 756 (1989).

[74]UNGAR, *supra* at 306.

[75]D. M. GILIMOR & J. A. BARRON, MASS COMMUNICATION LAW: CASES AND COMMENT (4th ed. 1984) 125.

[76]467 F.Supp. 990 (W.D. Wisc. 1979), *appeal dismissed as moot*, 610 F.2d 819 (7th Cir. 1979).

[77]42 U.S.C.A. 2011 *et seq.*

[78]*Id.* at 2014 (y).

[79]*Id.* at 2280.

[80]*U.S. v. The Progressive, Inc.*

[81]*Id.*

[82]*Id.*

[83]*Id.*

[84]The *Wisconsin State Journal* and the *Capital-Times*.

[85]*Nebraska Press Association v. Judge Hugh Stewart*, 427 U.S. 539, 96 S.Ct. 2791, 49 L.Ed.2d 683, 1 Med.L.Rptr. 1059 (1970).

[86]*See id.*

[87]*Id.*

[88]*Id.*

[89]*Id.*

[90]*Id.*

[91]*Id.*

[92]384 U.S. 333, 86 S.Ct. 1507, 16 L.Ed.2d 600 (1966).

[93]*Nebraska Press Association v. Judge Stuart, supra.*

[94]*Id.*

[95]*Id.*

[96]*Id.*

[97]*Id.*

[98]*Id.*

[99]236 U.S. 273, 35 S.Ct. 383, 59 L.Ed. 573 (1915).

[100]249 U.S. 47, 39 S.Ct. 247, 63 L.Ed. 470 (1919).

[101]*Id.*

[102]*Id.*

[103]*Id.*

[104]*Jacob Abrams v. U.S.*, 250 U.S. 616, 40 S.Ct. 17, 63 L.Ed. 1173 (1919).

[105]*Id.* (Holmes dissent).

[106]*Id.* (majority opinion).

[107]*Id.* (Holmes dissent).

[108]*See, for example, Jacob Frohwerk v. U.S.*, 249 U.S. 204 (1919); *Eugene V. Debs v. U.S.*, 249 U.S. 211 (1919); *Peter Schafer v. U.S.*, 251 U.S. 466 (1920); and *Clinton H. Pearce v. U.S.*, 252 U.S. 239 (1919).

[109]*Benjamin Gitlow v. New York*, 268 U.S. 652, 45 S.Ct. 625, 69 L.Ed. 1138 (1925).

[110]New York Penal Law §§ 160, 161 (as cited in *id.*).

[111]1: "nor shall any State deprive any person of life, liberty or property, without due process of law . . ."

[112]*Gitlow v. New York, supra.*

[113]*Id.*

[114]*Id.*

[115]*See* F. FRIENDLY & M. ELLIOTT, *supra*, at 79.

[116]274 U.S. 357, 47 S.Ct. 641, 71 L.Ed. 1095 (1927).

[117]*Id.*

[118]*Id.*

[119]*Id.*

[120]*Id.*

[121]*Clarence Brandenburg v. Ohio*, 395 U.S. 444, 89 S.Ct. 1827, 23 L.Ed.2d 430 (1969).

[122]*Id.*

[123]*Dirk DeJong v. Oregon*, 299 U.S. 353, 57 S.Ct. 255, 81 L.Ed. 278 (1937).

[124]F. FRIENDLY & M. ELLIOTT, *supra*, at 73. Chapter 5 is a well-researched and highly interesting account of the development of the case and the decision-making process involved in the U.S. Supreme Court.

[125]*Id.* at 72.

[126]315 U.S. 568, 62 S.Ct. 766, 86 L.Ed. 1031 (1942).

[127]*Id.*

[128]*Id.*

[129]*Daniel Niemotko v. Maryland* and *Neil W. Kelly v. Maryland,* 340 U.S. 268, 71 S.Ct. 303, 95 L.Ed. 295 (1951).

[130]*Irving Feiner v. New York,* 340 U.S. 315, 71 S.Ct. 303, 95 L.Ed. 295 (1951).

[131]*Id.*

[132]*Cox v. Louisiana* (Cox I), 379 U.S. 536, 85 S.Ct. 453, 13 L.Ed.2d 471 (1965).

[133]*Cox v. Louisiana* (Cox II), 379 U.S. 559, 85 S.Ct. 476, 13 L.Ed.2d 487 (1965).

[134]*Dennis v. United States,* 341 U.S. 494, 71 S.Ct. 857, 95 L.Ed. 1137 (1951).

[135]*Id.*

[136]*Id.*

[137]*Id.*

[138]*Nationalist Socialist Party v. Village of Skokie,* 432 U.S. 43 (1977).

[139]*See* F. FRIENDLY & ELLIOTT, *supra,* at 81. Chapter 5 gives a detailed and colorful account of the Skokie case.

[140]*National Socialist Party v. Skokie.*

[141]366 N.E.2d 347 (1977).

[142]373 N.E.2d 21 (1978).

[143]*United States v. Snepp,* 456 F.Supp. 176 (E.D. Va. 1978).

[144]*Snepp v. United States,* 595 F.2d 926 (4th Cir. 1979).

[145]*Frank W. Snepp II v. United States* and *United States v. Frank W. Snepp,* 444 U.S. 507, 100 S.Ct. 763, 62 L.Ed.2d 704 (1980).

[146]*Id.*

[147]*Id.*

[148]*Yetta Stromberg v. California,* 283 U.S. 359, 51 S.Ct. 532, 75 L.Ed. 1117 (1931).

[149]*Id.*

[150]*Id.*

[151]*Minersville School District v. Gobitis,* 310 U.S. 586 (1940).

[152]*Board of Education v. Barnette,* 319 U.S. 624 (1943).

[153]F. FRIENDLY & M. ELLIOTT, *supra,* at 115.

[154]*Board of Education v. Barnette.*

[155]391 U.S. 367, 88 S.Ct. 1673, 20 L.Ed.2d 672 (1968).

[156]Title 50 of the United States Code 462(b) (3) of the Universal Military Training and Service Act of 1948 and 12(b) (3) of the amendment.

[157]*United States v. O'Brien.*

[158]*Id.*

[159]*John F. Tinker v. Des Moines Independent Community School District,* 393 U.S. 503, 89 S.Ct. 733, 21 L.Ed.2d 731 (1969).

[160]*Id.*

[161]*Id.*

[162]*Id.*

[163]394 U.S. 576, 89 S.Ct. 1354, 22 L.Ed.2d 572 (1969).

[164]403 U.S. 15, 91 S.Ct. 1780, 29 L.Ed.2d 284 (1971).

[165]*Id.*

[166]*Id.*

[167]*Id.*

[168]*Id.*

[169]*Id.*

[170]*Spence v. Washington,* 418 U.S. 405, 94 S.Ct. 2727, 41 L.Ed.2d 842 (1974).

[171]*Id.*

[172]*Id.*

[173]*Hazelwood School District v. Kuhlmeier*, 484 U.S. 260, 108 S.Ct. 562, 98 L.Ed.2d 592, 14 Med.L.Rptr. 2081 (1988).

[174]*October 13: The Student Press's Turn*, 3 STUDENT PRESS L. CENTER REP. 3 (Winter 1987–1988).

[175]*Kuhlmeier v. Hazelwood School District*, 607 F.Supp. 1450 (1988).

[176]*Id.*

[177]*Tinker v. Des Moines School District.*

[178]*Kuhlmeier v. Hazelwood School District*, 795 F.2d 1368 (8th Cir. 1986).

[179]*Hazelwood School District v. Kuhlmeier.*

[180]*Tinker v. Des Moines School District.*

[181]*Hazelwood School District v. Kuhlmeier.*

[182]*Id.*

[183]*Id.*

[184]*See Hazelwood: A Complete Guide to the Supreme Court Decision*, 9 STUDENT PRESS L. CENTER REP. 3 (Spring 1988) for a detailed analysis of the decision, including "Model Guidelines for Student Publications."

[185]P. Parsons, *Student Press Censorship Reborn Within Hours of* Hazelwood *Ruling*, 15 MEDIA L. NOTES 12 (Winter 1988).

[186]Anderson, 11 PRESSTIME 6–7, 10 (February 1989).

[187]Johnson, Louisville (Ky.) Courier-Journal, November 13, 1988.

[188]Mead, *Student's Editorial on Sex Censored by Principal*, Lexington (Ky.) Herald-Leader, March 29, 1988, at A1, A5.

[189]*Id.* at A5.

[190]*Id.* and editorial, *Bad Lesson in Free Expression*, March 30, 1988.

[191]Dickson, *Attitudes of High School Principals About Press Freedom After Hazelwood*, 66 JOURNALISM Q. 169 (1989).

[192]Click & Kopenhaver, *Principals Favor Discipline More Than a Free Press*, 43 JOURNALISM EDUCATOR 48 (Summer 1988).

[193]L. A. Day & J. M. Butler, Hazelwood School District v. Kuhlmeier: *A Constitutional Retreat or Sound Public Policy?*, paper presented to the Annual Convention of the Association for Education in Journalism and Mass Communication, Portland, Oregon, July 1988.

[194]Note, *Only the News That's Fit to Print: Student Expressive Rights in Public School Communications Media After* Hazelwood v. Kuhlmeier, 11 HASTINGS COMM/ENT L. J. 35 (1988).

[195]*Id.* at 74.

[196]CAL. EDUC. CODE 48907 (West Supp. 1987).

[197]MASS. GEN. L. ch. 71, §§ 82, 86 (Supp. 1988).

[198]*Iowa Expression Law Loosens Hazelwood's Grasp*, 10 STUDENT PRESS L. CENTER 3 (fall 1989).

[199]*Id.* at 4.

[200]D. Spencer, *Faculty Advisor: A Road Not Taken*, 15 MEDIA L. NOTES 12 (Spring 1988).

[201]*Hazelwood v. Kuhlmeier* at n. 7.

[202]*Censorship and Selection: Issues and Answers for Schools* [summarized in] 76 THE QUILL 49 (October 1988).

[203]*United States v. Morison*, 604 F. Supp. 655 (D.Md. 1985).

[204]*See* C. Crystal, *Media Fights Man's Sentence in Navy 'Leaks' Case*, 1987–1988 SOCIETY OF PROFESSIONAL JOURNALISTS, SIGMA DELTA CHI FREEDOM OF INFORMATION REP. 24 AND M. Brenner, 1988–1989 SOCIETY OF PROFESSIONAL JOURNALISTS, SIGMA DELTA CHI FREEDOM OF INFORMATION REP. 20.

[205]18 U.S.C. §§ 641, 793 (1953).

[206]844 F.2d 1057, 15 Med.L.Rptr. 1369 (4th Cir. 1988).

[207]*Morison v. United States, cert. denied*, 488 U.S. 908 (1988).

[208]*Texas v. Johnson*, 491 U.S. 397, 109 S.Ct. 2533, 105 L.Ed.2d 342 (1989).

[209]A. Epstein, *High Court Upholds Right to Burn Flag*, Lexington (Ky.) Herald-Leader (Knight-Ridder News Service), June 22, 1989, at A1, col. 5.

[210]*Texas v. Johnson.*

[211]*Id.*

[212]*Id.*

[213]Media Access Project's Andy Schwartzman, quoted in *And the First Shall Be First*, 117 BROADCASTING 25–26 (July 3, 1989).

[214]*Texas v. Johnson.*

[215]George F. Will, *The Justices Are Wrong—But Keep Off the Constitution*, Washington Post syndicated column published in Lexington (Ky.) Herald-Leader, July 2, 1989, at F7, col. 1.

[216]James J. Kilpatrick, *First Amendment: It 'Ain't Broke,' so Don't Fix It*, Universal Press Syndicate column published in Lexington (Ky.) Herald-Leader, June 29, 1989, at A19, col. 1.

[217]*Id.*

[218]103 Stat. 777, 18 U.S.C.A. § 700 (Supp. 1990).

[219]*Id.*

[220]*United States v. Eichman et al.* and *United States v. Haggerty et al.*, 496 U.S., 110 S.Ct. 2404, 110 L.Ed.2d 287 (1990).

[221]*Id.*

[222]*United States v. Noriega*, 752 F.Supp. 1045 (S.D. Fla. 1990).

[223]*In re Cable News Network, Inc.*, 917 F.2d 1543 (11th Cir. 1990).

[224]*In re Cable News Network, Inc.*, cert. denied, 111 S.Ct. 451 (1990).

[225]*United States v. Noriega.*

[226]*Rust v. Sullivan*, 111 S.Ct. 1759, 114 L.Ed.2d 233, 59 U.S.L.W. 4451 (1991).

[227]Epstein, *Court Upholds Ban on Clinics' Abortion Advice*, Lexington (Ky.) Herald-Leader (Knight-Ridder News Service), at A1, col. 5.

[228]*Rust v. Sullivan.*

[229]*See*, for example, the debate between Bruce Fein and James F. Fitzpatrick in *Outlook: Rust v. Sullivan*, 9 COMMUNICATIONS LAWYER 1 (Fall 1991).

[230]111 S.Ct. 2720, 115 L.Ed.2d 888, 59 U.S.L.W. 4858 (1991).

[231]*Id.*

[232]112 S.Ct. 501, 116 L.Ed.2d 476, 19 Med.L.Rptr. 1609, 60 U.S.L.W. 4029 (1991).

[233]*Id.*

[234]*R.A.V. v. City of St. Paul*, 60 U.S.L.W. 4667 (1992).

[235]St. Paul, Minn. Legis. Code § 292.02 (1990).

[236]*In re* Welfare of R.A.V., 464 N.W.2d 507 (Minn. 1991).

[237]*Chaplinsky v. New Hampshire*, 315 U.S. 568 (1942).

[238]*R.A.V. v. City of St. Paul.*

[239]R. C. Dickeson, *Why Chavez Isn't Speaking* ("Other Opinions"), Greeley (Colo.) Tribune, May 10, 1990, at A12, col. 1.

[240]*First the Peace Sign, Next Geometry—Oh, Where Will It All End?*, Lexington (Ky.) Herald-Leader ("People" column compiled from wire services), June 23, 1989, at A18, col. 1.

[241]*End of School Year Halts Pupils' Preaching*, The Atlanta Journal and Constitution (United Press International), June 5, 1988, at A7, col. 4.

[242]Presser, *Article Brings Disciplinary Charges*, 77 A.B.A. J. 30 (July 1991).

[243]*Selling with Sex: The Real Outrage*, Lexington (Ky.) Herald-Leader (editorial), October 12, 1989, at A12, col. 1.

[244]*Sheila Shea's Dead, But She Is Still Speaking Her Mind*, Lexington (Ky.) Herald-Leader ("People" column compiled from wire services), June 26, 1988, at A2, col. 1.

CHAPTER 5

[1]McCann Erickson Worldwide Insider's Report (June 1993).

[2]1992 Leo Burnett Media Costs and Coverage at 1–2.

[3]*USA Snapshots: Growth in Political Ads*, USA Today, March 21, 1989, at A1.

[4]492 U.S. 469, 109 S.Ct. 3028 (1989).

[5]316 U.S. 52, 62 S.Ct. 920, 86 L.Ed. 1262, 1 Med.L.Rptr. 1907 (1942).

[6]*Id.*

[7]318 U.S. 413, 63 S.Ct. 920, 86 L.Ed. 1262, 1. Med.L.Rptr. 1907 (1942).

[8]*Id.*

[9]319 U.S. 105, 63 S.Ct. 870, 87 L.Ed. 1292 (1943).

[10]*Id.*

[11]319 U.S. 141, 63 S.Ct. 862, 87 L.Ed. 1313 (1943).

[12]319 U.S. 157, 63 S.Ct. 877, 87 L.Ed. 1324 (1943).

[13]376 U.S. 254, 84 S.Ct. 710, 11 L.Ed.2d 686, 1 Med.L.Rptr. 1527 (1964).

[14]*Id.*

[15]*Id.*

[16]*Roe v. Wade*, 410 U.S. 113, 93 S.Ct. 705, 35 L.Ed.2d 147 (1973).

[17]*Pittsburg Press Co. v. The Pittsburg Commission on Human Relations*, 413 U.S. 376, 93 S.Ct. 2553, 37 L.Ed.2d 669, 1 Med.L.Rptr. 1908 (1973).

[18]*Id.*

[19]*Id.*

[20]*Id.*

[21]*Id.*

[22]*Id.*

[23]*Bigelow v. Virginia*, 421 U.S. 809, 96 S.Ct.2222, 44 L.Ed.2d 600, 1 Med.L.Rptr. 1919 (1975).

[24]*Roe v. Wade.*

[25]*Bigelow v. Virginia.*

[26]*Id.*

[27]*Virginia State Board of Pharmacy v. Virginia Citizens' Consumer Council*, 425 U.S. 748, 96 S.Ct. 1817, 48 L.Ed.2d 346, 1 Med.L.Rptr. 1930 (1976).

[28]*Id.*

[29]*Id.*

[30]*Id.*

[31]*Id.*

[32]*Id.*

[33]*Id.*

[34]*Id.*

[35]*Id.*

[36]*Linmark Associates, Inc. v. Willingboro*, 431 U.S. 85, 97 S.Ct. 1614, 52 L.Ed.2d 155 (1977).

[37]*Id.*

[38]*Hugh Carey v. Population Services International*, 431 U.S. 678, 97 S.Ct. 2010, 52 L.Ed.2d 675, 2 Med.L.Rptr. 1935 (1977).

[39]*Griswold v. Connecticut*, 381 U.S. 497, 85 S.Ct. 1678, 14 L.Ed.2d 510 (1965).

[40]*Bates v. State Bar of Arizona*, 433 U.S. 350, 97 S.Ct. 2691, 53 L.Ed.2d 810, 2 Med.L.Rptr. 2097 (1977).

[41]*Virginia State Board of Pharmacy.*

[42]*Bates v. State Bar of Arizona.*

[43]*Id.*

[44]*Id.*

[45]*Id.*

[46]*Id.*

[47]*Id.*

[48]*Ohralik v. Ohio State Bar Association*, 436 U.S. 447, 98 S.Ct. 1912, 56 L.Ed.2d 444 (1978) and *In re Primus*, 436 U.S. 412 (1978).

[49]*Id.*

[50]*Id.*

[51]*First National Bank of Boston v. Bellotti*, 435 U.S. 765, 98 S.Ct. 1407, 55 L.Ed.2d 707, 3 Med.L.Rptr. 2105 (1978).

[52]*Friedman v. Rogers*, 440 U.S. 1, 99 S.Ct. 887, 59 L.Ed.2d 100 (1979).

[53]*Consolidated Edison Co. v. Public Service Commission of New York*, 444 U.S. 530, 100 S.Ct. 2326, 65 L.Ed.2d 319, 6 Med.L.Rptr. 1518 (1980).

[54]*Central Hudson Gas & Electric Corp. v. Public Service Commission of New York*, 447 U.S. 557, 100 S.Ct. 2343, 65 L.Ed.2d 341, 6 Med.L.Rptr. 1497 (1980).

[55]*Consolidated Edison Corp.*

[56]*Id.*

[57]*Red Lion Broadcasting v. Federal Communications Commission*, 395 U.S. 367, 89 S.Ct. 1794, 23 L.Ed.2d 371, 1 Med.L.Rptr. 2053 (1969).

[58]*Consolidated Edison Corp.*

[59]*Central Hudson Gas & Electric Corp.*

[60]*Id.*

[61]*Id.*

[62]*Id.*

[63]*Id.*

[64]*Id.*

[65]*Id.*

[66]*In re R ____ M. J ____* , 455 U.S. 191, 102 S.Ct. 929, 71 L.Ed.2d 64 (1982).

[67]The bar rules permitted attorneys to send such announcements only to "lawyers, clients, former clients, personal friends and relatives."

[68]*American Medical Association v. Federal Trade Commission*, 638 F.2d 443 (2d Cir. 1980).

[69]*American Medical Association v. Federal Trade Commission*, 455 U.S. 676, 102 S.Ct. 1744, 71 L.Ed.2d 546 (1982).

[70]*Bolger v. Youngs Drug Products Corp.*, 463 U.S. 60, 103 S.Ct. 2875, 77 L.Ed. 2d 469 (1983).

[71]39 U.S.C.S. § 3001(e)(2)

[72]*Bolger v. Youngs Drug Products Corp.*

[73]*Id.*

[74]*Id.*

[75]*Id.*

[76]*Condom Makers Want Message on TV*, Lexington (Ky.) Herald-Leader (Knight-Ridder News Service), November 8, 1988, at D2, col. 1.

[77]*Id.*

[78]*Zauderer v. Office of Disciplinary Counsel*, 471 U.S. 626, 105 S.Ct. 2265, 85 L.Ed.2d 652 (1985).

[79]*Id.*

[80]Ky. Rules of the Supreme Court 3.135(5).

[81]*Shapero v. Kentucky Bar Association*, 486 U.S. 466, 108 S.Ct. 1916, 100 L.Ed.2d 475 (1988).

[82]*Id.*

[83]Curriden, *Making Airwaves*, A.B.A. J. 38, 40. (July 1989).

[84]Ky. Rules of the Supreme Court 3.135(5).

[85]Id. 3.135(6)

[86]*Peel v. Attorney Registration and Disciplinary Commission of Illinois*, 492 U.S. 917, 110 S.Ct. 2281 (1990).

[87]Gibbons, *Restriction on Lawyer Advertising May Fall*, A.B.A. J.58 (May 1990).

[88]*Attorneys and Advertising: Yellow Pages and Red Tape?*, YELLOW PAGES UPDATE, July–August 1988, at 6–8.

[89]*Id.*

[90]Marcotte, *Lawyer Ads—The Next Step*, A.B.A. J. (August 1988) at 17–18.

[91]Blodgett, *A Guide to Successful Marketing*, A.B.A. J. (August 1988) at 19–20.

[92]Reynoldson, *The Case Against Lawyer Advertising*, A.B.A. J. (January 1989) at 60–61.

[93]*Anonymous v. Grievance Committee for the Second and Eleventh Judicial Districts of the State of New York*, April 12, 1988.

[94]*Posadas de Puerto Rico Associates v. Tourism Co. of Puerto Rico*, 478 U.S. 328, 106 S.Ct. 2968, 92 L.Ed.2d 266, 13 Med.L.Rptr. 1033 (1986).

[95]*Id.*

[96]*Id.*

[97]*Id.*

[98]*Trustees of the State University of New York v. Fox.*

[99]*Id.*

[100]*City of Cincinnati v. Discovery Network*, 113 S.Ct. 1505, 21 Med.L.Rptr. 1161 (1993).

[101]38 Stat. 719 (1914).

[102]15 U.S.C.A. 12-27 (1914).

[103]15 U.S.C.A. 1-7 (1890).

[104]15 U.S.C.A. 13 (1936).

[105]*Federal Trade Commission v. Yagle*, 1 F.T.C. 13 (1916) and *Federal Trade Commission v. A. Theo. Abbot & Co.*, 1 F.T.C. 16 (1916).

[106]258 U.S. 483, 42 S.Ct. 384, 66 L.Ed. 729 (1922).

[107]283 U.S. 643, 51 S.Ct. 587, 75 L.Ed. 1324 (1931).

[108]*See* E. W. KITCH & H. S. PERLMAN, LEGAL REGULATION OF THE COMPETITIVE PROCESS (2nd ed. 1979) 177–181 for an historical overview of the Federal Trade Commission.

[109]52 Stat. 111 (1938).

[110]15 U.S.C.A. 45 (1975).

[111]FTC, WHAT'S GOING ON AT THE FTC? (1992) 2-3 and FTC, A GUIDE TO THE FEDERAL TRADE COMMISSION (1989) 13.

[112]Farhi, *They're Wacky, They're Zany, They're an Ad?*, Washington Post, November 6, 1992, at B1, col. 1.

[113]WHAT'S GOING ON AT THE FTC? 2-8.

[114]*Id.* at 2.

[115]*Charles of the Ritz Distributing Corp. v. FTC*, 143 F.2d 676 (1944).

[116]88 Stat. 2183, 15 U.S. 45 (1975).

[117]WHAT'S GOING ON AT THE FTC? 5-6.

[118]94 Stat. 374, 15 U.S.C.A. 45 (1980).

[119]K. J. MEIER, REGULATION: POLITICS, BUREAUCRACY, AND ECONOMICS 110 (1985).

[120]*Immigration and Naturalization Service v. Chadha*, 462 U. S. 919, 103 S.Ct. 2764, 77 L.Ed.2d 317 (1983).

[121]15 U.S.C.A. 45.

[122]*See* C.F.R. 1.1-1.4 (1986) for FTC authority to issue such opinions.

[123]16 C.F.R. 1.5 (1986).

[124]15 U.S.C.A. 2301.

[125]562 F.2d 749 (1977).

[126]*Cert. denied*, 435 U.S. 950 (1978).

[127]*In re ITT Continental Baking Co.*, 79 F.T.C. 248 (1971).

[126]*In re Ocean Spray Cranberries, Inc.*, 70 F. T. C. 975 (1972).

[129]*National Commission on Egg Nutrition v. FTC*, 570 F.2d 187 (7th Cir. 1977), *cert. denied*, 439 U. S. 821 (1978).

[130]*Id.*

[131]*Id.*

[13:]*J. B. Williams Co., Inc. v. FTC*, 381 F.2d 884 (6th Cir. 1967).

[133]*U.S. v. J. B. Williams Co., Inc.*, 498 F.2d 414 (6th Cir. 1974).

[134]*In re Pfizer, Inc.*, 81 F.T.C. 23 (1972).

[135]*Id.*

[136]*Id.*

[137]21 C.F.R. 201.200 and 202.1 (1989).

[138]16 C.F.R. 255.1 (1989).

[139]Epstein, *Imitation Becoming Sincerest Way to Litigation, Lexington (Ky.) Herald-Leader* (Knight-Ridder News Service), August 26, 1993, at A3, col. 2.

[140]*Midler v. Ford Motor Co.*, 849 F.2d 460, 15 Med.L.Rptr. 1620 (9th Cir. 1988), No. CV862683 AWT (GX) (C.D.Cal. 1989).

[141]*Singer Can Sue for Imitation of Voice*, TRIAL, October 1988, at 94–95.

[142]*Midler v. Ford Motor Co.*

[143]*Midler v. Ford Motor Co.*, 944 F.2d 909, 19 Med.L.Rptr. 2190 (9th Cir. 1991), *cert. denied*, 117 L.Ed. 2d 650 (1992).

[144]*Waits v. Frito-Lay Inc.*, 20 Med.L.Rptr. 1585 (9th Cir. 1992).

[145]*White v. Samsung Electronics America, Inc.* 971 F.2d. 1395, 20 Med.L.Rptr 1457 (9th Cir. 1992).

[146]*Miami Herald v. Tornillo*, 418 U. S. 241, 94 S.Ct. 2831, 41 L.Ed.2d 730, 1 Med.L.Rptr. 1898 (1974).

[147]Pasternack and Utt, *Newspapers' Policies on Rejection of Ads for Products and Services*, 65 JOURNALISM Q. 695 (1988).

[148]Id.

[149]Lexington (Ky.) Herald-Leader, Oct. 6, 1988, at B5, col. 1, and at B8, col. 1.

[150]Id.

[151]Federal Trade Commission, *Program-Length TV Commercials* ("Facts for Consumers"), July 1989.

[152]Lexington (Ky.) Herald-Leader, December 27, 1989, at D2, col. 3.

[153]*Id.*, citing Business Week.

[154]*Id.*

[155]Blodgett, *Lawn Care Firms: Let Us Spray*, 74 A.B.A. J. 20-21 (September 1988).

[156]*Id.*

[157]*Id.*

[158]*City of Cincinnati v. Discovery Network.*

[159]*Fane v. Edenfield*, 945 F.2d 1514 (11th Cir. 1991), *cert. granted*, 112 S.Ct. 2272 (1992).

CHAPTER 6

[1]FEDERAL COMMUNICATIONS COMMISSION (F.C.C.), BROADCASTING AND CABLE TELEVISION 3 (1988).

[2]M. HOFFMAN, THE WORLD ALMANAC AND BOOK OF FACTS 492 (1989).

[3]F.C.C. at 3.

[4]W. AGEE, P.H. AULT & E. EMERY, INTRODUCTION TO MASS COMMUNICATIONS 196 (9th ed. 1988).

[5]*Id.*

[6]*See* opinion in *National Broadcasting Co. (NBC) v. United States*, 319 U.S. 190, 63 S.Ct. 997, 87 L.Ed. 1344, 1 Med.L.Rptr. 1965 (1943).

[7]*NBC v. U.S.*

[8]Broadcast frequencies are now measured in *hertz* (kilo-, mega-, giga-, etc.), the international unit for cycles per second, in honor of Heinrich Hertz, discussed earlier in this chapter. Until the early 1990s, the designation was simply cycles per second (kilocycles, megacycles, etc.).

[9]F.C.C., *supra,* at 3.

[10]W. AGEE, P. H. AULT & E. EMERY, *supra,* at 197.

[11]*See NBC v. U.S.*

[12]*Hoover v. Intercity Radio Co.*, 52 App.D.C. 339, 286 F. 1003 (1925), (cited in *NBC v. U.S.*).

[13]*United States v. Zenith Radio Corp.*, 12 F.2d 614 (1926) (cited in *NBC v. U.S.*).

[14]35 Ops. Atty. Gen. 126 (1926) (cited in *NBC v. U.S.*).

[15]*See NBC v. U.S.*

[16]*Id.*

[17]F.C.C., *supra,* at 4.

[18]*Id.*

[19]47 U.S.C.A. 151.

[20]47 U.S.C.A. 307.

[21]*NBC v. U.S.*

[22]47 U.S.C.A. 305.

[23]47 U.S.C.A. 307(a). *See also NBC v. U.S.*

[24]Low-power television has actually been available since 1956 but under the guise of "satellite" or "translator" stations that simply retransmitted the signal of an existing full-power station to increase or improve the coverage area of the originating station.

[25]Knight-Ridder News Service, Lexington (Ky.) Herald-Leader, March 7, 1990, at A4, col. 1.

[26]*See* Robert A. Rankin, *Politics Could Put Development of New Phone on Hold*, Knight-Rider News Service, Lexington (Ky.) Herald-Leader, March 15, 1990, at A2, col. 1.

[27]*Id.*

[28]*Id.* at col. 6.

[29]47 U.S.C.A. 326.

[30]47 U.S.C.A. 315(9).

[31]528 F.2d 124 (7th Cir. 1975).

[32]60 F.C.C.2d 615 (1976).

[33]F.C.C., THE LAW OF POLITICAL BROADCASTING AND CABLECASTING: A POLITICAL PRIMER (hereinafter, 1984 F.C.C. *Primer*) at 5.

[34]*Id.* at 7

[35]*Sen. Eugene J. McCarthy*, 11 F.C.C. F.2d 511, 1 Med. L. Rptr. 2205 (1968); *aff'd*, 390 F.2d 471 (D.C. Cir. 1968).

[36]*Socialist Workers Party,* 39 F.C.C.2d 89 (1972).

[37]F.C.C., 1984 *Primer* at 14.

[38]*Adrian Weiss* (Ronald Reagan Films), 58 F.C.C.2d 342 (1976); *review denied*, 58 F.C.C.2d 1389 (1976).

[39]F.C.C., 1984 *Primer* at 14.

[40]*Petition of Aspen Institute and CBS, Inc.*, 55 F.C.C. 2d 697 (1975); *aff'd sub nom., Chisholm et al. v. F.C.C.*, 538 F.2d 349 (D.C. Cir., 1976), 1 Med.L.Rptr. 2207; *cert. denied*, 97 S.Ct. 247 (1976).

[41]*Chisholm et al. v. F.C.C.*, 1 Med.L.rptr. 2220.

[42]*Henry Geller*, 95 F.C.C.2d 1236 (1983); *aff'd sub nom., League of Women Voters v. F.C.C.*, 731 F.2d 995 (1984).

[43]*Id.*

[44]*Id.*

[45]*Id.*

[46]F.C.C., 1984 *Primer* at 33.

[47]*Id.* at 35

[48]*Socialist Workers Party*, 26 F.C.C.2d 485 (1970).

[49]F.C.C., 1984 *Primer* at 36.

[50]47 C.F.R. 73.1940(d).

[51]*Norman William Seemann, Esq.*, 40 F.C.C. 341 (1962)

[52]*See* 47 C.F.R. § 73.1940(e).

[53]*Id.*

[54]F.C.C., 1984 *Primer* at 61.

[55]*Id.*

[56]F.C.C. Report No. MM-319, *Mass Media Action*, March 24, 1988.

[57]F.C.C., 1984 *Primer* at 60.

[58]47 U.S.C.A. § 312 (a)(7).

[59]*Rockefeller for Governor Campaign (WAJR)*, 59 F.C.C.2d 646 (1976).

[60]*W. Roy Smith*, 18 F.C.C.2d 747 (1969).

[61]*Dan Walker (WMAQ)*, 57 F.C.C.2d 799 (1975).

[62]*Branch v. F.C.C.*, 824 F.2d 37 (D.C. Cir. 1987), 14 Med.L.Rptr. 1465; *cert. denied*, 108 S.Ct. 1220 (1988).

[63]*Id.*

[64]*Id.*

[65]Communications Act of 1934 § 315(b) (1)-(2).

[66]*See, for example*, F.C.C. Public Notice No. 88-269 (Aug. 4, 1988).

[67]F.C.C., 1984 *Primer* at 48.

[68]Codification of the Commission's Political Programming Policies, 7 F.C.C.Rcd. 678 (1991). *See also* Gross, *New Political Programming Policies of the FCC*, 10 COM. LAW. 3 (Fall 1992).

[69]*Farmers' Educational and Cooperative Union v. WDAY*, 360 U.S. 525, 79 S.Ct. 1302, 3 L.Ed. 1407 (1959).

[70]*Id.*

[71]*Id.*

[72]*Id.*

[73]*Atlanta NAACP*, 36 F.C.C.2d 635 (1972).

[74]395 U.S. 444. *See* discussion in Chapter 4.

[75]*Atlanta NAACP*.

[76]F.C.C, 1984 *Primer* at 44.

[77]*See* 47 C.F.R. 73.1930.

[78]*F.C.C. v. Pacifica Foundation*, 438 U.S. 726, 98 S.Ct. 3026, 57 L.Ed.2d 1073, 3 Med.L.Rptr. 2553 (1978).

[79]*Julian Bond*, 69 F.C.C.2d 943 (Bd. Bur. 1978).

[80]Radio Act of 1927, 29.

[81]Communications Act of 1934, 326.

[82]U.S. Criminal Code, 18 U.S.C. 1464.

[83]NATIONAL ASSOCIATION OF BROADCASTERS, BROADCAST REGULATION '89: A MID-YEAR REPORT 102 (1989).

[84]*See id.*

[85]*Sonderling Broadcasting Corp. (WGLD-FM)*, 27 R.R.2d 285 (F.C.C. 1973); *reaff'd*, 41 F.C.C. 777, 27 R.R.2d 1508 (1973).

[86]*Id.*

[87]*Illinois Citizens Committee for Broadcasting v. FCC*, 515 F.2d 397, 31 R.R.2d 1523 (D.C. Cir. 1974).

[88]NATIONAL ASSOCIATION OF BROADCASTERS at 103.

[89]*Pacifica Foundation*, 56 F.C.C.2d 94 (1975).

[90]*Pacifica Foundation v. FCC*, 556 F.2d 9 (D.C. Cir. 1979).

[91]*F.C.C. v. Pacifica Foundation*, 438 U.S. 726, 98 S.Ct. 3026, 57 L.Ed.2d 1073, 3 Med.L.Rptr. 2553 (1978).

[92]*Id.*

[93]For the curious, the words that will "curve your spine, grow hair on your hands and maybe even bring us . . . peace without honor . . . and a bourbon," according to Carlin, are *shit, piss, fuck, cunt, cocksucker, motherfucker* and *tits.* References to *shit* and *fuck* comprise a major portion of the 12-minute skit.

[94]A. WALLGREN, VIDEO PROGRAM DISTRIBUTION AND CABLE TELEVISION: CURRENT POLICY ISSUES AND RECOMMENDATIONS (Report No. 88-233 of the U.S. National Telecommunications Information Agency, June 1988) at i.

[95]Wiley, *The Media and the Communications Revolution: An Overview of Developing Trends*, in 1 COMMUNICATIONS LAW (J. Goodale, ed. 1992).

[96]See E. KRASNOW, L.D. LONGLEY & H.A. TERRY, THE POLITICS OF BROADCAST REGULATION (3rd ed.) 42 (1982).

[97]*Fifty Years in Communications at 30* (1984).

[98]*WGBH Foundation*, 69 F.C.C.2d 1250, 43 R.R.2d 1436 (1978).

[99]*New Indecency Enforcement Standards to be Applied to All Broadcast and Amateur Licenses*, 2 F.C.C.Rcd. 2726, 62 R.R.2d 1218 (1987).

[100]*Matter of David Hildebrand*, 2 F.C.C.Rcd. 2708, 2712 n.9, 62 R.R.2d 1208, 1209-1210 n. 12 (1987). The FCC revoked the license even though the record showed there were only 66 hams under 17 in the whole Los Angeles area. *See* Feldman, *The FCC and Regulation of Broadcast Indecency: Is there a National Broadcast Standard in the Audience?* 41 FED.COM.L.J. 369 at n.69.

[101]*Pacifica Foundation*, 2 F.C.C.Rcd. 2698, 62 R.R.2d 1191 (1987). The U.S. Department of Justice has primary responsibility for enforcing 464 for specific violations, while the FCC can use violations in revoking or refusing to renew a broadcast license.

[102]*Regents of the University of California*, 2 F.C.C.Rcd. 2703, 62 R.R.2d 1199 (1987) and *Infinity Broadcasting Corp. of Pennsylvania*, 2 F.C.C.Rcd. 2705, 62 R.R.2d 1202 (1987).

[103]*See Raunch Radio Stirs Debate*, GANNETTEER, July–August 1987, at 14–15.

[104]*More Competition is Goal of Sikes as Head of FCC*, St. Louis Post Dispatch, August 8, 1989.

[105]*Id.*

[106]*See Indecency, "Marketplace" Issues Dominate FCC Confirmation Scene*, TELEVISION-/RADIO AGE, August 7, 1989, at 12, 14.

[107]*Infinity Broadcasting*, 2 F.C.C.Rcd. 2705 (1987).

[108]Quoted in *Perspectives* ("Overheard"), NEWSWEEK, May 4, 1987, at 17.

[109]*Infinity Broadcasting Corp. of Pennsylvania* (Reconsideration Order), 3 F.C.C.Rcd. 930, 64 R.R.2d 211 (1987).

[110]413 U.S. 15. *See* discussion in Chapter 14.

[111]*Reconsideration Order* at 933.

[112]*Id.*

[113]*Id.* at n. 47.

[114]852 F.2d 1332, 65 R.R.2d 45, 15 Med.L.Rptr. 1907 (1988).

[115]Lexington (Ky.) Herald-Leader (Associated Press story), January 13, 1988, at A1, col. 3.

[116]Cincinnati Post (Associated Press Story), June 23, 1988, at A12, col. 1.

[117]*Action for Children's Television v. FCC.*

[118]*Id.*

[119]*Id.*

[120]*Id.*

[121]*FCC Fines Two South Florida Stations for Indecency*, THE BRECHNER REPORT, November 1989, at 1.

[122]Interview on National Public Radio's *All Things Considered* newscast, July 15, 1990.

[123]*Id.*

[124]*Action for Children's Television v. F.C.C.* (ACT II), 932 F.2d 1504 (D.C. Cir. 1991), *cert. denied*, 112 S.Ct. 1281 (1992).

[125]*Interview*, 8 COM.LAW 21, No. 1 (1990).

[126]*Id.*

[127]*Sable Communications of California Inc. v. F.C.C.*, 492 U.S. 115, 109 S.Ct. 2829, 16 Med.L.Rptr. 1961 (1989).

[128]*There's a Chill in the Airwaves*, Southline (Atlanta), July 29, 1987, at 6.

[129]Lexington (Ky.) Herald-Leader, March 24, 1989, at A18, col. 1.

[130]Public Telecommunications Act of 1993 § 16(a), 106 Stat. 949.

[131]*See* C.T. & P.G. NORBACK, TV GUIDE ALMANAC 484–496 (1980), for a copy of the NAB Television Code.

[132]*Program Standards (Family Viewing Considerations)*, NAB Television Code (1978).

[133]P.L. 86-274, 73 Stat. 557 (1959).

[134]*Red Lion Broadcasting v. F.C.C.* and *U.S. v. Radio Television News Directors' Association*, 395 U.S. 367, 89 S.Ct. 1794, 23 L.Ed.2d 371, 1 Med.L.Rptr. 2053 (1969).

[135]*Id.*

[136]*Id.*

[137]*Syracuse Peace Council*, 99 F.C.C.2d 1389 (1984); *recon. denied*, 59 R.R.2d(P&F) 179 (1985); *remanded sub nom.*, *Meredith Corp. v. F.C.C.*, 809 F.2d 863 (D.C. Cir. 1987).

[138]*Report Concerning General Fairness Doctrine Obligations of Broadcast Licensees*, 102 F.C.C.2d 143 (1985).

[139]*Syracuse Peace Council.*

[140]*Telecommunications Research and Action Center (TRAC) v. F.C.C.*, 801 F.2d 501; *rehearing denied*, 806 F.2d 1115 (D.C. Cir. 1986); *cert. denied*, 107 S.Ct. 3196 (1987).

[141]*TRAC v. F.C.C.*, 806 F.2d 1115 (D.C. Cir. 1986).

[142]*See* fn. 11 & 12 in *F.C.C. v. League of Women Voters of California*, 468 U.S. 364, 104 S.Ct. 3106, 82 L.Ed.2d 278, 10 Med.L.Rptr. 1937 (1984).

[143]*Radio Television News Directors' Association v. F.C.C.*, 809 F.2d 860 and *Meredith Corp. v. F.C.C*, 809 F.2d 863 (D.C. Cir. 1987).

[144]*FCC Ends Enforcement of Fairness Doctrine*, Report No. MM-265, August 4, 1987. *See* Memorandum Opinion and Order (F.C.C. 87–266).

[145]*FCC Reaffirms Decision to End Enforcement of Fairness Doctrine; Denies Various Requests for Reconsideration*, Report No. MM-319, March 24, 1988. *See* Memorandum Opinion and Order (F.C.C. 88–131).

[146]*Syracuse Peace Council v. F.C.C.* (Consolidated with *Geller v. F.C.C.*), 867 F.2d 654 (D.C. Cir. 1989).

[147]Gibbons, *Broadcasters: The Fairness Doctrine Just Not Needed*, GANNETTEER, March–April 1990, at 16–17.

[148]Markey, *The Fairness Doctrine, Congress and the FCC*, 6 COM.L. 1, No. 3 (1988).

[149]Dunklee, *The Fairness Doctrine is for the Public*, 77 THE QUILL 10, No. 8 (August 1989).

[150]Sanford, *The Politics of Fairness*, 77 THE QUILL 7, (January 1989).

[151]F.C.C., BROADCASTING AND CABLE TELEVISION 11 (1988).

[152]Shales, *The Great American Cable Tangle* (Outlook), The Washington Post, June 10, 1990, at C1, col. 1.

[153]Hobson, *Does the 1984 Cable Act Franchise 'Video Programming'?* 8 COM.L. 3, No. 2 (1990).

[154]Cable Communications Policy Act of 1984, Pub.L. 98-549, 98 Stat. 2779, 47 U.S.C.A. § 521-559.

[155]Cable television Consumer protection and Competition Act of 1992, 47 U.S.C.A. § 325, 521, 534, 535, 543, and 548.

[156]*Turner Broadcasting System, Inc. v. F.C.C.*, 819 F.Supp. 32 (D.D.C. 1993).

[157]*United Video Inc. v. F.C.C.*, 800 F.2d 1173, 66 R.R.2d 1865 (D.C. Cir. 1989).

[158]*Quincy Cable TV. Inc. v. F.C.C.*, 768 F.2d 1434 (D.C. Cir. 1985); *cert. denied*, 106 S.Ct. 2889 (1986).

[159]*Century Communications Corp. v. F.C.C.*, 835 F.2d 292 (D.C. Cir. 1987); clarified, 837 F.2d 517 (D.C. Cir. 1988); *cert. denied*, 108 S.Ct. 2014 (1988).

[160]*See* Wiley at 615 for a detailed overview of the ownership rules.

[161]*See* 47 C.F.R. § 73.659–73.671.

[162]*Schurz Communications v. F.C.C.*, 982 F.2d 1043 (7th Cir. 1992).

[163]*See* 47 C.F.R. § 73.658.

[164]Halpert, *High-Definition Television Will Alter Commerce as Well as Entertainment*, Lexington (Ky.) Herald-Leader (Knight-Ridder News Service), April 9, 1989, at E1, col. 4.

CHAPTER 7

[1]For the uninitiated, a *hornbook* is a book examining the fundamentals in a given field, whether it be in law or any other discipline. In law, they are particularly useful for anyone who wants a basic overview of a particular area such as torts. Both appellate and trial courts occasionally refer to "hornbook law" to demonstrate that a particular legal theory or principle has become widely accepted.

[2]PROSSER, LAW OF TORTS 737 (1971).

[3]*New York Times Co. v. L. B. Sullivan* and *Ralph D. Abernathy et al. v. L. B. Sullivan*, 376 U.S. 454, 84 S.Ct. 710, 11 L.Ed.2d 686, 1 Med.L.Rptr. 1527 (1964).

[4]Hansen & Moore, *Chilling the Messenger: The Impact of Libel on Community Newspapers*, 11(2) NEWSPAPER RESEARCH J. 86 (1990).

[5]Hansen & Moore, *Public Attitudes Toward Libel: Do Newspaper Readers and Editors See Eye to Eye?*, 13(3) NEWSPAPER RESEARCH J. 2 (1992).

[6]*See Survey: Juries Hiking Libel Penalties*, EDITOR & PUBLISHER, September 5, 1992, at 13.

[7]*Id.*

[8]PROSSER, *supra.*

[9]*Id.*

[10]Gartner, *Spreading the Word on Libellus*, Hartford Courant, August 9, 1991, at C3, col. 4.

[11]SANFORD, LIBEL AND PRIVACY: THE PREVENTION AND DEFENSE OF LITIGA-TION 15 (1992). Consult Chapter 2 in this excellent treatise by one of the foremost First Amendment attorneys in the country for a very enlightening review of the development of libel law. This work, which is updated occasionally, is a superb reference source for professional journalists.

[12]*See* TEDFORD, FREEDOM OF SPEECH IN THE UNITED STATES 14 (1985), for an informative discussion of the history of each of these types of libel.

[13]*See* TEETER & LE DUC, LAW OF MASS COMMUNICATIONS 23 (1992), excerpted from 3 Howell's State Trials 561 (1632-3).

[14]*See id.* at 24, excerpted from Howell's State Trials 513 (1663).

[15]*See* Tedford at 16–21 for a discussion of the history of each of these four types of libel.

[16]RESTATEMENT (SECOND) OF TORTS § 568A (1977).

[17]*See* GA. CODE ANN. (1992).

[18]*See* KY. REV. STAT. § 411.051, 411,061 and 411.062 (1992).

[19]The Kentucky Revised Statutes, for instance, makes a distinction between "newspaper libel" and "actions against a radio or television broadcasting station" for "a defamatory statement" in the process of making a qualifying correction (retraction).

[20]R. Sack, *Common Law Libel and the Press: A Primer*, in 1 COMMUNICATIONS LAW 1992 45 (J. C. Goodale ed. 1992).

[21]Delaware, Iowa, Minnesota, Mississippi, New Jersey, Pennsylvania, Texas, Vermont and Washington.

[22]Sack at 41.

[23]*See Superpowers Collide*, Lexington (Ky.) Herald-Leader (wire service), May 9, 1991, at A18, col. 1.

[24]*See Pitcher Says ESPN Remarks Were Off Base*, Lexington (Ky.) Herald-Leader (wire service), October 1, 1990, at B2, col. 2.

[25]*See Ex-Beatle v. Globe*, Lexington (Ky.) Herald-Leader (wire services), December 11, 1991, at A10, col. 2.

[26]B. SANFORD, SYNOPSIS OF THE LAW OF LIBEL AND THE RIGHT OF PRIVACY (3rd ed. 1984). It is interesting how the defamatory character of words can change within even a relatively short period of time. For instance, *communist* is listed as a "Red Flag" word, as it was in the 1980s, but with the demise of communist governments from Poland to the Soviet Union, the word probably has little defamatory meaning left.

[27]*Mitchell v. Globe International Publishing, Inc.*, 773 F.Supp. 1235 (W.D. Ark. 1991). *See also Woman, 96, Is Awarded $1.5 Million in Sun Libel Suit*, Lexington (Ky.) Herald-Leader (Associated Press), December 6, 1991, at A6, col. 1.

[28]*See The Truth Is Lies Are No Defense*, 14 PRESSTIME 60, January 1992 (No. 1).

[29]*E. W. Scripps Co., The Kentucky Post and Al Salvato v. Louis A. Ball*, 801 S.W.2d 684, 18 Med.L.Rptr. 1545 (Ky. 1990), cert. denied, _____ U.S. _____ (1991).

[30]*See A. America, Anatomy of a Libel Suit*, 13 (5) PRESSTIME 6–10, May 1991.

[31]*Id*. at 8.

[32]*Id*.

[33]*Id*.

[34]*Harte-Hanks Communications, Inc. v Daniel Connaughton*, 491 U.S. 657, 109 S.Ct. 2678, 105 L.Ed.2d 562, 16 Med.L.Rptr. 1881 (1989).

[35]*Bose Corp. v. Consumers Union of the U.S., Inc.*, 466 U.S. 485, 104 S.Ct. 1949, 80 L.Ed.2d 502, 10 Med.L.Rptr. 1625 (1984).

[36]*E. W. Scripps Co. v. Louis A. Ball*

[37]*See A. America, Anatomy of a Libel Suit, supra*.

[38]*See id.* for a thought-provoking account of the impact of the *Ball* libel suit on the *Kentucky Post*.

[39]RESTATEMENT (SECOND) OF TORTS § 558 (1977).

[40]*Curtis Publishing Co. v. Wallace Butts* and *Associated Press v. Edwin A. Walker*, 388 U.S. 130, 87 S.Ct. 1975, 18 L.Ed.2d 1094, 1 Med.L.Rptr. 1568 (1967).

[41]*Elmer Gertz v. Robert Welch, Inc.*, 418 U.S. 323, 94 S.Ct. 2997, 41 L.Ed.2d 789, 1 Med.L.Rptr. 1633 (1974).

[42]*Time, Inc. v. Mary Alice Firestone*, 424 U.S. 448, 96 S.Ct. 958, 47 L.Ed.2d 154, 1 Med.L.Rptr. 1665 (1976).

[43]*Dun & Bradstreet, Inc. v. Greenmoss Builders, Inc.*, 472 U.S. 749, 105 S.Ct. 2939, 86 L.Ed.2d 593, 11 Med.L.Rptr. 2417 (1985).

[44]*Greenbelt Cooperative Publishing Assoc. v. Charles S. Bresler*, 398 U.S. 6, 90 S.Ct. 1537, 1 Med.L.Rptr. 1589 (1970).

[45]*Hustler Magazine and Larry C. Flynt v. Jerry Falwell*, 485 U.S. 46, 108 S.Ct. 876, 99 L.Ed.2d 41, 14 Med.L.Rptr. 2281 (1988).

[46]*New York Times v. Sullivan*.

[47]*Philadelphia Newspapers, Inc. et al. v. Maurice S. Hepps et al.*, 475 U.S. 767, 106 S.Ct. 1558, 89 L.Ed.2d 783, 12 Med.L.Rptr. 1977 (1986).

[48]*New York Times v. Sullivan*.

[49]*Id.* See also SMOLLA, SUING THE PRESS: LIBEL, THE MEDIA & POWER 26–52 (1986) and A. LEWIS, MAKE NO LAW: THE SULLIVAN CASE AND THE FIRST AMENDMENT (1991) for insightful accounts of the *Sullivan* case. Lewis includes the first draft of Associate Justice William Brennan's unanimous opinion, which is rather interesting to compare with the final version.

[50]*Id.*

[51]*New York Times v. Sullivan.*

[52]*Id.*

[53]*Id.*

[54]*Id.*

[55]*Id.*

[56]*Id.*

[57]*Pring v. Penthouse International, Ltd.*, 7 Med.L.Rptr. 1101 (D. Wyo. 1981), *rev'd*, 695 F.2d 438, 8 Med.L.Rptr. 2409 (10th Cir. 1982), *cert. denied*, 103 S.Ct. 3112 (1983). The author, Philip Cioffari, Ph.D., was a professor of English at a New Jersey university.

[58]*Pring v. Penthouse International, Ltd.*, 695 F.2d 438, 8 Med.L.Rptr. 2409 (10th Cir. 1982).

[59]*Id.*

[60]*Paul Bindrim v. Gwen Davis Mitchell et al.*, 155 Cal.Rptr. 29, 5 Med.L.Rptr. 1113 (Cal. App. 1979), *cert. denied*, 444 U.S. 984, *rehearing denied*, 444 U.S. 1040 (1980).

[61]*Carson's Dentist Jokes Bring $5 Million Lawsuit*, Lexington (Ky.) Herald-Leader (wire services), September. 4, 1987, at A2, col. 1.

[62]*Film's Jokes Bring $10 Million Suit*, Lexington (Ky.) Herald-Leader (Associated Press), July 27, 1983, at 8B, col. 1.

[63]*Mansour v. Fanning*, 6 Med.L.Rptr. 2055, 506 F.Supp. 186 (D.C. N.Cal. 1980).

[64]*Id.*

[65]*Kentucky Fried Chicken, Inc. v. Sanders*, 563 S.W.2d 8 (Ky. 1978).

[66]*See* Prosser, *supra*, at 750.

[67]*Jim Garrison v. Louisiana*, 379 U.S. 64, 85 S.Ct. 209, 13 L.Ed.2d 125, 1 Med.L.Rptr. 1548 (1964).

[68]LEWIS COPELAND, THE WORLD'S BEST JOKES (1936).

[69]Note, *A Communitarian Defense of Group Libel Laws*, 101 HARV. L. REV. 682 (1988).

[70]*See* KANE, ERRORS, LIES, AND LIBEL 113–120 (1992) for an informative account of how the case developed.

[71]*Green v. Alton Telegraph Printing Co.*, No. 77–66 (Madison County, Ill. 1980).

[72]*See* Kane, *supra*, at 118.

[73]Since then there have been even larger jury awards, including a 1991 verdict against WFAA-TV in Dallas, Texas, for $58 million in a case involving a former district attorney whom a reporter accused of accepting bribes in DUI cases. This is the largest jury award thus far, although entertainer Wayne Newton won more than $19 million in compensatory and punitive damages plus almost $3.5 million in prejudgment interest in 1987 against NBC-TV, only to have the entire award overturned by the Ninth Circuit U.S. Court of Appeals. *See Newton v. NBC*, 677 F.Supp. 1066, 14 Med.L.Rptr. 1914 (D. Nev. 1987), *rev'd*, 930 F.2d 662, 18 Med.L.Rptr. 1001 (9th Cir. 1990). In 1990, a Philadelphia jury awarded a local attorney $34 million in damages for libel against the *Philadelphia Inquirer*. In 1993 the U.S. Supreme Court denied certiorari in a case in which a Maryland trial court judge had dismissed a $44 million suit against the weekly *Rockville* (MD) *Gazette* by a candidate for city council. The state appellate courts had earlier allowed the dismissal to stand.

[74]*Alton Telegraph Printing Co. v. Green*, 438 N.E.2d 203, 8 Med.L.Rptr. 1345 (1982).

[75]Kane, *supra*, at 120.

[76]*See* Christopher Maloney, *Presidential Politics Interrupt House Floor Proceedings*, C-SPAN UPDATE, October. 10, 1988.

[77]*Ronald R. Hutchinson v. William Proxmire and Morton Schwartz,* 443 U.S. 111, 99 S.Ct. 2675, 61 L.Ed.2d 411, 5 Med.L.Rptr. 1279 (1979).

[78]*Hutchinson v. Proxmire,* 431 F. Supp. 1311, 2 Med.L.Rptr. 1769 (W.D Wis. 1977).

[79]*Id.*

[80]*Hutchinson v. Proxmire,* 579 F.2d 1027, 4 Med.L.Rptr. 1016 (7th Cir. 1978).

[81]*Hutchinson v. Proxmire* (1979).

[82]*Id.*

[83]*Farmers' Educational and Cooperative Union of America v. WDAY,* 360 U.S. 525, 79 S.Ct. 1302, 3 L.Ed.2d 1407 (1959).

[84]*Time, Inc. v. Mary Alice Firestone.*

[85]*Id.,* quoting the trial court judge's decision.

[86]*Id.*

[87]*Id.*

[88]*Id.*

[89]Hansen & Moore, *Public Attitudes Toward Libel: Do Newspaper Readers and Editors See Eye to Eye?*

[90]Smolla, *supra,* at 33.

[91]Lewis, *supra,* at 25-26.

[92]*Id.* at 27.

[93]*Id.* at 25-26.

[94]*New York Times v. Sullivan,* quoting the trial court judge.

[95]*Id.*

[96]*Id.*

[97]*Id.*

[98]*Id.*

[99]*Jim Garrison v. Louisiana,* 379 U.S. 64, 85 S.Ct. 209, 13 L.Ed.2d 125, 1 Med.L.Rptr. 1548 (1964).

[100]Yes, this is the same Jim Garrison portrayed in Oliver Stone's movie, *JFK.*

[101]See ALEXANDER, A BRIEF NARRATIVE OF THE CASE AND TRIAL OF JOHN PETER ZENGER 1 (1963), for an enlightening account of Zenger's trial and its impact on sedition in this country.

[102]*Steve Ashton v. Kentucky,* 384 U.S. 195, 86 S.Ct. 1407, 16 L.Ed.2d 469 (1966).

[103]*Id.*

[104]*Alfred D. Rosenblatt v. Frank P. Baer,* 383 U.S. 75, 86 S.Ct. 669, 15 L.Ed.2d 597, 1 Med.L.Rptr. 1558 (1966).

[105]*Id.*

[106]*Curtis Publishing Co. v. Wallace Butts* and *Associated Press v. Edwin A. Walker* (1967).

[107]*Id.*

[108]*Id.*

[109]*Beckley Newspapers Corp. v. C. Harold Hanks,* 389 U.S. 81, 88 S.Ct. 197, 19 L.Ed.2d 248, 1 Med.L.Rptr. 1585 (1967).

[110]*Phil A. St. Amant v. Herman A. Thompson,* 390 U.S. 727, 88 S.Ct. 1323, 20 L.Ed.2d 262, 1Med.L.Rptr. 1586 (1968).

[111]*Greenbelt Cooperative Publishing Assoc. v. Charles S. Bresler* (1970).

[112]*Monitor Patriot Co. v. Roselle A. Roy,* 401 U.S. 265, 91 S.Ct. 621, 28 L.Ed.2d 35, 1 Med.L.Rptr. 1619 (1971).

[113]Id.

[114]*Time, Inc. v. Frank Pape,* 401 U.S. 265, 91 S.Ct. 633, 28 L.Ed.2d 45, 1 Med.L.Rptr. 1627 (1971).

[115]*Ocala Star-Banner Co. v. Leonard Damron,* 401 U.S. 295, 91 S.Ct. 628, 1 Med.L.Rptr. 1624 (1971).

[116]*George A. Rosenbloom v. Metromedia*, 403 U.S. 29, 91 S.Ct. 1811, 29 L.Ed.2d 296, 1 Med.L.Rptr. 1597 (1971).

[117]*Elmer Gertz v. Robert Welch, Inc.* (1974).

[118]*Id.*

[119]*See* John B. McCroy, Robert C. Bernius, Robert D. Sack, Robert E. Malchman & Timothy B. Shavers, *Constitutional Privilege in Libel Law*, in 1 COMMUNICATIONS LAW 1992 553-559 (J. C. Goodale ed. 1992).

[120]*Elmer Gertz v. Robert Welch, Inc.* (1974).

[121]*Id.*

[122]*Id.*

[123]*Id.*

[124]*Dun & Bradstreet, Inc. v. Greenmoss Builders, Inc.*

[125]*Harte-Hanks Communications, Inc. v. Connaughton.*

[126]*Id.*

[127]*Bose Corp. v. Consumers Union of the U.S., Inc.* (1984).

[128]*Milkovich v. Lorain Journal Co.*, 497 U.S. 1, 110 S. Ct. 2695, 111 L.Ed.2d 1, 17 Med.L.Rptr. 2009 (1990). Milkovich later settled out of court with the newspaper.

[129]*Id.*

[130]*Id.*

[131]*See* Harold W. Fuson, *A Yawn for Milkovich*, 79 THE QUILL 23, (July–Aug. 1991).

[132]*Masson v. New Yorker Magazine, Inc.*, 111 S.Ct. 2419, 18 Med.L.Rptr. 2241 (1991).

[133]*See*, Sack, *supra*, at 84–85.

[134]*See Brown & Williamson Tobacco Corp. v. Jacobson*, 827 F.2d 1119, 14 Med.L.Rptr. 1497 (7th Cir. 1987), cert. denied, 108 S.Ct. 1302 (1988).

[135]*Hustler Magazine and Larry C. Flynt v. Jerry Falwell* (1988).

[136]*Id.*

[137]*Newton v. NBC, supra*, at n. 73.

[138]*Philadelphia Newspapers, Inc. v. Hepps* (1986).

[139]*Reggie Warford v. Lexington Herald-Leader et al.*, 789 S.W. 2d 758, 17 Med.L.Rptr. 1785 (Ky. 1990), *cert. denied*, 111 S.Ct 754 (1991).

[140]*Kathy Keeton v. Hustler Magazine, Inc.*, 465 U.S. 770, 104 S.Ct. 1473, 79 L.Ed.2d 790, 10 Med.L.Rptr. 1405 (1984).

[141]*Id.*

[142]*Iain Calder and John South v. Shirley Jones*, 465 U. S. 783, 104 S.Ct. 1482, 79 L.Ed.2d 804, 10 Med.L.Rptr. 1401 (1984).

[143]*See, for example*, LIBEL REFORM PROJECT OF THE ANNENBERG WASHINGTON PROGRAM, PROPOSAL FOR THE REFORM OF LIBEL LAW 9-10 (1988) and GANNETT CENTER FOR MEDIA STUDIES, THE COST OF LIBEL: ECONOMIC AND POLICY IMPLICATIONS (Conference Report) 1 (1986).

[144]*Edwards v. National Audubon Society* 556 F.2d 113 (2d Cir. 1977), *cert. denied, sub. nom. Edwards v. New York Times*, 434 U.S. 1002 (1977).

[145]*See McCroy et al., supra*, at 591-592.

CHAPTER 8

[1]DeBenedictis, *Automobile Intrigue*, A.B.A. J. 28 (March 1990).

[2]*Id.*

[3]Rice, *Back from the Eye of the Media Hurricane, 'The Woman in Question' Writes About the Perils of the Press*, DATELINE, April 19, 1988, at 20-21.

[4]*Journalistic Soul-Searching Follows Snub by Donna Rice*, Cincinnati Post, November 19, 1988, at A1, col. 4.

[5]Boyd, *Deprived of Privacy*, Lexington (Ky.) Herald-Leader (Knight-Ridder News Service), July 8, 1990, at E1, col. 1.

[6]*FBI Pays Widow of U.S. Communist for 1984 Frame-Up*, Lexington (Ky.) Herald-Leader, October 27, 1987, at A3, col. 1.

[7]*Id.*

[8]The poll was part of an annual fall survey conducted by the University of Kentucky Survey Research Center. The questions on privacy were submitted by the author of this textbook. Respondents were interviewed at random by phone during October 28–December 2, 1987. All interviews were conducted by paid professionals, and all data were analyzed by the center. More specific results are available from the author.

[9]*See* Boyd, *Deprived of Privacy, supra.* The survey of 2,254 adults was conducted between January 11–February 11, 1990.

[10]*Id.*

[11]*See* Gnotto, *Spy Gadgets Thrive in High-Tech, Low-Trust World*, Lexington (Ky.) Herald-Leader (Knight-Ridder News Service), December 25, 1989, at F1, col. 1.

[12]U.S. Criminal Code, 18 U.S.C. § 2512 (1)-(2).

[13]*See* Boyd, *Private Eyes Put Technology on the Case*, Lexington (Ky.) Herald-Leader (Knight-Ridder News Service), July 24, 1990, at A2, col. 1.

[14]*Id.*

[15]*Id.*

[16]*Id.*

[17]*Id.*

[18]Boyd, *A Matter of Privacy*, Lexington (Ky.) Herald-Leader (Knight-Ridder News Service), June 10, 1990, at F1, col. 2.

[19]*Id.*

[20]*Id.*

[21]*See* Endejan, 8 COM. L. 6, No. 2 (1990) for a thorough discussion of the impact of CID.

[22]*See* I. Altman, *Privacy Regulation: Culturally Universal or Culturally Specific?*, 33 J. SOCIAL ISSUES 66 (No. 3, 1977).

[23]*Id.* at 72–77.

[24]S. D. Warren & L. D. Brandeis, *The Right to Privacy*, 4 HARV. L. REV. 193 (1890).

[25]W. AGEE, P. AULT & E. EMERY, INTRODUCTION TO MASS COMMUNICATIONS 83–89 (9th ed. 1988).

[26]*Id.* at 83.

[27]Warren & Brandeis, *supra.*

[28]*Roberson v. Rochester Folding Box Co.*, 171 N.Y. 538, 64 N.E. 442 (1902).

[29]New York Civil Rights Law § 50–51 (current law).

[30]*Pavesich v. New England Life Insurance Co.*, 122 Ga. 190, 50 S.E. 68 (1905).

[31]BLACK'S LAW DICTIONARY 1075 (5th ed. 1979).

[32]W. PROSSER & W. KEETON, HANDBOOK OF THE LAW OF TORTS 851–866 (5th ed. 1984).

[33]*Burger King Learns Fast Lesson from Mr. Rogers*, Lexington (Ky.) Herald-Leader (Associated Press), May 9, 1984, at B15, col. 1.

[34]*See Allen v. National Video*, 610 F. Supp. 612 (S.D. N.Y. 1985).

[35]*See White v. Samsung Electronics America, Inc.*, 20 Med.L.Rptr. 1457 (9th Cir. 1992).

[36]Lexington (Ky.) Herald-Leader, June 10, 1989, at A12, col. 1.

[37]*Hugo Zacchini v. Scripps-Howard Broadcasting Co.*, 433 U.S. 562, 97 S.Ct. 2849, 53 L.Ed.2d 965, 2 Med.L.Rptr. 1199 (1977).

[38]*Id.*

[39]*Time, Inc. v. James J. Hill*, 385 U.S. 374, 87 S.Ct. 534, 17 L.Ed.2d 456, 1 Med.L.Rptr. 1791 (1967).

[40]*Hugo Zacchini v. Scripps-Howard Broadcasting Co.*

[41]*Factors Etc., Inc. v. Pro Arts, Inc.*, 579 F.2d 215 (2d Cir. 1978), 4 Med.L.Rptr. 1144, *cert. denied*, 440 U.S. 908 (1979).

[42]*Memphis Development Corp. v. Factors Etc.*, 3 Med.L.Rptr. 2012 (1977).

[43]*Price v. Hal Roach Studies, Inc.*, 400 F.Supp. 836 (S.D. N.Y. 1975).

[44]BLACK'S LAW DICTIONARY 1377.

[45]*Price v. Hal Roach Studios, Inc.* at 844.

[46]*Memphis Development Corp. v. Factors Etc.*, 5 Med.L.Rptr. 2521 (1980).

[47]TENN. CODE ANN. § 47-25-1101 et seq. ("The Personal Rights Protection Act of 1984").

[48]*Elvis Presley Enterprises v. Elvisly Tours*, 14 Med.L.Rptr. 1053 (1987).

[49]*See* State ex rel. *Presley v. Crowell*, 733 S.W.2d 89 (Tenn. App.), 14 Med.L.Rptr. 1043 (1987). Had the Tennessee court *not* recognized a *common law right* that existed prior to the state statute in 1984, there would be a question of whether Presley's name and image had protection from the date of his death in 1977 to the effective date of the statute—a period of about seven years.

[50]*Estate of Elvis Presley v. Russen*, 513 F.Supp. 1339 (D. N.J. 1981).

[51]*Martin Luther King, Jr. Center for Social Change, Inc., v. American Heritage Products, Inc.*, 250 Ga. 135, 296 S.E.2d 697, 8 Med.L.Rptr. 2377 (1982).

[52]*Carson v. Here's Johnny Portable Toilets, Inc.*, 698 F.2d 831 (6th Cir.), 9 Med.L.Rptr. 1153 (1983).

[53]*Id.*

[54]*Cher v. Forum International, Ltd.*, 7 Med.L.Rptr. 2593 (C.D. Cal. 1982).

[55]*Cher v. Forum International, Ltd.*, 692 F.2d. 634, 8 Med.L.Rptr. 2484 (9th Cir. 1982), *cert. denied*, 462 U.S. 1120 (1982).

[56]*Time, Inc. v. Hill* .

[57]The photographs were nonobscene poses of Shields nude in a bathtub. Shields made no claim that they were pornographic.

[58]*Shields v. Gross*, 451 N.Y.S.2d 419 (App. Div. 1982), 58 N.Y.2d 338, 448 N.E.2d 108 (N.Y. 1983).

[59]*See Mary Jane Russell v. Marlboro Books*, 183 N.Y.S.2d 8 (1959).

[60]*Douglass v. Hustler Magazine*, 759 F.2d. 1128 (7th Cir. 1985), cert. denied, 109 S.Ct. 377 (1988).

[61]*Id.*

[62]*Hugo Zacchini v. Scripps-Howard Broadcasting.*

[63]*Id.*

[64]*Id.*

[65]*Namath v. Sports Illustrated*, 371 N.Y.S.2d 10 (N.Y. Sup. Ct. App. Div. 1962).

[66]*Id.*

[67]*Booth v. Curtis Publishing Co.*, 15 A.D.2d 343, 223 N.Y.S.2d 737 (N.Y. Sup. Ct. App. Div. 1962).

[68]*See* M. Ament & R. J. Emmett, *The Right of Publicity in Thoroughbreds: An Issue of Dollars and Horse Sense*, 10 LOUISVILLE LAW. 14 (No. 2, 1990).

[69]*Id.*

[70]*Dietemann v. Time, Inc.*, 449 F.2d 245, 1 Med.L.Rptr. 2417 (9th Cir. 1971).

[71]*Dietemann v. Time, Inc.*, 284 F.Supp. 925 (1968).

[72]*Dietemann v. Time, Inc.* (1971).

[73]*Id.*

[74]*Pearson v. Dodd*, 410 F.2d 701 (D.C. Cir.), 1 Med.L.Rptr. 1809, *cert. denied*, 395 U.S. 947 (1969).

[75]*Pearson v. Dodd*, 410 F.2d 701 (D.C. Cir.).

[76]*Id.*

[77]*Id.*

[78]*Florida Publishing Co. v. Fletcher*, 340 So.2d 914, 2 Med.L.Rptr. 1088 (Fla. 1976), *cert. denied*, 431 U.S. 930 (1977).

[79]*Id.*

[80]*Id.*

[81]*Id.*

[82]Reporters Committee for Freedom of the Press, *Photographers' Guide to Privacy*, NEWS MEDIA & L. (Summer 1986), at 2 (insert).

[83]Wisnia, *Private Grief, Public Exposure*, THE QUILL, 28 (July 1989).

[84]*See id.* at 29.

[85]*See* Society of Professional Journalists Code § V.2 in Appendix.

[86]*See* Radio Television News Directors Association Code § 3 in Appendix.

[87]*See Le Mistral v. Columbia Broadcasting System*, 61 A.D.2d 491, 402 N.Y.S.2d 815, 3 Med.L.Rptr. 1913 (1978).

[88]*Dietemann v. Time, Inc.* (1971).

[89]RESTATEMENT (SECOND) OF TORTS § 6521 comment c (1977).

[90]*Galella v. Onassis*, 353 F.Supp. 196 (S.D. N.Y. 1972), aff'd, 487 F.2d 986, 1 Med.L.Rptr. 2425 (2d Cir. 1973).

[91]*Id.*

[92]*Id.*

[93]*Id.*

[94]*Id.*

[95]*Galella v. Onassis*, 533 F.Supp. 1076 (S.D. N.Y. 1982).

[96]*Cefalu v. Globe Newspaper Co.*, 391 N.E.2d 935, 5 Med.L.Rptr. 1940, (Mass. App. Ct. 1979).

[97]*Id.*

[98]U.S. CONST. amend. IV.

[99]*California v. Acevedo*, 111 S.Ct. 1982, 114 L.Ed.2d 619 (1991).

[100]*Carroll v. United States*, 267 U.S. 132 (1925).

[101]*Griswold v. Connecticut*, 381 U.S. 479, 85 S.Ct. 1678 (1965).

[102]*Id.*

[103]U.S. CONST. amend. IX.

[104]*Bowers v. Hardwick*, 478 U.S. 186 (1986).

[105]*Webster v. Reproductive Health Services*, 109 S.Ct. 3040 (1989).

[106]*Roe v. Wade*, 410 U.S. 113 (1975).

[107]*Planned Parenthood of Southeastern Pennsylvania v. Casey*, 60 U.S.L.W. 4795 (1992).

[108]18 U.S.C. § 2510–2521.

[109]*Id.* at § 2511(4).

[110]*Id.* at § 2512(1).

[111]*Id.* at § 2511(2) (d).

[112]*Boddie v. American Broadcasting Cos.*, 731 F.2d 333, 10 Med.L.Rptr. 1923 (6th Cir. 1984).

[113]*Boddie v. American Broadcasting Cos.*, 694 F.Supp. 1304, 16 Med.L.Rptr. 1100 (N.D. Ohio 1988), aff'd 881 F.2d 267 (6th Cir. 1989).

[114]*Id.*

[115]California, Florida, Illinois, Maryland, Massachusetts, Montana, New Hampshire, Oregon, Pennsylvania and Washington.

[116]86 F.C.C.2d 313 (1981) and 64 RAD. REG.2d (P & F) 444 (1988).

[117]*Shevin v. Sunbeam Television Corp.*, 351 So.2d 723 (Fla. 1977), appeal dismissed, 435 U.S. 920, reh'g denied, 435 U.S. 1018, 3 Med.L.Rptr. 1312 (1978).

[118]*Id.*

[119]*Cassidy v. American Broadcasting Cos.*, 60 Ill.App.3d 831, 17 Ill.Dec. 936, 377 N.E.2d 126, 3 Med.L.Rptr. 2449 (1978).

[120]*Id.*

[121]*See What Really Happens in War*, PARADE, June 9, 1991, at 4.

[122]RESTATEMENT (SECOND) OF TORTS § 652D (1977).

[123]Video Privacy Protection Act of 1988.

[124]Hughes, *A Photo that Had to Be Used*, 1 FINELINE 3, No. 7 (1989).

[125]*Barger v. Louisville Courier-Journal*, 20 Med.L.Rptr. 1189 (1992).

[126]*Cox Broadcasting v. Cohn*, 420 U.S. 469, 43 L.Ed.2d 328, 95 S.Ct. 1029, 1 Med.L.Rptr. 1819 (1975).

[127]*Id.*

[128]*Florida Star v. B.J.F.*, 491 U.S. 524, 109 S.Ct. 2603, 105 L.Ed.2d 443, 16 Med.L.Rptr. 1801 (1989).

[129]*Oklahoma Publishing Co. V. Oklahoma County District Court*, 430 U.S. 308, 2 Med.L.Rptr. 1456 (1977).

[130]*Smith v. Daily Mail Publishing Co..* 443 U.S. 97 (1979).

[131]*Id.*

[132]*Florida Star v. B.J.F.*

[133]Donnelly, *To Name or Not To Name Alleged Victim*, Lexington (Ky.) Herald-Leader (Knight-Ridder News Service), April 18, 1991, at A3, col. 2.

[134]Janis, *Behind Every Pulitzer, There's Another Story: The Winner's*, GANNETTEER, June 1991, at 2.

[135]*Florida v. Globe Communications., Inc.*, No. 91–11008, slip op. (Palm Beach County Ct., October 24, 1991).

[136]Poore, *Judge Rejects Bid To Block Lottery Winner's Spending*, Lexington (Ky.) Herald-Leader, June 21, 1991, at C2, col. 5.

[137]*See* Rhoden, *Tennis Great Arthur Ashe Reveals That He Has AIDS*, Lexington (Ky.) Herald-Leader (New York Times News Service), April 9, 1992, at Al, col. 1; Ashe, *Why I Was Forced To Make a Choice* (Commentary), Lexington (Ky.) Herald-Leader (Washington Post News Service), April 14, 1992, at C1, col. 2; and *The Burden of Truth*, People, April 20, 1992, at 51.

[138]*Educator Seen in Adult Bookstore Resigns*, Lexington (Ky.) Herald-Leader (wire services), July 15, 1992, at A4, col. 1.

[139]Wolf, Thomason & LaRoeque, *The Right to Know v. the Right of Privacy: Newspaper Identification of Crime Victims*, 63 JOURNALISM Q. 503 (1986).

[140]*Briscoe v. Reader's Digest*, 4 Cal.3d 529, 483 P.2d 34, 1 Med.L.Rptr. 1845 (Cal. Sup. Ct. 1971).

[141]*Id.*

[142]*Briscoe v. Reader's Digest*, 1 Med.L.Rptr. 1852 (U.S. D.C. C.D. Cal., 1972).

[143]*Id.*

[144]*Virgil v. Time*, 527 F.2d 1122, 1 Med.L.Rptr. 1835 (9th Cir. 1975).

[145]*Id.*

[146]*Id.*

[147]*Cert. denied*, 425 U.S. 998, 96 S.Ct. 2215 (1976).

[148]*Virgil v. Sports Illustrated*, 424 F.Supp. 1286 (S.D. Cal. 1976).

[149]*Sidis v. F-R Publishing Corp.*, 113 F.2d 806, 1 Med.L.Rptr. 1775 (2d Cir. 1940).

[150]*Id.*

[151]*Id.*

[152]*Roshto v. Hebert*, 439 So.2d 428, 9 Med.L.Rptr. 2417 (La. 1983).

[153]*Howard v. Des Moines Register and Tribune Co.*, 3 Med.L.Rptr. 2304 (Iowa D.C. 1978).

[154]*Howard v. Des Moines Register and Tribune Co.*, 283 N.W.2d 289, 5 Med.L.Rptr. 1667 (Iowa 1979), *cert. denied*, 445 U.S. 904 (1980).

[155]*Howard v. Des Moines Register and Tribune Co.* (1979).

[156]*Id.*

[157]*Sipple v. Chronicle Publishing Co.*, 154 Cal.App.3d 1040, 201 Cal. Rptr. 665, 10 Med.L.Rptr. 1690 (1984).

[158]*Id.*

[159]*Id.*

[160]Blonston, *Most News outlets Refuse to Release Name of Alleged Gay at Pentagon*, Lexington (Ky.) Herald-Leader (Knight-Ridder News Service), August 7, 1991, at A3, col. 2.

[161]RESTATEMENT (SECOND) OF TORTS § 652E (1981).

[162]*Time, Inc. v. Hill*, 385 U.S. 374, 87 S.Ct. 534, 17 L.Ed.2d 456, 1 Med.L.Rptr. 1791 (1967).

[163]*Id.*

[164]*New York Times v. Sullivan*, 376 U.S. 254, 11 L.Ed.2d 686, 84 S.Ct. 710, 1 Med.L.Rptr. 1527 (1954).

[165]*Cantrell v. Forest City Publishing Co.*, 419 U.S. 245, 95 S.Ct. 465, 42 L.Ed.2d 419, 1 Med.L.Rptr. 1815 (1974).

[166]*Id.*

[167]*Id.*

[168]*Id.*

[169]*Id.*

[170]*Id.*

[171]*Id.*

[172]*Id.*

[173]*Id.*

[174]*Time v. Hill.*

[175]*Id.*

[176]18 U.S.C. § 2511(4) (b) (ii) (1989).

CHAPTER 9

[1]*See, for example, Reynolds v. United States*, 98 U.S. 145 1878, in which the Court, in affirming the constitutionality of a federal law making bigamy a crime in the territories, rejected a motion for a new trial on the ground that the trial judge had allowed an individual to serve on the jury who, it was asserted, " 'believed' he had formed an opinion which he had never expressed, and which he did not think would influence his verdict on hearing the testimony."

[2]*Richmond Newspapers, Inc. v. Virginia*, 448 U.S. 555, 100 S.Ct. 2814, 65 L.Ed.2d 973, 6 Med.L.Rptr. 1833 (1980).

[3]*Paul M. Branzburg v. John P. Hayes, In the Matter of Paul Pappas*, and *U.S. v. Earl Caldwell*, 408 U.S. 665, 92 S.Ct. 2646, 33 L.Ed.2d 626, 1 Med.L.Rptr. 2617 (1972).

[4]*Gannett Co., Inc. v. Daniel A. DePasquale*, 443 U.S. 368, 99 S.Ct. 2898, 61 L.Ed.2d 608, 5 Med.L.Rptr. 1337 (1979).

[5]*Thomas L. Houchins, Sheriff of the County of Alameda, Calif., v. KQED, Inc.*, 438 U.S. 1, 98 S.Ct. 2588, 57 L.Ed.2d 553, 3 Med.L.Rptr. 2521 (1978).

[6]*Gannett v. DePasquale.*

[7]*Id.*

[8]*J. M. Near v. Minnesota*, 283 U.S. 697, 51 S.Ct. 625, 75 L.Ed. 1357, 1 Med.L.Rptr. 1001 (1931)

[9]*Nebraska Press Association v. Judge Hugh Stuart*, 427 U.S. 539, 96 S.Ct. 2791, 49 L.Ed.2d 683, 1 Med.L.Rptr. 1059 (1976).

[10]*Id.*

[11]Minow and Cates, *Who Is an Impartial Juror in an Age of Mass Media?*, 40 AM. U. L. REV. 631 (1991).

[12]*Id.*

[13]*Murphy v. Florida*, 421 U.S. 794, 95 S.Ct. 2031, 44 L.Ed.2d 589, 1 Med.L.Rptr. 1232 (1975).

[14]*Irvin v. Dowd*, 366 U.S. 717, 81 S.Ct. 1639, 6 L.Ed.2d 751, 1 Med.L.Rptr. 1178 (1961).

[15]*Rideau v. Louisiana*, 373 U.S. 723, 83 S.Ct. 1417, 10 L.Ed.2d 663, 1 Med.L.Rptr. (1963).

[16]*Estes v. Texas*, 381 U.S. 532, 85 S.Ct. 1628, 14 L.Ed.2d, 1 Med.L.Rptr. 1187 (1965).

[17]*Sheppard v. Maxwell*, 384 U.S. 333, 86 S.Ct. 1507, 16 L.Ed.2d 600, 1 Med.L.Rptr. 1220 (1966).

[18]*Murphy v. Florida.*

[19]*Id.*

[20]*Irvin v. Dowd.*

[21]While the judge banned live broadcasting during most of the trial, the opening and closing arguments of the prosecutor, the return of the jury's verdict and the receipt of the verdict by the judge were broadcast live. Other portions of the trial were recorded by a camera behind a camouflaged booth and broadcast later as clips during the local newscasts. News photographers were also restricted to the booth area.

[22]*Estes v. Texas.*

[23]*Noel Chandler and Robert Granger v. Florida*, 449 U.S. 560, 101 S.Ct. 802, 66 L.Ed.2d 740, 7 Med.L.Rptr. 1041 (1981).

[24]*Estes v. Texas.*

[25]*Richmond Newspapers, Inc. v. Virginia.*

[26]*Id.*

[27]*Id.*

[28]*Id.*

[29]*Sheppard v. Maxwell.*

[30]The old network TV series, "The Fugitive" (starring the late David Jansen), which still lives in syndication on the Arts and Entertainment Cable Network was loosely based on the Sheppard Story.

[31]*Sheppard v. Maxwell.*

[32]*Id.*

[33]*Pell v. Procunier*, 417 U.S. 817, 94 S.Ct. 2800, 41 L.Ed.2d 495 (1974).

[34]*William B. Saxbe v. The Washington Post Co.*, 417 U.S. 843, 94 S.Ct. 2811, 41 L.Ed.2d 514 (1974).

[35]*Pell v. Procunier.*

[36]*William B. Saxbe v. The Washington Post Co.*

[37]*Branzburg v. Hayes.*

[38]*Richard Nixon v. Warner Communications*, 435 U.S. 589, 98 S.Ct. 1306, 55 L.Ed.2d 570, 3 Med.L.Rptr. 2074 (1978).

[39]*Thomas L. Houchins v. KQED*, 438 U.S. 1, 98 S.Ct. 2588, 57 L.Ed.2d 553, 3 Med.L.Rptr. 2521 (1977).

[40]*Id.*

[41]*Robert K. Smith v. Daily Mail Publishing Co.*, 443 U.S. 97, 99 S.Ct. 2667, 61 L.Ed.2d 399, 5 Med.L.Rptr. 1305 (1979).

[42]*Id.*

[43]*Id.*

[44]*Landmark Communications, Inc. v. Commonwealth of Virginia*, 435 U.S. 829, 98 S.Ct. 1535, 56 L.Ed.2d 1, 3 Med.L.Rptr. 2153 (1978).

[45]*Cox Broadcasting Corp. et al. v. Martin Cohn*, 420 U.S. 469, 95 S.Ct. 1029, 43 L.Ed.2d 328, 1 Med.L.Rptr. 1819 (1975).

[46]*Oklahoma Publishing Co. v. District Court in and for Oklahoma County*, 430 U.S. 308, 97 S.Ct. 1045, 51 L.Ed.2d 355, 2 Med.L.Rptr. 1456 (1977).

[47]*Landmark Communications v. Virginia.*

[48]*Id.*

[49]*Cox Broadcasting v. Cohn.*

[50]*Oklahoma Publishing v. District Court.*

[51]*Globe Newspaper Co. v. Norfolk County Superior Court*, 457 U.S. 596, 102 S.Ct. 2613, 73 L.Ed.2d 248, 8 Med.L.Rptr. 1689 (1982).

[52]*Id.*

[53]*Id.*

[54]*Press Enterprise Co. v. Riverside County Superior Court* ("Press Enterprise I"), 464 U.S. 501, 104 S.Ct. 819, 78 L.Ed.2d 629, 10 Med.L.Rptr. 1161 (1984).

[55]*Press Enterprise Co. v. Riverside County Superior Court* ("Press Enterprise II"), 478 U.S. 1, 106 S.Ct. 2735, 92 L.Ed.2d 1, 13 Med.L.Rptr. 1001 (1986).

[56]*Press Enterprise I.*

[57]*Press Enterprise II.*

[58]*Branzburg v. Hayes.*

[59]N.J.S.A. 2A:170-29(2)(b).

[60]*New Jersey v. Lashinsky*, 81 N.J. 1, 404 A.2d 1121, 5 Med.L.Rptr. 1418 (1979).

[61]*Id.*

[62]*Authorities Seized Videotapes, Film at Train Derailment Site*, Lexington (Ky.) Herald-Leader (Associated Press), August 3, 1991, at A6, col. 3.

[63]*Id.*

[64]*State of Oklahoma v. Benjamin Bernstein et al.*, 5 Med.L.Rptr. 2313, aff'd, Stahl v. Oklahoma, 665 P.2d 839, 9 Med.L.Rptr. 1945 (Okl. Crim. 1983), *cert. denied*, 464 U.S. 1069, 104 S.Ct. 973 (1984).

[65]*Stahl v. Oklahoma.*

[66]See E. DENNIS, D. STEBENNE, J. PAVLIK et al., THE MEDIA AT WAR: THE PRESS AND THE PERSIAN GULF CONFLICT (Hereinafter, *Report of the Gannett Foundation*) (1991).

[67]*Id.*

[68]*Id.*

[69]J. DeParle, *Control of Press Grew in Increments*, Lexington (Ky.) Herald-Leader (New York Times News Service), May 7, 1991, at A3, col. 2.

[70]*See id.*

[71]T. Weiner, *Illusion Was Allies' Secret Weapon*, Lexington (Ky.) Herald-Leader (Knight-Ridder News Service), July 14, 1991, at A1, col. 1, and at A13, col. 1.

[72]T. B. Rosenstiel, *Fooling Media Misled Iraqis, Too*, Lexington (Ky.) Herald-Leader (Los Angeles Times News Service), March 28, 1991, at D14, col. 2.

[73]*See id.*

[74]*See* K. Seelye & D. Polman, *Military Reined in Media, Held Tight*, Lexington (Ky.) Herald-Leader (Knight-Ridder News Service), March 28, 1991, at D14, col. 2.

[75]*See id.*

[76]*Report of the Gannett Foundation* at 96.

[77]*Id.*

[78]*Id.* at xii.

[79]*See Access to Places: A Guide for Reporters and Photographers Gathering News*, 10 NEWS MEDIA & L. 1, No. 3 (1986)

[80]Three particularly good sources for more information are: (1) YOUR RIGHT TO FEDERAL RECORDS, U.S. GENERAL SERVICES ADMINISTRATION AND U.S. DEPARTMENT OF JUSTICE (Joint publication) (no date), (2) INVESTIGATIVE REPORTERS AND EDITORS, THE REPORTER'S HANDBOOK: AN INVESTIGATOR'S GUIDE TO DOCUMENTS AND

TECHNIQUES (1991) and (3) AMERICAN BAR ASSOCIATION, A JOURNALIST'S PRIMER ON LOCATING LEGAL DOCUMENTS (1990). The IRE handbook is very comprehensive and ought to be read by every reporter and editor who deals with public materials, while the ABA booklet and the federal pamphlet provide succinct summaries of the rights under the Freedom of Information Act. The government publication also includes the text of the FOIA and an overview of the Privacy Act of 1974. You should also consult the Society of Professional Journalist's Annual FOI Report published as a special edition of THE QUILL magazine (November/December).

[81]5 U.S.C. § 552, as amended by Pub. L. No. 99-570, 1801-1804 (1986).

[82]5 U.S.C. § 552a, as amended by Pub. L. 97-365, 96 Stat. 1749 (1982).

[83]5 U.S.C. § 552a(4) (A) (iii).

[84]5 U.S.C. § 552a(4) (A) (ii).

[85]*See* 5 U.S.C. § 552a(6) (C) (b) (1-9).

[86]5 U.S.C. § 552a(6) (C).

[87]*See Environmental Protection Agency v. Mink*, 410 U.S. 73, 93 S.Ct. 827, 35 L.Ed.2nd 119, 1 Med.L.Rptr. 2448 (1973).

[88]Pub. L. No. 93-502, 88 Stat. 1561 (1974).

[89]Exec. Order No. 12,356, 3 C.F.R. § (1983).

[90]During his term, President Jimmy Carter, in contrast, issued an Executive Order that mandated a review of all classified material every 20 to 30 years, whereas the Reagan order required that a classified document be reviewed once—at the time the initial classification occurs.

[91]*Department of the Air Force et al. v. Michael T. Rose et al.*, 425 U.S. 352, 96 S.Ct. 1592, 48 L.Ed.2d 11, 1 Med.L.Rptr. 2509.

[92]*Id.*

[93]*Consumer Product Safety Commission v. GTE Sylvania, Inc.*, 447 U.S. 102, 100 S.Ct. 2051, 64 L.Ed.2d 766 (1980).

[94]*CIA v. Sims*, 471 U.S. 159, 105 S.Ct. 1881, 85 L.Ed.2d 173 (1985).

[95]The MKULTRA project lasted from 1953–1966.

[96]*CIA v. Sims.*

[97]*Chrysler Corp. v. Harold Brown, Secretary of Defense*, 441 U.S. 281, 99 S.Ct. 1705, 60 L.Ed.2d 208, 4 Med.L.Rptr. 218 (1979).

[98]Executive Order No. 12600 (1986).

[99]*Federal Open Market Committee v. David R. Merrill*, 443 U.S. 340, 99 S.Ct. 2800, 61 L.Ed.2d 587 (1979).

[100]*Id.*

[101]*Federal Trade Commission v. Grolier, Inc.*, 462 U.S. 19, 103 S.Ct. 2209, 76 L.Ed.2d 387, 9 Med.L.Rptr. 1737 1983).

[102]*U.S. Department of State v. Washington Post Co.*, 456 U.S. 595, 102 S.Ct. 1957, 72 L.Ed.2d 358, 8 Med.L.Rptr. 1521 (1982).

[103]*New York Times Co. v. National Aeronautics and Space Administration*, 852 F.2d 602, 15 Med.L.Rptr. 2012 (D.C. Cir. 1988).

[104]*Id.*

[105]*Id.*

[106]*New York Times Co. v. National Aeronautics and Space Administration*, 920 F.2d 1002, 18 Med.L.Rptr. 1465 (D.C. Cir. 1990) (*en banc*); 782 F.Supp. 628, 19 Med.L.Rptr. 1688 (D.D.C. 1991).

[107]*Department of Justice v. Reporters Committee for Freedom of the Press*, 109 S.Ct. 1468, 103 L.Ed.2d 774, 16 Med.L.Rptr. 1545 (1989).

[108]*Id.*

[109]*Id.*

[110]*National Labor Relations Board v. Robbins Tire and Rubber Co.*, 437 U.S. 214, 98 S.Ct. 2311, 57 L.Ed.2d 159 (1978).

[111]*Federal Bureau of Investigation v. Howard S. Abramson*, 456 U.S. 615, 102 S.Ct. 2054, 72 L.Ed.2d 376 (1982).

[112]*Critical Mass Energy Project v. Nuclear Regulatory Commission*, 975 F.2d 871 (D.C. Cir. 1992), *Cert. denied*, 113 S.Ct. 1579 (1993).

[113]5 U.S.C.A. § 552b.

CHAPTER 10

[1]Pub. L. No. 98-417 (1984) & Pub. L. No. 100-670 (1988).

[2]*See* 35 U.S.C. § 101.

[3]*See* 35 U.S.C. § 161.

[4]*See* 35 U.S.C. § 171.

[5]35 U.S.C. § 103.

[6]Write the Patent and Trademark Office, U.S. Department of Commerce, Washington, D.C. 20231 or call (703) 557-INFO.

[7]*Polaroid v. Eastman Kodak*, 789 F.2d 1556, 229 U.S.P.Q. 561 (Fed Cir. 1986), *Cert. denied*, 479 U.S. 850.

[8]KING, THE GENERAL/CORPORATE LEGAL PRACTITIONER'S ROLE IN PRO-TECTING INTELLECTUAL PROPERTY RIGHTS 29 (1990). This manual and related appendices are available from the University of Kentucky, College of Law, Office of Continuing Legal Education, Lexington, Ky. 40506. While the materials are geared to attorneys, they are also useful for laypersons, including journalists, who need a good overview of intellectual property law.

[9]U.S. DEPT. OF COMMERCE, PATENT & TRADEMARK OFFICE, BASIC FACTS ABOUT TRADEMARKS (1989).

[10]Pub. L. No. 100-667 (1988).

[11]15 U.S.C. § 1051.

[12]Goldstein, THE ASSOCIATED PRESS STYLEBOOK AND LIBEL MANUAL 211 (Fully updated Ed. 1992).

[13]*Mead Data Central, Inc. v. Toyota Motor Sales, U.S.A., Inc.*, 875 F.2d 1026, 10 U.S.P.Q.2d 1961 (2nd Cir. 1989). *Also see* Prather, *How Toyota Got "Lexus" for Name of New Car*, Lexington (Ky.) Herald-Leader, January 11, 1989, at Al, col. 1.

[14]*G. Heileman Brewing Co., Inc. v. Anheuser-Busch, Inc.*, Nos. 88-1223, 88-1309, 88-1310 (April 26, 1989); *see LA Law*, 75 A. B. A. J. 92 (August 1989).

[15]*L. L. Bean, Inc. v. Drake Publishers, Inc.*, 811 F.2d 26, 13 Med.L.Rptr. 2009 (1st Cir. 1987).

[16]*San Francisco Arts and Athletics, Inc. v. United States Olympic Committee*, 107 S.Ct. 925 (1987).

[17]*Cereal Name to Change*, Lexington (Ky.) Herald-Leader, July 10, 1991, at A3, col. 1.

[18]*Procter & Gamble Redesigns Controversial Product Logo that Prompted Devil Rumors*, Lexington (Ky.) Herald-Leader (Associated Press), July 11, 1991, at B4, col. 3.

[19]*Id.*

[20]KITCH & PERLMAN, LEGAL REGULATION OF THE COMPETITIVE PROCESS 622 (1979).

[21]17 U.S.C. § 102 (a) (1991).

[22]*Id.*

[23]17 U.S.C. § 102 (b) 1991.

[24]17 U.S.C. § 101 (1991).

[25]*Id.*

[26]17 U.S.C. § 101 (1991).

[27]17 U.S.C. § 106 (1991).

[28]17 U.S.C. § 102 (a) (1991).

[29]17 U.S.C. § 101 (1991).

[30]*See id.*

[31]*Id.*

[32]*Id.*

[33]*Community for Creative Non-Violence v. Reid,* 490 U.S. 730 109 S.Ct. 2166, 104 L.Ed.2d 811, 16 Med.L.Rptr. 1769 (1989).

[34]*Id.*

[35]*Id.*

[36]*Id.*

[37]*Id.*

[38]*Id.*

[39]17 U.S.C. § 101 (1991).

[40]Because neither party sought review of the appellate court's remand order, the Supreme Court did not determine whether joint authorship was applicable in this case.

[41]K. Middleton, *Freelance Photographers and Publishers: The Need for a Contract to Establish Joint Authorship in Commissioned Works,* paper presented to the Association for Education in Journalism and Mass Communication Southeast Regional Colloquium, Orlando, Florida, April 1991, at 23.

[42]*Id.*

[43]17 U.S.C. § 102 (1991).

[44]U.S. COPYRIGHT OFFICE, COPYRIGHT BASICS (Circular 1) (1992), at 3.

[45]*Hoehling v. Universal City Studios, Inc.,* 618 F.2d 972, 6 Med.L.Rptr. 1053 (2d Cir. 1980), *cert. denied* 449 U.S. 841 (1980).

[46]*Id.*

[47]*Id.*

[48]17 U.S.C. § 105 (1991).

[49]*See* U.S. COPYRIGHT OFFICE, COPYRIGHT BASICS at 5.

[50]*Miller v. Universal City Studios, Inc.,* 650 F.2d 1365, 7 Med.L.Rptr. 1735 (5th Cir. 1981).

[51]*Miller v. Universal City Studios, Inc.,* 460 F.Supp. 984 (S.D. Fla. 1978).

[52]*Id.*

[53]*Id.*

[54]*See* 15 U.S.C. § 1125(a), which was strengthened by the Trademark Law Revision Act of 1988. This section provides civil liability for the use of any goods or services in commerce with a "false designation of origin, false or misleading description of fact, or false or misleading representation of fact . . ." likely to cause confusion, mistake or deception about the origin, sponsorship or approval of the goods or services.

[55]*International News Service v. Associated Press,* 248 U.S. 215, 39 S.Ct. 68, 63 L.Ed. 211 (1918).

[56]The International News Service merged with United Press in 1958 to become United Press International, which is still operating.

[57]*Id.*

[58]SOCIETY OF PROFESSIONAL JOURNALISTS CODE OF ETHICS (1987) § III(1). *See* Appendix A.

[59]Public Laws 87–668, 89–142, 90–141, 90–416, 91–147, 91–555, 92–170, 92–566 and 93–573.

[60]17 U.S.C. § 304(b) (1991).

[61]17 U.S.C. § 303 (1991).

[62]*Against Her Will* ("People" section), Lexington (Ky.) Herald-Leader (wire services), May 7, 1991, at A[8], col. 1.

[63]*See* 17 U.S.C. § 305 (1991).

[64]Berne Convention Implementation Act of 1988, Pub. L. 100–568, 102 Stat. 2853.

[65]17 U.S.C. § 405 and 406 (1991).

[66]*See* U.S. COPYRIGHT OFFICE, COPYRIGHT NOTICE (Circular 3) (1992), at 5.

[67]17 U.S.C. § 405(b) (1991).

[68]17 U.S.C. § 401(d) and 402(d) (1991).

[69]17 U.S.C. § 401(a) (1991).

[70]17 U.S.C. § 402(a) (1991).

[71]17 U.S.C. § 401(b) (1991).

[72]*See* 37 C.F.R. § 201.20 for the complete regulations. They are also reprinted in Circular 96 § 201.20 ("Methods of Affixation and Positions of the Copyright Notice on Various Types of Works") (1985) of the Copyright Office and summarized in Circular 3 ("Copyright Notice") (1992) at 4–5 of the Copyright Office.

[73]17 U.S.C. § 401(c) (1991).

[74]*Id.*

[75]17 U.S.C. § 402(c) (1991).

[76]*See* 37 C.F.R. § 201.20(d)and U.S. COPYRIGHT OFFICE, COPYRIGHT NOTICE (Circular 3) (1992), at 4.

[77]17 U.S.C. § 501(a) (1991).

[78]*Chicago Catholics Lose Copyright Case*, ("National Digest" section), Atlanta Journal (wire reports), April 20, 1984, at A1, col. 1.

[79]*Jagger Gets Satisfaction in Lawsuit Over Song*, Lexington (Ky.) Herald-Leader (Associated Press), April 27, 1988, at A2, col. 3.

[80]*Before You Wish Upon A Star, Better Check the Copyright*, ("People" section), Lexington (Ky.) Herald-Leader (wire services), May 1, 1989, at A12, col. 1.

[81]Blodgett, *West, Mead Data Central Settle*, A.B.A. J.36 (September 1988).

[82]*Garrison Keillor Settles Suit with National Public Radio* ("People" section), Cincinnati Post, June 24, 1988, at A2, col. 3.

[83]Hild, *Piracy and Protection*, EDITOR & PUBLISHER, September 2, 1989, at 22PC.

[84]*Id.* at 39PC.

[85]*Id.*

[86]Maatta & Brennan, 10 HASTINGS COMM/ENT L.J. 1081 (1988).

[87]Joseph, *'Batman' Takes on Those Villainous Video Purloiners*, Lexington (Ky.) Herald-Leader (Orlando Sentinel), August 18, 1989, at B10, col. 1.

[88]Maatta & Brennan, *supra*, at 1084.

[89]*Id.* at 1083.

[90]Shearer, *Piracy Prices*, Parade Magazine, November 22, 1987, at 16.

[91]*Id.*

[92]*Disney Sheds Nice-Guy Image To Get Tough With Asian Forgers*, Lexington (Ky.) Herald-Leader (Associated Press), at E5, col. 4.

[93]Joseph, *supra*.

[94]*Id.*

[95]See U.S. COPYRIGHT OFFICE, HIGHLIGHTS OF U.S. ADHERENCE TO THE BERNE CONVENTION (Circular 93) (1989).

[96]*See* U.S. COPYRIGHT OFFICE, INTERNATIONAL COPYRIGHT RELATIONS (Circular 38a) (usually updated annually) for a complete list of countries having copyright agreements with the United States,

[97]17 U.S.C. § 205 (1991).

[98]*Constructive notice* is a legal term implying or imputing that the public has been notified in the eyes of the law by being provided a means for learning such information. In other words, by recording the agreement in the Copyright Office, the transferor and transferee have met any public notice requirements since anyone who examined the copies of the documents in the Copyright Office would know the terms of the agreement. This is in contrast to *actual notice* in which the parties have formally provided other parties with actual copies of the documents.

[99]*See* 17 U.S.C. § 205(c) (1)-(2) (1991).

[100]*See* 17 U.S.C. § 205(d) and (e) (1991).

[101]*See* U.S. COPYRIGHT OFFICE, RECORDATION OF TRANSFERS AND OTHER DOCUMENTS (Circular 12) (1991) at 4.

[102]*Id.*

[103]17 U.S.C. § 205 (1991).

[104]17 U.S.C. § 203 (a) (3) (1991).

[105]17 U.S.C. § 203 (b) (1) (1991).

[106]17 U.S.C. § 111 (1991).

[107]17 U.S.C. § 111 (a) (1) (1991).

[108]17 U.S.C. § 802 (1991).

[109]In July 1990 Congress reduced the number of CRT Commissioners from five to three and increased their salaries by giving them a higher federal employment classification. *See* Public Law 101-319 ("Copyright royalty Tribunal Reform and Miscellaneous Pay Act of 1989), approved July 3, 1990. Commissioners serve for seven-year terms, with the chair serving in that position for one year. The three are appointed by the President with the advice and consent of the Senate.

[110]*See Fortnightly Corp. v. United Artists Television, Inc.*, 392 U.S. 390, 88 S.Ct. 2084, 20 L.Ed.2d 1176 (1968) and *Teleprompter Corp. v. CBS, Inc.*, 415 U.S. 394, 94 S.Ct. 1129, 39 L.Ed.2d 415 (1974).

[111]*See* Fields, *Copyright Royalty Tribunal: Keeping It Fat and Happy Clue to Compulsory License,* TELEVISION/RADIO AGE, August 7, 1989, at 74.

[112]17 U.S.C. § 111(c)(3) (1991).

[113]*Cablevision Sys. Dev. Co. v. Motion Picture Ass'n of Am.*, 641 F. Supp. 1154 (D. D.C. 1986), *rev'd in part, and remanded in part*, 836 F.2d 599 (D.C. Cir.), *cert. denied*, 108 S.Ct. 2901 (1988).

[114]17 U.S.C. § 111(a)(4) (1991).

[115]17 U.S.C. § 119(a)(2)(B) (1991).

[116]17 U.S.C. § 119(d)(10) (1991).

[117]Cate, *Cable Television and the Compulsory Copyright License*, 42 FED. COM. L. J. 236 (1990).

[118]*Id.* at 238.

[119]17 U.S.C. § 116 (1991).

[120]Another licensing agency is SESAC, Inc. (which was once known as the Society of European State Authors and Composers), but ASCAP and BMI dominate the field.

[121]*See Buffalo Broadcasting Co., Inc. V. American Society of Composers, Authors and Publishers*, 744 F.2d 917 (2d Cir. 1984), *cert. denied*, 469 U.S. 1211, 105 S.Ct. 1181, 84 L.Ed.2d 329 (1985).

[122]*Id.*

[123]*Id.*

[124]*Id.*

[125]*Id.*

[126]*Sailor Music v. Gap Stores, Inc.*, 668 F.2d 84 (2d Cir. 1981), *cert. denied*, 456 U.S. 945 (1982).

[127]U.S. COPYRIGHT OFFICE, COPYRIGHT BASICS (Circular 1) (1992), at 3.

[128]17 U.S.C. § 507(a) (1991).

[129]17 U.S.C. § 507(b) (1991).

[130]*$25 Million Deal Includes Ownership of Birthday song,* Lexington (Ky.) Herald-Leader (New York Times News Service), December 20, 1988, at A4, col. 4.

[131]*For A Song: "Happy Birthday to You" May Sell for $12 Million,* Lexington (Ky.) Herald-Leader (New York Times News Service), October 20, 1988, at A2, col. 5.

[132]*$25 Million Deal Includes Ownership of Birthday Song, supra.*

[133]*Id.*

[134]*Id.*

[135]H.R. Rep. No. 94-1476, 94th Cong., 2nd Sess. 65 (1976). Excerpts are reproduced in U.S. COPYRIGHT OFFICE, REPRODUCTION OF COPYRIGHTED WORKS BY EDUCATORS AND LIBRARIANS (Circular 21) (1992), at 8-9.

[136]17 U.S.C. § 107 (1991).

[137]*Id.*

[138]H.R. Rep. No. 94-1476, supra.

[139]*Time, Inc. v. Bernard Geis Associates*, 293 F.Supp. 130 (S.D. N.Y. 1968).

[140]Bernard Geis Associates had offered all profits from the book to Time, Inc. in return for a license to use the copyrighted frames in the book, but the magazine publisher rejected the offer.

[141]*Time, Inc. v. Bernard Geis Associates.*

[142]*Id.*

[143]*Harper & Row Publishers, Inc. and The Reader's Digest Association, Inc. v. Nation Enterprises*, 471 U.S. 539, 105 S.Ct. 2218, 88 L.Ed.2d 588, 11 Med.L.Rptr. 1969 (1985).

[144]*Id.*

[145]*Id.*

[146]*Id.*

[147]*Id.*

[148]*Id.*

[149]Vittor, *"Fair Use" of Unpublished Materials: "Widow Censors," Copyright and the First Amendment*, COM. LAW, Fall 1989, at 1.

[150]*Harper & Row v. Nation Enterprises.*

[151]*Cohen v. Cowles*, 111 S.Ct. 2513, 115 L.Ed.2d 586, 18 Med.L.Rptr. 2273 (1991).

[152]*Masson v. New Yorker*, 111 S.Ct. 2419, 115 L.Ed.2d 447 18 Med.L.Rptr. 2241 (1991).

[153]*Salinger v. Random House*, 811 F.2d 90, 13 Med.L.Rptr. 1954 (2d Cir. 1987), *cert. denied*, 108 s.Ct. 213 (1987).

[154]*Id.*

[155]*Id.*

[156]*New Era Publications International v. Henry Holt & Co.*, 873 F.2d 576, 16 Med.L.Rptr. 1559 (2d Cir. 1989).

[157]*Id.*

[158]*Id.*

[159]*New Era Publications International v. Henry Holt & Co.*, *reh'g denied*, 884 F.2d 659, 16 Med.L.Rptr. 2224 (2d Cir. 1989).

[160]*New Era Publications International v. Carol Publishing Group*, 904 F.2d 152, 17 Med.L.Rptr. 1913 (2d Cir. 1990).

[161]*Id.*

[162]*See* Kaplan, *The End of History? A Copyright Controversy Leads to Self-Censorship*, NEWSWEEK, December 25, 1989, at 80.

[163]Public Law 102-492 (Oct. 24, 1992).

[164]*American Geophysical Union et al. v. Texaco, Inc.*, 85 Civ. 3446, 802 F. Supp. 1 (S.D. N.Y. 1992).

[165]*Basic Books, Inc. v. Kinko's Graphics Corp.*, 758 F.Supp. 1522 (S.D. N.Y. 1991).

[166]*See* Watkins, *Photocopying Chain Found in Violation of Copyright Law*, THE CHRONICLE OF HIGHER EDUCATION, April 3, 1991, at A1, col. 2, and at A19, col. 1.

[167]March 29, 1991, letter from Paul J. Orfalea, Chairperson of Kinko's distributed to university and college professors.

[168]The Eleventh Amendment (adopted in 1798) says: "The Judicial power of the United States shall not be construed to extend to any suit in law or equity, commenced or prosecuted against one of the United States by Citizens of another State, or by Citizens of Subjects of any Foreign State."

[169]*BV Engineering v. University of California at Los Angeles*, 858 F.2d 1394 (9th Cir. 1988).

[170]*See* DeLoughry, *Court Will Not Hear Case Accusing UCLA of Copying Software,* THE CHRONICLE OF HIGHER EDUCATION, March 28, 1989, at A1, col. 2, and at A18, col. 2.

[171]Copyright Remedy Clarification Act of 1990, Pub. L. No. 101-553, 17 U.S.C. § 501(a) and 511 (1991).

[172]17 U.S.C. § 501(a) (1991).

[173]17 U.S.C. § 511(a) (1991).

[174]17 U.S.C. § 511(b) (1991).

[175]*Court Clips Wings of Atlanta Video Clipping Service,* BROADCASTING, June 10, 1991, at 63, 65.

[176]Thompson, *Ruling on Right to Copy TV News Clips Decides Little,* Atlanta Journal, October 14, 1983, at A16, col. 1.

[177]*Court Clips Wings of Atlanta Video Clipping Service, supra.*

[178]*Lish v. Harper's Magazine Foundation,* 807 F. Supp. 1090, 20 Med.L.Rptr. 2073, (S.D. N.Y. 1992). *See* Reske, *Gordon Lish's $2,000 Letter,* 79 A.B.A. J. 28 (February 1993).

[179]*Acuff-Rose Music, Inc. v. Campbell,* 972 F.2d 1429 (6th Cir. 1992), *cert. granted,* 113 S.Ct. 1642 (1993).

[180]*Stewart v. Abend,* 110 S.Ct. 1750, 109 L.Ed.2d 184 (1990).

[181]*See* Epstein, *Court Ruling Could Pull Classic Videos from Shelves,* Lexington (Ky.) Herald-Leader (Knight-Ridder News Service), April 25, 1990, at Al, col. 1. By 1990, the rerelease had generated more than $12 million worldwide.

[182]*Rohauer v. Killiam Shows,* 551 F.2d 484 (2d Cir. 1977), *cert. denied,* 431 U.S. 949 (1977).

[183]Epstein, *supra.*

[184]*Steward v. Abend.*

[185]*See* Epstein, *supra.*

[186]*See Jagger Gets Satisfaction in Lawsuit Over Song,* Lexington (Ky.) Herald-Leader (Associated Press), April 27, 1988, at A2, col. 3.

[187]*Id.*

[188]*Sid and Marty Krofft Television Productions, Inc. v. McDonald's Corp.,* 562 F.2d 1157 (9th Cir. 1977).

[189]*Universal City Studios, Inc. v. Film Ventures International, Inc.,* 543 F.Supp. 1134 (C.D. Calif. 1982).

[190]*Id.*

[191]*Ruolo v. Russ Berrie & Co.,* 886 F.2d 931 (7th Cir. 1989).

[192]Abramson, *"Look and Feel" of Computer Software,* 95 CASE AND COMMENT 3 (January–February 1990).

[193]*Id.*

[194]17 U.S.C. § 503(b) (1991).

[195]17 U.S.C. § 504(b) (1991).

[196]Pub. L. No. 100-568, 102 Stat. 2853, 2860 (1988)

[197]The amounts prior to the October 31, 1988, enactment of the new law were $250 and $10,000, respectively.

[198]17 U.S.C. § 504(c)(2) (1991).

[199]*Id.*

[200]*Id.*

[201]*Id.*

[202]17 U.S.C. § 505 (1991).

[203]*See* 17 U.S.C. § 506 (1991) and 18 U.S.C. § 2319(b)(1)(A) (1991).

[204]18 U.S.C. § 2319(b)(1)−(3) (1992), as amended by Public Law 102-561.

[205]18 U.S.C. § 2318 (1991).

[206]*Sony Corp. of America v. Universal City Studios, Inc.,* 465 U.S. 1112, 104 S.Ct. 1619, 80 L.Ed.2d 1480 (1984).

[207]At the time of the Court's decision these devices were called video tape recorders or VTRs, but the terminology has now changed to videocassette recorders (VCRs).

[208]Betamax VCRs used the Beta format, which since then has lost out to the VHS format, but at the time of the suit, Beta was the dominant format. Even Sony has now abandoned Beta for VHS in its VCRs for home use. Although some technical experts still argue that the Beta format was superior to VHS, VHS won the battle, primarily because manufacturers of VHS recorders outmaneuvered the Beta folks in the marketplace.

[209]*Sony Corp. of America v. Universal City Studios, Inc.*

[210]*Id.*

[211]*See Television*, 56 CONSUMER REP. 576 (citing Cable TV Investor, A.C. Nielsen data) (1991).

[212]*Industries Reach Accord on Digital Recorders*, Lexington (Ky.) Herald-Leader (Associated Press), July 11, 1991, at B7, col. 1.

[213]17 U.S.C. § 1001 − § 1010 (1992), as amended by Public Law 102-563 (1992).

[214]There are only two special circumstances under which registration is required. First, if a work was published with a copyright notice before January 1, 1978, a renewal registration must be filed before the initial 28-year copyright term expires or the work goes into the public domain. Second, § 405 and 406 require that a work first published before January 1, 1989, be registered to maintain its copyright if the copyright notice was omitted or an erroneous year was indicated on the notice. Otherwise, registration is not required.

[215]*See* U.S. COPYRIGHT OFFICE, COPYRIGHT REGISTRATION FOR COMPUTER PROGRAMS (Circular 61) (1991) at 3.

[216]*See* U.S. COPYRIGHT OFFICE, COPYRIGHT REGISTRATION FOR AUTOMATED DATA DATABASES (Circular 65) (1992) at 2.

[217]The Copyright Act defines a "compilation" as "a work formed by the collection and assembling of preexisting materials or of data that are selected, coordinated, or arranged in such a way that the resulting work as a whole constitutes an original work of authorship." *See* 17 U.S.C. § 101 (1991).

[218]Pub. L. No. 98-62 (1984), effective November 8, 1984.

[219]17 U.S.C. § 908(a) (1991). These provisions are **not** part of the Copyright Law.

[220]*See* U.S. COPYRIGHT OFFICE, FEDERAL STATUTORY PROTECTION FOR MASK WORKS (Circular 100) (1991) for more information.

[221]U.S. COPYRIGHT OFFICE, THE UNITED STATES JOINS THE BERNE CONVENTION (Circular 93a) (1989) at 3.

[222]*Id.*

[223]*Gilliam v. American Broadcasting Cos., Inc.*, 538 F.2d 14 (2d Cir. 1976).

[224]*Donahue: Nun Essay Used False Names But Real People*, Lexington (Ky.) Herald-Leader (Associated Press), July 3, 1991, at A10, col. 1.

[225]*Id.*

[226]*Boston U. Dean Resigns*, Lexington (Ky.) Herald-Leader (wire services), July 13, 1991, at A3, col. 1.

CHAPTER 11

[1]For example, in a 1987 statewide poll the *Louisville Courier-Journal* found that two-thirds of Kentuckians felt communities should have the right to restrict access of adults to sexually explicit materials, but 83 percent indicated that adults should have the right to read or view such materials. Nevertheless, there is a sizable group (about one-fifth of the population) that favors banning all three of the major types of sexually oriented materials—those showing sexual violence between

adults, those showing adult sexual nonviolent activities and those displaying adult nudity only. *See Opinions Mixed on Explicit Material*, Lexington (Ky.) Herald-Leader (Associated Press), April 5, 1987, at B2, col. 3.

[2]47 U.S.C. § 559 (1984).

[3]Public Law 100-690, 102 Stat. 4181, November 18, 1988.

[4]*See Cuomo Refuses Extradition of Programming Execs*, ONSAT, July 22, 1990, at 8, col. 2; *HDO Pleads Guilty*, ONSAT, December 9, 1990, at 105, col. 1; and *HDO Pleads Guilty to Federal Charges*, ONSAT, January 6, 1991, at 6, col. 1. *See also Porn Case Fine Is $150,000*, Lexington (Ky.) Herald-Leader (Wire Services), February 16, 1991, at A3, col. 1.

[5]*HDO Pleads Guilty to Federal Charges, supra.*

[6]*Regina v. Hicklin*, L.R., 3 Q.B. 360 (1868).

[7]THE CONCISE COLUMBIA ENCYCLOPEDIA 189 (1983).

[8]*Regina v. Hicklin.*

[9]*United States v. One Book Called "Ulysses,"* 5 F.Supp. 182 (S.D.N.Y. 1933).

[10]*United States v. One Book Called "Ulysses,"* 72 F.2d 705 (1934).

[11]R. J. WAGMAN, THE FIRST AMENDMENT BOOK 203 (1991).

[12]*Alfred E. Butler v. State of Michigan*, 352 U.S. 380, 77 S.Ct. 524, 1 L.Ed.2d 412 (1957).

[13]*Id.*

[14]*Samuel Roth v. United States* and *David S. Alberts v. California*, 354 U.S. 476, 77 S.Ct. 1304, 1 L.Ed.2d 1498, 1 Med.L.Rptr. 1375 (1957).

[15]*Id.*

[16]*Near v. Minnesota*, 283 U.S. 697, 51 S.Ct. 625, 75 L.Ed. 1357, 1 Med.L.Rptr. 1001 (1931).

[17]*Roth v. United States* and *Alberts v. California.*

[18]*Id.*

[19]*Id.*

[20]*Id.*

[21]*Eleazar Smith v. California*, 361 U.S. 147, 80 S.Ct. 215, 4 L.Ed.2d 205 (1959).

[22]*Id.*

[23]KY. REV. STAT. § 531.020 (1992).

[24]GA. CODE ANN. § 26-2101 (a) (1992).

[25]*Manual Enterprises, Inc. v. Day, Postmaster General of the United States*, 370 U.S. 478, 82 S.Ct. 1432 (1962).

[26]*Nico Jacobellis v. Ohio*, 378 U.S. 184, 84 S.Ct. 1676, 12 L.Ed.2d 793 (1964).

[27]*A Quantity of Books et al. v. Kansas*, 378 U.S. 205, 84 S.Ct. 1723, 12 L.Ed.2d 809 (1964).

[28]*Ronald L. Freedman v. Maryland.* 380 U.S. 51, 85 S.Ct. 734, 13 L.Ed.2d 649 (1965).

[29]*Id.*

[30]*Id.*

[31]*A Book Named* John Cleland's Memoirs of a Woman of Pleasure *et al. v. Attorney General of Massachusetts*, 383 U.S. 413, 86 S.Ct. 975, 16 L.Ed.2d 1, 1 Med.L.Rptr. 1390 (1966).

[32]*Id.*

[33]*Ralph Ginzburg et al. v. U.S.*, 383 U.S. 463, 86 S.Ct. 942, 16 L.Ed.2d 31, 1 Med.L.Rptr. 1409 (1966).

[34]*Id.*

[35]*Id.*

[36]*Edward Mishkin v. New York*, 383 U.S. 502, 86 S.Ct. 958, 16 L.Ed.2d 56 (1966).

[37]*Marvin Miller v. California*, 413 U.S. 15, 93 S.Ct. 2607, 37 L.Ed.2d 419, 1 Med.L.Rptr. 1441 (1973).

[38]*Robert Redrup v. New York, William L. Austin v. Kentucky* and *Gent et al. v. Arkansas*, 386 U.S. 767, 87 S.Ct. 1414, 18 L.Ed.2d 515 (1967).

[39]*Ginsberg v. New York*, 390 U.S. 629, 88 S.Ct. 1274, 1 Med.L.Rptr. 1424 (1968).

[40]*Interstate Circuit, Inc. v. Dallas* and *United Artists Corp. v. Dallas*, 390 U.S. 676, 88 S.Ct. 1298, 20 L.Ed.2d 225 (1968).

[41]*Id.*

[42]*Robert Eli Stanley v. Georgia*, 394 U.S. 557, 89 S.Ct. 1243, 22 L.Ed.2d 542 (1969).

[43]*Id.*

[44]*United States v. Reidel*, 402 U.S. 351 (1971).

[45]*United States v. Thirty-Seven Photographs*, 402 U.S. 363 (1971).

[46]*Paris Adult Theatre I et al. v. Lewis R. Slaton, District Attorney, Atlanta Judicial Circuit, et al.*, 413 U.S. 49, 93 S.Ct. 2628, 37 L.Ed.2d 445, 1 Med.L.Rptr. 1454 (1973).

[47]*Id.*

[48]*Marvin Miller v. California*, 413 U.S. 15, 93 S.Ct. 2607, 37 L.Ed.2d 419, 1 Med.L.Rptr. 1441 (1973).

[49]*Id.*

[50]*Id.*

[51]*Paris Adult Theatre I.*

[52]*Id.*

[53]*William L. Hamling et al. v. U.S.*, 418 U.S. 87, 94 S.Ct. 2887, 41 L.Ed.2d 590, 1 Med.L.Rptr. 1479 (1974).

[54]*Id.*

[55]*Billy Jenkins v. Georgia*, 418 U.S. 153, 94 S.Ct. 2750, 1 Med.L.Rptr. 1479 (1974).

[56]*Id.*

[57]Penal Law, Art. 263, § 263.05ff (1977).

[58]Protection of Children Against Sexual Exploitation Act of 1977, P.L. 95-225, 18 U.S.C. § 2251-2253.

[59]*New York v. Paul Ira Ferber*, 458 U.S. 747, 102 S.Ct. 3348, 73 L.Ed.2d 1113, 8 Med.L.Rptr. 1809 (1982).

[60]*City of Renton et al. v. Playtime Theatres, Inc., et al.*, 475 U.S. 41, 106 S.Ct. 925, 89 L.Ed.2d 29 (1986).

[61]*Richard Arcara, District Attorney of Erie County v. Cloud Books, Inc.*, 478 U.S. 697 (1986).

[62]Attorney General's Commission on Pornography: Final Report (July 1986).

[63]*See* McDonald, *Sex Crimes, Porno Linked, Report Says*, Atlanta Constitution, July 10, 1986, at A2, col. 1.

[64]*Id.*

[65]*Id.*

[66]Racketeer Influenced and Corrupt Organizations (RICO) Act of 1970, 18 U.S.C. § 1961-68 (1991).

[67]*See* Blodgett, *RICO v. First Amendment*, 73 A.B.A. J. 17 (November 1987).

[68]*Fort Wayne Books, Inc. v. Indiana*, 489 U.S. 46, 109 S.Ct. 916, 16 Med.L.Rptr. 1337 (1989).

[69]*Id.*

[70]*Richard Pope and Charles G. Morrison v. Illinois*, 481 U.S. 497, 107 S.Ct. 1918, 95 L.Ed.2d 439, 14 Med.L.Rptr. 1001 (1987).

[71]*Id.*

[72]*Id.*

[73]*New York v. Paul Ira Ferber.*

[74]*Osborne v. Ohio*, 110 S.Ct. 1691 (1990).

[75]*Id.*

[76]*Id.*

[77]*Virginia v. American Booksellers Association*, 484 U.S. 383 (1988).

[78]Before remanding the case, the U.S. Supreme Court had the Virginia Supreme Court respond to the certified questions regarding statutory construction.

[79]*American Booksellers Association v. Virginia*, 882 F.2d 125 (4th Cir. 1989).

[80]*American Booksellers Association v. Virginia, cert. denied*, 110 S.Ct. 1525 (1990).

[81]*See State Offers Pee-wee Deal for Plea of No Contest*, Lexington (Ky.) Herald-Leader (Associated Press) October 30, 1991, at A8, col. 1.

[82]*See* McFadden, *Experts Shocked by Obscenity Decision*, Lexington (Ky.) Herald-Leader (New York Times News Service), June 9, 1990, at A2, col. 1; Parker, *Federal Judge Finds Rap LP Obscene*, Washington Post, June 7, 1990, at A1, col. 3.

[83]*Skyywalker Records, Inc. v. Navarro*, 739 F.Supp. 578, 17 Med.L.Rptr. 2073 (S.D. Fla. 1990).

[84]*Id.*

[85]*See Man Arrested for Selling Controversial Rap Record*, Lexington (Ky.) Herald-Leader (Associated Press), June 9, 1990, at A2, col. 5.

[86]*See* Parker, *Rap Singers Charged with Obscenity*, Washington Post, June 11, 1990, at A1, col. 1.

[87]*See 2 Live Crew Beats Obscenity Rap*, Lexington (Ky.), Herald-Leader (Associated Press), October 21, 1990, at A10, col. 3.

[88]*See Performers Arrested Over "Nasty" Songs*, Lexington (Ky.) Herald-Leader (Associated Press), August 12, 1990, at A10, col. 3.

[89]*Luke Records, Inc. v. Navarro*, 960 F.2d 134, 20 Med.L.Rptr. 1114 (11th Cir. 1992).

[90]*See* Andrews, *Recording Industry Unveils Warning Sticker*, Lexington (Ky.) Herald-Leader (Associated Press), May 10, 1990, at A1, col. 1.

[91]*See* Harrington, *In the Wake of 2 Live Crew*, Washington Post, June 8, 1990, at B1, col. 1.

[92]*See* Master, *Cincinnati Gallery, Director Acquitted of Mapplethorpe Obscenity Charges*, Lexington (Ky.) Herald-Leader (The Washington Post), at A1, col. 2.

[93]*Obscenity Verdict Hasn't Changed Cincinnati Chief's Outlook*, Lexington (Ky.) Herald-Leader (Associated Press), November 12, 1990, at A5, col. 1.

[94]*See* Kinney, *Cincinnati Arts Center Backed on Photo Fight*, Lexington (Ky.) Herald-Leader (Associated Press), at C1, col. 6.

[95]*Contemporary Arts Center v. Ney*, 735 F.Supp. 743 (S.D. Ohio 1990).

[96]*See* Curriden, *Obscenity on Wheels*, 76 A.B.A. J. 30 (June 1990).

[97]*FCC v. Pacifica Foundation*, 438 U.S. 726, 98 S.Ct. 3026, 57 L.Ed.2d 1073, 2 Med.L.Rptr. 1465 (1978).

[98]In the Matter of Infinity Broadcasting Corp. of Pennsylvania, 3 FCC 930, 62 RR2d 1202, *aff'd in part sub. nom.*, *Action for Children's Television v. FCC*, 852 F.2d 1332 (D.C. Cir. 1988).

[99]*Id.*

[100]*Id.*

[101]*Action for Children's Television v. FCC*, 852 F.2d 1332 (D.C. Cir. 1988).

[102]*Action for Children's Television v. FCC*, 932 F.2d 1504 (D.C. Cir. 1991).

[103]Paredes-Japa, *FCC Fails in Bid to "Bleep" Indecency from Television*, QUILL, October 1991, at 29.

[104]*Sable Communications of California v. FCC*, 492 U.S. 115, 109 S.Ct. 2829, 106, L.Ed.2d. 93 (1989).

[105]*Courts Approve Restrictions on "Dial-A-Porn,"* NEWS MEDIA & THE LAW, Fall 1991, at 40-41.

[106]*Dial Information Services Corp. of New York v. Thornburgh*, 938 F.2d 1535 (2nd Cir. 1991).

[107]Richard Carelli, *Clampdown on Dial-A-Porn Calls Upheld*, Lexington (Ky.) Herald-Leader (Associated Press), January 28, 1992, at A1, col. 5.

[108]*Phone Porn Restraints Are Upheld for Children*, Lexington (Ky.) Herald-Leader (Associated Press), July 17, 1991, at B5, col. 2.

[109]*Adams Newark Theatre Co. v. Newark*, 354 U.S. 931 (1956).

[110]*California v. LaRue*, 409 U.S. 109 (1972).

[111]*See, for example, New York State Liquor Authority v. Bellanca*, 452 U.S. 714 (1981) and *City of Newport v. Iacobucci*, 479 U.S. 92 (1986).

[112]*Doran v. Salem Inn, Inc.*, 422 U.S. 922 (1975).

[113]*Barnes v. Glen Theatre, Inc.*, 111 S.Ct. 2456, 115 L.Ed.2d 594 (1991).

[114]See *William Kennedy Smith Trial Boosts CNN Ratings*, Lexington (Ky.) Herald-Leader

(Knight-Ridder News Service), December 14, 1991, at B3, col. 1. Diane Sawyer's interview with Bowman helped "PrimeTime Live" get its highest ratings ever. *See Bowman Nets Top TV Rating*, Lexington (Ky.) Herald-Leader (wire services), December 21, 1991, at A3, col. 1.

[115]*See Papers Run Obscenity Ads to Comply with Law*, PRESSTIME, May 1991, at 46.

[116]*Id.*

[117]*Id.*

[118]*Herceg v.* Hustler, 814 F.2d 1017 (5th Cir. 1987). *See* Diamond and Primm, *Rediscovering Traditional Tort Typologies to Determine Media Liability for Physical Injuries: From the Mickey Mouse Club to* Hustler *Magazine*, 10 HASTINGS COMM/ENT L. J. 969-997 (1988) for an insightful analysis of this decision and other claims of liability for physical injuries caused by media publication.

[119]*Penthouse International v. Hinson McAuliffe*, 702 F.2d 925, 7 Med.L.Rptr. 1798 (N.D. Ga. 1981); *aff'd by evenly divided court*, 717 F.2d 517 (11th Cir. 1983).

[120]*Id.*

[121]From a story in the *Houston Chronicle* by Joe Abernathy on June 10, 1990, received via Electronic mail by the author.

[122]O'Connell, *Future Computers Will Turn Sexual Fantasy into "Reality,"* Lexington (Ky.) Herald-Leader (The Orlando Sentinel), May 6, 1991, at B3, col. 2.

Appendix A:
Society of Professional
Journalists
Code of Ethics*

SOCIETY of Professional Journalists, believes the duty of journalists is to serve the truth.

We BELIEVE the agencies of mass communication are carriers of public discussion and information, acting on their Constitutional mandate and freedom to learn and report the facts.

We BELIEVE in public enlightenment as the forerunner of justice, and in our Constitutional role to seek the truth as part of the public's right to know the truth.

We BELIEVE those responsibilities carry obligations that require journalists to perform with intelligence, objectivity, accuracy, and fairness.

To these ends, we declare acceptance of the standards of practice here set forth:

I. RESPONSIBILITY:

The public's right to know of events of public importance and interest is the overriding mission of the mass media. The purpose of distributing news and enlightened opinion is to serve the general welfare. Journalists who use their professional status as representatives of the public for selfish or other unworthy motives violate a high trust.

II. FREEDOM OF THE PRESS:

Freedom of the press is to be guarded as an inalienable right of people in a free society. It carries with it the freedom and the responsibility to discuss, question, and challenge actions and utterances of our government and of our public and private institutions. Journalists uphold the right to speak unpopular opinions and the privilege to agree with the majority.

III. ETHICS:

Journalists must be free of obligation to any interest other than the public's right to know the truth.

1. Gifts, favors, free travel, special treatment or privileges can compromise the integrity of journalists and their employers. Nothing of value should be accepted.

2. Secondary employment, political involvement, holding public office, and service in community organizations should be avoided if it compromises the integrity of journalists and their employers. Journalists and their employers should conduct their personal lives in a manner that protects them from conflict of interest, real or apparent. Their responsibilities to the public are paramount. That is the nature of their profession.

3. So-called news communications from private sources should not be published or broadcast without substantiation of their claims to news values.

4. Journalists will seek news that serves the public interest, despite the obstacles. They will make constant efforts to assure that the public's business is conducted in public and that public records are open to public inspection.

5. Journalists acknowledge the newsman's ethic of protecting confidential sources of information.

6. Plagiarism is dishonest and unacceptable.

IV. ACCURACY AND OBJECTIVITY:

Good faith with the public is the foundation of all worthy journalism.

1. Truth is our ultimate goal.

2. Objectivity in reporting the news is another goal that serves as the mark of an experienced professional. It is a standard of performance toward which we strive. We honor those who achieve it.

3. There is no excuse for inaccuracies or lack of thoroughness.

4. Newspaper headlines should be fully warranted by the contents of the articles they accompany. Photographs and telecasts should give an accurate picture of an event and not highlight and incident out of context.

5. Sound practice makes clear distinction between news reports and expressions of opinion. News reports should be free of opinion or bias and represent all sides of an issue.

6. Partisanship in editorial comment that knowingly departs from the truth violates the spirit of American journalism.

7. Journalists recognize their responsibility for offering informed analysis, comment, and editorial opinion on public events and issues. They accept the obligation to present such material by individuals whose competence, experience, and judgment qualify them for it.

8. Special articles or presentations devoted to advocacy or the writer's own conclusions and interpretations should be labeled as such.

V. FAIR PLAY:

Journalists at all times will show respect for the dignity, privacy, rights, and well-being of people encountered in the course of gathering and presenting the news.

1. The news media should not communicate unofficial charges affecting reputation or moral character without giving the accused a chance to reply.

2. The news media must guard against invading a person's right to privacy.

3. The media should not pander to morbid curiosity about details of vice and crime.

4. It is the duty of news media to make prompt and complete correction of their errors.

5. Journalists should be accountable to the public for their reports and the public should be encouraged to voice its grievances against the media. Open dialogue with our readers, viewers, and listeners should be fostered.

VI. MUTUAL TRUST:

Adherence to this code is intended to preserve and strengthen the bond of mutual trust and respect between American journalists and the American people.

The Society shall—by programs of education and other means—encourage individual journalists to adhere to these tenets, and shall encourage journalistic publications and broadcasters to recognize their responsibility to frame codes of ethics in concert with their employees to serve as guidelines in furthering these goals.

CODE OF ETHICS

(Adopted 1926; revised 1973, 1984, 1987)

Appendix B:
National Press Photographers Association, Inc. Code of Ethics*

The National Press Photographers Association, a professional society dedicated to the advancement of photojournalism, acknowledges concern and respect for the public's natural-law right to freedom in searching for the truth and the right to be informed truthfully and completely about public events and the world in which we live.

We believe that no report can be complete if it is not possible to enhance and clarify the meaning of words. We believe that pictures, whether used to depict news events as they actually happen, illustrate news that has happened or to help explain anything of public interest, are an indispensable means of keeping people accurately informed; that they help all people, young and old, to better understand any subject in the public domain.

Believing the foregoing we recognize and acknowledge that photojournalists should at all times maintain the highest standards of ethical conduct in serving the public interest. To that end the National Press Photographers Associations sets forth the following Code of Ethics which is subscribed to by all of its members:

1. The practice of photojournalism, both as a science and art, is worthy of the very best thought and effort of those who enter into it as a profession.
2. Photojournalism affords an opportunity to serve the public that is equalled by few other vocations and all members of the profession should strive by example and influence to maintain high standards of ethical conduct free of mercenary considerations of any kind.

---

3. It is the individual responsibility of every photojournalist at all times to strive for pictures that report truthfully, honestly and objectively.

4. Business promotion in its many forms is essential, but untrue statements of any nature are not worthy of a professional photojournalist and we severely condemn any such practice.

5. It is our duty to encourage and assist all members of our profession, individually and collectively, so that the quality of photojournalism may constantly be raised to higher standards.

6. It is the duty of every photojournalist to work to preserve all freedom-of-the-press rights recognized by law and to work to protect and expand freedom-of-access to all sources of news and visual information.

7. Our standards of business dealings, ambitions and relations shall have in them a note of sympathy for our common humanity and shall always require us to take into consideration our highest duties as members of society. In every situation in our business life, in every responsibility that comes before us, our chief thought shall be to fulfill that responsibility and discharge that duty so that when each of us is finished we shall have endeavored to lift the level of human ideals and achievement higher than we found it.

8. No Code of Ethics can prejudge every situation, thus common sense and good judgement are required in applying ethical principles.

Appendix C:
American Society of
Newspaper Editors
A Statement of Principles*

PREAMBLE

The First Amendment, protecting freedom of expression from abridgment by any law, guarantees to the people through their press a constitutional right, and thereby places on newspaper people a particular responsibility.

Thus journalism demands of its practitioners not only industry and knowledge but also the pursuit of a standard of integrity proportionate to the journalist's singular obligation.

To this end the American Society of Newspaper Editors sets forth this Statement of Principles as a standard encouraging the highest ethical and professional performance.

ARTICLE I—Responsibility

The primary purpose of gathering and distributing news and opinion is to serve the general welfare by informing the people and enabling them to make judgments on the issues of the time. Newspapermen and women who abuse the power of their professional role for selfish motives or unworthy purposes are faithless to that public trust.

The American press was made free not just to inform or just to serve as a

---

forum for debate but also to bring an independent scrutiny to bear on the forces of power in the society, including the conduct of official power at all levels of government.

ARTICLE II—Freedom of the Press

Freedom of the press belongs to the people. It must be defended against encroachment or assault from any quarter, public or private.

Journalists must be constantly alert to see that the public's business is conducted in public. They must be vigilant against all who would exploit the press for selfish purposes.

ARTICLE III—Independence

Journalists must avoid impropriety and the appearance of impropriety as well as any conflict of interest or the appearance of conflict. They should neither accept anything nor pursue any activity that might compromise or seem to compromise their integrity.

ARTICLE IV—Truth and Accuracy

Good faith with the reader is the foundation of good journalism. Every effort must be made to assure that the news content is accurate, free from bias and in context, and that all sides are presented fairly. Editorials, analytical articles and commentary should be held to the same standards of accuracy with respect to facts as news reports.

Significant errors of fact, as well as errors of omission, should be corrected promptly and prominently.

ARTICLE V—Impartiality

To be impartial does not require the press to be unquestioning or to refrain from editorial expression. Sound practice, however, demands a clear distinction for the reader between news reports and opinion. Articles that contain opinion or personal interpretation should be clearly identified.

ARTICLE VI — Fair Play

Journalists should respect the rights of people involved in the news, observe the common standards of decency and stand accountable to the public for the fairness and accuracy of their news reports.

Persons publicly accused should be given the earliest opportunity to respond.

Pledges of confidentiality to news sources must be honored at all costs, and therefore should not be given lightly. Unless there is clear and pressing need to maintain confidences, sources of information should be identified.

These principles are intended to preserve, protect and strengthen the bond of trust and respect between American journalists and the American people, a bond that is essential to sustain the grant of freedom entrusted to both by the nation's founders.

Originally adopted in 1922 as the "Canons of Journalism," the document was revised and renamed "Statement of Principles" on October 23, 1975.

Appendix D:
Standards of Practice of the American Association of Advertising Agencies*

We hold that a responsibility of advertising agencies is to be a constructive force in business.

We hold that, to discharge this responsibility, advertising agencies must recognize an obligation, not only to their clients, but to the public, the media they employ, and to each other. As a business, the advertising agency must operate within the framework of competition. It is recognized that keen and vigorous competition, honestly conducted, is necessary to the growth and the health of American business. However, unethical competitive practices in the advertising agency business lead to financial waste, dilution of service, diversion of manpower, loss of prestige, and tend to weaken public confidence both in advertisements and in the institution of advertising.

We hold that the advertising agency should compete on merit and not by attempts at discrediting or disparaging a competitor agency, or its work, directly or by inference, or by circulating harmful rumors about another agency, or by making unwarranted claims of particular skill in judging or prejudging advertising copy.

To these ends, the American Association of Advertising Agencies has adopted the following *Creative Code* as being in the best interests of the public, the advertisers, the media, and the agencies themselves. The A.A.A.A. believes the Code's provisions serve as a guide to the kind of agency conduct that experience has shown to be wise, foresighted, and constructive. In accepting membership, an agency agrees to follow it.

---

*© 1990 American Association of Advertising Agencies, Inc. Reprinted with permission First adopted October 16, 1924—Most recently revised September 18, 1990.

579

Creative Code

We, the members of the American Association of Advertising Agencies, in addition to supporting and obeying the laws and legal regulations pertaining to advertising, undertake to extend and broaden the application of high ethical standards. Specifically, we will not knowingly create advertising that contains:

a. False or misleading statements or exaggerations, visual or verbal

b. Testimonials that do not reflect the real opinion of the individual(s)involved

c. Price claims that are misleading

d. Claims insufficiently supported or that distort the true meaning or practicable application of statements made by professional or scientific authority

e. Statements, suggestions, or pictures offensive to public decency or minority segments of the population.

We recognize that there are areas that are subject to honestly different interpretations and judgment. Nevertheless, we agree not to recommend to an advertiser, and to discourage the use of, advertising that is in poor or questionable taste or that is deliberately irritating through aural or visual content or presentation.

Comparative advertising shall be governed by the same standards of truthfulness, claim substantiation, tastefulness, etc., as apply to other types of advertising.

These Standards of Practice of the American Association of Advertising Agencies come from the belief that sound and ethical practice is good business. Confidence and respect are indispensable to success in a business embracing the many intangibles of agency service and involving relationships so dependent upon good faith.

Clear and willful violations of these Standards of Practice may be referred to the Board of Directors of the American Association of Advertising Agencies for appropriate action, including possible annulment of membership as provided by Article IV, Section 5, of the Constitution and By-Laws.

Appendix E:
Code of Broadcast News Ethics
Radio-Television News
Directors Association*

The responsibility of radio and television journalists is to gather and report information of importance and interest to the public accurately, honestly and impartially.

The members of the Radio-Television News Directors Association accept these standards and will:

1. Strive to present the source or nature of broadcast news material in a way that is balanced, accurate and fair.
   A. They will evaluate information solely on its merits as news, rejecting sensationalism or misleading emphasis in any form.
   B. They will guard against using audio or video material in a way that deceives the audience.
   C. They will not mislead the public by presenting as spontaneous news any material which is staged or rehearsed.
   D. They will identify people by race, creed, nationality or prior status only when it is relevant.
   E. They will clearly label opinion and commentary.
   F. They will promptly acknowledge and correct errors.
2. Strive to conduct themselves in a manner that protects them from conflicts of interest, real or perceived. They will decline gifts or favors which would influence or appear to influence their judgments.
3. Respect the dignity, privacy and well-being of people with whom they deal.

---

*© Radio-Television News Directors Association. Reprinted with permission.

4. Recognize the need to protect confidential sources. They will promise confidentiality only with the intention of keeping that promise.
5. Respect everyone's right to a fair trial.
6. Broadcast the private transmissions of other broadcasters only with permission.
7. Actively encourage observance of this code by all journalists, whether members of the Radio-Television News Directors Association or not.

Appendix F:
Statement of Principles, National Association of Broadcasters*

National Association of Broadcasters
1771 N Street, N.W.
Washington, D.C. 20036-2891
(202) 429-5350

IMMEDIATE RELEASE   88/90

NAB APPROVES VOLUNTARY PROGRAMMING PRINCIPLES

WASHINGTON, June 21, 1990 -- The National Association of Broadcasters' Joint Board of Directors this week approved a statement of principles for radio and television broadcasting that addresses four key areas: children's TV, indecency and obscenity, violence, and drugs and substance abuse.

The NAB statement said the programming guidelines are meant to "record and reflect what it believes to be the generally accepted standards of America's radio and television broadcasters." The statement noted broadcasters have "strived to present programming of the highest quality pursuant to standards of excellence and responsibility." The NAB statement added "broadcasters will continue to earn public trust and confidence by following the same principles that have served them well for so long."

NAB expressed hope the new standards "will be particularly useful at this time, given public concern about certain serious societal problems, notably violence and drug abuse," the statement said.

The NAB action is a response to a May 1990 request by the group's Executive Committee, which directed NAB staff to develop

- MORE -

*Reprinted with permission

the new voluntary standards. The statement was developed by
NAB's Legal Department staff, who consulted with numerous
broadcast attorneys about the legal and policy implications of
having standards.

In its document, NAB said there will be no interpretation or
enforcement of these provisions by NAB or other groups.
Similarly, it said the standards "are not in any way intended to
inhibit creativity in or programming of controversial, diverse
and sensitive subjects."

The NAB document reads:

STATEMENT OF PRINCIPLES
OF RADIO AND TELEVISION BROADCASTING

ISSUED BY
THE BOARD OF DIRECTORS OF THE
NATIONAL ASSOCIATION OF BROADCASTERS

Preface

The following Statement of Principles of radio and
television broadcasting is being adopted by the Board of
Directors of the National Association of Broadcasters on behalf
of the Association and the commercial radio and television
stations it represents.

America's free over-the-air radio and television
broadcasters have a long and proud tradition of universal, local
broadcast service to the American people. These broadcasters,
large and small, representing diverse localities and
perspectives, have strived to present programming of the highest
quality to their local communities pursuant to standards of
excellence and responsibility. They have done so and continue to
do so out of respect for their status as daily guests in the
homes and lives of a majority of Americans and with a sense of
pride in their profession, in their product and in their public
service.

The Board issues this statement of principles to record
and reflect what it believes to be the generally-accepted
standards of America's radio and television broadcasters. The
Board feels that such a statement will be particularly useful at
this time, given public concern about certain serious societal
problems, notably violence and drug abuse.

- MORE -

The Board believes that broadcasters will continue to earn public trust and confidence by following the same principles that have served them well for so long. Many broadcasters now have written standards of their own. All have their own programming policies. NAB would hope that all broadcasters would set down in writing their general programming principles and policies, as the Board hereby sets down the following principles.

PRINCIPLES CONCERNING PROGRAM CONTENT

Responsibly exercised artistic freedom

The challenge to the broadcaster often is to determine how suitably to present the complexities of human behavior without compromising or reducing the range of subject matter, artistic expression or dramatic presentation desired by the broadcaster and its audiences. For television and for radio, this requires exceptional awareness of considerations peculiar to each medium and of the composition and preferences of particular communities and audiences.

Each broadcaster should exercise responsible and careful judgment in the selection of material for broadcast. At the same time each broadcast licensee must be vigilant in exercising and defending its rights to program according to its own judgments and to the programming choices of its audiences. This often may include the presentation of sensitive or controversial material.

In selecting program subjects and themes of particular sensitivity, great care should be paid to treatment and presentation, so as to avoid presentations purely for the purpose of sensationalism or to appeal to prurient interests or morbid curiosity.

In scheduling programs of particular sensitivity, broadcasters should take account of the composition and the listening or viewing habits of their specific audiences. Scheduling generally should consider audience expectations and composition in various time periods.

Responsibility In Children's Programming

Programs designed primarily for children should take into account the range of interests and needs of children from informational material to a wide variety of entertainment material. Children's programs should attempt to contribute to the sound, balanced development of children and to help them achieve a sense of the world at large.

SPECIAL PROGRAM PRINCIPLES

1. Violence.

Violence, physical or psychological, should only be

- MORE -

portrayed in a responsible manner and should not be used exploitatively. Where consistent with the creative intent, programs involving violence should present the consequences of violence to its victims and perpetrators.

Presentation of the details of violence should avoid the excessive, the gratuitous and the instructional. The use of violence for its own sake and the detailed dwelling upon brutality or physical agony, by sight or by sound, should be avoided.

Particular care should be exercised where children are involved in the depiction of violent behavior.

2.   Drugs and Substance Abuse.

The use of illegal drugs or other substance abuse should not be encouraged or shown as socially desirable.

Portrayal of drug or substance abuse should be reasonably related to plot, theme or character development. Where consistent with the creative intent, the adverse consequences of drug or substance abuse should be depicted.

Glamorization of drug use and substance abuse should be avoided.

3.   Sexually Oriented Material.

In evaluating programming dealing with human sexuality, broadcasters should consider the composition and expectations of the audience likely to be viewing or listening to their stations and/or to a particular program, the context in which sensitive material is presented and its scheduling.

Creativity and diversity in programming that deals with human sexuality should be encouraged. Programming that purely panders to prurient or morbid interests should be avoided.

Where significant child audiences can be expected, particular care should be exercised when addressing sexual themes.

Obscenity is not constitutionally-protected speech and is at all times unacceptable for broadcast.

All programming decisions should take into account current federal requirements limiting the broadcast of indecent matter.

Endnote

This statement of principles is of necessity general and advisory rather than specific and restrictive. There will be no interpretation or enforcement of these principles by NAB or

- MORE -

others. They are not intended to establish new criteria for programming decisions, but rather to reflect generally-accepted practices of America's radio and television programmers. They similarly are not in any way intended to inhibit creativity in or programming of controversial, diverse or sensitive subjects.

Specific standards and their application and interpretation remain within the sole discretion of the individual television or radio licensee. Both NAB and the stations it represents respect and defend the individual broadcaster's First Amendment rights to select and present programming according to its individual assessment of the desires and expectations of its audiences and of the public interest.

NAB serves and represents America's radio and television broadcast stations, and all the major networks.

- 30 -

E1-4;F1;H1-2;I1-2;M1;O1;T1;V1   Contact: Susan Kraus/
                                              Walt Wurfel
                                              (202) 429-5350

Table of Cases

Index